Lecture Notes in Computer Science 1520

Edited by G. Goos, J. Hartmanis and J. van Leeuwen

Springer
Berlin
Heidelberg
New York
Barcelona
Hong Kong
London
Milan
Paris
Singapore
Tokyo

Michael Maher   Jean-Francois Puget (Eds.)

Principles and Practice of Constraint Programming – CP98

4th International Conference, CP98
Pisa, Italy, October 26-30, 1998
Proceedings

Springer

Series Editors

Gerhard Goos, Karlsruhe University, Germany
Juris Hartmanis, Cornell University, NY, USA
Jan van Leeuwen, Utrecht University, The Netherlands

Volume Editors

Michael Maher
School of Computing and Information Technology
Griffith University
Nathan, Queensland 4111, Australia
E-mail: M.Maher@cit.gu.edu.au

Jean-Francois Puget
ILOG S.A.
9, rue de Verdun, BP 85, F-94253 Gentilly Cedex, France
E-mail: puget@ilog.fr

Cataloging-in-Publication data applied for

Die Deutsche Bibliothek - CIP-Einheitsaufnahme

Principles and practice of constraint programming : 4th international conference ; proceedings / CP '98, Pisa, Italy, October 26 - 30, 1998. Michael Maher ; Jean-Francois Puget (ed.). - Berlin ; Heidelberg ; New York ; Barcelona ; Hong Kong ; London ; Milan ; Paris ; Singapore ; Tokyo : Springer, 1998
(Lecture notes in computer science ; Vol. 1520)
ISBN 3-540-65224-8

CR Subject Classification (1998): D.1, D.3.2-3, I.2.3-4, F.3.2, F.4.1, I.2.8

ISSN 0302-9743
ISBN 3-540-65224-8 Springer-Verlag Berlin Heidelberg New York

Typesetting: Camera-ready by author
SPIN 10692794 06/3142 – 5 4 3 2 1 0 Printed on acid-free paper

Preface

Constraints have emerged as the basis of a representational and computational paradigm that draws from many disciplines and can be brought to bear on many problem domains. This volume contains papers dealing with all aspects of computing with constraints. In particular, there are several papers on applications of constraints, reflecting the practical usefulness of constraint programming.

The papers were presented at the 1998 International Conference on Principles and Practice of Constraint Programming (CP'98), held in Pisa, Italy, 26–30 October, 1998. It is the fourth in this series of conferences, following conferences in Cassis (France), Cambridge (USA), and Schloss Hagenberg (Austria).

We received 115 high quality submissions. In addition, 7 abstracts submissions were not followed by a full paper, hence were not counted as submissions. The program committee selected 29 high quality papers after thorough refereeing by at least 3 experts and further discussion by committee members.

We thank the referees and the program committee for the time and effort spent in reviewing the papers. The program committee invited three speakers:

- Joxan Jaffar
- Peter Jeavons
- Patrick Prosser

Their papers are in this volume.

In addition to the invited and contributed talks, the conference also contained a poster session, which provided attendees with a wider view of the active research in constraint programming. One-page abstracts of the posters appear at the end of this volume. The program also contained four tutorials, presented by Alexander Bockmayr and Thomas Kasper, Rina Dechter, Claude Le Pape and Mark Wallace, and Makoto Yokoo. Following the conference there were five workshops on a range of constraint-based computing topics.

This year, a pre-conference competition was run for the best use of constraints to tackle telecommunication applications. The competition was sponsored by Telecom Italia. The judges were Henry Kautz, Ora Lassila, Claude Le Pape, Michael Maher, Remo Pareschi, and Jean-Francois Puget. The winning entry was: "Optimal placement of base stations in wireless indoor telecommunications" by Thom Fruewirth and Pascal Brisset. This application was presented in the program of the conference and a summary appears in this proceedings.

The success of a conference depends primarily on organization. We thank Francesca Rossi, the conference chair, for the excellent job she did organizing the conference, and for her cooperation and proactive support in preparing the conference program. We also thank Stefano Bistarelli for his work as publicity chair and local organizer, and Roland Yap for his work as workshop chair.

CP'98 was organized in cooperation with AAAI and EATCS. The conference was jointly sponsored by AI*IA, APT Pisa, Compulog Net, Cosytec, ILOG, Prologia, SINTEF, ToscoDati, and GNIM-CNR.

September 1998

Michael Maher
Jean-Francois Puget
CP'98 Program Co-Chairs

Organization

Conference Chair

Francesca Rossi (U. Pisa, Italy)

Program Committee

Peter van Beek (U. Alberta, Canada)
Christian Bessiere (LIRMM-CNRS, France)
Alexander Bockmayr (Max Planck Institute, Germany)
Alex Brodsky (George Mason U., USA)
Yves Caseau (Bouygues, France)
Philippe Codognet (INRIA and Sony CSL, France)
Rina Dechter (U. California - Irvine, USA)
Yves Deville (U. Catholique de Louvain, Belgium)
Boi Faltings (EPFL, Switzerland)
Maurizio Gabbrielli (U. Pisa, Italy)
Ian Gent (U. Strathclyde, UK)
Nevin Heintze (Bell Laboratories, USA)
Manolis Koubarakis (UMIST, UK)
Jimmy Lee (The Chinese U. Hong Kong, China)
Alan Mackworth (U. British Columbia, Canada)
Michael Maher (Griffith U., Australia), Co-Chair
Kim Marriott (Monash U., Australia)
Wim Nuijten (ILOG, France)
Catuscia Palamidessi (Pennsylvania State U., USA)
Jean-Francois Puget (ILOG, France), Co-Chair
Francesca Rossi (U. Pisa, Italy)
Helmut Simonis (Cosytec, France)
Barbara Smith (U. Leeds, UK)
Peter Stuckey (U. Melbourne, Australia)
Ralf Treinen (U. Paris - Sud, France)
Michel Van Caneghem (U. Marseilles and Prologia, France)
Dirk Van Gucht (Indiana U., USA)
Makoto Yokoo (NTT, Japan)

Workshop Chair

Roland Yap (National U. Singapore, Singapore)

Publicity Chair

Stefano Bistarelli (U. Pisa, Italy)

Organizing Committee

Alan Borning (U. of Washington)
Jacques Cohen (Brandeis U.)
Alain Colmerauer (U. of Marseille)
Eugene Freuder (U. of New Hampshire), Executive Chair
Herve Gallaire (Xerox)
Jean-Pierre Jouannaud (U. of Paris Sud)
Jean-Louis Lassez (New Mexico Tech)
Ugo Montanari (U. of Pisa)
Anil Nerode (Cornell U.)
Vijay Saraswat (AT&T Research)
Gert Smolka (DFKI and U. des Saarlandes)
Ralph Wachter (Office of Naval Research)

Referees

A. Aggoun
Akira Aiba
Chris Beck
Nicolas Beldiceanu
B. Bennett
F.S. de Boer
Alan Borning
Eric Bourreau
J.T. Buchanan
Jim Caldwell
Witold Charatonik
A.G. Cohn
Andrew Davenport
Bruce Davey
Romuald Debruyne
O. Delerue
Denys Duchier
Hani El Sakkout
Sandro Etalle
Laurent Fribourg
Daniel Frost
Y. Georget
James Harland
Warwick Harvey
Martin Henz
Ulrich Junker
Kalev Kask
Philip Kilby
Alvin Kwan
Philippe Laborie
Cosimo Laneve
Javier Larrosa
Michel Leconte
Michel Lemaitre
Ho-fung Leung
Vassilis Liatsos
Fabrizio Luccio
Claude Marché
Jean-Luc Massat
Maria Chiara Meo
Rene Moreno
Tobias Müller
Martin Müller
Lee Naish
Joachim Niehren
Dino Oliva
Christine Paulin-Mohring
Laurent Perron
Gilles Pesant
Andreas Podelski
Frederic Poncin
E. Poupart
Patrick Prosser
Jean-Charles Regin
Jean-Hugues Rety
Jon G. Riecke
Irina Rish
Jerome Rogerie
P. Roy
Peter Schachte
Ralf Scheidhauer
Tomas Schiex
Christian Schulte
Spiros Skiadopoulos
Kostas Stergiou
Paul Strooper
Takayuki Suyama
Vincent Tam
Peter Van Roy
Gerard Verfaillie
Marco Verhoeven
Marie-Catherine Vilarem
Paolo Volpe
Uwe Waldmann
Toby Walsh
Herbert Wiklicky
Christos Zaroliagis
Neng-Fa Zhou

Table of Contents

Invited Papers

Submitted Papers

Posters

Telecommunication application

Open Constraint Programming

Joxan Jaffar and Roland H.C. Yap

Department of Computer Science
School of Computing
National University of Singapore
Republic of Singapore 119260
{joxan,ryap}@comp.nus.edu.sg

Constraint Programming (CP) has proven useful in several areas, and though the initial impetus came from logic programming frameworks like CLP and CCP, the use of CP and constraint solving is obtaining wider appeal. We suggest that the limiting features of traditional CP are a dependence on a (logic) language, the need for monotonicity in the constraint system, and, to a lesser extent, the lack of an independent mechanism for agents to specify concurrent interaction with constraint solvers.

Some background and examples: the ILOG constraint libraries serve to provide constraint based search using a finite-domain solver for programs written in C++, and not a logic programming language. The Oz language is not rule-based; it uses a finite domain solver for search problems (though instead of backtracking, an encapsulated search mechanism is used). In addition, the concurrent part of Oz borrows from CCP in using entailment of term and feature constraints for synchronization. Further afield, the "glass box" approach to finite-domain constraint solving uses constraints on indexicals which are non-monotonic. Deductive and constraint databases define a store intensionally, but updates are non-monotonic. In shared-memory languages for parallel programming, the model is one of a global flat store equipped with various synchronization primitives. Coordination based models like Actors/Blackboards/Linda use a structured global store and more sophisticated synchronization primitives on the store. In summary, the issues covered here include: a global store, logical structure vs local structure, monotonic vs non-monotonic operations, facilities for control and search. The point is, we need them all.

Here we introduce a model in which agents and constraint solvers interact. Details of agents are of no interest here; they may be written in any (sequential or concurrent) programming language. We employ a more pragmatic definition of constraint system, but more importantly, there is a framework for specifying how agents and solvers interact. What emerges is a general facility which has the traditional advantages of CP, and much more.

Constructing Constraints

Peter Jeavons

Department of Computer Science, Royal Holloway, University of London, UK
e-mail: p.jeavons@dcs.rhbnc.ac.uk

Abstract. It is well-known that there is a trade-off between the expressive power of a constraint language and the tractability of the problems it can express. But how can you determine the expressive power of a given constraint language, and how can you tell if problems expressed in that language are tractable? In this paper we discuss some general approaches to these questions.
We show that for languages over a finite domain the concept of an 'indicator problem' gives a universal construction for any constraint within the expressive power of a language. We also discuss the fact that all known tractable languages over finite domains are characterised by the presence of a particular solution to a corresponding indicator problem, and raise the question of whether this is a universal property of tractable languages.

1 What is a constraint?

A constraint is a way of specifying that a certain relationship must hold between the values taken by certain variables. There are very few "textbook" definitions of this concept (because there are very few textbooks), but the definition given in [22] is that a constraint is a set of *labelings*, and a labeling is a set of variable-value pairs. For example, the constraint that says that the variables X and Y must be assigned different values from the set $\{R, G, B\}$ would be expressed by the following set of labelings

$$\{\{(X,R),(Y,G)\},\{(X,R),(Y,B)\},\{(X,G),(Y,R)\},\\ \{(X,G),(Y,B)\},\{(X,B),(Y,R)\},\{(X,B),(Y,G)\}\}.$$

This interpretation of the notion of constraint is convenient for some types of analysis, but for our purposes, it is important to separate out more clearly two aspects of a constraint which are rather mixed together in this definition. These two aspects are the *relation* which must hold between the values, and the particular variables over which that relation must hold. We therefore prefer to use the following definition of constraints (which is similar to the definition used by many authors, see, for example, [1, 4]).

Definition 1. A constraint C is a pair (s, R), where s is a tuple of variables of length m, called the *constraint scope*, and R is a relation of arity m, called the *constraint relation*.

Note that a relation of arity m is simply a subset of the set of all m-tuples of elements from some set, say D, called the *domain*. In this paper, tuples will be written in the form $\langle d_1, d_2, \ldots, d_m \rangle$, and the set of all tuples of length m will be denoted D^m. The tuples in the constraint relation R indicate the allowed combinations of simultaneous values for the corresponding variables in the scope s. The length of these tuples, m, will be called the *arity* of the constraint. In particular, unary constraints specify the allowed values for a single variable, and binary constraints specify the allowed combinations of values for a pair of variables.

Using this definition, the constraint that says that the variables X and Y must be assigned different values from the set $\{R, G, B\}$ would be expressed by the pair

$$(\langle X, Y \rangle, \{\langle R, G \rangle, \langle R, B \rangle, \langle G, R \rangle, \langle G, B \rangle, \langle B, R \rangle, \langle B, G \rangle\}).$$

Alternatively, we might specify the constraint relation implicitly, and write this constraint as

$$(\langle X, Y \rangle, \ \{\langle c_1, c_2 \rangle \mid c_1, c_2 \in \{R, G, B\}, c_1 \neq c_2\}).$$

By using implicit specifications of relations in this way we can easily define constraints over both finite and infinite sets.

Satisfying a constraint means choosing a tuple of values for the variables in the scope that is a member of the constraint relation.

A constraint satisfaction problem, $\mathbf{P}$, is given by a set of variables, V, a domain of possible values, D, and a set of constraints. A solution to $\mathbf{P}$ is a mapping from V to D whose restriction to each individual constraint scope satisfies that constraint.

2 What is a constraint language?

Separating out the notions of the constraint *scope* and the constraint *relation* by using the definition above allows us to study each of these aspects independently. For example, the *scopes* of the constraints determine the structure of the constraint satisfaction problem, or, in other words, the way that the constraints overlap. The structure associated with a given problem is often described as the "constraint graph", or "constraint hypergraph", associated with a given problem. By imposing restrictions on the possible scopes of the constraints we can define classes of problems with restricted structures. There are many results in the literature about the tractability of constraint satisfaction problems that have certain forms of restricted structure, such as a tree-structure [6, 20], or some generalisation of a tree-structure [3, 7, 9, 20].

On the other hand, the constraint *relations* determine the kinds of constraints that are involved in our constraint satisfaction problem. By imposing restrictions on the possible constraint relations we are allowed to use we can define the notion of a "constraint language". For example, if we take all relations that can be specified by linear equations over the real numbers, then we have the language of linear equations. If we take just binary relations that can be specified by a disequality, as in the examples above, then we have the language of graph-colouring.

Definition 2. A *constraint language* is a set, $\mathcal{L}$, of relations.

For any constraint language $\mathcal{L}$, the class of all constraint satisfaction problems in which all the constraint relations are elements of $\mathcal{L}$ will be denoted CSP($\mathcal{L}$).

Example 1. Let $\mathcal{L}$ be the set containing the single binary relation $R_{\leq 1}$ over the real numbers, $\mathcal{R}$, defined as follows:

$$R_{\leq 1} = \{\langle a, b\rangle \mid a, b \in \mathcal{R}, a - b \leq 1\}$$

One element of CSP($\mathcal{L}$) is the constraint satisfaction problem $\mathbf{P}$, which has 4 constraints, $\{C_1, C_2, C_3, C_4\}$, defined as follows:

- $C_1 = (\langle v_1, v_2\rangle, R_{\leq 1})$;
- $C_2 = (\langle v_2, v_3\rangle, R_{\leq 1})$;
- $C_3 = (\langle v_3, v_2\rangle, R_{\leq 1})$;
- $C_4 = (\langle v_3, v_4\rangle, R_{\leq 1})$.

The structure of this problem is illustrated in Figure 1.

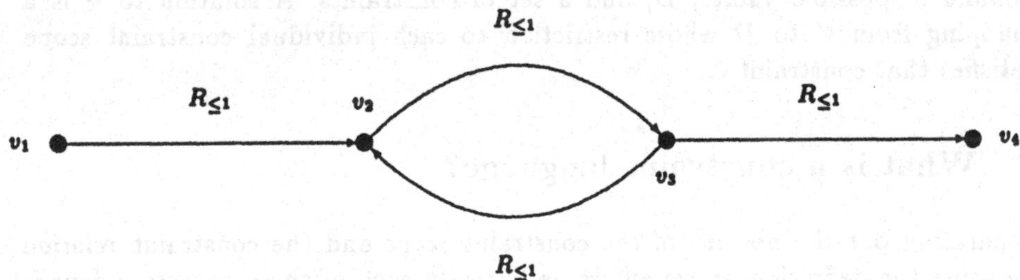

Fig. 1. The CSP defined in Example 1

3 What is expressive power?

Some constraint languages are more powerful than others because they allow us to express a larger collection of problems. For example, if we are dealing with applications involving real-valued variables, then it is possible to express more numerical relationships using arbitrary polynomial equations than if we were restricted to using just linear equations. Similarly, if we are dealing with applications involving Boolean variables, then it is possible to express more logical relationships using ternary clauses than if we were restricted to using just binary clauses.

Of course, the penalty for increased expressive power is generally an increase in computational complexity. For example, the satisfiability problem with ternary clauses is NP-complete [8], whereas the satisfiability problem involving only binary clauses can be solved in polynomial time [8]. More generally, the finite constraint satisfaction problem with arbitrary constraints is known to be NP-complete [19], whereas many families of restricted constraints have been identified which give rise to tractable problem classes [2, 13, 16, 15, 18, 20, 23, 24],

For any given application, it would be very useful to be able to select a constraint language which has sufficient expressive power to express the desired constraints, but is sufficiently restrictive to allow an efficient solution technique. However, it is not immediately clear how to determine what can be expressed in a given language, or whether a language is tractable. These are the questions that we address in this paper.

First, we need to define exactly what it means to "express" a constraint using a constraint language. To clarify this idea, note that in any constraint satisfaction problem some of the required relationships between variables are given explicitly in the constraints, whilst others generally arise implicitly from interactions of different constraints. For any problem in CSP($\mathcal{L}$), the explicit constraint relations must be elements of $\mathcal{L}$, but there may be implicit restrictions on some subsets of the variables for which the corresponding relations are not elements of $\mathcal{L}$, as the next example indicates.

Example 2. Reconsider the constraint satisfaction problem **P**, defined in Example 1.

Note that there is no explicit constraint on the pair $\langle v_1, v_3\rangle$. However, it is clear that the possible pairs of values which can be taken by this pair of variables are precisely the elements of the relation $R_{\leq 2} = \{\langle a, b\rangle \mid a, b \in \mathcal{R}, a - b \leq 2\}$.

Similarly, the pairs of values which can be taken by the pair of variables $\langle v_1, v_4\rangle$ are precisely the elements of the relation $R_{\leq 3} = \{\langle a, b\rangle \mid a, b \in \mathcal{R}, a - b \leq 3\}$.

Finally, note that there are two constraints on the pair of variables $\langle v_2, v_3\rangle$. The possible pairs of values which can be taken by this pair of variables are precisely the elements of the relation $R'_{\leq 1} = \{\langle a, b\rangle \mid a, b \in \mathcal{R}, -1 \leq (a - b) \leq 1\}$.

We now define exactly what it means to say that a constraint relation can be expressed in a constraint language.

Definition 3. A relation R can be *expressed* in a constraint language $\mathcal{L}$ if there exists a problem **P** in CSP($\mathcal{L}$), and a list, s, of variables, such that the solutions to **P** when restricted to s give precisely the tuples of R.

Example 3. Reconsider the language $\mathcal{L}$ containing the single binary relation $R_{\leq 1}$, defined in Example 1.

It was shown in Example 2 that the relations $R_{\leq 2}$, $R_{\leq 3}$ and $R'_{\leq 1}$ can all be expressed in this language.

For any constraint language $\mathcal{L}$, the set of *all* relations which can be expressed in $\mathcal{L}$ will be called the *expressive power* of $\mathcal{L}$, and will be denoted $\mathcal{L}^+$.

4 Simple constructions for binary relations

Note that for any binary relation R which belongs to a language $\mathcal{L}$, the relation

$$R^{\cup} = \{\langle a, b\rangle \mid \langle b, a\rangle \in R\},$$

which is called the "converse" of R, can also be expressed in $\mathcal{L}$.

The next example indicates some standard ways to obtain new binary relations which can be expressed using a given set of binary relations.

Example 4. Let $\mathcal{L}$ be a constraint language, and let R_1 and R_2 be any two binary relations in $\mathcal{L}$ (not necessarily distinct).

The class of problems CSP($\mathcal{L}$) contains the problem $\mathbf{P}_{\text{series}}$ with just two constraints C_1 and C_2 where $C_1 = (\langle v_1, v_2\rangle, R_1)$ and $C_2 = (\langle v_2, v_3\rangle, R_2)$.

The possible solutions to $\mathbf{P}_{\text{series}}$ on the variables v_1 and v_3 are exactly the elements of the following relation:

$$\{\langle c_1, c_2\rangle \mid \exists x, \langle c_1, x\rangle \in R_1 \text{ and } \langle x, c_2\rangle \in R_2\}$$

which is called the "composition" of R_1 and R_2 and denoted $R_1; R_2$. Hence, $R_1; R_2$ can be expressed in the language $\mathcal{L}$.

Furthermore, the class of problems CSP($\mathcal{L}$) contains the problem $\mathbf{P}_{\text{parallel}}$ with just two constraints C'_1 and C'_2 where $C'_1 = (\langle v_1, v_2\rangle, R_1)$ and $C'_2 = (\langle v_1, v_2\rangle, R_2)$.

The possible solutions to $\mathbf{P}_{\text{parallel}}$ on the variables v_1 and v_2 are exactly the elements of the relation $R_1 \cap R_2$, the intersection of R_1 and R_2. Hence, $R_1 \cap R_2$ can be expressed in the language $\mathcal{L}$.

We have now seen three ways to express new binary relations using given binary relations: converse, composition and intersection. By repeatedly applying these three operations to the relations of $\mathcal{L}$ we can obtain a large number of new relations, in general.

Definition 4. For any constraint language $\mathcal{L}$, the set of relations that can be obtained from the elements of $\mathcal{L}$ using some sequence of converse, composition and intersection operations will be denoted $\widehat{\mathcal{L}}$.

Example 5. Reconsider the language $\mathcal{L}$ defined in Example 1, which contains the single binary relation $R_{\leq 1}$ over the real numbers defined as follows:

$$R_{\leq 1} = \{\langle a, b\rangle \mid a, b \in \mathcal{R}, a - b \leq 1\}$$

By generalising the constructions given in Example 2, it can be shown that $\widehat{\mathcal{L}}$ contains all relations of the form

$$\{\langle a, b\rangle \mid a, b \in \mathcal{R},\ -n_1 \leq (a-b) \leq n_2\}$$

where n_1 and n_2 are arbitrary positive integers, or ∞.

Hence all of these relations can be expressed in the language $\mathcal{L}$.

At first sight, it might appear that the language $\widehat{\mathcal{L}}$ will contain *all* the binary relations that can be expressed in the language $\mathcal{L}$. It is therefore natural to ask whether there are any languages $\mathcal{L}$ in which we can express any binary relations which are *not* in $\widehat{\mathcal{L}}$.

To answer this question, we note that the definition of $\widehat{\mathcal{L}}$ allows us to express a relation using an arbitrary sequence of converse, composition and intersection operations. The latter two operations correspond to "series" and "parallel" constructions in the constraint graph of the corresponding constraint satisfaction problem. However, it is well-known in graph theory that not every graph can be obtained by a sequence of series and parallel constructions [5]. This suggests that it may be possible to express more constraints by considering constraint satisfaction problems whose constraint graphs cannot be constructed in this way.

The next example shows that for some languages $\mathcal{L}$ it is indeed possible to express relations that are not contained in $\widehat{\mathcal{L}}$.

Example 6. Let $\mathcal{L}$ be the set containing the single binary disequality relation, $\neq_D$, over the set $D = \{R, G, B\}$, defined as follows:

$$\neq_D = \{\langle a, b\rangle \mid a, b \in D, a \neq b\}$$

Note that

$$\neq_D^{\cup} = \neq_D$$

$$\neq_D ; \neq_D = D^2.$$

Hence, the language $\widehat{\mathcal{L}}$ contains just two relations, $\neq_D$ and D^2.

One element of CSP($\mathcal{L}$) is the constraint satisfaction problem **P**, which has 5 constraints, $\{C_1, C_2, C_3, C_4, C_5\}$, defined as follows:

- $C_1 = (\langle v_1, v_2\rangle, \neq_D)$;
- $C_2 = (\langle v_1, v_3\rangle, \neq_D)$;
- $C_3 = (\langle v_2, v_3\rangle, \neq_D)$;
- $C_4 = (\langle v_2, v_4\rangle, \neq_D)$.
- $C_5 = (\langle v_3, v_4\rangle, \neq_D)$.

The structure of this problem is illustrated in Figure 2. Note that there is no explicit constraint on the pair $\langle v_1, v_4\rangle$. However, by considering all solutions to **P**, it can be shown that the value taken by the variable v_1 is always equal to the value taken by the variable v_4. Hence, the possible pairs of values which can be taken by this pair of variables are precisely the elements of the relation $\{\langle a, b\rangle \mid a, b \in \{R, G, B\}, a = b\}$, and this relation is *not* an element of $\widehat{\mathcal{L}}$.

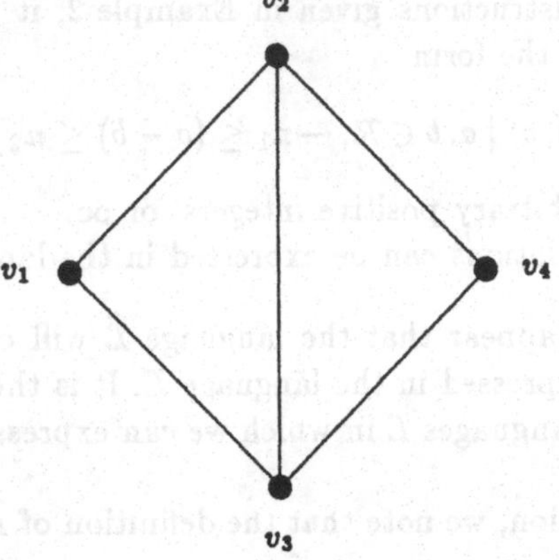

Fig. 2. The constraint graph of the CSP defined in Example 6

Example 7. Let $\mathcal{L}$ be the set containing the single binary relation, $R_\times$, over the set $D = \{0, 1, 2\}$, defined as follows:

$$R_\times = \{\langle 0,0\rangle, \langle 0,1\rangle, \langle 1,0\rangle, \langle 1,2\rangle, \langle 2,1\rangle, \langle 2,2\rangle\}$$

Note that

$$R_\times^\cup = R_\times$$
$$R_\times ; R_\times = D^2.$$

Hence, the language $\widehat{\mathcal{L}}$ contains just two relations, $R_\times$ and D^2.

One element of CSP($\mathcal{L}$) is the constraint satisfaction problem **P**, which has 5 constraints, $\{C_1, C_2, C_3, C_4, C_5\}$, defined as follows:

- $C_1 = (\langle v_1, v_2\rangle, R_\times)$;
- $C_2 = (\langle v_1, v_3\rangle, R_\times)$;
- $C_3 = (\langle v_2, v_3\rangle, R_\times)$;
- $C_4 = (\langle v_2, v_4\rangle, R_\times)$.
- $C_5 = (\langle v_3, v_4\rangle, R_\times)$.

Note that there is no explicit constraint on the pair $\langle v_1, v_4\rangle$. However, by considering all solutions to **P**, it can be shown that the possible pairs of values which can be taken by this pair of variables are precisely the elements of the relation $R'_\times$, which is defined as follows

$$\{\langle 0,0\rangle, \langle 0,1\rangle, \langle 1,0\rangle, \langle 1,1\rangle, \langle 1,2\rangle, \langle 2,1\rangle, \langle 2,2\rangle\}$$

and this relation is *not* an element of $\widehat{\mathcal{L}}$.

Examples 6 and 7 show that for some languages $\mathcal{L}$, the language $\widehat{\mathcal{L}}$ does not contain all of the binary relations which can be expressed in $\mathcal{L}$, or in other words $\widehat{\mathcal{L}} \neq \mathcal{L}^+$. In fact, this is a well-known result in the literature on algebraic properties of binary relations [17]. Hence, in order to calculate the true expressive power of a constraint language, we need to consider more general ways of constructing constraints, even when we consider only binary constraints.

Furthermore, the definitions of the converse and composition operations given above are specific to binary relations, so we also need a more general approach to determine the expressive power of languages containing non-binary relations.

In the next section, we show that for any language of relations over a finite set, there is a single, universal, family of constructions which can be used to obtain all of the relations that can be expressed in that language.

5 A universal construction

Definition 3 states that a relation R can be expressed in a language $\mathcal{L}$ if there is some problem in CSP($\mathcal{L}$) which imposes that relation on some of its variables. We now show that for any language over a finite domain, and any relation, it is only necessary to consider one particular form of problem. In other words, for finite domains, there is a "universal construction" which can be used to express any relation that it is possible to express in a given language.

Definition 5. Let $\mathcal{L}$ be a set of relations over a finite set D.

For any natural number $m \geq 1$, the *indicator problem* of order m for $\mathcal{L}$ is defined to be the constraint satisfaction problem $\mathbf{IP}(\mathcal{L}, m)$ with set of variables D^m, domain of values D, and set of constraints $\{C_1, C_2, \ldots, C_q\}$, where $q = \sum_{R \in \mathcal{L}} |R|^m$, and the constraints C_i are defined as follows. For each $R \in \mathcal{L}$, and for each sequence $t_1, t_2, \ldots, t_m$ of tuples from R, there is a constraint $C_i = (s_i, R)$ with $s_i = (v_1, v_2, \ldots, v_n)$, where n is the arity of R and $v_j = \langle t_1[j], t_2[j], \ldots, t_m[j] \rangle$ for $j = 1$ to n.

Note that for any set of relations $\mathcal{L}$ over a set D, $\mathbf{IP}(\mathcal{L}, m)$ has $|D|^m$ variables, and each variable corresponds to an m-tuple over D. Some examples of indicator problems are given below, and more examples can be found in [14].

Theorem 6. *Let $\mathcal{L}$ be a set of relations over a finite set D, let $R = \{t_1, t_2, \ldots, t_m\}$ be any relation over D, and let n be the arity of R.*

The relation R can be expressed in the language $\mathcal{L}$ if and only if R is equal to the solutions to $\mathbf{IP}(\mathcal{L}, m)$ restricted to the variables $v_1, v_2, \ldots, v_n$, where $v_j = \langle t_1[j], t_2[j], \ldots, t_m[j] \rangle$ for $j = 1$ to n.

Proof. If R is equal to the solutions to $\mathbf{IP}(\mathcal{L}, m)$ restricted to some list of variables, then R can obviously be expressed in $\mathcal{L}$, by Definition 3.

To prove the converse, consider the relation R' whose tuples are given by the solutions to $\mathbf{IP}(\mathcal{L}, m)$ restricted to $v_1, v_2, \ldots, v_n$.

By the definition of the indicator problem, we have $R \subseteq R'$. Hence, if $R' \neq R$, then there must be at least one solution, s, to $\mathbf{IP}(\mathcal{L}, m)$ whose restriction to $v_1, v_2, \ldots, v_n$ is not contained in R.

However, it is shown in [15] that the solutions to $\mathbf{IP}(\mathcal{L}, m)$ are *closure operations*[1] on $\mathcal{L}$, and that every relation in $\mathcal{L}^+$ is closed under all of these operations.

Hence, if $R' \neq R$, then R cannot be expressed in $\mathcal{L}$, which gives the result.

Example 8. Reconsider the relation $R_\times$ over $D = \{0, 1, 2\}$, defined in Example 7.

The indicator problem for $\{R_\times\}$ of order 1, $\mathbf{IP}(\{R_\times\}, 1)$, has 3 variables and 6 constraints. The set of variables is

$$\{\langle 0\rangle, \langle 1\rangle, \langle 2\rangle\},$$

and the set of constraints is

$$\begin{aligned} \{\ & ((\langle 0\rangle, \langle 0\rangle), R_\times), \\ & ((\langle 0\rangle, \langle 1\rangle), R_\times), \\ & ((\langle 1\rangle, \langle 0\rangle), R_\times), \\ & ((\langle 1\rangle, \langle 2\rangle), R_\times), \\ & ((\langle 2\rangle, \langle 1\rangle), R_\times), \\ & ((\langle 2\rangle, \langle 2\rangle), R_\times)\ \}. \end{aligned}$$

This problem has has 6 solutions, which may be expressed in tabular form as follows:

	Variables		
	$\langle 0\rangle$	$\langle 1\rangle$	$\langle 2\rangle$
Solution 1	0	0	0
Solution 2	0	1	0
Solution 3	0	1	2
Solution 4	2	1	0
Solution 5	2	1	2
Solution 6	2	2	2

Note that the restriction of this set of solutions to any sequence of variables gives more than one tuple, so by Theorem 6, the language $\{R_\times\}$ cannot express any relation containing exactly one tuple.

Example 9. Reconsider the relation $R_\times$ over $D = \{0, 1, 2\}$, defined in Example 7.

The indicator problem for $\{R_\times\}$ of order 2, $\mathbf{IP}(\{R_\times\}, 2)$, has 9 variables and 36 constraints. The set of variables is

$$\{\langle 0,0\rangle, \langle 0,1\rangle, \langle 0,2\rangle, \langle 1,0\rangle, \langle 1,1\rangle, \langle 1,2\rangle, \langle 2,0\rangle, \langle 2,1\rangle, \langle 2,2\rangle\},$$

[1] Sometimes called *polymorphisms* [10]

and the set of constraints is

$$\begin{aligned}\{\, & ((\langle 0,0\rangle,\langle 0,0\rangle),R_{\times}),\ ((\langle 0,0\rangle,\langle 0,1\rangle),R_{\times}),\ ((\langle 0,0\rangle,\langle 1,0\rangle),R_{\times}),\ ((\langle 0,0\rangle,\langle 1,1\rangle),R_{\times}),\\ & ((\langle 0,1\rangle,\langle 0,0\rangle),R_{\times}),\ ((\langle 0,1\rangle,\langle 0,2\rangle),R_{\times}),\ ((\langle 0,1\rangle,\langle 1,0\rangle),R_{\times}),\ ((\langle 0,1\rangle,\langle 1,2\rangle),R_{\times}),\\ & ((\langle 0,2\rangle,\langle 0,1\rangle),R_{\times}),\ ((\langle 0,2\rangle,\langle 0,2\rangle),R_{\times}),\ ((\langle 0,2\rangle,\langle 1,1\rangle),R_{\times}),\ ((\langle 0,2\rangle,\langle 1,2\rangle),R_{\times}),\\ & ((\langle 1,0\rangle,\langle 0,0\rangle),R_{\times}),\ ((\langle 1,0\rangle,\langle 0,1\rangle),R_{\times}),\ ((\langle 1,0\rangle,\langle 2,0\rangle),R_{\times}),\ ((\langle 1,0\rangle,\langle 2,1\rangle),R_{\times}),\\ & ((\langle 1,1\rangle,\langle 0,0\rangle),R_{\times}),\ ((\langle 1,1\rangle,\langle 0,2\rangle),R_{\times}),\ ((\langle 1,1\rangle,\langle 2,0\rangle),R_{\times}),\ ((\langle 1,1\rangle,\langle 2,2\rangle),R_{\times}),\\ & ((\langle 1,2\rangle,\langle 0,1\rangle),R_{\times}),\ ((\langle 1,2\rangle,\langle 0,2\rangle),R_{\times}),\ ((\langle 1,2\rangle,\langle 2,1\rangle),R_{\times}),\ ((\langle 1,2\rangle,\langle 2,2\rangle),R_{\times}),\\ & ((\langle 2,0\rangle,\langle 1,0\rangle),R_{\times}),\ ((\langle 2,0\rangle,\langle 1,1\rangle),R_{\times}),\ ((\langle 2,0\rangle,\langle 2,0\rangle),R_{\times}),\ ((\langle 2,0\rangle,\langle 2,1\rangle),R_{\times}),\\ & ((\langle 2,1\rangle,\langle 1,0\rangle),R_{\times}),\ ((\langle 2,1\rangle,\langle 1,2\rangle),R_{\times}),\ ((\langle 2,1\rangle,\langle 2,0\rangle),R_{\times}),\ ((\langle 2,1\rangle,\langle 2,2\rangle),R_{\times}),\\ & ((\langle 2,2\rangle,\langle 1,1\rangle),R_{\times}),\ ((\langle 2,2\rangle,\langle 1,2\rangle),R_{\times}),\ ((\langle 2,2\rangle,\langle 2,1\rangle),R_{\times}),\ ((\langle 2,2\rangle,\langle 2,2\rangle),R_{\times})\,\}.\end{aligned}$$

This problem has 32 solutions, which may be expressed in tabular form as follows:

	Variables								
	$\langle 0,0\rangle$	$\langle 0,1\rangle$	$\langle 0,2\rangle$	$\langle 1,0\rangle$	$\langle 1,1\rangle$	$\langle 1,2\rangle$	$\langle 2,0\rangle$	$\langle 2,1\rangle$	$\langle 2,2\rangle$
Solution 1	0	0	0	0	0	0	0	0	0
Solution 2	0	0	0	0	0	0	0	1	0
Solution 3	0	0	0	0	0	1	0	0	0
Solution 4	0	0	0	0	1	0	0	0	0
Solution 5	0	0	0	0	1	0	0	1	0
Solution 6	0	0	0	0	1	1	0	0	0
Solution 7	0	0	0	1	0	0	0	0	0
Solution 8	0	0	0	1	0	1	0	0	0
Solution 9	0	0	0	1	1	0	0	0	0
Solution 10	0	0	0	1	1	1	0	0	0
Solution 11	0	0	0	1	1	1	2	2	2
Solution 12	0	1	0	0	0	0	0	0	0
Solution 13	0	1	0	0	0	0	0	1	0
Solution 14	0	1	0	0	1	0	0	0	0
Solution 15	0	1	0	0	1	0	0	1	0
Solution 16	0	1	2	0	1	2	0	1	2
Solution 17	2	1	0	2	1	0	2	1	0
Solution 18	2	1	2	2	1	2	2	1	2
Solution 19	2	1	2	2	1	2	2	2	2
Solution 20	2	1	2	2	2	2	2	1	2
Solution 21	2	1	2	2	2	2	2	2	2
Solution 22	2	2	2	1	1	1	0	0	0
Solution 23	2	2	2	1	1	1	2	2	2
Solution 24	2	2	2	1	1	2	2	2	2
Solution 25	2	2	2	1	2	1	2	2	2
Solution 26	2	2	2	1	2	2	2	2	2
Solution 27	2	2	2	2	1	1	2	2	2
Solution 28	2	2	2	2	1	2	2	1	2
Solution 29	2	2	2	2	1	2	2	2	2
Solution 30	2	2	2	2	2	1	2	2	2
Solution 31	2	2	2	2	2	2	2	1	2
Solution 32	2	2	2	2	2	2	2	2	2

Note that the restriction of this set of solutions to the pair of (identical) variables $\langle 0,2\rangle$ and $\langle 0,2\rangle$ gives the tuples $\langle 0,0\rangle$ and $\langle 2,2\rangle$. Hence, by Theorem 6, the relation $\{\langle 0,0\rangle,\langle 2,2\rangle\}$ can be expressed in the language $\{R_\times\}$.

Conversely, note that the restriction of this set of solutions to the variables $\langle 0,0\rangle$ and $\langle 0,1\rangle$ gives the tuples $\langle 0,0\rangle,\langle 0,1\rangle,\langle 2,1\rangle$ and $\langle 2,2\rangle$. Hence, by Theorem 6, the relation $\{\langle 0,0\rangle,\langle 0,1\rangle\}$ *cannot* be expressed in the language $\{R_\times\}$.

Theorem 6 states that in order to determine whether a relation R can be expressed in a language $\mathcal{L}$, it is sufficient to consider the indicator problem $\mathbf{IP}(\mathcal{L},m)$, where $m=|R|$. However, the size of these indicator problems grows rapidly with m. In some cases it is not necessary to build the indicator problem $\mathbf{IP}(\mathcal{L},m)$ because the relation can be expressed using an indicator problem $\mathbf{IP}(\mathcal{L},m')$, where $m'<m$, as the next example illustrates.

Example 10. Reconsider the relation $R_\times$ over $D=\{0,1,2\}$, defined in Example 7.

The indicator problem for $\{R_\times\}$ of order 2, $\mathbf{IP}(\{R_\times\},2)$, has 32 solutions, as shown in Example 9.

If we restrict the solutions to $\mathbf{IP}(\{R_\times\},2)$ to the variables $\langle 0,1\rangle$ and $\langle 1,1\rangle$, then we get the relation $R'_\times$, defined in Example 7, which contains 7 tuples. Hence, we have shown that $R'_\times$ can be expressed in the language $\{R_\times\}$ without building the indicator problem of order 7.

If we restrict the solutions to $\mathbf{IP}(\{R_\times\},2)$ to the variables $\langle 0,0\rangle$ and $\langle 0,1\rangle$, then we get the relation $R''_\times$ containing 4 tuples, defined as follows

$$R''_\times=\{\langle 0,0\rangle,\langle 0,1\rangle,\langle 2,1\rangle,\langle 2,2\rangle\}$$

Hence we have shown that $R''_\times$ can be expressed in the language $\{R_\times\}$ without building the indicator problem of order 4. (Note that $R''_\times$ is *not* symmetric, hence it also illustrates the fact that a language containing symmetric binary relations can express non-symmetric relations, in some cases).

6 Expressive power and complexity

In this section, we shall consider how the choice of constraint language, $\mathcal{L}$, affects the complexity of deciding whether the corresponding class of constraint satisfaction problems, CSP($\mathcal{L}$), has a solution. We shall therefore regard CSP($\mathcal{L}$) as a class of decision problems in which the question to be decided in each problem instance is the existence of a solution.

If there exists an algorithm which decides every instance in CSP($\mathcal{L}$) in polynomial time, then we shall say that $\mathcal{L}$ is a *tractable* constraint language. On the other hand, if CSP($\mathcal{L}$) is NP-complete, then we shall say that $\mathcal{L}$ is NP-complete.

Example 11. The binary inequality relation over a set D, denoted $\neq_D$, is defined as

$$\neq_D=\{\langle d_1,d_2\rangle\in D^2\mid d_1\neq d_2\}.$$

Note that CSP($\{\neq_D\}$) corresponds precisely to the GRAPH $|D|$-COLORABILITY problem [8]. This problem is tractable when $|D|\leq 2$ and NP-complete when $|D|\geq 3$. Hence, the language $\{\neq_D\}$ is tractable when $|D|\leq 2$, and NP-complete when $|D|\geq 3$.

The next result shows that if we can express a relation in a language, then we might as well add it to the language, because it will not change the complexity of the class of problems we are dealing with.

Proposition 7. *For any constraint language $\mathcal{L}$ and any relation R which can be expressed in $\mathcal{L}$,* CSP($\mathcal{L} \cup \{R\}$) *is reducible to* CSP($\mathcal{L}$) *in linear time and logarithmic space.*

Proof. Since R can be expressed in L we know that there is some problem $\mathbf{P}_R$ in CSP($\mathcal{L}$) for which the values of the solutions restricted to some list of variables, s, are precisely the elements of R.

Let $\mathbf{P}$ be any constraint satisfaction problem in CSP($\mathcal{L} \cup R$). We can reduce $\mathbf{P}$ to a constraint satisfaction problem in CSP($\mathcal{L}$) simply by examining each constraint C in turn, and whenever the constraint relation of C is R, then replacing C by (a disjoint copy of) the problem $\mathbf{P}_R$ described above, and then replacing each variable in s with the corresponding member of the scope of C.

Corollary 8. *For any constraint language $\mathcal{L}$, and any finite constraint language $\mathcal{L}_0$, if $\mathcal{L}_0 \subseteq \mathcal{L}^+$, then* CSP($\mathcal{L}_0$) *is reducible to* CSP($\mathcal{L}$) *in logarithmic space.*

Corollary 9. *Any constraint language $\mathcal{L}$ which can express all of the relations in some finite NP-complete language $\mathcal{L}_0$ is NP-complete.*

By using Corollary 9, together with Theorem 6, we can show that many languages are NP-complete by simply showing that they can express some known NP-complete language.

Example 12. The smallest known NP-complete language is the language containing the single relation $T = \{\langle 1,0,0\rangle, \langle 0,1,0\rangle, \langle 0,0,1\rangle\}$. The associated class of constraint satisfaction problems, CSP($\{T\}$), corresponds precisely to the ONE-IN-THREE SATISFIABILITY problem [21], which is NP-complete.

Hence, for any language $\mathcal{L}$, and any two domain elements d_0, d_1, if the solutions to $\mathbf{IP}(\mathcal{L}, 3)$, restricted to the variables $\langle d_1, d_0, d_0\rangle$, $\langle d_0, d_1, d_0\rangle$ and $\langle d_0, d_0, d_1\rangle$ is equal to $\{\langle d_1, d_0, d_0\rangle, \langle d_0, d_1, d_0\rangle, \langle d_0, d_0, d_1\rangle\}$, then $\mathcal{L}$ is NP-complete.

In particular, if $\mathbf{IP}(\mathcal{L}, 3)$ has only 3 solutions then $\mathcal{L}$ is NP-complete.

Note that this provides a purely mechanical procedure to establish NP-completeness of a constraint language, without having to design any specific reductions, or invent any new constructions.

Example 13. Reconsider the relation $R_\times$ over $D = \{0,1,2\}$, defined in Example 7.

The language $\{R_\times\}$ is clearly tractable, because any problem in CSP($\{R_\times\}$) has the trivial solution in which every variable takes the value 0.

However, if we consider the language $\mathcal{L}_0 = \{R_\times, R_0\}$, where $R_0 = \{\langle 0,1,2\rangle\}$ then we find that the indicator problem for $\mathcal{L}_0$ of order 3, $\mathbf{IP}(\mathcal{L}_0, 3)$, with 27 variables and 217 constraints, has only 3 solutions. Hence, $\mathcal{L}_0$ is NP-complete.

We can also conclude from Corollary 9 that if $\mathcal{L}$ is a tractable language, then it must be impossible to express in $\mathcal{L}$ any finite NP-complete language (assuming that P is not equal to NP). In view of Theorem 6, this means that tractable languages must have extra solutions to their indicator problems, in addition to the standard solutions that are present in all cases. The presence of these additional solutions provides an 'indicator' of tractability, and it is this which gives rise to the name 'indicator problem'[2].

Example 14. Let $\mathcal{L}$ be any Boolean constraint language (i.e. a set of relations over the domain $\{0, 1\}$).

In this case CSP($\mathcal{L}$) corresponds exactly to the GENERALISED SATISFIABILITY problem [8], for which all possible tractable constraint languages are known, and are fully described in [21]. The tractable languages fall into just 6 distinct classes, which are defined as follows:

Class 0a All relations in the language contain the tuple $\langle 0, 0, \ldots, 0\rangle$.
Class 0b All relations contain the tuple $\langle 1, 1, \ldots, 1\rangle$.
Class Ia All relations can be defined using Horn clauses.
Class Ib All relations can be defined using anti-Horn clauses[3].
Class II All relations can be defined using clauses with at most 2 literals.
Class III All relations can be defined using linear equations over the integers modulo 2.

If $\mathcal{L}$ does not fall into one of these 6 classes, then CSP($\mathcal{L}$) is NP-complete [21].

The indicator problem for $\mathcal{L}$ of order 3, **IP**($\mathcal{L}$, 3), has 8 variables, corresponding to the 8 possible Boolean sequences of length 3. It has 256 possible solutions, corresponding to the 256 possible assignments of Boolean values to these 8 variables.

Amongst these 256 possible solutions, we can identify 6 distinguished assignments as shown in the following table. It can be shown [11] that the language $\mathcal{L}$ falls into one of the 6 tractable classes described above if and only if **IP**($\mathcal{L}$, 3) has the corresponding solution, as shown in this table.

	Variables							
	$\langle 0,0,0\rangle$	$\langle 0,0,1\rangle$	$\langle 0,1,0\rangle$	$\langle 0,1,1\rangle$	$\langle 1,0,0\rangle$	$\langle 1,0,1\rangle$	$\langle 1,1,0\rangle$	$\langle 1,1,1\rangle$
Class 0a - Constant 0	0	0	0	0	0	0	0	0
Class 0b - Constant 1	1	1	1	1	1	1	1	1
Class Ia - Horn	0	0	0	0	0	0	1	1
Class Ib - Anti-Horn	0	0	1	1	1	1	1	1
Class II - 2-Sat	0	0	0	1	0	1	1	1
Class III - Linear	0	1	1	0	1	0	0	1

[2] Solutions to indicator problems can indicate other properties as well as tractability. For example, whether a certain level of local consistency is sufficient to ensure global consistency [12].

[3] An *anti-Horn* clause is a disjunction of literals, with at most one negative literal.

For larger finite domains it is still the case that all known maximal tractable constraint languages are characterised by the presence of a single additional solution to the indicator problem of order 3 [15]. This solution can be viewed as the 'signature' of that tractable language.

It is currently an open question whether all possible tractable languages are characterised by a single signature in this way. If this were true, it would mean that there are only a finite number of maximal tractable languages over any finite domain. However, with the current state of knowledge, it appears to be possible that there are tractable languages characterised only by the presence of more than one additional solution to the indicator problem of order 3, or by the presence of certain solutions to indicator problems of higher order, although none have so far been identified.

7 Conclusions and open problems

In this paper we have examined the notion of constraint languages, and the expressive power of constraint languages. We have shown that calculating the expressive power of a given language is not a trivial task, but for all languages over finite domains there is a universal construction involving the indicator problem which provides a complete algorithmic solution.

We have also examined how the complexity of a language can be related to the expressive power, and hence shown that the indicator problem can also be used to determine whether a language is NP-complete or tractable.

These investigations raise the following open questions:

1. Is there a more efficient universal construction to determine the expressive power of languages over finite domains?
2. Is there a universal construction for any language over an infinite domain?
3. Is every maximal tractable language over a finite domain characterised by a 'signature' solution to the indicator problem of order 3?
4. Is every constraint language either tractable or NP-complete?

Acknowledgements

This research was supported by EPSRC research grant GR/L09936. I am grateful to Dave Cohen and Victor Dalmau for many helpful discussions.

References

1. S. Bistarelli, U. Montanari, and F. Rossi. Semiring-based constraint solving and optimisation. *Journal of the ACM*, 44:201–236, 1997.
2. M.C. Cooper, D.A. Cohen, and P.G. Jeavons. Characterising tractable constraints. *Artificial Intelligence*, 65:347–361, 1994.
3. R. Dechter and J. Pearl. Tree clustering for constraint networks. *Artificial Intelligence*, 38:353–366, 1989.

4. R. Dechter and P. van Beek. Local and global relational consistency. *Theoretical Computer Science*, 173(1):283–308, 1997.
5. R.J. Duffin. Topology of series-parallel networks. *Journal of Mathematical Analysis and Applications*, 10:303–318, 1965.
6. E.C. Freuder. A sufficient condition for backtrack-free search. *Journal of the ACM*, 29(1):24–32, 1982.
7. E.C. Freuder. A sufficient condition for backtrack-bounded search. *Journal of the ACM*, 32:755–761, 1985.
8. M. Garey and D.S. Johnson. *Computers and Intractability: A Guide to the Theory of NP-Completeness.* Freeman, San Francisco, CA., 1979.
9. M. Gyssens, P.G. Jeavons, and D.A. Cohen. Decomposing constraint satisfaction problems using database techniques. *Artificial Intelligence*, 66(1):57–89, 1994.
10. T. Ihringer and R. Pöschel. Collapsing clones. *Acta Sci. Math. (Szeged)*, 58:99–113, 1993.
11. P.G. Jeavons and D.A. Cohen. An algebraic characterization of tractable constraints. In *Computing and Combinatorics. First International Conference COCOON'95 (Xi'an,China,August 1995)*, volume 959 of *Lecture Notes in Computer Science*, pages 633–642. Springer-Verlag, 1995.
12. P.G. Jeavons, D.A. Cohen, and M.C. Cooper. Constraints, consistency and closure. *Artificial Intelligence*, 101(1-2):251–265, 1998.
13. P.G. Jeavons, D.A. Cohen, and M. Gyssens. A unifying framework for tractable constraints. In *Proceedings 1st International Conference on Constraint Programming—CP'95 (Cassis, France, September 1995)*, volume 976 of *Lecture Notes in Computer Science*, pages 276–291. Springer-Verlag, 1995.
14. P.G. Jeavons, D.A. Cohen, and M. Gyssens. A test for tractability. In *Proceedings 2nd International Conference on Constraint Programming—CP'96 (Boston, August 1996)*, volume 1118 of *Lecture Notes in Computer Science*, pages 267–281. Springer-Verlag, 1996.
15. P.G. Jeavons, D.A. Cohen, and M. Gyssens. Closure properties of constraints. *Journal of the ACM*, 44:527–548, 1997.
16. P.G. Jeavons and M.C. Cooper. Tractable constraints on ordered domains. *Artificial Intelligence*, 79(2):327–339, 1995.
17. B. Jónsson. The theory of binary relations. In *Algebraic Logic (Budapest, Hungary 1988)*, volume 54 of *Colloq. Math. Soc. Janos Bolyai*, pages 245–292. North-Holland, 1991.
18. L. Kirousis. Fast parallel constraint satisfaction. *Artificial Intelligence*, 64:147–160, 1993.
19. A.K. Mackworth. Consistency in networks of relations. *Artificial Intelligence*, 8:99–118, 1977.
20. U. Montanari. Networks of constraints: Fundamental properties and applications to picture processing. *Information Sciences*, 7:95–132, 1974.
21. T.J. Schaefer. The complexity of satisfiability problems. In *Proceedings 10th ACM Symposium on Theory of Computing (STOC)*, pages 216–226, 1978.
22. E. Tsang. *Foundations of Constraint Satisfaction.* Academic Press, London, 1993.
23. P. van Beek and R. Dechter. On the minimality and decomposability of row-convex constraint networks. *Journal of the ACM*, 42:543–561, 1995.
24. P. van Hentenryck, Y. Deville, and C-M. Teng. A generic arc-consistency algorithm and its specializations. *Artificial Intelligence*, 57:291–321, 1992.

The Dynamics of Dynamic Variable Ordering Heuristics

Patrick Prosser

Department of Computer Science, University of Strathclyde, Glasgow G1 1XH, Scotland. E-mail: pat@cs.strath.ac.uk

Abstract. It has long been accepted that dynamic variable ordering heuristics outperform static orderings. But just how dynamic are dynamic variable ordering heuristics? This paper examines the behaviour of a number of heuristics, and attempts to measure the entropy of the search process at different depths in the search tree.

1 Introduction

Many studies have shown that dynamic variable ordering (dvo [9]) heuristics out perform static variable ordering heuristics. But just how dynamic are dynamic variable ordering heuristics? This might be important because if we discover that some dvo heuristic H_1 results in less search effort than heuristic H_2 and H_1 is more dynamic than H_2 then we might expect that we can make a further improvement by increasing the dynamism of H_1. Conversely if we discover that H_1 is better and less dynamic then we might plan to make H_1 even more ponderous. But how do we measure the dynamism of a heuristic? To investigate this we first look inside the search process, and define our measure of entropy. We then measure entropy for a variety of heuristics. A further examination of the search process reveals that the different heuristics have different *signatures*, distributing their search effort over different depths of the search tree.

2 Inside Search

Tabulated below is the number of selections of each variable at each depth in the search tree, for a single instance of a randomly generated binary csp, $\langle 20, 10, 0.5, 0.37\rangle$[1], as seen by a forward checking routine with a dynamic variable ordering heuristic. Each row corresponds to a depth in search (20 in all) and each column represents a variable (again, 20 in all, with the first column entry being row/depth number). Looking at row 3 for example we see that variable V_3 was selected 8 times, variable V_7 selected once, V_8 selected 3 times, and so on. A variable V_i is *selected* at depth d if at depth $d-1$ the current variable is consistently instantiated and the next variable selected by the heuristic at depth d is V_i. The data below corresponds to a single soluble instance.

[1] The problem has 20 variables, each with a domain of 10 values. The proportion of constraints in the graph is 0.5, and the proportion of possible pairs of values in conflict across a constraint is 0.37.

	Visits at Depth	Entropy
1	1 0 0 0 0 0 0 0 0 0 0 0 0 0 0 0 0 0 0 0	0.0
2	0 0 0 0 0 0 0 0 0 0 0 0 0 0 0 0 3 0 0 0	0.0
3	0 0 8 0 0 0 1 3 0 0 2 0 0 0 1 1 0 0 1 0	2.28
4	0 7 5 1 0 0 8 3 0 0 1 0 4 0 0 11 0 0 3 0	2.85
5	0 2 5 2 2 0 6 4 7 0 3 0 3 0 0 5 0 0 11 0	3.24
6	0 3 1 2 0 0 3 2 2 0 2 0 3 0 2 4 0 0 5 1	3.44
7	0 4 0 0 1 1 1 1 0 2 0 0 2 2 0 0 0 0 0 3	2.98
8	0 0 0 0 2 0 1 0 0 3 1 0 1 0 1 0 0 1 0 1	2.85
9	0 1 0 1 1 0 0 0 0 1 0 0 0 0 0 0 0 0 0 0	2.0
10	0 0 0 1 0 0 0 0 1 0 0 0 0 0 0 0 0 0 0 0	1.0
11	0 0 0 0 0 0 0 0 0 0 0 0 0 1 0 0 0 0 0 0	0.0
12	0 0 0 0 0 0 0 0 0 0 0 0 0 0 0 1 0 0 0 0	0.0
13	0 0 0 0 0 0 0 0 0 0 0 1 0 0 0 0 0 0 0 0	0.0
14	0 0 0 0 0 0 0 0 0 0 0 0 1 0 0 0 0 0 0 0	0.0
15	0 0 0 0 0 0 0 0 0 0 1 0 0 0 0 0 0 0 0 0	0.0
16	0 0 0 0 0 1 0 0 0 0 0 0 0 0 0 0 0 0 0 0	0.0
17	0 0 0 0 0 0 1 0 0 0 0 0 0 0 0 0 0 0 0 0	0.0
18	0 0 0 0 0 0 0 0 0 0 0 0 0 0 1 0 0 0 0 0	0.0
19	0 1 0 0 0 0 0 0 0 0 0 0 0 0 0 0 0 0 0 0	0.0
20	0 0 0 0 1 0 0 0 0 0 0 0 0 0 0 0 0 0 0 0	0.0

The column out to the right is the measured value of *entropy* for the data in that row.

3 Entropy

Entropy is a measure of the disorder within a system, or the information within the system (i.e. the number of bits required to represent that system). If the system is totally ordered, we will require few bits of information to represent the system, and it will have low entropy. If the system is very disordered we will require many bits to describe the system, and it will have high entropy. Therefore, we might measure the entropy resulting from the variable ordering heuristic at each depth in the search tree. If the heuristic is static, always selecting the same variable at a given depth, then entropy will be a minimum. If the heuristic is very dynamic, selecting freely any future variable at a given depth, entropy should be a maximum.

From thermodynamics, entropy is $k.log(w)$ where k is Boltzmann's constant and w is the *disorder* parameter, the probability that the system will stay in its current state rather than any other state. For our application we measure entropy at depth d as

$$\sum_{i=1}^{n} -p_{d,i}.log_2(p_{d,i}) \tag{1}$$

where $p_{d,i}$ is the probability of selecting variable V_i at depth d. Looking at the tabulation above, for the first row $d = 1$, only one variable is selected at this depth (the root of the search tree) and entropy is zero. At depth $d = 2$ we see that only V_{17} is visited, but three times. Again $p_{2,17} = 1$ and entropy is again zero. The third row $d = 3$, there are 17 visits at this depth, variable V_3 is visited 8 times, consequently $p_{3,3} = 8/17$, $p_{3,7} = 1/17$, $p_{3,8} = 3/17$, and so on. The entropy at depth $d = 3$ is then

```
-[8/17.log(8/17) + 1/17.log(1/17) + 3/17.log(3/17) +
  2/17.log(2/17) + 1/17.log(1/17) + 1/17.log(1/17) +
  1/17.log(1/17)]
= 2.28
```

If all the n variables are selected the same number of times at depth d, then the entropy at that depth is $log_2(n)$, and this is a maximum, the number of bits required to represent the n variables selected. Conversely if only 1 variable is ever selected at depth d then entropy at that depth is zero (we require no bits to represent this). If a dvo heuristic is highly dynamic at a certain depth we expect a correspondingly high entropy, and if the variable ordering is static we have zero entropy.

4 Entropy at Depth

Experiments were carried out on 100 instances of $\langle 20, 10, 0.5, 0.37 \rangle$ problems (from the crossover point [7]). Of these, 54 were soluble and 46 insoluble. The search algorithm used was forward checking with conflict-directed backjumping (fc-cbj [8]). Five heuristics were investigated:

- FF, fail-first, choosing the variable with smallest current domain, tie breaking randomly [6, 9].
- BZ, Brelaz heuristic, essentially FF tie breaking on the variable with most constraints acting into the future subproblem, and tie breaking further randomly [1].
- GEL, Geelen's combined variable and value ordering heuristic, selecting the most promising value for the least promising variable [2].
- KP, the minimise-κ heuristic, selecting the variable that leaves the future subproblem with the lowest κ value [5].
- RAND, a random selection at each point. When a variable is selected we pick at random from the future variables. RAND is the *straw man* to show just what effect natural dynamism has on entropy at depth.

We might say that as we move from FF to BZ to KP to GEL we move towards more informed heuristics.

Figure 1 shows average entropy at depth (on the left) for the 54 soluble instances, and (on the right) for the 46 insoluble instances. A contour is given for each of the heuristics. The contour for RAND (our straw man) shows that at depths 5 to about 12 entropy is constant at about 4.2, and this corresponds closely to what theory predicts. That is, at depth 1 a variable has been selected and is withdrawn from future selections. Consequently greater depths can select

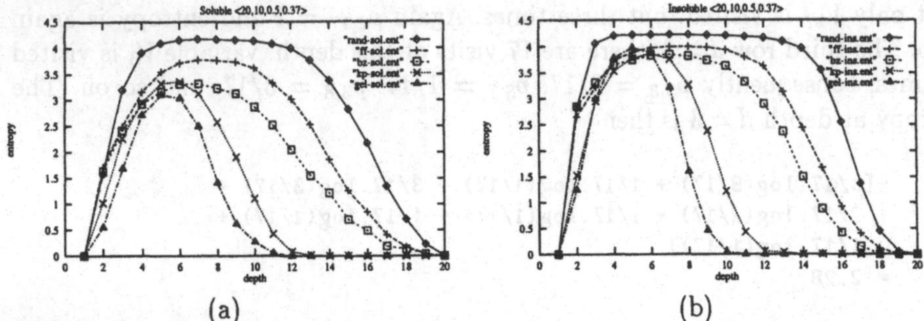

Fig. 1. Entropy at Depth for ⟨20, 10, 0.5, 0.37⟩ problems; on the left (a) 54 soluble problems, and on the right (b) 46 insoluble problems. Note that the tail of the contours in (b) for RAND, FF, and BZ have relatively small sample sizes.

from at most 19 variables. If each variable is selected at a given depth with equal probability entropy will be $log_2(19) \approx 4.25$, and this is what we observe.

The FF heuristic is significantly different from RAND; entropy is generally lower at all depths, and entropy falls away at a shallower depth. More generally, what we see is less entropic behaviour as heuristics become more informed. This pattern appears to hold, but maybe to a lesser extent over insoluble problems (Figure 1(b)).

5 Effort inside search

We now investigate how effort is distributed across the depths of search. First we tabulate the overall performance of the heuristics, in terms of consistency checks and nodes visited.

	Soluble		Insoluble	
	Checks	Nodes	Checks	Nodes
RAND	444.8	29.7	1216.7	80.3
FF	29.1	1.1	68.8	2.7
BZ	15.4	0.6	34.8	1.3
KP	16.8	0.7	37.8	1.6
GEL	16.8	0.7	59.6	2.6

The table above shows for each heuristic the performance measured as the average number of consistency checks (measured in thousands) for the soluble and the insoluble problems, and nodes visited (again in thousands). No claims are drawn from the above results, for example that one heuristic is better than another, because the sample size is too small and the problem data too specific[2].

[2] For example, we will get a different ranking of the heuristics if we vary problem features[3].

The contours in Figure 2 show, for the RAND heuristic, the average number of consistency checks performed at varying depths in the search tree, nodes visited, and variables selected. Note that the y-axis is a logscale. The curves look quite natural, with the peak in search effort taking place in the first third of search.

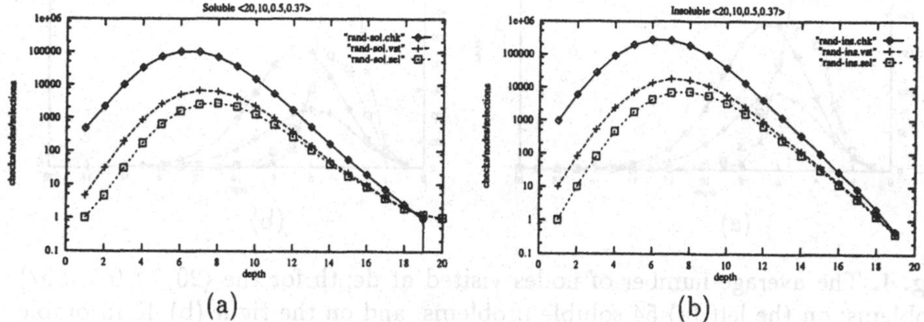

Fig. 2. Average Checks, Nodes Visited and Variables Selected at Depth for ⟨20, 10, 0.5, 0.37⟩ problems using RAND dvo; on the left (a) 54 soluble problems, and on the right (b) 46 insoluble problems.

Figure 3 shows average consistency checks only, for the four dvo's: FF, BZ, KP, and GEL. The contours are very different from RAND, compressing the search effort into a relatively narrow band at shallow depth. Also note that KP and GEL typically dispense with search after depth 9, thereafter walking to the solution without backtracking. Figure 3 suggests that each heuristic has a different signature. KP and GEL appear to squeeze all the search effort up to a shallow depth, and are reminiscent of the different signatures of forward checking and mac-based algorithms [10].

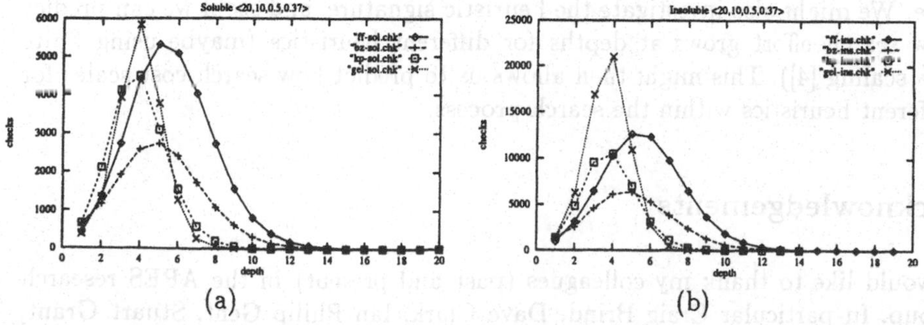

Fig. 3. Average Checks at Depth for ⟨20, 10, 0.5, 0.37⟩ problems; on the left (a) 54 soluble problems, and on the right (b) 46 insoluble problems.

Figure 4 shows the average number of nodes visited by each of the heuristics (excluding RAND) at various depths. These contours are very similar to those in Figure 3, as expected, showing that consistency checks correlate with visits.

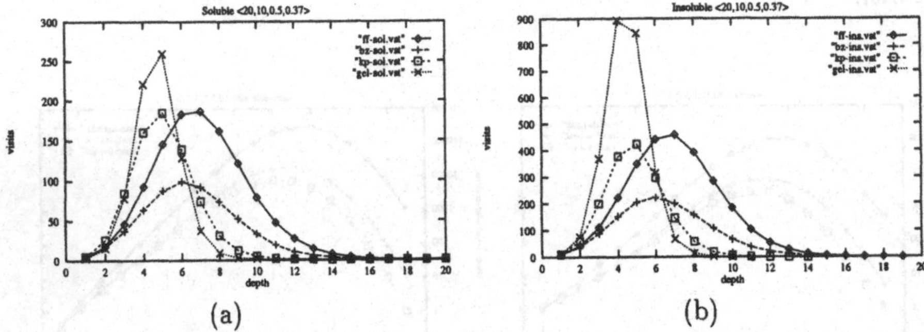

Fig. 4. The average number of nodes visited at depth for the $\langle 20, 10, 0.5, 0.37 \rangle$ problems; on the left (a) 54 soluble problems, and on the right (b) 46 insoluble problems.

6 Conclusion

A small empirical study has been presented, investigating the behaviour of dynamic variable ordering heuristics. We have attempted to measure the dynamism of dvo heuristics using entropy, and it appears that the more informed a heuristic the less entropic/dynamic its behaviour. We also see that the heuristics examined have markedly different signatures, moving the search effort to different depths in the search tree.

Further work should be done, in particular different ways of measuring entropy should be explored. Rather than measure it across depths in the search tree, maybe it can be measured along paths, or maybe just arcs in the search tree. We might also investigate the heuristic signature, and see if we can predict how search effort grows at depths for different heuristics (maybe using finite size scaling [4]). This might then allows us to predict how search cost scales for different heuristics within the search process.

Acknowledgements

I would like to thank my colleagues (past and present) in the APES research group. In particular Craig Brind, Dave Clark, Ian Philip Gent, Stuart Grant, Phil Kilby, Ewan MacIntyre, Andrea Prosser, Paul Shaw, Barbara Smith, Kostas Stergiou, Judith Underwood, and Toby Walsh. I would also like to thank Peter van Beek for encouraging us to ask such interesting questions.

References

1. D. Brelaz. New methods to color the vertices of a graph. *JACM*, 22(4):251–256, 1979.
2. P.A. Geelen. Dual viewpoint heuristics for the binary constraint satisfaction problem. In *Proc. ECAI92*, pages 31–35, 1992.
3. I.P. Gent, E. MacIntyre, P. Prosser, B.M. Smith, and T. Walsh. An empirical study of dynamic variable ordering heuristics for constraint satisfaction problems. In *Proc. CP96*, pages 179–193, 1996.
4. I.P. Gent, E. MacIntyre, P. Prosser, and T. Walsh. Scaling effects in the CSP phase transition. In *Principles and Practice of Constraint Programming*, pages 70–87. Springer, 1995.
5. I.P. Gent, E. MacIntyre, P. Prosser, and T. Walsh. The constrainedness of search. In *Proc. AAAI-96*, 1996.
6. R.M. Haralick and G.L. Elliott. Increasing tree search efficiency for constraint satisfaction problems. *Artificial Intelligence*, 14:263–313, 1980.
7. T. Hogg, B.A. Huberman, and C.P. Williams. Phase transitions and the search problem (editorial). *Artificial Intelligence*, 81(1-2):1–15, 1996.
8. P. Prosser. Hybrid algorithms for the constraint satisfaction problem. *Computational Intelligence*, 9(3):268–299, 1993.
9. P.W. Purdom. Search rearrangement backtracking and polynomial average time. *Artificial Intelligence*, 21:117–133, 1983.
10. D. Sabin and E.C. Freuder. Contradicting conventional wisdom in constraint satisfaction. In *Proc. ECAI-94*, pages 125–129, 1994.

On Completion of Constraint Handling Rules

Slim Abdennadher and Thom Frühwirth

Computer Science Institute, University of Munich
Oettingenstr. 67, 80538 München, Germany
{Slim.Abdennadher, Thom.Fruehwirth}@informatik.uni-muenchen.de

Abstract. Constraint Handling Rules (CHR) is a high-level language for writing constraint solvers either from scratch or by modifying existing solvers. An important property of any constraint solver is confluence: The result of a computation should be independent from the order in which constraints arrive and in which rules are applied. In previous work [1], a sufficient and necessary condition for the confluence of terminating CHR programs was given by adapting and extending results about conditional term rewriting systems. In this paper we investigate so-called completion methods that make a non-confluent CHR program confluent by adding new rules. As it turns out, completion can also exhibit inconsistency of a CHR program. Moreover, as shown in this paper, completion can be used to define new constraints in terms of already existing constraints and to derive constraint solvers for them.

1 Introduction

Constraint Handling Rules (CHR) is our proposal to allow more flexibility and application-oriented customization of constraint systems. CHR is a declarative language extension especially designed for writing user-defined constraints. CHR is essentially a committed-choice language consisting of multi-headed guarded rules that rewrite constraints into simpler ones until they are solved. CHR defines both *simplification* of and *propagation* over user-defined constraints. Simplification replaces constraints by simpler constraints while preserving logical equivalence. Propagation adds new constraints, which are logically redundant but may cause further simplification.
As a special-purpose language for constraints, CHR aims to fulfill the promise of user-defined constraints as described in [4]: "For the theoretician meta-theorems can be proved and analysis techniques invented once and for all; for the implementor different constructs (backward and forward chaining, suspension, compiler optimization, debugging) can be implemented once and for all; for the user only one set of ideas need to be understood, though with rich (albeit disciplined) variations (constraint systems)."
We have already shown in previous work [1] that analysis techniques are available for an important property of any constraint solver, namely confluence: The result of a computation should be independent from the order in which constraints arrive and in which rules are applied. For confluence of terminating CHR programs we were able to give a sufficient and necessary condition by adapting and extending work done in conditional term rewriting systems (TRS).

In this paper we investigate so-called completion methods as known from TRS [12]. Completion is the process of adding rules to a non-confluent set of rules until it becomes confluent. Once again, we have to adapt and extend the results from TRS to be applicable for CHR. As it turns out, our completion method for CHR can also exhibit inconsistency of the logical meaning of a CHR program.
A practical application of our completion method lies in software development. Completion can be used to define new constraints in terms of already existing ones and to derive constraint solvers for them. Furthermore, completion can be used as a method to provide generic answers given as a set of rules. In this way, completion helps the CHR programmer to extend, modify and specialize existing solvers instead of having to write them from scratch.
This paper is organized as follows. In Section 2 we define the CHR language and summarize previous confluence results. Section 3 presents our completion method for CHR, including a fair algorithm, a correctness theorem and a theorem relating completion and consistency. In Section 4 we give further examples for the use of our completion method. Finally, we conclude with a summary.

2 Preliminaries

In this section we give an overview of syntax and semantics as well as confluence results for CHR. More detailed presentations can be found in [1, 2]. We assume some familiarity with (concurrent) constraint (logic) programming [14, 11, 13].

2.1 Syntax of CHR

A *constraint* is a first order atom. We use two disjoint kinds of predicate symbols for two different classes of constraints: One kind for *built-in* constraints and one kind for *user-defined* constraints. Built-in constraints are those handled by a predefined constraint solver that already exists as a certified black-box solver. Typical built-in constraints include *true*, *false* and =. User-defined constraints are those defined by a CHR program.
A *CHR program* is a finite set of rules. There are two basic kinds of rules[1].
A *simplification rule* is of the form

$$Rulename\ @\ H \Leftrightarrow C \mid B.$$

A *propagation rule* is of the form

$$Rulename\ @\ H \Rightarrow C \mid B,$$

where *Rulename* is a unique identifier of a rule, the head H is a non-empty conjunction of user-defined constraints, the guard C is a conjunction of built-in constraints and the body B is a conjunction of built-in and user-defined constraints. Conjunctions of constraints as in the body are called *goals*. A guard "*true*" is usually omitted together with the vertical bar.

[1] Their syntax is inspired by concurrent logic programming languages like GHC.

2.2 Declarative Semantics of CHR

The logical meaning of a simplification rule is a logical equivalence provided the guard holds

$$\forall \bar{x} \, (C \rightarrow (H \leftrightarrow \exists \bar{y} \, B)).$$

The logical meaning of a propagation rule is an implication if the guard holds

$$\forall \bar{x} \, (C \rightarrow (H \rightarrow \exists \bar{y} \, B)),$$

where $\bar{x}$ is the list of variables occuring in H or in C and $\bar{y}$ are the variables occuring in B only.
The logical meaning $\mathcal{P}$ of a CHR program P is the conjunction of the logical meanings of its rules united with a (consistent) constraint theory CT that defines the built-in constraints. We require CT to define $=$ as syntactic equality.

2.3 Operational Semantics of CHR

The operational semantics of CHR is given by a transition system.
A *state* is a triple

$$<G, C_U, C_B>,$$

where G is a conjunction of user-defined and built-in constraints called *goal store*. C_U is a conjunction of user-defined constraints. C_B is a conjunction of built-in constraints. C_U and C_B are called *user-defined* and *built-in (constraint) stores*, respectively. An empty goal or user-defined store is represented by $\top$. An empty built-in store is represented by *true*.
Given a CHR program P we define the transition relation $\longmapsto$ by introducing four kinds of computation steps (Figure 1). In the figure, all meta-variables stand for conjunctions of constraints. An equation $c(t_1, \ldots, t_n) = d(s_1, \ldots, s_n)$ of two constraints stands for $t_1 = s_1 \wedge \ldots \wedge t_n = s_n$ if c and d are the same predicate symbol and for *false* otherwise. An equation $(p_1 \wedge \ldots \wedge p_n) = (q_1 \wedge \ldots \wedge q_m)$ stands for $p_1 = q_1 \wedge \ldots \wedge p_n = q_n$ if $n = m$ and for *false* otherwise. Note that conjuncts can be permuted since conjunction is associative and commutative.[2]
In the **Solve** computation step, the built-in solver produces a new normalized constraint store C'_B that is logically equivalent (according to the constraint theory CT) to the conjunction of the new constraint C and the old constraint store C_B. **Introduce** transports a user-defined constraint H from the goal store into the user-defined constraint store. There it can be handled with other user-defined constraints by applying CHR.
To **Simplify** user-defined constraints H' means to remove them from the user-defined store and to add the body B of a fresh variant of a simplification rule $(R \; @ \; H \Leftrightarrow C \mid B)$ to the goal store and the equation $H = H'$ and the guard C to the built-in store, provided H' matches the head H and the guard C is implied by the built-in constraint store C_B. Note that "matching" means that

[2] For technical reasons, we consider conjunctions of constraints not to be idempotent.

Solve

$$\frac{C \text{ is a built-in constraint} \quad CT \models C_B \land C \leftrightarrow C'_B}{<C \land G, C_U, C_B> \mapsto <G, C_U, C'_B>}$$

Introduce

$$\frac{H \text{ is a user-defined constraint}}{<H \land G, C_U, C_B> \mapsto <G, H \land C_U, C_B>}$$

Simplify

$(R\,@\,H \Leftrightarrow C \mid B)$ is a fresh variant of a rule in P with the variables $\bar{x}$

$$\frac{CT \models C_B \rightarrow \exists \bar{x}(H{=}H' \land C)}{<G, H' \land C_U, C_B> \mapsto <G \land B, C_U, C \land H{=}H' \land C_B>}$$

Propagate

$(R\,@\,H \Rightarrow C \mid B)$ is a fresh variant of a rule in P with the variables $\bar{x}$

$$\frac{CT \models C_B \rightarrow \exists \bar{x}(H{=}H' \land C)}{<G, H' \land C_U, C_B> \mapsto <G \land B, H' \land C_U, C \land H{=}H' \land C_B>}$$

Fig. 1. Computation Steps

it is only allowed to instantiate variables of H but not variables of H'. In the logical notation this is achieved by existentially quantifying only over the fresh variables $\bar{x}$ of the rule to be applied.

The **Propagate** transition is similar to the **Simplify** transition, but retains the user-defined constraints H' in the user-defined store. Trivial nontermination caused by applying the same propagation rule again and again is avoided by applying a propagation rule at most once to the same constraints. A more complex operational semantics that addresses this issue can be found in [1].

An *initial state* for a goal G is of the form $<G, \top, \mathit{true}>$. A *final state* is either of the form $<G, C_U, \mathit{false}>$ (such a state is called *failed*) or of the form $<\top, C_U, C_B>$ with no computation step possible anymore and C_B not *false* (such a state is called *successful*).

A *computation* of a goal G is a sequence $S_0, S_1, \ldots$ of states with $S_i \mapsto S_{i+1}$ beginning with the initial state for G and ending in a final state or diverging. $\mapsto^*$ denotes the reflexive and transitive closure of $\mapsto$.

Example 1. We define a user-defined constraint for a (partial) order $\leq$ that can handle variable arguments.

```
r1 @ X ≤ X ⇔ true.
r2 @ X ≤ Y ∧ Y ≤ X ⇔ X=Y.
r3 @ X ≤ Y ∧ Y ≤ Z ⇒ X ≤ Z.
r4 @ X ≤ Y ∧ X ≤ Y ⇔ X ≤ Y.
```

The CHR program implements reflexivity (r1), antisymmetry (r2), transitivity (r3) and idempotence (r4) in a straightforward way. The reflexivity rule r1 states that X≤X is logically true. The antisymmetry rule r2 means that if we find X≤Y as well as Y≤X in the current store, we can replace them by the logically equivalent X=Y. The transitivity rule r3 propagates constraints. It states that the conjunction of X≤Y and Y≤Z implies X≤Z. Operationally, we add the logical consequence X≤Z as a redundant constraint. The idempotence rule r4 absorbs multiple occurrences of the same constraint.
In the following computation constraints which are considered in the current computation step are underlined:

$$\begin{array}{ll}
 & <\underline{A \leq B} \wedge \underline{C \leq A} \wedge \underline{B \leq C}, \top, \mathbf{true}> \\
\mapsto^{*}_{\mathbf{Introduce}} & <\top, \underline{A \leq B} \wedge \underline{C \leq A} \wedge B \leq C, \mathbf{true}> \\
\mapsto_{\mathbf{Propagate}} & <\underline{C \leq B}, A \leq B \wedge C \leq A \wedge B \leq C, \mathbf{true}> \\
\mapsto_{\mathbf{Introduce}} & <\top, A \leq B \wedge C \leq A \wedge \underline{B \leq C} \wedge \underline{C \leq B}, \mathbf{true}> \\
\mapsto_{\mathbf{Simplify}} & <\underline{B = C}, A \leq B \wedge C \leq A, \mathbf{true}> \\
\mapsto_{\mathbf{Solve}} & <\top, \underline{A \leq B} \wedge \underline{C \leq A}, B = C> \\
\mapsto_{\mathbf{Simplify}} & <\underline{A = B}, \top, B = C> \\
\mapsto_{\mathbf{Solve}} & <\top, \top, A = B \wedge B = C>
\end{array}$$

2.4 Confluence

The confluence property of a program guarantees that any computation starting from an arbitrary initial state, i.e. any possible order of rule applications, results in the same final state. Due to space limitations, we can just give an overview on confluence where some definitions are left informal. Detailed confluence results for CHR can be found in [1, 2, 3]. The papers adopt and extend the terminology and techniques of conditional TRS [8] about confluence. Our extensions enable handling of propagation rules, global context (the built-in constraint store) and local variables.
We require that states are normalized so that they can be compared syntactically in a meaningful way. Basically, we require that the built-in constraints are in a (unique) normal form, where all syntactical equalities are made explicit and are propagated to all components of the state. The normalization also has to make all failed states syntactically identical.

Definition 1. A CHR program is called *confluent* if for all states S, S_1, S_2: If $S \mapsto^* S_1$ and $S \mapsto^* S_2$ then S_1 and S_2 are joinable. Two states S_1 and S_2 are called *joinable* if there exists a state T such that $S_1 \mapsto^* T$ and $S_2 \mapsto^* T$.

To analyze confluence of a given CHR program we cannot check joinability starting from any given ancestor state S, because in general there are infinitely many such states. However one can construct a finite number of "minimal" states where more than one rule is applicable (and thus more than one transition possible) based on the following observations: First, adding constraints to the components of the state cannot inhibit the application of a rule as long as the

built-in constraint store remains consistent (monotonicity property). Second, joinability can only be destroyed if one rule inhibits the application of another rule. Only the removal of constraints can affect the applicability of another rule, in case the removed constraint is needed by the other rule.
By monotonicity, we can restrict ourselves to ancestor states that consist of the head and guards of two rules. To possibly destroy joinability, at least one rule must be a simplification rule and the two rules must *overlap*, i.e. have at least one head atom in common in the ancestor state. This is achieved by equating head atoms in the state.

Definition 2. Given a simplification rule R_1 and an arbitrary (not necessarily different) rule R_2, whose variables have been renamed apart. Let G_i denote the guard ($i = 1, 2$). Let H_i^c and H_i be a partition of the head of the rule R_i into two conjunctions, where H_i^c is nonempty. Then a *critical ancestor state* S *of* R_1 *and* R_2 is

$$<\top, H_1^c \wedge H_1 \wedge H_2, (H_1^c = H_2^c) \wedge G_1 \wedge G_2>,$$

provided $(H_1^c = H_2^c) \wedge G_1 \wedge G_2$ is consistent in CT.

The application of R_1 and R_2, respectively, to S leads to two states that form the so-called *critical pair*.

Definition 3. Let S be a critical ancestor state of R_1 and R_2. If $S \mapsto S_1$ using rule R_1 and $S \mapsto S_2$ using rule R_2 then the tuple (S_1, S_2) is the *critical pair* of R_1 and R_2. A critical pair (S_1, S_2) is *joinable*, if S_1 and S_2 are joinable.

Example 2. Consider the program for $\leq$ of Example 1. The following critical pair stems from the critical ancestor state[3] $<\top, \mathtt{X} \leq \mathtt{Y} \wedge \mathtt{Y} \leq \mathtt{X} \wedge \mathtt{Y} \leq \mathtt{Z}, \mathtt{true}>$ of r2 and r3:

$$(S_1, S_2) := (<\mathtt{X} = \mathtt{Y}, \mathtt{Y} \leq \mathtt{Z}, \mathtt{true}>, <\mathtt{X} \leq \mathtt{Z}, \mathtt{X} \leq \mathtt{Y} \wedge \mathtt{Y} \leq \mathtt{Z} \wedge \mathtt{Y} \leq \mathtt{X}, \mathtt{true}>)$$

It is joinable. A computation beginning with S_1 proceeds as follows:

$$\begin{array}{ll} & <\underline{\mathtt{X} = \mathtt{Y}}, \mathtt{Y} \leq \mathtt{Z}, \mathtt{true}> \\ \mapsto_{\mathbf{Solve}} & <\top, \mathtt{X} \leq \mathtt{Z}, \mathtt{X} = \mathtt{Y}> \end{array}$$

A computation beginning with S_2 results in the same final state:

$$\begin{array}{ll} & <\underline{\mathtt{X} \leq \mathtt{Z}}, \mathtt{X} \leq \mathtt{Y} \wedge \mathtt{Y} \leq \mathtt{Z} \wedge \mathtt{Y} \leq \mathtt{X}, \mathtt{true}> \\ \mapsto_{\mathbf{Introduce}} & <\top, \mathtt{X} \leq \mathtt{Z} \wedge \underline{\mathtt{X} \leq \mathtt{Y}} \wedge \mathtt{Y} \leq \mathtt{Z} \wedge \underline{\mathtt{Y} \leq \mathtt{X}}, \mathtt{true}> \\ \mapsto_{\mathbf{Simplify}} & <\underline{\mathtt{X} = \mathtt{Y}}, \mathtt{X} \leq \mathtt{Z} \wedge \mathtt{Y} \leq \mathtt{Z}, \mathtt{true}> \\ \mapsto_{\mathbf{Solve}} & <\top, \underline{\mathtt{X} \leq \mathtt{Z}} \wedge \underline{\mathtt{X} \leq \mathtt{Z}}, \mathtt{X} = \mathtt{Y}> \\ \mapsto_{\mathbf{Simplify}} & <\top, \mathtt{X} \leq \mathtt{Z}, \mathtt{X} = \mathtt{Y}> \end{array}$$

Definition 4. A CHR program is called *terminating*, if there are no infinite computations.

---

[3] Variables from different rules already identified to have an overlap; for readability.

For most existing CHR programs it is straightforward to prove termination using simple well-founded orderings. Otherwise it seems impossible without relying on implementational details [10].
The following theorem from [1] gives a decidable, sufficient and necessary criterion for confluence of a terminating program:

Theorem 5. A terminating CHR program is confluent iff all its critical pairs are joinable.

3 Completion

The idea of completion as developed for term rewriting systems (TRS) is to derive a rule from a non-joinable critical pair that would allow a transition from one of the critical states into the other one, thus re-introducing confluence [12]. In analogy to completion algorithms for TRS [5], our algorithm for CHR maintains a set C of critical pairs and a set P of rules. These sets are manipulated by four inference rules (Figure 2). Terminology is taken from TRS. We write $(C, P) \longmapsto (C', P')$ to indicate that the pair (C', P') can be obtained from (C, P) by an application of an inference rule.

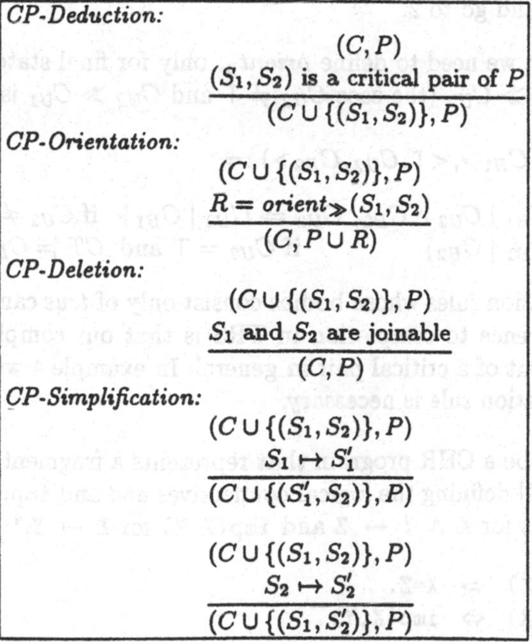

CP-Deduction:

$$\frac{(C,P) \quad (S_1,S_2) \text{ is a critical pair of } P}{(C\cup\{(S_1,S_2)\},P)}$$

CP-Orientation:

$$\frac{(C\cup\{(S_1,S_2)\},P) \quad R = orient_{\gg}(S_1,S_2)}{(C,P\cup R)}$$

CP-Deletion:

$$\frac{(C\cup\{(S_1,S_2)\},P) \quad S_1 \text{ and } S_2 \text{ are joinable}}{(C,P)}$$

CP-Simplification:

$$\frac{(C\cup\{(S_1,S_2)\},P) \quad S_1 \mapsto S_1'}{(C\cup\{(S_1',S_2)\},P)}$$

$$\frac{(C\cup\{(S_1,S_2)\},P) \quad S_2 \mapsto S_2'}{(C\cup\{(S_1,S_2')\},P)}$$

Fig. 2. Inference rules of completion

The rule *CP-Deduction* permits to add critical pairs to C. *CP-Orientation* removes a critical pair from C and adds new rules to P, provided the critical pair can be oriented with respect to the termination ordering $\gg$. In contrast to completion methods for TRS, we need - as examplified below - more than one rule to make a critical pair joinable. With the inference rules *CP-Deletion* and *CP-Simplification*, C can be simplified. The rule *CP-Deletion* removes a joinable critical pair. The rule *CP-Simplification* replaces state in a critical pair by its successor state.
Different versions of completion differ in which critical pair they "orient" first and in how they keep track of critical pairs that still need to be processed. A version of completion is *fair* if it does not avoid processing any critical pair infinitely often. One simple fair version of completion is to use the following strategy:

1. Set $i := 0$ and begin with the set of the rules $P_0 := P$ and their non-joinable critical pairs C_0.
2. If $C_i = \emptyset$, stop successfully with $P' = P_i$.
3. Let C_i be $C \cup \{(S_1, S_2)\}$. Then $(C \cup \{(S_1, S_2)\}, P_i) \longmapsto^*_{CP-Simplification} (C \cup \{(T_1, T_2)\}, P_i)$, such that T_1 and T_2 are final states. If $R = orient_{\gg}(T_1, T_2)$, then $P_{i+1} := P_i \cup R$. Otherwise abort unsuccessfully.
4. Form all critical pairs between a rule of R and all rules of P_{i+1} by the inference rule *CP-Deduction*. To produce C_{i+1}, add these critical pairs to C_i and then remove all (in P_{i+1}) joinable critical pairs by the inference rule *CP-Deletion*.
5. Set $i := i + 1$ and go to 2.

With this strategy, we need to define $orient_{\gg}$ only for final states. For the case $C_{U1} \neq \top$ and $C_{U1} \gg C_{U2}$ (the case $C_{U2} \neq \top$ and $C_{U2} \gg C_{U1}$ is analogous) we define
$orient_{\gg}(<\top, C_{U1}, C_{B1}>, <\top, C_{U2}, C_{B2}>) :=$

$$\begin{cases} \{C_{U1} \Leftrightarrow C_{B1} \mid C_{U2} \wedge C_{B2},\ C_{U2} \Rightarrow C_{B2} \mid C_{B1}\} & \text{if } C_{U2} \neq \top \\ \{C_{U1} \Leftrightarrow C_{B1} \mid C_{B2}\} & \text{if } C_{U2} = \top \text{ and } CT \models C_{B1} \leftrightarrow C_{B2} \end{cases}$$

Note that propagation rules whose bodies consist only of *true* can be eliminated. One obvious difference to completion in TRS is that our completion for CHR derives *two* rules out of a critical pair in general. In example 4 we show why the additional propagation rule is necessary.

Example 3. Let P be a CHR program that represents a fragment of the Boolean constraint solver [9] defining the logical connectives and and imp. The constraint and(X,Y,Z) stands for X ∧ Y ↔ Z and imp(X,Y) for X → Y.[4]

```
and1 @ and(X,X,Z) ⇔ X=Z.
and2 @ and(X,Y,X) ⇔ imp(X,Y).
```

[4] In the solver, imp is used as an ordering relation which explains the binary notation in contrast to the ternary and.

```
and3 @ and(X,Y,Z) ∧ and(X,Y,Z1) ⇔ and(X,Y,Z) ∧ Z=Z1.

imp1 @ imp(X,Y) ∧ imp(Y,X) ⇔ X=Y.
```

We choose the termination ordering:

$C_1 \gg C_2$ iff C_2 is a conjunct of C_1 or C_1 is `and(X,Y,Z)` and C_2 is `imp(X,Y)`.

The completion procedure results in the following sequence; critical pairs which are considered in the current inference step are underlined.

$$
\begin{aligned}
P_0 = \; & P \\
C_0 = \; & \{\underline{(<\mathtt{imp(X,X)}, \top, \mathtt{true}>, <\mathtt{X} = \mathtt{X}, \top, \mathtt{true}>)}, \\
& \underline{(<\mathtt{X} = \mathtt{Z}, \mathtt{and(X,Y,X)}, \mathtt{true}>, <\mathtt{imp(X,Y)}, \mathtt{and(X,Y,Z)}, \mathtt{true}>)}, \\
& \underline{(<\mathtt{X} = \mathtt{Z}, \mathtt{and(X,Y,Z)}, \mathtt{true}>, <\mathtt{imp(X,Y)}, \mathtt{and(X,Y,Z)}, \mathtt{true}>)}\}
\end{aligned}
$$

$$
\begin{aligned}
P_1 = \; & P \cup \{\mathtt{r1@imp(X,X)} \Leftrightarrow \mathtt{true}\} \\
C_1 = \; & \{\underline{(<\mathtt{X} = \mathtt{Z}, \mathtt{and(X,Y,X)}, \mathtt{true}>, <\mathtt{imp(X,Y)}, \mathtt{and(X,Y,Z)}, \mathtt{true}>)}, \\
& \underline{(<\mathtt{X} = \mathtt{Z}, \mathtt{and(X,Y,Z)}, \mathtt{true}>, <\mathtt{imp(X,Y)}, \mathtt{and(X,Y,Z)}, \mathtt{true}>)}\}
\end{aligned}
$$

$$
\begin{aligned}
P_2 = \; & P_1 \cup \{\mathtt{r2@imp(X,Y)} \wedge \mathtt{and(X,Y,Z)} \Leftrightarrow \mathtt{imp(X,Y)} \wedge \mathtt{X} = \mathtt{Z}\} \\
C_2 = \; & \{\underline{(<\mathtt{X} = \mathtt{X} \wedge \mathtt{imp(X,Y)}, \top, \mathtt{true}>, <\mathtt{imp(X,Y)}, \mathtt{imp(X,Y)}, \mathtt{true}>)}\}
\end{aligned}
$$

$$
\begin{aligned}
P_3 = \; & P_2 \cup \{\mathtt{r3@imp(X,Y)} \wedge \mathtt{imp(X,Y)} \Leftrightarrow \mathtt{imp(X,Y)}\} \\
C_3 = \; & \emptyset
\end{aligned}
$$

Let c.p. stand for critical pair from now on. The first, underlined c.p. of C_0 comes from equating the heads of rules **and2** and **and1**. This c.p. becomes joinable by adding rule **r1** to P. The second c.p. of C_0 comes from equating the head of rule **and2** with the first head constraint of **and3**. It becomes joinable by adding rule **r2**. The third c.p. of C_0 comes from equating the head of **and2** with the second head constraint of **and3**. It also becomes joinable due to **r2**. A non-joinable c.p. is added in the third step, which comes from equating the head of **and2** and the second head constraint of **r2**. For the sake of simplicity we dropped all new propagation rules generated by *orient*, since they were trivial, i.e. their bodies consisted only of `true`.
The result of the completion procedure is $P' = P_3$:

```
% rules and1, and2, and3, imp1 together with

r1 @ imp(X,X)  ⇔  true.
r2 @ imp(X,Y) ∧ and(X,Y,Z)  ⇔  imp(X,Y) ∧ X=Z.
r3 @ imp(X,Y) ∧ imp(X,Y)  ⇔  imp(X,Y).
```

The new rules derived by completion reveal some interesting properties of `imp`, e.g. `r1` states that "`X` implies `X`" is always true. P' is terminating (see Theorem 9 for correctness) and all its critical pairs are joinable, therefore P' is confluent.

The next example shows that in general it is not sufficient to derive only simplification rules as in completion for TRS, in order to join a non-joinable critical pair.

Example 4. Let P be the following CHR program, where p, q and r are user-defined constraints and $\geq$, $\leq$ are built-in constraints.

```
r1 @ p(X,Y)  ⇔  X ≥ Y ∧ q(X,Y).
r2 @ p(X,Y)  ⇔  X ≤ Y ∧ r(X,Y).
```

P is not confluent, since the c.p. stemming from r1 and r2

$$(<\mathtt{q(X,Y)} \wedge \mathtt{X} \geq \mathtt{Y}, \top, \mathtt{true}>, <\mathtt{r(X,Y)} \wedge \mathtt{X} \leq \mathtt{Y}, \top, \mathtt{true}>)$$

is non-joinable. The corresponding final states are

$$<\top, \mathtt{q(X,Y)}, \mathtt{X} \geq \mathtt{Y}>, <\top, \mathtt{r(X,Y)}, \mathtt{X} \leq \mathtt{Y}>.$$

Let r(X,Y) $\gg$ q(X,Y). Then the completion procedure derives:

```
r3 @ r(X,Y)  ⇔  X ≤ Y | q(X,Y) ∧ X ≥ Y.
r4 @ q(X,Y)  ⇒  X ≥ Y | X ≤ Y.
```

The following computations show that it is necessary to derive the propagation rule to P to join the c.p. above:

$$
\begin{array}{ll}
 & <\mathtt{r(X,Y)} \wedge \mathtt{X} \leq \mathtt{Y}, \top, \mathtt{true}> \\
\mapsto_{\mathbf{Solve}} & <\mathtt{r(X,Y)}, \top, \mathtt{X} \leq \mathtt{Y}> \\
\mapsto_{\mathbf{Introduce}} & <\top, \mathtt{r(X,Y)}, \mathtt{X} \leq \mathtt{Y}> \\
\mapsto_{\mathbf{Simplify}} & <\mathtt{q(X,Y)} \wedge \mathtt{X} \geq \mathtt{Y}, \top, \mathtt{X} \leq \mathtt{Y}> \\
\mapsto_{\mathbf{Solve}} & <\mathtt{q(X,Y)}, \top, \mathtt{X} = \mathtt{Y}> \\
\mapsto_{\mathbf{Introduce}} & <\top, \mathtt{q(X,Y)}, \mathtt{X} = \mathtt{Y}> \\
\mapsto_{\mathbf{Propagate}} & <\mathtt{X} \leq \mathtt{Y}, \mathtt{q(X,Y)}, \mathtt{X} = \mathtt{Y}> \\
\mapsto_{\mathbf{Solve}} & <\top, \mathtt{q(X,Y)}, \mathtt{X} = \mathtt{Y}>
\end{array}
$$

Without the application of the propagation rule the computation below would result in a different final state:

$$
\begin{array}{ll}
 & <\mathtt{q(X,Y)} \wedge \mathtt{X} \geq \mathtt{Y}, \top, \mathtt{true}> \\
\mapsto_{\mathbf{Solve}} & <\mathtt{q(X,Y)}, \top, \mathtt{X} \geq \mathtt{Y}> \\
\mapsto_{\mathbf{Introduce}} & <\top, \mathtt{q(X,Y)}, \mathtt{X} \geq \mathtt{Y}> \\
\mapsto_{\mathbf{Propagate}} & <\mathtt{X} \leq \mathtt{Y}, \mathtt{q(X,Y)}, \mathtt{X} \geq \mathtt{Y}> \\
\mapsto_{\mathbf{Solve}} & <\top, \mathtt{q(X,Y)}, \mathtt{X} = \mathtt{Y}>
\end{array}
$$

As is the case for TRS our completion procedure cannot be always successful. We distinguish three cases:

1. The algorithm stops successfully and returns a program P'.

2. The algorithm aborts unsuccessfully, if a critical pair cannot be transformed into rules for one of three reasons:
   - The program remains terminating if new rules are added but the termination ordering is too weak to detect this.
   - The program loses termination if new rules are added.
   - The critical pair consists exclusively of built-in constraints.
3. The algorithm does not terminate, because new rules produce new critical pairs, which require again new rules, and so on.

In the next section we show that when the algorithm stops successfully, the returned program P' is confluent and terminating.

3.1 Correctness of the Completion Algorithm

We now show that the completion procedure applied to a CHR program results in an equivalent program. For the proof to go through, every rule has to satisfy a *range-restriction* condition: Every variable in the body or the guard appears also in the head. In practice, in almost all solvers, rules with local variables (variables that occur on the right-hand side of a rule only) can be rewritten to be range-restricted. One introduces interpreted function symbols for the local variables and extends the equality theory in CT accordingly.
Some definitions are necessary before we go further.

Definition 6. Let P_1 and P_2 be CHR programs and let CT be the appropriate constraint theory. P_1 and P_2 are *equivalent*, if their logical meanings $\mathcal{P}_1$ and $\mathcal{P}_2$ are equivalent:

$$CT \models \mathcal{P}_1 \leftrightarrow \mathcal{P}_2$$

Definition 7. Let S be a state $<Gs, C_U, C_B>$, which appears in a computation of G. The *logical meaning* of S is the formula

$$\exists \bar{x}\ Gs \wedge C_U \wedge C_B,$$

where $\bar{x}$ are the (local) variables appearing in S and not in G. A *computable constraint* of G is the logical meaning of a state which appears in a computation of G.

Lemma 8. Let P be a CHR program and G be a goal. Then for all computable constraints C_1 and C_2 of G the following holds:

$$P \cup CT \models \forall\, (C_1 \leftrightarrow C_2).$$

Proof. See [2].

Theorem 9. Let P be a range-restricted CHR program respecting a termination ordering $\gg$ and C be the set of the non-joinable critical pairs of P. If, for inputs $C_0 = C$, $P_0 = P$ and $\gg$, the completion procedure generates a successful derivation of the form $(C_0, P_0) \longmapsto \ldots \longmapsto (\emptyset, P')$, then P' is terminating with respect to $\gg$, confluent and equivalent to P.

Proof. Omitted from the final version for space reasons. See [2].

3.2 Consistency

Another property of completion is that it can exhibit inconsistency of the program to complete.

Definition 10. A constraint theory CT is called *complete*, if for every constraint c either $CT \models \forall c$ or $CT \models \forall \neg c$ holds.

Theorem 11. Let P be a CHR program and CT a complete theory. If the completion procedure aborts unsuccessfully, because the corresponding final states of a critical pair consist only of differing built-in constraints, then the logical meaning of P is inconsistent.

Proof. Let C_{B1}, C_{B2} be the built-in constraints of the final states. According to Lemma 8, the following holds

$$\mathcal{P} \cup CT \models \forall\, (\exists \bar{x}_1 C_{B1} \leftrightarrow \exists \bar{x}_2 C_{B2}),$$

where $\bar{x}_1, \bar{x}_2$ are the local variables of the final states.
We prove the claim by contradiction. Assume that $\mathcal{P}$ is consistent. Then $\mathcal{P} \cup CT$ is consistent. Therefore $CT \models \forall\, (\exists \bar{x}_1 C_{B1} \leftrightarrow \exists \bar{x}_2 C_{B2})$ holds, since CT is complete. Then according to the normalization function C_{B1} and C_{B2} have a unique form. This contradicts the prerequisite that the states are different. □

Example 5. Let P be the following CHR program trying to implement the constraint `maximum(X,Y,Z)`, which holds, if `Z` is the maximum of `X` and `Y`, and where $\leq$ and $=$ are built-in constraints. Note that there is a typo in the body of the second rule, since `Y` should have been `Z`:

```
r1 @ maximum(X,Y,Z) ⇔ X ≤ Y | Z = Y.
r2 @ maximum(X,Y,Z) ⇔ Y ≤ X | Y = X.
```

The c.p.

$$(\texttt{<Z = Y}, \top, \texttt{X} \leq \texttt{Y} \wedge \texttt{Y} \leq \texttt{X>}, \texttt{<Y = X}, \top, \texttt{X} \leq \texttt{Y} \wedge \texttt{Y} \leq \texttt{X>})$$

stemming from `r1` and `r2` is not joinable. The states of the c.p. consist only of built-in constraints. Thus the completion procedure aborts unsuccessfully.
The logical meaning of this CHR program is the theory

```
∀ X,Y,Z (X ≤ Y → (maximum(X,Y,Z) ↔ Z = Y))
∀ X,Y,Z (Y ≤ X → (maximum(X,Y,Z) ↔ Y = X))
```

together with an appropriate constraint theory describing $\leq$ as an order relation and $=$ as syntactic equality. The logical meaning $\mathcal{P}$ of this program is not a consistent theory. This can be exemplified by the atomic formula maximum(1, 1, 0), which is logically equivalent to 0=1 (and therefore *false*) using the first formula. Using the second formula, however maximum(1, 1, 0) is logically equivalent to 1=1 (and therefore *true*). This results in $\mathcal{P} \cup CT \models$ *false*$\leftrightarrow$*true*.

4 More Uses of Completion

The first example shows that the completion method can be used - to some extent – to specialize constraints.

Example 6. We define the constraint < as a special case of $\leq$. If we extend the CHR program for $\leq$ of Example 1 by the simplification rule

`r5 @ X ≤ Y ⇔ X ≠ Y | X < Y.`

then the resulting program is not confluent anymore. With the termination ordering

$C_1 \gg C_2$ iff C_2 is a conjunct of C_1 or C_1 is `X ≤ Y` and C_2 is `X < Y`,

the completion procedure derives the following rules:

```
r6 @ X < Y ∧ Y < X   ⇔ X ≠ Y | false.
r7 @ X < Y ∧ X < Y  ⇔  X ≠ Y | X < Y.
```

where `r6` comes from a c.p. of `r2` and `r5`,

$$(<\mathtt{X}=\mathtt{Y},\top,\mathtt{X}\neq\mathtt{Y}>,<\mathtt{X}<\mathtt{Y},\mathtt{Y}\leq\mathtt{X},\mathtt{X}\neq\mathtt{Y}>).$$

`r7` comes from a c.p. of `r4` and `r5`,

$$(<\top,\mathtt{X}\leq\mathtt{Y},\mathtt{X}\neq\mathtt{Y}>,<\mathtt{X}<\mathtt{Y},\mathtt{Y}\leq\mathtt{X},\mathtt{X}\neq\mathtt{Y}>).$$

`r6` obviously defines the antisymmetry of < and `r7` idempotence. Irreflexivity of < could not be derived, since the definition of < by rule `r5` already presupposes that `X≠Y`. However, completion can derive irreflexivity from rule `r1` and the rule

`r8 @ X ≤ Y ∧ Y< X ⇔ false.`

since the resulting c.p.

$$(<\mathtt{X}<\mathtt{X},\top,\mathtt{true}>,<\mathtt{false},\top,\mathtt{true}>).$$

leads to the simplification rule

`r9 @ X < X    ⇔ false.`

The next example shows how completion can be used as a method to provide generic answers, even if a constraint cannot further be simplified. This retains some of the power of logic languages like Prolog, where several answers can be given. Our approach is similar to the ones that related Prolog and TRS computation methods [7, 6].

Example 7. A CHR formulation of the classical Prolog predicate `member` as a user-defined constraint is ($\neq$ is built-in):

```
r1 @ member(X,[]) ⇔ false.
r2 @ member(X,[X|_]) ⇔ true.
r3 @ member(X,[H|T]) ⇔ X ≠ H | member(X,T).
```

Using CHR, the goal `member(X,[1,2,3])` delays. However Prolog generates three solutions `X=1`, `X=2` and `X=3`. If we add

```
r4 @ member(X,[1,2,3]) ⇔ answer(X).
```

to P, then the program is non-confluent. Our completion procedure derives:

```
a1 @ answer(1) ⇔ true.
a2 @ answer(2) ⇔ true.
a3 @ answer(3) ⇔ true.
a4 @ answer(X) ⇔ X ≠ 1 ∧ X ≠ 2 ∧ X ≠ 3 | false.
```

The rules `a1`, `a2` and `a3` correspond to the answers of the Prolog program, while the last rule `a4` makes explicit the closed world assumption underlying Clark's completion semantics of Prolog.

Completion can also derive recursively defined constraints.

Example 8. Let P be the following CHR program

```
r1 @ append([],L,L) ⇔ true.
r2 @ append([X|L1],Y,[X|L2]) ⇔ append(L1,Y,L2).
```

defining the well-known ternary append predicate for lists as a simple constraint, which holds if its third argument is a concatenation of the first and the second argument. P is confluent since there are no critical pairs. When we add the rule

```
r3 @ append(L1,[],L3) ⇔ new(L1,L3).
```

confluence is lost. Completion derives a constraint solver for `new`:

```
r4 @ new([],[]) ⇔ true.              % joins c.p. of r1 and r3
r5 @ new([A|B],[A|C]) ⇔ new(B,C).  % joins c.p. of r2 and r3
```

Our completion procedure has uncovered that `append(L1,[],L3)` holds exactly if `L1` and `L2` are the same list, as tested by the generated, recursive constraint `new`. Note that the rules represent in a finite way the infinitely many answers that would be generated by the corresponding program in Prolog.

5 Conclusions

We introduced a completion method for Constraint Handling Rules (CHR). Completion methods make a non-confluent CHR program confluent by adding new rules. We have shown that our proposed completion procedure is correct and can exhibit inconsistency of a CHR program. We also gave various examples to show that completion can be used as a method to provide generic answers and to define new constraints from existing ones and to derive constraint solvers for them. The latter helps the CHR programmer to extend, modify and specialize existing solvers instead of having to write them from scratch. We currently investigate using our completion method on larger real-life solvers for easing their modification and for giving more informative answers. An interesting direction for future work is to explore the relationship of completion to partial evaluation.

References

1. S. Abdennadher. Operational semantics and confluence of constraint propagation rules. In *Third International Conference on Principles and Practice of Constraint Programming, CP'97*, LNCS 1330. Springer-Verlag, 1997.
2. S. Abdennadher. *Analyse von regelbasierten Constraintlösern (in German)*. PhD thesis, Computer Science Institute, LMU Munich, February 1998.
3. S. Abdennadher, T. Frühwirth, and H. Meuss. On confluence of constraint handling rules. In *2nd International Conference on Principles and Practice of Constraint Programming, CP'96*, LNCS 1118. Springer-Verlag, August 1996. Revised and extended version to appear in the Constraints Journal.
4. ACM. The constraint programming working group. Technical report, ACM-MIT SDRC Workshop, Report Outline, Draft, September 1996.
5. L. Bachmair and N. Dershowitz. Commutation, transformation, and termination. In J. H. Siekmann, editor, *Proceedings of the Eighth International Conference on Automated Deduction (Oxford, England)*, LNCS 230. Springer-Verlag, July 1986.
6. M. P. Bonacina and J. Hsiang. On rewrite programs: Semantics and relationsship with PROLOG. *Journal of Logic Programming*, 14:155–180, 1992.
7. N. Dershowitz and N. A. Josephson. Logic programming by completion. In Sten-Åke Tärnlund, editor, *Proceedings of the Second International Conference on Logic Programming*, Uppsala, 1984.
8. N. Dershowitz, N. Okada, and G. Sivakumar. Confluence of conditional rewrite systems. In J.-P. Jouannaud and S. Kaplan, editors, *Proceedings of the 1st International Workshop on Conditional Term Rewriting Systems*, LNCS 308, 1988.
9. T. Frühwirth. Constraint handling rules. In A. Podelski, editor, *Constraint Programming: Basics and Trends*, LNCS 910. Springer-Verlag, March 1995.
10. T. Frühwirth. *A Declarative Language for Constraint Systems: Theory and Practice of Constraint Handling Rules*. Habilitation, Computer Science Institute, LMU Munich, 1998. Shortened version to appear in Journal of Logic Programming, Special Issue on Constraint Logic Programming, P. Stuckey and K. Marriot, editors.
11. J. Jaffar and M. J. Maher. Constraint logic programming: A survey. *Journal of Logic Programming*, 20, 1994.
12. D. E. Knuth and P. B. Bendix. Simple word problems in universal algebra. In J. Leech, editor, *Computational Problems in Abstract Algebra*. Pergamon Press, 1970.
13. K. Marriott and P. Stuckey. *Programming with Constraints: An Introduction*. The MIT Press, 1998.
14. V. A. Saraswat. *Concurrent Constraint Programming*. MIT Press, Cambridge, 1993.

Error-Correcting Source Code

Yasuhiro Ajiro, Kazunori Ueda*, Kenta Cho**

Department of Information and Computer Science
Waseda University
4-1, Okubo 3-chome, Shinjuku-ku, Tokyo 169-8555, Japan
{ajiro,ueda}@ueda.info.waseda.ac.jp

Abstract. We study how constraint-based static analysis can be applied to the automated and systematic debugging of program errors.
Strongly moding and constraint-based mode analysis are turning to play fundamental roles in debugging concurrent logic/constraint programs as well as in establishing the consistency of communication protocols and in optimization. Mode analysis of Moded Flat GHC is a constraint satisfaction problem with many simple mode constraints, and can be solved efficiently by unification over feature graphs. We have proposed a simple and efficient technique which, given a non-well-moded program, diagnoses the "reasons" of inconsistency by finding minimal inconsistent subsets of mode constraints. Since each constraint keeps track of the symbol occurrence in the program that imposed the constraint, a minimal subset also tells possible sources of program errors. The technique is quite general and can be used with other constraint-based frameworks such as strong typing.
Based on the above idea, we study the possibility of *automated debugging in the absence of mode/type declarations.* The mode constraints are usually imposed redundantly, and the constraints that are considered correct can be used for correcting wrong symbol occurrences found by the diagnosis. As long as bugs are near-misses, the automated debugger can propose a rather small number of alternatives that include the intended program. Search space is kept small because constraints effectively prune many irrelevant alternatives. The paper demonstrates the technique by way of examples.

1 Introduction

This paper proposes a framework of automated debugging of program errors under static, constraint-based systems for program analysis, and shows how and why program errors can be fixed in the absence of programmers' declarations. The language we are particularly interested in is Moded Flat GHC [7][8] proposed in 1990. Moded Flat GHC is a concurrent logic (and consequently, a concurrent constraint) language with a constraint-based mode system designed by one of

* Supported in part by the Ministry of Education (grant No. 09245101) and Japan Information Processing Development Center (JIPDEC).

** Currently with Toshiba Corp.

the authors, where modes prescribe the information flow that may be caused by the execution of a program.

Languages equipped with strong typing or strong moding[3] enable the detection of a type/mode errors by checking or reconstructing types or modes. The best-known framework for type reconstruction is the Hindley-Milner type system [3], which allows us to solve a set of type constraints obtained from program text efficiently as a unification problem.

Similarly, the mode system of Moded Flat GHC allows us to solve a set of mode constraints obtained from program text as a constraint satisfaction problem. Without mode declarations or other kinds of program specification given by programmers, mode reconstruction statically determines the read/write capabilities of variable occurrences and establishes the consistency of communication protocols between concurrent processes [8]. The constraint satisfaction problem can be solved mostly (though not entirely) as a unification problem over feature graphs (feature structures with cycles) and can be solved in almost linear time with respect to the size of the program [1]. As we will see later, types also can be reconstructed using a similar (and simpler) technique.

Compared with abstract interpretation usually employed for the precise analysis of program properties, constraint-based formulation of the analysis of basic properties has a lot of advantages. Firstly, thanks to its incremental nature, it is naturally amenable to separate analysis of large programs. Secondly, it allows simple and general formulations of various interesting applications including error diagnosis.

When a concurrent logic program contains bugs, it is very likely that mode constraints obtained from the erroneous symbol occurrences are incompatible with the other constraints. We have proposed an efficient algorithm that finds a minimal inconsistent subset of mode constraints from an inconsistent (multi)set of constraints [2]. A minimal inconsistent subset can be thought of as a minimal "explanation" of the reason of inconsistency. Furthermore, since each constraint keeps track of the symbol occurrence(s) in the program that imposed the constraint, a minimal subset tells possible sources (i.e., symbol occurrences) of program errors. Our technique can locate multiple bugs at once. The technique is quite general and can be used with other constraint-based frameworks such as strong typing.

Since the conception of the above framework of program diagnosis and some experiments, we have found that the multiset of mode constraints imposed by a program usually has redundancy and it usually contains more than one minimal inconsistent subset when it is inconsistent as a whole. Redundancy comes from two reasons:

1. A non-trivial program contains conditional branches or nondeterministic choices. In (concurrent) logic languages, they are expressed as a set of rewrite rules (i.e., program clauses) that may impose the same mode constraints on the same predicate.

[3] Modes can be thought of as "types in a broad sense," but in this paper we reserve the term "types" to mean sets of possible values.

2. A non-trivial program contains predicates that are called from more than one place, some of which may be recursive calls. The same mode constraint may be imposed by different calls.

We can often take advantage of the redundancies and pinpoint a bug (Sect. 3) by assuming that redundant modes are correct. The next step worth trying is *automated error correction*. We can estimate the intended mode of a program from the parts of the program that are considered correct, and use it to fix small bugs, which is the main focus of this paper.

Bugs that can be dealt with by automated correction are necessarily limited to near-misses, but still, automated correction is worth studying because:

– serious algorithm errors cannot be mechanically corrected anyway,
– if the algorithm for a program has been correctly designed, the program is usually "mostly correct" even if it doesn't run at all, and
– real-life programs are subject to a number of revisions, upon which small errors are likely to be inserted.

Our idea of error correction can be compared with error-correcting codes in coding theory. Both attempt to correct minor errors using redundant information. Unlike error-correcting codes that contain explicit redundancies, programs are usually not written in a redundant manner. However, programs interpreted in an abstract domain may well have *implicit* redundancies. For instance, the `then` part and the `else` part of a branch will usually compute a value of the same type, which should also be the same as the type expected by the reader of the value. This is exactly why the multiset of type or mode constraints usually has redundancies.

It is not obvious whether such redundancies can be used for automated error correction, because even if we correctly estimate the type/mode of a program, there may be many possible ways of error correction that are compatible with the estimated type/mode. The usefulness of the technique seems to depend heavily on the choice of a programming language and the power of the constraint-based static analysis. We have obtained promising results using Moded Flat GHC and its mode system, with the assistance of type analysis and other constraints.

The other concern in automated debugging is search space. Generate-and-test search, namely the generation of a possible correction and the computation of its principal mode (and type), can involve a lot of computation, but we can prune much of the search space by using 'quick-check' mode information to detect non-well-modedness. Types are concerned with aspects of program properties that are different from modes, and can be used together with modes to improve the quality of error correction.

2 Strong Moding and Typing in Concurrent Logic Programming

We first outline the mode system of Moded Flat GHC. The readers are referred to [8] and [9] for details.

In concurrent logic programming, modes play a fundamental role in establishing the safety of a program in terms of the consistency of communication protocols. The mode system of Moded Flat GHC gives a polarity structure (that determines the information flow of each part of data structures created during execution) to the arguments of predicates that determine the behavior of goals. A mode expresses this polarity structure, which is represented as a mapping from the set of *paths* to the two-valued codomain $\{in, out\}$. Paths here are strings of pairs, of the form $\langle symbol, arg \rangle$, of predicate/function symbols and argument positions, and are used to specify possible positions in data structures. Formally, the set P_{Term} of paths for terms and the set P_{Atom} of paths for atomic formulae are defined using disjoint union as:

$$P_{Term} = (\sum_{f \in Fun} N_f)^*, \; P_{Atom} = (\sum_{p \in Pred} N_p) \times P_{Term} ,$$

where $Fun/Pred$ are the sets of function/predicate symbols, and N_f/N_p are the sets of possible argument positions (numbered from 1) for the symbols f/p. The purpose of mode analysis is to find the set of all modes (each of type $P_{Atom} \rightarrow \{in, out\}$) under which every piece of communication is cooperative. Such a mode is called a *well-moding*. Intuitively, *in* means the inlet of information and *out* means the outlet of information. A program does not usually define a unique well-moding but has many of them. So the purpose of mode analysis is to compute the set of all well-modings in the form of a *principal* (i.e., most general) mode. Principal modes can be expressed naturally by mode graphs, as described later in this section.

Given a mode m, we define a *submode* m/p, namely m viewed at the path p, as a function satisfying $(m/p)(q) = m(pq)$. We also define IN and OUT as submodes returning *in* and *out*, respectively, for any path. An overline '$-$' inverts the polarity of a mode, a submode, or a mode value.

A Flat GHC program is a set of clauses of the form h :- G | B, where h is an atomic formula and G and B are multisets of atomic formulae. Constraints imposed by a clause h :- G | B are summarized in Fig. 1. Rule (BU) numbers unification body goals because the mode system allows different body unification goals to have different modes. This is a special case of mode polymorphism that can be introduced into other predicates as well [2], but in this paper we will not consider general mode polymorphism because whether to have polymorphism is independent of the essence of this work.

For example, consider a quicksort program defined as follows:

```
quicksort(Xs,Ys) :- true | qsort(Xs,Ys,[]).
qsort([],   Ys0,Ys ) :- true | Ys=₁Ys0.
qsort([X|Xs],Ys0,Ys3) :- true |
  part(X,Xs,S,L), qsort(S,Ys0,Ys1), Ys1=₂[X|Ys2], qsort(L,Ys2,Ys3).
part(_,[],     S, L ) :- true | S=₃[], L=₄[].
part(A,[X|Xs],S0,L ) :- A>=X | S0=₅[X|S], part(A,Xs,S,L).
part(A,[X|Xs],S, L0) :- A< X | L0=₆[X|L], part(A,Xs,S,L).
```

(HF) $m(p) = in$, for a function symbol occurring in h at p.

(HV) $m/p = IN$, for a variable symbol occurring more than once in h at p and somewhere else.

(GV) If some variable occurs both in h at p and in G at p', $\forall q \in P_{Term}\,(m(p'q) = in \Rightarrow m(pq) = in)$.

(BU) $m/\langle =_k, 1\rangle = \overline{m/\langle =_k, 2\rangle}$, for a unification body goal $=_k$.

(BF) $m(p) = in$, for a function symbol occurring in B at p.

(BV) Let v be a variable occurring exactly $n\,(\geq 1)$ times in h and B at $p_1, \ldots, p_n$, of which the occurrences in h are at $p_1, \ldots, p_k$ $(k \geq 0)$. Then

$$\begin{cases} \mathcal{R}(\{m/p_1, \ldots, m/p_n\}), & \text{if } k = 0; \\ \mathcal{R}(\{\overline{m/p_1}, m/p_{k+1}, \ldots, m/p_n\}), & \text{if } k > 0; \end{cases}$$

where the unary predicate $\mathcal{R}$ over finite *multisets* of submodes represents "cooperative communication" between paths and is defined as

$$\mathcal{R}(S) \stackrel{\text{def}}{=} \forall q \in P_{Term}\, \exists s \in S\, (s(q) = out \wedge \forall s' \in S \backslash \{s\}\, (s'(q) = in)).$$

Fig. 1. Mode constraints imposed by a program clause h :- G | B or a goal clause :- B.

From the entire definition, we obtain 53 constraints which are consistent. We could regard these constraints themselves as representing the principal mode of the program, but the principal mode can be represented more explicitly in terms of a mode graph (Fig. 2). Mode graphs are a kind of feature graphs [1] in which

1. a path (in the graph-theoretic sense) represents a member of P_{Atom},
2. the node corresponding to a path p represents the value $m(p)$ ($\downarrow = in$, $\uparrow = out$),
3. each arc is labeled with the pair ⟨*symbol*, *arg*⟩ of a predicate/function symbol and an argument position, and may have a "negative sign" (denoted "•" in Fig. 2) that inverts the interpretation of the mode values of the paths beyond that arc, and
4. a binary constraint of the form $m/p_1 = m/p_2$ or $m/p_1 = \overline{m/p_2}$ is represented by letting p_1 and p_2 lead to the same node.

Mode analysis proceeds by merging many simple mode graphs representing individual mode constraints. Thus its decidability is guaranteed by the decidability of the unification algorithm for feature graphs. The principal mode of a well-moded program, represented as a mode graph, is uniquely determined, as long as all the mode constraints imposed by the program are unary (i.e., constraint on the mode value of, or the submode at, a particular path) or binary (i.e.,

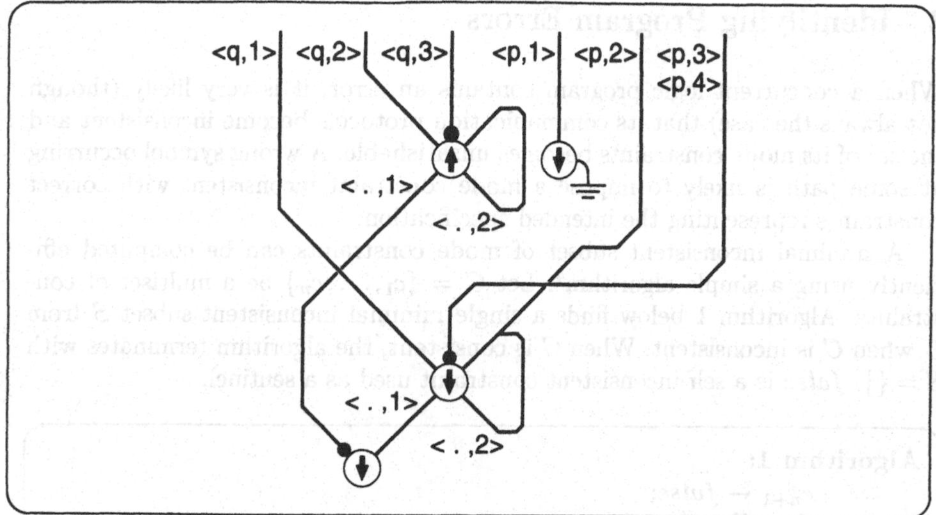

Fig. 2. The mode graph of a quicksort program. **q** stands for **qsort** and **p** stands for **part**. The mode information of the toplevel predicate and unification goals is omitted.

constraint between the submodes at two particular paths). Space limitations do not allow us to explain further details, which can be found in [9].

A type system for concurrent logic programming can be introduced by classifying a set *Fun* of function symbols into mutually disjoint sets $F_1, \ldots, F_n$. A type here is a function from P_{Atom} to the set $\{F_1, \ldots, F_n\}$. Like principal modes, principal types can be computed by unification over feature graphs. Constraints on a well-typing τ are summarized in Fig. 3. The choice of a family of sets $F_1, \ldots, F_n$ is somewhat arbitrary. This is why moding is more fundamental than typing in concurrent logic programming.

Mode and type analyses have been implemented as part of *klint*, a static analyzer for KL1 programs [11].

(HBF$_\tau$) $\tau(p) = F_i$, for a function symbol occurring at p in h or B.

(HBV$_\tau$) $\tau/p = \tau/p'$, for a variable occurring both at p and p' in h or B.

(GV$_\tau$) $\forall q \in P_{Term}\big(m(p'q) = in \Rightarrow \tau(pq) = \tau(p'q)\big)$, for a variable occurring both at p in h and at p' in G.

(BU$_\tau$) $\tau/\langle =_k, 1\rangle = \tau/\langle =_k, 2\rangle$, for a unification body goal $=_k$.

Fig. 3. Type constraints imposed by a program clause h :- G | B or a goal clause :- B.

3 Identifying Program Errors

When a concurrent logic program contains an error, it is very likely (though not always the case) that its communication protocols become inconsistent and the set of its mode constraints becomes unsatisfiable. A wrong symbol occurring at some path is likely to impose a mode constraint inconsistent with correct constraints representing the intended specification.

A minimal inconsistent subset of mode constraints can be computed efficiently using a simple algorithm[4]. Let $C = \{c_1, \ldots, c_n\}$ be a multiset of constraints. Algorithm 1 below finds a single minimal inconsistent subset S from C when C is inconsistent. When C is consistent, the algorithm terminates with $S = \{\}$. *false* is a self-inconsistent constraint used as a sentinel.

Algorithm 1:

```
c_{n+1} ← false;
S ← {};
while S is consistent do
  D ← S; i ← 0;
  while D is consistent do
    i ← i + 1; D ← D ∪ {c_i}
  end while;
  S ← S ∪ {c_i}
end while;
if i = n + 1 then S ← {}
```

The readers are referred to [2] for a proof of the minimality of S, as well as various extensions of the algorithm. Note that the algorithm can be readily extended to finding multiple bugs at once. That is, once we have found a minimal subset covering a bug, we can reapply the algorithm to the rest of the constraints.

In the algorithm, the merging of constraint sets and the checking of their consistency are realized mostly as the unification of mode graphs and the checking of its success/failure. Although the algorithm is quite general, its efficiency hinges upon the fact that there is a pair of efficient algorithms for computing the union of constraint sets and checking its consistency.

Our experiment shows that the average size of minimal inconsistent subsets is less than 4, and we have not yet found a minimal inconsistent subset with more than 11 elements. The size of minimal subsets turns out to be independent of the total number of constraints, and most inconsistencies can be explained by constraints imposed by a small range of program text.

Because we are dealing with near-misses, we can assume that most of the mode constraints obtained from a program represent an intended specification and that they have redundancies in most cases. In this case, one can often pinpoint a bug either

[4] The algorithm described here is a revised version of the one proposed in [2] and takes into account the case when C is consistent.

1. by computing a maximal consistent subset of size $n-1$ and taking its complement, or
2. by computing several overlapping minimal inconsistent subsets and taking their intersection.

Algorithm 2 described below combines these two alternative policies of pinpointing. To reduce the amount of computation, we do not compute all minimal subsets; instead, for each element (say s_i) of the initial inconsistent subset S, we execute Algorithm 1 after removing s_i from C, which will lead to another minimal subset if it exists. Thus Algorithm 2 simultaneously computes constraints suspected by the two policies.

Let $S = \{s_1, \ldots, s_m\}$ be a minimal subset obtained by Algorithm 1, and **getminimal**(C) be a function which computes a minimal inconsistent subset from a multiset C of constraints using Algorithm 1 above:

Algorithm 2:

```
T ← S;
for j ← 1 to m do
  S' ← getminimal(C\{s_j});
  if S' = {} then
    output {s_j} as a solution of Policy 1
  else T ← T ⊍ S';
end for
```

Here, T is a *multiset* of constraints what serves as counters of the numbers of constraints occurring in S and (various versions of) S', and $\uplus$ is a multiset union operator. T records how many times each constraint occurred in different minimal subsets. Under Policy 2, constraints with more occurrences in T are more likely to be related to the source of the error.

Algorithm 2 is useful in locating multiple bugs at once. That is, once we have obtained a minimal inconsistent subset S, we can apply Algorithm 2 to refine the subset and remove only those constraints in the refined subset from C.

When Policy 1 outputs a single constraint imposed by an erroneous symbol occurrence, we need not consider Policy 2. However, there are cases where Policy 1 outputs no constraints or more than one constraint, in which case Policy 2 may better tell which constraints to suspect first.

Algorithm 2 is not always able to refine the initial set S, however. For instance, when S is the only minimal inconsistent subset, the algorithm will output all the elements of S by Policy 1 and will find no alternative subset by Policy 2. Fortunately, this is not a serious problem because S is usually quite small.

4 Automated Debugging Using Mode Constraints

Constraints that are considered wrong can be corrected by

– replacing the symbol occurrences that imposed those constraints by other symbols, or
– when the suspected symbols are variables, by making them have more occurrences elsewhere (cf. Rule (BV) of Fig. 1).

In this paper, we focus on programs with a small number of errors in variables and constants; that is, we focus on errors in terminal symbols in abstract syntax trees. This may seem restrictive, but concurrent logic programs have quite flat syntactic structures (compared with other languages) and instead make heavy use of variables. Our experience tells that a majority of simple program errors arise from the erroneous use of variables, for which the support of a static mode system and debugging tools are invaluable.

An algorithm for automated correction is basically a search procedure whose initial state is the erroneous program, whose operations are the rewriting of the occurrences of variables or constants, and whose final states are well-moded programs[5]. This can be regarded also as a form of *abductive reasoning* which, from a presumably correct mode constraint B and the moding rules of the form "if A then B" (or "B for A") as shown in Fig. 1, infers a syntactic constraint A that is considered correct.

The symbols to be substituted in the correction are chosen from the constants or other variables occurring in the same clause. When the symbol to be rewritten occurs in the head, we should also consider replacement by a fresh variable. We don't have to try to form the mode graphs of all the alternative programs; from the set $C \setminus S$, we can derive a *replacement guideline*, namely simple constraints to be satisfied by the substituted symbol. Any replacement that violates the guideline will not lead to a well-moded program and can be rejected immediately.

Error correction may require the rewriting of more than one symbol occurrence. We perform iterative-deepening search with respect to the number of rewritings, because the assumption of near-misses implies that a simpler correction is more likely to be the intended one. These ideas have been partially implemented in the *kima* analyzer for KL1 programs [10].

5 Using Constraints Other Than Modes

When error correction requires the rewriting of more than one symbol occurrence, the iterative-deepening search may report a large number of alternative solutions, though they always include an intended one.

Using both the mode system and the type system reduces the number of alternatives greatly. Modes and types capture different aspects of a program, and rather few of well-formed programs are both well-moded and well-typed. We can expect that there are only a small number of well-moded and well-typed program syntactically in the 'neighborhood' of the given near-miss program.

---

[5] Here, we assume that errors can be corrected without changing the shape of the abstract syntax tree, though we could extend our technique and allow occurrences of terminal symbols to be simply added or deleted.

The reason why a type system alone is insufficient should become clear by considering programs that are simple in terms of types such as numerical programs. The mode system is sensitive to the number of occurrences of variables (rule (BV) in Fig. 1) and can detect many errors that cannot be found by type analysis. However, even when the programs are simple in terms of types, types can be useful for inferring what constant should replace the wrong symbol.

Other heuristics from our programming experiences can reinforce the framework as well:

1. A singleton variable occurring in a clause body is highly likely to be an error.
2. A solution containing a variable occurring more than once in a clause head is less likely to be an intended one.

These heuristics are not as *ad hoc* as it might look; indeed they can be replaced by a unified rule on *constraint strength*:

- A well-moded solution with weaker mode constraints is more likely to be an intended one.

A singleton variable occurring at p in a clause body imposes a constraint $m/p = OUT$, which is much stronger than $m(p) = out$. Similarly, a variable occurring more than once at $p_1, p_2, \ldots$ in a clause head imposes a constraint $m/p_i = IN$.

We could use more surface-level heuristics such as the similarity of variable names, but this is outside the scope of this paper.

6 Experiments and Examples

We show some experimental results and discuss two examples of automated debugging. The examples we use are admittedly simple but that can be justified. First, we must anyway start with simple examples. Second, we have found that most inconsistencies can be explained by constraints imposed by a small range of program text, as we pointed out in Sect. 3. So we strongly expect that the total program size does not make much difference in the performance or the quality of automated debugging.

6.1 Experiments

We applied the proposed technique to programs with one mutation in variable occurrences. We systematically generated near-misses (each with one wrong occurrence of a variable) of three programs (there are many ways of inserting a bug) and examined how many of them became non-well-moded, whether automated correction reported an intended program, and how many alternatives were reported. Table 1 shows the results. In the table, the column "total cases" shows the numbers of cases examined, and the column "detected cases" shows how many cases lead to non-well-moded programs. For non-well-moded programs, we examined how many well-moded alternatives were proposed by the automated debugger by depth-1 search. In this experiment, we did not apply Algorithm 2 to refine a minimal inconsistent subset.

The programs we used are list concatenation (append), the generator of a Fibonacci sequence, and quicksort. We used the definitions of predicates only, that is, we did not use the constraints that might be imposed by the caller of these programs.

The row "mode only" indicates the results using mode constraints only, except that when correcting errors we regarded singleton variables in clause bodies as erroneous. In this experiment, minimal inconsistent subsets, when found, always included constraints imposed by the wrong symbol occurrence, and the original, intended programs were always included in the sets of the alternatives proposed by the algorithm.

Table 1. Single-error detection and correction

Program	Analysis	Total cases	Detected cases	Proposed alternatives 1	2	3	4	5	6	7	≥8
`append`	mode only	57	33	16	4	1	0	5	4	2	1
	new variable	13	11	7	0	0	1	1	2	0	0
	mode & type	57	44	19	3	2	5	1	3	0	0
`fibonacci`	mode only	84	43	28	7	0	0	0	2	3	3
	new variable	15	14	6	3	0	0	0	2	2	1
	mode & type	84	57	34	2	0	2	2	3	0	0
`quicksort`	mode only	245	148	84	33	2	3	1	8	7	10
	new variable	45	43	24	2	0	3	2	4	3	5
	mode & type	245	189	93	33	5	9	0	5	2	1

A bug due to a wrong variable occurrence often results from misspelling (say the confusion of `YS` and `Ys`), in which case the original variable is likely to be replaced by a variable not occurring elsewhere in the clause. The row "new variable" shows the statistics of this case, which tells most errors were detected by mode analysis.

The row "mode & type" shows the improvement obtained by using types as well. The column "detected cases" shows that some of the well-moded erroneous programs were newly detected as non-well-typed. Note that the experiments did not consider the automated correction of well-moded but non-well-typed programs. For `fibonacci` and `quicksort`, we assumed that integers and list constructors belonged to different types. For append, we employed a stronger notion of types and assumed that the type of the elements of a list could not be identical to the type of the list itself.

The results show that the use of types was effective in reducing the number of alternatives. More than half of non-well-moded near-misses were uniquely restored to the original program. Thus, programmers can benefit much from the support of constraint-based static analysis by writing programs in a well-moded and well-typed manner.

6.2 Example 1 — Append

As an example included in the above experiment, we discuss an append program with a single error. This example is simple and yet instructive.

R_1 : append([], Y,Z) :- true | Y=$_1$Z.
R_2 : append([A|Y],Y,Z0) :- true | Z0=$_2$[A|Z], append(X,Y,Z).
(The head should have been append([A|X],Y,Z0))

Algorithm 1 computes the following minimal inconsistent subset of mode constraints:

	Mode constraint	Rule	Source symbol
(a)	$m/\langle \mathbf{append}, 1\rangle\langle ., 2\rangle = IN$	(HV)	Y in R_2
(b)	$m/\langle \mathbf{append}, 1\rangle = OUT$	(BV)	X in R_2

This tells that we should suspect the variables X and Y in Clause R_2. The search first tries to rewrite one of the occurrences of these variables (iterative-deepening), and finds six well-moded alternatives:

(1) R_2 : append([A|X],Y,Z0) :- true | Z0=$_2$[A|Z], append(X,Y,Z).
(2) R_2 : append([A|Y],X,Z0) :- true | Z0=$_2$[A|Z], append(X,Y,Z).
(3) R_2 : append([A|Y],Y,Z0) :- true | Z0=$_2$[A|Z], append(Y,Y,Z).
(4) R_2 : append([A|Y],Y,Z0) :- true | Z0=$_2$[A|Z], append(Z0,Y,Z).
(5) R_2 : append([A|Y],Y,Z0) :- true | Z0=$_2$[A|Z], append(A,Y,Z).
(6) R_2 : append([A|Y],Y,Z0) :- true | Z0=$_2$[A|Z], append(Z,Y,Z).

Types do not help much in this example, though Alternative (5) can be eliminated by an implicit type assumption described in Sect. 6.1 that list constructors and the elements of the list cannot occupy the same path. Alternatives (3), (4), (5) and (6) are programs that cause reduction failure for most input data, and can be regarded as less plausible solutions because of the two occurrences of Y in the clause heads that impose stronger constraints than intended.

What are Alternatives (1) and (2)? Alternative (1) is the intended program, and Alternative (2) is a program that merges two input lists by taking their elements alternately. It's not 'append', but is a quite meaningful program compared with the other alternatives!

In this example, Algorithm 2, if applied, will detect Constraint (b) as the unique result of Policy 1. This means that there must be some problems with the variable X, which in turn means that X must either be removed or occur more than once. Search of well-moded programs finds the same number of alternatives, but the search space is reduced because we do not have to consider the rewriting between Y and variables other than X.

6.3 Example 2 — Quicksort

Next, we consider a quicksort program with two errors.

1: R_1 : `quicksort(Xs,Ys) :- true | qsort(Xs,Ys,[]).`
2: R_2 : `qsort([],     Ys0,Ys ) :- true | Ys=`$_1$`Ys0.`
3: R_3 : `qsort([X|Xs],Ys0,Ys3) :- true |`
4: `part(X,Xs,S,L), qsort(S,Ys0,Ys1),`
5: `Ys2=`$_2$`[X|Ys1], qsort(L,Ys2,Ys3).`
(the unification should have been `Ys1=`$_2$`[X|Ys2]`)

Algorithm 1 returns the following minimal inconsistent subset:

	Mode constraint	Rule	Source symbol
(a)	$m(\langle \texttt{qsort}, 3\rangle) = in$	(BF)	"`[]`" in R_1
(b)	$m/\langle =_1, 1\rangle = m/\langle \texttt{qsort}, 3\rangle$	(BV)	`Ys` in R_2
(c)	$m/\langle =_1, 2\rangle = m/\langle =_1, 1\rangle$	(BU)	$=_1$ in R_2
(d)	$m/\langle \texttt{qsort}, 2\rangle = m/\langle =_1, 2\rangle$	(BV)	`Ys0` in R_2
(e)	$m(\langle =_2, 2\rangle) = in$	(BF)	"." in R_3
(f)	$m/\langle =_2, 2\rangle = m/\langle =_2, 1\rangle$	(BU)	$=_2$ in R_3
(g)	$m/\langle =_2, 1\rangle = m/\langle \texttt{qsort}, 2\rangle$	(BV)	`Ys2` in R_3

This subset is inconsistent because two inconsistent constraints can be derived from it:

$$m(\langle \texttt{qsort}, 2\rangle) = out, \quad \text{by (a), (b), (c) and (d),}$$
$$m(\langle \texttt{qsort}, 2\rangle) = in, \quad \text{by (e), (f) and (g).}$$

It is worth noting that this example is rather difficult—the minimal subset is rather large and Algorithm 2 does not find an alternative minimal subset. That is, there is no redundancy of mode constraints in the formation of the difference list representing the result.

Thus we cannot infer the correct mode of the path $\langle \texttt{qsort}, 2\rangle$ and other paths, and automated debugging should consider both of the possibilities, $m(\langle \texttt{qsort}, 2\rangle) = in$ and $m(\langle \texttt{qsort}, 2\rangle) = out$.

We consider the correction of both constants and variables here. It turns out that all depth-1 corrections are non-well-moded. There are six depth-2 corrections that are well-moded:

(1) Line 1: `quicksort(Xs,Ys) :- true | qsort(Xs,Zs,Zs).`
(2) Line 1: `quicksort(Xs,Ys) :- true | qsort(Zs,Ys,Zs).`
(3) Line 1: `quicksort(Xs,Ys) :- true | qsort(Xs,`c`,Ys).`
(4) Line 1: `quicksort(Xs,Ys) :- true | qsort(`c`,Ys,Xs).`
(5) Line 5: `Ys2=`$_2$`[X|Ys2], qsort(L,Ys1,Ys3).`
(6) Line 5: `Ys1=`$_2$`[X|Ys2], qsort(L,Ys2,Ys3).`

Here, c is some constant.

Typing doesn't help much for this example. The assumption that integers and list constructors should not occupy the same path does not exclude any of the above alternatives.

However, usage information will help. Suppose we know that `quicksort` is used as $m(\langle \texttt{quicksort}, 1\rangle) = in$ and $m(\langle \texttt{quicksort}, 2\rangle) = out$. This excludes

Alternatives (1), (2) and (4). We can also exclude Alternative (5) by static occur-check (`Ys2` occurs on both sides of unification).

Of the remaining, Alternative (6) is the intended program that sorts items in ascending order. It is interesting to see that Alternative (3) is a program for sorting items in *descending* order by choosing '`[]`', the simplest element of the list type, as the constant c. This is not an intended program, but is a reasonable and approximately correct alternative which should not be rejected in the absence of program specification.

7 Related Work

Most previous work on the mode analysis of (concurrent) logic languages was based on abstract interpretation, and focused mainly on the reasoning of program properties assuming that the programs were correct. In contrast, constraint-based mode analysis can be used for diagnosis as well as optimization by assuming that correct programs are well-moded.

Analysis of malfunctioning systems based on their intended logical specification has been studied in the field of artificial intelligence [4] and known as model-based diagnosis. Model-based diagnosis has similarities with our work in the ability of searching minimal explanations and multiple faults. However, the purpose of model-based diagnosis is to analyze the differences between intended and observed behaviors. Our mode system does *not* require that the intended behavior of a program be given as mode declarations, and still locates bugs quite well.

Wand proposed an algorithm for diagnosing non-well-typed functional programs [12]. His approach was to extend the unification algorithm for type reconstruction to record which symbol occurrence imposed which constraint. In contrast, our framework is built outside any underlying framework of constraint solving. We need not modify the constraint-solving algorithm but just call it. Besides its generality, our approach has an advantage that static analysis does not incur any overhead for well-moded/typed programs. Furthermore, the diagnosis guarantees the minimality of the explanation and often refines it further.

Comparison between Moded Flat GHC and other concurrent logic/constraint languages with some notions of moding can be found in [2].

8 Conclusions and Future Work

We studied how constraint-based static analysis could be applied to the automated and systematic debugging of program errors in the absence of mode/type declarations. We showed that, given a near-miss Moded Flat GHC program, our technique could in many cases report a unique solution or a small number of reasonable solutions that included the intended program.

If a programmer declares the mode and/or type of a program, that information can be used as constraints that are considered correct. In general, such constraints are useful in obtaining smaller minimal inconsistent subsets. However, our observation is that constraints implicitly imposed by the assumption of well-modedness (and well-typedness) is strong enough for automatic debugging to be useful.

It is a subject of future work to extend our framework to the correction of non-terminal program symbols (i.e., function and predicate symbols), mainly in terms of search space. It is yet to see whether the proposed framework works well for other programming paradigms such as typed functional languages and procedural languages, but we would claim that the concurrent logic/constraint programming paradigm benefits enormously from static mode/type systems.

Acknowledgment

The authors are indebted to Norio Kato for his comments on an earlier version of this paper.

References

1. Aït-Kaci, H. and Nasr, R., LOGIN: A Logic Programming Language with Built-In Inheritance. *J. Logic Programming*, Vol. 3, No. 3 (1986), pp. 185–215.
2. Cho, K. and Ueda, K., Diagnosing Non-Well-Moded Concurrent Logic Programs, In *Proc. 1996 Joint Int. Conf. and Symp. on Logic Programming (JICSLP'96)*, The MIT Press, 1996, pp. 215–229.
3. Milner, R., A Theory of Type Polymorphism in Programming. *J. of Computer and System Sciences*, Vol. 17, No. 3 (1978), pp. 348–375.
4. Reiter, R., A Theory of Diagnosis from First Principles. *Artificial Intelligence*, Vol. 32 (1987), pp. 57–95.
5. Somogyi, Z., Henderson, F. and Conway, T., The Execution Algorithm of Mercury, An Efficient Purely Declarative Logic Programming Language. *J. Logic Programming*, Vol. 29, No. 1–3 (1996), pp. 17–64.
6. Ueda, K., I/O Mode Analysis in Concurrent Logic Programming. In *Proc. Int. Workshop on Theory and Practice of Parallel Programming*, LNCS 907, Springer, 1995, pp. 356–368.
7. Ueda, K. and Morita, M., A New Implementation Technique for Flat GHC. In *Proc. Seventh Int. Conf. on Logic Programming (ICLP'90)*, The MIT Press, 1990, pp. 3–17.
8. Ueda, K. and Morita, M., Moded Flat GHC and Its Message-Oriented Implementation Technique. *New Generation Computing*, Vol. 13, No. 1 (1994), pp. 3–43.
9. Ueda, K., Experiences with Strong Moding in Concurrent Logic/Constraint Programming. In *Proc. Int. Workshop on Parallel Symbolic Languages and Systems*, LNCS 1068, Springer, 1996, pp. 134–153.
10. Ueda, K. and Cho, K. *kima* — Analyzer of Ill-moded KL1 Programs. Available from `http://www.icot.or.jp/AITEC/FGCS/funding/itaku-H8-index-E.html`, 1997.
11. Ueda, K., *klint* — Static Analyzer for KL1 Programs. Available from `http://www.icot.or.jp/AITEC/FGCS/funding/itaku-H9-index-E.html`, 1998.
12. Wand, M., Finding the Source of Type Errors, In *Proc. 13th ACM Symp. on Principles of Programming Languages*, ACM, 1986, pp. 38–43.

Optimized Q-pivot for Exact Linear Solvers

David-Olivier Azulay and Jean-François Pique

Laboratoire d'Informatique de Marseille, ESA CNRS 6077, Université de la Méditerranée, Faculté des Sciences de Luminy, Marseille, France
azulay@lim.univ-mrs.fr, pique@lim.univ-mrs.fr

Abstract. We use Q-matrices to efficiently solve incremental linear systems over $\mathbb{R}$, using integer computations. An algorithm optimized for the Q-pivot operation of Q-matrices is described, allowing a noticeable improvement in the efficiency of linear constraint solvers with infinite precision. We then present a coding of Q-matrices suitable for this algorithm and give some performance measurements.

1 Introduction

We will discuss algorithms for the resolution of linear systems in PROLOG-like constraint languages. Present implementations solve these systems either using infinite precision computations with rational numbers, which allows to guarantee the correctness of proofs and solutions (PROLOG III, CHIP, ATHENA, ...), or using floating point computations which allows to handle big problems with a reasonable computation time (CLP(R), CLAIRE, ...). Unfortunately the strong point of each method is the weak point of the other one. In constraint solvers the loss of precision is worsened by the fact that computations cannot be ordered, due to the incremental nature of the resolution process. In a decision procedure, the loss of precision can have very adverse effects even for algorithms, such as the revised simplex, which are known to be more immune to cumulative errors.

Present algorithms for the resolution of linear systems are constructions, sometimes very sophisticated, built upon the basic principle of the pivot described by Gauss. Starting from equations of the form $ax + by + cz \cdots = 0$, pivots (e.g. linear combinations of equations) are applied in order to express some variables as a function of the others ($x = -\frac{b}{a}y - \frac{c}{a}z \ldots$). In a matrix representation $A.x = 0$ of the system of equations[1], a pivot means a combination of rows. We will stick to the following initial system for our examples :

Example 1.

$$\text{Let } A.x = \begin{matrix} \\ l_1 \\ l_2 \\ l_3 \end{matrix} \begin{matrix} \begin{matrix} c_1 & c_2 & c_3 & c_4 & c_5 \end{matrix} \\ \begin{bmatrix} 2 & -4 & 5 & 6 & 7 \\ 1 & 0 & 1 & -4 & 5 \\ 6 & -8 & 9 & 0 & 1 \end{bmatrix} \end{matrix} . \begin{bmatrix} x_1 \\ x_2 \\ x_3 \\ x_4 \\ x_5 \end{bmatrix} = 0 \text{ such that } \forall i \in \{1,2,3,4,5\}\ x_i \in \mathbb{Q}.$$

[1] In a simplex with bounded variables, constant b_i can be represented by a variable x_i with bounds $[b_i, b_i]$.

This way of expressing solutions is more "natural" than the other one consisting in expressing some amount of a variable x as a function of the others ($ax = by + cz \ldots$), in order to only have integer coefficients. However computing on such coefficients is much faster than computing with rationals for which the reduction of the common factors between the numerator and the denominator is very costly. As a matter of fact, symbolic computation softwares are using algorithms with integer computations [3, 4] in order to solve such systems; unfortunately these algorithms only apply to static systems and cannot be used by the incremental solvers needed in constraint logic programming languages.

The formalism of Q-matrices (see [9]) palliates this defect and facilitates the expression of any manipulation of the equations by an operation over the domain of integer matrices. Since Q-matrices are integer matrices, computing with them is faster than with rationals by at least an order of magnitude ([16]). In this paper we present an optimized implementation of the Q-pivot (which is the pivot used with Q-matrices, cf. [9]) and we describe the incremental operations which are needed to implement a linear solver with Q-matrices. Section two is a reminder of the definition of a Q-matrix. In section three, after a discussion of the different pivots, we describe precisely our optimized Q-pivot. Section four presents the incremental operations for Q-matrices. Section five is a description of a data structure suitable for the described algorithm. In section six an evaluation of the efficiency of the algorithm is given, and we conclude in section seven.

2 Definition of a Q-matrix

We will call matrix a *set* of coefficients each of which being associated with a couple formed respectively from a row and column set of indices. In order to avoid complex denotations, we will stay in an intuitive context and will sometimes leave out the rigorous notation of row and column indices. We will denote L the set of row indices of a matrix A, and C the set of its column indices. When there are no ambiguities, we will say "the set B of columns" instead of "the set of columns whose indices are member of set B of column indices". Let us introduce in an informal way the denotations used to define Q-matrices; given A a matrix of size $m \times n$:

- we denote A_B the submatrix of size $|L| \times |B|$ formed from the columns of A with an index in a subset B of its column indices C;
- a square submatrix whose rows have been renamed with B, the column indices, and such that $|B| = |L|$ is denoted $A_{\overline{B}}$;
- a ***basis*** B of A, is a set of size $|L|$ of the column indices of A such that $\det(A_{\overline{B}}) \neq 0$;
- the concatenation of two matrices of size $m \times n$ and $m \times n'$ is denoted $\left[A | A' \right]$, a matrix of size $m \times (n + n')$;
- the matrix $A_{\overline{B}}$ such that the coefficients of *column* i have been replaced by the coefficients of *column* j of A is denoted $A_{\overline{B}} - i + j$.

Definition 1. *For any basis B of A, the Q-matrix $Q(A,B)$ is the matrix whose columns are named the same as the columns of A, whose rows are named with the elements of set B and such that each coefficient of $Q(A,B)$ is $q_{i,j} = \det(A_B^{\neg} - i + j)$.*

Property 1. *If A is an integer matrix, then $Q(A,B)$ is also an integer matrix for any basis B.*

From its definition a Q-matrix $Q(A,B)$ has a square submatrix with all diagonal coefficients equal to $\det(A_B)$; if we name I_D an identity matrix with $(i,j) \in D \times D$, then $Q(A,B)_B = \det(A_B^{\neg}) \times I_D$ (in this case $D = B$). More interestingly, if we call A' the matrix obtained by applying m classical pivots on a set B of m columns of a matrix A, $Q(A,B) = \det(A_B^{\neg}) \times A'$. The main difference is that the common denominator $\det(A_B^{\neg})$ does not show up with reduced fractions.

Example 2.

$$Q(A,\{c_1,c_2,c_3\}) = \begin{bmatrix} -12 & 0 & 0 & 64 & 32 \\ 0 & -12 & 0 & 30 & -78 \\ 0 & 0 & -12 & -16 & -92 \end{bmatrix}, \ \det(A_B^{\neg}) = \begin{vmatrix} 2 & -4 & 5 \\ 1 & 0 & 1 \\ 6 & -8 & 9 \end{vmatrix} = -12$$

Property 2. *If I_D is the identity matrix, obviously we have $Q([\,A|I_D\,], D) = [\,A|I_D\,]$.*

Any matrix which has a set of columns forming an identity matrix is a Q-matrix if the basis is set to these columns and the rows are renamed accordingly. We therefore have at our disposal a simple means to build a Q-matrix from an arbitrary integer matrix: it suffices to concatenate to it an identity matrix (augmenting in the meantime the size of the matrix).

3 The Q-pivot

The Q-pivot is the pivot operation for Q-matrices. Let us remind the definition.

Definition 2. *A Q-pivot for an element $q_{l,c}$ of a Q-matrix $Q(A,B)$, noted $Q(A,B) \circlearrowleft (l,c)$, results in a new Q-matrix $Q' = Q(A,(B - \{l\}) \cup \{c\}))$ such that for each of its coefficients*

$$q'_{i,j} = (q_{l,c}q_{i,j} - q_{i,c}q_{l,j})/\det(A_B^{\neg}) \quad \textit{if } i \neq l, \ q'_{i,j} = q_{i,j} \quad \textit{otherwise} . \qquad (1)$$

Since by construction $q_{l,c}$ is the determinant of matrix $A_B^{\neg} - l + c$, it is also the determinant of the basis of Q'. On the next Q-pivot, $q_{l,c}$ will be the common divisor of all row combinations as we will explain it later.

In the standard simplex method the Q-pivot replaces the Gauss-Jordan pivot. In the revised simplex method the Q-pivot is used to update the complementary matrix (which is the inverse of the basis, up to a factor product). The efficiency of the Q-pivot is therefore a crucial point : the data structure and the algorithm described in the remaining have been designed to optimize it.

3.1 Analysis of Alternative Pivots

A pivot is a tool which allows us to express some variables with respect to the others in the process of solving a system of linear equations. The best known pivot is the Gauss-Jordan pivot which, applied to a matrix A, computes a new matrix A' with coefficients

$$a'_{i,j} = (a_{l,c}a_{i,j} - a_{i,c}a_{l,j})/a_{l,c} \text{ if } i \neq l, \qquad a'_{i,j} = a_{i,j}/a_{l,c} \text{ otherwise .} \tag{2}$$

With this pivot computations are made on rationals, which has a serious defect with exact arithmetic : the reduction of fractions by GCDs accounts for a noticeable part of the total computation time (up to 80 % of time in PROLOG III).

The cost of the reduction can be avoided with the so-called ***division free pivot*** which allows to only handle integer values; this is the same algorithm with the division dropped out. Thus the new matrix A' is the matrix whose coefficients are obtained from the formula

$$a'_{i,j} = a_{l,c}a_{i,j} - a_{i,c}a_{l,j} \text{ if } i \neq l, \qquad a'_{i,j} = a_{i,j} \text{ otherwise .} \tag{3}$$

It is clear that in this case numbers are never "reduced" and in the worst case one can observe an exponential growth of their size with respect to the number of pivots. This algorithm is therefore unusable just as it is; however, in order to diminish the size of the coefficients, it is possible to complement it with the reduction of rows by GCDs, which does not alter the meaning of the equations. It's faster to compute a GCD for all integer coefficients than a numerator–denominator GCD for each rational coefficient. As a matter of fact this first combination is quite efficient and is one of the most attractive solution, more especially as there exists efficient algorithms to compute a common divisor for several numbers (see [6]).

There is an algorithm which is closed to the Q-pivot, called ***fraction free pivot***. A fraction free pivot applied to a matrix A leads to a matrix A' whose coefficients are :

$$a'_{i,j} = (a_{l,c}a_{i,j} - a_{i,c}a_{l,j})/p \text{ if } i \neq l, \qquad a'_{i,j} = a_{i,j} \text{ otherwise .} \tag{4}$$

Where p is a common divisor for all coefficients of matrix A. It turns out that p is the value of the coefficient which has been used for the previous fraction free pivot. It is well known that in that case we have ***exact divisions***, e.g. all dividends are multiple of the divisor p (see [11][2]). In practice people use a division free pivot associated with a GCD reduction. If we classify the different pivots by increasing performance, we obtain the following schema which comes from experience:

division free pivot < Gauss-Jordan pivot (rational) < fraction free pivot ≈ normal Q-pivot < division free pivot +GCD < optimized Q-pivot.

[2] According to Bareiss, Jordan (1838-1922) already knew this operation.

Notice however that only Q-matrices allow an easy definition of incremental operations such as the Q-increment or Q-decrement by a row or column. ***Given a Q-matrix $Q(A,B)$, each coefficient can be expressed in a simple way as the determinant of a submatrix of the initial matrix A.*** With this property in mind it is possible to define specialized operations on Q-matrices.

3.2 Row Factors

Remember that each coefficient in a Q-matrix is expressed as the determinant of an $m \times m$ square matrix: in general they will be much "greater" than the coefficients of the initial matrix. From property 2, a Q-matrix can be obtained from any matrix A by adjoining to it an identity matrix I_D. Then it is easy to obtain the Q-matrix of $\left[A|I_D\right]$ for any basis of A by applying Q-pivots. This method however has the defect to increase the size of the initial matrix and, therefore, to augment the number of computations (compare example 2 with example 3).

Example 3.

$$Q(\left[A|I_D\right], D) = \left[A|I_D\right] \qquad D = \{l_1, l_2, l_3\}$$

$$Q(\left[A|I_D\right], \{c_1, c_2, c_3\}) = \left[\begin{array}{rrrrr|rrr} -12 & 0 & 0 & 64 & 32 & 8 & -4 & -4 \\ 0 & -12 & 0 & 30 & -78 & -3 & -12 & 3 \\ 0 & 0 & -12 & -16 & -92 & -8 & -8 & 4 \end{array}\right]$$

The m added columns are only there to constitute a full basis for the first Q-pivots. Since the columns of the basis have always the same structure, to represent them it is sufficient to memorize the determinant of the current basis in an auxiliary variable. For any integer matrix, it suffices to set this auxiliary value to 1 to "virtually" adjoin it an identity matrix. In this configuration, ***a fraction free pivot on a Q-matrix is a Q-pivot.*** The main difference is that the Q-matrix form exhibits on the basis diagonal the common divisor for the next Q-pivot. This one is also a multiple of all the denominators of the (rational) coefficients in the solution expressed with current basis.

In the following we will be interested in reducing the size of the computations operands by a factorization of row coefficients. As we just have said, it is not necessary to represent the coefficients of the basis columns, since they all are the same. However, if we factorize, keeping them on each row will allow us to simplify the computations. We denote $q', q'', q''', \ldots$ the coefficients obtained from successive pivots on $q_{l,c}, q'_{l',c'}, q''_{l'',c''}, \ldots$ As an analogy and to simplify notations, we will denote $'q_{'l,'c}$ the coefficient of a pivot on $('l,'c)$ which lead us to a Q-matrix with general coefficient $q_{i,j}$ (notice the prime ***ahead*** to denote the previous pivot coefficient). Since the pivot row is unaltered in a Q-pivot, we always have $q'_{l,c} = q_{l,c}$, $'q_{'l,'c} = q_{'l,'c}$.

Let λ_i ($\lambda_i > 0$) be a common factor for all coefficients in row i, and let $\dot{q}_{i,j}$ be the corresponding reduced coefficient. From now on, we will write our matrix coefficients as $q_{i,j} = \lambda_i\, \dot{q}_{i,j}$, represented in two separate matrices. We will denote $\dot{Q}$ the matrix formed with the $\dot{q}_{i,j}$ coefficients and we will call it *reduced matrix*. We will denote λ the vector formed with the row factors. Thus a matrix Q will be denoted $\lambda \otimes \dot{Q}$ where $\otimes$ is an operator with the lowest priority which intuitively means that each coefficient $\dot{q}_{i,j}$ should be multiplied by its respective row factor λ_i.

In order to better highlight the basis coefficients, we will denote β_i the determinant of the current basis divided by the factor of row i. Therefore for each row of the factorized Q-matrix $\dot{Q}$ we have:

$$\beta_i \equiv \dot{q}_{i,i} = q_{i,i}/\lambda_i = \det(A_B^{\rightharpoondown})/\lambda_i.$$

Example 4.

$$Q([A|I_D],\{c_1,c_2,c_3\}) = \begin{bmatrix}2\\3\\4\end{bmatrix} \otimes \left[\begin{array}{ccccc|ccc} -6 & 0 & 0 & 32 & 16 & 4 & -2 & -2 \\ 0 & -4 & 0 & 10 & 26 & -1 & -4 & 1 \\ 0 & 0 & -3 & -4 & 23 & -2 & -2 & 1 \end{array}\right]$$

To better understand the way computations are simplified, let us consider what happens on row i of $Q(A,B)$ for a Q-pivot with pivot $q_{l,c}$ when the pivot column coefficient is zero ($q_{i,c} = 0$ in our formulation). The Q-pivot formula 1 transforms into[3]:

$$\begin{aligned} q'_{i,j} &= \frac{q_{i,j} \times q_{l,c}}{{}'q_{'l,'c}} \\ &= \frac{\lambda_i\, \dot{q}_{i,j} \times q_{l,c}}{\lambda_i\, \beta_i} \\ &= \frac{\dot{q}_{i,j} \times q_{l,c}}{\beta_i} \end{aligned}$$

Observe that the ratio $q_{l,c}/\beta_i$ is invariant for all coefficients in a same row. We can decrease the size of the operands and the number of computations by extracting the common factor $a = \gcd(q_{l,c}, \beta_i)$ from these two operands. Stating that $\beta_i = a \times f$ and $q_{l,c} = a \times b$, we have:

$$q'_{i,j} = \frac{\dot{q}_{i,j}}{f} \times b$$

If β_i is a divisor of $q_{l,c}$, we have $f = 1$ and no operation is required on row coefficients, it suffices to consider b as the new row factor. If β_i and $q_{l,c}$ do have a common factor, the size of the operands, already diminished from row factor λ_i, is in addition reduced of factor f. In practice, it is often the case that the computations do simplify.

[3] Notice that in a Q-matrix $Q(A,B)$, owing to the renaming of rows, we have $q_{i,i} = {}'q_{'l,'c} = \lambda_i \beta_i\ \forall i \in B$.

Let us consider now the general formula for a Q-pivot, exhibiting the invariant terms for a row i:

$$\begin{aligned}\lambda_i'\dot{q}_{i,j}' &= \frac{\lambda_l\dot{q}_{l,c}\,\underline{\lambda_i\dot{q}_{i,j}} - \underline{\lambda_i}\dot{q}_{i,c}\,\lambda_l\dot{q}_{l,j}}{\underline{\lambda_i}\beta_i} \\ &= \frac{\lambda_l(\dot{q}_{l,c}\dot{q}_{i,j} - \dot{q}_{i,c}\dot{q}_{l,j})}{\beta_i} \end{aligned} \tag{5}$$

When the coefficients of a given row i are computed it is obvious that the two products $\lambda_l\dot{q}_{l,c}$ and $\lambda_l\dot{q}_{i,c}$ are invariant and need only be computed once. Let us list the most interesting variations of row factors. We know that:

- the row factor of the pivot row stay unchanged;
- row factors of rows such as the coefficient in the pivot column is zero are modified as described above;
- row factors of rows with a non zero coefficient in the pivot column and such that λ_l is a multiple of β_i are set to λ_l/β_i. In that case none of the general formula divisions is performed. Notice that whenever λ_l is not a multiple of β_i but there exists a common divisor different from one, this divisor becomes the row factor and operations are done with smaller operands.

The key point here is that *the β_i coefficients are now not necessarily equals* and therefore it is now necessary to express the value of β_i for each line (see example 4). One of the extra cost brought by this data structure is one or two GCD for each line, in order to detect the existence of common divisors between the numerator and denominator of this factors. See section 3.4 for a precise case analysis.

3.3 Auxiliary Basis and Truncated Q-matrix

From now on, we will always use the value β_i to divide the linear combinations of row i. We define a new binary operator $\sim$ whose right operand is a vector of size m, a compact form of a square diagonal matrix, and whose left operand is a matrix of size $m \times n$. The result of this operation is a new matrix of size $m \times (m+n)$ which is the matrix formed with this unpacked diagonal matrix adjoined to the matrix A. A Q-matrix can then be written with the two introduced operators: $Q = \lambda \otimes \dot{Q} \sim \beta$, where β is a vector filled with the reduced values β_i for $i \in B$. For a general matrix, these values are initialized to 1 to obtain $\left[A|I_D\right]$. An "auxiliary basis" β can be linked permanently to any matrix doing so.

Example 5.

$$\left[A|I_D\right] = \begin{bmatrix}1\\1\\1\end{bmatrix} \otimes \begin{bmatrix}2 & -4 & 5 & 6 & 7\\ 1 & 0 & 1 & -4 & 5\\ 6 & -8 & 9 & 0 & 1\end{bmatrix} \sim \begin{bmatrix}1\\1\\1\end{bmatrix} = \left[\begin{array}{ccccc|ccc}2 & -4 & 5 & 6 & 7 & 1 & 0 & 0\\ 1 & 0 & 1 & -4 & 5 & 0 & 1 & 0\\ 6 & -8 & 9 & 0 & 1 & 0 & 0 & 1\end{array}\right]$$

We will call "truncated Q-matrices" a Q-matrix which does not contain the totality of its basis columns: as an example the complementary matrix contains none of its basis columns, and a general matrix which has been fraction-free pivoted only contains a few of its basis columns.

We note that we avoid m^2 computations of useless coefficients at each iteration on the column set D of the real Q-matrix $Q([A|I_D],B)$. These m columns are not needed for a standard resolution of linear systems.

Example 6.

$$\left(Q([A|I_D],D) \circlearrowleft (l_1,c_1)\right)_C = \begin{bmatrix}1\\1\\2\end{bmatrix} \otimes \begin{bmatrix}2 & -4 & 5 & 6 & 7\\0 & 4 & -3 & -14 & 3\\0 & 4 & 6 & -18 & 20\end{bmatrix}$$

3.4 Optimized Q-pivot Algorithm

In the following algorithm, we have decided to minimize the number of elementary operations even if we execute a few more computations in the worst case. The main idea is to detect constant terms for a whole row in order to take their common factors into account (the underlined term corresponds to the row factor). Most of the optimized Q-pivot algorithm is simply handling +1 or −1 cases specially but in a cumulative way: this means that this algorithm produces reduced factors from reduced factors and so on ... Notice that the formula on the right describes the pivot formula obtained after the simplifications corresponding to the conditions on the left side. Notice that all divisions are known to be exact divisions.

general formula: $(\lambda_l(\dot{q}_{l,c}\dot{q}_{i,j} - \dot{q}_{i,c}\dot{q}_{l,j}))/\beta_i$

If the coefficient of the column pivot is zero ($q_{i,c} = 0$)

do $a \leftarrow |\gcd(\lambda_l\dot{q}_{l,c},\beta_i)|$, $b \leftarrow (\lambda_l\dot{q}_{l,c})/a$, $f \leftarrow \beta_i/a$

$(\lambda_l\dot{q}_{l,c}\dot{q}_{i,j})/\beta_i$ simplifies into $(ab\dot{q}_{i,j})/(af)$ $= b\dot{q}_{i,j}/f \ \underline{\times 1}$

if $b < 0$ do $b \leftarrow -b$, $f \leftarrow -f$

case $f =$

(A) +1: do $\lambda_i' \leftarrow b$, $\dot{q}_{i,j}' \leftarrow \dot{q}_{i,j}$ — $\dot{q}_{i,j} \ \underline{\times b}$

(B) −1: do $\lambda_i' \leftarrow b$, $\dot{q}_{i,j}' \leftarrow -\dot{q}_{i,j}$ — $-\dot{q}_{i,j} \ \underline{\times b}$

other: do $\lambda_i' \leftarrow +1$

(L) if $b = +1$ do $\dot{q}_{i,j}' \leftarrow \dot{q}_{i,j}/f$ — $\dot{q}_{i,j}/f \ \underline{\times b}$

(U) else $\dot{q}_{i,j}' \leftarrow b\dot{q}_{i,j}/f$ — $(b\dot{q}_{i,j})/f \ \underline{\times 1}$

If the coefficient of the column pivot is not zero ($q_{i,c} \neq 0$)

do $a \leftarrow |\gcd(\dot{q}_{l,c}, \dot{q}_{i,c})|$, $b \leftarrow \dot{q}_{l,c}/a$, $v \leftarrow \dot{q}_{i,c}/a$

do $d \leftarrow |\gcd(a\lambda_l, \beta_i)|$, $e \leftarrow a\lambda_l/d$, $f \leftarrow \beta_i/d$

$(\lambda_l(\dot{q}_{l,c}\dot{q}_{i,j} - \dot{q}_{i,c}\dot{q}_{l,j}))/\beta_i$ simplifies into $(de(b\dot{q}_{i,j} - v\dot{q}_{l,j}))/(df)$ $= e(b\dot{q}_{i,j} - v\dot{q}_{l,j})/f$ $\underline{\times 1}$

if $f < 0$ do $e \leftarrow -e$, $f \leftarrow -f$

if $e < 0$ do $b \leftarrow -b$, $e \leftarrow -e$

else do $v \leftarrow -v$ — $e(b\dot{q}_{i,j} + v\dot{q}_{l,j})/f$ $\underline{\times 1}$

if $f = +1$

do $\lambda_i \leftarrow e$ — $b\dot{q}_{i,j} + v\dot{q}_{l,j}$ $\underline{\times e}$

case $b =$

+1: case $v =$ — $\dot{q}_{i,j} + v\dot{q}_{l,j}$ $\underline{\times e}$

(C) +1: $\dot{q}'_{i,j} \leftarrow \dot{q}_{i,j} + \dot{q}_{l,j}$ — $\dot{q}_{i,j} + \dot{q}_{l,j}$ $\underline{\times e}$

(D) −1: $\dot{q}'_{i,j} \leftarrow \dot{q}_{i,j} - \dot{q}_{l,j}$ — $\dot{q}_{i,j} - \dot{q}_{l,j}$ $\underline{\times e}$

(G) other: $\dot{q}'_{i,j} \leftarrow \dot{q}_{i,j} + v\dot{q}_{l,j}$ — $\dot{q}_{i,j} + v\dot{q}_{l,j}$ $\underline{\times e}$

−1: case $v =$ — $-\dot{q}_{i,j} + v\dot{q}_{l,j}$ $\underline{\times e}$

(E) +1: $\dot{q}'_{i,j} \leftarrow \dot{q}_{l,j} - \dot{q}_{i,j}$ — $-\dot{q}_{i,j} + \dot{q}_{l,j}$ $\underline{\times e}$

(F) −1: $\dot{q}'_{i,j} \leftarrow -(\dot{q}_{i,j} + \dot{q}_{l,j})$ — $-\dot{q}_{i,j} - \dot{q}_{l,j}$ $\underline{\times e}$

(H) other: do $\dot{q}'_{i,j} \leftarrow v\dot{q}_{l,j} - \dot{q}_{i,j}$ — $-\dot{q}_{i,j} + v\dot{q}_{l,j}$ $\underline{\times e}$

other: case $v =$

(I) +1: $\dot{q}'_{i,j} \leftarrow b\dot{q}_{i,j} + \dot{q}_{l,j}$ — $b\dot{q}_{i,j} + \dot{q}_{l,j}$ $\underline{\times e}$

(J) −1: $\dot{q}'_{i,j} \leftarrow b\dot{q}_{i,j} - \dot{q}_{l,j}$ — $b\dot{q}_{i,j} - \dot{q}_{l,j}$ $\underline{\times e}$

(K) other: $\dot{q}'_{i,j} \leftarrow b\dot{q}_{i,j} + v\dot{q}_{l,j}$ — $b\dot{q}_{i,j} + v\dot{q}_{l,j}$ $\underline{\times e}$

else — $(de(b\dot{q}_{i,j} - v\dot{q}_{l,j}))/(df)$

do $h \leftarrow be$, $w \leftarrow ve$, $\lambda'_i \leftarrow +1$ — $= (h\dot{q}_{i,j} + w\dot{q}_{l,j})/f$ $\underline{\times 1}$

case $h =$

+1: case $w =$ — $(\dot{q}_{i,j} + w\dot{q}_{l,j})/f$ $\underline{\times 1}$

(M) +1: $\dot{q}'_{i,j} \leftarrow (\dot{q}_{i,j} + \dot{q}_{l,j})/f$ — $(\dot{q}_{i,j} + \dot{q}_{l,j})/f$ $\underline{\times 1}$

(N) −1: $\dot{q}'_{i,j} \leftarrow (\dot{q}_{i,j} - \dot{q}_{l,j})/f$ — $(\dot{q}_{i,j} - \dot{q}_{l,j})/f$ $\underline{\times 1}$

(Q) other: $\dot{q}'_{i,j} \leftarrow (\dot{q}_{i,j} + w\dot{q}_{l,j})/f$ — $(\dot{q}_{i,j} + w\dot{q}_{l,j})/f$ $\underline{\times 1}$

−1: case $w =$ — $(-\dot{q}_{i,j} + w\dot{q}_{l,j})/f$ $\underline{\times 1}$

(O) +1: $\dot{q}'_{i,j} \leftarrow (\dot{q}_{l,j} - \dot{q}_{i,j})/f$ — $(-\dot{q}_{i,j} + \dot{q}_{l,j})/f$ $\underline{\times 1}$

(P) −1: $\dot{q}'_{i,j} \leftarrow (\dot{q}_{i,j} + \dot{q}_{l,j})/-f$ — $(-\dot{q}_{i,j} - \dot{q}_{l,j})/f$ $\underline{\times 1}$

(R) other: $\dot{q}'_{i,j} \leftarrow (w\dot{q}_{l,j} - \dot{q}_{i,j})/f$ — $(-\dot{q}_{i,j} + w\dot{q}_{l,j})/f$ $\underline{\times 1}$

other: case $w =$

(S) +1: $\dot{q}'_{i,j} \leftarrow (h\dot{q}_{i,j} + \dot{q}_{l,j})/f$ — $(h\dot{q}_{i,j} + \dot{q}_{l,j})/f$ $\underline{\times 1}$

(T) −1: $\dot{q}'_{i,j} \leftarrow (h\dot{q}_{i,j} - \dot{q}_{l,j})/f$ — $(h\dot{q}_{i,j} - \dot{q}_{l,j})/f$ $\underline{\times 1}$

(V) other: $\dot{q}'_{i,j} \leftarrow (h\dot{q}_{i,j} + w\dot{q}_{l,j})/f$ — $(h\dot{q}_{i,j} + w\dot{q}_{l,j})/f$ $\underline{\times 1}$

We detail the maximal supplementary cost induced by this algorithm for a simplification; it happens for case T. Detecting this case requires 3 sign tests, 1 assignment to 1, 5 comparisons with 1 or −1, 5 negations, 2 products, 4 exact divisions and 2 computations of common divisors. But, in case T, only one multiplication is computed for each calculation of a new coefficient. In fact, the supplementary operations due to this phase of common factors calculations are absorbed by the avoided computation on each coefficient.

The only case for which this phase doesn't lead to an increased performance is case V, which is the case where no simplifications have been detected and where we have to compute all the calculations specified for the Q-pivot.

3.5 Efficiency

It's interesting to clarify for each case the exact number of operations required. The division performed here is an exact division, which means a division for which we know that the dividend is a multiple of the divisor. This division is of course faster than a generic one is (see [15]).

	Assignments			Negations			Additions			Multiplications			Divisions
Case	†	††	†††	†	††	†††	†	††	†††	†	††	†††	
A	—			—			—			—			—
B	0			1			—			—			—
C	1	0	0	0	0	0	0	0	1	—			—
D	0	0	0	1	0	0	0	0	1	—			—
E	1	0	0	0	1	0	0	0	1	—			—
F	0	0	0	1	1	1	0	0	1	—			—
G	0	0	0	0	0	0	0	0	1	1	0	1	—
H	0	0	0	0	1	0	0	0	1	1	0	1	—
I	1	0	0	0	0	0	0	0	1	0	1	1	—
J	0	0	0	1	0	0	0	0	1	0	1	1	—
K	—			—			0	0	1	1	1	2	—
L	—			—			0			0			1
M	—			—			0	0	1	0			1
N	—			—			0	0	1	0			1
O	—			—			0	0	1	0			1
P	—			—			0	0	1	0			1
Q	—			—			0	0	1	1	0	1	1
R	—			—			0	0	1	1	0	1	1
S	—			—			0	0	1	0	1	1	1
T	—			—			0	0	1	0	1	1	1
U	—			—			0			1			1
V	—			—			0	0	1	1	1	2	1

† : $q_{i,j} = 0, q_{l,j} \neq 0$ | †† : $q_{i,j} \neq 0, q_{l,j} = 0$ | ††† : $q_{i,j} \neq 0, q_{l,j} \neq 0$

The numbers induced by the Q-pivot are bounded by a constant as it is proven in [8]: elementary operations are therefore considered as constant time operations.

4 Incremental Modifications of a Q-matrix

4.1 Q-decrement by a Column

The Q-decrement by a column is used when we want to eliminate a variable from the constraints system. As the coefficients $q_{i,j}$ of a Q-matrix are equals to $\det(A_B^{\neg} - i + j)$, these remain unchanged if the basis columns are unchanged. So we have $Q(A - A_j, B) = Q(A, B)_{C-\{j\}}$ if $j \notin B$.

Definition 3. *The Q-decrement by a column c is the operation calculating Q', the Q-matrix associated to matrix A leaving out column c. To obtain $Q' = Q(A - A_c, B)$ we just remove column c of $Q(A, B)$.*

Example 7.

$$Q(\begin{bmatrix} 2 & -4 & 5 & 7 \\ 1 & 0 & 1 & 5 \\ 6 & -8 & 9 & 1 \end{bmatrix}, \{c_1, c_2, c_3\}) = \begin{bmatrix} -12 & 0 & 0 & 32 \\ 0 & -12 & 0 & 78 \\ 0 & 0 & -12 & -92 \end{bmatrix}$$

Thanks to the auxiliary basis β, we note that we can avoid the Q-pivot needed to bring it out of the basis when we remove such a column, since $q_{i,i} = \beta_i$: we can truncate Q-matrices without any restriction.

4.2 Q-decrement by a Row

To remove a constraint from our constraints system, and to quickly compute the modifications to be applied to the Q-matrix, we need the *complementary matrix*. The complementary matrix of a square matrix A_B, denoted $\widetilde{A_B}$, is the transposed matrix of the cofactors, that is to say $\widetilde{A_B} = \det A_B^{\neg} \times A_B^{-1}$. Matrix $\widetilde{A_B}$ is the square submatrix $Q([A|I_D], B)_D$, whatever the basis B is[4].

Definition 4. *The Q-decrement of a Q-matrix $Q(A, B)$ by a row c is done by adjoining the column of $\widetilde{A_B}$ whose name is the name of the row that we want to remove (the column is arbitrarily renamed). We then calculate a Q-pivot for the element which is on the row we want to remove. Finally, we remove this column and row c of the matrix to obtain matrix Q'.*

If l is the row of A which has been renamed c in the Q-matrix $Q(A, B)$, Q' is the matrix $Q(A - {}_lA, B\text{-}\{c\})$[5].

As the complementary matrix $\widetilde{A_B}$ is the truncated Q-matrix $Q([A|I_D], B)_D$, it has been computed by the application of the same Q-pivots which allowed us to calculate $Q(A, B)$ from A. More precisely, $Q(A, B) = Q([A|I_D], B)_C$ is obtained from $Q([A|I_D], D)$ with m Q-pivots. As a consequence the row factors of $Q(A, B)$ and $\widetilde{A_B}$ are the same. So when we adjoin the column of the complementary matrix, we adjoin the reduced coefficients. For the same reason,

[4] In fact, we have here one of the method to compute the inverse of a matrix.

[5] The notation ${}_lA$ refers the row l of matrix A

it is trivial that the concatenation of a Q-matrix $Q(A, B)$ with one or more of the columns of its complementary matrix is a Q-matrix by construction.

The complexity of the Q-decrement by a row is equal to the complexity of the Q-pivot $m \times n$ (note that it's not necessary to effectively include the column of the complementary matrix in the Q-matrix).

Example 8.

$$\left[\begin{array}{ccccc|c} -12 & 0 & 0 & 64 & 32 & -4 \\ 0 & -12 & 0 & 30 & -78 & 3 \\ \hline 0 & 0 & -12 & -16 & -92 & \boxed{4} \end{array}\right] \rightarrow \begin{bmatrix} 4 & 0 & 4 & -16 & 20 & 0 \\ 0 & 4 & -3 & -14 & 3 & 0 \\ 0 & 0 & -12 & -16 & -92 & 4 \end{bmatrix}$$

$$Q(\begin{bmatrix} 2 & -4 & 5 & 6 & 7 \\ 1 & 0 & 1 & -4 & 5 \end{bmatrix}, \{c_1, c_2\}) = \begin{bmatrix} 4 & 0 & 4 & -16 & 20 \\ 0 & 4 & -3 & -14 & 3 \end{bmatrix}$$

4.3 Q-increment by a Column

When we want to add a variable to our linear system, its Q-matrix is modified. We describe here how to use the current Q-matrix to calculate the new one.

Definition 5. *The Q-increment of $Q(A, B)$ by a column s corresponds to the adjunction of column s to A. The new matrix $Q' = Q([\,A|s\,], B)$ is calculated thus: the columns of $Q(A, B)$ remain the same in Q', and the new column of Q' is equal to the product of the complementary matrix of A_B by s:*

$$Q([\,A|s\,], B) = \left[\,Q(A, B) | \widetilde{A_B}.s\,\right].$$

The complementary matrix is a truncated Q-matrix that we can therefore represent using reduced coefficients (see 4.2). Let's write the formula of the product of this matrix by a vector

$$\widetilde{A_B}.s = b \Rightarrow \forall i \in C,\ b_i = \sum_{j \in L} \dot{\tilde{a}}_{i,j} \times s_j = \sum_{j \in L} \lambda_i \dot{\tilde{a}}_{i,j} \times s_j = \lambda_i \sum_{j \in L} \dot{\tilde{a}}_{i,j} \times s_j.$$

The complexity of the Q-increment by a column is equal to the complexity of the product: $m \times n$.

Example 9.

$$A_B = \begin{bmatrix} 2 & -4 & 5 \\ 1 & 0 & 1 \\ 6 & -8 & 9 \end{bmatrix} \Rightarrow \widetilde{A_B} = \begin{bmatrix} 8 & -4 & -4 \\ -3 & -12 & 3 \\ -8 & -8 & 4 \end{bmatrix}$$

$$Q(\left[\begin{array}{ccccc|c} 2 & -4 & 5 & 6 & 7 & -1 \\ 1 & 0 & 1 & -4 & 5 & 3 \\ 6 & -8 & 9 & 0 & 1 & 7 \end{array}\right], B) = \left[\begin{array}{ccccc|c} -12 & 0 & 0 & 64 & 32 & 8 \\ 0 & -12 & 0 & 30 & -78 & -54 \\ 0 & 0 & -12 & -16 & -92 & -44 \end{array}\right]$$

4.4 Q-increment by a Row

If we add a constraint to our initial system, its associated Q-matrix is modified: its basis includes a new column and all its coefficients are updated. We are going to describe how to compute efficiently this new Q-matrix while keeping advantage of the presented data structure.

Definition 6. *A Q-increment of $Q(A,B)$ by a row r and for an extension $c \in C - B$ of basis B leads to a matrix Q' with row set $B \cup \{c\}$ and column set C and represents the following operations: multiply row r by $\det(A_B^{\neg})$, and for each row $i \in B$ of $Q(A,B)$ substract r_i times row i from this row r. This row r will be renamed c in Q' for a choice $c \in C - B$ such as $q'_{c,c} \neq 0$. Then, for each row $i \in B$ of $Q(A,B)$, substract $q_{i,c}$ times row c of Q' from $q'_{c,c}$ times row i of $Q(A,B)$ in order to get a row which, divided by $\det(A_B^{\neg})$, is row i of Q'.*

The matrix Q' is the Q-matrix $Q(\left[\frac{A}{r}\right], B \cup \{c\})$.

We can rewrite more intuitively this definition with elementary steps. We'll denote l_{m+1} the index of the row r we are adding, and we'll call A' the augmented matrix. To compute the new Q-matrix of size $(m+1) \times n$ which is associated to A', we start from the Q-matrix $Q(A,B)$ which is already calculated:

1. we add row r to $Q(A,B)$;
2. we multiply all the coefficients of the new row l_{m+1} by the determinant of $A_B^{\neg}$ in order to obtain Q'^1;
3. we apply a Q-pivot on each coefficient (i,i) with $i \in B$ to calculate the matrix Q'^2 (note that only the last row is modified at each iteration);
4. on row l_{m+1} we choose a non null element in a column $c_k \notin B$;
5. the wanted Q-matrix Q' is calculated by a Q-pivot on this element.

We can apply a Q-pivot on Q'^1 because Q'^1 is a truncated Q-matrix. This can be understood from the following property[6]:

$$Q(\left[\begin{array}{c|c|c} A & A_{B\to*} & 0 \\ \hline r & 0 & 1 \end{array}\right], D) = \left[\begin{array}{c|c} \dfrac{Q(A,B)}{\det(A_B^{\neg}) \times r} & \det(A_B^{\neg}) \times I_n \end{array}\right].$$

As the Q-matrix Q' is obtained from Q'^1 with m Q-pivots on the columns of B and a last one on column c_k, Q' is the Q-matrix $Q(A', B \cup \{c_k\})$.

Example 10.

[6] The set D is formed with the last $m+1$ column indices and the notation $B \to *$ means that indices of set B have been renamed to avoid conflicts with indices of A.

$$A' = \left[\begin{array}{ccccc} 2 & -4 & 5 & 6 & 7 \\ 1 & 0 & 1 & -4 & 5 \\ 6 & -8 & 9 & 0 & 1 \\ \hline 0 & -3 & 0 & 2 & -6 \end{array}\right] \quad Q'^1 = \left[\begin{array}{ccccc} \boxed{-12} & 0 & 0 & 64 & 32 \\ 0 & \boxed{-12} & 0 & 30 & -78 \\ 0 & 0 & \boxed{-12} & -16 & -92 \\ \hline 0 & -36 & 0 & -24 & 72 \end{array}\right]$$

$$Q' = \left[\begin{array}{ccccc} 66 & 0 & 0 & 0 & -1040 \\ 0 & 66 & 0 & 0 & 24 \\ 0 & 0 & 66 & 0 & 722 \\ 0 & 0 & 0 & 66 & -162 \end{array}\right] = Q(A', \{c_1, c_2, c_3, c_4\})$$

In order to multiply by $\det(A_{\overline{B}})$ all coefficients in the new row, we only need to update its row factor. Then we apply m Q-pivots on each coefficient $q_{j,j}$ with $j \in B$. This will only modify the last row (besides we'll note that it is useless to calculate a Q-pivot on columns where coefficient (l_{m+1}, j) is zero). In this particular case, the cost of each Q-pivot is n; the last Q-pivot requires $m \times n$ operations. The global complexity of the Q-increment by a row is therefore $m \times n$.

4.5 Update of the Complementary Matrix

Calculating the complementary matrix $\widetilde{A_B}$ from scratch requires m^3 operations, which means m Q-pivots on $\left[A_B | I_D\right]$. But updating it only requires m^2 in the worst case. The complementary matrix is a square matrix that is to say it must be increased (or decreased) simultaneously by a column and a row. If it augments, we must first add the column, then the row. Since it is the truncated Q-matrix $Q(\left[A_B | I_D\right], B)_D$[7], for a complementary matrix, we can say that:

- a Q-increment by a row is realized as explained above;
- a Q-increment by a column is calculated by multiplying the complementary matrix with the vector which is to be added;
- a Q-decrement by a row is easier to program because the column we should have added and removed is already in $\widetilde{A_B}$;
- a Q-decrement by a column is unchanged.

When the complementary matrix is decreased, we just have to execute a Q-pivot for the element which is at the intersection of the row and the column we want to remove, and then to remove this row and this column. When the basis of $Q(A, B)$ changes, the complementary matrix is also modified. The new coefficients are computed with this scheme:

$$\left[Q(A, B') \middle| \widetilde{A_{B'}}\right] = \left[Q(A, B) \middle| \widetilde{A_B}\right] \circlearrowleft q_{l,c} \text{ with } B' = B - \{l\} \cup \{c\}.$$

[7] From this fact, the complementary matrix required for some of the operations on the complementary matrix is itself; remember that $Q(\left[A_B | I_D\right], B) = \left[\det(A_{\overline{B}}) \times I_B \middle| \widetilde{A_B}\right]$.

5 Data Structure

In linear programs, matrices are generally sparse and coded accordingly: only the values different from zero are stored. In addition to the memory saving, we avoid all the tests with zeros by using a linked lists of non null coefficients. In good implementations, a well thought imbrication of loops allows to benefit from the sparsity of both rows and columns and leads to a very important improvement compared to a naive implementation. Row factors are stored in an array to allow an immediate access.

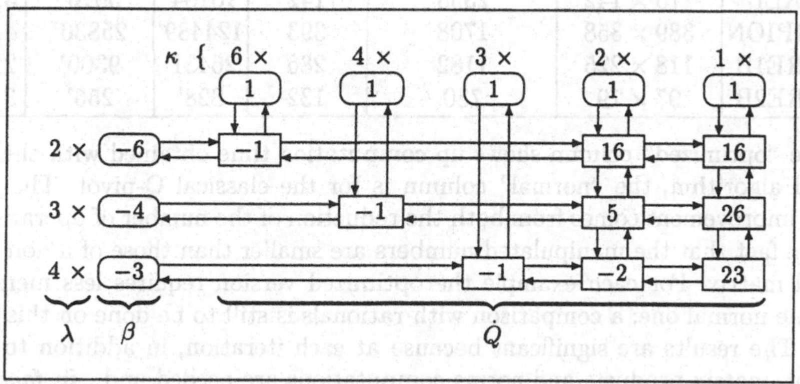

Fig. 1. Coding the Q-matrix $Q(A, \{c_1, c_2, c_3\})$

We also code a column with a linked list coupled to a column factor κ_j: a coefficient $a_{i,j}$ is therefore expressed as $\lambda_i \times \kappa_j \times \dot{a}_{i,j}$. To obtain this decomposition, it is better to execute first with the row factorization, and then with the column factorization in order to increase the probability of common divisors in the optimized Q-pivot algorithm.

One can verify that the introduction of column factors implies only one more multiplication in the formulation of the optimized Q-pivot. With such a structure, left or right matrix products are computed in the best way.

6 Compared Efficiencies

All the coefficients are coded in exact precision using a multi-precision library (GNU MP implemented by [13]). The results presented here have been obtained with the described data structure. The solver use the revised simplex method (see [7]); pivot choice is done with the "steepest-edge" method (cf. [12]). All problems are issued from the NETLIB library[8]. Times are indicated in CPU ticks

[8] These problems are available at *netlib.att.com/lp/data*.

(1'≈ 1/100 second). It is not an optimal implementation of the revised simplex method, without LU factorization nor "partial pricing"; since we start with the full problem, incremental operations are not used here. The first Table displays the whole computation time, while the second considers only the Q-pivot time (in a revised simplex the Q-pivot is applied to the complementary matrix).

Problem	Size of the pb	Coefficients $\neq 0$	Iterations	Normal	Optimized	Gain
AGG	489×163	11127	155	21610'	5127'	4,21
AGG2	517×302	4515	160	33920'	10107'	3,35
AGG3	517×302	4531	159	42120'	13511'	3,11
BRANDY	221×249	2150	1039	293031'	100912'	2,90
ISRAEL	175×142	2358	142	16104'	5016'	3,21
SCORPION	389×358	1708	393	124489'	25836'	4,81
SHARE1B	118×225	1182	286	26431'	9300'	2,84
SHARE2B	97×79	730	132	828'	255'	3,24

The "optimized" column shows up computation time obtained with the described algorithm, the "normal" column is for the classical Q-pivot. The efficiency improvement comes from both the reduction of the number of operations, and the fact that the manipulated numbers are smaller than those of a non factorized matrix. For each example the optimized version requires less memory than the normal one; a comparison with rationals is still to be done on this last point. The results are significant because at each iteration, in addition to the Q-pivot, matrix products and norms computations are needed and , ***in fact, all operations on Q-matrices benefit from the optimized structure.***

Below you will find a study of the sole Q-pivot performance with a measurement of the frequency of two extreme cases: the percentage of row pivots where case A (a simple update of the row factor) or case V (no simplification) have been detected. For comparison we indicate the number of rows which have been processed.

		Normal	Optimized			
	Nb of row pivoted	Time	Time	Case A	Case V	Gain
AGG	314272	5648'	1064'	86,10%	1,76%	5,30
AGG2	349332	7690'	695'	89,75%	4,94%	11,06
AGG3	348816	9811'	936'	90,93%	0,93%	10,48
BRANDY	277200	81753'	33108'	44,35%	35,23%	2,46
ISRAEL	55158	4884'	1566'	64,28%	24,29%	3,11
SCORPION	303416	51678'	2117'	77,36%	0,08%	24,41
SHARE1B	47268	6514'	1857'	51,91%	15,29%	3,50
SHARE2B	21984	135'	108'	70,64%	14,97%	1,25

For each NETLIB problem, fractional values have been represented exactly by multiplying each row with 10^{f_i}, where f_i is the smallest value for row i such that all floats on the row are expressed as integers. The gain resulting from the use of integer computations instead of rational computations can be consulted in [16]: in the average it is around a factor of 10 with a non optimized Q-pivot.

7 Conclusion

We have described a set of algorithms allowing the incremental exact resolution of linear systems coded with integer coefficients. These algorithms, based on the formalism of Q-matrices, have the property to maintain integer coefficients while reducing them. Using integers instead of rationals allows by itself a great improvement in the efficiency of exact solvers. A tight optimization of the Q-pivot with an adequate data structure has been described, which leads to a further improvement in the performance for any operation related to Q-matrices (product, comparison, addition, ...). In particular the described incremental operations, which are all based on the Q-pivot, fully benefit from the improvement.

We have demonstrated the efficiency of the optimized Q-pivot on NETLIB problems. A future work is to incorporate these new algorithms in a logic programming constraint solver to demonstrate their effective capabilities.

References

[1] David-Olivier Azulay. Du côté des Q-matrices. Mémoire de D.E.A., Juillet 1994.

[2] David-Olivier Azulay and Jean-François Pique. Q-matrix operators for incremental resolution of linear systems. Technical report, Laboratoire d'Informatique de Marseille, 1998.

[3] Erwin H. Bareiss. Sylvester's identity and multistep integer-preserving gaussian elimination. *Mathematics and Computation*, 22:565–578, 1968.

[4] Erwin H. Bareiss. Computational solutions of matrix problems over an integral domain. *J. Inst. Maths Applics*, 10:68–104, 1972.

[5] W. A. Blankinship. A new version of the euclidian algorithm. *American Math Monthly*, 70:742–745, 1963.

[6] Gordon H. Bradley. Algorithm and bound for the greatest common divisor of n integers. *Communication of the ACM*, 13(7):433–436, July 1970.

[7] Vašek Chvátal. *Linear programming.* W. H. Freeman and Company, 1983.

[8] Jack Edmonds. Systems of distinct representatives and linear algebra. *Journal of research of the National Bureau of Standards*, 71B(4):241–245, 1967.

[9] Jack Edmonds. Exact pivoting. For ECCO VII, February 1994.

[10] Jack Edmonds and Jean-François Maurras. Notes sur les Q-matrices d'Edmonds. *RAIRO*, 31(2):203–209, 1997.

[11] Keith O. Geddes, Stephen R. Czapor, and Georges L. Labahn. *Algorithms for computer algebra.* Kluwer Academic Publishers, 1992.

[12] D. Goldfarb and J.K. Reid. A practicable steepest-edge simplex algorithm. *Mathematical Programming*, 12:361–371, 1977.

[13] Torbjön Granlund. *The GNU Multiple Precision Arithmetic Library*, 2.0.2 edition, June 1996.

[14] Martin L. Griss. The algebraic solution of sparse linear systems via minor expansion. *ACM Transactions on Mathematical Software*, 2(1):31–49, 1976.

[15] Tudor Jebelean. An algorithm for exact division. *Journal of symbolic computation*, 15(2):169–180, 1993.

[16] Jean-François Pique. Un algorithme efficace pour l'implantation de contraintes arithmétiques en précision infinie. In J.C. Bajard, D. Michelucci, J.M. Moreau, and J.M. Muller, editors, *Real Numbers and Computers Conferences*, pages 289–293, Saint-Étienne, France, Avril 1995.

Constraint Techniques for Solving the Protein Structure Prediction Problem

Rolf Backofen

Institut für Informatik/LMU München
Oettingenstraße 67, D-80538 München
backofen@informatik.uni-muenchen.de

Abstract. The protein structure prediction problem is one of the most (if not *the most*) important problem in computational biology. This problem consists of finding the conformation of a protein (i.e., a sequence of amino-acids) with minimal energy. Because of the complexity of this problem, simplified models like Dill's HP-lattice model [12] have become a major tool for investigating general properties of protein folding. Even for this simplified model, the structure prediction problem has been shown to be NP-complete [3, 5].
We describe a constraint formulation of the HP-model structure prediction problem, present the basic constraints and search strategy. We then introduce a novel, general technique for excluding geometrical symmetries in constraint programming. To our knowledge, this is the first general and declarative technique for excluding symmetries in constraint programming that can be added to an existing implementation. Finally, we describe a new lower bound on the energy of an HP-protein. Both techniques yield an efficient pruning of the search tree.

1 Introduction

The protein structure prediction problem is specified as follows: Given a protein by its sequence of amino acids, what is its native structure? Many results in the past have shown the problem to be NP-hard. But the situation is even worse, since one does not know the general principles why natural proteins fold into a native structure. E.g., these principles are interesting if one wants to design artificial proteins (for drug design). For the time being, one problem there is that artificial proteins usually don't have a native structure.

To attack this problem, simplified models have been introduced, which became a major tool for investigating general properties of protein folding. An important class of simplified models are the so-called lattice models. The simplest used lattice is the cubic lattice, where every conformation of a lattice protein is a self-avoiding walk in $\mathbb{Z}^3$. A discussion of lattice proteins can be found in [6]. There is a bunch of groups working with lattice proteins. Examples of how lattice proteins can be used for predicting the native structure or for investigating principles of protein folding are [17, 1, 8, 16, 11, 9, 2, 13].

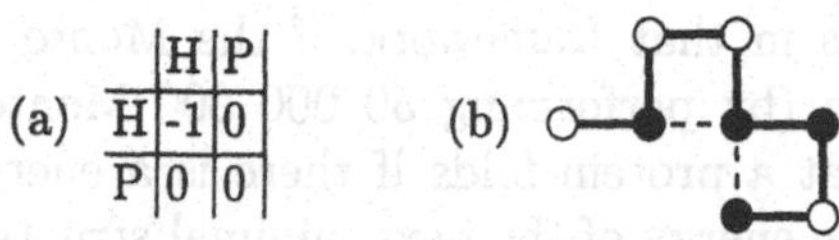

Fig. 1. Energy matrix and sample conformation for the HP-model

An important representative of lattice models is the HP-model, which has been introduced by [12]. In this model, the 20 letter alphabet of amino acids is reduced to a two letter alphabet, namely H and P. H represents *hydrophobic* amino acids, whereas P represent *polar* or hydrophilic amino acids. The energy function for the HP-model is given by the matrix as shown in Figure 1(a). It simply states that the energy contribution of a contact between two monomers is -1 if both are H-monomers, and 0 otherwise. Two monomers form a *contact* in some specific conformation if they are not connected via a bond, and the euclidian distance of the positions is 1. A conformation with *minimal energy* (called *optimal conformation*) is just a conformation with the maximal number of contacts between H-monomers. Just recently, the structure prediction problem has been shown to be NP-complete even for the HP-model [3,5].

A sample conformation for the sequence PHPPHHPH in the two-dimensional lattice with energy -2 is shown in Figure 1(b). The white beads represent P, the black ones H monomers. The two contacts are indicated via dashed lines.

An example of the use of lattice models is the work by Šali, Shakhnovich and Karplus [17].[1] They investigate under which conditions a protein folds into its native structure by performing the following computer experiment:

1.) generate 200 random sequences of length 27.

2.) find the minimal structures on the $3 \times 3 \times 3$-cube. The reason for using a sequence length of 27 is that the $3 \times 3 \times 3$-cube has exactly 27 position.[2]

3.) simulate protein folding on the lattice model using a Monte Carlo method with Metropolis criteria. The Monte Carlo method is as follows. Initially, a random conformation of the sequence is generated. Starting from this initial conformation, the algorithm performs so-called Monte Carlo steps in order to search for the minimal conformation. A single Monte Carlo step consists of the following operations: First, a local move is selected at random until a move is found that produces a valid conformation (i.e., a self-avoiding conformation). Two examples of allowed moves are

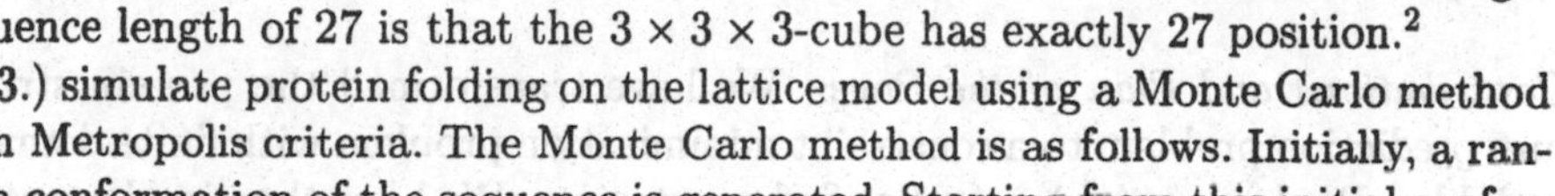

Here, the positions of the shaded monomers are changed. Second, the resulting conformation is evaluated according to the Metropolis criterion. If the energy of the result is lower than the energy of the previous one, then the conformation is always accepted. Otherwise, the conformation is accepted by random, where the probability depends on the energy difference.

[1] The same lattice model is used by several other people, e.g., [1, 16, 2, 9].
[2] In a later paper [8], the authors considered proteins of length 125.

Now a protein folds in that framework, if the Monte Carlo method finds its native conformation (by performing 50 000 000 Monte Carlo steps). The authors have found that a protein folds if there is a energy gap between the native structure and the energy of the next minimal structure.

In performing such experiments, it is clear that the quality of the predicted principle depends on several parameters. The first is the quality of the used lattice and energy function. The second, and even more crucial point, is the ability for finding the native structure as required by Step 2. For the energy function used by [17], there is no *exact* algorithm for finding the minimal structure. To be computational feasible, they have restricted in [17] the search for the native structure on the $3 \times 3 \times 3$-cube as indicated in Step 2.

Previous Work In the literature, several algorithms were proposed for the HP-model. E.g., there are heuristic approaches such as the hydrophobic zipper [7], the genetic algorithm by Unger and Moult [15] and the chain growth algorithm by Bornberg-Bauer [4]. Another example is an approximation algorithm as described in Hart and Istrail [10], which produces a conformation, whose energy is known to be at least $\frac{3}{8}$ of the optimal energy, in linear time. And there is one exact algorithm, namely the CHCC of Yue and Dill [18], which finds all optimal conformations. There are two differences between the CHCC-algorithm and ours. First, the motivation for development of CHCC was to find *all* minimal conformations in the HP-model, whereas we are only interested in finding the minimal energy. Second, we want to provide a declarative formulation of the problem that can be used for other models as well (currently, we are working on an extension of the HP-model). The CHCC algorithm is designed in a way that is only suited for the HP-model.

Contributions and Plan of the Paper We have transformed the protein structure prediction problem to a constraint minimisation problem with finite domain variables, Boolean variables, and reified constraints. We have then implemented this constraint problem using the language Oz [14]. The main problem we where faced with was the existence of 47 geometrical symmetries. One possible way for excluding symmetries is to use an appropriate modeling. Although this results in an efficient implementation in general, this approach has some drawbacks. Despite the fact that one often does not find a modeling that excludes the symmetries (as in our case), this approach is inflexible. Usually, such a model cannot be extended without doing a complete re-modeling.

For this reason, we have searched for a declarative way of excluding symmetries. In our approach, we consider binary branching search trees. The symmetries are excluded by adding at the right branch (which is visited after the left branch) constraints which enforce the right branch to exclude all solution for which a symmetric solution has been found in the left branch. These exclusion constraints are defined by just using general properties of the symmetries considered. There are several advantages. First, it is a general method that can be used with any kind of symmetries that can be defined using constraint expressions. Second, it can be added to an existing implementation, since this technique is applied on the level of the search tree, and uses existing constraint expressions. And third, it does not impose any restrictions on the search strategy. To our knowledge, there is no existing method for excluding symmetries declaratively.

Another way to prune the search tree was the use of a new lower bound on the surface of all H-monomers given their distribution to planes described by the equation $x = c$. This results in an upper bound on the number of contacts. The lower bound on the surface uses a property of lattice models, namely that for any sequence s and any conformation of s in $\mathbb{Z}^3$, two monomers $1 \leq i, j \leq \text{length}(s)$ can form a contact iff $|i - j| > 1$, and i is even and j is odd, or vice versa.

In Section 2.1, we introduce the basic definitions for the structure prediction problem. In Section 2.2, we introduce the constraint minimisation problem modeling the structure prediction problem and describe the search strategy. We then introduce in Section 2.3 the technique for excluding symmetries in a declarative way, and apply the introduced technique to our lattice problem. In the following Section 2.4, we explain the new lower bound on the surface. Finally, in Section 3, we present results for some HP-sequences taken from the literature, show search times and number of search steps with and without symmetry exclusion.

2 Constraint Formulation

2.1 Basic Definitions

A sequence is an element in $\{H, P\}^*$. With s_i we denote the ith element of a sequence s. We say that a monomer with number i in s is even (resp. odd) if i is even (resp. odd). A conformation c of a sequence s is a function $c : [1..|s|] \to \mathbb{Z}^3$ such that

1. $\forall 1 \leq i < |s| : ||c(i) - c(i+1)|| = 1$ (where $|| \cdot ||$ is the euclidic norm on $\mathbb{Z}^3$)
2. and $\forall i \neq j : c(i) \neq c(j)$.

Given a conformation c of a sequence s, the number of contacts $\text{Contact}_s(c)$ in c is defined as the number of pairs (i, j) with $i + 1 < j$ such that

$$s_i = H \land s_j = H \land ||c(i) - c(j)|| = 1.$$

The energy of c is just $-\text{Contact}_s(c)$. With $\boldsymbol{e}_x$, $\boldsymbol{e}_y$ and $\boldsymbol{e}_z$ we denote $(1,0,0)$, $(0,1,0)$ or $(0,0,1)$, respectively. We say that two points $\boldsymbol{p}, \boldsymbol{p}' \in \mathbb{Z}^3$ are *neighbors* if $||\boldsymbol{p} - \boldsymbol{p}'|| = 1$. Then the *surface* $\text{Surf}_s(c)$ is defined as the number of pairs of neighbor positions, where the first position is occupied by an H-monomer, but the second not. I.e.,

$$\text{Surf}_s(c) = \left|\{\, (c(i), \boldsymbol{p}) \,\middle|\, s_i = H \;\land\; ||\boldsymbol{p} - c(i)|| = 1 \land \forall j : (s_j = H \Rightarrow c(j) \neq \boldsymbol{p}) \,\}\right|$$

Now Yue and Dill [18] made the observation that there is a simple linear equation relating surface and energy. This equation uses the fact that every monomer has 6 neighbors, each of which is in any conformation either filled with either an H-monomer, a P-monomer, or left free. Let n_H^s be the number of H-monomers in s. Then we have for every conformation c that

$$6 \cdot n_H^s = 2 \cdot [\mathrm{Contact}_s(c) + \mathrm{HHBonds}(s)] + \mathrm{Surf}_s(c), \tag{1}$$

where HHBonds(s) is the number of bonds between H-monomers (i.e., the number of H-monomers whose successor in s is also a H-monomer). Since HHBonds(s) is constant for all conformations c of s, this implies that minimizing the surface is the same as maximizing the number of contacts.

In a later section, we will consider a lower bound on the surface given partial knowledge about a conformation c. Given the above, the lower bound on the surface yields an upper bound on the number of contacts (which generates in fact a lower bound on the energy since the energy is defined as $-\mathrm{Contact}_s(c)$).

Given a conformation, the *frame* of the conformation is the minimal rectangular box that contains all H-monomers of the sequence. Given a vector $\boldsymbol{p}$, we denote with $(\boldsymbol{p})_{\mathrm{x}}$, $(\boldsymbol{p})_{\mathrm{y}}$ and $(\boldsymbol{p})_{\mathrm{z}}$ the x-,y- and z-coordinate of $\boldsymbol{p}$, respectively. The *dimensions* (fr_x, fr_y, fr_z) of the frame are the numbers of monomers that can be placed in x-, y- and z-direction within the frame. E.g., we have

$$fr_x = \max\{|(c(i) - c(j))_{\mathrm{x}}| \mid 1 \leq i,j \leq \mathrm{length}(s) \wedge s_i = H \wedge s_j = H\} + 1.$$

2.2 Constraints and Search Strategy

A frame is uniquely determined by its dimension and its starting point. Yue and Dill [18] provided a method to calculate a lower bound on the surface when all H-monomers are packed within a specific frame. Thus, there are usually a few frames to be searched through to find the optimal conformation, since often bigger frames have a higher lower bound for the surface than an optimal conformation found in a smaller frame. For all examples in [18], there is even only one frame that has to be searched through. Note that also some of the P-monomers must be included within this frame, namely those P-monomers whose left and right neighbors in chain are H-monomers. The reason is just that one cannot include the surrounding H-monomers into the core without also including the middle P-monomer. These P-monomers are called *P-singlets* in [18]. A position $p \in \mathbb{Z}^3$ is a *caveat in a conformation c of s* if p is contained in the hull (over $\mathbb{Z}^3$) of the set of positions occupied by H-monomers in c

Our constraint problem consists of finite domain variables. We use also Boolean constraint and reified constraints. With reified constraints we mean a constraint $\mathrm{x} =: (\phi)$, where ϕ is a finite domain constraint. x is a Boolean variable which is 1 if the constraint store entails ϕ, and 0 if the constraint store disentails ϕ. A constraint store entails a constraint ϕ if every valuation that makes the constraint store valid also makes ϕ valid. We use also entailment constraints of the form $\phi \rightarrow \psi$, which are interpreted as follows. If a constraint store entails ϕ, then ψ is added to the constraint store. We have implemented the problem using the language Oz [14], which supports finite domain variables, Boolean constraints, reified constraints, entailment constraints and a programmable search module. The latter was used for the implementation of the symmetry exclusion.

`Caveats`	Boolean; is 0 if the conformation contains no caveats
`Frx, Fry, Frz`	dimension of the frame
X_i, Y_i, Z_i	x-,y-, and z-coordinate of the ith monomer
E_j`.seh`, E_j`.soh`	number of even and odd H-monomers of the jth x-plane (or x-layer) in the frame, respectively (where $1 \leq j \leq$ `Frx`);
$\mathtt{Elem}_j^i$	membership of H-monomer i in the jth x-layer
P_k`.ctp`	type of the kth position of the frame (where $1 \leq k \leq \mathtt{Frx} \cdot \mathtt{Fry} \cdot \mathtt{Frz}$); the core type P_k`.ctp` of the kth position is either 1, if it is occupied by an H-monomer, and 0 otherwise
O_i^k	for every position k of the frame and every monomer i; O_i^k has boolean value (i.e., 0 or 1), and is 1 iff monomer i occupies the kth position of the frame.
$\mathtt{Surf}_k^l$	surface contribution between neighbour positions k and l under the condition, that k is occupied by an H-monomer. Thus, k is in the frame, and l is in the frame or within distance 1 from the frame
`Surface`	complete surface of the conformation

Fig. 2. The variables and their description

Given a specific sequence s, the main variables of our constraint problem are listed in Figure 2. We use constraint optimization to minimize the variable `Surface`. There are additional variables and constraints used for pruning the search tree, which we have suppressed for simplicity.

The basic constraints, which describe basic properties of self-avoiding walks, are the following. W.l.o.g., we can assume that we have for every $1 \leq i \leq \text{length}(s)$:

$$X_i \in [1..(2 \cdot \text{length}(s)] \wedge Y_i \in [1..(2 \cdot \text{length}(s)] \wedge Z_i \in [1..(2 \cdot \text{length}(s)]$$

The self-avoidingness is just $(X_i, Y_i, Z_i) \neq (X_j, Y_j, Z_j)$ for $i \neq j$.[3]

For expressing that the distance between two successive monomers is 1, we introduce for every monomer i with $1 \leq i < \text{length}(s)$ three variables $\mathtt{Xdiff}_i$, $\mathtt{Ydiff}_i$ and $\mathtt{Zdiff}_i$. The value range of these variables is [0..1]. Then we can express the unit-vector distance constraint by

$$\mathtt{Xdiff}_i =: |X_i - X_{i+1}| \qquad \mathtt{Zdiff}_i =: |Z_i - Z_{i+1}|$$
$$\mathtt{Ydiff}_i =: |Y_i - Y_{i+1}| \qquad 1 =: \mathtt{Xdiff}_i + \mathtt{Ydiff}_i + \mathtt{Zdiff}_i.$$

The other constraints are as follows. Clearly, we must have

$$\sum_{j=1}^{\mathtt{Frx}} E_j.\mathtt{soh} =: |\{i \mid i \text{ odd and } s_i = H\}| \quad \sum_{j=1}^{\mathtt{Frx}} E_j.\mathtt{seh} =: |\{i \mid i \text{ even and } s_i = H\}|$$

[3] This cannot be directly encoded in Oz [14], but we reduce these constraints to difference constraints on integers.

Then we have for every layer j that $\texttt{E}_j\texttt{.soh}+\texttt{E}_j\texttt{.seh}+ \leq \texttt{Fry}\cdot\texttt{Frz}$. Using reified constraints, $\texttt{Elem}_j^i$ can be defined by

$$\texttt{Elem}_j^i =: (\texttt{X}_i =: j-1 + \text{x-coordinate of starting point of frame}).$$

Then $\texttt{E}_j\texttt{.seh} =: \sum_{i \text{ even},\, s_i = H} \texttt{Elem}_j^i$, and $\texttt{E}_j\texttt{.soh}$ can be defined analogously.

We can state that whenever two monomers i and $i+3$ are in the same layer, then $i+1$ and $i+2$ must also be in one layer due to the condition that we must fold into a lattice conformation. I.e., for every $1 \leq j \leq \texttt{Frx}$ we have

$$(\texttt{Elem}_j^i =: 1 \wedge \texttt{Elem}_j^{i+3} =: 1) \to \texttt{X}_{i+1} =: \texttt{X}_{i+2}$$

Furthermore, there is a special treatment of P-singlets, which may not be buried into the core without forming a caveat. Thus we have for every P-singlet i that

$$(\texttt{Elem}_j^i =: 1 \wedge \texttt{Elem}_j^{i+1} =: 0 \wedge \texttt{Caveats} =: 0) \to \texttt{Elem}_j^{i-1} =: 1$$
$$(\texttt{Elem}_j^i =: 1 \wedge \texttt{Elem}_j^{i-1} =: 0 \wedge \texttt{Caveats} =: 0) \to \texttt{Elem}_j^{i+1} =: 1.$$

At some stage of the search we have to assign monomers to frame positions. A monomer i is assigned the position k by setting $\texttt{O}_i^k$ to 1 in one branch (which has just the effect that $\texttt{Y}_i$ and $\texttt{Z}_i$ is set to the y- and z-coordinate of the position k), and 0 in the other. Self-avoidingness is achieved by $\texttt{Sum}[\texttt{O}_1^k, \ldots, \texttt{O}_{\text{length}(s)}^k] =<: 1$.

But there are additional constraints which restrict the core type and the monomers that can be placed at some position. Let $\{i_1, \ldots, i_n\}$ be the set of all H-monomers in s. If at some stage no monomer in $\{i_1, \ldots, i_n\}$ can be placed at some position k, then the core type must be 0. This is implemented by

$$\texttt{P}_k\texttt{.ctp} =: (\texttt{Sum}[\texttt{O}_{i_1}^k, \ldots, \texttt{O}_{i_n}^k] >: 0).$$

Finally, we have constraints relating core types of positions and surface contributions. Of course, we get $\texttt{Surface} =: \sum_{k,l} \texttt{Surf}_k^l$, where k, l ranges over all neighbor positions. If l is a position outside the frame (i.e., if its x-,y- or z-coordinate is outside the frame), then $\texttt{Surf}_k^l =: \texttt{P}_k\texttt{.ctp}$. Otherwise we have $\texttt{Surf}_k^l =: (\texttt{P}_k\texttt{.ctp} =: 1 \wedge \texttt{P}_l\texttt{.ctp} =: 0)$. Now the surface contributions and the Caveats variable can be related using reified constraints. For every line li in $\mathbb{Z}^3$ parallel to one of the coordinate axis, which intersects with the frame, we define the Boolean variable $\texttt{Caveat}_{\text{li}}$ by

$$\texttt{Caveat}_{\text{li}} =: (\textstyle\sum_{k \neq l \text{ on li}} \texttt{Surf}_k^l >: 2).$$

Then $\texttt{Caveats} =: (\sum_{\text{lines li}} \texttt{Caveat}_{\text{li}} >: 1)$.

Our search strategy is as follows. We select the variables according to the following order (from left to right)

$$\texttt{Caveats} < \begin{matrix}\texttt{Frx}\\ \texttt{Fry}\\ \texttt{Frz}\end{matrix} < \begin{matrix}\texttt{E}_j\texttt{.seh}\\ \texttt{E}_j\texttt{.soh}\end{matrix} < \texttt{Elem}_j^i < \texttt{O}_i^k < \begin{matrix}\texttt{X}_i\\ \texttt{Y}_i\\ \texttt{Z}_i\end{matrix}$$

It is a good strategy to set `Caveats` to 0 in the first branch, since in almost every case there is an optimal conformation without a caveat. The frame dimensions are chosen ordered by surface according to the lower bound given in [18]. After having determined the variables $\mathtt{E}_j\mathtt{.seh}$ and $\mathtt{E}_j\mathtt{.soh}$, we calculate a lower bound on the surface, which will be described in Section 2.4. If all H-monomers and P-singlets are assigned to layers, we search for the positions of these monomers within the frame. Finally, we place the remaining monomers.

2.3 Excluding Geometric Symmetries

We fix a first-order signature Σ including the equality $\doteq$ with a set of variables $\mathcal{V}$. Constraints are literals, and constraint formulae are quantifier-free formulae over Σ. We identify $t \doteq t'$ with $t' \doteq t$. $\mathcal{C}$ denotes the set of all constraints. A set of constraints $C \subseteq \mathcal{C}$ is interpreted as the conjunction of the constraints contained in C, and we will freely mix set notation and conjunction. We fix a standard interpretation $\mathcal{A}$ with domain $\mathcal{D}^{\mathcal{A}}$, which describes our constraint theory. An *assignment* α *in* $\mathcal{A}$ is a partial function $\alpha : \mathcal{V} \rightarrow \mathcal{D}^{\mathcal{A}}$. A *propagation operator* $\mathcal{P}$ for $\mathcal{A}$ is a monotone function $\mathcal{P} : \mathcal{C} \mapsto \mathcal{C}$ with $\mathcal{A} \models (C \Leftrightarrow \mathcal{P}(C))$. The propagation operator $\mathcal{P}$ characterises the constraint solver and will be fixed. A constraint set C *determines* a set of variables $\mathcal{X}$ *to an assignment* α iff for all $x \in \mathcal{X}$ there is ground term t such that $\alpha(t) = \alpha(x)$ and $x \doteq t \in C$.

In the following, we assume a fixed constraint set C_{Pr} describing the problem to be solved. Furthermore, our constraint problem has the property, that there is a subset of variables $\mathcal{X} \subseteq \mathcal{V}$ consisting of the monomer position variables $\mathtt{X}_i, \mathtt{Y}_i, \mathtt{Z}_i$, whose valuation completely determines the valuation of the other variables. Since we want to define the symmetries on these variables, we define

$$\|C\| = \{\alpha \mid \mathrm{dom}(\alpha) = \mathcal{X} \wedge \mathcal{A}, \alpha \models C\}.$$

where $\mathcal{A}, \alpha \models C$ means that there is a uniquely defined $\alpha' \supseteq \alpha$ total that satisfies C in $\mathcal{A}$. Furthermore, we write $\phi \models \psi$ for entailment, i.e. $\|\phi\| \subseteq \|\psi\|$.

A *symmetry* s *for* C_{Pr} is a bijection $s : \|C_{\mathrm{Pr}}\| \rightarrow \|C_{\mathrm{Pr}}\|$. A *symmetry set* $\mathcal{S}$ *for* C_{Pr} is a set of symmetries operating on $\|C_{\mathrm{Pr}}\|$, which is closed under inversion. We denote the identity function on $\|C_{\mathrm{Pr}}\|$ with $\mathrm{id}_{C_{\mathrm{Pr}}}$ (which is a symmetry by definition). Clearly, one can consider the set of all symmetries for C_{Pr} (which even form a group). But in general, we do not want to consider all symmetries, since either there are too many of them, or some of them do not have an intuitive characterisation.

Definition 1 (Search Tree). *Let t be a finite, binary, rooted, ordered tree, whose edges are labelled by literals, and whose nodes are labelled by triples of constraint sets. The tree t is a* search tree *for C_{Pr} if 1.) the root node v_r has the label $(\emptyset, \emptyset, \mathcal{P}(C_{\mathrm{Pr}}))$, and 2.) every binary node has the form*

$$\begin{array}{ccc} & (C_p, C_n, C_{\mathrm{prop}}) & \\ {}^{c}\swarrow & & \searrow^{\neg c} \\ (C_p \wedge c, C_n, C^l_{\mathrm{prop}}) & & (C_p, C_n \wedge \neg c, C^r_{\mathrm{prop}}) \end{array}$$

with $C^l_{\text{prop}} \supseteq \mathcal{P}(C_{\text{prop}} \wedge c)$ *and* $C^r_{\text{prop}} \supseteq \mathcal{P}(C_{\text{prop}} \wedge \neg c)$

Given a node v in t with label $(C_p, C_n, C_{\text{prop}})$, we set $\|v\| = \|C_{\text{prop}}\|$. For every tree t, we denote with $\prec_t$ the partial ordering of nodes induced by t.

Definition 2 (Expanded, C_{Pr}-Complete w.r.t $\mathcal{S}$ and $\mathcal{S}$-Reduced Trees). *The search tree t is* completely expanded *if every leaf $v = (C_p, C_n, C_{\text{prop}})$ satisfies either 1.)* $\|v\| = \{\alpha\}$ and C_{prop} determines $\mathcal{X}$ to α, *or 2.)* $\perp \in \mathcal{P}(C_{\text{prop}})$. *Let $\mathcal{S}$ be a symmetry set for C_{Pr}. A search tree is C_{Pr}-*complete w.r.t. $\mathcal{S}$ *if for every $\alpha \in \|C_{\text{Pr}}\|$ there is a leaf v such that*

$$\|v\| = \{\alpha\} \ \vee \ \exists s \in \mathcal{S} \backslash \{\text{id}_{C_{\text{Pr}}}\} : \|v\| = \{s(\alpha)\}.$$

A search tree is $\mathcal{S}$-reduced *if for every leaf v with $\|v\| = \{\alpha\}$ we have that $\forall s \in \mathcal{S}\ \forall v' \neq v : (\|v'\| = \{\alpha'\} \Rightarrow s(\alpha') \neq \alpha)$.*

In our case, the symmetries are rotations and reflections. These are affine mappings $S : \mathbb{Z}^3 \to \mathbb{Z}^3$ with $S(\boldsymbol{x}) = A_S\boldsymbol{x} + \boldsymbol{v}_S$ that map the $\mathbb{Z}^3$ onto $\mathbb{Z}^3$. I.e., the matrix A_S is an orthogonal matrix with the property that the columns $\boldsymbol{v}_1$, $\boldsymbol{v}_2$ and $\boldsymbol{v}_3$ of A_S satisfy $\forall i \in [1..3] : \boldsymbol{v}_i \in \{\pm \boldsymbol{e}_x, \pm \boldsymbol{e}_y, \pm \boldsymbol{e}_z\}$. Since the dimension of A_S must be 3, we have $6 \times 4 \times 2$ matrices, and henceforth 47 non-trivial symmetries. The problem is that the vector $\boldsymbol{v}_S$ is not yet fixed. Now in our case, the use of the frame surrounding the core monomers allows one to fix this vector. As an example, we use $\mathbb{Z}^2$ with a rectangular frame. For every symmetry s, we have to fix $\boldsymbol{v}_S$ such that the frame is mapped to itself. If this is not possible, then the corresponding symmetry is excluded by the frame dimension. Consider a frame in $\mathbb{Z}^2$ with starting point $(0,0)$ and dimensions $\texttt{Frx} = 4$ and $\texttt{Fry} = 3$.[4] Then the top left point of the frame is $(3,2)$. Furthermore, consider the three symmetries reflection at the y-axis, rotation by 90° and rotation by 180°, which we will name S_1, S_2 and S_3 in the following. The corresponding matrices are

$$A_{S_1} = \begin{pmatrix} -1 & 0 \\ 0 & 1 \end{pmatrix} \quad A_{S_2} = \begin{pmatrix} 0 & -1 \\ 1 & 0 \end{pmatrix} \quad A_{S_3} = \begin{pmatrix} -1 & 0 \\ 0 & -1 \end{pmatrix}, \tag{2}$$

and the corresponding mappings are

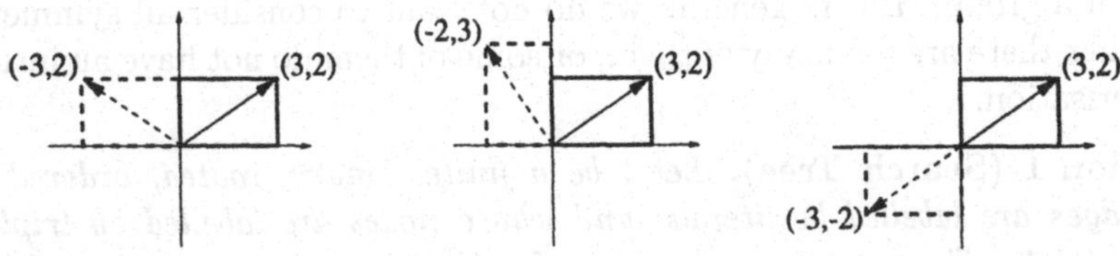

A symmetry S is compatible with the frame dimensions $(\texttt{Frx}, \texttt{Fry})$ if the frame is mapped to itself, i.e., if $\{\boldsymbol{v} \mid \boldsymbol{0} \leq \boldsymbol{v} \leq (\texttt{Frx} - 1, \texttt{Fry} - 1)\} = \{S(\boldsymbol{v}) \mid \boldsymbol{0} \leq$

[4] If we define an appropriate symmetry S for a frame with starting point $(0,0)$, then we get a symmetry for a frame with the same dimension and starting point $\boldsymbol{s}$ by using the affine mapping $S'(\boldsymbol{x}) = S(\boldsymbol{x} - \boldsymbol{s}) + \boldsymbol{s} = S(\boldsymbol{x}) + \boldsymbol{s} - A_S\boldsymbol{s}$.

$v \leq (\mathtt{Frx}-1, \mathtt{Fry}-1)\}$. For a given matrix A_S, there exists a v_S such that $S(x) = A_S x + v_S$ satisfies this condition if and only if A_S satisfies

$$A_S(\mathtt{Frx}-1, \mathtt{Fry}-1) = (a_x, a_y) \text{ and } |a_x| = \mathtt{Frx}-1 \wedge |a_y| = \mathtt{Fry}-1. \quad (3)$$

For the matrices A_{S_1}, A_{S_2} and A_{S_3}, we get $(-3,2)$, $(-2,3)$ and $(-3,-2)$, which excludes the symmetry characterised by A_{S_2}.

Given a symmetry characterised by an orthogonal matrix A_S which is compatible according to (3), then $v_S = (v_x, v_y)$ is defined by

$$v_x = \begin{cases} -a_x \text{ if } a_x < 0 \\ 0 \quad \text{else} \end{cases} \quad \text{and} \quad v_y = \begin{cases} -a_y \text{ if } a_y < 0 \\ 0 \quad \text{else} \end{cases},$$

where a_x and a_y are defined by (3). The extension to three dimension is straightforward.

Now the symmetries are excluded by adding at the right branch (which is visited after the left branch) constraints which enforce the right branch to exclude all solutions for which a symmetric solution has been found in the left branch. For this purpose, we need the notion of *symmetric constraints*. As an example, we use reflection along the x-axis S^{rx} in three dimensions. Furthermore, assume that we have selected a frame with the dimensions $(\mathtt{Frx}, \mathtt{Fry}, \mathtt{Frz}) = (4,3,3)$ with starting point $(0,0,0)$. Then the frame is of the form

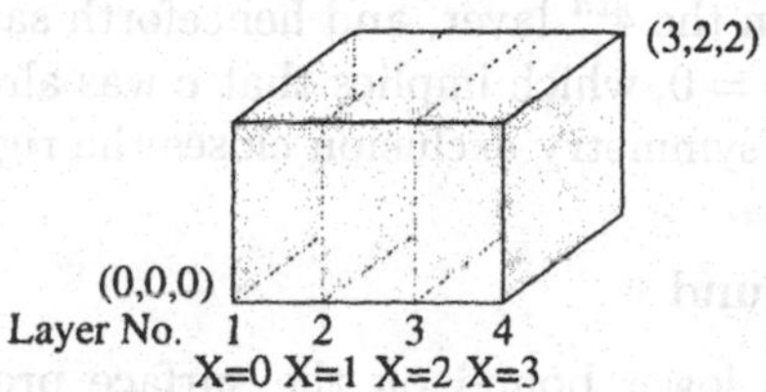

Using the above outlined method, S^{rx} is defined by

$$S^{\mathrm{rx}}(x) = \begin{pmatrix} -1\,0\,0 \\ 0\,1\,0 \\ 0\,0\,1 \end{pmatrix} x + \begin{pmatrix} -(-(\mathtt{Frx}-1)) \\ 0 \\ 0 \end{pmatrix} = \begin{pmatrix} -1\,0\,0 \\ 0\,1\,0 \\ 0\,0\,1 \end{pmatrix} x + \begin{pmatrix} 3 \\ 0 \\ 0 \end{pmatrix}$$

Now consider the constraint $\mathtt{Elem}_j^i =: b$, where $b \in \{0,1\}$. $\mathtt{Elem}_j^i =: b$ is defined by a reified constraint $\mathtt{Elem}_j^i =: (\mathtt{X}_i =: j-1)$. We first want to calculate the S^{rx}-symmetric constraint $S^{\mathrm{rx}}_{con}(\mathtt{X}_i =: j-1)$. Given some conformation c satisfying the constraint $\mathtt{X}_i =: j-1$, we know that the coordinates of the ith monomer are $(j-1, y_i, z_i)$ for some y_i, z_i. Furthermore, we know that these coordinates are mapped to $S^{\mathrm{rx}}(j-1, y_i, z_i)$ in the S^{rx}-symmetric conformation c' of c. Hence, we know that c' satisfies the constraint $\mathtt{X}_i =: a$, where a is the x-coordinate of $S^{\mathrm{rx}}(j-1, y_i, z_i)$. Since the x-coordinate of $S^{\mathrm{rx}}(x,y,z)$ is $-x+3$, we can conclude that the symetric constraint $S^{\mathrm{rx}}_{con}(\mathtt{X}_i =: j-1)$ is $\mathtt{X}_i =: 3-(j-1)$, which is equivalent to $\mathtt{X}_i =: 4-j$. Now we can use this to define the symmetric constraint $S^{\mathrm{rx}}_{con}(\mathtt{Elem}_j^i =: b)$ for $\mathtt{Elem}_j^i =: b$. Since $\mathtt{X}_i =: 4-j$ is equivalent to

$\mathtt{X}_i =: (5-j)-1$, and $\mathtt{X}_i =: k-1$ is equivalent to $\mathtt{Elem}^i_k =: 1$, we get that the S^{rx}-symmetric constraint to $\mathtt{Elem}^i_j =: b$ is

$$\mathtt{Elem}^i_{5-j} =: b.$$

This states if the ith H-monomer is in the 1st layer of the frame, then the ith H-monomer must be in the 4th layer in the conformation produced by S^{rx}. Using this construction for generating symmetric constraints, we can present an example of a (partial) $\{S^{\text{rx}}\}$-excluded search tree. Here, the constraints added by the symmetry exclusion algorithm are indicated by a leading *and*:

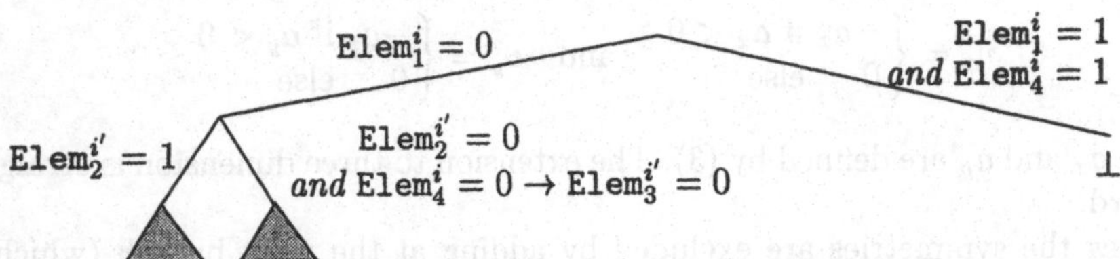

In the right-most branch, we have added the constraint $\mathtt{Elem}^i_4 = 1$, which is the same as $\neg S^{\text{rx}}_{con}(\mathtt{Elem}^i_1 = 0)$. Together with $\mathtt{Elem}^i_1 = 1$, this yields an immediate contradiction. The reason is simply the following. Consider any conformation satisfying $\mathtt{Elem}^i_1 = 1$ (the label of the right-most branch). Then we know that the monomer i is in the 1st layer. Consider an arbitrary conformation c which is generated from a conformation c' satisfying $\mathtt{Elem}^i_1 = 1$ by reflection at the x-axis. Then c has monomer i in the 4th layer, and henceforth satisfies $\mathtt{Elem}^i_4 = 1$. But $\mathtt{Elem}^i_4 = 1$ implies $\mathtt{Elem}^i_1 = 0$, which implies that c was already found in the left branch. Henceforth, the symmetry exclusion closes the right-most branch.

2.4 A new lower bound

We will now describe a lower bound on the surface provided that know the distribution of H-monomers to x-layers. For the rest of this section, let $\mathtt{E}_j.\mathtt{seh}$ (resp. $\mathtt{E}_j.\mathtt{soh}$) be the number of even (resp. odd) H-monomers in the jth x-layer. Given a conformation c, we distinguish between x-surface and yz-surface of c. The x-surface of c is defined by

$$\text{Surf}^x_s(c) = \left|\{\, (c(i),p) \,|\, s_i = H \;\wedge\; p - c(i) = \pm e_x \wedge \forall j : (s_j = H \Rightarrow c(j) \neq p) \,\}\right|$$

The yz-surface of c is just $\text{Surf}_s(c) - \text{Surf}^x_s(c)$. For the lower bounds on x-surface and yz-surface, we use a special property of the cubic lattice, namely that even H-monomers can form contacts only with odd H-monomers. Given a point $(x,y,z) \in \mathbb{Z}^3$, we say that (x,y,z) is *odd* (resp. *even*) if $x+y+z$ is odd (resp. even). We write $(x,y,z) \equiv (x',y',z')$ iff $x+y+z \equiv x'+y'+z' \mod 2$. Then we have for every conformation c of s that $c(i) \equiv c(j)$ iff $i \equiv j \mod 2$. Using this property, we get the following a lower bound on the x-surface:

$$\begin{aligned}\text{Surf}^x_s(c) \geq\; & \mathtt{E}_1.\mathtt{soh} + \mathtt{E}_1.\mathtt{seh} + \mathtt{E}_{\mathtt{Frx}}.\mathtt{soh} + \mathtt{E}_{\mathtt{Frx}}.\mathtt{seh} \\ & + \sum_{1 \leq j < \mathtt{Frx}} \left(|\mathtt{E}_j.\mathtt{soh} - \mathtt{E}_{j+1}.\mathtt{seh}| + |\mathtt{E}_j.\mathtt{seh} - \mathtt{E}_{j+1}.\mathtt{soh}|\right)\end{aligned}$$

For a lower bound on the yz-surface, we consider the surface contribution in the different x-layers. Now let the jth x-layer be defined by the equation $x = a_j$, and let $P(x = a_j)$ be the set of points in the plane $x = a_j$. We define the yz-surface of this layer by

$$\mathrm{Surf}^s_j(c) = \left| \left\{ (c(i), p) \in P(x = a_j)^2 \,\middle|\, \begin{array}{l} s_i = H \wedge p - c(i) \in \{\pm e_y, \pm e_z\} \\ \wedge \forall j : (s_j = H \Rightarrow c(j) \neq p) \end{array} \right\} \right|$$

The first lower bound is given in [18], where it was found that the surface in layer j is given by the minimal rectangle enclosing the H-monomers in that layer. Thus, consider the following two conformations, where the positions occupied by H-monomers in the jth x-layer look as follows:

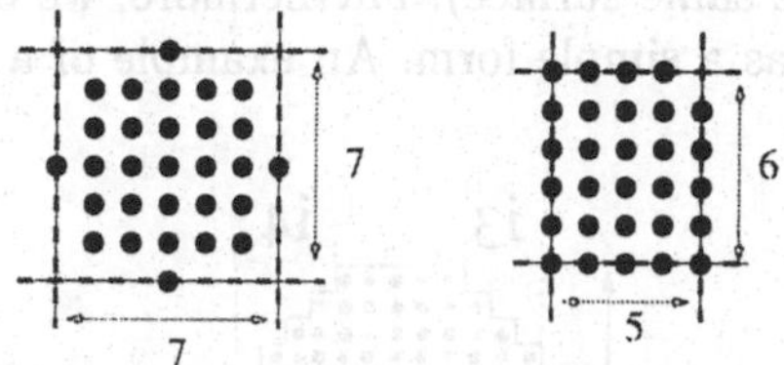

Both have the property that $\mathrm{E}_j.\mathtt{soh}+\mathrm{E}_j.\mathtt{seh} = 29$. But $\mathrm{Surf}^s_j(c)$ is $2\cdot 7+2\cdot 7 = 28$ for the first conformation, and $2 \cdot 5 + 2 \cdot 6 = 22$ for the second. Hence, given $n_H = \mathrm{E}_j.\mathtt{soh} + \mathrm{E}_j.\mathtt{seh}$, then a lower bound for $\mathrm{Surf}^s_j(c)$ is given by $2 \cdot a + 2 \cdot b$, where $a = \lceil \sqrt{n_H} \rceil$ and $b = \lceil \frac{n_H}{a} \rceil$.

But we can provide a better lower bound for $\mathrm{Surf}^s_j(c)$ by considering the different parity of H-monomers. For this purpose, we introduce the concept of a coloring as an abstraction of the points occupied by H-monomers in a conformation c. A *coloring* is a function $f : \mathbb{Z}^2 \to \{0,1\}$. We say that a point (x, y) is colored black by f iff $f(x,y) = 1$. In the following, we consider only colorings different from the empty coloring f_e (which satisfies $\forall p : f_e(p) = 0$). A point $(x, y) \in \mathbb{Z}^2$ is a *caveat in* f if (x, y) is contained in the hull (over $\mathbb{Z}^2$) of the points colored black in f. Given a coloring f, define $e(f) = |\{(x,y) \mid f(x,y) = 1 \text{ and } x + y \text{ even}\}|$ and $o(f) = |\{(x,y) \mid f(x,y) = 1 \text{ and } x + y \text{ odd}\}|$. The ***surface*** $\mathrm{Surf}(f)$ of a coloring f is defined analogously to the surface of a conformation, i.e., it is the number of pairs where the first point is colored black by f, and the second is colored white. Given a pair (e, o) of integers, we define $\mathrm{Surf}(e, o)$ to be $\min\{\mathrm{Surf}(f) \mid f \text{ colouring with } e(f) = e \wedge o(f) = o\}$. W.l.o.g, we can restrict ourself to cases where $e \leq o$. Thus, we have the following lemma.

Lemma 1. $\mathrm{Surf}^s_j(c) \geq \begin{cases} \mathrm{Surf}(\mathrm{E}_j.\mathtt{seh}, \mathrm{E}_j.\mathtt{soh}) & \textit{if } \mathrm{E}_j.\mathtt{seh} \leq \mathrm{E}_j.\mathtt{soh} \\ \mathrm{Surf}(\mathrm{E}_j.\mathtt{soh}, \mathrm{E}_j.\mathtt{seh}) & \textit{if } \mathrm{E}_j.\mathtt{soh} \leq \mathrm{E}_j.\mathtt{seh}. \end{cases}$

In the following theorem, we handle the simple case where $|e - o| \leq 1$. There, the lower bound on colorings agrees with the lower bound as given in [18].

Theorem 1. *Let* (e, o) *be a pair of integers with* $|e - o| \leq 1$. *Let* $a = \lceil \sqrt{e + o} \rceil$ *and* $b = \lceil \frac{e+o}{a} \rceil$. *Then* $\mathrm{Surf}(e, o) = 2a + 2b$.

The remaining case is to calculate $\mathrm{Surf}(e,o)$ where $e < o+1$. But it would be too time consuming to search through all possible colorings f in order to determine $\mathrm{Surf}(e,o)$. But this is not necessary, since we can consider a 'normal form' of colorings to which every coloring can be extended. The normal forms are kind of maximal colorings provided a given difference $d(f) = o(f) - e(f)$. We will handle only caveat-free colorings for simplicity reasons. Let f be a coloring. Then we define $\mathrm{length}(f)$ to be $\max\{|x - x'| \mid \exists y, y' : f(x,y) = 1 = f(x',y')\} + 1$, and $\mathrm{height}(f)$ to be $\max\{|y - y'| \mid \exists x, x' : f(x,y) = 1 = f(x',y')\} + 1$. The pair $(\mathrm{height}(f), \mathrm{length}(f))$ is called the *frame* of f. We define the partial order $\preceq$ on caveat-free colorings by $f \preceq f'$ if and only if $\mathrm{height}(f) = \mathrm{height}(f')$, $\mathrm{length}(f) = \mathrm{length}(f')$ and $d(f) = d(f')$. It is easy to see that $\mathrm{Surf}(f) = \mathrm{Surf}(f')$ given $f \preceq f'$. We can show that every f can be extended to a $\preceq$-maximal coloring f' (which must have the same surface). Furthermore, we can show, that every $\preceq$-maximal coloring f has a simple form. An example of a $\preceq$-maximal coloring f with $o(f) > e(f)$ is

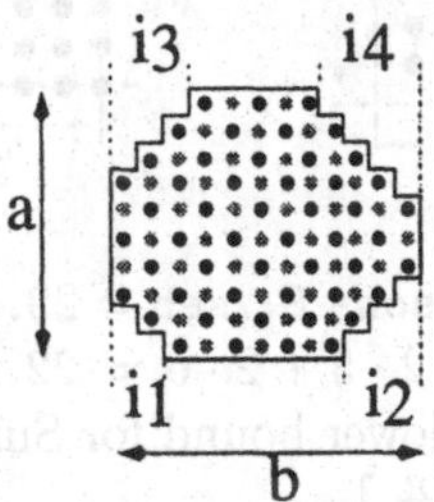

Here, we use black beads for odd positions (x,y) with $f(x,y) = 1$, and grey beads for even positions (x,y) with $f(x,y) = 1$. (a,b) is the frame of f, and $i_1, \ldots, i_4$ are the side length of triangles excluded at the corner. The tuple $(a, b, i_1, i_2, i_3, i_4)$ is called the characteristics of this coloring. In this case, the characteristics is $(10, 12, 2, 3, 3, 4)$.

Theorem 2. *Let f be a $\preceq$-maximal coloring. Then f has a unique characteristics $(a, b, i_1, i_2, i_3, i_4)$. Furthermore, we have $e(f) + o(f) = a \times b - \sum_{j=1}^{4} \frac{i_j(i_j+1)}{2}$, $d(f) = \frac{i_1+i_2+i_3+i_4}{2} + 1$ and $\mathrm{Surf}(f) = 2a + 2b$.*

3 Results

We have tested the program on all sequences presented in [18]. For all we found an optimal conformation. In Table 1, we have listed the test sequences together with the found optimal conformation, the sequence length and the optimal surface. For comparison, the runtimes (on a Sun4) of the algorithm in [18] for all optimal conformations are 1 h 38 min for L1, 1 h 14 min for L2, 5 h 19 min for L3, 5 h 19 min for L4 and 20 min for L5, respectively. There is a newer, more efficient version of this algorithm reported in [19], but there are no explicit runtime given for these or others sequences. In Table 2, we have listed the number of steps to find a first conformation (and a second, if the first was not optimal), the number of steps needed to prove optimality, and the runtime on a Pentium 180 Pro.

Sequence and Sample Conformation	Length	Optimal Surface
L1 HPPPPHHHHPPHPHPHHHPHPPHHPPH	27	40
RFDBLLFRFUBULBDFLUBLDRDDFU		
L2 HPPPHHHHPHPHHPPPHPHHPHPPPHP	27	38
RFDLLBUURFDLLBBRURDDFDBLUB		
L3 HPHHPPHHPPHHHHPPPHPPPHHHPPH	27	38
RFLDLUBBUFFFDFURBUBBDFRFDL		
L4 HHPHHPHHPHHHHHHPPHHHHHHPPHHHHHHH	31	52
RRFDBLDRFLLBUFLURFDDRFUBBUFRDD		
L5 PHPPHPPHPPHPPHPPHPPHPPHPPHPPHPPHPPHP	36	32
RFDBDRUFUBRBLULDLDRDRURBLDLULURBRFR		

Table 1. Test sequences. Below every sequence, we list an optimal conformation represented as a sequence of bond directions (R=right,L=left and so on).

Acknowledgement

I would like to thank Prof. Peter Clote, who got me interested in bioinformatics, and enabled and inspired this research. I would like to thank Prof. Martin Karplus for helpful discussions on the topic of lattice models, and for motivating me to apply constraint programming techniques to lattice protein folding. I would like to thank Dr. Erich Bornberg-Bauer, who initiated this research, too. I would like to thank him also for explaining me the biological background, and for many discussion and hints. Furthermore, I would like to thank Sebastian Will, who contributed on the section 'Exclusion of Geometrical Symmetries'.

References

1. V. I. Abkevich, A. M. Gutin, and E. I. Shakhnovich. Impact of local and non-local interactions on thermodynamics and kinetics of protein folding. *Journal of Molecular Biology*, 252:460–471, 1995.
2. V.I. Abkevich, A.M. Gutin, and E.I. Shakhnovich. Computer simulations of prebiotic evolution. In Russ B. Altman, A. Keith Dunker, Lawrence Hunter, and Teri E. Klein, editors, *PSB'97*, pages 27–38, 1997.
3. B. Berger and T. Leighton. Protein folding in the hydrophobic-hydrophilic (HP) modell is NP-complete. In *Proc. of the RECOMB'98*, pages 30–39, 1998.
4. Erich Bornberg-Bauer. Chain growth algorithms for HP-type lattice proteins. In *Proc. of the 1st Annual International Conference on Computational Molecular Biology (RECOMB)*, pages 47 – 55. ACM Press, 1997.
5. P. Crescenzi, D. Goldman, C. Papadimitriou, A. Piccolboni, and M. Yannakakis. On the complexity of protein folding. In *Proc. of STOC*, 1998. To appear. Short version in *Proc. of RECOMB'98*, pages 61–62.
6. K.A. Dill, S. Bromberg, K. Yue, K.M. Fiebig, D.P. Yee, P.D. Thomas, and H.S. Chan. Principles of protein folding – a perspective of simple exact models. *Protein Science*, 4:561–602, 1995.
7. Ken A. Dill, Klaus M. Fiebig, and Hue Sun Chan. Cooperativity in protein-folding kinetics. *Proc. Natl. Acad. Sci. USA*, 90:1942 – 1946, 1993.
8. Aaron R. Dinner, Andreaj Šali, and Martin Karplus. The folding mechanism of larger model proteins: Role of native structure. *Proc. Natl. Acad. Sci. USA*, 93:8356–8361, 1996.

Seq.	1st Conf.		2nd Conf.		total # Steps	Runtime
	# Steps	Surface	# Steps	Surface		
L1	519	40 (opt.)	—		921	3.85 sec
L2	1322	40	1345	38 (opt.)	5372	1 min 35 sec
L3	1396	38 (opt.)	—	—	1404	4.09 sec
L4	35	52 (opt.)	—	—	38	0.68 sec
L5	1081	32 (opt.)	—	—	1081	4.32 sec

Seq.	1st Conf.		2nd Conf.		total # Steps	Runtime
	# Steps	Surface	# Steps	Surface		
L1	139	40 (opt.)	—	—	159	3.35 sec
L2	43	38 (opt.)	—	—	61	1.53 sec
L3	217	38 (opt.)	—	—	218	1.17 sec
L4	28	52 (opt.)	—	—	28	1.05 sec
L5	25	32 (opt.)	—	—	25	440 ms

Table 2. Search time and number of search steps for the sample sequences. The first table contains the results for an implementation without symmetry exclusion, the second table for the current implementation containing symmetry exclusion. The main reduction in the number of search steps is due to the symmetry exclusion. Only for L4, the older implementation achieves a better result. The reason is that for this sequence, both implementations actually do not have to perform a search to find the optimal conformation. In this case, the symmetry exclusion is clearly an overhead.

9. S. Govindarajan and R. A. Goldstein. The foldability landscape of model proteins. *Biopolymers*, 42(4):427–438, 1997.
10. William E. Hart and Sorin C. Istrail. Fast protein folding in the hydrophobid-hydrophilic model within three-eighths of optimal. *Journal of Computational Biology*, 3(1):53 – 96, 1996.
11. David A. Hinds and Michael Levitt. From structure to sequence and back again. *Journal of Molecular Biology*, 258:201–209, 1996.
12. Kit Fun Lau and Ken A. Dill. A lattice statistical mechanics model of the conformational and sequence spaces of proteins. *Macromolecules*, 22:3986 – 3997, 1989.
13. Angel R. Ortiz, Andrzej Kolinski, and Jeffrey Skolnick. Combined multiple sequence reduced protein model approach to predict the tertiary structure of small proteins. In Russ B. Altman, A. Keith Dunker, Lawrence Hunter, and Teri E. Klein, editors, *PSB'98*, volume 3, pages 375–386, 1998.
14. Gert Smolka. The Oz programming model. In Jan van Leeuwen, editor, *Computer Science Today*, Lecture Notes in Computer Science, vol. 1000, pages 324–343. Springer-Verlag, Berlin, 1995.
15. R. Unger and J. Moult. Genetic algorithms for protein folding simulations. *Journal of Molecular Biology*, 231:75–81, 1993.
16. Ron Unger and John Moult. Local interactions dominate folding in a simple protein model. *Journal of Molecular Biology*, 259:988–994, 1996.
17. A. Šali, E. Shakhnovich, and M. Karplus. Kinetics of protein folding. *Journal of Molecular Biology*, 235:1614–1636, 1994.
18. Kaizhi Yue and Ken A. Dill. Sequence-structure relationships in proteins and copolymers. *Physical Review E*, 48(3):2267–2278, September 1993.
19. Kaizhi Yue and Ken A. Dill. Forces of tertiary structural organization in globular proteins. *Proc. Natl. Acad. Sci. USA*, 92:146 – 150, 1995.

Global Constraints for Partial CSPs: A Case-Study of Resource and Due Date Constraints

Philippe Baptiste[1,2], Claude Le Pape[2] and Laurent Peridy[3]

[1]UMR CNRS 6599, HEUDIASYC, U.T.C., Compiègne, BP 20529, F-60205
[2]Bouygues, Direction des Technologies Nouvelles
[3]Institut de Mathématiques Appliquées, Université Catholique de l'Ouest

E-mails: baptiste@utc.fr, lepape@dmi.ens.fr, laurent.peridy@ima.uco.fr

Abstract

This paper presents the results of a case study, concerning the propagation of a global disjunctive resource constraint, when the resource is over-loaded. The problem can be seen as a partial constraint satisfaction problem, in which either the resource constraint or the due dates of some jobs have to be violated. Global constraint propagation methods are introduced to efficiently deal with this situation. These methods are applied to a well-known operations research problem: minimizing the number of late jobs on a single machine, when jobs are subjected to release dates and due dates. Dominance criteria and a branch and bound procedure are developed for this problem. 960 instances are generated with respect to different characteristics (number of jobs, overload ratio, distribution of release dates, of due dates and of processing times). Instances with 60 jobs are solved in 23 seconds on average and 90% of the instances with 100 jobs are solved in less than 1 hour.

1. Introduction

In the recent years, various classes of global constraints have been developed to enable the resolution of computationally demanding problems, such as the Job-Shop Scheduling problem (see, *e.g.*, [Aggoun and Beldiceanu, 93], [Nuijten, 94], [Caseau and Laburthe, 95]) or the Car Sequencing problem [Régin and Puget, 97]. These global constraints have enabled the development of many industrial applications based on constraint programming. In parallel, a lot of academic work has been performed on over-constrained problems, and many extensions of the constraint satisfaction paradigm have been proposed (see, *e.g.*, [Freuder and Wallace, 92], [Bistarelli *et al.*, 95], [Schiex *et al.*, 95]). It appears that such extensions could be highly useful in practice. Indeed, industrial problems tend to include many "preference" constraints, that cannot be all satisfied at the same time. Consequently, one of the issues that the constraint programming community shall address is the embedding of global constraints in partial constraint satisfaction frameworks. This is not easy for (at least) two reasons.

- First, a global constraint often corresponds to multiple local constraints. For example, an "all-different" constraint between n variables corresponds, in a sense, to $n\ (n - 1) / 2$ binary different constraints. Consequently, one does not merely want to reason about whether the "all-different" constraint is satisfied or not, but also about its "degree" of satisfaction. A solution in which most of the variables are different is probably better than a solution where all variables are equal.

- Second, global constraints often rely on complex algorithms, derived from graph theory or operations research. Extensions of these algorithms to a partial constraint satisfaction framework are seldom if ever immediate.

In this situation, we decided to engage in a case study concerning a problem often encountered in practice, *i.e.*, the partial satisfaction of due-dates in a scheduling problem. The problem we chose as a starter is a variant of the One-Machine problem [Garey and Johnson, 79]. Given are a set of jobs $\{J_1, \ldots, J_n\}$ to be executed on a given machine. With each job is associated a release date r_i, before which the job cannot start, a due date d_i, at which one would like the job to be finished, and a processing time p_i (all integers). Each job must be executed without interruption and the machine can execute only one job at a time. When this problem has no solution, some due dates have to be relaxed (or some jobs have to be subcontracted, to be executed with other resources). We consider the simplest version of this problem, in which all jobs are equally important, and the goal is to perform as many jobs as possible within their due-dates. This problem is known as $(1| r_j |\Sigma U_j)$ in the scheduling community (*e.g.*, [Brucker, 95]).

An instance of the decision-variant of this problem [Garey and Johnson, 79] consists of a set of jobs, as described above, and an integer N. The problem is to find an assignment of start times to jobs such that:

- jobs do not overlap in time,
- each job starts after its release date,
- the number of jobs that end after their due date is lower than or equal to N.

Without loss of generality, we can suppose that $r_i + p_i \leq d_i$, for all i, since otherwise job J_i cannot be done on time. A job scheduled between its release date and its due date is "on-time". Conversely, a job that ends after its due date is "late" (or, equivalently, is subcontracted).

The $(1| r_j|\Sigma U_j)$ problem is NP-hard in the strong sense and is therefore unlikely to be solvable in polynomial time [Garey and Johnson, 79]. However, some special cases are solvable in polynomial time. Moore's well-known algorithm [Moore, 68] solves in $O(n \log(n))$ steps the special case where release dates are equal. Moreover, when release and due dates of jobs are ordered similarly ($r_i < r_j \Rightarrow d_i \leq d_j$), the problem is solvable in a quadratic amount of steps [Kise *et al.*, 78]. Lower bounding techniques have been developed for the general problem. [Dauzère-Pérès, 95] relies on the resolution of several linear programs to compute a lower bound of the number of late jobs. Another lower bound can be obtained by relaxing the non-preemption constraint (*i.e.*, jobs can be interrupted at any time). [Lawler, 90] describes an $O(n^5)$ algorithm (requiring a cubic amount of memory space) for solving this preemptive relaxation. [Baptiste, 98] proposes another dynamic programming algorithm that improves both time and space bounds to respectively $O(n^4)$ and $O(n^2)$. Few exact approaches have been made to solve the $(1| r_j|\Sigma U_j)$. [Dauzère-Pérès, 95] shows that the problem can be modeled by a Mixed Integer Program (MIP). Unfortunately, instances with more than 10 jobs could not be considered because of the size of the MIP.

We develop constraint propagation methods to deal with the partial satisfaction of due dates on a given disjunctive resource. These methods are then used as part of a branch and bound procedure to compute an optimal solution of the $(1| r_j|\Sigma U_j)$. The number of late jobs is represented by a constrained variable v whose domain is $[0, n]$. Each job J_i

is described by a binary variable ξ_i that states whether the job is on-time ($\xi_i = 1$) or late ($\xi_i = 0$) and by an integer variable σ_i (the start time), whose domain is $[r_i, d_i - p_i]$. The first constraint to satisfy is $\Sigma(1-\xi_i)=\nu$. Simple arc-consistency techniques can be used to propagate this constraint. The "classical" resource constraint is modified to work not only on the domains of the start time variables σ_i, but also on the job status variables ξ_i. It states that jobs which must be on-time cannot overlap in time: $\forall t, |\{J_i \text{ such that } \xi_i = 1 \text{ and } \sigma_i \le t < \sigma_i + p_i\}| \le 1$. To allow further pruning, the maximal value of ν and dominance relations between the job status variables (of the form $\xi_i \Rightarrow \xi_j$) can also be taken into account in this constraint. Constraint propagation reduces the domains of both the σ_i and ξ_i variables. To simplify notations, r_i always denotes the minimum value in the domain of σ_i and d_i the maximum value in the domain of σ_i+p_i. r_i and d_i will be referred to as the release date and the due date of J_i, even when modified by propagation. O denotes the set of jobs that have to be on-time (ξ_i has been bound to 1) and L denotes the set of jobs that have to be late ($\xi_i = 0$).
The constraint propagation methods are used in a branch and bound procedure for the $(1|\,r_j\,|\Sigma U_j)$. To reach an optimal solution, we solve several decision variants of the problem. More precisely, we rely on the following scheme.

1. Compute an initial lower bound of $(1|r_j|\Sigma U_j)$; set the minimum of ν to this value.
2. Try to bound ν to its minimal value N.
3. If there is a feasible schedule with N late jobs then stop (N is the optimum). Otherwise, provoke a backtrack, remove N from the domain of ν and go to step 2.

Beside the lower bound computation, our search strategy is based on three principles. First, at each node of the search tree, we verify that there exists a schedule of the jobs that have to be on-time (if not, a backtrack occurs). Such a verification is NP-hard in the strong sense but it turns out to be "easy" in practice. Second, given the above verification, our branching scheme simply consists in selecting an unbound variable ξ_i to instantiate either to 1 or 0. Third, we use several dominance properties (*cf.*, Section 3.2) that allow us to generate constraints of the form "if J_i is on-time then J_j is on-time" ($\xi_i \Rightarrow \xi_j$), which are in turn exploited as part of constraint propagation; for each job J_i, $O(J_i)$ is the set of jobs that have to be on time if J_i is on-time. Symmetrically, $L(J_i)$ is the set of jobs that have to be late if J_i is late ($J_i \in O(J_i)$and $J_i \in L(J_i)$).
The paper is organized as follows: Section 2 presents in details the propagation scheme that has been designed for the modified resource constraint; Section 3 describes both the search strategy and the dominance properties. Section 4 presents the experimental results obtained on 960 instances, ranging from 10 to 140 jobs, and proposes some further research directions.

2. Constraint Propagation

The propagation of the modified resource constraint consists of four interrelated parts.

1. In the first part, classical resource constraint propagation techniques are used on the on-time jobs: disjunctive constraint propagation and edge-finding are applied on O (see *e.g.*, [Carlier and Pinson, 90], [Baptiste and Le Pape, 95]).
2. In the second part, for each job J_i such that such that ξ_i is unbound, we try to add all jobs in $O(J_i)$ to the set O of jobs that must be on-time. The resource constraint is propagated as described in part 1. Two cases can occur. If an inconsistency is

triggered, then the job J_i has to be late (ξ_i can be set to 0); otherwise the release date r'_i and the due date d'_i obtained after the propagation are kept and imposed as the new release ($r_i = r'_i$) and as the new due date ($d_i = d'_i$) of the job. Notice that one pass of such a propagation scheme runs in $O(n^3)$ since for each job the edge-finding algorithm, itself running in $O(n^2)$, is called.

3. The third part described in Section 2.1 determines a lower bound for ν.
4. The fourth part described in Section 2.2 focuses on the ξ_i variables.

Of course, when the domain of a variable is modified by one of the four parts above, the overall propagation process restarts.

2.1. Lower Bound Computation

The One-Machine problem [Carlier, 82] is a special case of the $(1|\, r_j|\Sigma U_j)$ in which all jobs must be on-time. Its preemptive relaxation is polynomial. It is well known that there exists a feasible preemptive schedule if and only if over any interval $[r_j, d_k]$, the sum of the processing times of the jobs in $S(r_j, d_k) = \{J_i \mid r_j \le r_i \text{ and } d_i \le d_k\}$ is lower than or equal to $d_k - r_j$. As a consequence, the optimum of the following MIP is the minimum number of jobs that must be late on any preemptive schedule of the machine (hence, this optimum is a lower bound of the variable ν). The binary variable x_i is equal to 1 when a job is on-time, to 0 otherwise.

$$\min \sum_{i\in\{1,\cdots,n\}} (1 - x_i)$$

$$\forall r_j, \forall d_k > r_j, \quad \sum_{J_i \in S(r_j,d_k)} p_i x_i \le d_k - r_j \qquad (P)$$

$$\forall J_i \in O, x_i = 1 \text{ and } \forall J_i \in L, x_i = 0$$

$$\forall i \in \{1,\cdots,n\},\ x_i \in \{0,1\}$$

The first set of constraints of P represents the resource constraints. The notation (r_j, d_k) refers to the resource constraint over the interval $[r_j, d_k]$. In the following, we focus on the continuous relaxation CP of P. We claim that CP can be solved in $O(n^2\log(n))$ steps. To achieve this result, we first provide a characterization of one vector that realizes the optimum (Proposition 1). From now on, we suppose that jobs are sorted in increasing order of processing times.

Proposition 1. The largest vector (according to the lexicographical order) satisfying all the constraints of CP realizes the optimum of CP.

Proof. Let $Y = (Y_1, \ldots, Y_n)$ be the largest vector (according to the lexicographical order) satisfying all the constraints of CP, *i.e.*, Y_1 is maximal, Y_2 is maximal (given Y_1), Y_3 is maximal (given Y_1 and Y_2), …, Y_n is maximal (given $Y_1, \ldots, Y_{n-1}$). Moreover, let $X = (X_1, \ldots, X_n)$ be the largest (according to the lexicographical order) optimal solution of CP. Suppose that $X \ne Y$; let then u be the first index such that $X_u < Y_u$. Consider the set C of constraints that are saturated at X.

$$C = \{(r_j, d_k) \mid J_u \in S(r_j, d_k) \text{ and } \sum_{J_i \in S(r_j,d_k)} p_i X_i = d_k - r_j\}$$

If C is empty, then none of the constraints containing the variable x_u is saturated at the point X ($X_u < Y_u$ ensures that $X_u < 1$ and that x_u is not constrained to be equal to 0) and thus, X is not an optimum of CP. Hence C is not empty. Let then $(\rho_1, \delta_1) \in C$ be the pair such that ρ_1 is maximum and δ_1 is minimum (given ρ_1). Let $(\rho_2, \delta_2) \in C$ be the pair such that δ_2 is minimum and ρ_2 is maximum (given δ_2).

Suppose that $\rho_2 < \rho_1$. It is then obvious that $\rho_2 < \rho_1 \leq \rho_u < \delta_u \leq \delta_2 < \delta_1$. Let $A = S(\rho_2, \delta_2) - S(\rho_1, \delta_2)$ and let $B = S(\rho_1, \delta_1) - S(\rho_1, \delta_2)$. Because both (ρ_1, δ_1) and $(\rho_2, \delta_2) \in C$, we have:

$$\sum_{J_i \in A} p_i X_i + \sum_{J_i \in S(\rho_1,\delta_2)} p_i X_i = \delta_2 - \rho_2 \quad \text{and} \quad \sum_{J_i \in S(\rho_1,\delta_2)} p_i X_i + \sum_{J_i \in B} p_i X_i = \delta_1 - \rho_1$$

Since, the sets A, B and $S(\rho_1, \delta_2)$ are disjoint and since $A \cup B \cup S(\rho_1, \delta_2) \subseteq S(\rho_2, \delta_1)$,

$$\sum_{J_i \in S(\rho_2,\delta_1)} p_i X_i \geq \delta_2 - \rho_2 + \delta_1 - \rho_1 - \sum_{J_i \in S(\rho_1,\delta_2)} p_i X_i \geq \delta_1 - \rho_2$$

The inequality above cannot be strict hence (ρ_1, δ_2) belongs to C. This, together with $\rho_2 < \rho_1$ contradicts our hypothesis on the choice of δ_1.

Now suppose that $\rho_1 = \rho_2 = \rho$ and $\delta_1 = \delta_2 = \delta$. The pair (ρ, δ) is the unique minimal saturated constraint containing the variable x_u. We claim that among jobs in $S(\rho, \delta)$, there is one job, say J_v, such that $v > u$ and $X_v > 0$ and $J_v \notin O$ (otherwise we could prove, because $X_u < Y_u$, that X_u can be increased; which contradicts the fact that X is optimal). Consider now X' the vector defined as follows. $\forall\, i \notin \{u, v\}$, $X'_i = X_i$ and $X'_u = X_u + \varepsilon / p_u$ and $X'_v = X_v - \varepsilon / p_v$. Where $\varepsilon > 0$ is a small value such that $\varepsilon \leq p_u(1 - X_u)$, $\varepsilon \leq p_v X_v$ and such that for any non-saturated constraint (r_j, d_k),

$$\varepsilon \leq d_k - r_j - \sum_{J_i \in S(r_j,d_k)} p_i X_i$$

Since jobs are sorted in increasing order of processing times, $\varepsilon / p_u - \varepsilon / p_v \geq 0$ and thus, $\Sigma (1 - X'_i) \leq \Sigma (1 - X_i)$. Moreover, X' is "better" for the lexicographical order than X. Second, because of the definition of ε, the constraints that were not saturated for X are not violated for X'. Third, the saturated constraints (for the vector X) that contain the variable x_u all contain the variables in (ρ, δ). In particular, they contain both x_u and x_v. As a consequence they are also saturated for the vector X'. We have then proven that all constraints are satisfied. This contradicts our hypothesis on X. □

Proposition 1 induces a simple algorithm (Algorithm 1) to compute the optimum X of *CP*. Jobs J_i that do not have to be late or on-time are considered one after another. Each time, we compute the maximum resource constraint violation if the job is fully on-time (lines 4-11). Given this violation, the maximum value X_i that the variable x_i can take is computed (line 12). This algorithm runs in $O(n^4)$ since there are n jobs J_i and since for each of them $O(n^2)$ violations are computed, each of them in linear time.

Algorithm 1.

```
1  ∀ Ji, initialize Xi to 1.0 if Xi ∈ O, to 0.0 otherwise
2  for i = 1 to n
3     if Ji ∉ O and Ji ∉ L
4       Xi = 1.0, Violation = 0
5       for all constraint (rj, dk) such that Ji ∈ S(rj, dk)
6          sum = 0.0
7          for Jl ∈ S(rj, dk)
8            sum = sum + pl * Xl
9          end for
10         Violation = max(Violation, sum - dk - rj)
11      end for
12      Xi = (pi - Violation) / pi
13    end if
14 end for
```

We improve this algorithm thanks to Jackson's Preemptive Schedule (*JPS*), the One-Machine preemptive schedule obtained by applying the Earliest Due Date priority dispatching rule [Carlier and Pinson, 90]. A fundamental property of *JPS* is that it is feasible (*i.e.*, each job ends before its due date) if and only if there exists a feasible preemptive schedule.

The procedure "`ComputeJPS`" of Algorithm 2 is called for several values of i. It computes the *JPS* of the jobs, assuming that the processing time of $J_l (l \neq i)$ is $p_l X_l$ and that the processing time of J_i is p_i. "`EndTimeJPS[k]`" is the end time of J_k on *JPS*. *JPS* can be built in $O(n\log(n))$ [Carlier, 82]. Algorithm 2 then runs in $O(n^2\log(n))$.

Algorithm 2.

```
1  ∀ Ji, initialize Xi to 1.0 if Xi ∈ O, to 0.0 otherwise
2  for i = 1 to i = n
3    if Ji ∉ O and Ji ∉ L
4      ComputeJPS
5      ViolationJPS = 0
6      for all jobs Jk such that Xk > 0
7        ViolationJPS := max(ViolationJPS, EndTimeJPS[k] - dk)
8      end for
9      Xi = (pi - ViolationJPS) / pi
10   end if
11 end for
```

Proof of the correctness of Algorithm 2. By induction. Suppose that at the beginning of iteration i (line 2), the first coordinates $X_1, \ldots, X_{i-1}$ are exactly equal to those of Y, the maximal vector (according to the lexicographical order) satisfying the constraints of *CP*. Consider the case $Y_i = 1$ then, because of the structure of *CP*, there exists a feasible preemptive schedule of $J_1, \ldots, J_n$ (the processing time of job J_u being $p_u Y_u$) and thus, the *JPS* computed line 4 is also feasible; which means that no violation occurs. Hence, $X_i = 1$ (line 9). Consider now the case $Y_i < 1$.

- We first prove that $X_i \leq Y_i$. Since $Y_i < 1$, the violation computed by Algorithm 1 at step i is positive. Let then (r_j, d_k) be the constraint that realizes this violation. We then have $Y_i = 1 - \frac{1}{p_i}(p_i + \sum_{J_l \in S(r_j,d_k), l \neq i} p_l Y_l + r_j - d_k)$. Moreover, at step i of Algorithm 2, `EndTimeJPS[k]` $\geq p_i + \sum_{J_l \in S(r_j,d_k), l \neq i} p_l X_l + r_j$. Hence $X_i \leq Y_i$ (line 9).

- We now prove that $Y_i \leq X_i$. Let k be the index of the job such that the maximum violation on *JPS* is "`EndTimeJPS[k] - dk`". Such an index exists because we have proven that $X_i \leq Y_i < 1$ and thus, "`ViolationJPS`" is strictly positive. Let t be the largest time point lower than or equal to the end time of this job such that immediately before t, *JPS* is either idle or executing a job with a larger due date than d_k. According to the particular structure of *JPS*, t is a release date, say r_j. Notice that between r_j and d_k, *JPS* is never idle and the jobs that are processed are exactly those whose release date is greater than or equal to r_j and whose due date is lower than or equal to d_k. As a consequence, the end time of the kth job is $r_j + \sum_{J_l \in S(r_j,d_k), l \neq i} p_l X_l + p_i$. Hence, $X_i = 1 - \frac{1}{p_i}(r_j + \sum_{J_l \in S(r_j,d_k), l \neq i} p_l X_l + p_i - d_k) \geq Y_i$. □

Example 1.
The following table displays the characteristics of four jobs J_1, J_2, J_3 and J_4. The last column X is the value of the job variable at the end of Algorithm 2. The Gantt charts display the *JPS* computed at each step of Algorithm 2.

Job	r	p	d	X
J_1	7	2	10	2/2
J_2	4	3	9	3/3
J_3	1	5	6	4/5
J_4	4	7	12	2/7

2.2. A Filtering Algorithm

In this section, we propose an algorithm, which is able to detect that, given the domain of v, some jobs must be on time while some others must be late. To strengthen constraint propagation, we use a dominance property introduced in Section 1 and described in Section 3: For any job J_i, a set $O(J_i)$ of jobs that have to be on-time if J_i is on-time and a set $L(J_i)$ of jobs that have to be late if J_i is late can be computed.

Late Job Detection

From now on, we suppose that the optimum X of *CP* has been computed as described in the previous section. Consider a job J_j such that $J_j \notin O$ and $J_j \notin L$. Our objective is to compute efficiently a lower bound of the number of late jobs if J_j and $O(J_j)$ are on-time. If this lower bound is greater than the maximal value in the domain of v, then, J_j must be late. Algorithm 2 could be used to compute such a lower bound. However, this would lead to a high overall complexity of $O(n^3 \log(n))$. We propose to use a slightly weaker lower bound that can be computed in linear time, for a given job J_j. The overall filtering scheme then runs in $O(n^2)$.
Let *CPo* be the linear program *CP* to which the constraints $\forall J_i \in O(J_j), x_i = 1$ have been added. Moreover, let *Xo* be the optimal vector of *CPo* obtained by Algorithm 2 (*CPo* has a solution, otherwise part 2 of the propagation described at the beginning of Section 2 would have detected that $J_j \in L$). Propositions 2 and 3 exhibit two relations that X and *Xo* satisfy. These relations are used to compute a lower bound of $\sum Xo_i$.

Proposition 2. $\sum p_i Xo_i \leq \sum p_i X_i$

Proof. Let $G(Jobs, Time, E)$ be a bipartite graph, where $Jobs = \{Job_1, \ldots, Job_n\}$ is a set of vertices corresponding to the jobs, where $Time = \{T_t, \min_i r_i \leq t < \max_i d_i\}$ is a set of vertices corresponding to all the "relevant" time-intervals $[t, t+1]$ and where an edge $(Jobi, T_t)$ belongs to E if and only if J_i can execute in $[t, t+1]$ (*i.e.*, $r_i \leq t < d_i$). Consider the network flow (*cf.* Figure 1) built from G by adding:

- two vertices S, P and an edge (P, S),
- for each node Job_i an edge (S, Job_i) whose capacity is (1) upper bounded by either 0 if $J_i \in L$ or by p_i otherwise and (2) lower bounded by either p_i if $J_i \in O$ or by 0 otherwise,
- for each node T_t an edge (T_t, P) whose capacity is upper bounded by 1.

For any feasible flow, a vector satisfying all constraints of *CP* can be built (the ith coordinate of the vector is the value of the flow on (S, Job_i) divided by p_i). Since $\forall i, X_i * p_i$ is integer, a feasible flow can be derived from the *JPS* associated to X (when J_i executes in $[t, t+1]$ on *JPS*, set the value of the flow to 1 on the edge (Job_i, T_t)).

Suppose that $\sum p_i Xo_i > \sum p_i X_i$ then the flow corresponding to X is not maximal in G and thus there is an augmenting path from S to P. Let then X^+ be the vector corresponding to the augmented flow. Because of the structure of G, $\forall i, X^+_i \geq X_i$. On top of that there exists l such that $X^+_l > X_l$. This contradicts Proposition 1. □

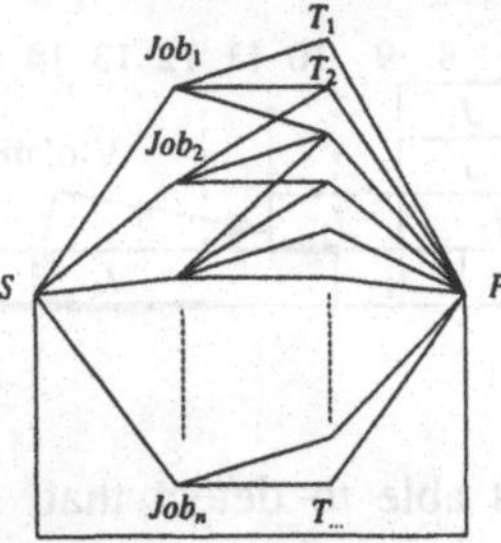

Figure 1. Network flow associated to G

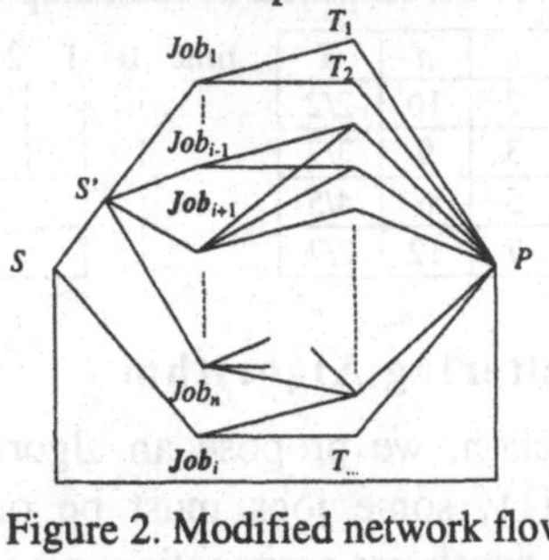

Figure 2. Modified network flow

Proposition 3. $\forall J_i \notin O(J_j), Xo_i \leq X_i$

Proof (sketch). Suppose the proposition does not hold. Let i be the first index such that $J_i \notin O(J_j)$ and $Xo_i > X_i$. We modify the instance of the problem by removing the jobs J_u with $u > i$ that do not belong to O nor to $O(J_j)$. The jobs that have been removed do not influence Algorithm 1 when computing the i first coordinates of X and of Xo (*i.e.*, for the modified instance, the i first coordinates of the optimum vector are exactly those of X). Now, consider the modified instance. We still have $J_i \notin O(J_j)$ and $Xo_i > X_i$. Moreover, the jobs that have a greater index than i belong to $O \cup O(J_j)$. Consider the modified network (Figure 2) built from the bipartite graph G by adding:

- three vertices S, S', P, and two edges, (S, S') and (P, S),
- for each node Job_u $(u \neq i)$ an edge (S', Job_u) whose capacity is (1) upper bounded by either 0 if $J_u \in L$ or by p_u otherwise and (2) lower bounded by either p_u if $J_u \in O$ or by 0 otherwise,
- an edge (S, Job_i) whose capacity is upper bounded by p_i and lower bounded by 0,
- for each node T_t an edge (T_t, P) whose capacity is upper bounded by 1.

For any feasible flow, a vector satisfying all constraints of CP can be built. Conversely, for any vector satisfying all constraints of CP, a feasible flow can be built. The flow corresponding to Xo is obviously feasible. Moreover the flow on (P, S) for vector X is greater than or equal to the one for Xo (see Proposition 2). Moreover, the flow on (S, Job_i) for Xo is greater than the one for X. Hence, because of the conservation law at S, the flow that goes over (S, S') is not maximal for Xo. As a consequence, there is an augmenting path from S' to S for the flow corresponding to Xo. Let then Xo^+ be the vector corresponding to the augmented flow. Because of the structure of G, $\forall u \neq i, Xo^+_u \geq Xo_u$. Hence, $\forall J_u \in O \cup O(J_j)$, $Xo^+_u = 1$ and then, Xo^+ satisfies all the constraints of CPo. Moreover it is better than Xo because:

- If the edge (P, S) is in the augmenting path then $\sum p_i Xo^+_i > \sum p_i Xo_i$.
- If the edge (Job_i, S) is in the augmenting path then we claim that Xo^+ is greater, for the lexicographical order, than Xo. Indeed, there is an edge from S' to a job, say Job_u, in the augmenting path. Hence, J_u neither belongs to O nor to $O(J_j)$ (otherwise, the edge would be saturated for Xo and it could not belong to the augmenting path). Consequently, $u < i$ and then $Xo^+_u > Xo_u$.

This contradicts the fact that Xo is optimal. □

Thanks to Propositions 2 and 3, we can add the constraints $\sum p_i Xo_i \le \sum p_i X_i$ and $\forall J_i \in O(J_j), x_i \le X_i$ to the linear program *CPo*. Since we are interested in a lower bound of *CPo*, we can also relax the resource constraints. As a consequence, we seek to solve the following program, that is solved in linear time by Algorithm 3.

$$\begin{aligned}
&\min \sum (1 - x_i) \\
&\sum p_i x_i \le \sum p_i X_i \\
&\forall J_i \notin o, x_i \le X_i \\
&\forall J_i \in O \cup O(J_j), x_i = 1 \text{ and } \forall J_i \in L, x_i = 0 \\
&\quad \forall i \in \{1, \cdots, n\},\ x_i \in [0,1]
\end{aligned}$$

Algorithm 3.

```
∀ Ji initialize Xoi to 1.0 if Ji∈O∪O(Jj), to 0.0 otherwise
MaxVal = Σ pi Xi - Σ pi Xoi
for all job Ji ∉ O∪O(Jj)
   Xoi = min(Xi, MaxVal / pi)
   MaxVal = MaxVal - pi * Xoi
End for
```

On-Time Job Detection

Let J_j be a job that is neither late nor on-time. We want to compute a lower bound of the number of late jobs if all jobs in $L(J_j)$ are late. Let X_l be the optimal vector of *CPl*, the linear program *CP* to which the constraints $\forall J_i \in L(J_j), x_i = 0$ have been added. We claim that $\Sigma p_i Xl_i \le \Sigma p_i X_i$ and that $\forall J_i \notin L(J_j), Xl_i \ge X_i$ (proofs are similar to the proofs of propositions 2 and 3). The same mechanism than for the late job detection then applies: The new constraints are entered in *CPl* while the resource constraints are removed. The resulting linear program can be also solved in linear time.

3. Search Strategy

We describe our branching scheme and then propose several dominance properties.

3.1. Branching Scheme

The search tree is built as follows. While all variables ξ_i are not instantiated,

1. select a job J_i such that ξ_i is not instantiated,
2. impose the fact that J_i must be on-time (if a backtrack occurs, J_i must be late),
3. apply dominance properties and propagate constraints
4. check that there exists a feasible One-Machine schedule of the jobs that must be on-time (if not, the problem is inconsistent and a backtrack occurs).

When the branch and bound succeeds, all variables ξ_i are instantiated and at most N of these variables are equal to 0 (because arc-consistency is enforced on the constraint $\Sigma(1 - \xi_i) = N$). Moreover there is a feasible One-Machine schedule of the on-time jobs (step 4). Since the late jobs can be scheduled anywhere, a solution schedule with less than N late jobs has been found. Let us detail the heuristic used for the job selection and the procedure that checks whether there is a feasible One-Machine schedule of the jobs that must be on-time.

Job Selection

Let *pmin* be the minimum processing time among jobs J_i such that ξ_i is not instantiated. Let then S be the set of jobs J_i such that ξ_i is not instantiated and such that $p_i \leq 1.1 * pmin$. Among jobs in S, we select a job whose time window is maximum (*i.e.*, $d_i - r_i$ maximum). This heuristic "bets" that it is better to schedule small jobs with large time windows rather than large jobs with tight time windows.

Solving the One-Machine Problem

A large amount of work has been carried on this problem (*e.g.*, [Carlier, 82]) because it serves as the basis for the resolution of several scheduling problems (*e.g.*, the Job-Shop problem [Carlier and Pinson, 90], [Baptiste and Le Pape, 95], [Peridy, 96]). Since the One-Machine resolution procedure is called at each node of the search tree, it has to be very fast. Following some initial experiments, it appeared that it is often easy to find a feasible schedule of the jobs in O. As a consequence, before starting an exhaustive search, we use a simple heuristic (the Earliest Due Date dispatching rule) to test whether the obtained schedule is feasible or not. [Carlier, 82] proposes an $O(n \log(n))$ algorithm to implement this heuristic. It appears that over all our experiments, this simple heuristic was able to find a feasible schedule for 97% of the One-Machine instances that had to be solved. For the remaining instances, the branch and bound procedure described below has been used.

To solve the One-Machine problem we use the edge-finding branching technique [Applegate and Cook, 91] combined with classical resource constraint propagation techniques (disjunctive constraint plus edge-finding bounding technique): at each node of the search tree, a job J_i which can be the first one to execute among unordered jobs in O is selected according to a given heuristic (Earliest Due Date in our implementation). The alternative is then: either J_i is the first to execute among unordered jobs (J_i is then marked as ordered and all remaining unordered jobs become candidates to be first), or J_i is not. The search stops when all jobs are ordered.

However, this branching scheme sometimes is inefficient. In particular, it is unable to focus early in the search tree on bottlenecks that occur late in time. To avoid this drawback and inspired by the ideas proposed in [Carlier, 82], we slightly modify the branching scheme as follows:

- If there are some time intervals $[r_j, d_k]$ such that (1) the resource can never be idle in $[r_j, d_k]$ (because the sum of the processing times of the jobs that have to execute after r_j and before d_k is equal to $d_k - r_j$) and such that (2) there is a job J_i that can start before r_j and that can end after d_k, then we select among these intervals one whose size is maximum. The branching decision is then: Either J_i ends before r_j or J_i starts after d_k.
- Otherwise, the edge-finding branching scheme is applied.

3.2. Dominance Properties

Dominance properties allow to reduce the search space to schedules that have a particular structure. The most important dominance property relies on the idea that "it is better to schedule small jobs with large time windows than large jobs with small time windows". We also propose two other dominance rules that respectively fix the start times of some jobs and split the problem into distinct sub-problems.

Dominance of Small Jobs with Large Time-Windows

We rely on the observation that on any solution, if a large job J_j is on-time and is scheduled inside the time window $[r_i, d_i]$ of a smaller job J_i that is late then, the jobs J_i and J_j can be "exchanged", *i.e.*, J_i becomes on-time and J_j becomes late. More formally our dominance property is based upon the binary job-relation "<".

$$\forall J_i, \forall J_j, J_i < J_j \Leftrightarrow \begin{cases} i < j \\ r_i + p_i \le r_j + p_j \\ d_j - p_j \le d_i - p_i \end{cases}$$

"<" is transitive and $\forall J_i$, $\forall J_j$, $J_i < J_j \Rightarrow J_i \neq J_j$. Thus, it defines a strict partial order on jobs. Proposition 4 is the theoretical basis of our dominance property.

Proposition 4. There is an optimal schedule such that

$$\forall J_i, \forall J_j, (\neg(J_i < J_j)) \vee (J_j \in L) \vee (J_i \in O)$$

Proof (sketch). Consider an optimal schedule such that the first index i, for which there exists a job J_j that violates the above equation, is maximum. We have

$$(J_i < J_j) \wedge (J_j \in O) \wedge (J_i \in L)$$

We build a new schedule obtained by "exchanging" J_i and J_j. More precisely, J_i is scheduled at the date $\max(\sigma_j, r_i)$ and J_j is scheduled after all other jobs (it then becomes late). It is obvious to verify that the new schedule is still feasible and that J_i is now on-time. Now, suppose that there exists a late job J_k such that $J_k < J_i$. We then have $J_k < J_i < J_j$. Moreover, J_k was also late on the initial schedule. Consequently, $k > i$ because of the choice of i. This contradicts our hypothesis on the choice of the initial schedule. □

Proposition 4 allows us to define $L(J_i) = \{J_j | J_i < J_j\} \cup \{J_i\}$ and $O(J_i) = \{J_j | J_j < J_i\} \cup \{J_i\}$. In addition, for any pair (J_i, J_j) with $i<j$, the following constraint can be added:

$$(r_i + p_i > \sigma_j + p_j) \vee (\sigma_j > d_i - p_i) \vee (\xi_j = 0) \vee (\xi_i = 1).$$

Arc-consistency is achieved on this new constraint. It allows to prove that some jobs must be late or on-time and it tightens the domains of the start variables.

Straight Scheduling Rule

We propose a simple dominance property which schedules automatically a set of jobs if they "fit" in a particular interval.

Proposition 5. Given a time-interval $[t_1, t_2]$, let $J(t_1, t_2) = \{J_i \notin L \mid t_1 < d_i \text{ and } r_i < t_2\}$ be the set of jobs that may execute (even partially) in $[t_1, t_2]$. Moreover, suppose that there exists a feasible schedule S_J of $J(t_1, t_2)$ that is idle before t_1 and after t_2. Then there exists an optimal overall schedule S such that between t_1 and t_2 the schedules S and S_J are identical.

Proof. Obvious. □

Consider now any time point t_1 and let $J(t_1)$ be the set of jobs J_i that do not have to be late and that can end after t_1 ($t_1 < d_i$). We use the following algorithm to look for a time-point t_2 that satisfies the conditions of Proposition 5. In this algorithm, we assume that $J(t_1)$ is not empty.

Algorithm 4.

```
1   S = J(t1), t2 = max(t1, min({ru, Ju ∈ S}))
2   stop = false, success = false
3   while (S ≠ Ø and stop = false)
4     Select a job Ji in S with ri ≤ t2 and with di minimal
5     S = S - Ji, t2 = t2 + pi
6     if (di < t2)
7       stop = true
8     else if (t2 ≤ min({ru, Ju ∈ S})
9       stop = true, success = true
10    end if
11  end while
```

At the end of Algorithm 4, if the Boolean "success" is true, the conditions of Proposition 5 hold for the points (t_1, t_2). Indeed, all jobs in $J(t_1)$ that can start strictly before t_2 are scheduled and do not end after their due date on this schedule (lines 6-10). These jobs are exactly those in $J(t_1, t_2)$. For a given value of t_1, Algorithm 4 runs in $O(n^2)$ since there are $O(n)$ jobs in S and since each time, "`min({ru, Ju ∈ S}`" has to be computed (line 8). Now remark that if t_1 is not a due date of a job then $J(t_1 - 1, t_2) = J(t_1, t_2)$ and a schedule that can fit in $[t_1, t_2]$ can also fit in $[t_1 - 1, t_2]$. Hence we decided to apply Algorithm 4 for $t_1 = \min_i(r_i)$ and for t_1 in $\{d_1, d_2, \ldots, d_n\}$. This leads to an overall complexity of $O(n^3)$.

Decomposition Rule

The basic idea of the decomposition is to detect some cases in which the problem can be split into two sub-problems. Each of them being solved independently.

Proposition 6. Let t_1 be a time point such that $\forall\ J_i \notin L$, either $d_i \leq t_1$ or $t_1 \leq r_i$. Any optimal schedule, is the "sum" of an optimal schedule of $\{J_i \notin L \mid d_i \leq t_1\}$ and of an optimal schedule of $\{J_i \notin L \mid t_1 \leq r_i\}$

Proof. Obvious because jobs of $\{J_i \notin L \mid d_i \leq t_1\}$ and of $\{J_i \notin L \mid t_1 \leq r_i\}$ do not compete for the machine. □

We only consider the values of t_1 that are release dates (if the problem can be decomposed at time t_1, it is easy to verify that it can also be decomposed at the next release date immediately after t_1). There are $O(n)$ distinct release dates and the decomposition test (at a given time point) obviously runs in linear time. Consequently, the overall decomposition test runs in $O(n^2)$.

Once the problem has been decomposed, the optimum of each sub-problem is computed and we simply have to verify that the sum of these optima is lower than or equal to N.

4. Experimental Results

Our implementation of the branch and bound is based on CLAIRE SCHEDULE [Le Pape and Baptiste, 97], a constraint-based library for preemptive and non-preemptive scheduling, itself implemented in CLAIRE [Caseau and Laburthe, 96], a high-level functional and object-oriented language. To test the efficiency of our branch and bound procedure, instances of the $(1 \mid r_j \mid \Sigma U_j)$ have been generated. Our intuition is that one shall pay attention to at least three important characteristics:

- The distribution of the processing times.

- The overall "*load*" of the machine; where the load is the ratio between the sum of the processing times of the jobs and (max d_i – min r_i).
- The margin $m_i = d_i - r_i - p_i$ of each job.

Our generation scheme is based on 4 parameters: The number of jobs n and the three statistical laws followed by the release dates, the processing times and the margins (given r_i, p_i and m_i, the due date can be immediately computed $d_i = m_i + r_i + p_i$).

- Processing times are generated from the uniform distribution $[p_{min}, p_{max}]$.
- Release dates are generated from the normal distribution $(0, \sigma)$.
- Margins are generated from the uniform distribution $[0, m_{max}]$

Given these parameters and relying on the fact that most of the release dates are in $[-2\sigma, 2\sigma]$, the load is approximately equal to $(0.5\,n\,(p_{min} + p_{max})) / (4\sigma + p_{max} + m_{max})$. Given n, p_{min}, p_{max}, m_{max} and *load*, this allows us to determine a correct value of σ. One instance has been generated for each of the 960 combinations of the parameters $(n, (p_{min}, p_{max}), m_{max}, load)$ in the Cartesian product $\{10, 20, 40, 60, \ldots, 140\} * \{(0, 100), (25, 75)\} * \{50, 100, 150, \ldots, 500\} * \{0.5, 0.8, 1.1, 1.4, 1.7, 2.0\}$.

Table 1 reports the results obtained for different values of n; each line corresponding to 120 instances. The column "%" provides the percentage of instances that have been solved within one hour of CPU time on a PC Dell OptiPlex GX Pro 200 MHz running Windows NT. The columns "Avg CPU" and "Max CPU" report respectively the average and the maximum CPU time in seconds required to solve the instances of each group (n = 10, n = 20, ..., n = 140) that could be solved within the time limit. The column "Late" reports the minimal and the maximal number of late jobs among the instances of the corresponding group. Figure 3 illustrates the (reasonable) loss of efficiency of our algorithm when the number of jobs increases. Instances are solved within a few amount of backtracks (35 backtracks on the average for n = 60, 154 for n = 100 and 259 for n = 140). The extensive use of pruning techniques can explain the good behavior of the algorithm. The large time spent per node is of course the drawback of such an approach.

Throughout our experiments, we discovered that the efficiency of the algorithm varies from one instance to another (which is not very surprising for an NP-complete problem). To characterize, from an experimental point of view, the instances that our algorithm found to hard to solve, we generated 25 instances of 60 jobs for each combination of the parameters $(p_{min}, p_{max}) \in \{(0,100), (25,75)\}$, $m_{max} \in \{25, 50, \ldots, 500\}$ and $load \in \{0.2, 0.3, 0.4, \ldots, 2.2\}$. 5 minutes have been allotted to each instance. Figure 4 reports the average CPU time required to solve the different group of instances (for the 2% of instances that could not be solved within the time limit, we decided to count 5 minutes when computing the average CPU time). The study of Figure 4 leads us to the following remarks:

- The tighter the processing time distribution is, the harder is the instance.
- The hardest instances seem to be those for which the *load* ratio is between 0.7 and 1.2 and when the margin parameter m_{max} varies in [275, 475] (for an average processing time of 50).
- When the *load* ratio becomes very high, instances are quite easy. An hypothesis is that the search tree becomes small (because very few jobs can be on-time and thus very few decisions have to be taken). Conversely, when the load ratio is very low, instances are easy (because few jobs are late on an optimal solution).

- When both *load* and m_{max} are low, the behavior of the algorithm is somewhat surprising. Further investigations have shown that for these instances the number of backtracks is kept very small but the time spent per node increases a lot. This is, we think, a side-effect of our current implementation: The decomposition rule is likely to be triggered very often for such instances. Hence, a large amount of (small and easy) sub-problems are solved one after another. This is a source of inefficiency because, in the current implementation, the data structures representing each sub-problem have to be initialized at each decomposition.

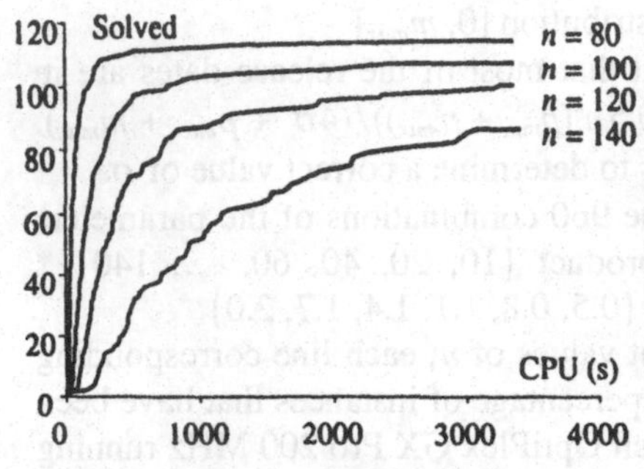

Figure 3. Number of instances solved within a time limit in seconds

n	%	Avg CPU	Max CPU	Late
10	100.0	0.0	0.1	0 / 6
20	100.0	0.2	0.7	0 / 13
40	100.0	3.1	27.5	0 / 23
60	100.0	23.2	184.5	0 / 33
80	96.7	117.3	2903.2	0 / 47
100	90.0	273.5	2395.3	0 / 55
120	84.2	538.2	3263.4	0 / 69
140	72.5	1037.3	3087.8	1 / 73

Table 1. Behavior of the algorithm for several sizes of instances

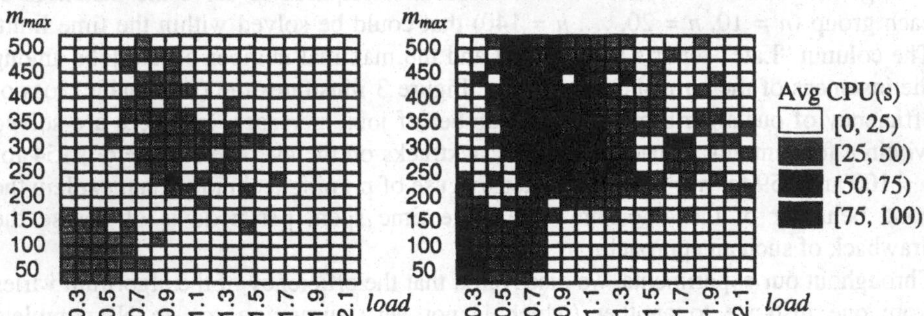

Figure 4. The behavior of the algorithm on 60-jobs instances with different characteristics. The left chart has been obtained on instances with $p_{min} = 0$ and $p_{max} = 100$ while the right one has been obtained on instances with $p_{min} = 25$ and $p_{max} = 75$.

We have proposed a set of techniques, including global constraint propagation, to solve a particular partial CSP. This is of course a first step and a lot of work remains to adapt and / or to develop global constraints in over-constrained frameworks. In particular, we think that a large part of the results presented in this paper can be extended to the cumulative case, *i.e.*, the case where jobs can execute in parallel. Studying the more general situations where all jobs do not have the same importance (*i.e.*, each job has a weight) or where some jobs have several due dates (with a different weight for each due date) are also exciting research directions.

Acknowledgments

The authors would like to thank Jacques Carlier, Eric Pinson, Emmanuel Néron, Stéphane Dauzère-Pérès and Marc Sevaux for many enlightening discussions on the topic of this paper.

References

A. Aggoun and N. Beldiceanu [1993], *Extending CHIP in Order to Solve Complex Scheduling and Placement Problems*, Mathematical and Computer Modeling 17:57-73.

D. Applegate and W. Cook [1991], *A Computational Study of the Job-Shop Scheduling Problem*, ORSA Journal on Computing 3(2):149-156.

Ph. Baptiste and C. Le Pape [1995], *A Theoretical and Experimental Comparison of Constraint Propagation Techniques for Disjunctive Scheduling*, Proc. 14th International Joint Conference on Artificial Intelligence.

Ph. Baptiste [1998], *An $O(n^4)$ Algorithm for Preemptive Scheduling of a Single Machine to Minimize the Number of Late Jobs*, Technical Report 98/98, Université de Technologie de Compiègne.

S. Bistarelli, U. Montanari and F. Rossi [1995], *Constraint Solving over Semirings*, Proc. 14th International Joint Conference on Artificial Intelligence.

P. Brucker [1995], *Scheduling algorithms*, Springer Lehrbuch.

J. Carlier [1982], *The One-Machine Sequencing Problem*, European Journal of Operational Research 11:42-47.

J. Carlier and E. Pinson [1990], *A Practical Use of Jackson's Preemptive Schedule for Solving the Job-Shop Problem*, Annals of Operations Research 26:269-287.

Y. Caseau and F. Laburthe [1995], *Disjunctive Scheduling with Task Intervals*, Technical Report, Ecole Normale Supérieure.

Y. Caseau and F. Laburthe [1996], *CLAIRE: A Parametric Tool to Generate C++ Code for Problem Solving*, Working Paper, Bouygues, Direction Scientifique.

S. Dauzère-Pérès [1995], *Minimizing Late Jobs in the General One Machine Scheduling Problem*, European Journal of Operational Research 81:134-142.

E. Freuder and R. Wallace [1992], *Partial Constraint Satisfaction*, Artificial Intelligence 58:21-70.

M. R. Garey and D. S. Johnson [1979], *Computers and Intractability. A Guide to the Theory of NP-Completeness*, W. H. Freeman and Company.

H. Kise, T. Ibaraki and H. Mine [1978], *A Solvable Case of the One-Machine Scheduling Problem with Ready and Due Times*, Operations Research 26(1):121-126.

E. L. Lawler [1990], *A Dynamic Programming Algorithm for Preemptive Scheduling of a Single Machine to Minimize the Number of Late Jobs*, Annals of Operations Research 26:125-133.

C. Le Pape and Ph. Baptiste [1997], *A Constraint Programming Library for Preemptive and Non-Preemptive Scheduling*, Proc. 3rd International Conference on the Practical Application of Constraint Technology.

J. M. Moore [1968], *An n job, one machine sequencing algorithm for minimizing the number of late jobs*, Management Science 15(1):102-109.

W. P. M. Nuijten [1994], *Time and Resource Constrained Scheduling: A Constraint Satisfaction Approach*, PhD Thesis, Eindhoven University of Technology.

L. Péridy [1996], *Le problème de job-shop : arbitrages et ajustements*, PhD Thesis, Université de Technologie de Compiègne, France (in French).

J-C. Régin and J-F. Puget [1997], *A Filtering Algorithm for Global Sequencing Constraints*, Proc. 3rd International Conference on Principles and Practice of Constraint Programming.

T. Schiex, H. Fargier and G. Verfaillie [1995], *Valued Constraint Satisfaction Problems: Hard and Easy Problems*, Proc. 14th International Joint Conference on Artificial Intelligence.

Using Graph Decomposition for Solving Continuous CSPs

Christian Bliek[1], Bertrand Neveu[2], and Gilles Trombettoni[1]

[1] Artificial Intelligence Laboratory, EPFL
CH-1015 Lausanne, Switzerland
{cbliek,trombe}@lia.di.epfl.ch
[2] CERMICS, équipe Contraintes
2004 route des lucioles, 06902 Sophia-Antipolis Cedex, B.P. 93, France
Bertrand.Neveu@sophia.inria.fr

Abstract. In practice, constraint satisfaction problems are often structured. By exploiting this structure, solving algorithms can make important gains in performance. In this paper, we focus on structured continuous CSPs defined by systems of equations. We use graph decomposition techniques to decompose the constraint graph into a directed acyclic graph of small blocks. We present new algorithms to solve decomposed problems which solve the blocks in partial order and perform intelligent backtracking when a block has no solution.

For under-constrained problems, the solution space can be explored by choosing some variables as input parameters. However, in this case, the decomposition is no longer unique and some choices lead to decompositions with smaller blocks than others. We present an algorithm for selecting the input parameters that lead to good decompositions.

First experimental results indicate that, even on small problems, significant speedups can be obtained using these algorithms.

1 Introduction

In the area of continuous CSPs, research has traditionally focused on techniques to enforce some form of local consistency. These techniques are used in combination with dichotomic search to find solutions. We use Numerica, a state of the art system for solving the specific type of CSPs considered in this paper [Hentenryck *et al.*, 1997].

In practice, constraint satisfaction problems are often structured. However, little has been done to exploit the structure of continuous CSPs to make gains in performance. In this paper, we focus on efficient solution strategies for solving structured CSPs. We will restrict our attention to CSPs which are defined by nonlinear equations and study the general case in which the system is not necessarily square. This paper brings together techniques to decompose constraint graphs with backtracking algorithms to solve the decomposed systems.

Although our approach is general, we have chosen to present 2D mechanical configuration examples. By doing so, we do not want to convey that our approach applies only to this type of problems. We mainly use these examples for didactical reasons; they are easy to understand and to illustrate.

2 The Dulmage and Mendelsohn Decomposition

In this paper, *a constraint graph* G is a bipartite graph (V, C, E) where V are the variables, C are the constraints and there is an arc between a constraint in C and each of its variables in V.

A *maximum matching* of a bipartite constraint graph includes a maximum number of arcs which share no vertex. A matching implicitly gives a direction to the corresponding constraint graph; a pair (v, c) corresponds to a directed arc from c to v and directed arcs from v to other matched constraints connected to v. The D&M decomposition is based on the following theorem.

Theorem 1 *(Dulmage and Mendelsohn, 1958) Any maximum-matching of a constraint graph G gives a canonical partition of the vertices in G into three disjoint subsets: the under-constrained part, the over-constrained part and the well-constrained part.*

Observe that one or two of the three parts may be empty in the general case.

Starting from any maximum matching of the graph, the over-constrained part is formed with all nodes reachable from any non matched constraint in C by a reverse path. The under-constrained part is formed with all nodes reachable from any non matched variable in V by a directed path. The well-constrained part is formed with the other nodes and yields a perfect matching of the corresponding subgraph. Figure 1 shows an example. Variables are represented by circles, constraints by rectangles; a pair in the matching is depicted by an ellipse. The well-constrained part can be further decomposed. The perfect matching of

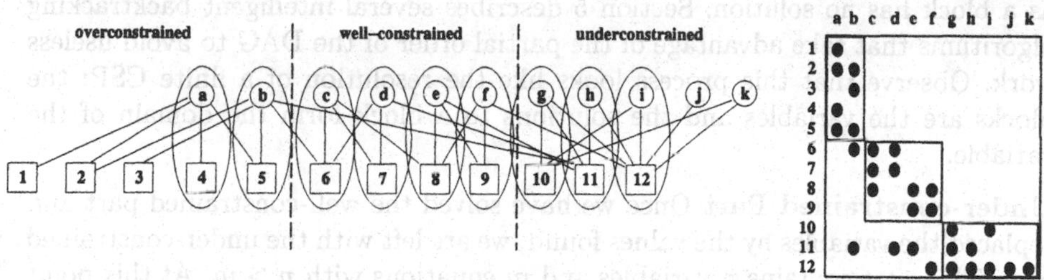

Fig. 1. The D&M decomposition of a constraint graph (left) and the equivalent matrix representation (right).

this part implicitly defines a directed graph. We then compute its strongly connected components, called *blocks*, to obtain a directed acyclic graph (DAG) of blocks.

It turns out that this decomposition, called the *fine* decomposition, is independent of the matching performed.

Theorem 2 *(König, 1916) Every perfect matching of a (square) bipartite graph leads to a unique decomposition into strongly connected components.*

Note that König's theorem does not apply in case of non perfect matching.

3 Overview

In this part, we give a general overview of the algorithms described in this paper and of how they work together. As input, we have a set of numeric equations which may be non-square. We make the general assumption that square $n \times n$ systems give a discrete set of solutions. This is in fact a basic assumption of Numerica [Hentenryck *et al.*, 1997], the tool we use to solve systems of equations. In a number of pathological cases, this assumption is not verified, then we can for example use probabilistic methods to diagnose the problem (see Section 7).

We first perform a D&M decomposition [Pothen and Chin-Fan, 1990] and handle the three parts, if present, in the order over-constrained, well-constrained and finally under-constrained part.

Over-constrained Part In this part, the number of equations m is greater than the number n of variables. If the corresponding equations are independent, the system has no solution. We can deal with this situation in a number of ways. First, through a backtrack-free selection process, we could let the user remove $m - n$ equations to make the part well-constrained[1]. Alternatively, the $m - n$ extra constraints might be kept as *soft* constraints. They are simply verified after the solution process. If the $m - n$ equations are redundant, we get solutions, otherwise there is no solution.

Well-constrained Part As explained in Section 2, for this part, we can perform a fine decomposition. The result is a DAG of blocks. Each block is solved by Numerica and, in the subsequent blocks, the implied variables are replaced by the values found. To ensure completeness, backtracking is performed as soon as a block has no solution. Section 5 describes several intelligent backtracking algorithms that take advantage of the partial order of the DAG to avoid useless work. Observe that this process looks like the resolution of a finite CSP: the blocks are the variables and the solutions to a block form the domain of the variable.

Under-constrained Part Once we have solved the well-constrained part and replaced the variables by the values found, we are left with the under-constrained part. This part contains n variables and m equations with $n > m$. At this point $r = n - m$ ***driving input variables*** (***divs***) must be given a value to obtain a $m \times m$ problem. There are a number of issues related to the selection of the r ***divs*** in the under-constrained part.

First, some sets of r input variables may lead to "badly-constrained" systems, that is, systems for which there exists no perfect matching. This means that we cannot arbitrarily choose r of the n variables as ***divs***. Section 6.1 presents a new algorithm which allows the selection of the r ***divs*** one by one and forbids certain future choices after each selection. This approach might be used for example in physical simulation [Serrano, 1987], where the user explicitly changes different parameters in order to understand the behavior of a system.

[1] This process is the dual of the one for removing variables in the under-constrained part as described in Section 6.1.

Second, König's theorem does not hold for the under-constrained part. That is, the DAG of blocks obtained is not unique and depends on the matching. In particular, certain choices of *divs* lead to decompositions with smaller blocks than others and are usually easier to solve. Section 6 presents new algorithms to find decompositions with small blocks. Interactive sketching applications (see [Bliek *et al.*, 1998]) should favor this type of decompositions.

4 Examples

In this section, we present 2 examples that will be used throughout this paper.

Didactic Example (Figure 2) Various points (white circles) are connected with

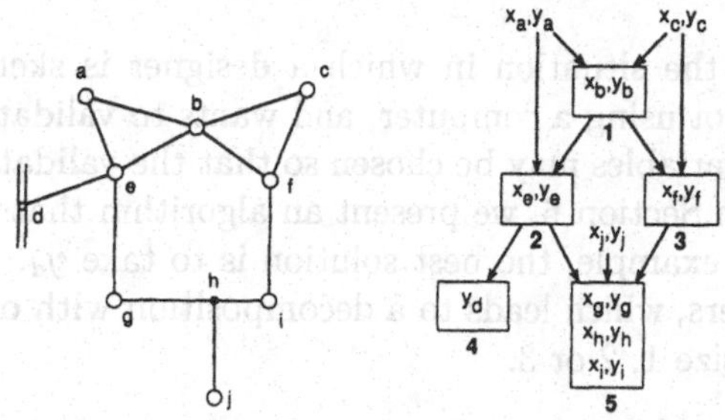

Fig. 2. Didactic problem and a corresponding DAG of blocks.

rigid rods (lines). Rods only impose a distance constraint between two points. Point h (black circle) differs from the others in that it is attached to the rod $\langle g, i\rangle$. Finally, point d is constrained to slide on the specified line. The problem is to find a feasible configuration of the points so that all constraints are satisfied.

Mini-robot (Figure 3) The triangle a–b–c represents the base and is fixed. Since the robot is symmetrical, let us describe the left half. Point d is the left shoulder. The rod $\langle a, d\rangle$ has a variable length r_s, and is used to rotate the rod $\langle c, d\rangle$. On this rod we have an arm mechanism whose length is variable and depends on the parameter r_a. The gray point e is constrained to slide on the rod $\langle c, d\rangle$. The black point f is attached to both the rod $\langle e, g\rangle$ and $\langle d, h\rangle$, and hereby forces these rods to act like a scissor. The position of the end point i of the arm can now be positioned by controlling r_a and r_s.

The decomposition shown in the right side of Figure 3 corresponds to the above description of the robot. That is, r_a, r'_a, r_s and r'_s are the driving inputs that control the endpoints. Suppose however that we want the robot to pick up an object. In this case the end points i and i' should go to a specific location. The question now is: what values should r_a, r'_a, r_s, r'_s take to get the two endpoints at the desired spot? The decomposition of this inverse problem is shown in the middle of Figure 3.

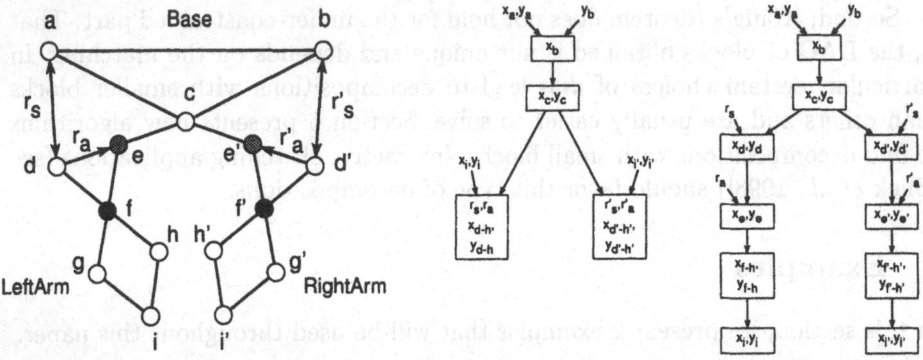

Fig. 3. Minirobot (left), DAG of inverse problem (middle) and driving problem (right).

Finally, consider the situation in which a designer is sketching the points and rods for this robot using a computer, and wants to validate his drawing. In this case, the input variables may be chosen so that the validation problem is as simple as possible. In Section 6, we present an algorithm that is designed to do exactly that. In this example, the best solution is to take y_d, y_b, x_i, x'_i, y'_e, x'_d, y'_d as input parameters, which leads to a decomposition with one block of size 5 and other blocks of size 1, 2 or 3.

5 Solving Well-Constrained Systems

5.1 Introduction

In case the D&M decomposition consists only of a well constrained part, we can perform a fine decomposition. By doing so we avoid to send the system as a whole to the solver. Indeed, we will only need to solve smaller systems which correspond to the blocks in the DAG. To see this, consider the decomposition shown in Figure 2 on the right. Respecting the order of the DAG, we first obtain a solution for block 1. We can now substitute the values for the corresponding variables appearing in the equations of block 2 and obtain a solution from the solver. Then we process block 3 in a similar fashion, followed by block 4 and 5.

When a block has no solution, one has to backtrack. A chronological backtracker goes back to the previous block. It tries a different solution for that block and restarts to solve the subsequent blocks. However, this approach is inefficient. Indeed, in the example above, suppose block 5 had no solution. Chronological backtracking would go back to block 4, find a different solution for it, and solve block 5 again. Clearly, the same failure will be encountered again in block 5.

A better strategy is to reconsider only those blocks which might have caused the problem. We could follow the approach used by Conflict Based Backjumping (CBJ) [Prosser, 1993]. When no solution is found for block 5, one would go back directly to block 3. However, when jumping back, CBJ erases all intermediate search information. Here, the solution of block 4 would be erased when jumping back to block 3. This is unfortunate; the solution of block 4 is still valid and the solver may have spent a considerable amount of time finding it.

This problem can be avoided by holding on to the intermediate search information. This approach is taken in dynamic backtracking (DB) [Ginsberg, 1993]. As CBJ, DB jumps back to the cause of the problem. However, when doing so, it does not erase intermediate nogoods. Instead, it moves the problem variable to the set of uninstantiated variables and removes only nogoods based on its assignment. By doing so, DB effectively reorders variables. Unfortunately, this reordering is incompatible with the partial order imposed by the DAG. We therefore need to resort to algorithms that keep intermediate search information but are also flexible enough to respect the partial order imposed by the decomposition. General Partial Order Backtracking (GPB) [Bliek, 1998] satisfies these requirements. Below we present a specific instance of GPB that can be used to solve decomposed problems.

5.2 Solving Partially Ordered Problems with GPB

We first briefly describe the GPB algorithm for solving discrete CSPs. At all times GPB maintains a complete set of assignments X which are incrementally modified until all constraints are satisfied. The search process is driven by the addition of new nogoods. A *nogood* γ is a subset of assignments of values to variables which are incompatible. X is modified incrementally so as to remain compatible with the current set of nogoods. When a new nogood is added, the value of one of its variables, say y, will be changed. By choosing y, γ becomes an ordered nogood, denoted by $\vec{\gamma}$. We call y the *conclusion* variable, denoted by $c(\vec{\gamma})$, and the remaining variables *antecedent* variables $a(\vec{\gamma})$. An ordered nogood $\vec{\gamma}$ defines an ordering relation $x < c(\vec{\gamma})$ for each antecedent $x \in a(\vec{\gamma})$.

Nogoods are generated when the current assignments violate a constraint. In this case the nogood is the constraint violation. Nogoods are also generated when for a domain of a given variable y, all values are ruled out by nogoods. In this case a new nogood $\beta(y)$ is inferred that contains the assignments of all the antecedent variables $a(\vec{\gamma}_i)$ appearing in every nogood $\vec{\gamma}_i$ with $y = c(\vec{\gamma}_i)$. In addition to the conclusion variables of a nogood, one may also modify the assignment of other variables in X, as long as the new values are acceptable. A value v is *acceptable* for the variable x if $x = v$ is compatible with the antecedents of any of the current nogoods and if v is in the live domain of x. The *live domain* of a variable is the set of values of its domain that is not ruled out by a conclusion of a nogood. When a new nogood with conclusion y is added, all nogoods $\vec{\gamma}_i$ for which $y \in a(\vec{\gamma}_i)$ are discarded. By doing so, an assignment is ruled out by at most one nogood. The space complexity of GPB is therefore polynomial. The problem has no solution when the empty nogood is inferred.

We now present an instance of GPB, called GPB_I. We will see that this algorithm can easily be adapted to solve decomposed continuous CSPs. Instead of modifying a complete set of assignments, GPB_I incrementally extends a consistent partial set of assignments. We therefore have a set of instantiated variables I and a set of uninstantiated variables U. To ensure termination, it is required that the selection of the conclusion of a nogood respects a partial order. In GPB_I we use an ordering scheme $<_I$ defined as follows. The variables in I respect the total order defined by the instantiation sequence and any variable in I precedes any variable in U. Abusing notation, we define the antecedents of a variable y as $a(y) = \{x \mid x < y\}$. The descendants of y are defined by $D(y) = \{x \mid y <_t x\}$, where $<_t$ is the transitive closure of $<$. With these definitions, we modify GPB to obtain GPB_I.

```
algorithm GPB_I
  Until U is empty or the empty nogood is inferred do
    Select a variable x ∈ U for which a(x) ⊆ I and
    assign an acceptable value v to x.
    if x = v violates some constraint with variables in I then
      Generate a nogood γ corresponding to the constraint violation and
      Backtrack(γ),
    else
      move x from U to I.
    end
  end
end.
procedure Backtrack (γ)
  Select y as conclusion of γ so that y follows a(γ⃗) in the ordering scheme and
  store γ⃗.
  Discard all nogoods γ⃗_i for which y ∈ a(γ⃗_i) and
  move y and the variables D(y) in I to U.
  if the live domain of y is empty then
    Backtrack(β(y)).
  end
end.
```

Algorithm 1: GPB_I

GPB_I is an instance of GPB and therefore terminates. It is also systematic since it satisfies an additional restriction on the assignments that may be changed. We refer the reader to [Bliek *et al.*, 1998] for a detailed discussion.

As described above, GPB_I halts as soon as it finds a solution. To find all solutions to a given CSP, the algorithm can be modified as follows. When a solution is found, it is reported and a new nogood is generated that rules out exactly this set of assignments. We then backtrack from this nogood and restart the search loop to find the next solution.

GPB_I solves discrete CSPs. We now adapt it to solve continuous problems that are decomposed into a DAG of blocks. Here the blocks take over the role of the variables. The discrete domain[2] of possible values for a block x is the set

[2] As stated earlier, we assume that we have a discrete set of solutions for each block.

of solutions, denoted by $\sigma(x)$, of the corresponding subproblem. Recall that, for a given block x, the solutions of the parent blocks, denoted by $p(x)$, are first substituted into the equations of block x. The resulting system is then solved over the continuous domains of the variables of the block. By solving the system, all values in the continuous domains are eliminated, except for $\sigma(x)$. One can view this as the addition of a nogood, denoted by $P(x)$, that has the given block x as conclusion and $p(x)$ as antecedent variables.

We can now modify GPB$_I$ to solve decomposed problems. The main difference is that the domain $\sigma(x)$ of a block x is not known *a priori* and has to be computed based on the values of $p(x)$. We therefore have to make sure that $\sigma(x)$ is recomputed every time any of the values of $p(x)$ changes. The resulting algorithm is called GPB$_\Delta$. The backtrack procedure remains the same. However,

```
algorithm GPB∆
  Until U is empty or the empty nogood is inferred do
    select a block x ∈ U for which a(x) ∪ p(x) ⊆ I
    if σ(x) is outdated with respect to p(x) then
      recompute σ(x) using the new values for p(x) and backtrack(P(x)),
    else
      assign an acceptable value v to x and move x from U to I.
    end
  end
end.
```

Algorithm 2: GPB$_\Delta$

in a practical implementation, care has to be taken to represent and handle the nogoods of the type $P(x)$.

In Figure 4, we illustrate GPB$_\Delta$ on the example of Figure 2. Suppose we solve block 1 and select first the solution where b is above a and c. Then we proceed to solve block 2 and select the solution where e is above a and b. We make a similar choice for f whose solutions are computed in block 3. Now, in block 4, we select one of the two possible locations for d. Finally, we reach block 5 to find out that there is no solution (dashed). This situation is shown on the left in Figure 4. At this point, we add a nogood $P(5)$ which is based on the solutions of blocks 2 and 3 and rules out all possible values for block 5. We find that the domain of 5 is empty and infer a nogood $\beta(5)$ which states that the solutions of block 2 and 3 are incompatible. Since block 3 was instantiated after block 2 we select block 3 as conclusion of this nogood. We now select the other solution for this block where point f is below b and c. Once again we find that block 5 has no solution (second picture in Figure 4) and backtrack to block 3. However, this time, both possible solutions of block 3 are ruled out by nogoods, so we continue backtracking. Since the two nogoods have block 2 as antecedent and $P(3)$ has block 1 as antecedent, we generate a new nogood stating that the solutions of

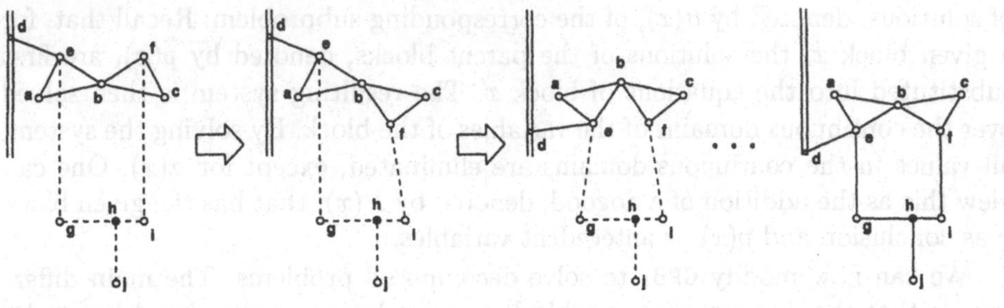

Fig. 4. Example problem.

block 1 and 2 are incompatible. As shown in the third picture in Figure 4, we now use the other solution for block 2. This search process continues until we reach the configuration, depicted on the right in Figure 4, that satisfies all constraints.

Observe that GPB$_\Delta$, did not erase the solutions of block 4 when it backtracked to block 3. However, they would have been erased by CBJ, which would later need to recompute them.

5.3 Examples

We found that, as compared to solving the system as a whole, the use of GPB$_\Delta$ on decomposed systems is very effective. Let us illustrate this point with some examples. As it is usually done when solving CSPs defined by systems of equations, we report the running times to find all solutions. All the tests were performed on a Sun SparcStation 5 with Ilog Numerica 1.0.

On the small didactic example of Figure 2, GPB$_\Delta$ needs only 2.9 seconds, while without decomposition Numerica needs 4.8 seconds. The speedups are more important when the examples are somewhat more complicated. Consider the mini-robot positioning problem shown in Figure 3. Without decomposing the problem, it takes Numerica 2153 seconds to solve the problem. Using the decomposition shown in the middle in Figure 3, with GPB$_\Delta$ this running time is reduced to 33.3 seconds.

In some cases very small blocks can be found. In this case, the backtrack search over the discrete sets of solutions is dominant. Figure 5 shows an example of such a situation. As before, arcs represent distance constraints and we have fixed the two coordinates, x_a and y_a, of point a as well as one coordinate, x_b, of point b. In addition to what is shown in the figure, there are two variables that measure the height of each of the legs defined as $r = (y_i + y_h)/2$ and $r' = (y_{i'} + y_{h'})/2$. We limited the possible range on these two variables to stay within the interval ρ shown in Figure 5. By doing so, there is only one solution which is the one shown in the figure. Without decomposition, it takes Numerica 2091 seconds to solve this problem. With the decomposition shown on the right in Figure 5, GPB$_\Delta$ solves the problem in 29 seconds.

6 Handling Structurally Under-constrained Problems

As discussed in Section 3, in this case, we need to find r *divs* such that the remaining constraint graph has a perfect matching. Two different approaches for

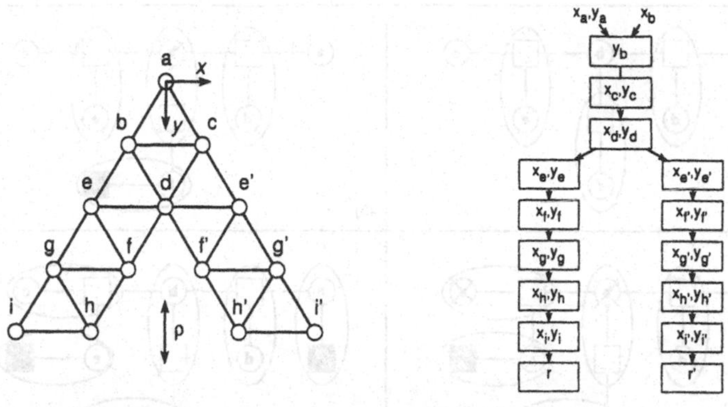

Fig. 5. A configuration of triangles corresponding to a pyramid tower.

doing so are presented below. Once the *divs* are selected, the problem becomes well-constrained and can be solved by GPB_{Δ}.

6.1 Backtrack-Free Driving Inputs' Selection

The algorithm shown below is based on the D&M properties. It allows to choose the *divs* one by one in a backtrack-free manner. The time complexity of the algo-

```
algorithm Free-divs-selection (a constraint graph; its D&M decomposition)
  while r divs have not been chosen do
    choose as div any variable v in the under-constrained part
    if v is matched in the current matching then
      – invert in the current matching an alternating path from v to an un-
        matched variable
      – apply a D&M decomposition on the new matching (which transfers
        some nodes from the under-constrained to the well-constrained part)
    end
  end
end.
```

Algorithm 3: The backtrack-free *div* selection

rithm is $O(r \times (n+m))$ for a constraint graph with n variables and m constraints. Indeed, one path inversion and one "D&M part retrieval" is necessary for each of the r *div* selections. Figure 6 illustrates this algorithm. The correctness of the backtrack-free *div* selection follows directly from the D&M properties. The proof can be found in the extended version of this paper [Bliek *et al.*, 1998].

6.2 Finding Small Blocks: $OpenPlan_{sb}$

We present below an algorithm called $OpenPlan_{sb}$[3] which finds decompositions with well-constrained square blocks whose largest block is of minimum size.

[3] *sb* stands for *small blocks.*

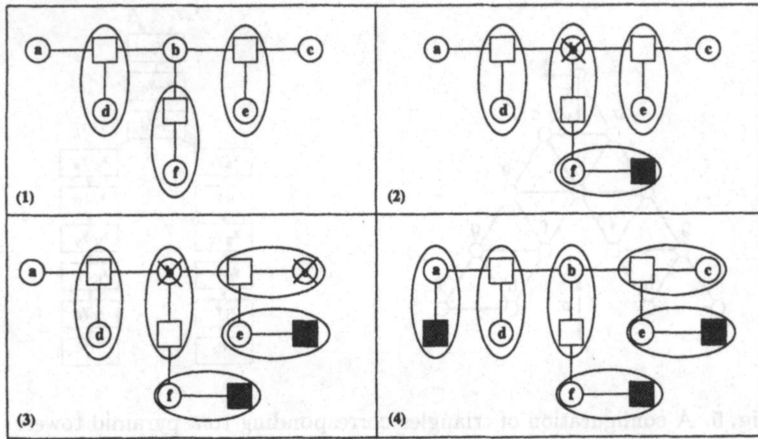

Fig. 6. Backtrack-free *div* selection. (1) Initial maximum matching. 3 *divs* are to be selected. (2) Selection of variable *f* as *div*: variable *b* is forbidden for further selection. (3) The selection of *e* forbids *c*. (4) The selection of *a* makes the problem well-constrained.

```
algorithm OpenPlan_sb (G: a constraint graph): a DAG of blocks
  let D be an empty DAG of blocks
  while constraints remain in the constraint graph do
     select-free-block_sb: select a free square block b of smallest size for which there
     exists a perfect matching
     add b in D (along with the corresponding directed arcs)
     remove b from G
  end
  return D
end.
```

Algorithm 4: OpenPlan$_{sb}$

OpenPlan$_{sb}$ is a specialized version of an algorithm called OpenPlan: the procedure *select-free-block* of OpenPlan can select any free block whereas *select-free-block$_{sb}$* imposes restrictions. OpenPlan is based on the PDOF algorithm used for maintaining constraints in interactive applications [Vander Zanden, 1996]. It builds a DAG of blocks in reverse order from the leaves to the roots. A *free* block has variables which are linked only to constraints within the block. Iteratively selecting and removing blocks which are free ensures that a DAG of blocks is built, that is, that no directed cycle can appear between blocks [Trombettoni, 1997].

We now detail how OpenPlan$_{sb}$ finds the best decomposition of the constraint graph of the didactic problem. The process is illustrated on the right side of Figure 7. First, the block $[c_7,y_d]$, a 1×1 free block, is selected and removed: x_d becomes a *div*. Now there is no more 1×1 free block available so that a 2×2 free block, for example $[c_1,c_3,x_a,y_a]$, is selected and removed. Then, the free block $[c_4,c_5,x_c,y_c]$ is selected and removed. This frees the block $[c_6,c_9,x_f,y_f]$ which is selected and removed. The block $[c_2,x_b]$ is now free; y_b becomes a *div*. In the

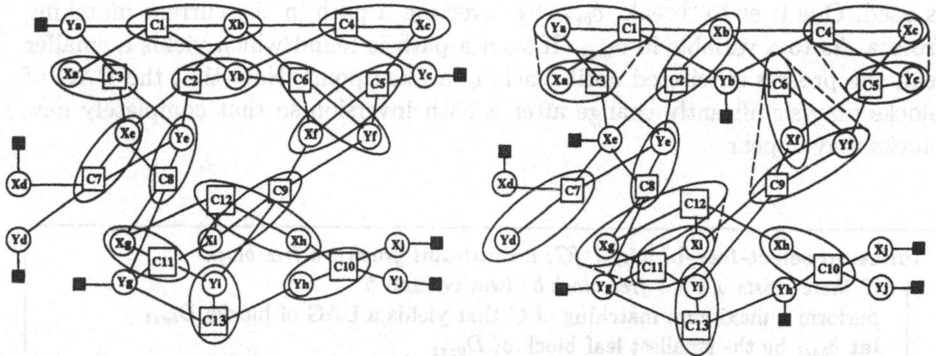

Fig. 7. A decomposition of the didactic problem with one 13×13 block (left) and a decomposition with four 2×2 blocks (a, b, f, (x_g, x_i)) and several 1×1 blocks (right).

same way, OpenPlan$_{sb}$ finally selects the blocks $[c_8,y_e]$, $[c_{11},c_{12},x_g,x_i]$, $[c_{13},y_i]$ and $[c_{10},x_h]$.

Proposition 1 *OpenPlan$_{sb}$ finds a decomposition whose largest block has a minimum size.*

The proof can be found in the extended paper [Bliek *et al.*, 1998].

Note that, as opposed to OpenPlan$_{sb}$, the maximum-matching algorithm finds decompositions with blocks of arbitrary size: both decompositions of Figure 7 could be indifferently obtained by maximum-matching whereas OpenPlan$_{sb}$ finds the one in the right.

Selecting a 1×1 free block is the only operation involved in the classical PDOF. This amounts to searching variables linked to only one constraint. However, if there is no 1×1 free block, *finding a well-constrained free block of minimum size is suspected to be NP-hard*, so that OpenPlan$_{sb}$ is exponential. Indeed, a naive algorithm which searches for a $k \times k$ valid block is $O(n^k)$, where n is the number of variables.

Nevertheless, this algorithm can sometimes be used for problems which may be numerically hard to solve. In this case, the overhead for obtaining the best decomposition can be neglected over the gain in solving small blocks. Our first experimental results presented in Section 6.4 seem to confirm this.

6.3 Finding Small Blocks: OpenPlan$_{hm}$

When the constraint graphs are large, we have to resort to heuristic methods to find good decompositions. To do so, another instance of OpenPlan, called OpenPlan$_{hm}$, is proposed for which the procedure select-free-block$_{hm}$ is a hill-climbing heuristic. If no 1×1 block has been found, a maximum matching of the constraint graph is performed. We consider first the smallest leaf b_{best} of this matching to be selected by *select-free-block$_{hm}$*. However, b_{best} is not the smallest possible free block, since other matchings could yield smaller leaves. Therefore, *select-free-block$_{hm}$* changes the matching so that a smaller leaf could appear. Instead of performing a full search over all matchings, a hill-climbing heuristic is used. One tries to "break" b_{best} by inverting a path in the current matching from a *div* to a variable in b_{best}. If such a path is found which yields a smaller leaf, the process is reitered until reaching a fixed point. Note that the DAG of blocks may significantly change after a path inversion so that completely new blocks may appear.

```
function select-free-block_hm (G: a constraint graph): a free block
  if there exists a 1 × 1 free block b then return b
  perform a maximum matching of G that yields a DAG of blocks D_best
  let b_best be the smallest leaf block of D_best
  while D_best is changing do
    let cdivs be the set of divs in D_best such that an alternating path exists from
    a div in cdivs to a variable in b_best
    D ← D_best; b ← b_best
    for every div d in cdivs and every variable v in b_best do
      invert an alternating path from d to v that yields a DAG of blocks D'
      if D' has a smaller leaf block b' than b then D ← D'; b ← b'
    end
    D_best ← D; b_best ← b
  end
  return b_best
end.
```

Algorithm 5: Heuristic method to select a small well-constrained free block

In Figure 7, we show how OpenPlan_{hm} obtains the best decomposition (right) starting from the matching corresponding to the worst one (left). *select-free-block$_{hm}$* first inverts the path from y_d to x_e, which yields the first free (1×1) block $[c_7, y_d]$. Then it selects the block $[c_1, c_3, x_a, y_a]$ by inverting the path from y_a to x_b. Now it can proceed until the best decomposition is obtained.

6.4 First Experimental Results

On the didactic problem, the *divs* on the left in Figure 7 lead to one unique block solved by Numerica in 10 s. With the *divs* in Figure 7 (right), the problem is solved by GPB_Δ in 3.3 s.

We also performed tests on a small distance problem in 3 D made of two tetrahedra and some additional rods shown in Figure 8.

The worst decomposition of this problem has two blocks of size 7. The best decomposition, obtained by both OpenPlan_{sb} and OpenPlan_{hm}, includes blocks of size 2 or 3 only. When the driving inputs correspond to the bad decomposition, Numerica takes 1284.8 s to solve the whole system. Solving the same problem with GPB_Δ takes 125.4 s. Now when the driving inputs correspond to the good decomposition, Numerica on the whole system takes 200 s whereas only 22.7 s are necessary to solve the same problem using GPB_Δ.

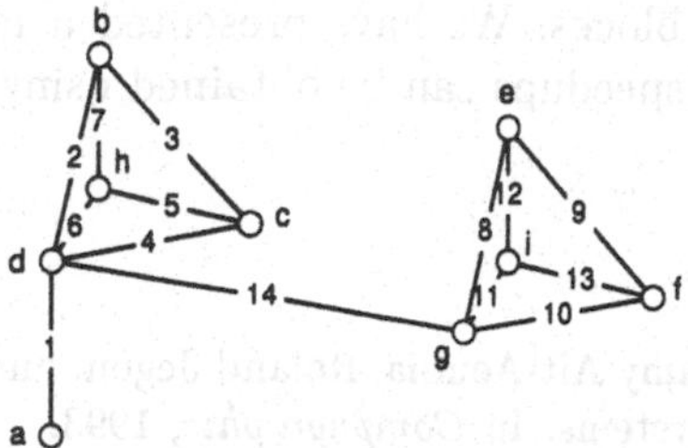

Fig. 8. A 3D linkage with two tetrahedra.

7 Related Work

To our knowledge, no existing system which performs graph decomposition combines complete numerical solvers with backtracking. The system presented in [Serrano, 1987] uses a maximum-matching algorithm to decompose general design problems. However, completeness is not achieved; blocks are solved using a traditional Newton-Raphson method and no backtracking is performed. Furthermore, this work is not based on the D&M decomposition. In particular, the driving inputs cannot be selected in a backtrack-free fashion.

In [Ait-Aoudia *et al.*, 1993], the D&M technique is used to study geometric constraints. However, no attention is paid to the solution aspects.

The D&M decomposition does not take into account the values of the coefficients of the equations. However, some problems, whose D&M decomposition is structurally well constrained, are in fact made of dependent equations. One way to detect redundancy in nonlinear systems of equations is to calculate the Jacobian at various randomly selected points [Lamure and Michelucci, 1997]. This information could then be used to properly decompose this type of systems.

In the case of mechanical configuration, there exist a number of techniques to discover subsystems that are rigid [Fudos and Hoffmann, 1997]. By replacing these rigid subsystems by smaller ones, gains in performance can be made. This technique is complementary to ours and could be used to further improve the performance of our algorithms on mechanical configuration problems.

8 Conclusion

In this paper, we have presented techniques to solve structured continuous CSPs. Our approach is based on decomposition techniques by Dulmage & Mendelsohn and König, that decompose structured problems into a directed acyclic graph of blocks. The contribution of this paper is twofold. First, we propose new algorithms for solving structurally well-constrained problems. They combine the use of existing solvers, for solving the blocks, with intelligent backtracking techniques that use the partial order of the DAG to avoid useless work. Second, we present new algorithms to handle under-constrained problems. These algorithms allow the selection of driving input variables, whose values are assumed to be set externally. Input variables can either be selected through an interactive backtrack-free selection or can be selected automatically using a new algorithm to obtain decompositions with small blocks. We have presented a number of examples to illustrate that significant speedups can be obtained using these algorithms.

References

[Ait-Aoudia *et al.*, 1993] Samy Ait-Aoudia, Roland Jegou, and Dominique Michelucci. Reduction of constraint systems. In *Compugraphic*, 1993.

[Bliek *et al.*, 1998] Christian Bliek, Bertrand Neveu, and Gilles Trombettoni. Using graph decomposition for solving continuous csps. Technical Report 98-287, E.P.F.L., Lausanne, Switzerland, 1998.

[Bliek, 1998] Christian Bliek. Generalizing dynamic and partial order backtracking. In *AAAI 98: Fifteenth National Conference on Artificial Intelligence*, pages 319–325, Madison, Wisconsin, July 1998.

[Fudos and Hoffmann, 1997] Ioannis Fudos and Christoph Hoffmann. A graph-constructive approach to solving systems of geometric constraints. *ACM Transactions on Graphics*, 16(2):179–216, 1997.

[Ginsberg, 1993] M.L. Ginsberg. Dynamic backtracking. *Journal of Artificial Intelligence Research*, 1:25–46, August 1993.

[Hentenryck *et al.*, 1997] Pascal Van Hentenryck, Laurent Michel, and Yves Deville. *Numerica : A Modeling Language for Global Optimization*. MIT Press, 1997.

[Lamure and Michelucci, 1997] Hervé Lamure and Dominique Michelucci. Qualitative study of geometric constraints. In Beat Brüderlin and Dieter Roller, editors, *Workshop on Geometric Constraint Solving and Applications*, pages 134–145, Technical University of Ilmenau, Germany, 1997.

[Pothen and Chin-Fan, 1990] Alex Pothen and Jun Chin-Fan. Computing the block triangular form of a sparse matrix. *ACM Transactions on Mathematical Software*, 16(4):303–324, 1990.

[Prosser, 1993] P. Prosser. Hybrid algorithms for the constraint satisfaction problem. *Computational Intelligence*, 9(3):268–299, August 1993.

[Serrano, 1987] D. Serrano. *Constraint Management in Conceptual Design*. PhD thesis, Massachusetts Institute of Technology, Cambridge, Massachusetts, October 1987.

[Trombettoni, 1997] Gilles Trombettoni. *Solution Maintenance of Constraint Systems Based on Local Propagation*. PhD thesis, University of Nice-Sophia Antipolis, 1997. In french.

[Vander Zanden, 1996] Bradley Vander Zanden. An incremental algorithm for satisfying hierarchies of multi-way, dataflow constraints. *ACM Transactions on Programming Languages and Systems*, 18(1):30–72, January 1996.

Anytime Lower Bounds for Constraint Violation Minimization Problems

Bertrand Cabon[1], Simon de Givry[2], and Gérard Verfaillie[3]

[1] MATRA MARCONI SPACE, 31 av. des Cosmonautes, 31402 Toulouse Cedex 4, France, Bertrand.Cabon@tls.mms.fr
[2] THOMSON LCR, Domaine de Corbeville, 91404 Orsay Cedex, France, degivry@thomson-lcr.fr
[3] ONERA-CERT, 2 avenue Edouard Belin, BP 4025, 31055 Toulouse Cedex 4, France, Gerard.Verfaillie@cert.fr

Abstract. *Constraint Violation Minimization Problems* arise when dealing with over-constrained *CSPs*. Unfortunately, experiments and practice show that they quickly become too large and too difficult to be optimally solved. In this context, multiple methods (limited tree search, heuristic or stochastic local search) are available to produce non-optimal, but *good* quality solutions, and thus to provide the user with anytime upper bounds of the problem optimum. On the other hand, few methods are available to produce anytime lower bounds of this optimum. In this paper, we explore some ways of producing such bounds. All of them are algorithmic variants of a *Branch and Bound* search. More specifically, we show that a new algorithm, resulting from a combination of the *Russian Doll Search* and *Iterative Deepening* algorithms, clearly outperforms five known algorithms and allows high lower bounds to be rapidly produced.

1 Constraint Violation Minimization Problems

In many decision tasks (planning, scheduling, resource allocation, design, diagnosis), the objective is to find a solution which satisfies a set of hard (or imperative) constraints, generally expressing physical limitations, and which, at the same time, satisfies as well as possible a set of soft (or relaxable) constraints, expressing costs, utilities, preferences, probabilities.

Such problems can be referred to as *Constraint Violation Minimization Problems*. *Max-CSPs* [6], *Weighted CSPs*, *Possibilistic CSPs* [15], *Fuzzy CSPs* [14, 4], and *Probabilistic CSPs*[14, 5] are some of the frameworks which have been defined to represent them. *Valued* and *Semiring CSPs* [16, 2, 1] are two more general frameworks, which include all of the above frameworks.

Although all of our work has been carried out in the general *Valued CSP* framework, for the sake of simplicity, we limit our presentation to *Weighted CSPs*. These problems can be defined as classical *CSPs*, with a weight associated with each constraint. The weight of a complete variable assignment is defined as the sum of the weights of the violated constraints, and the objective is to find a complete assignment whose weight is minimum. In *Max-CSPs*, all the constraints have the same weight, equal to 1, and the weight of a complete variable assignment is simply the number of violated constraints.

Remember that all of the algorithms which are presented in this paper can be easily extended to the *Valued CSP* framework, to take into account soft and hard constraints and to consider other violation aggregation functions.

2 Why produce anytime lower bounds?

It is known that the *Weighted CSP* and *Max-CSP* problems, which generalize the *Max-SAT* problem, are *NP-hard*. In addition, experiments, which have been carried out for example on randomly generated *Max-CSPs* [18], show that these problems are far more difficult to solve that the corresponding *CSPs*. Even small instances, involving only some tens of variables with ten values per variable, cannot be optimally solved in a reasonable time. The situation is naturally worse when one wants to solve instances which result from translating real-world problems and involve hundreds or thousands of variables.

In practice, when someone wants to solve such a problem, he uses any incomplete method (limited tree search, heuristic or stochastic local search) which is able to provide him with solutions of increasing quality, and thus with decreasing upper bounds of the problem optimum.

But some questions arise: What is the quality of the best solution found thus far? How far is its weight from the optimal weight? What gain can be expected from using more time or more resources to explore other solutions?

Producing lower bounds of the problem optimum can help to answer these questions. For example, if the lower bound equals the upper bound, optimality is proven and the search can stop. More generally, if the distance between the upper and lower bounds is small enough, the user or the system can decide to stop the search and to use time and ressources for other tasks. Conversely, if this distance remains large, he/it can decide to invest more time and ressources in finding better solutions or producing higher lower bounds.

In this paper we explore some ways of producing anytime increasing problem lower bounds, concurrently with the usual production of anytime decreasing problem upper bounds, in order to obtain a tighter and tighter bounding of the problem optimum.

Whereas any incomplete method can be used for producing upper bounds, producing lower bounds generally requires complete methods. This statement is consistent with the results of the *Complexity Theory* [12]: since producing an upper bound is an *NP* problem, a polynomial length certificate therefore exists; since producing a lower bound is a *Co-NP* problem, such a certificate may not exist (if $P \neq NP$).

After a quick overview of possible approaches for producing such lower bounds in the context of *Weighted CSPs* (see 3), we limit this paper to an exploration and a comparison of algorithmic variants of a *Branch and Bound* search, some of them well-known, others more recent (see 4). The main result is that a new algorithm, resulting from a combination of the *Russian Doll Search* [19] and *Iterative Deepening* [8] algorithms, clearly outperforms all the others and allows high lower bounds to be rapidly produced (see 5).

3 How produce anytime lower bounds?

3.1 Problem simplification

A first method to obtain a problem lower bound consists in solving completely a simplified problem: the optimum of the simplified problem, either is a lower bound of the original problem, or allows such a bound to be computed. Such a simplification is currently obtained by removing some constraints or by removing some forbidden tuples in some constraints. In [3], it is obtained by modifying the violation aggregation function to be minimized.

3.2 Objective simplification

Another method to obtain a problem lower bound consists in aiming at a simpler objective, like *Local Consistency*. For example, *Directed Arc Consistency* preprocessing [20] produces a problem lower bound. The sum of the weights of the constraints which must be relaxed, in order to obtain a classical *CSP*, whose *Arc Consistency* closure is non empty or, more generally, a classical *CSP* which satisfies any *Local Consistency* property, is also a problem lower bound[1].

3.3 Search simplification

A last method consists in performing a limited tree search, depending on the available time and ressources, and in exploiting the subproblem lower bounds, which are computed at each node of the tree, in order to produce a problem lower bound. This is the way we explore in this paper.

4 Using variants of a Branch and Bound search

We explored and compared six variants of a *Branch and Bound* search, each of them able to produce anytime problem lower bounds:

- *Recursive Best First* (*rbf*);
- *Iterative Deepening* (*id*);
- *Iterative Objective Relaxing* (*ior*);
- *Iterative Approximating* (*ia*);
- *Russian Doll Search* (*rds*);
- *Iterative Deepening + Russian Doll Search* (*idrds*).

For each algorithm, we give a well-known reference, a short informal description and the corresponding pseudo-code. Though these algorithms have been developped in various contexts and presented using various styles, we tried to present all the pseudo-codes in a uniform way in the *Weighted CSP* context.

[1] It is due to the fact that *Consistency* implies *Local Consistency*.

In each pseudo-code, both global variables *ub* and *lb* record the anytime problem upper and lower bounds. *ub* and *lb* are respectively initialized to $+\infty$ and 0.

In an application context, at any time, these bounds can be used to help the user or the system to decide about the continuation of the search. Note however that, while the six presented algorithms produce an anytime problem lower bound, only *rbf* and *ia* produce concurrently an anytime problem upper bound. The other four (*id*, *ior*, *rds* and *idrds*) produce no problem upper bound before the last step of the algorithm.

Whereas *rbf* uses a *Best First* search, the other five (*id*, *ior*, *ia*, *rds* and *idrds*) use a *Depth First* search.

Although all of them have been developed and tested with a dynamic value ordering and all of them, except the last two (*rds* and *idrds*), with a dynamic variable ordering (see 5), for the sake of simplicity, the pseudo-codes have been written assuming static variable and value orderings.

During the search, a global array A stores the current assignment. At the beginning, A is empty. n is the number of problem variables. $\text{DS}(j)$ returns the domain size of the variable j.

$\text{FC}(A, i, j)$ returns a lower bound of the subproblem, limited to the variables after i (i included) and constrained by the assignment A of the variables between i and j (i and j included). A *Forward Checking* method [6, 16] is used to compute this bound.

In a few words, if $\text{BC}(A, i, j)$ returns the sum of the weights of the constraints which are violated by the assignment A of the variables between i and j, and if $\Delta\text{BC}(A, i, j, l, k)$ returns the increment in BC, which would result from extending the assignment A with the assignment of the value k to the variable l, then:

$$\text{FC}(A, i, j) = \text{BC}(A, i, j) + \sum_{l=j+1}^{n} min_{k \in [1..\text{DS}(l)]} \Delta\text{BC}(A, i, j, l, k)$$

It is easy to establish that $\text{FC}(A, i, j)$:

- is really a subproblem lower bound;
- is monotonic: $i' \leq i, j \leq j' \Rightarrow \text{FC}(A, i, j) \leq \text{FC}(A, i', j')$;
- is exact *i.e.*, equal to the subproblem optimum, when $j = n$.

It can be also observed that FC takes into account only the constraints between assigned variables ($i \leq l \leq j$) and the constraints between assigned and unassigned variables ($j + 1 \leq l \leq n$). It does not take into account the constraints between unassigned variables. This fact will be used by *rds* and *idrds*.

Note that the second parameter i of the function FC is useful only with *rds* and *idrds*. It has been introduced for the sake of homogeneity and is systematically set to 1 with *rbf*, *id*, *ior* and *ia*.

Although the *Depth First Branch and Bound* algorithm, currently used for producing an anytime problem upper bound, produces no problem lower bound before ending, as an introduction, we present its pseudo-code in Figure 1.

```
DFBB()
   ub ← +∞
   lb ← 0
   SEARCH-DFBB(1)
   lb ← ub

SEARCH-DFBB(j)
   for k = 1 to DS(j)
      A[j] ← k
      llb ← FC(A, 1, j)
      if llb < ub
      then if j = n
           then ub ← llb
           else SEARCH-DFBB(j + 1)
```

Fig. 1. *Depth First Branch and Bound*

4.1 Recursive Best First

What we refer to as *rbf* (for *Recursive Best First*) is the recursive version of the classical *Best First Branch and Bound*, proposed in [9] in order to avoid the exponential space requirements of the original version. Whereas a node is explored only once by the original version, it may be explored several times by the recursive version. But, as the classical version, the recursive version explores the nodes in a *Best First* order. Thus the lower bound associated with the current node is a problem lower bound.

Although we implemented the full recursive version, we present in Figure 2 a simpler version (called *Simple Recursive Best First* in [9]). Note that BEST(j) returns the first child of the current node whose associated lower bound is minimum.

4.2 Iterative Deepening

What we refer to as *id* (for *Iterative Deepening*) is the first version of this algorithm, proposed in [8]. The search is limited to a depth h ($h \leq n$) and the minimum of the lower bounds associated with all the nodes at depth h is a problem lower bound. Increasing h from 1 to n produces an anytime problem lower bound (see Figure 3).

4.3 Iterative Objective Relaxing

What we refer to as *ior* (for *Iterative Objective Relaxing*) is the second version of the *Iterative Deepening* algorithm, proposed in [8]. The algorithm searches for an assignment whose weight equals the current problem lower bound. Initially, this lower bound equals 0. When the search fails, the minimum of the lower bounds associated with all the failing nodes is the new current problem lower bound. When it succeeds, the current problem lower bound is obviously the optimum (see Figure 4).

```
RBF()
    ub ← +∞
    lb ← 0
    SEARCH-RBF(1, +∞)

SEARCH-RBF(j, llb)
    for k = 1 to DS(j)
        A[j] ← k
        llb[j, k] ← FC(A, 1, j)
    k* ← BEST(j)
    if j = n
    then ub ← min(ub, llb[j, k*])
    while llb[j, k*] ≤ llb
        lb ← llb[j, k*]
        if j = n
        then stop
        llb' ← min(llb, min_{k≠k*} llb[j, k]))
        A[j] ← k*
        llb[j, k*] ← SEARCH-RBF(j + 1, llb')
        k* ← BEST(j)
    return llb[j, k*]
```

Fig. 2. *Recursive Best First*

```
ID()
    ub ← +∞
    lb ← 0
    for h = 1 to n
        lub ← +∞
        SEARCH-ID(1, h)
        lb ← lub

SEARCH-ID(j, h)
    for k = 1 to DS(j)
        A[j] ← k
        llb ← FC(A, 1, j)
        if llb < lub
        then if j = h
             then lub ← llb
                  if h = n
                  then ub ← lub
             else SEARCH-ID(j + 1, h)
```

Fig. 3. *Iterative Deepening*

```
IOR()
   ub ← +∞
   lb ← 0
   while ub = +∞
      lub ← +∞
      SEARCH-IOR(1, lb)
      lb ← lub

SEARCH-IOR(j, lb)
   for k = 1 to DS(j)
      A[j] ← k
      llb ← FC(A, 1, j)
      if llb ≤ lb
      then if j = n
           then ub ← lub ← llb
           else SEARCH-IOR(j + 1, lb)
      else lub ← min(lub, llb)
```

Fig. 4. *Iterative Objective Relaxing*

4.4 Iterative Approximating

What we refer to as *ia* (for *Iterative Approximating*) is referred to as A^*_ϵ in [13]. By replacing the backtrack condition of the classical *Depth First Branch and Bound* ($ub \leq \text{FC}(A, 1, j)$) by a weaker condition ($\epsilon.ub \leq \text{FC}(A, 1, j), 0 < \epsilon \leq 1$), we obtain at the end of the search a problem lower bound lb equal to $\epsilon.ub$. Increasing ϵ produces an anytime problem lower bound. For the sake of homogeneity with the other algorithms, we chose $\epsilon = \frac{i}{n}$, with i increasing from 1 to n (see Figure 5).

4.5 Russian Doll Search

Russian Doll Search, we refer to as *rds*, has been recently proposed in [19]. Assuming a static variable ordering, one searches for an optimum of the problem limited to the variables after i (i included). The optimum found is obviously a problem lower bound and decreasing i from n down to 1 provides an anytime problem lower bound.

More importantly, the successive optima are recorded (in the global array rds) and used in order to improve the lower bound associated with each node of the future searches: because they do not take into account the same constraints, $\text{FC}(A, 1, j)$ (resulting from *Forward Checking*) and $rds[j + 1]$ (resulting from previous searches) can be safely added to obtain a higher subproblem lower bound $\text{FC}(A, i, j) + rds[j + 1]$ (see Figure 6).

4.6 Iterative Deepening + Russian Doll Search

Iterative Deepening + Russian Doll Search, we refer to as *idrds*, results from a combination of *Iterative Deepening* and *Russian Doll Search*. With the original *Russian Doll*

```
IA()
    ub ← +∞
    lb ← 0
    for i = 1 to n
        SEARCH-IA(1, i)
        lb ← ub.(i/n)

SEARCH-IA(j, i)
    for k = 1 to DS(j)
        A[j] ← k
        llb ← FC(A, 1, j)
        if llb < ub.(i/n)
        then if j = n
             then ub ← llb
             else SEARCH-IA(j + 1, i)
```

Fig. 5. *Iterative Approximating*

```
RDS()
    ub ← +∞
    lb ← 0
    rds[n + 1] ← 0
    for i = n downto 1
        lub ← +∞
        SEARCH-RDS(i, i)
        lb ← rds[i] ← lub

SEARCH-RDS(j, i)
    for k = 1 to DS(j)
        A[j] ← k
        llb ← FC(A, i, j) + rds[j + 1]
        if llb < lub
        then if j = n
             then lub ← llb
                  if i = 1
                  then ub ← lub
             else SEARCH-RDS(j + 1, i)
```

Fig. 6. *Russian Doll Search*

Search, one searched for an optimum of the problem limited to the variables after i (i included). With the new algorithm, one only searches for a lower bound of this optimum, using an *Iterative Deepening* approach. The depth h of the search increases from 1 to n. For each value of h, i decreases from $n - h + 1$ down to 1.

As previously, these successive lower bounds are recorded (in the global array *lbrds*) and used in order to improve the lower bound associated with each node of the future searches: as with *rds* and for the same reasons, $\text{FC}(A, 1, j)$ and $lbrds[j+1]$ can be safely added to obtain a subproblem lower bound (see Figure 7). Note that, because $lbrds[j+1] \leq rds[j+1]$:

$$\text{FC}(A,i,j) \leq \text{FC}(A,i,j) + lbrds[j+1] \leq \text{FC}(A,i,j) + rds[j+1]$$

```
IDRDS()
    ub ← +∞
    lb ← 0
    lbrds[n + 1] ← 0
    for h = 1 to n
        for i = n − h + 1 downto 1
            lub ← +∞
            SEARCH-IDRDS(i, i, h)
            lbrds[i] ← max(lub, lbrds[i + 1])
            lb ← max(lub, lb)

SEARCH-IDRDS(j, i, h)
    for k = 1 to DS(j)
        A[j] ← k
        llb ← FC(A, i, j) + lbrds[j + 1]
        if llb < lub
        then if j = i + h − 1
             then lub ← llb
                  if h = n
                  then ub ← lub
             else SEARCH-IDRDS(j + 1, i, h)
```

Fig. 7. *Iterative Deepening + Russian Doll Search*

5 Experiments

For the first four algorithms (*rbf*, *id*, *ior* and *ia*), we used the following classical dynamic variable ordering: among the variables of minimum current domain size, choose the first of maximum degree. For the last two (*rds* and *idrds*), which only support a static variable ordering, we used a maximum degree ordering. For all the algorithms, *Forward Checking* allows us to use a dynamic minimum *Inconsistency Count* value ordering [6, 16]: choose for the variable l the first value k such that $\Delta\text{BC}(A, i, j, l, k)$ is minimum.

5.1 Randomly Generated Problems

We carried out first experiments on *Max-CSPs*, randomly generated according to the four parameter model described in [17]: a number n of variables, a domain size d constant for all the variables, a graph connectivity c, and a constraint tightness t constant for all the constraints.

The results we show have been obtained with $n = 30$, $d = 10$ and $c = 0.5$. Figures 8, 9 and 10 are respectively associated with $t = 0.5$, $t = 0.7$ and $t = 0.9$, with 100 problems for each t's value. All these problems are inconsistent and cannot be optimally solved within a reasonable time. The number of violated constraints in optimal solutions increases with t. Note that, unlike what occurs with classical *CSPs*, complexity also increases with t and decreases only when t becomes very close to 1 [19, 11]. Each figure shows the mean evolution, within 300 seconds, of the problem lower bound, computed by each of the six algorithms.

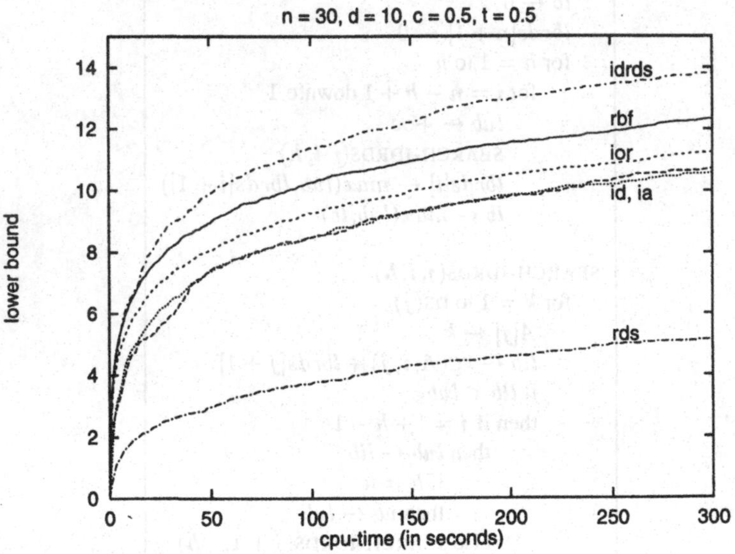

Fig. 8. Randomly generated problems. Tightness = 0.5

The three figures display the same traits:

- *rds* is not the right option for producing anytime lower bounds;
- *rbf*, *id*, *ior*, and *ia* have a similar behavior;
- *idrds* is systematically the best option.

The similarity between *rbf*, *id*, *ior*, and *ia*, as well as the relative efficiency of *idrds*, increases with constraint tightness. With $t = 0.9$, the mean lower bound produced by *rbf*, *id*, *ior*, and *ia*, within 300 seconds is about 50. Within the same time, the mean lower bound produced by *idrds* exceeds 100.

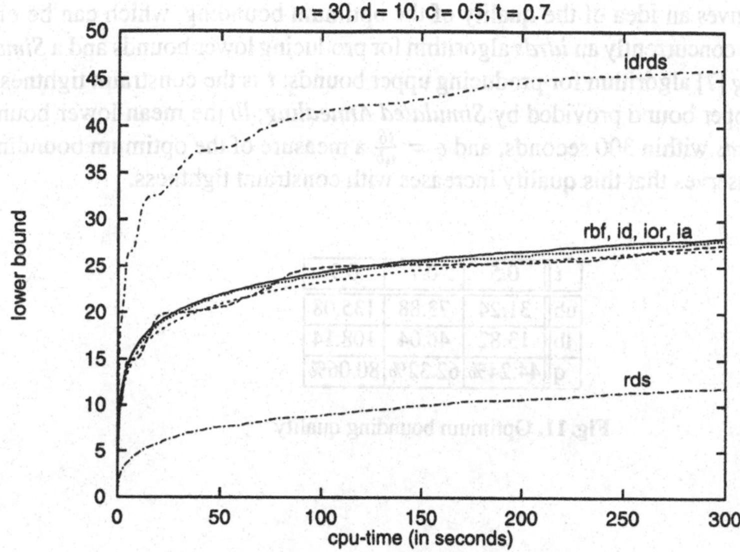

Fig. 9. Randomly generated problems. Tightness = 0.7

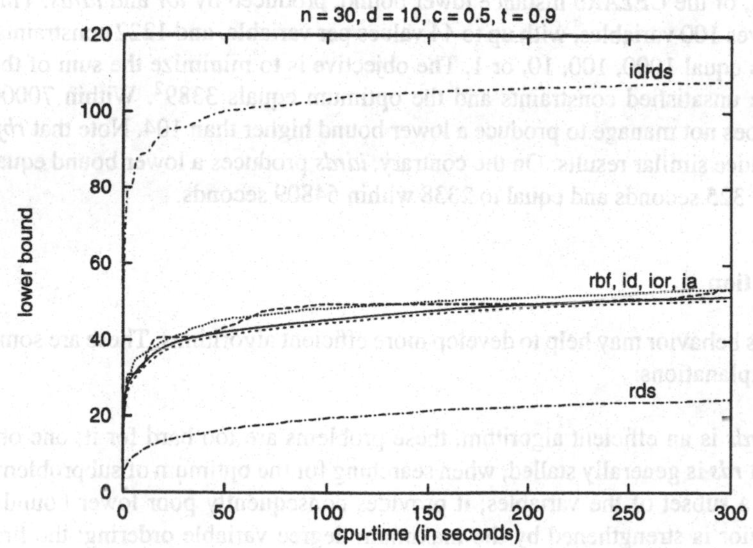

Fig. 10. Randomly generated problems. Tightness = 0.9

Figure 11 gives an idea of the quality of the optimum bounding, which can be obtained by using concurrently an *idrds* algorithm for producing lower bounds and a *Simulated Annealing* [7] algorithm for producing upper bounds: t is the constraint tightness, ub the mean upper bound provided by *Simulated Annealing*, lb the mean lower bound provided by *idrds* within 300 seconds, and $q = \frac{lb}{ub}$ a measure of the optimum bounding quality. One observes that this quality increases with constraint tightness.

t	0.5	0.7	0.9
ub	31.24	73.88	135.08
lb	13.82	46.04	108.14
q	44.24%	62.32%	80.06%

Fig. 11. Optimum bounding quality

5.2 Real World Problems

This behavior is made still clearer with larger, more difficult problems, like the *CELAR* instances of the *Radio Link Frequency Assignment Problem* (see ftp://ftp.cert.fr/pub/lemaitre/LVCSP/Pbs/CELAR/). Figure 12 shows the evolution, within 70000 seconds, of the *CELAR6* instance lower bound, produced by *ior* and *idrds*. This instance involves 100 variables, with up to 44 values per variable, and 1222 constraints, whose weights equal 1000, 100, 10, or 1. The objective is to minimize the sum of the weights of the unsatisfied constraints and the optimum equals 3389[2]. Within 70000 seconds, *ior* does not manage to produce a lower bound higher than 104. Note that *rbf*, *id*, and *ia* produce similar results. On the contrary, *idrds* produces a lower bound equal to 1314 within 325 seconds and equal to 2338 within 64809 seconds.

5.3 Explanation

Explaining this behavior may help to develop more efficient algorithms. These are some preliminary explanations:

- although *rds* is an efficient algorithm, these problems are too hard for it; one observes that *rds* is generally stalled, when searching for the optimum of subproblems involving a subset of the variables; it provides consequently poor lower bounds; this behavior is strengthened by the maximum degree variable ordering: the first considered variables are the least constrained; note that choosing the inverse order leads to worse results: solving subproblems is strongly penalized by a bad variable ordering;

[2] This optimum has been proven by producing a lower bound, equal to the best upper bound found (see [3]).

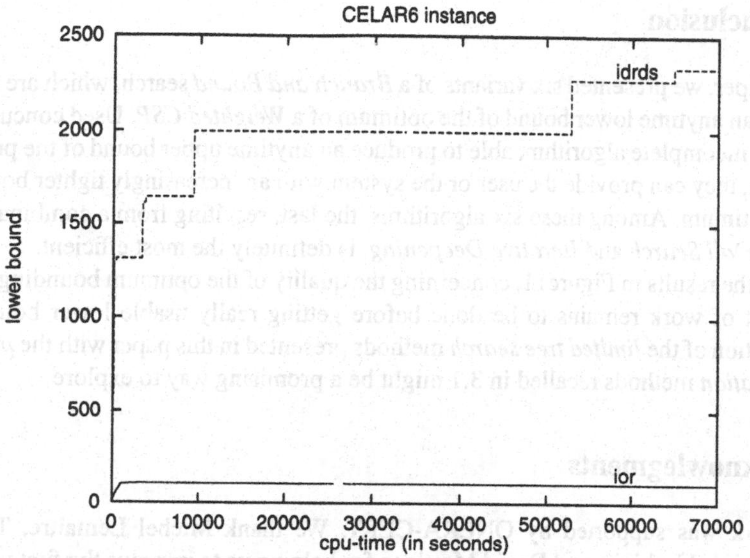

Fig. 12. Radio Link Frequency Assignment Problem

- the similar behavior of *rbf*, *id*, *ior*, and *ia* was unexpected; it may be due to the fact that these four algorithms use the same *Forward Checking* method for computing a subproblem lower bound at each node of the search; because *Forward Checking* takes into account only the constraints between assigned variables and between assigned and unassigned variables, the resulting lower bounds are poor, particularly when few variables are assigned; note that preliminary experiments with the same algorithms, improved by combining *Forward Checking* and *Directed Arc Consistency Counts* [20, 10], do not provide significantly better results;
- as to the efficiency of *idrds*, it may be due to an excellent cooperation between *id* and *rds*:
  - at the beginning of the search, with low values for h, the computed lower bounds, stored in the array *lbrds*, are poor, but searches are strongly limited; then progressively, as lower bounds increase, searches are less and less limited;
  - the main difference from *rds* lies in the fact that *idrds* is not stalled in the optimal solving of subproblems involving a subset of the variables; it rapidly considers the whole problem;
  - the main difference from *id* and the similar algorithms lies in the use of the results of the previous searches to improve the lower bound associated with each node of the current search;
  - finally, the fact that the efficiency of *idrds* increases with constraint tightness is certainly due to increasing subproblem lower bounds and a consequently increasing improvement of the lower bound associated with each node.

6 Conclusion

In this paper, we presented six variants of a *Branch and Bound* search, which are able to produce an anytime lower bound of the optimum of a *Weighted CSP*. Used concurrently with any incomplete algorithm, able to produce an anytime upper bound of the problem optimum, they can provide the user or the system with an increasingly tighter bounding of the optimum. Among these six algorithms, the last, resulting from a combination of *Russian Doll Search* and *Iterative Deepening*, is definitely the most efficient.

But, the results in Figure11, concerning the quality of the optimum bounding, recall that a lot of work remains to be done before getting really usable lower bounds. A combination of the *limited tree search* methods presented in this paper with the *problem simplification* methods recalled in 3.1 might be a promising way to explore.

7 Acknowlegments

This work was supported by ONERA-CERT. We thank Michel Lemaître, Thomas Schiex, Lionel Lobjois, and David Martinez for helping us to improve the first versions of this paper.

References

1. S. Bistarelli, H. Fargier, U. Montanari, F. Rossi, T. Schiex, and G. Verfaillie. Semiring-based CSPs and Valued CSPs: Basic Properties and Comparison. In M. Jampel, E. Freuder, and M. Maher, editors, *Over-Constrained Systems (LNCS 1106, Selected papers from the Workshop on Over-Constrained Systems at CP-95, reprints and background papers)*, pages 111–150. Springer, 1996.
2. S. Bistarelli, U. Montanari, and F. Rossi. Constraint Solving over Semirings. In *Proc. of the 14th International Joint Conference on Artificial Intelligence (IJCAI-95)*, pages 624–630, Montréal, Canada, 1995.
3. S. de Givry, G. Verfaillie, and T. Schiex. Bounding the Optimum of Constraint Optimization Problems. In *Proc. of the 3rd International Conference on Principles and Practice of Constraint Programming (CP-97)*, Schloss Hagenberg, Austria, 1997.
4. H. Fargier, D. Dubois, and H. Prade. Problèmes de satisfaction de contraintes flexibles: une approche égalitariste. *Revue d'Intelligence Artificielle*, 9(3):311–354, 1995.
5. H. Fargier and J. Lang. Uncertainty in Constraint Satisfaction Problems: a Probabilistic Approach. In *Proc. of the European Conference on Symbolic and Quantitavive Approaches of Reasoning under Uncertainty (ECSQARU-93)*, pages 97–104, Grenade, Spain, 1993.
6. E. Freuder and R. Wallace. Partial Constraint Satisfaction. *Artificial Intelligence*, 58:21–70, 1992.
7. S. Kirkpatrick, C. Gelatt, and M. Vecchi. Optimization by Simulated Annealing. *Science*, 220, 1983.
8. R. Korf. Depth-First Iterative Deepening: An Optimal Admissible Tree Search. *Artificial Intelligence*, 27:97–109, 1985.
9. R. Korf. Linear-space Best-first Search. *Artificial Intelligence*, 62:41–78, 1993.
10. J. Larrosa and P. Meseguer. Expoiting the Use of DAC in MAX-CSP. In *Proc. of the 2nd International Conference on Principles and Practice of Constraint Programming (CP-96, LNCS 1118)*, pages 308–322, Cambridge, MA, USA, 1996.

11. J. Larrosa and P. Meseguer. Phase Transition in MAX-CSP. In *Proc. of the 12th European Conference on Artificial Intelligence (ECAI-96)*, pages 190–194, Budapest, Hungary, 1996.
12. C. Papadimitriou. *Computational Complexity*. Addison-Wesley Publishing Company, 1994.
13. J. Pearl. *HEURISTICS, Intelligent Search Strategies for Computer Problem Solving*. Addison-Wesley Publishing Company, 1984.
14. A. Rosenfeld, R. Hummel, and S. Zucker. Scene Labeling by Relaxation Operations. *IEEE Transactions on Systems, Man, and Cybernetics*, 6(6):173–184, 1976.
15. T. Schiex. Possibilistic Constraint Satisfaction Problems or "How to handle soft constraints ?". In *Proc. of the 8th International Conference on Uncertainty in Artificial Intelligence (UAI-92)*, Stanford, CA, USA, 1992.
16. T. Schiex, H. Fargier, and G. Verfaillie. Problèmes de satisfaction de contraintes valués. *Revue d'Intelligence Artificielle*, 11(3):339–373, 1997.
17. B. Smith. Phase Transition and the Mushy Region in Constraint Satisfaction Problems. In *Proc. of the 11th European Conference on Artificial Intelligence (ECAI-94)*, pages 100–104, Amsterdam, The Netherlands, 1994.
18. G. Verfaillie and S. de Givry. Algorithmic problems and solutions in the Valued Constraint Satisfaction Problem framework. In *Proc. of the EUFIT-97 session on "Valued Constraint Satisfaction"*, Aachen, Germany, 1997.
19. G. Verfaillie, M. Lemaître, and T. Schiex. Russian Doll Search for Solving Constraint Optimization Problems. In *Proc. of the 13th National Conference on Artificial Intelligence (AAAI-96)*, pages 181–187, Portland, OR, USA, 1996.
20. R. Wallace. Directed Arc Consistency Preprocessing. In *Proc. of the ECAI-94 Workshop on Constraint Processing (LNCS 923)*, pages 121–137. Springer, 1994.

Introducing External Functions in Constraint Query Languages

Barbara Catania[1], Alberto Belussi[2], and Elisa Bertino[1]

[1] Dipartimento di Scienze dell'Informazione
University of Milano
Via Comelico, 39/41
20135 Milano, Italy
e-mail: {bertino,catania}@dsi.unimi.it

[2] Facoltà di Scienze Matematiche Fisiche e Naturali
Università degli Studi di Verona
Ca' Vignal, Strada Le Grazie
37134 Verona, Italy
e-mail: belussi@elet.polimi.it

Abstract. Constraint databases use constraints to model and query data. In particular, constraints allow a finite representation of infinite sets of relational tuples (also called generalized tuples). The choice of different logical theories to express constraints inside relational languages leads to the definition of constraint languages with different expressive power. Practical constraint database languages typically use linear constraints. This choice allows the use of efficient algorithms but, at the same time, some useful queries, needed by the considered application, may not be represented inside the resulting languages (for example, the convex hull cannot be computed [19]). These additional queries can only be modeled by changing the theory (thus, loosing the advantages of the linear theory), or extending the language, or using external functions. In this paper we consider the last approach and we propose an algebra and a calculus for constraint relational databases extended with external functions, formally proving their equivalence. In doing that, we use an approach similar to the one used by Klug to prove the equivalence between the relational algebra and the relational calculus extended with aggregate functions [14]. As far as we know, this is the first approach to introduce external functions in constraint query languages.

1 Introduction

Constraint programming is very attractive from a database point of view since it is completely declarative. The use of constraints to model data is based on the consideration that a relational tuple is a particular type of constraint [13]. More precisely, a tuple in traditional databases can be interpreted as a conjunction of equality constraints between attributes of the tuple and values on a given domain. The introduction of new logical theories to express relationships (i.e., constraints) between the attributes of a database item leads to the definition of *Constraint Databases* as a new research area [13].

Constraints can be added to relational database systems at different levels. At the data level, they finitely represent possibly infinite sets of relational tuples. A conjunction of constraints is typically called *generalized tuple*, a finite set of generalized tuples is called *generalized relation*, whereas the set of (multi-dimensional) points representing the solutions of a generalized tuple t is called *extension* of t. Constraints are a powerful mechanism for modeling spatial and temporal concepts [2, 4, 18], where often infinite information has to be represented. At the query language level, constraints increase the expressive power of simple relational languages by allowing mathematical computations.

Both the relational calculus and the relational algebra have been extended to deal with constraints [11–13, 18]. In order to guarantee a good trade-off between expressive power and computational complexity, the underlying theory should mediate between application requirements and efficiency. This consideration may lead us to use more efficient but less expressive theories, as for example the theory of linear polynomial inequalities (LPOLY), instead of less efficient but more expressive theories, as the theory of polynomial inequalities (POLY).

This approach is not always satisfactory because the chosen theory may not be adequate to support all the functionalities needed by the considered applications [1, 5, 17, 19–21]. For example, if we extend the relational calculus with LPOLY (obtaining FO + LPOLY), the distance between two points and the convex hull of n points cannot be computed and, as another example, collinearity cannot be decided [19].

This problem can be approached in at least three different ways:

- The most naive solution is to change the chosen theory, by adopting a more expressive one (for example POLY). In this case, an higher expressive power is obtained at the price of lower system performance. However, this solution is usually not satisfactory since all implementation advantages of the firstly chosen theory would be lost.
- A second approach maintains the chosen theory and extend the underlying language [1, 17]. Unfortunately, naive extensions of FO + LPOLY cease to remain sound with respect to linear queries (i.e., mapping between databases represented by LPOLY) and yield a language equivalent in expressive power to FO + POLY [1, 20]. Sounds ways to extend FO + LPOLY have been proposed but the significance of these extensions is not always clear [20].
- A third approach maintains the chosen theory and the chosen language but provides operators for integrating external functions in the base language. The use of external functions avoids the choice of a "complex" logical theory, with high computational complexity. Rather, it allows to adopt a "simple" logic, for example LPOLY, and to express specific functionalities by means of external functions. Moreover, it does not increase the syntactical complexity of the language, by introducing new operators.

In this paper we consider the last approach and we propose an algebra and a calculus for constraint databases extended with external functions. Note that while several approaches have been proposed to model aggregate functions inside constraint query languages [8,9,15], as far as we know, no approach has been proposed to deal with arbitrary external functions.

The considered algebra, called Extended Generalized Relational Algebra (EGRA for short), has been first presented in [3]. This algebra deals with generalized relations based on a nested semantics, by which each relation is interpreted as a finite set of possibly infinite sets of relational tuples, each represented by the extension of a generalized tuple. Thus, the nested semantics interprets a generalized relation as a one-level nested relation. A similar semantics has been used in the definition of the DEDALE system [11]. As we will see, the use of the nested semantics allows us to introduce external functions in a simple and meaningful way.

The extended generalized relational algebra is a typical procedural language. For this procedural language, similarly to what has been done for the relational model, it is useful to define an equivalent declarative language, i.e., a calculus. In this paper we introduce the Extended Generalized Relational Calculus (ECAL for short) as an extension of the relational calculus proposed by Klug [14]. The Klug's calculus deals with aggregate functions and explicitly introduces range expressions for variables. By using aggregate functions, new aggregate values, not contained in the input relations, may be created. This cannot happen by using the traditional Codd's calculus [10]. The ability to create new values makes the proof of the equivalence between the Klug's calculus and the relational algebra very different with respect to the one based on the Codd's calculus. Since external functions have some similarities with aggregate functions, in that they generate new values, the use of the Klug's calculus simplifies the proof of the equivalence between EGRA and ECAL.

Other extensions of the Klug's calculus have been already proposed. In [16] it has been extended to deal with relations containing sets of atomic values as tuple components and in [15] to deal with constraints. With respect to the calculus presented in [16], ECAL deals with constraint databases on an arbitrary theory, and external functions, instead of aggregated functions. Moreover, in our proposal, sets contain relational tuples. With respect to the calculus presented in [15], ECAL is extended with external functions and new terms representing generalized tuples.

After introducing the languages, we discuss the basic issues arising in proving their equivalence, assuming to deal with theories admitting variables elimination and external functions satisfying a particular property. Such property, called *uniformness property*, guarantees that each external function allows the same manipulation to be applied to different sets of variables of a given generalized relation.

The paper is organized as follows. In Section 2 the generalized relational model and the Extended Generalized Relational Algebra are introduced. The Extended Generalized Relational Calculus is presented in Section 3. The introduction of external functions in the proposed languages and the basic issues arising in proving their equivalence are discussed in Section 4. Finally, Section 5 presents some conclusions and outlines future work.

2 An extended algebra for constraint databases

The use of constraints to model data is based on the consideration that a relational tuple can be seen as a conjunction of equality constraints [13]. By adopting more general theories to represent constraints, the concept of relational tuple can be first generalized to be a conjunction of constraints on the chosen theory. More generally, the definition of a generalized tuple is affected by the set of logical connectives used to combine constraints. For example, the use of disjunction allows a generalized tuple to represent a concave set of points. This ability is an essential requirement for spatial and temporal applications. By taking this approach, the *Generalized Relational Model* on a decidable logical theory Φ on a domain $\mathcal{D}$ is defined as follows:

- A *generalized tuple* t over variables $X_1, ..., X_k$ in the logical theory Φ is a finite quantifier-free disjunction $\varphi_1 \vee ... \vee \varphi_N$, where each φ_i, $1 \leq i \leq N$, is a conjunction of constraints in Φ. The variables in each φ_i are among $X_1, ..., X_k$. We denote with $\alpha(t)$ the set $\{X_1, ..., X_k\}$ and with $ext(t)$ (or extension of t) the set of relational tuples, belonging to $\mathcal{D}^k$, which are represented by t. Two generalized tuples t_1 and t_2 are equivalent if $ext(t_1) = ext(t_2)$.
- A *generalized relation r of arity k* in Φ is a finite set $r = \{t_1, ..., t_M\}$ where each t_i, $1 \leq i \leq M$, is a generalized tuple over variables $X_1, ..., X_k$ and in Φ. We denote with $\alpha(r)$ the set $\{X_1, ..., X_k\}$.
- A *generalized database* is a finite set of generalized relations.

A generalized relation can be interpreted by a *relational semantics*, in this case representing an infinite set of relational tuples [13], or by a *nested semantics*, in this case representing a finite set of infinite sets of relational tuples [3]. Formally, let $r = \{t_1, ..., t_n\}$ be a generalized relation, the nested semantics of r, denoted by $nested(r)$, is the set $\{ext(t_1), ..., ext(t_n)\}$. In the following, generalized relations are interpreted by adopting the nested semantics. Given a decidable logical theory Φ, the resulting model is called *Extended Generalized Relational Model* on Φ and it is denoted by EGRM(Φ).

An algebra on EGRM(Φ) databases, called *Extended Generalized Relational Algebra* (EGRA for short), has been presented in [3]. This algebra is obtained by extending the generalized relational algebra presented in [12, 18] to deal with generalized relations interpreted under the nested semantics.

EGRA provides two groups of operators, representing two different types of data manipulation:

1. *Set operators.* They treat each generalized tuple as a single object and apply a certain computation to each object, i.e., to each generalized tuple, as a whole.
2. *Tuple operators.* They apply a certain computation to generalized relations interpreted as infinite sets of relational tuples, and assign a given nested representation to the result. Thus, these operators do not consider each generalized tuple as an object by itself.

Op. name	Syntax e	Semantics $r = \mu(e)(r_1, \ldots, r_n), n \in \{1, 2\}$[a] Restrictions
Tuple operators		
atomic relation	R_1	$r = r_1$
selection	$\sigma_P(R_1)$	$r = \{t \wedge P : t \in r_1, ext(t \wedge P) \neq \emptyset\}$
		$\alpha(P) \subseteq \alpha(R_1) \quad \alpha(e) = \alpha(R_1)$
renaming	$\varrho_{[A\mid B]}(R_1)$	$r = \{t[A \mid B] : t \in r_1\}$
		$A \in \alpha(e), B \notin \alpha(e)$
		$\alpha(e) = (\alpha(R_1) \setminus \{A\}) \cup \{B\}$
projection	$\Pi_{[X_{i_1},\ldots,X_{i_p}]}(R_1)$	$r = \{\pi_{[X_{i_1},\ldots,X_{i_p}]}(t) : t \in r_1\}$[b]
		$\alpha(R_1) = \{X_1, \ldots, X_m\}$
		$\alpha(e) = \{X_{i_1}, \ldots, X_{i_p}\} \quad \alpha(e) \subseteq \alpha(R)$
natural join	$R_1 \bowtie R_2$	$r = \{t_1 \wedge t_2 : t_1 \in r_1, t_2 \in r_2, ext(t_1 \wedge t_2) \neq \emptyset\}$
		$\alpha(e) = \alpha(R_1) \cup \alpha(R_2)$
complement	$\neg R$	$r = \{\bar{t}_1 \vee \ldots \vee \bar{t}_m : \bar{t}_1 \vee \ldots \vee \bar{t}_m$ is the disjunctive normal form of $\neg t_1 \wedge \ldots \wedge \neg t_n, r_1 = \{t_1, \ldots, t_n\}$, $ext(\bar{t}_i) \neq \emptyset, i = 1, \ldots, m\}$
		$\alpha(e) = \alpha(R)$
Set operators		
union	$R_1 \cup R_2$	$r = \{t : t \in r_1$ or $t \in r_2\}$
		$\alpha(R_1) = \alpha(R_2) = \alpha(e)$
set difference	$R_1 \setminus^s R_2$	$r = \{t : t \in r_1, \nexists t' \in r_2 : ext(t) = ext(t')\}$
		$\alpha(R_1) = \alpha(R_2) = \alpha(e)$
set complement	$\neg^s R_1$	$r = \{not\ t^c : t \in r_1, ext(not\ t) \neq \emptyset\}$
		$\alpha(e) = \alpha(R_1)$
set selection	$\sigma^s_{(Q_1,Q_2,\subseteq)}(R_1)$	$r = \{t : t \in r_1,$ $ext(Q_1(t)) \subseteq ext(\Pi_{[\alpha(Q_1)]}(Q_2(t)))\}$
		$\alpha(Q_1) \subseteq \alpha(Q_2) \quad \alpha(e) = \alpha(R_1)$
	$\sigma^s_{(Q_1,Q_2,\bowtie\neq\emptyset)}(R_1)$	$r = \{t : t \in r_1, ext(Q_1(t)) \cap ext(Q_2(t)) \neq \emptyset\}$
		$\alpha(Q_1) = \alpha(Q_2) \quad \alpha(e) = \alpha(R_1)$

[a] We assume that r_i does not contain inconsistent generalized tuples, $i = 1, \ldots, n$.

[b] $\pi_{[X_{i_1},\ldots,X_{i_p}]}(t)$ represents the operator eliminating variables $\alpha(t) \setminus \{X_{i_1}, \ldots, X_{i_p}\}$ from the formula corresponding to t.

[c] The expression *not t* represents the disjunctive normal form of the formula $\neg t$.

Table 1. EGRA operators

EGRA operators are presented in Table 1. Notice that tuple operators, except complement, applies a typical relational computation to possibly infinite sets of relational tuples [10]. The EGRA complement operator always returns a generalized relation containing just one generalized tuple representing the set of points that are not contained in the extension of the input relation. Among set operators, union and set difference identify typical operations on sets. The other operators have the following meaning:

1. *Set complement.* Given a generalized relation r, this operator returns a generalized relation containing a generalized tuple t' for each generalized tuple t contained in r; t' is the disjunctive normal form of the formula $\neg t$.
2. *Set selection.* This operator selects from a generalized relation all the generalized tuples satisfying a certain *condition*. The condition is of the form (Q_1, Q_2, θ), where $\theta \in \{\subseteq, (\bowtie \neq \emptyset)\}$ and Q_1 and Q_2 are either: a generalized tuple P of EGRM(Φ), or expressions generated by operators $\{t, \Pi_{[X_1,...,X_n]}\}$, where t represents the input generalized tuple and the interpretation of $\Pi_{[X_1,...,X_n]}$ is a function taking a generalized tuple t' and returning the projection of t' on variables $X_1, ..., X_n$.
   The set selection operator with condition (Q_1, Q_2, θ), applied on a generalized relation r, selects from r only the generalized tuples t for which there exists a relation θ between $ext(Q_1(t))$ and $ext(Q_2(t))$.[1] See Table 1 for a detailed description of the available conditions.

In order to guarantee the closure property, due to the presence of the projection and complement operators, EGRA operators can only be applied to generalized relations belonging to EGRM(Φ) generalized databases, where Φ is a logical theory admitting variable elimination and closed under complementation.[2]

Example 1. Consider two generalized relations R and S such that $\alpha(R) = \{ID_r, X, Y\}$ and $\alpha(S) = \{ID_s, X, Y\}$, where ID_r and ID_s represent object identifiers and X and Y represent the coordinates of the points belonging to the extension of the spatial objects.

- The EGRA expression to retrieve all spatial objects in R that intersect the region identified by a constraint P (*range intersection query*) is: $\sigma^s_{(\Pi_{[X,Y]}(t), P, (\bowtie \neq \emptyset))}(R)$, where $\alpha(P) = \{X, Y\}$.
- The EGRA expression to determine all pairs of identifiers of spatial objects (ID_r, ID_s) $r \in R$, $s \in S$, such that r intersects s (*spatial join intersection based*) is $\Pi_{[ID_r, ID_s]}(\sigma^s_c(R \bowtie \varrho_{[X|_{X'}, Y|_{Y'}]}(S)))$ where $c = (Q_1(t), Q_2(t), (\bowtie \neq \emptyset))$, $Q_1(t) = \Pi_{[X,Y]}(t)$, and $Q_2(t) = \varrho_{[X'|_X, Y'|_Y]}(\Pi_{[X',Y']}(t))$. ◇

3 An extended calculus for constraint databases

In the following, we introduce a calculus which represents the declarative counterpart of the algebra presented in Section 2. Such calculus is obtained by extending the Klug's calculus [14] to deal with constraints and with the extended generalized relational model.

[1] $Q_1(t)$ and $Q_2(t)$ denote the application of Q_1 and Q_2 to a single generalized tuple t.

[2] A theory admits variable elimination if each formula $\exists X F(X)$ of the theory is equivalent to a formula G, where X does not appear. A theory is closed under complementation if, when c is a constraint of Φ, then $\neg c$ is equivalent to another constraint c' of Φ.

3.1 Syntax of the Extended Generalized Relational Calculus

The *Extended Generalized Relational Calculus* ECAL is defined via mutual recursion on three types of expressions: terms, formulas, and alphas. Terms represent the objects on which computations are performed (in our case, atomic values and generalized tuples). Formulas express properties about terms, and alphas are used to create new relations, composed either of relational tuples (thus, defining a new generalized tuple) or of generalized tuples (thus, defining a new generalized relation).

In defining the calculus, it is more convenient to use a positional notation. Thus, in the following, an attribute of a relational tuple is not identified by its name but by its position inside the tuple.

In defining the above objects, we assume we deal with two sets of variables:
- a set $V = \{v, v_1, v_2, ...\}$ of variables representing relational tuples;
- a set $G = \{g, g_1, g_2, ...\}$ of variables representing generalized tuples.

By considering a logical theory Φ, having $\mathcal{D}$ as domain, calculus objects are formally defined as follows.

Terms. Terms are used to represent the objects on which computations are performed. They can be either:

- *simple*, if they represent values from a given domain, such as real numbers;
- *set*, if they represent sets of relational tuples, whose attribute values are taken from the considered domain. Each set variable is a set term. Moreover, for each natural value n, we introduce a particular set term, representing the set of all possible relational tuples on domain $\mathcal{D}$ having n attributes.

Definition 2 (Terms). A term has one of the following forms:

- c, such that $c \in \mathcal{D}$ (simple term);
- $v[A]$, where $v \in V$ and A is a column number (simple term);
- $\mathcal{D}^n$, representing all relational tuples with degree n, with values from $\mathcal{D}$ (set term);
- g, such that $g \in G$ (set term).
- $op(t_1, ..., t_n)$, where t_i are simple (set terms), $i = 1, ..., n$, and op is a function defined in Φ. □

No term is introduced to represent a single relational tuple since, due to the nested semantics, queries always manipulate (the extension of) generalized tuples.

Formulas. Formulas are used to express properties about terms. Atomic formulas are used to specify on which relation a generalized tuple or a relational tuple ranges, and to specify the relationship existing between two generalized tuples or some simple terms. Complex formulas are obtained by logically combining or quantifying other formulas. Both atomic and complex formulas can be either simple or set formulas. In the first case, they specify conditions on simple terms; in the second case, they specify conditions on set terms.

Definition 3 (Formulas). A formula has one of the following forms:

- *Atomic simple formula*:
  - $t(v)$, where $v \in V$ and t is a closed target alpha (see below) or a set term;
  - $\mu(t_1, ..., t_n)$, where μ is a constraint of Φ and $t_1, ..., t_n$ are simple terms.
- *Atomic set formulas*:
  - $\alpha(g)$, where α is a closed general alpha (see below) and $g \in G$;
  - $t_1 \theta t_2$, where t_1, t_2 are set terms and $\theta \in \{\subseteq, \supseteq, =, \neq, \bowtie = \emptyset, \bowtie \neq \emptyset\}$.
- *Complex formulas*:
  - $\psi_1 \wedge \psi_2$ and $\psi_1 \vee \psi_2$ where ψ_1 and ψ_2 are either simple formulas or set formulas; in the first case, they are simple formulas, in the second case, they are set formulas;
  - $\neg\psi$ is a simple (set) formula if ψ is a simple (set) formula;
  - $(\exists r_x)\psi$ is a simple (set) formula if ψ is a simple (set) formula and r_x is a range formula (see below) for x. The scope of $(\exists r_x)$ is ψ. □

Range formulas are particular formulas that are used to specify a range for either a simple variable or a set variable.

Definition 4 (Range formulas). A range formula has the form $\alpha_1(x) \vee ... \vee \alpha_k(x)$. A range formula is *simple* if $x \in V$ and $\alpha_1, ..., \alpha_k$ are either closed target alphas (see below) or set terms; a range formula is *set* if $x \in G$ and $\alpha_1, ..., \alpha_k$ are closed general alphas or atomic alphas (see below). □

Alphas. An alpha represents either a set of relational tuples, i.e., a new generalized tuple, or a set of generalized tuples, i.e., a new generalized relation. Atomic alphas are a particular type of alphas, represented by generalized relation symbols.

Definition 5 (Alphas). An alpha has one of the following forms:

- *Atomic alpha*: for each generalized relation symbol R, R is an alpha.
- *Target alpha*: if $t_1, ..., t_n$ are simple terms, $r_1, ..., r_m$ are simple range formulas for the free variables in $t_1, ..., t_n$, and ψ is a simple formula, then $((t_1, ..., t_n) : r_1, ..., r_m : \psi)$ is a target alpha.
- *General alpha*: if t is a target alpha or a set term, $r_1, ..., r_m$ are set range formulas for the free variables in t, and ψ is a formula, then $((t) . r_1, ..., r_m : \psi)$ is a general alpha.

In the last two cases, ψ is called the *qualifier* whereas $(t_1, ..., t_n)$ and t are called the *target*. □

From the previous definition it follows that in our calculus each generalized relation can be seen as a general alpha, i.e., as a unary relation, with a unique set attribute representing the generalized tuple extension.

When the target of a target alpha has the form $(v[1], ..., v[n])$, $v \in V$, and n is the arity of v, for the sake of simplicity we write v instead of $(v[1], ..., v[n])$.

The scope of a range formula in an alpha expression is the associated target and the qualifier of the alpha. Occurrence of a variable x is *free* if it is not bound by quantifiers or range formulas. A calculus object (term, formula, alpha) is *closed* if it has no free occurrences of any variable.

In the following, we denote with ECAL the language composed by all the closed set alphas generated by combining terms, formulas, and alphas, as explained before.

ECAL allows the representation of computations on generalized relations in two steps: first, conditions on generalized tuples are checked in the more external closed set alpha; then the more internal target alpha allows checking conditions on the extension of the selected generalized tuples.

Example 6. The ECAL expression $(v : \mathcal{D}^2(v) : v[1] + v[2] \leq 2 \wedge v[2] \geq 7)$ is a target alpha which represents the generalized tuple $X + Y \leq 2 \wedge Y \geq 7$. The range formula of the previous alpha specifies that we are interested in all relational tuples composed of two attributes. The qualifier specifies the relation that must hold between the attributes of v. We assume that X corresponds to the first attribute and Y to the second one. Finally, the target specifies that we want to return all relational tuples v satisfying the qualifier. $\diamond$

Example 7. Consider the spatial join (intersection based) query presented in Example 1. The corresponding calculus expression is

$$(((v_1[1], v_2[1]) : g_1(v_1), g_2(v_2) :) : R(g_1), S(g_2) : \alpha_1(\overline{g}_1) \wedge \alpha_2(\overline{g}_2) \wedge (\overline{g}_1 \bowtie\neq \emptyset\ \overline{g}_2))$$

where $\alpha_1 \equiv (((v[2], v[3]) : g_1(v) :) ::)$ and $\alpha_2 \equiv (((v[2], v[3]) : g_2(v) :) ::)$ respectively. In the previous expression, first the intersection between spatial objects (i.e., generalized tuples) is checked with respect to their X and Y variables (assuming that X has position 2 and Y has position 3 inside tuples) and then the result is constructed starting from the extensions of each pair of intersecting tuples. This second step is required since the resulting tuple has to be a new generalized tuple, obtained by considering the identifiers of each pair of intersecting objects. The range intersection query with respect to an object represented by P can be expressed as $(g_1 : R(g_1) : \alpha_1(g_2) \wedge (g_1 \bowtie\neq \emptyset\ g_2))$, where $\alpha_1 \equiv (t_P ::)$ and t_P is the target alpha representing P. $\diamond$

3.2 Interpretation of ECAL objects

In order to assign an interpretation to calculus objects introduced in the previous section, we follow the approach presented in [14], extended with set terms.

The result of the interpretation varies according to the type of the object under consideration: (a) the interpretation of a formula produces values *true* (1) or *false* (0); (b) the interpretation of a term is an atomic value or a set of relational tuples; (c) the interpretation of an alpha is a relation.

In order to establish the association between variables in a calculus object and tuples in the current instances of the corresponding relations, the notion of *model* is introduced. Formally, a model M for a calculus object q is a triple $\langle I, S, X\rangle$, where: (a) I is a database instance; (b) S (the *free list* for object q) is a list of ordered pairs $\langle u_i, S_i\rangle$, where $u_i \in V \cup G$ is a free variable occurring in q and S_i is the domain (the relation) over which u_i ranges; (c) X (the *valuation list* for q and D) is a list of pairs $\langle u_i, x_i\rangle$, where $u_i \in V \cup G$ is a free variable in q and $x_i \in S_i$ such that $\langle u_i, S_i\rangle \in S$.

Terms interpretation

$$c(M) = c \qquad v_i[A](M) = x_i[A] \qquad \mathcal{D}^n(M) = \mathcal{D}^n \qquad g_i(M) = x_i$$

Formula interpretation

$$\alpha(g_i)(M) = \begin{cases} 1 \text{ if } x_i \in \alpha(M) \\ 0 \text{ otherwise} \end{cases} \quad (t_1\theta t_2)(M) = \begin{cases} 1 \text{ if } t_1(M)\theta t_2(M) = 1 \\ 0 \text{ otherwise} \end{cases}$$

$$g_i(v_j)(M) = \begin{cases} 1 \text{ if } x_j \in x_i \\ 0 \text{ otherwise} \end{cases} \quad (\mu(t_1, ..., t_n))(M) = \begin{cases} 1 \text{ if } \mu(t_1(M), ..., \\ \quad t_n(M)) = 1 \\ 0 \text{ otherwise} \end{cases}$$

$$(\neg\psi)(M) = \begin{cases} 1 \text{ if } \psi(M) = 0 \\ 0 \text{ otherwise} \end{cases} \quad (\psi_1 \vee (\wedge)\psi_2)(M) = \begin{cases} 1 \text{ if } \psi_1(M) = 1 \text{ or (and)} \\ \quad \psi_2(M) = 1 \\ 0 \text{ otherwise} \end{cases}$$

$$((\exists r_{u_i})\psi)(M) = \begin{cases} 0 & \text{if } r_{u_i}(M) \text{ is empty} \\ MAX\{\psi(I, S', X') \mid u \in r_{u_i}(M)\} & \text{otherwise} \end{cases}$$

S' is similar to S except that the pair $\langle u_i, S_i\rangle$ is replaced in S' by $\langle u_i, r_{u_i}(M)\rangle$. X' is similar to X except that the pair $\langle u_i, u\rangle$ replaces $\langle u_i, x_i\rangle$.

Alpha interpretation

- $R_i(M) = r_i$ and r_i is the generalized relation named R_i in I.
- $((t_1, ..., t_n) : r_1, ..., r_m : \psi)(M) = \{(t_1(M'), ..., t_n(M')) \mid \psi(M') = 1\}$ where $M' = \langle I', S', X'\rangle$. S' is the same as S except that for those variables u_j ranging over r_k, $1 \leq k \leq m$, S' contains $\langle u_j, r_k(M)\rangle$. X' is the same as X except that for those variables u_j ranging over r_k, $1 \leq k \leq m$, S' contains $\langle u_j, u\rangle$, $u \in r_k(M)$.
- $((t) : r_1, ..., r_m : \psi)(M) = \{t(M') \mid \psi(M') = 1\}$ where $M' - \langle I', S', X'\rangle$. S' is the same as S except that for those variables u_j ranging over r_k, $1 \leq k \leq m$, S' contains $\langle u_j, r_k(M)\rangle$ (note that $u_j \in V \cup G$). X' is the same as X except that for those variables u_j ranging over r_k, $1 \leq k \leq m$, S' contains $\langle u_j, u\rangle$, $u \in r_k(M)$.

4 Introducing external functions in EGRA and ECAL

The introduction of external functions in database languages is an important topic. Functions increase the expressive power of database languages, relying on user defined procedures. External functions can be considered as library functions, completing the knowledge about a certain application domain. In the context of constraint databases, the use of external functions allows us to express all functionalities that cannot be expressed by using the underlying theory.

In constraint databases, external functions can be modeled as functions manipulating generalized tuples. Given a generalized tuple t, it is often useful to characterize an external function f with respect to the following features:

- The set of variables belonging to $\alpha(t)$ to which the manipulation is applied. Indeed, it may happen that function f only transforms a part of a generalized tuple. Formally, this means that function f projects the generalized tuple on such variables before applying the transformation.
  This set is called *input set* of function f and it is denoted by $is(f)$. Thus, $is(f) \subseteq \alpha(t)$.
  In order to make the function independent of $\alpha(t)$, we consider an ordering of $\alpha(t)$. Such ordering is a total function, denoted by $order_{\alpha(t)}$, from $\{1, ..., card(\alpha(t))\}$[3] to $\alpha(t)$. Using such an ordering, $is(f)$ can be characterized as a set of natural numbers: we assume that each number $i \in is(f)$ identifies variable $order_{\alpha(t)}(i) = X_i$.
- The set of variables, belonging to $\alpha(t)$, that are contained in $\alpha(f(t))$. This set of variables is called *local output set* and it is denoted by $los(f)$. Thus, $los(f) \subseteq is(t) \cap \alpha(f(t))$. Also $los(f)$ can be represented as a set of natural numbers.
  If $i \in is(f)$ but $i \notin los(f)$ this means that f uses variable X_i during its computation but it does not return any new value for X_i.
- The cardinality of set $\alpha(f(t)) \setminus \alpha(t)$, denoted by $n(f)$, representing the set of new variables introduced by the function in the generalized tuple. For simplicity, we assume that, if $card(\alpha(f(t)) \setminus \alpha(t)) = n$, the new variables are denoted by $New_1, ..., New_n$.

To preserve the closure of the language, an external function f must take a generalized tuple t defined on a given theory Φ and return a new generalized tuple t' over Φ, obtained by applying function f to t. We assume that each function is total on the set of generalized tuples defined on Φ. Functions satisfying the previous properties are called *admissible functions*.

Definition 8 (Admissible functions). Let Φ be a decidable logical theory. An admissible function f for Φ is a function from $DOM(\Phi, n_1)$[4] to $DOM(\Phi, n_2)$, such that $n_1 \geq max\{x | x \in is(f)\}$ and $n_2 = card(los(f)) + n(f)$. For any generalized tuple $t \in DOM(\Phi, n_1)$, associated with a given ordering $order_{\alpha(t)}$, function f returns a new generalized tuple $t' \in DOM(\Phi, n_2)$ such that $\alpha(t') = \{order_{\alpha(t)}(i) | i \in los(f)\} \cup \{New_1, ..., New_{n(f)}\}$. The ordering induced by function f to $f(t)$ first lists variables in $los(f)$ and then new variables. □

[3] Given a set S, $card(S)$ represents the cardinality of S.

[4] $DOM(\Phi, m)$ denotes the set of all the possible generalized tuples t on Φ, such that $card(\alpha(t)) = m$.

Example 9. To show some examples of external functions, we consider metric relationships in spatial applications. Metric relationships are based on the concept of Euclidean distance referred to the reference space $\mathcal{E}^2$. Since a quadratic expression is needed to compute this type of distance, metric relationships can be represented in EGRA only if proper external functions are introduced. For example the following two functions can be considered.

- *Distance*: given a constraint c with four variables (X, Y, X', Y'), representing two spatial objects, it generates a constraint $Dis(c)$ obtained from c by adding a variable New_1 which represents the minimum Euclidean distance between the two spatial objects. Thus, assuming $order_{\alpha(c)}(1) = X$, $order_{\alpha(c)}(2) = Y$, $order_{\alpha(c)}(3) = X'$, and $order_{\alpha(c)}(4) = Y'$, we have $is(Dis) = \{1,2,3,4\}$, $los(Dis) = \{1,2,3,4\}$, and $n(Dis) = 1$.
- *Distance'*: it is similar to the previous function. Given a constraint c with four variables (X, Y, X', Y'), representing two spatial objects, it generates a constraint $Dis'(c)$ representing the minimum Euclidean distance between the two spatial objects. In this case, $is(Dis') = \{1,2,3,4\}$, $los(Dis') = \emptyset$, and $n(Dis') = 1$. ◇

4.1 Introducing external functions in EGRA

Given a set of admissible external functions $\mathcal{F}$, new algebraic operators can be added to EGRA, obtaining the EGRA($\mathcal{F}$) language.

The family of *Apply Transformation* operators allows the application of an admissible function f to all generalized tuples contained in a generalized relation. Two different types of apply transformations can be defined:

- *Unconditioned apply transformation.*
$AT_f(r) = \{f(t) : t \in r\}$.
By using this operator, only the result of the function is maintained in the new relation.
- *Conditioned apply transformation.*
$AT_f^{\tilde{X}}(r) = \{\Pi_{[\tilde{X}]}(t) \bowtie f(t) : t \in r\}$, where $\tilde{X} \subseteq \alpha(r)$.
This transformation is called "conditioned" since the result of the application of function f to a generalized tuple t is combined with some information already contained in t. By changing $\tilde{X}$, we obtain different types of transformations.

Note that for each conditioned apply transformation $AT_f^{\tilde{X}}$ there exists an external functions f' such that, for any generalized relation r, $AT_f^{\tilde{X}}(r) = AT_{f'}(r)$. The main difference between the two approaches is that the conditioned approach is more flexible and reasonable from a practical point of view.

The second operator is the *Application dependent set selection*. It is similar to the set selection of Table 1; the only difference is that now queries, specified in the selection condition C_f, may contain apply transformation operators. The set operator is formally defined as follows:
$\sigma^s_{C_f}(r) = \{t : t \in r, C_f(t)\}$, where $\alpha(\sigma^s_{C_f}(r)) = \alpha(r)$.

Example 10. Consider the external functions introduced in Example 9. Given a generalized relation R with four variables, expressions $AT_{Dis}(R)$ and $AT^{\alpha(t)}_{Dis'}(R)$ are equivalent. Indeed, in the first case each generalized tuple contained in the input generalized relation r is replaced by a new generalized tuple representing the old generalized tuple and, by using a new variable, the distance between the objects represented in the considered generalized tuple. In the second case, the function only returns a new variable representing the distance between the two objects. The old objects are maintained due to the join performed by the $AT^{\alpha(t)}_{Dis'}(R)$ operator.

Given the relations introduced in Example 1, the *spatial join distance based*, retrieving for example all pairs $(r, s) \in R \times S$ such that the distance between r and s is less than 40 Km, together with the real distance between r and s, can be expressed as $\sigma^s_{New_1 \leq 40}(AT_{Dis}(R \bowtie S'))$, where $S' = \varrho_{[X|_{X'}, Y|_{Y'}]}(S)$. ◇

4.2 Introducing external functions in ECAL

In order to introduce external functions in ECAL, a new set term must be introduced in the language, representing the application of an external function to a generalized tuple. Given a set of admissible functions $\mathcal{F}$, the set term is
$f(g_i)$, where $f \in \mathcal{F}$ and $g_i \in G$.
Given a model M, the new set term is interpreted as follows:
$f(g_i)(M) = f(g_i(M))$.
This means that the interpretation of the application of a function to a generalized tuple variable is equivalent to applying function f to the interpretation of the generalized tuple variable. The resulting language is denoted by ECAL($\mathcal{F}$).

Example 11. Consider the spatial join distance based introduced in Example 10. In order to express this query in the calculus, first the alpha representing all pairs of spatial objects is generated; then, the distance is computed and, if it is lower than 40 Km, the pair is returned to the user. The expression is $(g : \alpha_1(g) : \exists\, g(v)\; v[5] \leq 40)$, where $\alpha_1 = (Dis(g) : \alpha_2(g) :)$ and $\alpha_2 = (((v_1, v_2) : g_1(v_1), g_2(v_2) :) : R(g_1), S(g_2) :)$. In the previous expression, α_2 represents all pairs of spatial objects (corresponding to the algebraic Cartesian product), α_1 applies function Dis to the pairs of objects and the outer alpha checks the condition about the distance, represented by the fifth column of the generalized tuples contained in α_1. As we can see, the previous expression allows us to represent the result in a "bottom-up" way, layering the different computations on different, but nested, alphas. ◇

4.3 Equivalence between EGRA($\mathcal{F}$) and ECAL($\mathcal{F}$)

The proof of the equivalence between EGRA($\mathcal{F}$) and ECAL($\mathcal{F}$) relies on the proof of the following results:

1. *Each EGRA expression can be represented in ECAL.*

To prove this result, for each algebraic expression $e \in \text{EGRA}(\mathcal{F})$, an equivalent closed alpha $\alpha \in \text{ECAL}(\mathcal{F})$ is presented such that for all generalized relational database instances I, $e(I) = \alpha(I)$.

2. *Each ECAL expression can be represented in EGRA.*
To prove this result, the set $\mathcal{F}$ cannot be completely arbitrary, as the set of aggregate functions considered in [14] was not arbitrary. As in [14], we require that, if there is a function in $\mathcal{F}$ which operates on a given set of attributes, there must be similar functions which operate on *all* other possible sets of columns. This property is known as *uniformness property*. Then, similarly to what has been done in [14, 16], a calculus object q is translated into an algebraic expression by translating each individual component of q recursively and then combining these translations. The uniformness property is used to prove that the calculus terms containing external functions can be translated into some equivalent algebraic expressions.

Due to space constraints, the complete proof of the equivalence cannot be presented. See [7] for additional details.

5 Concluding remarks

This paper has presented a new calculus (ECAL($\mathcal{F}$)) for constraint databases, extended with external functions. ECAL($\mathcal{F}$) is based on the Klug's calculus [14] and it has been proved to be equivalent to the algebra first presented in [3, 4]. Future work includes a detailed analysis of the expressive power and the complexity of the proposed languages, by using specific classes of external functions. A related problem is that of classifying admissible functions with respect to the considered theories. The detection of specific applications that may get advantages from the use of the proposed languages and the definition of optimization techniques are some other topics to be investigated.

References

1. F. Afrati, S.S. Cosmadakis, S. Grumbach, and G.M. Kuper. Linear vs. Polynomial Constraints in Database Query Languages. In *LNCS 874: Proc. of the 2nd Int. Workshop on Principles and Practice of Constraint Programming*, pages 181–192, 1994.
2. M. Baudinet, M Niezotte, and P. Wolper. On the Representation of Infinite Temporal Data and Queries. In *Proc. of the 10th ACM SIGACT-SIGMOD-SIGART Int. Symp. on Principles of Database Systems*, pages 280–290, 1991.
3. A. Belussi, E. Bertino, and B. Catania. An Extended Algebra for Constraint Databases. *IEEE Trans. on Knowledge and Data Engineering*, to appear.
4. A. Belussi, E. Bertino, and B. Catania. Manipulating Spatial Data in Constraint Databases. In *LNCS 1262: Proc. of the 5th Symp. on Spatial Databases*, pages 115–141, 1997.
5. M. Benedikt, G. Dong, L. Libkin, and L. Wong. Relational Expressive Power of Constraint Query Languages. In *Proc. of the 15th ACM SIGACT-SIGMOD-SIGART Symp. on Principles of Database Systems*, pages 5–16, 1996.

6. A. Brodsky. Constraint Databases: Promising Technology or Just Intellectual Exercize?. *Constraints Journal*, 2(1),1997. Also *ACM Computing Surveys*, 28(4) (online), 1997.
7. B. Catania. Constraint Databases: Data Models and Architectural Issues. Ph.D. Thesis, University of Milano, Italy, 1998.
8. J. Chomicki, D. Goldin, and G. Kuper. Variable Independence and Aggregation Closure. *Proc. of the 15th ACM SIGACT-SIGMOD-SIGART Int. Symp. on Principles of Database Systems*, pages 40–48, 1996.
9. J. Chomicki and G. Kuper. Measuring Infinite Relations. *Proc. of the 14th ACM SIGACT-SIGMOD-SIGART Int. Symp. on Principles of Database Systems*, pages 78–94, 1995.
10. E.F. Codd. A Relational Model of Data for Large Shared Data Banks. *Communications of the ACM*, 6(13):377–387, 1970.
11. S. Grumbach, P. Rigaux, and L. Segoufin. The DEDALE System for Complex Spatial Queries. In *Proc. of the ACM SIGMOD Int. Conf. on Management of Data*, pages 89–98, 1998.
12. P.C. Kanellakis and D.Q. Goldin. Constraint Programming and Database Query Languages. In *LNCS 789: Proc. of the Int. Symp. on Theoretical Aspects of Computer Software*, pages 96–120, 1994.
13. P. Kanellakis, G. Kuper, and P. Revesz. Constraint Query Languages. *Journal of Computer and System Sciences*, 51(1):25–52, 1995.
14. A. Klug. Equivalence of Relational Algebra and Relational Calculus Query Languages Having Aggregate Functions. *Journal of the ACM*, 29(3):699–717.
15. G.M. Kuper. Aggregation in Constraint Databases. In *Proc. of the 1st Int. Workshop on Principles and Practice of Constraint Programming*, pages 171–172, 1993.
16. G. Ozsoyoglu, Z.M. Ozsoyoglu, and V. Matos. Extending Relational Algebra and Relational Calculus with Set-Valued Attributes and Aggregated Functions. *ACM Transactions on Database Systems*, 12(4):566–592, 1987.
17. J. Paredaens, B. Kuijpers, G. Kuper, and L. Vandeurzen. Euclid, Tarski, and Engeler Encompassed. In *Proc. of the 1Int. Workshop on Database Programming Languages*, 1997.
18. J. Paredaens, J. Van den Bussche, and D. Van Gucht. Towards a Theory of Spatial Database Queries. In *Proc. of the 13th ACM SIGACT-SIGMOD-SIGART Int. Symp. on Principles of Database Systems*, pages 279–288, 1994.
19. L. Vandeurzen, M. Gyssens, and D. Van Gucht On the Desirability and Limitations of Linear Spatial Database Models. In *LNCS 951: Proc. of the Int. Symp. on Advances in Spatial Databases*, pages 14–28, 1995.
20. L. Vandeurzen, M. Gyssens, and D. Van Gucht On Query Languages for Linear Queries Definable with Polynomial Constraints. In *LNCS 1118: Proc. of the Second Int. Conference on Principles and Practice of Constraint Programming*, pages 468–481, 1996.
21. L. Vandeurzen, M. Gyssens, and D. Van Gucht An Expressive Language for Linear Spatial Database Queries. In *Proc. of the ACM SIGACT-SIGMOD-SIGART Int. Symp. on Principles of Database Systems*, pages 109–118, 1998.

A Note on Partial Consistencies over Continuous Domains

Hélène Collavizza, François Delobel, and Michel Rueher

Université de Nice-Sophia-Antipolis, I3S
ESSI, 930, route des Colles - B.P. 145
06903 Sophia-Antipolis, France
{helen,delobel,rueher}@essi.fr

Abstract. This paper investigates the relations among different partial consistencies which have been proposed for pruning the domains of the variables in constraint systems over the real numbers. We establish several properties of the filtering achieved by the algorithms based upon these partial consistencies. Especially, we prove that :
1) 2B–Consistency (or Hull consistency) algorithms actually yield a weaker pruning than Box-consistency;
2) 3B–Consistency algorithms perform a stronger pruning than Box-consistency.
This paper also provides an analysis of both the capabilities and the inherent limits of the filtering algorithms which achieve these partial consistencies.

1 Introduction

Partial consistencies are the cornerstones for solving non linear constraints over the real numbers [5, 21, 3, 14, 13, 1, 26].

A partial consistency is a *local* property which is enforced in order to prune the sets of possible values of a variable before searching for isolated solutions. *Arc–consistency* is a partial consistency which has widely been used in constraint solvers over finite domains [17, 25]. However, arc-consistency cannot be enforced when working with real numbers or floating point numbers. Thus, specific local consistencies have been proposed in order to prune intervals of real numbers [6, 11, 14, 1]. This paper investigates the relation between two of them : *2B–Consistency* and *Box–Consistency*. 2B–Consistency (or hull consistency) [1, 2, 5, 13, 14] is an approximation of arc–consistency which only requires the checking of arc–consistency property for each bound of the intervals; Box–Consistency [1, 26] is a coarser approximation of arc–consistency than 2B–Consistency. Roughly speaking, Box–Consistency consists of replacing all existentially quantified variables but one with their intervals in the definition of 2B–Consistency.

To limit the effects of a strictly local processing, higher order extensions of these two consistencies have been introduced :

- *3B–Consistency* [14] is an approximation of path consistency, a higher order extension of arc-consistency [17, 25]. Roughly speaking, 3B–Consistency

checks whether 2B–Consistency can be enforced when the domain of a variable is reduced to the value of one of its bounds in the whole system;
- *Bound-consistency* [26] applies the principle of 3B–Consistency to Box–Consistency : Bound-consistency checks whether Box–Consistency can be enforced when the domain of a variable is reduced to the value of one of its bounds in the whole system.

It has been stated in [16] without proof that :

- 2B–Consistency algorithms actually achieves a weaker filtering than Box–Consistency, especially when a variable occurs more than once in some constraint. This is due to the fact that 2B–Consistency algorithms require a decomposition of the constraints with multiple occurrences of the same variable;
- The filtering achieved by Box–Consistency algorithms is weaker than that computed by 3B–Consistency algorithms.

The main result of this paper is a proof of the above properties. If $\Phi_{cstc}(P)$ is the closure of a constraint system P computed by an algorithm ensuring consistency *cstc*, and P_{decomp} is a decomposition of P allowing 2B-consistency filtering, we then prove that the following relations hold :

$$\Phi_{Bound}(P) \preceq \Phi_{3B}(P_{decomp}) \preceq \Phi_{box}(P) \preceq \Phi_{2B}(P_{decomp})$$

This paper also provides an analysis of both the capabilities and the limits of the filtering algorithms which achieve these partial consistencies. We pay special attention to their ability to handle the so-called dependency problem[1].

Layout of the paper

Section 2 reviews some basic concepts of interval analysis required in the rest of the paper. Section 3 is devoted to the analysis of 2B–Consistency. Features and properties of Box–Consistency are the focus of Section 4. 3B–Consistency and Bound–Consistency are introduced in section 5. Section 6 mentions efficiency and precision issues.

2 Interval constraint solving

This section recalls some basics of interval analysis [1, 2, 11] and formally defines a constraint system over intervals of real numbers.

[1] The so-called *dependency problem* [9] is a fundamental problem in interval analysis : when a given variable occurs more than once in an interval computation it is treated as a different variable. For instance, $X \otimes SIN(X)$ is the same as $X \otimes SIN(Y)$ with Y equal to but independent of X. Suppose $X = [-5, 5]$ and $\otimes$ and SIN are respectively interval extensions of the multiplication over the reals and function *sinus*, then the value of $X \otimes SIN(X)$ is not $[-4.8, 1.9]$ but $[-5, 5]$. As shown by this example, the dependency problem often entails a widening of the computed intervals.

2.1 Notations

Throughout this paper, the following notations, possibly subscripted, are used :

- x, y, z denote variables over the reals; X, Y, Z denote variables over the intervals;
- $\mathcal{R}^\infty = \mathcal{R} \cup \{-\infty, +\infty\}$ denotes the set of real numbers augmented with the two infinity symbols. $\overline{\mathbb{F}}$ denotes a finite subset of $\mathcal{R}^\infty$ containing $\{-\infty, +\infty\}$[2];
- u, v, r denote constants in $\mathcal{R}$; a, b denote constants in $\overline{\mathbb{F}}$; a^+ (resp. a^-) corresponds to the smallest (resp. largest) number of $\overline{\mathbb{F}}$ strictly greater (resp. smaller) than a;
- f, g denote functions over the reals; F,G denote functions over the intervals;
- c denotes a constraint over the reals, C denotes a relation over the intervals; $Var(c)$ denotes the variables occuring in c;
- $\Phi_{cstc}(P)$ is the closure of P by consistency *cstc* (where *cstc* is *2B*, *Box*, *3B*, *Bound*).

2.2 Interval analysis

Definition 1 (Interval). *An interval* $[a, b]$ *with* $a, b \in \overline{\mathbb{F}}$ *is the set of real numbers* $\{r \in \mathcal{R} \mid a \leq r \leq b\}$.

Let r be a real number. $\tilde{r}$ denotes the smallest[3] (w.r.t. inclusion) interval of $\overline{\mathbb{F}}$ containing r. $\mathcal{I}$ denotes the set of intervals and is ordered by set inclusion. $\mathcal{U}(\mathcal{I})$ denotes the set of unions of intervals.

Definition 2 (Set Extension). *Let* S *be a subset of* $\mathcal{R}$. *The approximation of* S *—denoted* $\Box S$*— is the smallest interval* I *such that* $S \subseteq I$.

Definition 3 (Interval Extension [19, 9]).
• *An interval function* $F \;: \mathcal{I}^n \to \mathcal{I}$ *is an interval extension of function* $f \;: \mathcal{R}^n \to \mathcal{R}$ *iff :*

$$\forall I_1, \ldots, I_n \in \mathcal{I} \;: r_1 \in I_1, \ldots, r_n \in I_n \Rightarrow f(r_1, \ldots, r_n) \in F(I_1, \ldots, I_n).$$

• *An interval relation* $C \;: \mathcal{I}^n \to$ *Bool is an interval extension of relation* $c \;: \mathcal{R}^n \to$ *Bool iff :*

$$\forall I_1, \ldots, I_n \in \mathcal{I} \;: r_1 \in I_1, \ldots, r_n \in I_n \Rightarrow [c(r_1, \ldots, r_n) \Rightarrow C(I_1, \ldots, I_n)]$$

---

[2] Practically speaking, $\overline{\mathbb{F}}$ corresponds to the set of floating-point numbers used in the implementation of non linear constraint solvers.

[3] The term smallest subset (w.r.t. inclusion) must be understood here according to the precision of floating-point operations. In the rest of the paper, we consider —as in [13, 1]— that results of floating-point operations are outward-rounded to preserve the correctness of the computation. However, we assume that the largest computing error when computing a bound of a variable of the initial constraint system is always smaller than one float. This hypothesis may require the use of big floats [4] when computing intermediate results. Consequences of the relaxation of this hypothesis are examined in details in section 6.

For instance, the interval relation $\doteq$ defined as $I_1 \doteq I_2 \Leftrightarrow (I_1 \cap I_2) \neq \emptyset$ is an interval extension of the equality relation on real numbers.

Definition 4 (Natural Interval Extension [19, 20]). *An interval function $F : \mathcal{I}^n \rightarrow \mathcal{I}$ is the natural interval extension of $f : \mathcal{R}^n \rightarrow \mathcal{R}$ if F is the interval extension of f obtained by replacing in f each constant k with its natural interval extension $\tilde{k}$, each variable with an interval variable and each arithmetic operation with its optimal interval extension [19].*

Optimal interval extensions have been introduced by [19] for the basic interval operations. For instance, let $\odot$ be an operator in $\{+, -, \times, /\}$, and $[a, b] \odot [c, d] = \{x \odot y$ such that $a \leq x \leq b$ and $c \leq y \leq d\}$ then the optimal interval extensions for these four operations are :

- $[a, b] \ominus [c, d] = [a - d, b - c]$
- $[a, b] \oplus [c, d] = [a + c, b + d]$
- $[a, b] \otimes [c, d] = [min(ac, ad, bc, bd), max(ac, ad, bc, bd)]$
- $[a, b] \oslash [c, d] = [min(\frac{a}{c}, \frac{a}{d}, \frac{b}{c}, \frac{b}{d}), max(\frac{a}{c}, \frac{a}{d}, \frac{b}{c}, \frac{b}{d})]$ *if* $0 \notin [c, d]$

In the rest of this paper $\oplus, \ominus, \otimes, \oslash$ denote the optimal interval extensions of $+, -, \times, /$.

Optimal interval extensions can be defined in a similar way for *power* and almost all other elementary functions and relations [20].

Example 1. Let $f(x) = x + x^2 + 3$ be a function over the reals. Its natural interval extension is defined by $X \oplus X \nabla 2 \oplus \tilde{3}$ where ∇ is the optimal interval extensions of *power*.

We now recall a fundamental result of interval analysis with many consequences on efficiency and precision of interval constraint solving methods.

Proposition 1. *[19] Let $F : \mathcal{I}^n \rightarrow \mathcal{I}$ be the natural interval extension of $f : \mathcal{R}^n \rightarrow \mathcal{R}$ and let $f_{sol} = \Box\{f(v_1, \ldots, v_n) \mid v_1 \in I_1, \ldots, v_n \in I_n\}$. If each x_i occurs only once in f then $f_{sol} = F(I_1, \ldots, I_n)$ else $f_{sol} \subseteq F(I_1, \ldots, I_n)$.*

This result can be extended to k-ary relations over $\mathcal{R}^n$:

Proposition 2. *Let $C : \mathcal{I}^n \rightarrow Bool$ be the natural extension of an equation $c : \mathcal{R}^n \rightarrow Bool$ then, if each x_i occurs only once in c, then :*

$$C(I_1, \ldots, I_n) \Leftrightarrow (\exists v_1 \in I_1, \ldots, \exists v_n \in I_n \mid c(v_1, \ldots, v_n)).$$

Proof : We consider here constraints of the form $c : f(x_1, \ldots, x_n) = 0$. Thus, c holds if and only if the relation $(\exists v_1 \in I_{x_1}, \ldots, \exists v_n \in I_{x_n} \mid f(v_1, \ldots, v_n) = 0)$ holds. If no variable has multiple occurrences in c, then, by proposition 1, we have : $(\exists v_1 \in I_{x_1}, \ldots, \exists v_n \in I_{x_n} \mid f(v_1, \ldots, v_n) = 0) \Leftrightarrow F(X_1, \ldots, X_n) \doteq [0, 0]$, where $F(X_1, \ldots, X_n)$ is the natural interval extension of $f(x_1, \ldots, x_n)$ according to definition 4. So, property 2 holds since $F(X_1, \ldots, X_n) \doteq [0,0]$ is the interval extension of $f(x_1, \ldots, x_n) = 0$ ◇

It follows that only the sub-distributive law holds in interval analysis[4]:

$$I \otimes (J \oplus K) \subseteq I \otimes J \oplus I \otimes K$$

2.3 Interval constraint system

A k-ary constraint c is a relation over the reals. C denotes its natural interval extension.

Definition 5 (CSP). *A CSP [17] is a triple $(\mathcal{X}, \mathcal{D}, \mathcal{C})$ where $\mathcal{X} = \{x_1, \ldots, x_n\}$ denotes a set of variables, $\mathcal{D} = \{D_{x_1}, \ldots, D_{x_n}\}$ denotes a set of domains, D_{x_i} being the interval containing all acceptable values for x_i, and $\mathcal{C} = \{c_1, \ldots, c_m\}$ denotes a set of constraints.*

$P_\emptyset$ denotes an empty CSP, i.e., a CSP with at least one empty domain. $\mathcal{D}' \subseteq \mathcal{D}$ means $D'_{x_i} \subseteq D_{x_i}$ for all $i \in 1..n$. We define a CSP $P = (\mathcal{X}, \mathcal{D}, \mathcal{C})$ to be smaller than a CSP $P' = (\mathcal{X}, \mathcal{D}', \mathcal{C})$ if $\mathcal{D}' \subseteq \mathcal{D}$. We note $P \preceq P'$ this relation. By convention $P_\emptyset$ is the smallest CSP.

3 2B–Consistency

Most of the CLP systems over intervals (e.g., [21, 22, 2, 23]) compute an approximation of arc-consistency [17] called 2B–Consistency (or Hull consistency). In this section, we give the definition of 2B–consistency and explain why its computation requires a relaxation of the constraint system.

3.1 Definitions

2B–Consistency [14] states a local property on the bounds of the domains of a variable at a single constraint level. Roughly speaking, a constraint c is 2B–Consistent if for any variable x there exist values in the domains of all other variables which satisfy c when x is fixed to any bound of D_x.

Definition 6 (2B–Consistency). *Let $(\mathcal{X}, \mathcal{D}, \mathcal{C})$ be a CSP and $c \in \mathcal{C}$ a k-ary constraint over the variables $(x_1, \ldots, x_k)$. c is 2B–Consistent iff :*
$\forall i, D_{x_i} = \Box\{v_i \in D_{x_i} \mid \exists v_1 \in D_{x_1}, \ldots, \exists v_{i-1} \in D_{x_{i-1}}, \exists v_{i+1} \in D_{x_{i+1}}, \ldots, \exists v_k \in D_{x_k}$ such that $c(v_1, \ldots, v_{i-1}, v_i, v_{i+1} \ldots, v_k)$ holds $\}$.
A CSP is 2B–Consistent iff all its constraints are 2B–Consistent.

2B–Consistency is weaker than arc–consistency.

Example 2. Let $P_1 = (\{x_1, x_2\}, \{D_{x_1} = [1,4],\ D_{x_2} = [-2,2]\}, \{x_1 = x_2^2\})$ be a CSP. P_1 is 2B–Consistent but not arc–Consistent since there is no value in D_{x_1} which satisfies the constraint when $x_2 = 0$.

[4] Of course, commutative and associative laws are preserved.

Proposition 3. *Let $(\mathcal{X},\mathcal{D},\mathcal{C})$ be a CSP such that no variable occurs more than once in any constraint of $\mathcal{C}$. Let $c \in \mathcal{C}$ be a k-ary constraint over the variables $(x_1,\ldots,x_k)$. c is 2B–Consistent iff for all x_i in $\{x_1,\ldots,x_k\}$ such that $D_{x_i} = [a,b]$ the following relations hold :*

- $C(D_{x_1},\ldots,D_{x_{i-1}},[a,a^+),D_{x_{i+1}},\ldots,D_{x_k})$,
- $C(D_{x_1},\ldots,D_{x_{i-1}},(b^-,b],D_{x_{i+1}},\ldots,D_{x_k})$.

where $[a,a^+)$ and $(b^-,b]$ denote half-open intervals.

Proof : Assume that both $C(D_{x_1},\ldots,D_{x_{i-1}},[a,a^+),D_{x_{i+1}},\ldots,D_{x_k})$ and $C(D_{x_1},\ldots,D_{x_{i-1}},(b^-,b],D_{x_{i+1}},\ldots,D_{x_k})$ hold. By proposition 2 we have :

1. $\exists x_1 \in D_{x_1},\ldots,\exists x_{i-1} \in D_{x_i-1},\exists x_i \in [a,a^+),\exists x_{i+1} \in D_{x_i+1},\ldots,\exists x_k \in D_{x_k}$ such that $c(x_1,\ldots,x_{i-1},x_i,x_{i+1},\ldots,x_k)$ holds, and
2. $\exists x_1 \in D_{x_1},\ldots,\exists x_{i-1} \in D_{x_i-1},\exists x_i \in (b^-,b],\exists x_{i+1} \in D_{x_i+1},\ldots,\exists x_k \in D_{x_k}$ such that $C(x_1,\ldots,x_{i-1},x_i,x_{i+1},\ldots,x_k)$ holds.

Thus, $D_{x_i} = \Box\{x_i \in D_{x_i} \mid \exists v_1 \in D_{x_1},\ldots,\exists v_{i-1} \in D_{x_i-1},\exists v_{i+1} \in D_{x_i+1},\ldots,$ $\exists v_k \in D_{x_k}$ such that $c(v_1,\ldots,x_i,\ldots,v_k)$ holds $\}$.
The counterpart results from the definition of 2B–Consistency.◇

Definition 7 (Closure by 2B–Consistency). *[14] Closure by 2B–Consistency of a CSP $P = (\mathcal{X},\mathcal{D},\mathcal{C})$ is the CSP $P' = (\mathcal{X},\mathcal{D}',\mathcal{C})$ such that :*

- *P and P′ have the same solutions;*
- *P′ is 2B–Consistent;*
- *$\mathcal{D}' \subseteq \mathcal{D}$ and domains in $\mathcal{D}'$ are the largest ones for which P′ is 2B–Consistent.*

Closure by 2B–Consistency of a CSP always exists and is unique [15].

3.2 Computing 2B–Consistency

2B–Consistency is enforced by narrowing the domains of the variables. Using the above notations, the scheme of the standard interval narrowing algorithm — derived from AC3– can be written down as in figure 1. IN implements the computation of the closure by 2B-consistency of a CSP $P = (\mathcal{X},\mathcal{D},\mathcal{C})$. $narrow(c,\mathcal{D})$ is a function which prunes the domains of variables $Var(c)$ until c is 2B–consistent.

The approximation of the projection functions is the basic tool for narrowing domains in $narrow(c,\mathcal{D})$.

Let c be a k-ary constraint over $(x_1,\ldots,x_k)$, and $< I_1,\ldots,I_k > \in \mathcal{I}^k$: for each i in $1..k$, $\pi_i(c, I_1 \times \ldots \times I_k)$ denotes the projection over x_i of the solutions of c in the part of the space delimited by $I_1 \times \ldots \times I_k$.

Definition 8 (projection of a constraint).
$\pi_i(c, I_1 \times \ldots \times I_k) : (\mathcal{C},\mathcal{I}^k) \to \mathcal{U}(\mathcal{I})$ *is the projection of c on x_i iff :*
$\pi_i(c, I_1 \times \ldots \times I_k) = \{v_i \in I_i \mid \exists < v_1,\ldots,v_{i-1},v_{i+1},\ldots,v_k > \in I_1 \times \ldots \times I_{i-1} \times I_{i+1},\ldots \times I_k$ *such that* $c(v_1,\ldots,v_i,\ldots,v_k)$ *holds*$\}$

```
IN(in C, inout D)
    Queue ← C ;
    while Queue ≠ ∅
        c ← POP Queue;
        D' ← narrow(c, D);
        if D' ≠ D then  D ← D';
                            Queue ←Queue ∪ {c' ∈ C | Var(c) ∪ Var(c') ≠ ∅}
        endif
    endwhile
```

Fig. 1. Algorithm IN

Definition 9 (approximation of the projection).
$AP_i(c, I_1\times\ldots\times I_k)$: $(\mathcal{C},\mathcal{I}^k)\rightarrow\mathcal{I}$ is an approximation of $\pi_i(c, I_1\times\ldots\times I_k)$ iff $AP_i(c, I_1\times\ldots\times I_k) = \Box\,\pi_i(c, I_1\times\ldots\times I_k) = [Min\ \pi_i(c, I_1\times\ldots\times I_k), Max\ \pi_i(c, I_1\times\ldots\times I_k)]$.
In other words $AP_i(c, I_1\times\ldots\times I_k)$ is the smallest interval encompassing projection $\pi_i(c, I_1\times\ldots\times I_k)$.

The following proposition trivially holds :

Proposition 4. *Constraint c is 2B–Consistent on $< I_1,\ldots,I_k >$ iff for all i in $\{1,\ldots,k\}$, $I_i = AP_i(c, I_1\times\ldots\times I_k)$.*

In the general case, AP_i cannot be computed directly because it is difficult to define functions Min and Max, especially when c is not monotonic. For instance, if variable x has multiple occurrences in c, defining these functions would require x to be isolated[5]. Since such a symbolic transformation is not always possible, this problem is usually solved by decomposing the constraint system into a set of basic constraints for which the AP_i can easily be computed [16]. Basic constraints are generated syntactically by introducing new variables.

Definition 10 (decomposition of a constraint system).
Let $P = (\mathcal{X},\mathcal{D},\mathcal{C})$ be a CSP and $c\in\mathcal{C}$ a constraint. We define $\mathcal{M}_c\subseteq\mathcal{X}$ as the set of variables having multiple occurrences in c. decomp(c) is the set of constraints obtained by substituting in c each occurrence of variables $x\in\mathcal{M}_c$ by a new variable y with domain $D_y = D_x$ and by adding a constraint $x = y$. $New_{(x,c)}$ is the set of new variables introduced to remove multiple occurrences of variable x in c, $\mathcal{X}_{New} = \bigcup\{New_{(x,c)}\mid x\in\mathcal{X}$ and $c\in\mathcal{C}\}$. P_{decomp} is the CSP $(\mathcal{X}',\mathcal{D}',\mathcal{C}')$ where $\mathcal{X}' = \mathcal{X}\cup\mathcal{X}_{New}$, $\mathcal{D}' = \mathcal{D}\cup\{D_y\mid y\in\mathcal{X}_{New}\}$ and $\mathcal{C}' = \{decomp(c)\mid c\in\mathcal{C}\}$.

[5] B. Faltings [6] has recently introduced a new method for computing the projection without defining projection function. However, this method requires a complex analysis of constraints in order to find extrema.

Decomposition does not change the semantics of the constraint system : P and P_{decomp} have the same solutions since P_{decomp} just results from a rewriting[6] of P. However, a *local* consistency like Arc–Consistency is not preserved by such a rewriting. Thus, P_{decomp} is a *relaxation* of P when computing an approximation of Arc–Consistency.

Example 3 (decomposition of the constraint system). Let $c \;: x_1 + x_2 - x_1 = 0$ be a constraint and $D_{x_1} = [-1, 1]$, $D_{x_2} = [0, 1]$ the domains of x_1 and x_2. Since x_1 appears twice in c, its second occurrence will be replaced with a new variable x_3 : *decomp*$(c) = \{x_1 + x_2 - x_3 = 0, x_1 = x_3\}$.

In this new constraint system, each projection can easily be computed with interval arithmetic. For instance, $AP_1(x_1 + x_2 - x_3 = 0, D_{x_1}, D_{x_2}, D_{x_3})$ is $D_{x_1} \cap (D_{x_3} \ominus D_{x_2})$.

However, this decomposition increases the locality problem : the first constraint is checked independently of the second one and so x_1 and x_3 can take distinct values. More specifically, the initial constraint c is not 2B–Consistent since there is no value of x_1 which satisfies c when $x_2 = 1$. On the contrary, *decomp*(c) is 2B–Consistent since the values $x_1 = -1$ and $x_3 = 0$ satisfy $x_1 + x_2 - x_3 = 0$ when $x_2 = 1$. On the initial constraint, 2B–Consistency reduces D_{x_2} to [0,0] while it yields $D_{x_1} = [-1, 1], D_{x_2} = [0, 1]$ for *decomp*(c).

Remark 1. Example 3 like almost all other examples in this paper trivially can be simplified. However, the reader can more easily check partial consistencies on such examples than on non–linear constraints where the same problems occur.

4 Box–Consistency

Box–Consistency [1, 26] is a coarser approximation of arc-consistency than 2B–Consistency. It mainly consists of replacing every existentially quantified variable but one with its interval in the definition of the 2B–Consistency. Thus, Box–Consistency generates a system of univariate functions which can be tackled by numerical methods such as Newton. Contrary to 2B–Consistency, Box–Consistency does not require any constraint decomposition and thus does not amplify the locality problem. Moreover, Box–Consistency can tackle some dependency problems when each constraint of a CSP contains only one variable which has multiple occurrences.

4.1 Definition and properties of Box–Consistency

Definition 11 (Box–Consistency). *Let $(\mathcal{X}, \mathcal{D}, \mathcal{C})$ be a CSP and $c \in \mathcal{C}$ a k-ary constraint over the variables $(x_1, \ldots, x_k)$. c is Box-Consistent if, for all x_i*

[6] In practice, c is decomposed into binary and ternary constraints for which projection functions are straightforward to compute. Since there are no multiple occurrences in *decomp*(c) and interval calculus is associative, this binary and ternary constraint system has the same solutions as P_{decomp}.

in $\{x_1, \ldots, x_k\}$ *such that* $D_{x_i} = [a, b]$, *the following relations hold :*
1. $C(D_{x_1}, \ldots, D_{x_{i-1}}, [a, a^+), D_{x_{i+1}}, \ldots, D_{x_k})$,
2. $C(D_{x_1}, \ldots, D_{x_{i-1}}, (b^-, b], D_{x_{i+1}}, \ldots, D_{x_k})$.

Closure by Box–Consistency of P is defined similarly to closure by 2B–Consistency of P, and is denoted by $\Phi_{Box}(P)$.

Proposition 5. $\Phi_{2B}(P) \preceq \Phi_{Box}(P)$ *and* $\Phi_{2B}(P) \equiv \Phi_{Box}(P)$ *when no variable occurs more than once in the constraints of* C.

Proof : From the definitions of 2B–Consistency, Box–Consistency and interval extension of a relation, it results that $\Phi_{2B}(P) \preceq \Phi_{Box}(P)$. By proposition 2 the equivalence holds when no variable occurs more than once in the constraints of C. ⋄

It follows that any CSP which is 2B–Consistent is also Box–Consistent. On the contrary a CSP which is Box–Consistent may not be 2B–Consistent (see example 4).

Example 4. Example 3 is not 2B–Consistent for x_2 but it is Box–Consistent for x_2 since $([-1,1] \oplus [0, 0^+] \ominus [-1,1]) \cap [0,0]$ and $([-1,1] \oplus [1^-, 1] \ominus [-1,1]) \cap [0,0]$ are non-empty.

The decomposition of a constraint system amplifies the limit due to the local scope of 2B–Consistency. As a consequence, 2B–Consistency on the decomposed system yields a weaker filtering than Box–Consistency on the initial system :

Proposition 6. $\Phi_{Box}(P) \preceq \Phi_{2B}(P_{decomp})$

Proof : The different occurrences of the same variable are connected by the existential quantifier as stated in the definition of the 2B–Consistency. However, the decomposition step breaks down the links among these different occurrences and generates a CSP P_{decomp} which is a relaxation of P for the computation of a local consistency. It follows that $\Phi_{Box}(P) \preceq \Phi_{Box}(P_{decomp})$. By proposition 5 we have : $\Phi_{Box}(P_{decomp}) \equiv \Phi_{2B}(P_{decomp})$, and thus $\Phi_{Box}(P) \preceq \Phi_{2B}(P_{decomp})$⋄

Example 5. Let c be the constraint $x_1 + x_2 - x_1 - x_1 = 0$ and $D_{x_1} = [-1, 1]$ and $D_{x_2} = [0.5, 1]$ the domains of its variables. c is not Box–Consistent since $[-1, -1^+] \oplus [0.5, 1] \ominus [-1, -1^+] \ominus [-1, -1^+] \cap [0, 0]$ is empty. But *decomp*(c) is 2B–Consistent for D_{x_1} and D_{x_2}.

Box–Consistency can tackle some dependency problems in a constraint c which contains only one variable occuring more than once. More precisely, Box–Consistency enables to reduce domain D_x if variable x occurs more than once in c and if D_x contains inconsistent values. For instance, in example 5, filtering by Box–consistency reduces the domain of x_1 because value -1 of D_{x_1} has no support in domain D_{x_2}.

However, Box–Consistency may fail to handle the dependency problem when the inconsistent values of constraint c are in the domain of variable x_i while a variable x_j $(j \neq i)$ occurs more than once in c. For instance, in example 3, value 1 of D_{x_2} has no support in domain D_{x_1} but Box–Consistency fails to detect the inconsistency because $[-1,1] \oplus [1^-,1] \ominus [-1,1] \cap [0,0]$ holds.

4.2 Computing Box–Consistency

The Box–Consistency filtering algorithm proposed in [1, 26, 27] is based on an iterative narrowing operation using the interval extension of the Newton method. Computing Box–Consistency follows the generic algorithm IN (see figure 1) used for computing 2B–Consistency[7]. The function $narrow(c, \mathcal{D})$ prunes the domains of the variables of c until c is Box–consistent. Roughly speaking, for each variable x of constraint c, an interval univariate function F_x is generated from c by replacing all variables but x with their intervals. The narrowing process consists in finding the leftmost and rightmost zeros of F_x. Figure 2 shows function LNAR which computes the leftmost zero of F_x for initial domain I_x of variable x (this procedure is given in [27]).

```
function LNAR (IN: F_x, I_x, return Interval)
    r ← right(I_x)
    if  0 ∉ F_x(I_x) then return ∅
        else  I ← NEWTON(F_x, I_x)
              if 0 ∈ F_x([left(I), left(I)^+]) then return [left(I), r]
                 else  SPLIT(I, I_1, I_2)
                       L_1 ← LNAR(F_x, I_1)
                       if L_1 ≠ ∅ then return [left(L_1), r]
                          else return [left(LNAR(F_x, I_2)), r]
                       endif
              endif
    endif
```

Fig. 2. Function LNAR

Function LNAR first prunes interval I_x with function NEWTON which is an interval version of the classical Newton method. However, depending on the value of I_x, Newton may not reduce I_x enough to make I_x Box–Consistent. So, a split step is applied in order to ensure that the left bound of I_x is actually a zero. Function SPLIT divides interval I in two intervals I_1 and I_2, I_1 being the left part of the interval. The splitting process avoids the problem of finding

[7] In [26], a branch process is combined with this filtering algorithm in order to find all the isolated solutions

a safe starting box for Newton (see [12]). As mentioned in [27], even if F_x is not differentiable, the function LNAR may find the leftmost zero thanks to the splitting process (in this case, the call to function NEWTON is just ignored). Notice that Box–consistency can be computed in such a way because it is defined on interval constraints whereas the existential quantifiers in the definition of 2B–consistency require the use of projection functions.

5 3B–Consistency and Bound–Consistency

2B–Consistency is only a partial consistency which is often too weak for computing an accurate approximation of the set of solutions of a CSP. In the same way that arc-consistency has been generalized to higher consistencies (e.g., path consistency [17]), 2B–Consistency and Box–Consistency can be generalized to higher order consistencies [14].

5.1 3B–Consistency

Definition 12 (3B–Consistency). *[14] Let $P = (\mathcal{X}, \mathcal{D}, \mathcal{C})$ be a CSP and x a variable of $\mathcal{X}$ with domain $[a, b]$. Let also be :*

- $P_{D_x^1 \leftarrow [a,a^+)}$ *the CSP derived from P by substituting D_x in $\mathcal{D}$ by $D_x^1 = [a, a^+)$;*
- $P_{D_x^2 \leftarrow (b^-,b]}$ *the CSP derived from P by substituting D_x in $\mathcal{D}$ by $D_x^2 = (b^-, b]$.*

D_x is 3B–Consistent iff $\Phi_{2B}(P_{D_x^1}) \neq P_\emptyset$ and $\Phi_{2B}(P_{D_x^2}) \neq P_\emptyset$.
A CSP is 3B–Consistent iff all its domains are 3B–Consistent.

It results from this definition that any CSP which is 3B–Consistent is also 2B–Consistent ([14]). The generalization of the 3B–Consistency to kB–Consistency is straightforward and is given in [14, 16]. Closure by kB–Consistency of P is defined in a similar way to closure by 2B–Consistency of P, and is denoted by $\Phi_{kB}(P)$.

Proposition 7. *Let $\mathcal{P} = (\mathcal{X}, \mathcal{D}, \mathcal{C})$ be a CSP. If P_{decomp} is 3B–Consistent then P is Box–Consistent.*

Proof : Since Box-consistency is a local consistency we just need to show that the property holds for a single constraint.
Assume c is a constraint over $(x_1, ..., x_k)$, x is one of the variables occuring more than once in c, $D_x = [a, b]$ and $New_{(x,c)} = (x_{k+1}, \ldots, x_{k+m})$ is the set of variables introduced for replacing the multiple occurrences of x in c. Suppose that P_{decomp} is 3B–Consistent for D_x .
Consider P_1 the CSP derived from P_{decomp} by reducing domain D_x to $[a, a^+)$. P_1 is 2B–Consistent for D_x and thus the domain of all variables in $new_{(x,c)}$ is reduced to $[a, a^+)$; this is due to the equality constraints added when introducing new variables. From proposition 3, it results that the following relation holds:
$C'(D_{x_1}, \ldots, D_{x_{i-1}}, [a, a^+), D_{x_{i+1}}, \ldots, D_{x_k}, [a, a^+), \ldots, [a, a^+), D_{x_{k+m}}, \ldots, D_{x_n})$
C' is the very same syntactical expression as C up to variable renaming.

$(D_{x_{k+m}},\ldots,D_{x_n})$ are the domains of the variables introduced for replacing the multiple occurrences of $\mathcal{M}_c \setminus \{x\}$. As the natural interval extension of a constraint is defined over the intervals corresponding to the domains of the variables, relation $C(D_{x_1},\ldots,D_{x_{i-1}},[a,a^+),D_{x_{i+1}},\ldots,D_{x_k})$ holds too.

The same reasoning can be applied when x is replaced with its upper bound $(b^-,b]$. So we conclude that D_x is also Box–Consistent. ◇

Example 6. [8] Let $\mathcal{C} = \{x_1 + x_2 = 100, x_1 - x_2 = 0\}$ and $\mathcal{D} = \{[0,100],[0,100]\}$ be the constraints and domains of a given CSP P. $\Phi_{3B}(P_{decomp})$ reduces the domains of x_1 and x_2 to the interval [50,50] whereas Φ_{Box}(P) does not achieve any pruning (P is Box–Consistent).

The following proposition is a direct consequence of proposition 7 :

Proposition 8. *$\Phi_{3B}(P_{decomp}) \preceq \Phi_{Box}(P)$.*

Thus, 3B–Consistency allows to tackle at least the same dependency problems as Box–consistency. However, 3B–Consistency is not effective enough to tackle the dependency problem in general (see example 7).

Example 7. Let c_0 be the constraint $x_1 * x_2 - x_1 + x_3 - x_1 + x_1 = 0$ and $D_{x_1} = [-4,3], D_{x_2} = [1,2]$ and $D_{x_3} = [-1,5]$ the domains of its variables. *decomp*(c) $= \{x_1 * x_2 - x_4 + x_3 - x_5 + x_6 = 0, x_1 = x_4 = x_5 = x_6\}$. c is not 2B–Consistent since there are no values in D_{x_1} and D_{x_2} which verify the relation when $x_3 = 5$. However, *decomp*(c) is 3B–Consistent. Indeed, the loss of the link between the two occurrences of x_1 prevents the pruning of x_3.

A question which naturally arises is that of the relation which holds between Φ_{2B}(P) and $\Phi_{3B}(P_{decomp})$: example 8 shows that $\Phi_{2B}(P) \preceq \Phi_{3B}(P_{decomp})$ does not hold and example 7 shows that $\Phi_{3B}(P_{decomp}) \preceq \Phi_{2B}(P)$ does not hold, even if only one variable occurs more than once in each constraint of P. It follows that no order relation between $\Phi_{3B}(P_{decomp})$ and Φ_{2B}(P) can be exhibited.

Example 8. Let P be a CSP defined by $\mathcal{C} = \{x_1 + x_2 = 10; x_1 + x_1 - 2 \times x_2 = 0\}$, $D_{x_1} = D_{x_2} = [-10,10]$. *decomp*$(x_1 + x_1 - 2 \times x_2 = 0) = \{x_1 + x_3 - 2 \times x_2 = 0, x_3 = x_1\}$. P is 2B–Consistent but P_{decomp} is not 3B–Consistent : Indeed, when x_1 is fixed to 10, $\Phi_{2B}(P_{D_{x_1} \leftarrow [10^-,10]}) = P_\emptyset$ since D_{x_2} is reduced to $\emptyset$. In this case, the link between x_1 and x_3 is preserved and 3B–Consistency reduces D_{x_2} to [5,5].

---

[8] One may also notice that :

- Neither the initial constraint nor the decomposed system in example 3 are 3B–Consistent but both of them are Box–Consistent;
- Constraint c in example 7 is not 2B–Consistent but it is Box–Consistent

5.2 Bound–Consistency

Bound-consistency was suggested in [16] and was formally defined in [26]. Informally speaking, Bound-consistency applies the principle of 3B–Consistency to Box–Consistency : it checks whether Box–Consistency can be enforced when the domain of a variable is reduced to the value of one of its bounds in the whole system.

Definition 13 (Bound–Consistency). *Let $(\mathcal{X},\mathcal{D},\mathcal{C})$ be a CSP and $c \in \mathcal{C}$ a k-ary constraint over the variables $(x_1,\ldots,x_k)$. c is Bound-Consistent if for all $x_i \in (x_1,\ldots,x_k)$ such that $D_{x_i} = [a,b]$, the following relations hold :*
1. $\Phi_{Box}(C(D_{x_1},\ldots,D_{x_{i-1}},[a,a^+),D_{x_{i+1}},\ldots,D_{x_k})) \neq P_\emptyset$,
2. $\Phi_{Box}(C(D_{x_1},\ldots,D_{x_{i-1}},(b^-,b],D_{x_{i+1}},\ldots,D_{x_k})) \neq P_\emptyset$.

Since $\Phi_{Box}(\mathrm{P}) \preceq \Phi_{2B}(P_{decomp})$ it is trivial to show that $\Phi_{Bound}(P) \preceq \Phi_{3B}(P_{decomp})$. Bound–Consistency achieves the same pruning as 3B–Consistency when applied to examples 6 and 3.

6 Discussion

This paper has investigated the relations among 2B–Consistency, 3B–Consistency, Box–Consistency and Bound–Consistency. The advantage of Box–Consistency is due to the fact that it generates univariate functions which can be tackled by numerical methods such as Newton, and which do not require any constraint decomposition. On the other hand, 2B–Consistency algorithms require a decomposition of the constraints with multiple occurrences of the same variable. This decomposition increases the limitations due to the local nature of 2B-Consistency

As expected, higher consistencies — e.g., 3B–Consistency and Bound–Consistency — can reduce the drawbacks due to the local scope of the inconsistency detection.

Experimental results of `Numerica` and `Newton` are very impressive [1,27]. However, other experimental results [8] show that Box–Consistency is not always better than 2B–Consistency, and that combining these two kinds of partial consistencies is clearly a promising approach. It is nevertheless important to notice that the precision of the computations is a very critical issue when one is comparing different filtering algorithms.

Up until now, we assumed that the largest computing error when computing a bound of a variable of the initial system is always smaller than one float. However, as this hypothesis may entail a significant computing cost overhead, it is relaxed in most implementations. Moreover, for efficiency reasons kB–Consistency and Box–Consistency algorithms usually stop the propagation process before normal termination : when the restriction of a domain is less than ϵ —relative or absolute— no pruning is achieved. kB(w)–Consistency and Box(w)–Consistency have been introduced to characterize such filtering algorithms [14,8]

Formally, 2B(w)–Consistency can be defined in the following way :

Definition 14. *Let $(\mathcal{X},\mathcal{D},\mathcal{C})$ be a CSP, $x \in \mathcal{X}$, $D_x = [a,b]$, w a positive integer. D_x is 2-B(w)-consistent if for all $C(x,x_1,\ldots,x_k)$ in $\mathcal{C}$, the following relations hold :*
1) $\exists v \in [a, a^{+w}]$, $\exists v_1,\ldots,v_k \in D_{x_1} \times \ldots \times D_{x_k} \mid c(v,v_1,\ldots,v_k)$
2) $\exists v' \in [b^{-w}, b]$, $\exists v'_1,\ldots,v'_k \in D_{x_1} \times \ldots \times D_{x_k} \mid c(v',v'_1,\ldots,v'_k)$
where a^{+w} (resp.a^{-w}) denotes the wth float after (resp. before) a.

Definition of kB(w)–Consistency and Box(w)–Consistency is straightforward.

Of course, if the result of any elementary arithmetic operation which is not a float is rounded to the previous (or next) float, then there is no guarantee on the unicity of the result; the fixed-point computed by filtering algorithms will depend on the order of evaluation of the terms in an expression, or even on the order of evaluation of constraints when a weaker precision than one float is used to stop propagation (e.g. w in [14]). So, it becomes hard to set the properties of the intervals computed by filtering algorithms.

In other words, the major problem when comparing kB(w)–Consistency and Box(w)–Consistency comes from the fact that the confluency of the filtering algorithms is lost : the final values of the domains depend on the propagation strategy. Thus, no relation can be established : neither among the different kB(w)–Consistencies themselves, nor between kB(w)–Consistency and Box(w)–Consistency.

Acknowledgements

Thanks to Olivier Lhomme, Christian Bliek and Bertrand Neveu for their careful reading and helpful comments on earlier drafts of this paper. Thanks also to Frédéric Goualard, and Laurent Granvilliers for interesting discussions and email correspondence.

References

1. F. Benhamou, D. Mc Allester, and P. Van Hentenryck. CLP(Intervals) Revisited. in *Proc. Logic Programming : Proceedings of the 1994 International Symposium*, MIT Press, (1994).
2. F. Benhamou and W. Older. Applying interval arithmetic to real, integer and boolean constraints. *Journal of Logic Programming*, (1997).
3. C. Bliek. Computer Methods for Design Automation. PhD thesis, Massachusetts Institute of Technology, 1992.
4. R.P. Brent. A FORTRAN multiple-precision arithmetic package *ACM Trans. on Math. Software*, 4, no 1, 57-70, 1978.
5. J.C. Cleary. Logical arithmetic. *Future Computing Systems*, 2(2) :125–149, 1987.
6. B. Faltings. Arc–consistency for continuous variables. *Artificial Intelligence*, vol. 65, pp. 363–376, 1994.
7. E. C. Freuder. Synthesizing constraint expressions. *Communications of the ACM*, 21 :958–966, November 1978.

8. L. Granvilliers. On the combination of Box–consistency and Hull-consistency. Workshop " Non binary constraints", ECAI-98, Brighton, 23-28 August 1998.
9. E. Hansen. Global optimization using interval analysis. *Marcel Dekker*, NY, 1992.
10. Hoon Hong and Volker Stahl. Safe starting regions by fixed points and tightening. *Computing*, 53 :323–335, 1994.
11. E. Hyvőnen. Constraint reasoning based on interval arithmetic : the tolerance propagation approach. *Artificial Intelligence*, vol. 58, pp. 71–112, 1992.
12. H. Hong, V. Stahl . *Safe Starting Regions by Fixed Points and Tightening.* Computing, vol. 53, pp 323-335, 1994.
13. J. H. M. Lee and M. H. van Emden. Interval computation as deduction in CHIP. *Journal of Logic Programming*, 16 :3–4, pp.255–276, 1993.
14. O. Lhomme. Consistency techniques for numeric CSPs. in *Proc. IJCAI93, Chambery, (France)*, pp. 232–238, (August 1993).
15. O. Lhomme. Contribution à la résolution de contraintes sur les réels par propagation d'intervalles. PhD Thesis, University of Nice Sophia Antipolis - CNRS, Route des Colles, B.P. 145, 06903 Sophia Antipolis Cedex, France, 1994.
16. O. Lhomme and M. Rueher. Application des techniques CSP au raisonnement sur les intervalles. *RIA (Dunod)*,vol. 11 :3, pp. 283–312, 1997.
17. A. Mackworth. Consistency in networks of relations. *Artificial Intelligence*, vol. 8, no. 1, pp. 99–118, 1977.
18. U. Montanari. Networks of constraints : Fundamental properties and applications to picture processing. *Information Science*, 7(2) : 95–132, 1974.
19. R. Moore, Interval Analysis. *Prentice Hall*, 1966.
20. A. Neumaier. Interval methods for systems of equations. *Cambridge University Press*, 1990.
21. W.J. Older and A. Velino. Extending prolog with constraint arithmetic on real intervals. In *Proc. of IEEE Canadian conference on Electrical and Computer Engineering.* IEEE Computer Society Press, 1990.
22. W. Older and A. Vellino. Constraint arithmetic on real intervals. in *Constraint Logic Programming : Selected Research*, eds., Frédéric Benhamou and Alain Colmerauer. MIT Press, (1993).
23. Prologia *PrologIV Constraints inside.* Parc technologique de Luminy - Case 919 13288 Marseille cedex 09 (France), 1996.
24. M. Rueher, C. Solnon. Concurrent Cooperating Solvers within the Reals. *Reliable Computing.* Kluwer Academic Publishers, Vol.3 :3, pp. 325-333, 1997.
25. E. Tsang. Foundations of Constraint Satisfaction. *Academic Press*, 1993.
26. P. Van Hentenryck, Y. Deville, and L. Michel. *Numerica. A modeling language for global optimization.* MIT Press, 1997.
27. P. Van Hentenryck, D. McAllester, and D. Kapur. *Solving Polynomial Systems Using a Branch and Prune Aprroach.* SIAM Journal (forthcomming).

Consistency Techniques in Ordinary Differential Equations

Yves Deville[1], Micha Janssen[1], Pascal Van Hentenryck[2]

[1] Université catholique de Louvain,
Pl. Ste Barbe 2, B-1348 Louvain-la-Neuve, Belgium
[2] Brown University, Box 1910, Providence, RI 02912, USA
{yde,mja}@info.ucl.ac.be pvh@cs.brown.edu

Abstract. This paper studies the application of interval analysis and consistency techniques to ordinary differential equations. It presents a unifying framework to extend traditional numerical techniques to intervals. In particular, it shows how to extend explicit methods to intervals. The paper also took a fresh look at the traditional problems encountered by interval techniques and studied how consistency techniques may help. It proposes to generalize interval techniques into a two-step process: a forward process that computes an enclosure and a backward process that reduces this enclosure. In addition, the paper studies how consistency techniques may help in improving the forward process and the wrapping effect.

1 Introduction

Differential equations (DE) are important in many scientific applications in areas such as physics, chemistry, and mechanics to name only a few. In addition, computers play a fundamental role in obtaining solutions to these systems.

THE PROBLEM A (first-order) *ordinary differential equation* (ODE) system $\mathcal{O}$ is a n-dimensional system $u' = f(t, u)$. Given an initial condition $u(t_0) = u_0$ and assuming existence and uniqueness of solution, the solution of $\mathcal{O}$ is a function $s^* : \Re \rightarrow \Re^n$ satisfying $\mathcal{O}$ and the initial condition $s^*(t_0) = u_0$. Note that differential equations of order p (i.e. $f(t, u, u', u'', \ldots, u^p) = 0$) can always be transformed into an ODE by introduction of new variables. Although an ODE system can potentially be transformed into autonomous ODE ($u' = f(u)$) by the addition of a new function $u_{n+1}(t)$ (with $u'_{n+1}(t) = 1$ and $u_{n+1}(t_0) = t_0$), we prefer to keep the time variable explicit for a clearer presentation of some of our novel techniques. However, the autonomous form is more appropriate for some treatment such as automatic differentiation.

There exist different mathematical methods for proving the existence and uniqueness of a solution of an ODE system with initial value. But, in practice, a system is generally required, not only to prove existence, but also to produce numerical values of the solution $s^*(t)$ for different values of variable t. If, for some classes of ODE systems, the solution can be represented in closed form (i.e. combination of elementary functions), it is safe to say that most ODE systems cannot be solve explicitly [Hen62]. For instance, the innocent-looking equation $u' = t^2 + u^2$ cannot be solved in terms of elementary functions!

Discrete variable methods aim to approximate the solution $s^*(t)$ of *any* ODE system, not over a continuous range of t, but only at some points $t_0, t_1, \ldots, t_m$. Discrete variable methods include *one-step methods* (where $s^*(t_j)$ is approximated from the approximation u_{j-1} of $s^*(t_{j-1})$) and *multistep methods* (where $s^*(t_j)$ is approximated from the approximation $u_{j-1}, \ldots, u_{j-p}$ of $s^*(t_{j-1}), \ldots, s^*(t_{j-p})$). In general, these methods do not guarantee the existence of a solution within a given bound and may suffer from traditional numerical problems of floating-point systems.

INTERVAL ANALYSIS IN ODE Interval techniques for ODE systems were introduced by Moore [Moo66]. (See [BBCG96] for a description and a bibliography of the application of interval analysis to ODE systems.) These methods provide numerically reliable enclosures of the exact solution at points $t_0, t_1, \ldots, t_m$. To achieve this result, they typically apply a one-step Taylor interval method and make extensive use of automatic differentiation to obtain the Taylor coefficients [Moo79, Ral81, Cor88, Abe88]. The major problem of interval methods on ODE systems is the explosion of the size of resulting boxes at points $t_0, t_1, \ldots, t_m$. There are mainly two reasons for this explosion. On the one hand, step methods have a tendency to accummulate errors from point to point. On the other, the approximation of an aribitrary region by a box, called the wrapping effect, may introduce considerable imprecision after a number of steps. One of the best systems in this area is Lohner's AWA [Loh87, Sta96]. It uses the Picard iteration to prove existence and uniqueness and to find a rough enclosure of the solution. This rough enclosure is then used to compute correct enclosures using a mean value method and the Taylor expansion on a variational equation on global errors. It also applies coordinate transformations to reduce the wrapping effect.

GOAL OF THE PAPER This paper mainly serves two purposes. First, it provides a unifying framework to extend traditional numerical techniques to intervals. In particular, the paper shows how to extend explicit methods to intervals. Second, the paper attempts to take a fresh look at the traditional problems encountered by interval techniques and to study how consistency techniques may help. It proposes to generalize interval techniques into a two-step process: a forward process that computes an enclosure and a backward process that reduces this enclosure. In addition, the paper studies how consistency techniques may help in improving the forward process and the wrapping effect.

The new techniques proposed in this paper should be viewed as defining an experimental agenda to be carried out in the coming years. The techniques are reasonably simple mathematically and algorithmically and were motivated by the same intuitions as the techniques at the core of the NUMERICA system [VHLD97]. In this respect, they should complement well existing methods. But, as it was the case for NUMERICA, only extensive experimental evaluation will determine which combinations of these techniques is useful in practice and which application areas they are best suited for. Very preliminary experimental results illustrate the potential benefits.

The rest of this paper is organized as follows. Section 2 provides the necessary background and notations. Section 3 presents the generic algorithm that can be instantiated to produce the various methods. Section 4 describes how to find bounding box. Section 5 describes step methods used in the forward phase. Section 6 describes the backward pruning based on box-consistency. Section 7 discusses the wrapping effect. Section 8 presents some experimental results. Section 9 concludes the paper.

2 Background and Definitions

This paper uses rather standard notations of interval programming. $\mathcal{F}$ denotes the set of $\mathcal{F}$-numbers, $\mathcal{D}$ the set of boxes $\subseteq \Re^n$ whose bounds are in $\mathcal{F}$, $\mathcal{I}$ the set of intervals $\subseteq \Re$ whose bounds are in $\mathcal{F}$, and D (possibly subscripted) denotes a box in $\mathcal{D}$. Given a real r and a subset A of $\Re^n$, $\bar{r}$ denotes the smallest interval in $\mathcal{I}$ containing r and $\Box A$ the smallest box in $\mathcal{D}$ containing A. If g is a function, $\hat{g}$ and G denote interval extensions of g. We also use $g_i(x)$ and $G_i(D)$ to denote the ith component of $g(x)$ and $G(D)$.
The solution of an ODE system can be formalized mathematically as follows.

Definition 1 Solution of an ODE System with Initial Value. A *solution* of an ODE system $\mathcal{O}$ with initial conditions $u(t_0) = u_0$ is a function $s^*(t) : \Re \rightarrow \Re^n$ satisfying $\mathcal{O}$ and the initial conditions $s^*(t_0) = u_0$.

In this paper, we restrict attention to ODE systems that have a unique solution for a given initial value. Techniques to verify this hypothesis numerically are given in the paper. Moreover, in practice, as mentioned, the objective is to produce (an approximation of) the values of the solution function s^* of the system $\mathcal{O}$ at different points $t_0, t_1, \ldots, t_m$. It is thus useful to adapt the definition of a solution to account for this practical motivation.

Definition 2 Solution of an ODE System. The *solution* of an ODE system $\mathcal{O}$ is a function $s(t_0, u_0, t_1) : \Re \times \Re^n \times \Re \rightarrow \Re^n$ such that $s(t_0, u_0, t_1) = s^*(t_1)$, where s^* is the solution of $\mathcal{O}$ with initial conditions $u(t_0) = u_0$.

The solution of an ODE system $\mathcal{O}$ can be used to obtain the solution of $\mathcal{O}$ at *any* point for *any* initial value. It is useful to extend our definition to sets of values.

Definition 3 Set Solution of an ODE System. Let s be the solution of an ODE system $\mathcal{O}$. The *set solution* $\mathcal{O}$ at t_1 wrt t_0 and D is the set $s(t_0, D, t_1) = \{s(t_0, u, t_1) \mid u \in D\}$.

The interval techniques presented in this paper aim at approximating set solutions as tightly as possible. The next definition introduces the concept of bounding box that is fundamental to prove the existence and the uniqueness of a solution to an ODE system over a box and to bound the errors.

Definition 4 Bounding Box. Let s be the solution of an ODE system $\mathcal{O}$. A box B is a *bounding box* of s in $[t_0, t_1]$ wrt D if, forall $t \in [t_0, t_1]$, $s(t_0, D, t) \subseteq B$.

Informally speaking, a bounding box is thus an enclosure of the solution on the *whole interval* $[t_0, t_1]$. The following theorem is an interesting topological property of solutions.

Theorem 5. *Let $\mathcal{O}$ be an ODE system $u' = f(t,u)$ with $f \in \mathcal{C}$, let s be the solution of $\mathcal{O}$ (i.e. existence and uniqueness), and let $Fr(A)$ denote the frontier of set A. Then, (1) $s(t_0, D, t_1)$ is a closed set; and (2) $s(t_0, Fr(D), t_1) = Fr(s(t_0, D, t_1))$.*

Proof. (Sketch) Under the given hypothesis, $s \in \mathcal{C}$ [Har64]. Thesis (2) can then be proven by showing that if $x \in Fr(D)$ then $s(t_0, x, t_1) \in Fr(s(t_0, D, t_1))$ and if $x \in D \setminus Fr(D)$ then $s(t_0, x, t_1) \notin Fr(s(t_0, D, t_1))$ [DJVH98]. □

As a consequence, $s(t_j, D_j, t_{j+1})$ can be computed by considering the frontier of D_j only.

3 The Generic Algorithm

The interval methods described in this paper can be viewed as instantiations of a generic algorithm. It is useful to present the generic algorithm first and to describe its components in detail in the rest of the paper. The generic algorithm is parametrized by three procedures: a procedure to compute a bounding box, since bounding-boxes are fundamental in obtaining enclosures, a step procedure to compute forward, and a procedure to prune by using step procedures backwards. Procedure BoundingBox computes a bounding box of an ODE system in an interval for a given box. Procedure Step computes a box approximating the value of $s^*(t_j)$ given the approximations of $s^*(t_k)$ $(1 \le k \le j-1)$ and the bounding boxes $B_1, \ldots, B_{j-1}$. Procedure Prune prunes the boxes D_j at t_j using the box D_{j-1} at t_{j-1}. The intuition underlying the basic step of the generic algorithm is illustrated in Figure 1. The next three sections review these three components. Note however that it is possible to use several step procedures, in which case the intersection of their results is also an enclosure.

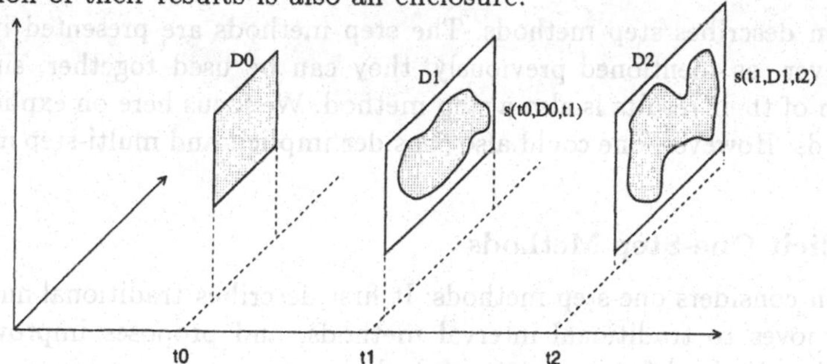

Fig. 1. Computing correct enclosures of the solution

```
solve(𝒪, D_0, < t_0, ..., t_m >)
begin
   forall(j in 1..n)
   begin
      B_j  := BoundingBox(𝒪, D_{j-1}, t_{j-1}, t_j);
      D_j  := Step(𝒪, < D_0, ..., D_{j-1} >, < t_0, ..., t_j >, < B_0, ..., B_j >);
      D_j  := Prune(𝒪, D_{j-1}, t_{j-1}, D_j, t_j, B_j);
   end;
end;
```

4 The Bounding Box

This section considers how to obtain a bounding box for an ODE system. As will become clear later on, bounding boxes are fundamental to obtain reliable solutions to ODE systems. The traditional interval techniques to obtain bounding boxes are based on Picard operator [Har64, Moo79].

Theorem 6 (Picard Operator). *Let D_0 and B be two boxes such that $D_0 \subseteq B$, let $[t_0, t_1] \in \mathcal{I}$, and let $h = t_1 - t_0$. Let $\mathcal{O}$ be an ODE system $u' = f(t, u)$, where f is continuous and has a Jacobian (i.e first-order partial derivatives) over $[t_0, t_1]$. Let Φ be the transformation (Picard Operator)*

$$\Phi(B) = D_0 + [0, h]F([t_0, t_1], B)$$

where F is an interval extension of f. If $\Phi(B) \subseteq B$, then (1) The $\mathcal{O}$ system with initial value $u(t_0) \in D_0$ has a unique solution s; and (2) $\Phi(B)$ is a bounding box of s in $[t_0, t_1]$ wrt D_0.

Theorem 6 can be used for proving existence and uniqueness of a solution and for providing a bounding box [Loh87, Cor95]. A typical algorithm starts from an approximation $B^0 = D_0$ and applies Picard operator. If $\Phi(B^0) \not\subseteq B$, the algorithm widens B^0 into B^1 (e.g., by doubling its size) and iterates the process. The algorithm can also narrow the step size. Note that the existence of Jacobian(f) can be checked numerically by evaluating its interval extension over the box. Note also that the Picard operator uses a Taylor expansion of order 1. It can be generalized for higher orders, which is interesting to increase the step sizes.

5 The Step Methods

This section describes step methods. The step methods are presented in isolation. However, as mentioned previously, they can be used together, since the intersection of their results is also a step method. We focus here on explicit one-step methods. However, one could also consider implicit and multi-step methods [DJVH98].

5.1 Explicit One-Step Methods

This section considers one-step methods: It first describes traditional numerical methods, moves to traditional interval methods, and proposes improvements which can be obtained from consistency techniques.

TRADITIONAL NUMERICAL METHODS To understand traditional interval methods, it is useful to review traditional numerical methods. In explicit one-step methods, the solution s of an ODE system $\mathcal{O}$ is viewed as the summation of two functions:

$$s(t_0, u_0, t_1) = sc(t_0, u_0, t_1) + e(t_0, u_0, t_1). \tag{1}$$

where the function sc can always be computed while the function e cannot. As a consequence, a traditional numerical method based on an explicit one-step method is an algorithm of the form

```
forall(i in 1..n)    u_i := sc(t_{i-1}, u_{i-1}, t_i);
```

This algorithm approximates the solution $s^*(t)$ for an initial value $u(t_0) = u_0$.

Example 1 Taylor Method. The Taylor method is one of the best known explicit one-step methods where the function sc is given by the Taylor expansion of a given order p, i.e.,

$$sc_T(t_0, u_0, t_1) = u_0 + hf^{(0)}(t_0, u_0) + \ldots + \frac{h^p}{p!} f^{(p-1)}(t_0, u_0)$$

INTERVAL METHODS The key idea underlying (explicit or implicit) one-step interval methods is to define an extension of the interval solution s.[3]

Definition 7 Interval Solution of an ODE System. Let s be the solution of an ODE system $\mathcal{O}$. An *interval solution* of $\mathcal{O}$ is an interval extension S of s, i.e.

$$\forall t_0, t_1 \in \mathcal{F}\ ,\ D_0 \in \mathcal{D} : s(t_0, D_0, t_1) \subseteq S(t_0, D_0, t_1)$$

As a consequence, a traditional interval method based on an one-step method is an algorithm of the form

```
D0 = ū0;
forall(i in 1..n)
    Di := S(ti-1, Di-1, ti);
```

This algorithm provides safe intervals for $s^*(t_1), \ldots, s^*(t_m)$, i.e.,

$$s^*(t_i) \in D_i \quad (1 \leq i \leq m).$$

DIRECT INTERVAL EXTENSIONS Traditionally, interval solutions are often constructed by considering an explicit one-step function $s(t_0, u_0, t_1) = sc(t_0, u_0, t_1) + e(t_0, u_0, t_1)$, by taking an interval extension SC of sc and by using a bounding box to bound the error function e to obtain a function of the form $S(t_0, D_0, t_1) = SC(t_0, D_0, t_1) + E(t_0, D_0, t_1)$.

Definition 8 Direct Explicit One-Step Interval Extension. Let s be an explicit one-step solution of an ODE system $\mathcal{O}$ of the form

$$s(t_0, u_0, t_1) = sc(t_0, u_0, t_1) + e(t_0, u_0, t_1)$$

A direct explicit one-step interval extension of s is an interval solution S of the form

$$S(t_0, D_0, t_1) = SC(t_0, D_0, t_1) + E(t_0, B_0, t_1).$$

where SC is an interval extension of sc, B_0 is a bounding box of s in $[t_0, t_1]$ wrt D_0, and E is an interval extension of e.

Possible examples are the Taylor and Runge-Kutta methods.

Example 2 Taylor Interval Solution. The Taylor Interval Solution of order p of an ODE system $\mathcal{O}$ is defined as

$$S_T(t_0, D_0, t_1) = D_0 + hF^{(0)}(t_0, D_0) + \ldots + \frac{h^p}{p!} F^{(p-1)}(t_0, D_0) + \frac{h^{p+1}}{(p+1)!} F^{(p)}([t_0, t_1], B)$$

where $h = t_1 - t_0$, B is a bounding box of s in $[t_0, t_1]$ wrt D_0, and the interval functions $F^{(j)}$ are interval extensions of functions $f^{(j)}$ which can be obtained by automatic differentiation. More information on automatic generation of the value of these functions can be found in [Moo79, Ral80, Ral81, Cor88, Abe88].

---

[3] As usual, interval solutions could also be defined on particular subsets of $\mathcal{F}$ and $\mathcal{D}$.

MEAN VALUE FORM STEP METHODS Mean value forms have been proposed to use contraction characteristics of functions and may return smaller intervals. From Equation 1, we may apply the mean value theorem on $sc(t_0, u, t_1)$ (on variable u) to obtain

$$s(t_0, u, t_1) = sc(t_0, m, t_1) + \sum_{i=1}^{n} \left(\frac{\partial sc}{\partial (u)_i}\right)(t_0, \xi, t_1)\,(u_i - m_i) + e(t_0, u, t_1)$$

for some ξ between u and m. As a consequence, any interval solution of s, may serve as a basis to define a new interval solution.

Definition 9. Let D be a box $\langle I_1, \ldots, I_n \rangle$, m_i be the center of I_i, and $S_M = SC_M + E_M$ be an interval solution of an ODE system $\mathcal{O}$. The MVF solution of $\mathcal{O}$ in D wrt SC_M, denoted by $\tau_M(t_0, D, t_1)$, is the interval function

$$SC_M(t_0, \langle \overrightarrow{m_1}, \ldots, \overrightarrow{m_n} \rangle, t_1) + \sum_{i=1}^{n} \widehat{\left(\frac{\partial sc}{\partial (u)_i}\right)}(I_i)\,(I_i - \overrightarrow{m_i}) + E_M(t_0, D_0, t_1)$$

In the above definiton, the interval function $\widehat{\left(\frac{\partial sc}{\partial (u)_i}\right)}(I_i)$ can be evaluated by automatic differentiation, during the evaluation of $SC(t_0, I_i, t_1)$. extensions.

PIECEWISE INTERVAL EXTENSIONS Direct interval techniques propagate entire boxes through interval solutions. As a consequence, errors may tend to accummulate as computations proceed. This section investigates a variety of techniques inspired by, and using, consistency techniques that can be proposed to reduce the accummulation of errors. The main idea, which is used several times in this paper and was inspired by box-consistency, is to propagate small boxes as illustrated in Figure 2.

Definition 10 Piecewise Explicit One-Step Interval Extension. Let s be a solution to an ODE system $\mathcal{O}$ of the form

$$s(t_0, u_0, t_1) = sc(t_0, u_0, t_1) + e(t_0, u_0, t_1).$$

A piecewise explicit one-step interval extension of s is a function $S(t_0, D, t_1)$ defined as

$$S(t_0, D_0, t_1) = \Box\{SC(t_0, \bar{u}_0, t_1) \mid u_0 \in D_0\} + E(t_0, B_0, t_1)$$

where SC is an interval extension of sc, B_0 is a bounding box of s in $[t_0, t_1]$ wrt D_0, and E is an interval extension of e.

Piecewise interval extensions of an ODE system are not only a theoretical concept: they can in fact also be computed. The basic idea here is to express piecewise interval extension as unconstrained optimization problems.

Proposition 11. *Let s be a solution to an ODE system $\mathcal{O}$ of the form*

$$s(t_0, u_0, t_1) = sc(t_0, u_0, t_1) + e(t_0, u_0, t_1).$$

A piecewise explicit one-step interval extension of s is a function $S(t_0, D, t_1)$ defined as

$$S_i(t_0, D_0, t_1) = [min_{u \in D_0} SC_i(t_0, u, t_1), max_{u \in D_0} SC_i(t_0, u, t_1)] + E_i(t_0, B_0, t_1)$$

where $1 \leq i \leq n$, SC is an interval extension of sc, B_0 is a bounding box of s in $[t_0, t_1]$ wrt D_0, and E is an interval extension of e.

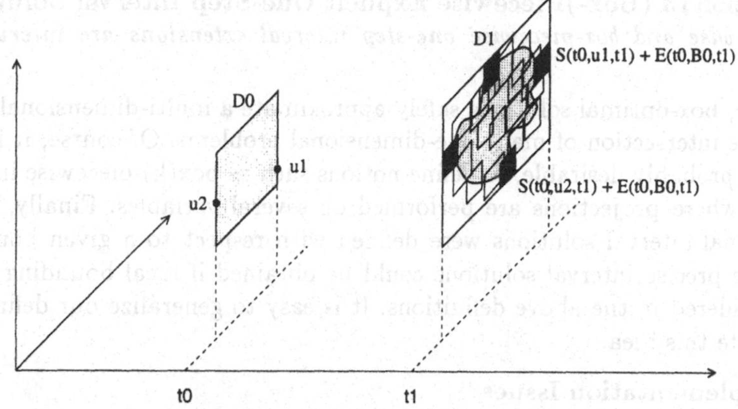

Fig. 2. A Piecewise Interval Solution

Note that these minimization problems must be solved globally to guarantee reliable solutions. The implementation section discusses how a system like NUMERICA may be generalized to solve these problems. The efficiency of the system of course depends on the step size, on the size of D_0, and on the desired accuracy. It is interesting to observe that the function SC does not depend on the error term and hence methods that are not normally considered in the interval community (e.g., Runge-Kutta method) may turn beneficial from a computational standpoint. It is of course possible to sacrifice accuracy for computation time by using projections, the fundamental idea behind consistency techniques. For instance, interval methods are generally very fast on one-dimensional problems, which partly explains why consistency techniques have been successful to solve systems of nonlinear equations.

Definition 12 Box-Piecewise Explicit One-Step Interval Extension. Let s be a solution to an ODE system $\mathcal{O}$ of the form

$$s(t_0, u_0, t_1) = sc(t_0, u_0, t_1) + e(t_0, u_0, t_1).$$

A box-piecewise explicit one-step interval extension of s wrt dimension i is a function $S_i(t_0, D, t_1)$ defined as

$$S_i(t_0, < I_1, \ldots, I_n >, t_1) = \Box\{SC(t_0, < I_1, \ldots, I_{i-1}, \bar{r}, I_{i+1}, \ldots, I_n >, t_1) \mid r \in I_i\} \\ + E(t_0, B_0, t_1)$$

where SC is an interval extension of sc, B_0 is a bounding box of s in $[t_0, t_1]$ wrt D_0, and E is an interval extension of e. The box-piecewise explicit one-step interval extension of s wrt E and B is the function

$$S(t_0, D_0, t_1) = \cap_{i \in 1..n} S_i(t_0, D_0, t_1)$$

Each of the interval solutions reduces to a one-dimensional (interval) unconstrained optimization problem. The following property is a direct consequence of interval extensions.

Proposition 13 (Box-)Piecewise Explicit One-Step Interval Solution. *The piecewise and box-piecewise one-step interval extensions are interval solutions.*

In essence, box-optimal solutions safely approximate a multi-dimensional problem by the intersection of many one-dimensional problems. Of course, it is possible, and probably desirable, to define notions such as box(k)-piecewise interval solutions where projections are performed on several variables. Finally, notice that optimal interval solutions were defined with respect to a given bounding box. More precise interval solutions could be obtained if local bounding boxes were considered in the above definitions. It is easy to generalize our definitions to integrate this idea.

5.2 Implementation Issues

Several of the novel techniques proposed in this section can be reduced to unconstrained optimization problems. In general, interval techniques for unconstrained optimization problems require the function to satisfy a stability requirement (i.e., the optimum is not on the frontier of the box defining the search space). This requirement is not guaranteed in this context since, by Theorem 5, we know that the minimum of function s is on the frontier of D_0, and we minimize function sc, an approximation of s.

Definition 14 min-stability. A function g is *min-stable* for box $K = \langle K_1, \ldots, K_n \rangle \subseteq \Re^n$ if there exists some $\epsilon > 0$ such that

$$min(g(K)) = min(g(K'))$$

with $K' = \langle K_1 + [-\epsilon, \epsilon], \ldots, K_n + [-\epsilon, \epsilon] \rangle$.

Let $K = \langle K_1, \ldots, K_n \rangle \subseteq \Re^n$ be a box and $g : \Re^n \to \Re$ be a function to minimize in K. Here are some necessary conditions for a point d in K to be a minimum when the function is not min-stable.

$\frac{\partial g}{\partial x_i}(d) = 0$ if d_i is in the interior of K_i ($left(K_i) < d_i < right(K_i)$)
$\frac{\partial g}{\partial x_i}(d) \geq 0$ if $d_i = left(K_i)$
$\frac{\partial g}{\partial x_i}(d) \leq 0$ if $d_i = right(K_i)$

Traditional interval algorithms for unconstrained minimization can be generalized to include the interval meta-constraints

$$left(I_i) \neq left(K_i) \wedge right(I_i) \neq right(K_i) \Rightarrow \widehat{\left(\frac{\partial g}{\partial x_i}\right)}(D) = 0$$

$$left(I_i) = left(K_i) \wedge right(I_i) \neq right(K_i) \Rightarrow \widehat{\left(\frac{\partial g}{\partial x_i}\right)}(D) \geq 0$$

$$left(I_i) \neq left(K_i) \wedge right(I_i) = right(K_i) \Rightarrow \widehat{\left(\frac{\partial g}{\partial x_i}\right)}(D) \leq 0$$

with $\widehat{\left(\frac{\partial g}{\partial x_i}\right)}$ an interval extension of $\left(\frac{\partial g}{\partial x_i}\right)$, and $D = \langle I_1, \ldots, I_n \rangle$. The search can also be restricted to the frontier by adding the redundant constraint

$$\bigvee_{1 \leq i \leq n} left(I_i) = left(K_i) \vee right(I_i) = right(K_i)$$

and applying techniques such as constructive disjunction [VHSDar]. Note that combining these two necessary conditions require some extra care to preserve correctness.

6 Backwards Pruning: Box-Consistency for ODE

This section proposes another technique to address the growth of intervals in the step methods. The fundamental intuition here is illustrated in Figure 3. We know that all the solutions at t_{j-1} are in D_{j-1}. If, in D_j, there is some box H such that $S(t_j, H, t_{j-1}) \cap D_{j-1} = \emptyset$, then we know that the box H is *not* part of the solution at t_j. In other words, it is possible to use the step methods backwards to determine whether pieces of the box can be pruned away. This section formalizes this idea in terms of box-consistency.

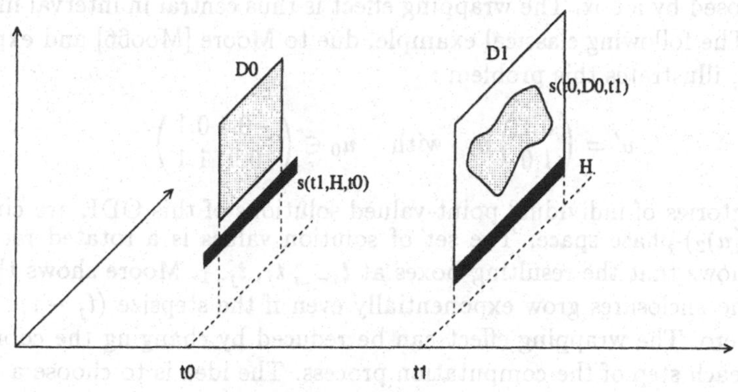

Fig. 3. Pruning

Box consistency aims at reducing a box D_j at t_j given that the solution at t_{j-1} are known to be in D_{j-1}.

Definition 15 Interval Projection of an ODE System. An *interval projection ODE* $\langle S, i\rangle$ is the association of an interval solution S and of an index i $(1 \le i \le n)$.

Definition 16 Box Consistency of an ODE System. Let S be an interval solution of an ODE system $\mathcal{O}$. An interval projection ODE $\langle S, i\rangle$ is *box-consistent* at t_1, D_1 wrt t_0, D_0 if

$$I_i = \square\{\, r_i \in I_i \mid \emptyset \neq D_0 \cap S(t_1, \langle I_1, ..., I_{i-1}, \overline{r_i}, I_{i+1}, ..., I_n\rangle, t_0)\}$$

where $D_1 = \langle I_1, \ldots, I_n\rangle$. An interval solution is *box-consistent* at t_1, D_1 wrt t_0, D_0 if its projections are box-consistent at t_1, D_1 wrt t_0, D_0.

Proposition 17. *Let* $D_1 = \langle I_1, \ldots, I_n\rangle$, *and* $I_i = [l_i, r_i]$. *An interval projection ODE* $\langle S, i\rangle$ *is* box-consistent *at* t_1, D_1 *wrt* t_0, D_0 *iff, when* $l_i \neq r_i$,

$$\begin{aligned} &\emptyset \neq D_0 \cap S(t_1, \langle I_1, ..., I_{i-1}, [l_i, l_i^+], I_{i+1}, ..., I_n\rangle, t_0) \\ \wedge\ &\emptyset \neq D_0 \cap S(t_1, \langle I_1, ..., I_{i-1}, [r_i^-, r_i], I_{i+1}, ..., I_n\rangle, t_0) \end{aligned}$$

and, when $l_i = r_i$,

$$\emptyset \neq D_0 \cap S(t_1, \langle I_1, ..., I_{i-1}, [l_i, l_i], I_{i+1}, ..., I_n\rangle, t_1).$$

Traditional propagation algorithms can now be defined to enforce box-consistency of ODE systems.

7 The Wrapping Effect

The wrapping effect is the name given to the error resulting from the enclosure of a region (which is not a box) by a box. It only occurs for multidimensional function. In one dimension, a perfect interval extension of a continuous function g always yields the correct interval. However, a perfect interval extension of a multidimensional function g introduces overestimations in the resulting box, because the set $g(D) = \{g(d) | d \in D\}$ is not necessarily a box. This effect is especially important when the enclosure is used for finding a new region which is also enclosed by a box. The wrapping effect is thus central in interval methods for ODE. The following classical example, due to Moore [Moo66] and explained in [Cor95] , illustrates this problem :

$$u' = \begin{pmatrix} 0 & 1 \\ 1 & 0 \end{pmatrix} u \quad \text{with} \quad u_0 \in \begin{pmatrix} -0.1 & 0.1 \\ 0.9 & 1.1 \end{pmatrix}$$

The trajectories of individual point-valued solutions of this ODE are circles in the $((u)_1, (u)_2)$-phase space. The set of solution values is a rotated rectangle. Figure 4 shows that the resulting boxes at t_{j-1}, t_j, t_{j+1}. Moore shows that the width of the enclosures grow exponentially even if the stepsize $(t_j - t_{j-1})$ converges to zero. The wrapping effect can be reduced by changing the coordinate system at each step of the computation process. The idea is to choose a coordinate system more appropriate to the shape of $s(t_{j-1}, D_{j-1}, t_j)$, hence reducing the overestimation of the box representation of this set (Figure 5).

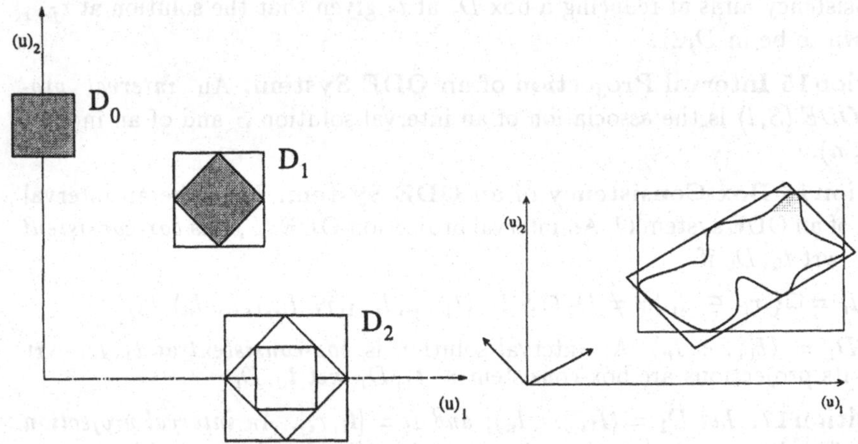

Fig. 4. The Wrapping Effect

Fig. 5. Reducing the Overestimation by Coordinate Transformation

An appropriate coordinate system has to be chosen at each step. Assuming that such coordinate systems are given by mean of (invertible) matrices M_j, a naive approach, based on an explicit one-step method, would consist of computing

$$D_j := S(t_{j-1}, M_{j-1}.D'_{j-1}, t_j) \;;$$
$$D'_j := M_j^{-1} D_j$$

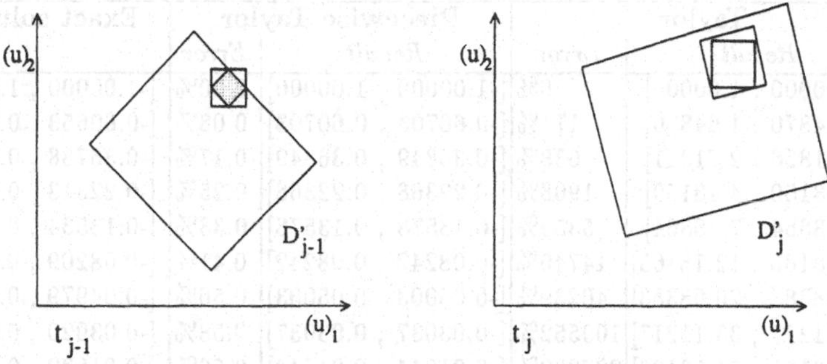

Fig. 6. Coordinate transformation on ϵ-boxes

where D'_j and D'_{j-1} are the boxes at t_j and t_{j-1} in their local coordinate system. This approach is naive since it introduces three wrapping effects: in $M_{j-1}D'_{j-1}$ to restore the original coordinate system needed to compute S, in the computation of S, and in the computation of $M_j^{-1}D_j$ to produce the result in the new coordinate system. To remedy this limitation, more advanced techniques (see, for instance, [Loh87, Ste71, DS76]) have been proposed but they are all bound to a specific step procedure. For instance, Lohner merges the two naive steps together using a mean value form and use associativity in the matrix products to try eliminating the wrapping effect. More precisely, the key term to be evaluated in his step method is of the form $(M_j^{-1}JM_{j-1})D'_{j-1}$ and the goal is to choose M_j^{-1} so that $M_j^{-1}JM_{j-1}$ is close to an identity matrix.

Piecewise interval extensions, however, reduce the wrapping effect in the naive method substantially, as illustrated in Figure 6. The overestimations of $M_{j-1}.D'_{j-1}$ and $M_j^{-1}D_j$ on ϵ-boxes introduce wrapping effects that are small compared to the overall size of the box and to the benefits of using piecewise interval extensions. In addition, this reduction of the wrapping effect is not tailored to a specific step method. The basic idea is thus (1) to find a linear approximation of $s(t_{j-1}, M_{j-1}.D'_{j-1}, t_j)$; (2) to compute the matrix M_j^{-1} from the linear relaxation; (3) to apply the naive method on ϵ-boxes. Step (1) can be obtained by using, for instance, a Taylor extension, while Step (2) can use Lohner's method that consists of obtaining a QR factorization of the linear relaxation. Lohner's method has the benefit of being numerically stable.

8 Experimental Results

This section compares some standard techniques with piecewise interval extensions. This goal is to show that consitency techniques can bring substantial gain in precision. The results were computed with Numerica with a precision of `1e-8`, using optimal bounding boxes.

Consider the ODE $u'(t) = -u(t)$ for an initial box [-1,1] at $t_0 = 0$. Table 1 compares the results obtained by an interval Taylor method of order 4 with step size 0.5, the results obtained by the piecewise interval extension of the same method, and the exact solutions. Relative errors on the size of the boxes are also

t	Taylor Result	Taylor Error	Piecewise Taylor Result	Piecewise Taylor Error	Exact solution
0.0	[-1.00000 , 1.00000]	0%	[-1.00000 , 1.00000]	0.00%	[-1.00000 , 1.00000]
0.5	[-1.64870 , 1.64870]	171%	[-0.60703 , 0.60703]	0.08%	[-0.60653 , 0.60653]
1.0	[-2.71826 , 2.71821]	638%	[-0.36849 , 0.36849]	0.17%	[-0.36788 , 0.36788]
1.5	[-4.48150 , 4.48150]	1908%	[-0.22368 , 0.22368]	0.25%	[-0.22313 , 0.22313]
2.0	[-7.38864 , 7.38864]	5359%	[-0.13578 , 0.13578]	0.33%	[-0.13534 , 0.13534]
2.5	[-12.18163 , 12.18163]	14740%	[-0.08242 , 0.08242]	0.41%	[-0.08209 , 0.08209]
3.0	[-20.08383 , 20.08383]	40239%	[-0.05003 , 0.05003]	0.50%	[-0.04979 , 0.04979]
3.5	[-33.11217 , 33.11217]	109552%	[-0.03037 , 0.03037]	0.58%	[-0.03020 , 0.03020]
4.0	[-54.59196 , 54.59196]	297962%	[-0.01844 , 0.01844]	0.66%	[-0.01832 , 0.01832]

Table 1. ODE $u'(t) = -u(t)$

t	Taylor MVF Result	Taylor MVF Error	Piecewise Taylor Result	Piecewise Taylor Error	Exact solution
0.0	[0.10000 , 0.40000]	0.00%	[0.10000 , 0.40000]	0.00%	[0.10000 , 0.40000]
0.5	[0.06798 , 0.37635]	29.52%	[0.09511 , 0.33344]	0.10%	[0.09524 , 0.33333]
1.0	[0.03884 , 0.36099]	65.37%	[0.09075 , 0.28583]	0.14%	[0.09091 , 0.28571]
1.5	[0.01027 , 0.35316]	110.31%	[0.08679 , 0.25010]	0.16%	[0.08696 , 0.25000]
2.0	[-0.02004 , 0.35314]	168.68%	[0.08318 , 0.22231]	0.18%	[0.08333 , 0.22222]
2.5	$[-\infty, +\infty]$		[0.07985 , 0.20007]	0.19%	[0.08000 , 0.20000]
3.0			[0.07678 , 0.18188]	0.19%	[0.07692 , 0.18182]
3.5			[0.07394 , 0.16672]	0.20%	[0.07407 , 0.16667]
4.0			[0.07131 , 0.15389]	0.21%	[0.07143 , 0.15385]
4.5			[0.06885 , 0.14290]	0.21%	[0.06897 , 0.14286]
5.0			[0.06656 , 0.13337]	0.21%	[0.06667 , 0.13333]

Table 2. ODE $u'(t) = -u^2(t)$

given. As can be seen, the intervals of the traditional Taylor method grow quickly, although this function is actually contracting. The piecewise interval extension, on the other hand, is close to the exact solutions and is able to exploit the contraction characteristics of the function.

Consider now the ODE $u'(t) = -u^2(t)$ for an initial box $[0.1, 0.4]$ at $t_0 = 0$. Table 2 compares the results obtained by a mean value form of a Taylor method of order 4, the results obtained by the piecewise interval extension of the Taylor method of order 4, and the exact solutions. Once again, it can be seen that the standard method leads to an explosion of the size of the intervals, while the piecewise interval extension is close to the exact results. Note that the Taylor method of order 4 also behaves badly on this ODE.

Consider now the system

$$\begin{cases} u_1'(t) = -u_1(t) - 2u_2(t) \\ u_2'(t) = -3u_1(t) - 2u_2(t) \end{cases}$$

for an initial box ([5.9,6.1],[3.9,4.1]) at $t_0 = 0$. Table 3 compares the results obtained by an interval Taylor method of order 4, the results obtained by the piecewise interval extension of the same method, and the exact solutions. Once again, similar results can be observed.

t	dim	Taylor		Piecewise Taylor		Exact solution
		Result	*Error*	*Result*	*Error*	
0.0	u1	[5.90000 , 6.10000]	0.0%	[5.90000 , 6.10000]	0.00%	[5.90000 , 6.10000]
	u2	[3.90000 , 4.10000]	0.0%	[3.90000 , 4.10000]	0.00%	[3.90000 , 4.10000]
0.1	u1	[4.75414 , 5.02917]	24.4%	[4.78106 , 5.00225]	0.07%	[4.78111 , 5.00214]
	u2	[1.70100 , 1.92226]	0.1%	[1.70100 , 1.92226]	0.10%	[1.70106 , 1.92210]
0.2	u1	[4.05742 , 4.42291]	49.6%	[4.11788 , 4.36246]	0.12%	[4.11798 , 4.36226]
	u2	[0.06566 , 0.44081]	53.6%	[0.13089 , 0.37558]	0.17%	[0.13103 , 0.37531]
0.3	u1	[3.65219 , 4.15688]	86.9%	[3.76933 , 4.03975]	0.17%	[3.76951 , 4.03948]
	u2	[-1.19270 , -0.59227]	122.4%	[-1.02776 , -0.75721]	0.21%	[-1.02754 , -0.75757]
0.4	u1	[3.43316 , 4.14938]	140.1%	[3.64179 , 3.94076]	0.20%	[3.64205 , 3.94042]
	u2	[-2.23853 , -1.30590]	212.6%	[-1.92176 , -1.62266]	0.25%	[-1.92145 , -1.62309]
0.5	u1	[3.32116 , 4.35646]	214.0%	[3.67355 , 4.00407]	0.24%	[3.67391 , 4.00366]
	u2	[-3.19776 , -1.77303]	332.1%	[-2.65071 , -2.32006]	0.27%	[-2.65030 , -2.32056]
⋮						
0.8	u1	[2.96130 , 6.26697]	642.7%	[4.39089 , 4.83740]	0.32%	[4.39158 , 4.83669]
	u2	[-6.63827 , -1.77474]	992.7%	[-4.42981 , -3.98317]	0.34%	[-4.42906 , -3.98396]
0.9	u1	[2.57376 , 7.48325]	898.0%	[4.78171 , 5.27530]	0.34%	[4.78254 , 5.27446]
	u2	[-8.39440 , -1.11612]	1379.6%	[-5.00212 , -4.50839]	0.37%	[-5.00122 , -4.50930]
1.0	u1	[1.85766 , 9.16200]	1243.6%	[5.23702 , 5.78264]	0.36%	[5.23800 , 5.78165]
	u2	[-10.76604 , 0.11270]	1901.0%	[-5.59955 , -5.05378]	0.39%	[-5.59850 , -5.05484]

Table 3. ODE $u_1'(t) = -u_1(t) - 2u_2(t)$ and $u_2'(t) = -3u_1(t) - 2u_2(t)$

9 Conclusion

This paper studied the application of interval analysis and consistency techniques to ordinary differential equations. It presented a unifying framework to extend traditional numerical techniques to intervals showing, in particular, how to extend explicit one-step methods to intervals. The paper also took a fresh look at the traditional problems encountered by interval techniques and studied how consistency techniques may help. It proposed to generalize interval techniques into a two-step process: a forward process that computes an enclosure and a backward process that reduces this enclosure. In addition, the paper studied how consistency techniques may help in improving the forward process and the wrapping effect. Very preliminary results indicate the potential benefits of the approach. Our current work focuses on the full implementation and experimental evaluation of the techniques proposed in this paper in order to determine which combinations of these techniques will be effective in practice. Future work will also be devoted to the application of consistency techniques to ODE systems with boundary values, since interval analysis and consistency techniques are particularly well-adapted when compared to traditional methods (as observed by several members of the community).

Acknowledgment

Many thanks to Philippe Delsarte and Jean Mawhin for fruitfull discussions. This research is partially supported by the *Actions de recherche concertées (ARC/95/00-187)* of the Direction générale de la Recherche Scientifique – Communauté Française de Belgique and by an NSF NYI award.

References

[Abe88] Oliver Aberth. *Precise Numerical Analysis.* William Brown, Dubuque, Iowa, 1988.

[BBCG96] Martin Berz, Christian Bischof, George Corliss, and Andreas Griewank, editors. *Computational Differentiation: Techniques, Applications, and Tools.* SIAM, Philadelphia, Penn., 1996.

[Cor88] George F. Corliss. Applications of differentiation arithmetic. In Ramon E. Moore, editor, *Reliability in Computing*, pages 127–148. Academic Press, London, 1988.

[Cor95] G.F. Corliss. *Theory of Numerics in Ordinary and Partial Diffential Equations (W.A. Light, M. Machetta (Eds)*, volume Vol IV, chapter Guaranteed Error Bounds for Ordinary Differential Equations, pages 1–75. Oxford University Press, 1995.

[DJVH98] Y. Deville, M. Janssen, and P. Van Hentenryck. Consistency Techniques in Ordinary Differential Equations. Technical Report TR98-06, Université catholique de Louvain, July 1998.

[DS76] D.P. Davey and N.F. Stewart. Guaranteed Error Bounds for the Initial Value problem Using Polytope Arithmetic. *BIT*, 16:257–268, 1976.

[Har64] Ph. Hartman. *Ordinary Differential Equations.* Wiley, New York, 1964.

[Hen62] P. Henrici. *Discrete Variable Methods in Ordinary Differential Equations.* John Wiley & Sons, New York, 1962.

[Loh87] Rudolf J. Lohner. Enclosing the solutions of ordinary initial and boundary value problems. In Edgar W. Kaucher, Ulrich W. Kulisch, and Christian Ullrich, editors, *Computer Arithmetic: Scientific Computation and Programming Languages*, pages 255–286. Wiley-Teubner Series in Computer Science, Stuttgart, 1987.

[Moo66] R.E. Moore. *Interval Analysis.* Prentice-Hall, Englewood Cliffs, NJ, 1966.

[Moo79] R.E. Moore. *Methods and Applications of Interval Analysis.* SIAM Publ., 1979.

[Ral80] Louis B. Rall. Applications of software for automatic differentiation in numerical computation. In Götz Alefeld and R. D. Grigorieff, editors, *Fundamentals of Numerical Computation (Computer Oriented Numerical Analysis)*, Computing Supplement No. 2, pages 141–156. Springer-Verlag, Berlin, 1980.

[Ral81] Louis B. Rall. *Automatic Differentiation: Techniques and Applications*, volume 120 of *Lecture Notes in Computer Science.* Springer-Verlag, Berlin, 1981.

[Sta96] O. Stauning. Enclosing Solutions of Ordinary Differential Equations. Technical Report Tech. Report IMM-REP-1996-18, Technical University Of Denmark, 1996.

[Ste71] N.F. Stewart. A Heuristic to Reduce the Wrapping Effect in the Numerical Solution of ODE. *BIT*, 11:328–337, 1971.

[VHLD97] P. Van Hentenryck, M. Laurent, and Y. Deville. *Numerica, A Modeling Language for Global Optimization.* MIT Press, 1997.

[VHSDar] P. Van Hentenryck, V. Saraswat, and Y. Deville. The Design, Implementation, and Evaluation of the Constraint Language cc(FD). *Journal of Logic Programming (Special Issue on Constraint Logic Programming)*, 1998 (to appear).

Early Projection in CLP($\mathcal{R}$)

Andreas Fordan[1] and Roland H.C. Yap[2]

[1] GMD-FIRST Berlin, Germany, fordan@gmd.de
[2] School of Computing, National University of Singapore, ryap@comp.nus.edu.sg

Abstract. During the evaluation of a constraint logic program, many local variables become inaccessible, or *dead*. In Prolog and other programming languages, the data bound to local variables can be removed automatically by garbage collection. The case of CLP is more complex, as the variables may be involved in several constraints. We can consider dead variables to be existentially quantified. Removing an existential variable from a set of constraints is then a problem of *quantifier elimination*, or *projection*. Eliminating variables not only allows recovery of space but also can decrease the cost of further consistency tests. Surprisingly, the existing systems do not exploit these advantages. Instead, the primary use of projection is as a mechanism for obtaining answer constraints. In this paper, we will give a general system architecture for automatic early projection and specify the heuristics for CLP($\mathcal{R}$) together with an in-situ removal method. We then show the effectiveness of early projection by applying it to some practical planning problems.

1 Introduction

The CLP framework [10], gives a scheme for integrating constraint and logic programming where the logic programming component provides the underlying inference engine and programming capabilities and the constraint system provides the fundamental constraint operations over some chosen domain. An important aspect of a CLP language/system is the requirement to detect during evaluation if a system of constraints is infeasible. In this paper, we will show that constraint projection is another useful operation in the evaluation of a CLP program. Linear arithmetic constraint domains provide complete solving methods as well as complete projection methods. Most of the existing systems with real arithmetic constraints like CLP($\mathcal{R}$) [14, 4] and ECL^{i}PS^e [6] make use of a projection on the query variables. The purpose of the projection is to present the answer constraints in a concise and 'nice' form. For every query, only a single projection is done to obtain the answer constraints.[1] These systems basically employ variants of the Fourier method [18, 11] for that purpose.

Projection however can be applied to more than just producing answer constraints. It is a powerful instrument for removing existentially quantified variables from the constraint store during execution. The major reasons why an early projection can be advantageous are to:

[1] CLP($\mathcal{R}$) also provides dump which projects the constraint store onto a set of variables.

- reduce the size of the constraint store giving space savings,
- speedup constraint solving due to the store having fewer constraints,
- enable more efficient answer projection.

Consider the CLP clause below (let $\boldsymbol{t_i}$ denote a sequence of terms, $C(\boldsymbol{t_0})$ a set of constraints and p, p_i predicate symbols):

$$p(\boldsymbol{t}) \quad \leftarrow \quad C(\boldsymbol{t_0}),\ p_1(\boldsymbol{t_1}),\ \ldots, p_n(\boldsymbol{t_n}) \tag{1}$$

The local variables in the clause are conventionally considered to be existentially quantified. When they become inaccessible, or *dead*, they can be eliminated from the store. Nevertheless, there are several reasons why it may be inappropriate or not possible to perform elimination. Firstly, the store is not always decreased or simplified by this operation. Secondly, the variable may be referred to again because of backtracking. Thirdly, for some domains[2] there may not be any efficient elimination algorithm or perhaps variable removal is not possible.

In this paper, we shall develop a general architecture of early projection. We classify elimination heuristics into conservative and progressive, taking the above considerations into account. A conservative system will avoid risky projections, thus be more transparent to the user. The aspect of control is more strongly emphasized in progressive systems, the user is responsible for the order and time of eliminations.

Consider the following CLP($\mathcal{R}$) example, from [2], which illustrates how extraneous local variables in the store can be costly:

```
p(0,X) :- X<=1.
p(N,X) :- N>0, p(N-1,Y), X<=Y.
```

The time for the evaluation of `:- p(500,X).` is about 12 seconds in CLP($\mathcal{R}$) 1.2 running on a Sun 5. If we enforce a projection after every rule application, it is about 100 times faster. For a given memory size where the largest `N` for a query is 500, applying early projection allows `N` to increase to 11,000. This example illustrates how projection can give both faster constraint solving during evaluation and faster answer projection because of the smaller store. Applying early projection means that the maximum number of inequalities during evaluation is two, without projection the number grows linearly with `N`.[3]

In section 2, we investigate when local variables become inaccessible and safety properties for elimination. Section 3 presents a framework for automatic early projection in CLP(X). We give a general system architecture of automatic early projection. The aspect of control is discussed. Section 4 applies this framework to CLP($\mathcal{R}$). We specify suitable heuristics and tackle the problem of in-situ elimination. Finally, we apply early projection to two practical planning problems that involve expensive projections.

[2] The important case of Finite Domains is discussed in [3].

[3] At every iteration of the second rule, we get $Y \leq 1, X \leq 1$.

1.1 Related Work

Techniques for the projection of linear constraints have been developed for CLP, see [8,9,7]. In CLP($\mathcal{R}$), answer constraints was developed in [14,11] which dealt with projection (linear and others) and other presentation issues. The above elimination techniques are suited in principle for early projection as well.

The present work does not give a new elimination method, rather we present a framework for early projection. The interplay between the Prolog engine, the solver, and the projection is defined. A general CLP system architecture for automatic elimination is developed. The closest related work is [17] which uses static program analysis to determine dead variables at compile time. A CLP($\mathcal{R}$) program analyzer and compiler is described in [15,16] which provides dead variable removal as one optimization among others. The advantage of the program analysis approach is that no runtime overhead is imposed for dead variable detection. However, the effectiveness will depend on the accuracy of the analysis in detecting dead variables. Thus, it is complementary to our approach of dynamic run-time detection and removal.[4] In [15,16], the optimizations concentrate on the case of variable removal in linear equations. In this paper, we consider the general case of variable removal and also specifically linear inequalities.

2 Quantifiers in Resolution

Projection is an important vehicle for simplifying problems by reducing their dimension. The eliminated variables can be considered to be existentially quantified. Thus these variables only occur temporarily during the lifetime of evaluation. In programming languages, such temporary variables are often called *local*. (Constraint) logic programming provides for an automatic allocation and deallocation of data in the scope of local procedure variables.

Definition 1. *The local variables of a (constraint) clause (1) (cf. introduction) are those which occur in the body but not in the head:* $\bigcup_{i=1}^{n} vars(\boldsymbol{t_i}) \setminus vars(\boldsymbol{t})$.

2.1 Dead Variables

We start with the basic definitions of resolution:

Definition 2. *A subgoal, written as S, is either an atom or a constraint. A constraint goal G is of the form $S_1, \ldots, S_m$. Let A denote an atom. A constraint clause is a formula $A \leftarrow G$.*

Definition 3. *Let $S_1, \ldots, S_m$ be a constraint goal and C a constraint. The pair $\langle G', C'\rangle$ is said to be derived from $\langle S_1, \ldots, S_m; C\rangle$ if the underlying computation rule R selects $R(S_1, \ldots, S_m) = S_k$, and*

- *if S_k is a constraint, $C' = C \wedge S_k$, $\mathcal{D} \models \exists C'$ and $G' = S_1, \ldots, S_{k-1}, S_{k+1}, \ldots, S_m$.*

[4] Combining analysis with our approach is possible but beyond the scope of this paper.

– *if S_k is an atom, $A \leftarrow G$ a constraint clause, $C' = C \wedge A = S_k$, $\mathcal{D} \models \exists C'$, and $G' = S_1, \ldots, S_{k-1}, G, S_{k+1}, \ldots, S_m$.*

A derivation is a sequence $\langle G_1, C_1\rangle, \ldots, \langle G_n, C_n\rangle$ where $\langle G_i, C_i\rangle$ is derived from $\langle G_{i-1}, C_{i-1}\rangle$. It is called successful if G_n is empty. In this case, C_n is the computed answer of the derivation.

As local variables are implicitly existentially quantified, it may be possible to remove them after the clause has been completely evaluated. For top-down evaluation, the elimination can often be committed earlier.

Definition 4. *A variable x in a derivation $\langle G_1, C_1\rangle, \ldots, \langle G_k, C_k\rangle$ is called textually dead at step k if x occurs in some goal $G_2, \ldots, G_{k-1}$ but not in G_1 and not in G_k.*

Variables in G_1 are query variables and by definition not dead. A textually dead variable x is then, a variable which is neither a query variable nor does it occur in any further derivation. Once a variable becomes textually dead, it remains so in further derivations. Observe that k is not required to be the earliest time when x becomes dead. This allows some flexibility in deciding when to eliminate x (see Section 3). The textually dead condition is not sufficient to prevent x from being accessed again, for example, if x is aliased because it occurs in some syntactical equations, the binding of some other alive variable can potentially access x after step k.

Definition 5. *A variable x is said to be shared with another variable y if $y = t$ is implied by the constraint store C where t is a term containing x (including just x). Let SHARED(x) denote the set of all variables y in C that x is shared with.*

Definition 6. *Let C_k be the constraint store at a derivation step k and x be textually dead at step k. If the variables in SHARED(x) are also textually dead, then x is called access dead, or simply dead.*

Note that the definition here differs from [17] which also considers delayed non-linear constraints in CLP($\mathcal{R}$). We treat non-linears using the elimination buffer heuristics (section 3.3), which allows more generality for specific CLP implementations.

Proposition 1. *A dead variable x may be removed from C_k without affecting the derivation.*

Definition 7. *Let x be a dead variable at step k with $1 < k \leq n$ in the derivation $\langle G_1, C_1\rangle, \ldots, \langle G_n, C_n\rangle$. Replacing C_k by a C'_k equivalent to $\exists x\ C_k$ in the course of the derivation is referred to as early projection. If x is eliminated in C_n, the process is called answer projection.*

However, the removal of dead variables is not always desirable:

- The elimination may conflict with the need to restore the constraint store during backtracking, cf. section 2.2.
- For some domains such as non-linear real constraints, no general efficient elimination method is known. Even elimination in linear arithmetic constraints bears certain risks. A heuristic might indicate when an elimination is too expensive. With syntactic terms equations, elimination is not possible, in general.

In such cases, x remains in C_k.

2.2 Safe Variables

Before some variable is going to be eliminated, the interaction between projection and backtracking should be considered. Backtracking means that the projection done may create unnecessary work. A method to *undo* the projection is also required. In general, this can be expensive since we would be forced to save the constraint state before the projection[5] to be able to restore it. We now define when to eliminate variables safely taking backtracking into account.

Definition 8. *The (historical) subgoal sequence of a derivation* $\langle G_1, C_1\rangle, \ldots, \langle G_n, C_n\rangle$ *is the sequence* $S_1, \ldots, S_n = R(G_1), \ldots, R(G_n)$ *of those subgoals selected for resolution by the underlying computation rule R. Assuming an ordering on a procedure's clauses, we call an atom* S_i *backtrackable if the selected clause in the derivation is not the last clause selected from the predicate* S_i *of the form* $S_i \leftarrow G$*. A subgoal sequence is successful if the corresponding derivation is successful. The constraint (store) of a subgoal sequence is*

$$\bigwedge_{1 \le i \le n,\ S_i \text{ is a constraint}} S_i.$$

Note that the constraint store of a successful subgoal sequence is equivalent to the computed answer of the corresponding derivation.

The subgoal sequence reflects the order in which the subgoals are resolved. For example, consider the goal `:- p(X,A), A=2.` with the following program:

```
p(X,A) :- Y<=A, q(A), X=2*Y.        q(1).      q(2).
```

The historical subgoal sequence starts as follows: `p(X,A)`^{1}, `Y<=A`^{2}, `q(A)`^{3}, `A=1`^{4}, `X=2*Y`^{5}. The superscripts give the historical order. As `Y` is dead after goal 5, we may wish to eliminate it from the store. Thus, we replace the three constraints `Y<=A`^{2}, `A=1`^{4} and `X=2*Y`^{5} by `A=1,X<=2`. Execution proceeds with `A=2`^{6} which initiates backtracking. Prolog execution has a choice point for goal 3. Backtracking then requires that we recover the constraint store from goals 3 to 5. Suppose that the constraint store is not saved during elimination, we now cannot distinguish between the constraints in the store that come from goals no. 4/5 with

[5] Nevertheless, this is done in the answer presentation of CLP($\mathcal{R}$). In this special case it is reasonable because only one step is necessary.

that from no. 2. In undoing goals 4 and 5, we can only choose to delete `X<=2` or not. But after `r(A)` has been backtracked, both decisions lead to the difficulty that reprocessing `X=2*Y` at the new goal no. 5 relates to the variable `Y`, which does not exist anymore. The following definition generalizes this prohibiting effect. We could of course save the constraint store for backtracking but this would mean that using elimination could possibly be more expensive than not using elimination.

Definition 9. *We call a variable x unsafe in a derivation if the corresponding subgoal sequence is of the form $S_1, \ldots, L, \ldots, B, \ldots, R, \ldots, S_n$, where B is backtrackable, and L, R are constraints on x. If x is not unsafe and x is dead at a certain step of the derivation, x is called safe (to eliminate) at this step.*

Definition 10. *The elimination of x in a subgoal sequence $S_1, \ldots, S_n$ is as follows. Let $S_{i_1}, \ldots, S_{i_s}$ be those constraints from $S_1, \ldots, S_n$ containing x. Let P be equivalent to $\exists x: S_{i_1} \wedge \ldots \wedge S_{i_s}$. Replace S_{i_1} by P and drop S_{i_j} for $j \neq 1$.*[6]

Theorem 1. *The elimination of a safe variable x in a subgoal sequence $\mathcal{S}$ obtaining $\mathcal{S}'$ yields equivalent constraint stores after undoing the subgoals to the right of the last backtrackable goal in $\mathcal{S}$ respectively $\mathcal{S}'$.*

Proof. It is enough to consider the constraints $S_{i_1}, \ldots, S_{i_s}$ with $1 < i_1 \leq \cdots \leq i_s \leq k$ in the store which contain x. Let S_b be the last backtrackable goal. As x is safe, either $b < i_1$ or $i_s < b$ holds. If $i_s < b$ then x is not affected by the undoing. If $b < i_1$, then all $S_{i_1}, \ldots, S_{i_s}$ are deleted simultaneously in $\mathcal{S}$, which is equivalent to removing S'_{i_s} which was defined equivalent to $\exists x: S_{i_1} \wedge \ldots \wedge S_{i_s}$ in $\mathcal{S}'$. □

3 Automatic Early Projection

Once we are able to quickly detect the candidates for early elimination, heuristics must be found to decide whether elimination is wise. We will give a system architecture suited to initialize the projection. We will argue for certain forms of heuristics and discuss some aspects of control.

3.1 Detection of Dead Variables

Dead variables can be statically detected using program analysis techniques. One such approach for CLP($\mathcal{R}$) using abstract interpretation is given in [17]. Such an approach has to be tailored for a specific CLP domain and implementation.

We propose an alternate approach which extends the WAM to provide runtime support for detecting dead variables dynamically. Due to the lack of space, the extension is only sketched using an example. We add to the WAM a mechanism for detecting when variables are dead, subject to some safety conditions. These variables are then reported to the elimination module of the solver which chooses to project some or all such reported dead variables away. Consider the **`sumprod/3`** program from [17] below.

[6] Note that the S_{i_j} are not necessarily contiguous.

```
sumprod(0, [], 0).
sumprod(S, L, N) :-
    L = [H|L1], try_elim(L),
    S = T + S1, try_elim(S),
    T = H * N, elim(T), elim(H),
    N1 = N - 1, try_elim(N),
    release(S1), release(L1), release(N1), sumprod(S1, L1, N1).
```

The three new WAM instructions, in italics above, illustrate how the last use of a variable is reported to the solver elimination module. Every rule variable is treated by exactly one of these commands at its last textual occurrence in the rule body. Initially a variable is *blocked* from elimination. The last occurrence of a local variable, which is in a constraint, is reported using *elim/1*. This instruction reports a variable even if it is blocked (this saves a *release/1* in contrast to *try_elim/1*). If instead the variable is in an atom, we use *release/1* to unblock the local variable before the call. The last occurrences of head variables are annotated with *try_elim/1* which only reports if the variable is unblocked.

The scheme above only provides for detection of textually dead variables. In order to recognize whether x is dead, another mechanism is required to decide if x has any sharing with non-dead variables. Most CLP systems would use a Prolog style unification/binding mechanism, which separates Herbrand variables where term equation constraints are implemented by variable binding from other constraint domain variables. In other words, a textually dead variable x is dead if and only if it is not multiply referenced. One possible solution to detect if a variable/term is no longer referenced is to use reference counting.[7] Cells on the heap are extended with a reference count which is incremented by the WAM whenever a reference to this cell occurs in unification.

The *elim(x)* command then decrements the reference count of x. If x is safe (section 2.2) and no longer referenced now (count=0), it is reported to the elimination module. If x is a structure $f(c_1, \ldots, c_n)$ on the heap, *elim/1* is called recursively for all $c_1, \ldots, c_n$. Note that this method gives a form of garbage collection.

3.2 Detection of Safe Variables

We now address a run-time detection mechanism for detecting safe variables based on the WAM. We assume that there is some means of keeping track of the historical order of the solver variables. For example, the abstract machine of CLP($\mathcal{R}$), the CLAM [12], associates historical subscripts to the solver variables.

We introduce a flag to each solver variable x to mark its backtrack state. Initially, x is unmarked. The WAM maintains some data fields per choice point *CP*. We introduce a new field btk_svar to reference the most recent solver variable at the time of *CP*'s creation. If the abstract machine encounters a constraint on x and x is older than btk_svar of the most recent choice point, then x is marked.

[7] We assume that terms are only finite, thus there are no cyclic structures to complicate reference counting.

So far, we did not consider backtracking. The trail in the CLAM is modified to a 'tagged value trail', as not only logical variable bindings have to be undone but also certain constraint operations. We use such a tagged trail to introduce a new type of trail data, *unmarkers*. When a (previously unmarked) solver variable x is marked, an unmarker referencing to x is pushed on the trail. During the undoing phase, any unmarker popped from the trail simply unmarks the variable.

Proposition 2. *Unmarked dead variables are safe.*

3.3 System Architecture

As before, we assume a modern CLP system based on an abstract WAM-like machine extended with mechanisms for detecting dead and safe variables. We also assume that the constraint solver has a mechanism for doing projection.

Next, we introduce a new system module, called the *elimination buffer*, containing a memory for dead variables and heuristics. Heuristics may initiate the elimination of some variable in the buffer, or prevent this. Fig. 1 illustrates the system architecture of a CLP system extended by an elimination buffer. The elimination buffer keeps all reported variables that occur actually in the constraint store. Elimination heuristics decide when it is wise to eliminate (a group of) variables. In this case, the solver is commanded to perform the projection. We propose two kinds of heuristics:

- A conservative approach. We may take the viewpoint that the user should not know about the automatic projection. In this case, the slow-down must be minimal. Only some projections which are known to be computationally cheap can be performed. For example with inequalities, the number of constraints is decreased by eliminating x, if x occurs at most once with positive (negative) coefficient in the store.
- A progressive approach. We might argue that the user has to know about the projection anyway, e.g. because the answer projection can consume considerable time. Moreover, a constraint clause can be interpreted as a command to eliminate the dead variables after the rule application. Thus, we should

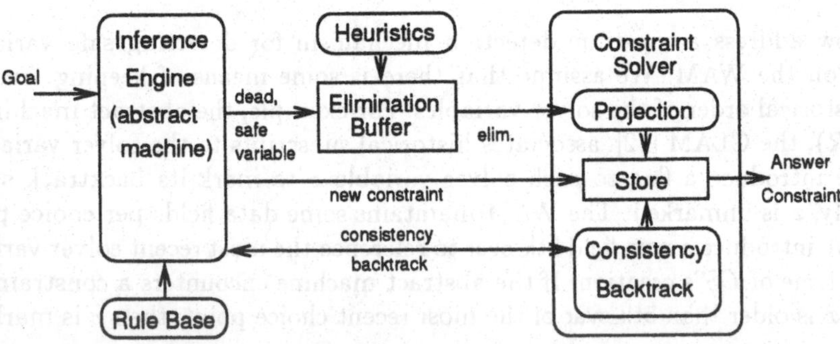

Fig. 1. Extended architecture

eliminate any variable we can. The user has a language-inherent means of control to prevent CLP($\mathcal{R}$) from elimination: the variable can be included in the head of the clause.[8]

Note that it can be useful to perform projection only from time to time, for instance, the Fourier algorithm does not apply to the Simplex solved form directly.

3.4 Controlling Automatic Projection

A clause containing existential variables can be considered as a command for an automatic deduction system to eliminate those variables after use. Unfortunately, this can be very inefficient in some cases. It could be advantageous to defer the elimination to a more suitable time, or even to preserve the existential quantifier in the answer. A system providing automatic early projection can try to predict the best time following some conservative or progressive guidelines. In some cases, it may be clear that an elimination is not wise.

For example, suppose that a program has a variable to represent a global error function which could be involved in most of the constraints. Its elimination using the Fourier or other projection methods could therefore be expensive. In this case, it is natural that the error variable is not eliminated.

Remark 2 *The user can always prevent variables from being eliminated. In cases of doubt, the program can be rewritten, such that those variables are included in the relevant rule heads, i.e. they are made target variables.*

In practice, we will not eliminate all dead variables but only the safe ones (cf. Def. 9), as otherwise handling backtracking introduces additional costs. We have introduced a mechanism for the efficient detection of safe variables not requiring any undoing of the projection, in section 3.2. But the price to pay for this efficiency is that it might be sometimes unpredictable for the programmer to know when a certain variable is eliminated, or when it is unsafe. In this section, we try to give the programmer an intuition whether and how a variable can be purposely made safe.

Note there are problems for which no program with only safe variables exists. For instance compute the constraint for $z = xy$ where $(x \geq -1 \lor x \leq 1) \land (y \geq -2 \lor y \leq 2)$. One program for this is:

```
p(Z) :- q(X), r(Y), Z=X*Y.
```

with corresponding definitions for `q/1` and `r/1`. There is no permutation of the three subgoals such that z is a safe variable during the execution.

The user has often an intuition whether a predicate is deterministic or not. A predicate is deterministic if for any call, only one answer is generated. If we want to make a local variable x of some rule body safe, it is better if we order the subgoals in the rule bodies as follows:

[8] Annotations to block a variable can also be added for convenience.

Definition 11. *A local variable x in a clause body is called (quasi-)syntactically safe if x is not contained in an (indeterministic) atom or in two constraints separated by an (indeterministic) atom.*

Theorem 3. *Variables in the binding of a (quasi-)syntactically safe variable x in a clause are safe to eliminate after the application of that clause, if they are not shared.*

Proof. Suppose that the clause has been already applied. Then the subgoal sequence $\langle G_i, C_i\rangle, \ldots, \langle G_j, C_j\rangle$ produced for the derivation of the body has the following properties. First, $G_i, \ldots, G_j$ are the only possible subgoals of the overall sequence referring to x. Thus x is textually dead at step $j+1$. Second, there is no indeterministic evaluation between two constraints on x and hence no backtrackable goal. □

Note that a syntactically safe variable guarantees safe variables only in the sense that these are *textually* dead after the application of the clause, but not necessarily access dead. This is intuitive as we would not expect that a variable is eliminated and then further referred to in the program.

4 Early Projection in CLP($\mathcal{R}$)

After presenting the case for a general architecture and mechanism for early projection in CLP, we now turn to CLP($\mathcal{R}$) as a driving example for applying early projection to the real number domain.

4.1 Heuristics

Elimination heuristics have to estimate the cost of an elimination. The cost of (Gaussian) elimination can be estimated from the number of occurrences of the variable in the constraint store and whether the variable is parametric or non-parametric ([17] emphasizes the non-parametric case which is cheap). Since linear equation solving is typically less expensive than inequalities, we would often prefer the elimination of a variable which is only involved in linear equations, particularly if it is non-parametric.

As for the linear inequalities, the cost of a Fourier elimination step can be estimated by the number of constraints generated resp. removed. Let N and P be the number of inequalities in the equalities $\mathcal{C}$ which contain the variable x with positive, resp. negative coefficient. The special case $N = 0$ or $P = 0$ is called *trivial* step and should be preferred to all other eliminations.

The elimination of x generates NP constraints deleting $N + P$ ones. Thus we define $measure(\mathcal{C}, x) = NP - N - P$. A conservative heuristic could be $measure(\mathcal{C}, x) < 0$. The conservative case holds if $P \leq 1$ or $N \leq 1$. We could also decide to include the case $N = P = 2$ tantamount to $measure(\mathcal{C}, x) = 0$.

When a variable enters the elimination buffer, its occurrences in the store are counted and the variable is annotated by the values N and P. We propose to categorize the variables into four classes: (1) the trivial Fourier variables, (2) variables occurring in the equations, (3) the conservative buffer, (4) the progressive buffer. During the elimination, N, P and the mapping of the variables to the four categories is realized.

A progressive heuristic could be e.g. unconditional elimination, similar to the existing answer projection [11]. Unfortunately, this may lead to a very suboptimal elimination order of the variables. Such eliminations should not be enforced. In some rare cases, it could still be advantageous when most of the generated constraints are removed by some redundancy check afterwards. Nevertheless, generation plus removal represent considerable expense which conflicts somewhat with the goal of *early* projection to save time and space. A weaker progressive condition would be, e.g., $N \leq 2$ or $P \leq 2$.

CLP($\mathcal{R}$) delays non-linear constraints until they become linear. This means that as in [11], such variables in non-linears are not eliminable even if they are textually dead. In CLP($\mathcal{R}$), this can be easily checked (using the non-linear hard constraint data structures [13]) to prevent any reported variable which is involved in non-linears from being removed. Some removal is possible by examining the form of the non-linears. This heuristic can be generalised to any system which utilises an incomplete solver and also systems which provide delayed predicates such as **freeze**.

4.2 In-Situ Removal

Early projection in CLP($\mathcal{R}$) faces the problem that the inequalities in the constraint store are in solved form, i.e. in a simplex tableau form, while the Fourier algorithm applies only to the canonical form. Of course, it is possible to regain this form by a sequence of suitable pivot operations as with answer projection [11]. The essential disadvantage of this general strategy is that after the projection, the constraints—although trivially feasible—have to be 'solved' anew since the new constraints generated by projection are no longer in solved form.

For the conservative case (see above) however, we are able to perform the elimination *in situ*, i.e. directly in the tableau. Due to lack of space, we can only give an informal description. In the following, we assume familiarity with the simplex algorithm. We distinguish the two conservative cases (1) $N=0$ called *trivial* case and (2) $N = 1$ called *single* case (cases $P = 0$ resp. $P = 1$ are omitted here w.l.o.g.).

Consider the trivial case first. All occurrences of our variable x are positive. Let $s_1, \ldots, s_P$ denote the slack variables of the corresponding inequalities. Eliminating x clearly mounts to remove all these inequalities. Assume that s_i is a basic variable. Dropping the corresponding row will remove the corresponding inequality from the store. If s_i is non-basic, we compute, similar to the simplex algorithm, an exit equation for s_i that preserves the solved form and make s_i basic using one pivot operation. When $s_1, \ldots, s_P$ are removed, the column of x will be empty and can be dropped.

Now consider the single case. Let s denote the slack variable associated to the single occurrence and $s_1, \ldots, s_P$ be defined as above. Assume that x is basic and

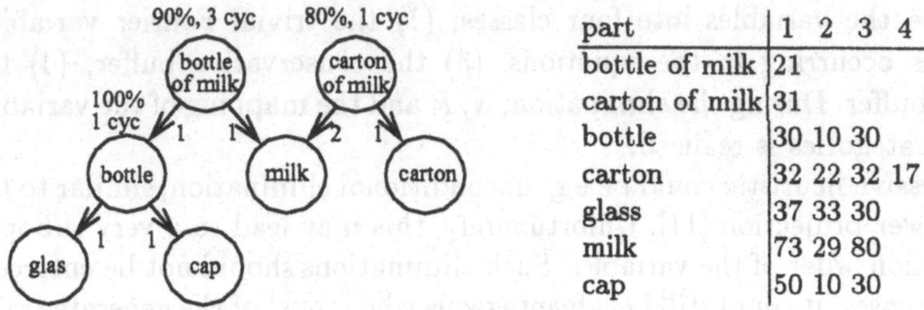

part	1	2	3	4
bottle of milk	21			
carton of milk	31			
bottle	30	10	30	
carton	32	22	32	17
glass	37	33	30	
milk	73	29	80	
cap	50	10	30	

Fig. 2. BOM and availabilities of a dairy farm

s is non-basic. Dropping the row of x eliminates x from the system but does not decrease the constraints. Dropping the column of s in the tableau is equivalent to setting $s = 0$, i.e. the inequality associated to s becomes an equality. This corresponds exactly to what the Fourier algorithm does in this case: replacing x in the multiple occurrence using the single occurrence. If x is non-basic, we can apply the technique mentioned for the trivial case to make it basic. If s is basic, we can either decide to defer the removal or to run a simplex (which never required more than one pivot operation in our experience) to make it non-basic.

The above strategies presuppose that s and $s_1, \ldots, s_P$ are known. Unfortunately, they are not efficiently derivable from the tableau. In order to keep track of x's occurrences, a copy of the original inequalities is maintained (the detection of implicit equalities uses these anyway [19]) and Fourier is performed on them in parallel for the conservative cases. Note that those variables that do not meet the conservative condition are kept in the elimination buffer as they might become conservative in the course of the projection.

5 Practical Examples

Recall the toy example from the introduction. Early projection has given both desired effects, acceleration of solving as well as answer generation. In this simple case, conservative and progressive elimination obtain the same result. This section investigates more complex problems.

5.1 Materials Requirements Planning

The Can-Build problem was defined in [5, 2]. It is an availability-controlled model of materials requirements planning. The availabilities are seen as the hardest constraints on a production plan. Given a bill of material (BOM) and a table of availabilities[9] as in Fig. 2, we can construct a generalized production plan, i.e. a non-ground constraint representing the possible plans.

In order to construct the plan of a part, the plans of its components must be known. For instance, glass and cap are used to construct the bottle. The milk

[9] The table denotes that e.g. 50 caps are available in day 1, 60 in day 2, etc.

as a shared part is split before used for the two products. Note that most of the variables used in this process are redundant. When the plan for the bottle is finished, the plans of glass and cap become redundant. This will intuitively be expressed using local variables in any CLP($\mathcal{R}$) modeling of Can-Build. It is essential to remove them from the store since afterwards, an analysis tool will perform many expensive computations using the generalized production plan.

The following table shows some benchmarks on the effects of conservative early projection[10] on the performance of Can-Build problems:

	early projection			answer projection		
instance	solving	output	solver nodes	solving	output	solver nodes
dairy	0.06s	0.01s	574	0.03s	0.03s	2213
dairy2	0.46s	0.07s	3725	0.23s	0.32s	12645
dairy3	0.66s	0.18s	4229	0.33s	0.80s	16741
dairy4	1.86s	0.28s	9539	0.60s	2.62s	35786

The projection does not accelerate the solver. This is due to the particular format of Can-Build constraints which are trivially feasible and hardly require any pivot operations. The overall computation time (solving+output) is improved by early projection, especially for large examples. The main effect however is the recovery of solver space. The space consumption for the used example was approximately reduced to 1/4. Obviously, this helps solving much bigger Can-Build instances.

5.2 Flow-Show Scheduling

The FAKOS system developed at Daimler-Benz Research Labs Berlin is a flow shop scheduling system from the Mercedes automobile production plant in Sindelfingen. Fig. 3 illustrates a possible scenario which is close to a realistically sized problem [1]. The nodes of the graph are *production units* denoted by capital letters. The lower case letters represent different *types* of the products. A unit may provide only a subset of the types but every *column* must serve the whole type set abcdefgh. Neighbored columns may have links from left to right indicating the direction of the production. Units P and Q deliver the finished products (cars). Every unit has its *normal* and its *maximum capacity*. The *orders* specify the outcome of the rightmost column per type. The task is (1) to ensure that the orders can be fulfilled, i.e. every unit works below its maximum capacity (feasibility test), and (2) to optimize fairness between the production units. The second task, the optimization, is modelled by means of an error function. One of various possibilities is the sum of the column errors $E = \sum_{1 \leq i \leq 7} E_i$. The error of a column is greater than or equal to the errors of the units of that column (U_i be the set of units of column i; n_u be the normal capacity and q_u the quota of unit u) $E_i \geq E_u$ for all $u \in U_i$, where $E_u = |n_u - q_u|$. A deviation from the normal capacity is considered to be costly and within a column, the worst error is dominant. Repeated error minimization yields instantiations for all unit quotas, i.e. the plan.

[10] A prototype implementation of in-situ elimination has been used.

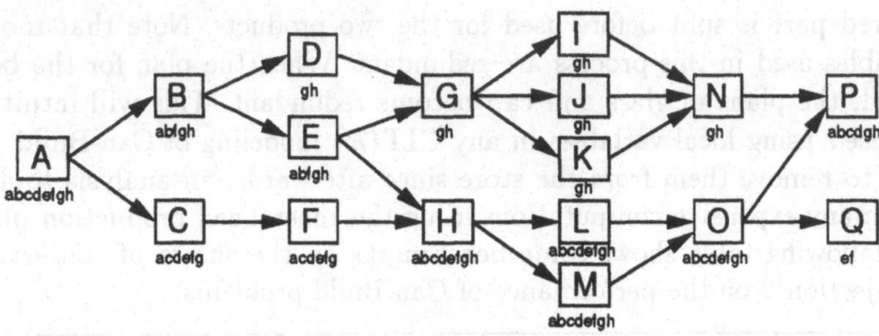

Fig. 3. An example factory

Assume we would try to find the minimal error value by projecting on the variable representing the error. We applied a progressive early projection to the initial constraint system and/or after any of the seven columns during the imposing of the constraints representing the error. The execution times for the generation of the plan taken on a Sun 5 are given in the table below.

		error construction	
		late	early
initial system	late	too big	0.23s
	early	8.17s	0.22s

The main benefit of the early projection lies in the influence on the elimination order here. The times obtained using progressive early projection are several orders of magnitude smaller than those in [1].

6 Conclusion

We have designed a framework for automatic projection in CLP, obtaining two benefits. Conservative early projection efficiently supports a CLP solver in the case when there is a significant amount of existential redundancy and helps accelerate the answer projection. This can be seen as an optimization. Progressive projection enhances the expressivity of CLP by adding a new but inherently implicit instrument that provides the power to simplify problems involving existential variables. CLP($\mathcal{R}$) as the prime application of these techniques has shown promising results in a prototype implementation.

References

1. Hartwig Baumgärtel. Distributed constraint processing for production logistics. In *Proceedings of the Third International Conference on the Practical Application of Constraint Technology (PACT'97)*, Blackpool, Lancashire, UK, 1997. The Practical Application Company.
2. A. Fordan, U. Geske, and A. Nareyek. Optimizing constraint-intensive problems using early projection. In *Proceedings of the JICSLP Conference, Poster-Session.* The MIT Press. Also appeared as GMD-Studie Nr. 296, 1996.
3. Andreas Fordan. Linear projection in CLP(FD). Arbeitspapiere der GMD 1099, Gesellschaft für Mathematik und Datenverarbeitung, Berlin, Germany, 1997.
4. N. Heintze et al. The CLP($\mathcal{R}$) programmer's manual, version 1.2. Technical report, IBM, Yorktown Heights, USA, November 1992.
5. Hewlett-Packard, Bristol. *BTS Models / BTS Requirements Specification*, May 1992.
6. Christian Holzbaur. Ofai clp(Q,R). Manual, Austrian Research Institute for Artificial Intelligence, Vienna, 1995.
7. Tien Huynh and Jean-Louis Lassez. Practical issues on the projection of polyhedral sets. Technical Report RC 15872 (#70560), IBM Research Division, June 1990.
8. J-L. Imbert. Redundancy, variable elimination and linear disequations. In *International Symposium on Logic Programming (ILPS)*, pages 139–153, 1994.
9. Jean-Louis Imbert. Fourier's elimination: Which to choose? In *Principles and Practice of Logic Programming.* The MIT Press, 1995.
10. J. Jaffar and J-L. Lassez. Constraint logic programming. In *Proceedings of the 14th ACM POPL Conference*, pages 111–119, January 1987.
11. J. Jaffar, M.J. Maher, P.J. Stuckey, and R.H.C. Yap. Projecting CLP($\mathcal{R}$) constraints. *New Generation Computing*, 11(3 & 4):449–469, 1993.
12. Joxan Jaffar, Spiro Michaylov, Peter Stuckey, and Roland Yap. An abstract machine for CLP($\mathcal{R}$). In *Proceedings of the ACM SIGPLAN Symposium on Programming Language Design and Implementation (PLDI), San Francisco*, pages 128–139, June 1992.
13. Joxan Jaffar, Spiro Michaylov, and Roland H.C. Yap. A methodology for managing hard constraints in CLP systems. In *Proceedings of the ACM-SIGPLAN Conference on Programming Language Design and Implementation.* ACM Press, 1991.
14. Joxan Jaffar, Spiro Michayov, Peter Stuckey, and Roland Yap. The CLP($\mathcal{R}$) language and system. *ACM Transactions on Programming Languages and Systems*, 14(3):339–395, July 1992.
15. A.D. Kelly, A.D. Macdonald, K. Marriott, H. Søndergaard, P.J. Stuckey, and R.H.C. Yap. An optimizing compiler for CLP($\mathcal{R}$). In *First International Conference on Principles and Practice of Constraint Programming*, pages 222–239, 1995.
16. A.D. Kelly, A.D. Macdonald, K. Marriott, P.J. Stuckey, and R.H.C. Yap. Effectiveness of optimizing compilation for CLP($\mathcal{R}$). In *JICSLP'96: Joint International Symposium on Logic Programming*, pages 37–51, 1996.
17. Andrew D. MacDonald, Peter Stuckey, and Roland Yap. Redundancy of variables in CLP($\mathcal{R}$). In *ILPS'93: Proceedings 3rd International Logic Programming Symposium*, Vancouver, 1993.
18. A. Schrijver. *Theory of Linear and Integer Programming.* John Wiley & Sons, 1986.
19. Peter J. Stuckey. Incremental linear arithmetic constraint solver and detection of implicit equalities. *ORSA Journal of Comput.*, 3(4), 1991.

Suggestion Strategies for Constraint-Based Matchmaker Agents *

Eugene C. Freuder and Richard J. Wallace

University of New Hampshire
Durham, NH 03824

Abstract. In this paper we describe a paradigm for content-focused matchmaking, based on a recently proposed model for constraint acquisition and satisfaction. Matchmaking agents are conceived as constraint-based solvers that interact with other, possibly human, agents (Customers). The Matchmaker provides potential solutions ("suggestions") based on partial knowledge, while gaining further information about the problem itself from the other agent through the latter's evaluation of these suggestions. The dialog between Matchmaker and Customer results in iterative improvement of solution quality, as demonstrated in simple simulations. We also show empirically that this paradigm supports "suggestion strategies" for finding acceptable solutions more efficiently *or* for increasing the amount of information obtained from the Customer. This work also indicates some ways in which the tradeoff between these two metrics for evaluating performance can be handled.

1 Introduction

Intelligent matchmakers can be regarded as a third generation tool for Internet accessibility, where hypertext constitutes the first generation, and search engines the second. "Content-focused matchmaker" agents can provide advice to internet consumers (people or other agents) about complex products [3]. The reigning paradigm for such agents is apparently the "deep interview", as embodied in the PersonaLogic website [4]. Here the primary mode of interaction is the Matchmaker query, which is essentially a multiple-choice question about product features. We propose a constraint-based paradigm, with a very different form of interaction.

In this paradigm, the primary mode of interaction is the *suggestion* made by the Matchmaker to the Customer. This suggestion is made in the form of a product. The secondary mode of communication is the *correction*, made by the Customer to the Matchmaker, indicating how the suggested product fails to meets the Customer's needs. We believe this form of interaction is more natural and shifts more of the burden from the Customer (who may be a person) to the Matchmaker.

* This material is based on work supported by the National Science Foundation under Grant No. IRI-9504316.

The Matchmaker could be an impartial matchmaker or a vendor. The product could be a physical product, e.g. a car, or an information source, e.g. a web page. The Customer could also be a computer agent, and indeed in our experiments we use a computer agent to simulate a Customer. In future work on multi-agent systems we envision Matchmakers playing the role of Customer with other Matchmakers to procure information for their clients, and Matchmakers seeking compromise solutions for multiple clients.

We model the intelligent matchmaker paradigm using formal methods drawn from the study of constraint satisfaction problems (CSPs). The Matchmaker's knowledge base and Customer's needs are both modeled as a network of constraints. A suggestion corresponds to a solution of a CSP. A correction specifies Customer constraints that the proposed solution violates. Repeating the cycle of suggestion and correction allows the Matchmaker to improve its picture of the Customer's problem until a suggestion constitutes a satisfactory solution. The problem of both acquiring and solving a CSP has been termed the "constraint acquisition and satisfaction problem" (CASP) in [1], where the basic suggestion/correction model was suggested but not implemented. (Although derived independently, this model has points of contact with earlier work on incremental models for building queries in Prolog [5] [7].)

The constraint network representation supports the computation of suggestions and easily incorporates corrections. In computing suggestions the constraint solving process infers the implications of corrections in a manner which avoids the need to make all constraints explicit. We believe that this form of model-based representation will be easier to build and maintain than the rule or decision tree based representation that presumably underlies a deep interview matchmaker.

The objective here is to model a situation in which Customers do not enter the interaction with a fully explicit description of their needs. They may be unfamiliar with what is available in the marketplace. They recognize their constraints during the interaction with the Matchmaker. They cannot list all their requirements up front, but they can recognize what they do not want when they see it (cf. [7] for a similar argument in a different context). We believe this to be a common form of customer conduct:- picture yourself browsing through a store or a catalogue, or interacting with a salesclerk.

The Matchmaker can facilitate this process by an appropriate choice of suggestions, or tentative solutions. For example, some suggestion strategies may lead to a satisfactory solution more easily for the user than others, e.g. with fewer iterations of the suggestion/correction cycle. In this paper we present experiments that provide empirical evaluation of some simple suggestion strategies.

Ease of use is not the only evaluation criteria. We consider one other here. In an environment in which the Matchmaker has an ongoing relationship with the Customer, it can be desirable for the Matchmaker to learn as much as possible about the Customer's constraints, to facilitate future interactions. In our implementation it is possible, in fact it proves experimentally the norm, for the Matchmaker to come up with a satisfactory solution *before* acquiring all of the

Customer constraints. (Some constraints will be fortuitously satisfied by the suggestion.) Thus we use the number of Customer constraints acquired by the Matchmaker as another performance metric when comparing suggestion strategies.

Notice that this latter metric is somewhat antithetical to ease of use criteria. Acquiring many Customer constraints can be viewed as good, because it facilitates future interaction; however, it also might be viewed as bad, because it requires more Customer effort (in the form of corrections). There is a similarly double-edged situation, analogous to one encountered in the classical information-retrieval literature, that we plan to pursue in future research: we would like to model the situation in which some suggestions lead to a satisfactory solution quickly, while others lead to a more satisfactory solution, but at greater "cost" to the Customer. However, even with our simple initial model of the matchmaker process we encounter some interesting empirical behavior.

The contributions of this paper are:

- A new matchmaker agent paradigm.
- A constraint-based implementation of this paradigm.
- Basic suggestion strategies for complete and stochastic matchmakers.
- Basic metrics for strategy evaluation.
- Experimental evaluation of suggestion strategies.

2 Background: CSPs and CASPs

A constraint satisfaction problem (CSP) involves assigning values to *variables* that satisfy a set of *constraints*. Each constraint is a relation based on the Cartesian product of the *domains*, or allowable assignments, of a subset of variables. In the present work all constraints are binary, i.e., they are based on the domains of two variables. A binary CSP is associated with a constraint graph whose nodes represent variables and arcs represent constraints.

CSPs have four basic types of parameter: number of variables, number of values in a domain or domain size, number of constraints, and number of value tuples in a constraint. In practice, if the domain size is the same for all variables, we refer to it as the value of a single domain size parameter. Otherwise, we often use an aggregate measure like the mean as a representative parameter value. Number of constraints is usually expressed in relation to the total number of possible constraints in a graph of n variables and is referred to as problem density. Most often constraint sizes are expressed in a complementary way, as the (relative) number of unacceptable tuples, or *tightness* of a constraint. Again, if tightness varies among constraints, we refer to average tightness as a representative value.

In a constraint acquisition and satisfaction problem (CASP) the constraint solver must acquire information about the constraints before it can solve the problem. The situation can be conceptualized by assuming some universe of constraints, i.e., all the constraints which can possibly be part of the CASP.

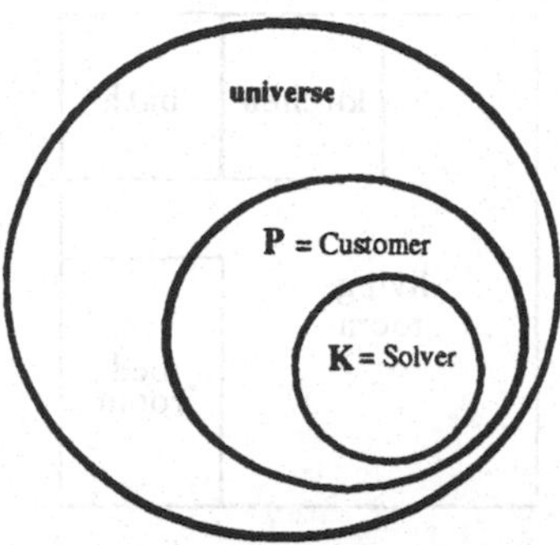

Fig. 1. The three classes of constraints that set the scene for a Matchmaking dialog: those initially known to both Solver and Customer (K), those known (perhaps implicitly) to the Customer (P), and the universal set of constraints, which includes all those that might have been part of the problem.

(In the extreme case, this would be the complete graph based on the known variables.) A certain set of constraints within this universe forms the current problem, P. The CSP solver (here the Matchmaker) knows a subset of the constraints in P at the outset, call it K, but it must in fact solve problem P. It will, therefore, have to acquire knowledge about the remaining constraints in P before it can find a satisfactory solution in a reasonable amount of time.

3 CASPs, Agents, and Matchmaking

Matchmaking based on the CASP paradigm involves two agents, the CASP Solver and the Customer. In this situation, the Customer 'knows' the problem to be solved, but not so explicitly that it can tell the Solver outright. The Solver elicits some of this Customer knowledge by suggesting a solution based on the constraints that it (the Solver) knows about. The Customer then evaluates the solution to determine whether there are constraints of concern that are violated. These violations are communicated to the Solver, which incorporates this information as constraints between the variables involved in each violation. The Solver then solves the new CSP and presents this solution as a new suggestion to the Customer. This communication cycle is repeated until the solution is fully satisfactory to the Customer, i.e., none of the latter's constraints are violated.

To get some idea of how this might work in practice, we will consider the following example. A customer comes into a real estate office looking for an apartment. She knows that she wants a one-bedroom apartment within a certain price range. The agent has several apartments available, so they decide to go and have a look at them. The first apartment they visit has this layout:

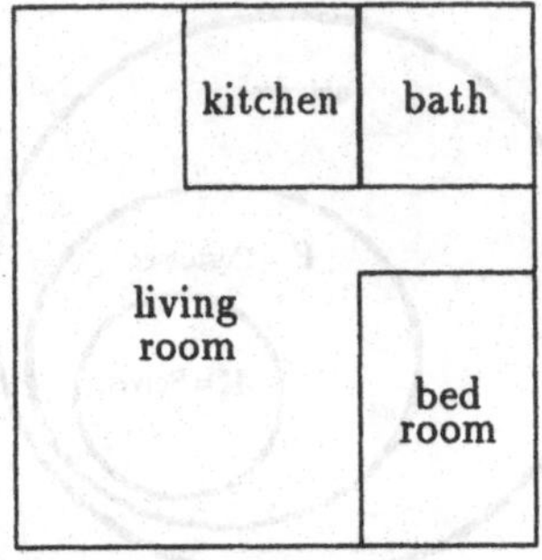

On looking it over, the customer immediately realizes that the kitchen is much too small. So they go to another apartment:

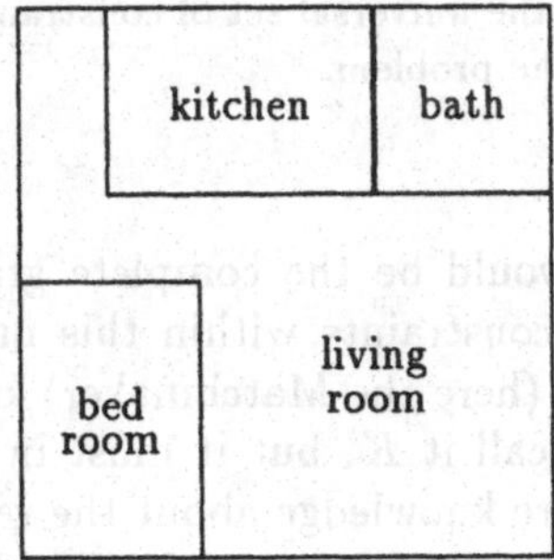

The customer finds the kitchen satisfactory, but now she realizes she prefers having the bathroom next to the bedroom, as it was in Apt. 1. So they look at a third apartment:

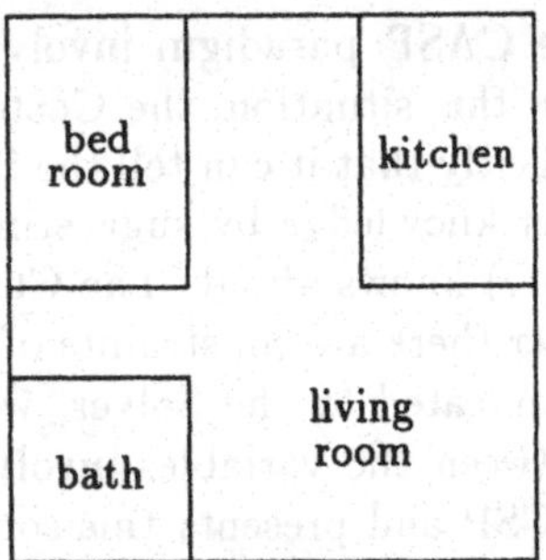

This apartment satisfies all the customer's constraints, so she deems it acceptable.

4 Suggestion Strategies

In the situation just described, the agent might have chosen to show the apartments in a different order. In particular, after showing Apt. 1, he might have taken the customer to see Apt. 3. In this case, the customer's problem would have been solved in two steps rather than three. However, in this case the constraint involving the locations of the bedroom and bathroom would have been satisfied fortuitously. By showing Apt. 2, the agent discovered this constraint, thus learning more about the customer's problem. This is, of course, an example of the tradeoff between efficiency and information gain that was described in the Introduction.

Examples like this give us reason to expect that the two goals of efficiently solving the Customer's problem and making that problem explicit are potentially divergent. Because of this, we would like to examine heuristics from the CSP domain that bear on this question. In so doing we will consider the situation in more abstract terms, even if some of the strategies we consider are not directly applicable to an example such as the one above, e.g. because they put too great demands on the Customer.

To begin the analysis of suggestion strategies for matchmaking, we will simplify the Dialog between Solver and Customer in the following ways. We assume that both the Solver's and the Customer's constraints are drawn from the same universe; hence, when the Solver is apprised of a constraint violation it does not have to decide what the constraint actually is, i.e., the set of acceptable tuples. Further, constraints known to the Solver are assumed to be a proper subset of the Customer's (implicit) constraints (Figure 1). In terms of the CASP definition in Section 2, the former is set K, and the latter can be identified with P. (In an overall Customer-Solver Dialog, the constraints in K might be determined by preliminary questioning – what kind of apartment are you looking for?, what price range? – before the first solution is presented.) We also assume that on each iteration of the communication cycle, the Customer gives the Solver the complete set of constraints violated by the last solution. While this may seem unrealistic when many constraints are considered at once, as in the experiments to be described, in other cases the simplicity of the problem or of the focal problem of the dialog suggest that it is not always such an extreme assumption. (Think of all the constraints involved in an apartment layout that do not have to be discussed in a dialog like the one in the example above.)

If our goal is to limit the number of iterations in the suggestion-correction cycle, there are two approaches we might take. One is to try to find solutions more likely to satisfy constraints between variables, even if these constraints are not presently in the Solver's representation. This policy is, therefore, one of maximizing satisfaction, specifically, the number of satisfied constraints. An alternative, possibly more perverse, approach is to maximize constraint violations. Here, the policy is to find solutions that violate as many constraints as possible so that more constraints are incorporated into the Solver's set from the start.

Fairly straightforward methods for finding solutions under either policy can be derived from current knowledge of constraint satisfaction. These methods depend on the kind of procedure used in the solution process. For algorithms that use complete or exhaustive search, selecting values less likely to be in conflict with values in other variables is a promising method for maximizing satisfaction. For hill-climbing or heuristic repair methods, a strategy in the same spirit is solution reuse, i.e., starting each search with the solution obtained earlier, after revising the information about conflicts based on the last Customer communication. A complete search strategy that conforms to the policy of maximizing violations is the converse of the satisfaction strategy: choose values *most* likely to be in conflict. A corresponding hill-climbing strategy is to search each time from a new location, i.e., with a new set of initial values.

If our goal is to learn as much as possible about the Customer, where "learning about the Customer" means learning his or her constraints, then intuitively, maximization strategies do not appear well-suited to this goal, but violation strategies should serve this purpose at least as well as that of maximizing efficiency. This in turn suggests that satisfaction strategies will be subject to a tradeoff between the two different goals, while violation strategies might overcome it. On the other hand, it is not clear which kind of strategy will be most efficient in finding an acceptable solution. If a satisfaction method is much better than any others, then it may be necessary to consider this tradeoff carefully.

To better understand how different procedures chosen with the above goals in mind will perform in practice and the degree to which the tradeoffs discussed here are important, we now turn to empirical investigations of suggestion strategies.

5 Experimental Evaluation of Suggestion Strategies

5.1 Methods

Tests were made with random problems; for brevity, we concentrate on one problem set and mention results for other sets of problems in passing. This set included ten problems with 50 variables and a constant domain size of 5. A fully connected graph of constraints was obtained in all cases by first generating a random spanning tree for the variable set. The density, in terms of edges added to the spanning tree, was fixed at 0.25 (giving 343 constraints). There was a fixed probability of including a tuple in a constraint, and the average tightness was almost exactly equal to the stipulated probability of 0.18. Problems with these parameters are in or near the critical region for computational complexity.

Two kinds of algorithms were tested: (i) a complete CSP algorithm, forward checking with conflict-directed backjumping and dynamic ordering by domain size [6], (ii) a heuristic repair method, min-conflicts augmented with a random walk strategy [8]. In the latter procedure, after a variable in conflict has been chosen, a value is chosen at random from the domain with probability p, while the usual min-conflicts procedure is followed with probability $1 - p$.

For the complete algorithm, suggestion strategies were devised by ordering domain values in specific ways prior to search. To maximize constraint satisfaction, values in each domain were ordered by maximum averaged promise (max-promise), where "promise" is the relative number of supporting values in each adjacent domain [2], and these proportions are averaged across all adjacent domains. In this work, promise was based on the universal constraint set for each problem. A violation strategy was obtained by reversing this order for each domain, which gave an ordering by minimum averaged promise (min-promise). Another violation strategy was to 'shuffle' the domains before each search, i.e., to order each domain by random sequential selection of its values. Lexical ordering of values served as a control.

For the heuristic procedure, a possible maximization strategy is *solution reuse*: each iteration after the first begins with the solution obtained at the end of the last iteration. Two kinds of suggestion strategy were tested as candidate violation strategies. In one case the walk probability was raised from 0.10 to 0.35; since the latter allows more random selection of values, a greater variety of solutions might be found, leading to more violations. The other kind of strategy was a *restart* strategy: each iteration begins with an initial assignment generated from scratch. In addition, restarting was combined with three different preprocessing strategies: (i) min-conflicts greedy preprocessing based on a single variable ordering, where for each successive variable a value is chosen that minimizes conflicts with existing assignments of values to variables, (ii) greedy preprocessing based on a different, randomly selected, variable ordering for each iteration, (iii) hill-climbing from an initial random assignment on each iteration, i.e., for each variable a value is chosen at random and its conflicts with previous assignments recorded. Since the walk strategy is independent of the restart strategies, all combinations of the two were tested.

For each Matchmaking Dialog, the constraint set of the original CSP was the universal set. From this universe, constraints were chosen by random methods to be in K and P. At the beginning of each dialog, the full constraint set was scanned and, with probability p_k, a given constraint was added to *both* the Solver's and the Customer's constraint sets. (These constraints, therefore, comprise K.) If the constraint was not chosen, then with probability p_p, it was added to the Customer's set, P. Four sets of values were used for p_k and p_p, respectively, in the procedure just described: 0.2 and 0.4, 0.2 and 0.8, 0.4 and 0.4, 0.4 and 0.8.

5.2 Experimental Results

Representative results for the different value orderings used with the complete CSP algorithm are shown in Table 1. The same pattern of results was found with 0.4, 0.4 and with 0.4, 0.8 for p_k and p_p, and for other sets of random problems.

In one case (0.2, 0.4), the satisfaction strategy, max-promise, found acceptable solutions after fewer iterations in comparison with either the lexical ordering or the constraint violation strategies. But with more Customer constraints in relation to Solver constraints, a violation strategy, min-promise, was more efficient in this respect than max-promise. In both cases, min-promise was the most effective in uncovering violations quickly, as reflected in the measure of violations per iteration. On the other hand, the shuffling procedure found more violations across the whole dialog.

The tradeoff expected with max-promise was very much in evidence, since this procedure uncovered far fewer Customer constraints than any other. This

Table 1. Matchmaking Dialog Statistics for Different Value Orderings

constr probs*	val ord	iterats to sol	violats /iter	undisc constr	sol sim	time (sec)
.2, .4						
	lex	8	8	59	.72	.03
	max	6	5	85	.83	.02
	min	8	11	37	.61	.02
	shuf	14	8	15	.22	.02
.2, .8						
	lex	12	14	69	.54	.55
	max	15	9	105	.65	.43
	min	11	17	47	.48	.53
	shuf	19	11	21	.24	.41

Notes. Means based on 10 problems and five dialogs, or initial K and P, per problem. Algorithm is FC-CBJ with dynamic ordering by domain size. * prob(shared constraint), prob(Customer constraint). *iterats* are number of iterations before a solution was found. *violats* are mean number of violations discovered by Customer on one iteration. *undisc constr* are mean number of undiscovered Customer constraints at end of a run. *sol sim* is mean similarity (proportion of common values) of successive solutions found during a run. *time* is run time for entire dialog. Expected numbers of shared and Customer-only constraints are 69 and 110 for the 0.2, 0.4 condition and 69 and 220 for the 0.2, 0.8 condition.

tradeoff was also found for the shuffling procedure: while it was the least efficient ordering, it uncovered more constraints than any other procedure.

Interestingly, the min-promise ordering required relatively few iterations, while finding more violations per iteration on average than the other orderings. In this respect it tended to overcome the tradeoff between efficiency and constraint discovery. In fact, when there were more Customer constraints not in the initial Solver set, this ordering was better than the satisfaction ordering, max-promise, on both metrics.

These relations are made clearer if we consider trends during an entire dialog, as for the number of undiscovered constraints (Figure 2). The curves in Figure 2 are for one problem, but the qualitative differences seen here were found with all problems tested. During the early iterations, both min-promise and shuffle discover many constraints, but the curve for the former levels out more quickly, and this procedure also finds a completely satisfactory solution more quickly, so its curve is shorter. Consequently, the curve for shuffle falls below the other curve on the eighth iteration, but it continues on for some time before finding a satisfactory solution. The curve for max-promise remains well above the other two throughout the dialog. And it requires even more iterations than shuffle to find a fully satisfactory solution.

From these results alone, one would conclude that max-promise should be

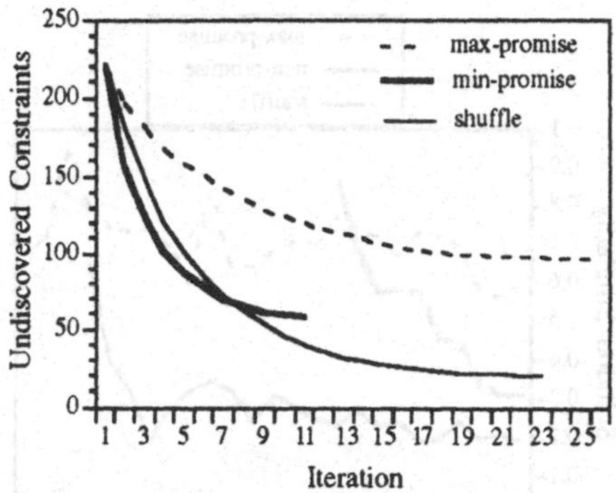

Fig. 2. Undiscovered Customer constraints after successive iterations with three value orderings. Condition involved inclusion probabilities of 0.2 and 0.8 (cf. explanation under Methods). Means based on five dialogs with one problem.

chosen to maximize efficiency if the difference between the number of Customer and Solver constraints is small, but min-promise is preferrable when the difference is large. If one wants to maximize constraint discovery overall, then the shuffle should be chosen. But for the best tradeoff between efficiency and constraint discovery, min-promise should be chosen.

Unfortunately, perhaps, the picture changes when efficiency is measured in terms of time instead of iterations. For overall time to complete a dialog, max-promise is better than min-promise, especially when there are more Customer constraints (the reverse of what was found when we considered iterations). This difference may be due to the greater time required to find a solution when starting from the least supported values. Surprisingly, shuffle is as fast as max-promise. (For the 0.4, 0.8 case, where times were twice as long as for 0.2, 0.8, shuffle was somewhat slower, but both shuffle and max-promise were almost twice as fast as the other two orderings.)

These results show that, when efficiency is measured in units of time rather than iterations, max-promise is generally the best strategy in terms of efficiency. However, now it is shuffle, rather than min-promise, that best overcomes the tradeoff between efficiency and constraint discovery. This does not leave us with a simple decision, since either measure of efficiency may be more appropriate in different contexts. In particular, a small increase in summed search time may be much more palatable than presentation of several additional solutions.

Trends for solution similarity across successive iterations are also of interest, since solution similarity may be important psychologically in interactions with a human customer. This measure tends to increase in the course of a dialog regardless of the ordering (Figure 3; Again, the same trends were found for all ten problems.) For min-promise, successive similarity is fairly low at first, but it rises sharply. Similarity values for max-promise are high throughout the dialog. In contrast, similarity values for shuffle are fairly low through most of the dialog.

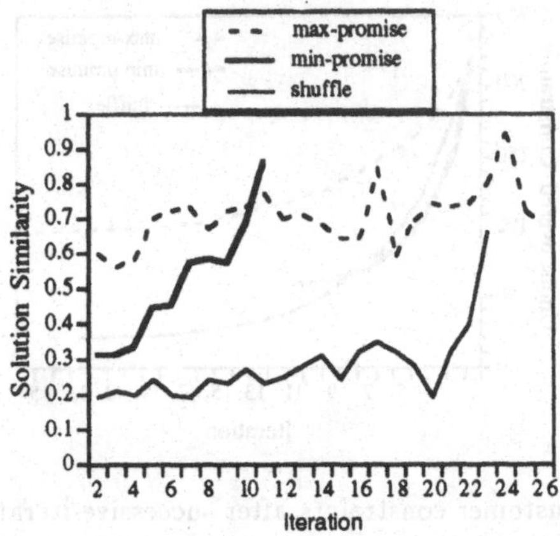

Fig. 3. Similarity of successive solutions during a dialog, for three value orderings. Same condition and problem as in Figure 2.

In experiments with heuristic repair (Table 2), some of the same differences are seen between satisfaction and violation strategies, and to some degree there are similar kinds of tradeoffs. Solution reuse, the satisfaction strategy, finds acceptable solutions after fewer iterations, and after less time, than any of the violation strategies. On the other hand, all of the latter are more successful in discovering Customer constraints. The most successful is the restart strategy that uses a different random value assignment at the beginning of each search; this procedure discovers as many constraints as the shuffled ordering with the complete algorithm. Unfortunately, success in discovering constraints is purchased with a considerable increase in runtime, and none of the procedures really overcomes this tradeoff. However, there is a partial mitigation in that the best restart strategies are just as successful with the lower walk probability as with the higher, although the runtime is much lower in the former case.

6 Application

These results give us some clearcut ideas about organizing a matchmaking dialog. In practice, we may have to modify the strategies to accomodate a human customer, but the basic strategies examined here and the relations between strategies and metrics for efficiency or information gain that were demonstrated in the previous section should still be relevant, as suggested by our discussion of the apartment-hunting scenario.

Currently we are building an application based on these ideas within a real estate domain, specifically, home buying. This was chosen in part because of the possibility of working with an actual real estate agency, which may provide the opportunity to field this project in a real-life setting. In addition, product

Table 2. Matchmaking Dialog Statistics for Hill-Climbing Strategies

restart proced	walk probs	iterat	violat / iter	undisc constr	sol sim	time (sec)
	0.2, 0.4 constraint probs.					
no restart (solution reuse)						
	0.10	6	9	70	.83	.18
	0.35	7	9	65	.81	.22
restart - mincon preproc						
	0.10	9	7	61	.74	.60
	0.35	9	7	57	.70	.65
restart - random var mincon						
	0.10	14	6	35	.47	1.03
restart - random value						
	0.10	14	8	15	.22	1.26
	0.2, 0.8 constraint probs.					
no restart (solution reuse)						
	0.10	14	12	76	.71	2.12
	0.35	15	13	47	.55	8.12
restart - mincon preproc						
	0.10	18	11	41	.43	17.0
	0.35	18	11	32	.36	28.6
restart - random var mincon						
	0.10	18	12	29	.31	15.3
restart - random value						
	0.10	18	12	24	.27	14.5

Notes. Same problems as in Table 1, five dialogs per problem. Minconflicts hill-climbing with random walk. Restart procedures described in text; for randomized orderings both walk probabilities gave almost identical results except for runtimes. Other abbreviations as in Table 1.

listings are readily available which can provide the necessary information for the data base.

The system being designed will read information from a data base and construct a CSP representation, taking as its variables the data base attributes and deriving constraints from the data base entries. Each solution of the CSP will be associated with a specific listing, which can then be scanned and viewed. Customer responses will be made via menu selection. The system is being written in Java so it can be fielded on the Web.

7 Concluding Comments

This work introduces a new strategy for Customer-Matchmaker interaction based on software agents performing the Matchmaker functions (and possibly playing the role of Customer as well). We have evaluated several strategies that may be useful in this context. We have also identified an important and interesting tradeoff between the goals of efficient problem solving and knowledge acquisition, and we have discovered a non-obvious method for ameliorating the situation.

This work also carries the implication that a multi-agent system may be well-suited for solving the Constraint Acquisition and Satisfaction Problem. There is an obvious division of labor between the information acquisition and CSP-solving aspects of CASPs, and it is likely that this can be mapped directly onto different agents in many situations.

References

1. E. C. Freuder. Active learning for constraint satisfaction. In *Active Learning. AAAI-95 Fall Symposium Series, Working Notes*, pp. 34–35, 1995.
2. P. A. Geelen. Dual viewpoint heuristics for binary constraint satisfaction problems. In *Proceedings ECAI-92*, pp. 31–35, 1992.
3. J. Gomez, D. E. Weisman, V. B. Trevino, and C. A. Woolsey. Content-focused matchmakers (excerpt). In *Money & Technology Strategies*, volume 2(3). Forrester Research, Inc., 1996.
4. M. Krantz. The web's middleman. *Time*, pp. 67–68, February 17, 1997.
5. M. Okhi, A. Takeuchi, and K. Furukawa. A framework for interactive problem solving based on interactive query revision. In *Logic Programmming '86*, LNCS Vol. 264, pp. 137–146. Springer-Verlag, Berlin, 1987.
6. P. Prosser. Hybrid algorithms for the constraint satisfaction problem. *Computational Intelligence*, 9:268–299, 1993.
7. M. H. van Emden, M. Ohki, and A. Takeuchi. Spreadsheets with incremental queries as a user interface for logic programming. *New Generation Computing*, 4:287–304, 1986.
8. R. J. Wallace. Analysis of heuristic methods for partial constraint satisfaction problems. In E. C. Freuder, editor, *Principles and Practice of Constraint Programming - CP'96*, LNCS Vol. 1118, pp. 482–496. Springer, Berlin, 1996.

Compiling Semiring-Based Constraints with clp(FD,S)

Yan Georget, Philippe Codognet*

INRIA-Rocquencourt, BP 105, 78153 Le Chesnay, France
{Yan.Georget,Philippe.Codognet}@inria.fr

Abstract. In some recent works, a general framework for finite domains constraint satisfaction has been defined, where classical CSPs, fuzzy CSPs, weighted CSPs, partial CSPs and others can be easily cast. This framework, based on a semiring structure, allows, under certain conditions, to compute arc-consistency. Restricting to that case and integrating semiring-based constraint solving in the Constraint Logic Programming paradigm, we have implemented a generic language, clp(FD,S), for semiring-based constraint satisfaction. In this paper, we describe the kernel of the language: the SFD system and our implementation of clp(FD,S). We also give some performance results on various examples.

1 Introduction

In [1, 2], a general framework for finite domains constraint satisfaction and optimization has been defined, where classical CSPs [15, 13, 14], fuzzy CSPs [16, 9, 17], partial CSPs [10] and others can be easily cast. This framework is based on a semiring structure. Moreover, the authors show that local consistency algorithms can be used, provided that certain conditions on the semiring operations are satisfied. Restricting to that case and integrating semiring-based constraint solving in the Constraint Logic Programming paradigm, our goal was to implement a generic language, clp(FD,S), for semiring-based constraint satisfaction using arc-consistency. In order to achieve that goal, we define, as it as been done in [3, 4] for finite domain constraints, a general scheme for compiling semiring-based constraints. The kernel of clp(FD,S), is called SFD and is generic with respect to the semiring. Hence, we are able to generate new languages by specifying semirings, the rest of the implementation being unchanged.

The work the most related to ours is LVCSP [12], a lisp library for constraint solving which is based on the VCSP formalism [18]. An important difference, as stated in [2], is that the semiring-based framework is more general than the VCSP framework because it allows to deal with partial orders. It is also worth mentioning that, in clp(FD,S), the semiring-based solving techniques have been integrated and implemented in a full Constraint Logic Programming (CLP) language, meaning that incrementality is a key feature of the solver. CLP has proved

* currently on sabbatical leave at:
SONY Computer Science Laboratory, 6, rue Amyot, 75 005 Paris, France

to be very useful for expressing problems in a concise and natural way and for easily implementing extensions such as optimization predicates.

The rest of the paper is organized as follows: In Section 2, we recall some definitions and results about semiring-based constraint satisfaction. We specialize some results to the case of arc-consistency in Section 3. We introduce the SFD system in Section 4 and give some examples of its use in Section 5. Then, Section 6 describes the implementation while Section 7 presents performances evaluation. Conclusion and perspectives are addressed in Section 8.

2 Semiring-based Constraint Satisfaction

The purpose of this section is to describe briefly the semiring-based framework. For more details, and also for the proofs of the properties, the reader should refer to [2].

2.1 Semirings

Definition 1 semiring. A semiring S is a tuple $\langle A, +, \times, \mathbf{0}, \mathbf{1}\rangle$ such that: A is a set and $\mathbf{0}, \mathbf{1} \in A$; $+$ is closed, commutative, associative, $\mathbf{0}$ is its unit element; $\times$ is closed, associative, distributes over $+$, $\mathbf{1}$ is its unit element, $\mathbf{0}$ is its absorbing element.

In the following, we will consider semirings with additional properties. Such semirings will be called c-semirings where c stands for constraints, meaning that they are the natural structures to be used when handling constraints.

Definition 2 c-semiring. A c-semiring S is a semiring $\langle A, +, \times, \mathbf{0}, \mathbf{1}\rangle$ such that: $+$ is idempotent, $\mathbf{1}$ is its absorbing element.

We can now define a partial ordering over the set A. For a c-semiring S as defined above, let us consider relation $\leq_S$ over A such that $a \leq_S b$ iff $a + b = b$. Then:

- $\leq_S$ is a partial order,
- $+$ and $\times$ are monotone on $\leq_S$,
- $\mathbf{0}$ is its minimum and $\mathbf{1}$ its maximum,
- $\langle A, \leq_S\rangle$ is a complete lattice and $+$ is its lub.

Additional properties are indeed needed to make it possible to compute local consistency, of which Arc-Consistency (AC [13]) is an instance.

Definition 3 lc-semiring. A lc-semiring S is a c-semiring $\langle A, +, \times, \mathbf{0}, \mathbf{1}\rangle$ such that: A is finite; $\times$ is idempotent.

With the last definition, we get the following results:

- $+$ distributes over $\times$,
- $\langle A, \leq_S\rangle$ is a complete distributive lattice and $\times$ is its glb.

2.2 Constraints

In the following, we suppose given: a c-semiring $S = \langle A, +, \times, \mathbf{0}, \mathbf{1}\rangle$, an ordered set of variables V and a finite set D. We recall the most important definitions of [2].

Definition 4 constraint. A constraint is a pair $\langle def, con\rangle$ where $con \subseteq V$ (*type* of the constraint) and $def : D^{|con|} \rightarrow A$.

A constraint specifies the involved variables and the values "allowed" for them. More precisely, for each tuple of values for the involved variables, a corresponding element of A is given, which can be interpreted as the tuple's weight, or cost, or level of confidence, or anything.

Definition 5 constraint problem. A constraint problem is a pair $\langle C, con\rangle$ where $con \subseteq V$ and C is a set of constraints.

In the following, we will assume that there are not two constraints with the same type (without this hypothesis the results would be a little more complicated).

Definition 6 tuple projection. Assuming that V is ordered via ordering $\prec$, consider any k-tuple $t = \langle t_1, \ldots, t_k\rangle$, of values of D and two sets $W = \{w_1, \ldots, w_k\}$ and $W' = \{w'_1, \ldots, w'_m\}$ such that $W' \subseteq W \subseteq V$ and $w_i \prec w_j$ if $i \leq j$ and $w'_i \prec w'_j$ if $i \leq j$. The projection of t from W to W', written $t \downarrow^{W}_{W'}$, is defined as the tuple $t' = \langle t'_1, \ldots, t'_m\rangle$ with $t'_i = t_j$ if $w'_i = w_j$.

Definition 7 combination. Given two constraints $c_1 = \langle def_1, con_1\rangle$ and $c_2 = \langle def_2, con_2\rangle$, their combination $c_1 \otimes c_2$ is the constraint $\langle def, con\rangle$ defined by $con = con_1 \cup con_2$ and $def(t) = def_1(t \downarrow^{con}_{con_1}) \times def(t \downarrow^{con}_{con_2})$

Definition 8 projection. Given a constraint $c = \langle def, con\rangle$ and a subset I of V, the projection of c over I, written $c \Downarrow_I$ is the constraint $\langle def', con'\rangle$ where $con' = con \cap I$ and $def'(t') = \sum_{t/t \downarrow^{con}_{I \cap con} = t'} def(t)$.

Definition 9 solution. The solution of the problem $P = \langle C, con\rangle$ is the constraint $Sol(P) = (\bigotimes C) \Downarrow_{con}$.

In words, the solution is the constraint induced on the variables in *con* by the whole problem.

Definition 10 best level of consistency. The best level of consistency of the problem P is defined by $blevel(P) = Sol(P) \Downarrow_{\emptyset}$. We say that:

- P is α-consistent if $blevel(P) = \alpha$,
- P is consistent if there exists $\alpha >_S \mathbf{0}$ such that P is α-consistent,
- P is inconsistent if it is not consistent.

Informally, the best level of consistency gives us an idea of how much we can satisfy the constraints of the problem. Note that the best level of consistency of a problem is, in the general case, an upper bound of the values associated with the tuples of its maximal solutions.

Definition 11 maximal solutions. Given a constraint problem P, consider $Sol(P) = \langle def, con\rangle$. A maximal solution of P is a pair $\langle t, v\rangle$ satisfying:

- $def(t) = v$,
- there is no t' such that $v <_S def(t')$.

Definition 12 constraint ordering. Consider two constraints $c_1 = \langle def_1, con\rangle$ and $c_2 = \langle def_2, con\rangle$, with $|con| = k$. Then $c_1 \sqsubseteq_S c_2$ if for all k-tuples t, $def_1(t) \leq_S def_2(t)$.

The relation $\sqsubseteq_S$ is a partial order.

Definition 13 problem ordering and equivalence. Consider two problems P_1 and P_2. Then $P_1 \sqsubseteq_P P_2$ if $Sol(P_1) \sqsubseteq_S Sol(P_2)$. If $P_1 \sqsubseteq_P P_2$ and $P_2 \sqsubseteq_P P_1$, then they have the same solution, thus we say that they are equivalent and we write $P_1 \equiv P_2$.

The relation $\sqsubseteq_P$ is a preorder. Moreover $\equiv$ is an equivalence relation. Consider two problems $P_1 = \langle C_1, con\rangle$ and $P_2 = \langle C_1 \cup C_2, con\rangle$. Then $P_2 \sqsubseteq_P P_1$ and $blevel(P_2) \leq_S blevel(P_1)$.

2.3 Local Consistency

In the following, we suppose given: a lc-semiring $S = \langle A, +, \times, \mathbf{0}, \mathbf{1}\rangle$, an ordered set of variables V and a finite set D.

Definition 14 local inconsistency. We say that the problem $P = \langle C, con\rangle$ is locally inconsistent if there exist $C' \subseteq C$ such that $blevel(C') = \mathbf{0}$.

Consider a set of constraints C and $C' \subseteq C$. If C is α-consistent then C' is β-consistent with $\alpha \leq_S \beta$. As a corollary: if a problem is locally inconsistent, then it is not consistent.

Definition 15 location. A typed location l is a set of variables. Given a problem $P = \langle C, con\rangle$, the value $[l]_P$ of the location l in P is $\langle def, l\rangle$ if it belongs to C, $\langle \mathbf{1}, l\rangle$ otherwise. The value $[\{l_1, \ldots, l_n\}]_P$ of the set of locations $\{l_1, \ldots, l_n\}$ is the set $\{[l_1]_P, \ldots, [l_n]_P\}$.

Definition 16 assignment. An assignment is a pair $l := c$ where $c = \langle def, l\rangle$. Given a problem $P = \langle C, con\rangle$, the result of the assignment $l := c$ is defined as $[l := c](P) = \langle \{\langle def', con'\rangle \in C / con' \neq l\} \cup c, con\rangle$.

Definition 17 local consistency rule. A local consistency rule is $l \leftarrow L$ where l is a location, L a set of locations and $l \notin L$.

Definition 18 rule application. The result of applying the rule $l \leftarrow L$ to the problem P is $[l \leftarrow L](P) = [l := Sol(\langle [L \cup \{l\}]_P, l \rangle)](P)$. The application of a sequence of rules $r; R$ is defined by $[r; R](P) = [R]([r](P))$.

Observe that, given a problem P and a rule r, $P \equiv [r](P)$.

Definition 19 stable problem. Given a problem P and a set R of rules for P, P is said to be stable w.r.t R if, for each $r \in R$, $[r](P) = P$.

Definition 20 strategy. Given a set R of rules, a strategy for R is an infinite sequence of R^∞. A strategy T is fair if each rule of R occurs in T infinitely often.

Definition 21 local consistency algorithm. Given a problem P, a set of rules R and a fair strategy T for R, a local consistency algorithm applies to P the rules in R in the order given by T. The algorithm stops when the current problem is stable w.r.t R. In that case, we note $lc(P, R, T)$ the resulting problem.

The following theorems are proven in [2]. The application of a local consistency algorithm terminates. If $P' = lc(P, R, T)$ then $P \equiv P'$. $lc(P, R, T)$ does not depend on T. Given a problem P and a value v assigned to a tuple in a constraint of P, consider $P' = lc(P, R, T)$ and the value v' assigned to the same tuple of the same constraint in P', then $v' \leq_S v$.

3 Application to Arc-Consistency

In this section, we will instantiate the results concerning local consistency to the particular case of AC.

3.1 Formal Approach

We suppose given a problem $P = \langle C, con \rangle$. Because we want to compute AC, we are interested only in the application of rules of the form:

$$r = \{x\} \leftarrow \{\{x, y_1, \ldots, y_n\}, \{y_1\}, \ldots, \{y_n\}\}$$

where $x, y_1, \ldots, y_n \in con$. We call such a rule an AC-rule, we note AC the set of AC-rules and $ac(P) = lc(P, AC)$. For the AC-rule r previously considered, we have:

$$[r](P) = [\{x\} := Sol(\langle [\{\{x\}, \{x, y_1, \ldots, y_n\}, \{y_1\}, \ldots, \{y_n\}\}]_P \rangle)](P)$$

Noting $C' = \{[\{x, y_1, \ldots, y_n\}]_P, [\{x\}]_P, [\{y_1\}]_P, \ldots, [\{y_n\}]_P\}$, this reduces to:

$$[r](P) = [\{x\} := Sol(\langle C', \{x\} \rangle)](P)$$

Or equivalently:

$$[r](P) = [\{x\} := (\bigotimes C') \Downarrow_{\{x\}}](P)$$

We note $[\{x, y_1, \ldots, y_n\}]_P = \langle def, \{x, y_1, \ldots, y_n\}\rangle$, $[\{x\}]_P = \langle def_x, \{x\}\rangle$ and $\forall i \in [1, n], [\{y_i\}]_P = \langle def_{y_i}, \{y_i\}\rangle$. We assume $x \prec y_1 \prec \cdots \prec y_n$. Finally, the application of the rule r reduce to replacing def_x by its product with:

$$\lambda i_x. \sum_{i_{y_1}, \ldots, i_{y_n}} def(i_x, i_{y_1}, \ldots, i_{y_n}) \times def_{y_1}(i_{y_1}) \times \ldots \times def_{y_n}(i_{y_n})$$

Note that the previous formula is a generalization of Zadeh's extension principle for fuzzy logic [11, 21].

3.2 Exploiting The Shape Of Constraints

The previous formula involves heavy computations. We show that these computations can be simplified for certain types of constraints.

Let us consider, for example, three constraints $c_E = \langle def_E, E\rangle$, with $E \in \{\{x\}, \{y\}, \{x, y\}\}$, $x \prec y$, $def_{\{x,y\}}(i, j) = \alpha$ (resp. β) if $i \geq j$ (resp. $i < j$), and $\alpha \geq_S \beta$.

The constraints $c_{\{x\}}$ and $c_{\{y\}}$ define the domains of x and y, while $c_{\{x,y\}}$ can be seen as $x \geq y$ with values α and β[2]. Here, we are interested in computing one step of AC over variable x. Using the formula of 3.1, the new domain of x is defined by:

$$def_{\{x\}}(i) \times (\sum_j def_{\{x,y\}}(i, j) \times def_{\{y\}}(j))$$

$$= def_{\{x\}}(i) \times (\alpha \times \sum_{j \leq i} def_{\{y\}}(j) + \beta \times \sum_j def_{\{y\}}(j))$$

Hence, the new domain of x is easily computed using $\lambda i. \sum_{j \leq i} def_{\{y\}}(j)$ and $\sum_j def_{\{y\}}(j)$. This means that it is possible to specialize the computation to the particular shape of the constraint. This principle can be used for every mathematical relation or function with a "regular shape". We will now design a language of operators well-suited for the encoding of such simple-shaped constraints, but where, more generally, any kind of multi-valued constraint can be cast, by combining primitive operators.

4 The SFD System

Let us now detail the set of indexicals and operators (the SFD system) that allows the compilation of usual mathematical constraints.

---

[2] It extends the classical arithmetic constraint by replacing the boolean truth values with value α for satisfaction and β for violation, while keeping the shape of the constraint. This scheme will be used in Section 5.1 for encoding high-level constraint.

4.1 Syntax Of The Language

Definition 22 valued domain. A *valued domain* (or domain) is a function from D to A.

Definition 23 range. Let $\mathcal{V}$ be a set of variables. A *range* is a syntactic domain defined by Table 1, where $Y \in \mathcal{V}$.

Definition 24 constraint. Let $\mathcal{V}$ be a set of variables. A *constraint* is a formula of the form X in r where $X \in \mathcal{V}$ and r is a range.

Table 1. Syntax of SFD constraints.

c ::= X in r		r ::= def(Y)	(indexical *def*)
		cut_R(r,at)	(cut)
		keep_R(r,at)	(keep)
		r + r	(+ operation)
it ::= i	(integer)	r * r	(× operation)
infinity	(greatest value)	r + at	(+ operation)
C	(integer parameter)	r * at	(× operation)
		it..it	(interval)
		comp(it)	(exclusion)
		d(r)	(different)
at ::= a	(semiring value)	le(r)	(less or equal)
at + at	(+ operation)	l(r)	(less)
at * at	(× operation)	ge(r)	(greater or equal)
pi(Y)	(indexical *pi*)	g(r)	(greater)
sigma(Y)	(indexical *sigma*)	add(r,r)	(addition)
A	(value parameter)	sub(r,r)	(substraction)
		mul(r,r)	(multiplication)
		div(r,r)	(division)
		add(r,it)	(addition)
		sub(r,it)	(substraction)
		mul(r,it)	(multiplication)
		div(r,it)	(division)

4.2 Semantics Of The Constraint Language

In the following, r will be a valued domain and r_i the semiring value associated to integer i. Note that all the indexes take their values in D. Let us first detail the operators and indexicals appearing in the category of ranges:

- The indexical **def** gives the valued domain of a variable.
- The following classes of operators are used for optimization:
  - Given a relation R over the semiring: r' =**cut_**R(**r**, α) is defined by $r'_j = \mathbf{0}$ if $R(r_j, \alpha)$, $r'_j = r_j$ otherwise.
  - Given a relation R over the semiring: r' =**keep_**R(**r**, α) is defined by $r'_j = r_j$ if $R(r_j, \alpha)$, $r'_j = \mathbf{0}$ otherwise.
- Semiring operations (between ranges and between a range and a semiring value):
  - $r'' = r + r'$ is defined by $r''_j = r_j + r'_j$.
  - $r'' = r \times r'$ is defined by $r''_j = r_j \times r'_j$.
  - $r' = r + a$ is defined by $r'_j = r_j + a$.
  - $r'' = r \times a$ is defined by $r'_j = r_j \times a$.
- Two operators are used to build domains from integers:
  - An operator for building intervals : $r = \mathtt{i_1..i_2}$ is defined by $r_j = \mathbf{1}$ if $j \in [i_1, i_2]$, $r_j = \mathbf{0}$ if $j \notin [i_1, i_2]$.
  - An operator for excluding one index : $r = \mathtt{comp(i)}$ is defined by $r_j = \mathbf{1}$ if $j \neq i$, $r_j = \mathbf{0}$ is $j = i$.
- We have the functional versions of usual relations:
  - Less or equal : $r' = \mathtt{le(r)}$ is defined by $r'_j = \sum_{k \leq j} r_k$.
  - Less : $r' = \mathtt{l(r)}$ is defined by $r'_j = \sum_{k<j} r_k$.
  - Greater or equal : $r' = \mathtt{ge(r)}$ is defined by $r'_j = \sum_{k \geq j} r_k$.
  - Greater : $r' = \mathtt{g(r)}$ is defined by $r'_j = \sum_{k>j} r_k$.
  - Different : $r' = \mathtt{d(r)}$ is defined by $r'_j = \sum_{k \neq j} r_k$.
- Arithmetic operations (between ranges and between a range and an integer):
  - $r'' = \mathtt{add(r,r')}$ is defined by $r''_j = \sum_{k+k'=j} r_k \times r'_{k'}$.
  - $r'' = \mathtt{sub(r,r')}$ is defined by $r''_j = \sum_{k-k'=j} r_k \times r'_{k'}$.
  - $r'' = \mathtt{mul(r,r')}$ is defined by $r''_j = \sum_{kk'=j} r_k \times r'_{k'}$.
  - $r'' = \mathtt{div(r,r')}$ is defined by $r''_j = \sum_{k=jk'} r_k \times r'_{k'}$.
  - For each **op** in {**add**, **sub**, **mul**, **div**} `op(r,i)` is defined by `op(r,r')` where $r'_i = \mathbf{1}$ and $r'_j = \mathbf{0}$ if $j \neq i$.

Let us details the indexicals appearing in the category of semiring values:

- The indexical **sigma** is defined by: **sigma**(Y)= $\sum_i Y_i$. **sigma**(Y) is an upper bound of the truth value of Y. As the truth values can only decrease during the (monotonic) computation, this is also an upper bound of the truth value that variable Y will have when instantiated.
- The indexical **pi** is defined by: **pi**(Y)= $\prod_{i/Y_i \neq 0} Y_i$. **pi**(Y) is a lower bound of the truth value of Y. Observe that, for the same reason as above, this is not a lower bound of the truth value that variable Y will have when instantiated.

5 Using The SFD System

5.1 Encoding High-Level Constraints

Using the SFD language, it is very easy to encode high-level constraints. Given a classical CSP constraint c (i.e. defined on a boolean semiring), we can derive a semiring constraint with the same shape but with value α for satisfaction and β for violation ($\alpha \geq_S \beta$), noted $c : (\alpha, \beta)$. In Section 3.2 for instance, we have defined the constraint $x \geq y : (\alpha, \beta)$, that could be expressed using SFD as follows:

```
X in ge(def(Y))*Alpha + sigma(Y)*Beta
Y in le(def(X))*Alpha + sigma(X)*Beta
```

We can define other arithmetic constraints similarly.
The constraint $x = y + c : (\alpha, \beta)$ is encoded by:

```
X in add(def(Y),C)*Alpha + sigma(Y)*Beta
Y in sub(def(X),C)*Alpha + sigma(X)*Beta
```

The constraint $x \leq y + z : (\alpha, \beta)$ is encoded by:

```
X in le(add(def(Y),def(Z)))*Alpha + sigma(Y)*sigma(Z)*Beta
Y in ge(sub(def(X),def(Z)))*Alpha + sigma(X)*sigma(Z)*Beta
Z in ge(sub(def(X),def(Y)))*Alpha + sigma(X)*sigma(Y)*Beta
```

More generally, it is possible to encode all the n-ary constraints involving a relation among ($\leq, <, =, >, \geq, \neq$) and two expressions built with operators among ($+, -, \times, /$). Moreover, other types of constraints can be defined (as in **clp(FD)**), such as, for instance, a weak form of constructive disjunction between constraints [4].

5.2 Computing Maximal Solutions

We will now focus on the computation of maximal solutions.

We suppose given a problem $P = \langle C, con \rangle$. We assume that $con = \{x_1, \ldots, x_n\}$ with $x_1 \prec \cdots \prec x_n$. In the following, we will note $c_{x,i,v}$ the constraint $\langle def_x, \{x\} \rangle$ such that $def_x(j) = v$ if $j = i$ and $def_x(j) = \mathbf{0}$ otherwise. Note that $c_{x,i,v}$ instantiate x to i with truth value v.

We follow the same approach as in traditional CLP: for each n-tuple t, we are going to solve the subproblem $P_t = \langle C_t, con \rangle$ where $C_t = C \cup \{c_{x_i, t_i, \mathbf{1}} / i \in [1, n]\}$. It is easy to prove that the maximal solutions of P can be found among those of the subproblems. For each t, we have to compute $Sol(P_t)$. Let $c_{x_i, t_i, v_i^t} = [\{x_i\}]_{ac(P_t)}$; because of the AC-computation, constraints c_{x_i, t_i} may have been replaced, so we get c_{x_i, t_i, v_i^t} instead of $c_{x_i, t_i, \mathbf{1}}$. It is easy to prove that $Sol(P_t) = \langle def, \{x_1, \ldots, x_n\} \rangle$ with $def(t') = \prod_i v_i^t$ if $t' = t$ and $def(t') = \mathbf{0}$ otherwise. Thus, the unique maximal solution of P_t is $\langle t, \prod_i v_i \rangle = \langle t, blevel(P_t) \rangle$. Note also that: $\prod_i v_i >_S v \Rightarrow \forall i, v_i >_S v$.

The two last results can be used to find a maximal solution of P efficiently: given t_1 and t_2, we can discard P_{t_2} as soon as one of the $v_i^{t_2}$ is not strictly greater than $blevel(P_{t_1})$.

Because we have the full power of a CLP language, it is very easy to write an optimization predicate that computes a maximal solution of given problem. Here is a definition, using a Prolog syntax:

```
maximal_solution(Vars) :-
    semiring_zero(Zero),
    g_assign(max,Zero),

    % first, computes the blevel (proof of optimality)
    repeat,                          % creates a choice point
    g_read(max,Alpha),
    (keep(greater,Vars,Alpha), % for each V in Vars:
                               % V in keep_greater(def(X),Alpha)
    labeling(Vars)
    ->
        blevel(Vars,Blevel),
        g_assign(max,Blevel),
        fail
    ;
        !,
        % then, computes the maximal solutions
        g_read(max,Beta),
        keep(greater_or_equal,Vars,Beta),
        labeling(Vars)).
```

Note that this optimization predicates is fully generic (it does not depend on the semiring).

6 Implementation

Let us first define an abstract encoding scheme for the semiring and then go into the implementation details.

6.1 Semiring Representation

In order to have a generic implementation, we have chosen to work on a representation of the semiring. Consider a c-semiring $S = \langle A, +, \times, \mathbf{0}, \mathbf{1}\rangle$ and:

- $B = [0, |A| - 1]$, i.e. the integer range between 0 and $|A| - 1$,
- ϕ a bijective function from A to B,
- $+_\phi = \lambda xy.\phi(\phi^{-1}(x) + \phi^{-1}(y))$ and
- $\times_\phi = \lambda xy.\phi(\phi^{-1}(x) \times \phi^{-1}(y))$.

Then, $S' = \langle B, +_\phi, \times_\phi, \phi(\mathbf{0}), \phi(\mathbf{1})\rangle$ is a c-semiring and ϕ is a morphism from A to B. We call S' a representation of S.

For example, since binary numbers with 3 bits range from 0 to 7, $\langle\mathcal{P}(\{a,b,c\}),\cup,\cap,\emptyset,\{a,b,c\}\rangle$ can be represented by $\langle[0,7],|,\&,0,7\rangle$ (where | and & are the C bitwise operators over integers).

Hence, if the user wants to use the semiring S, he has to:

- define S' (actually, knowing $|A|$, $+_\phi$ and $\times_\phi$ is sufficient),
- recompile a small part of the system (this could be avoided, but we have chosen this solution for efficiency reasons),
- then, he can write his `clp(FD,S)` programs using the semiring S'.

With this approach, the implementation remains totally generic. Moreover, the same example (and same code!) can be tested using different semirings.

6.2 Implementation Of X in r

We describe very briefly the implementation of X **in** r constraints in `clp(FD,S)`. This implementation is very close to the one of X **in** r constraints in `clp(FD)`. Thus, for more details, the reader should refer to [4]. Let us detail the three main data structures used to manage X **in** r constraints:

Constraint Frame: A constraint frame is created for every constraint. The informations recorded in a constraint frame are: the address of the associated code, the address of the FD variable it constrains, and the pointer to the environment in which to evaluate its range. The environment is just a list of as many arguments as are in the range of the constraint: each argument may be an integer, a semiring value, a (pointer to a) FD variable or a (pointer to a) range.

FD Variable Frame: The frame associated to an FD variable X is divided into two main parts: the valued domain (it is stored in a bit vector, but, as soon as X is instantiated, we switch to another representation, which is a pair index-value) and a dependency list pointing to the constraint frames of the constraints depending on X. These two parts are modified at different times during computation: the dependency lists are created when the constraints are *installed* and then are never changed, while the domain can be updated during execution. Actually, several distinct dependency lists are used:
- one related to **def**,
- one related to **sigma**,
- one related to **pi**,
- one related to **sigma** and **pi**.

This helps avoiding useless propagation.

Propagation Queue: The propagation phase consists of awakening and executing some constraints that could themselves select some new constraints to be awaken. To do this, we maintain an explicit propagation queue. A simple optimization consists in not pushing constraints but only pairs of the form $< X, mask >$ where X is the variable causing the propagation (that is, the one whose domain has been changed) and *mask* is a bit-mask of dependency lists to awake.

Finally, the implementation of SFD is very small: 5000 C lines and 500 Prolog lines in addition to the code for the Prolog compiler and run-time engine, taken from the original `clp(FD)` system.

7 Examples

In this section, we will test some of the instances of `clp(FD,S)`, using the following lc-semirings:

- $Bool = \langle\{false, true\}, \vee, \wedge, false, true\rangle$,
- $Fuzzy = \langle\{0.0, 0.1, \ldots, 1.0\}, max, min, 0.0, 1.0\rangle$,
- $Set = \langle\mathcal{P}(U), \cup, \cap, \emptyset, U\rangle$.

7.1 Boolean Examples

We compare `clp(FD,`*Bool*`)` and `clp(FD)`. We consider the problems `five` (Lewis Carroll's Zebra puzzle), originally presented in [19], and `cars` (a car sequencing problem), originally presented in [8]. We have run both implementations on a Sun Sparc 5. The results[3], given in Table 2, show that `clp(FD,`*Bool*`)` is slower than `clp(FD)`. The slow-down results from the loss of some specific optimizations, e.g. optimized boolean operations on bit-vectors. Observe also that, since `clp(FD)` indeed uses partial AC (propagating minimal and maximal values of domains), it could be much faster than `clp(FD,S)` on benchmarks heavily using arithmetic constraints, viz. linear equations. We plan to integrate a similar technique in `clp(FD,S)` in the future.

Table 2. `clp(FD)` versus `clp(FD,`*Bool*`)`

Problem	Time in ms using:	
	clp(FD)	clp(FD,*Bool*)
100×five	310	680
cars	20	70

7.2 Fuzzy Examples

We compare `clp(FD,`*Fuzzy*`)` and CON'*FLEX*, a system dedicated to fuzzy constraint solving [7]. We consider the problems `cantatrice` and `menu` given

[3] `five` has been run a hundred times.

with the CON'*FLEX* distribution. Both clp(FD,*Fuzzy*) and CON'*FLEX* have been run on a Pentium Pro 200. The results, given in Table 3, show that clp(FD,*Fuzzy*) performs well compared to a dedicated system.

Table 3. CON'*FLEX* versus clp(FD,*Fuzzy*)

Problem	Time in ms using: CON'*FLEX*	clp(FD,*Fuzzy*)
cantatrice	60	10
menu	30	10

7.3 Set-based Examples

We used clp(FD,*Set*) to solve time-tabling problems with preferences [5]. More precisely, we used the set-based framework to encode global preferences. We compare our results with those of [5]. Caseau and Laburthe use a global constraint, based on the Hungarian method, dedicated to weighted matching problems and additional redundant constraints (CLAIRE2), they also provide results using simple constraint propagation (CLAIRE1). Both clp(FD,*Set*) and the CLAIRE [6] codes have been run on a Sun Sparc 5. The results are given in Table 4. Our method is more efficient than simple constraint propagation for the three problems (both in time and backtrack number), it is more efficient than the weighted matching technique for problems 1 and 3 (both in time and backtrack number) but less efficient for problem 2 (for which the satisfiability is easier).

Table 4. CLAIRE versus clp(FD,*Set*).

Problem	CLAIRE1 Backtracks	Time (s)	CLAIRE2 Backtracks	Time (s)	clp(FD,*Set*) Backtracks	Time (s)
1	189000	1541	3500	29	899	18.6
2	286000	1040	234	2.6	31921	254
3	43000	246	17000	120	1797	9.7

8 Conclusion

We have defined a generic scheme for compiling semiring-based constraints. Using this kernel and a semiring representation, we can generate a new solver dedicated to the chosen semiring. Because of the generality of our approach, we lose some optimizations that could be introduced in the solver (for example, in the "boolean" one) but we still are efficient with respect to dedicated systems (this is due to the fact that we have captured the essential notions of the computation). Another important point is that we can now imagine (and trivially implement!) new solvers (for example, by combining different semirings).

Future work will focus on extending the expressive power of the SFD system and introducing partial AC (instead of the exact computation of AC which might be too costly in arithmetic examples). This roughly means moving from AC-3 to AC-5 [20] as in `clp(FD)`. The problem in our case is to find a good and generic approximation of a valued domain.

Finally, note that the `clp(FD,S)` system is freely available by:

`http://pauillac.inria.fr/~georget/clpfds.html`.

Acknowledgments

We would like to thank Daniel Diaz, Francesca Rossi and Stefano Bistarelli for fruitful discussions and comments.

References

1. S. Bistarelli, U. Montanari and F. Rossi. Constraint Solving over Semirings. In *Proceedings of IJCAI'95*, Morgan Kaufman, 1995.
2. S. Bistarelli, U. Montanari and F. Rossi. Semiring-based Constraint Solving and Optimization. Journal of ACM, vol.44, n.2, pp. 201-236, March 1997.
3. P. Codognet and D. Diaz. A Minimal Extension of the WAM for `clp(FD)`. In *Proceedings of ICLP'93, 10th Int. Conf. on Logic Programming*, Budapest, Hungary, MIT Press 1993.
4. P. Codognet and D. Diaz. Compiling Constraints in `clp(FD)`. *Journal of Logic Programming*, vol. 27, no. 3, 1996.
5. Y. Caseau and F. Laburthe. Solving Various Weighted Matching Problems with Constraints. In *Proceedings of CP'97, 3rd Int. Conf. on Constraint Programming*, Springer Verlag, 1997.
6. Y. Caseau and F. Laburthe. The Claire documentation. LIENS Report 96-15, Ecole Normale Superieure, Paris, 1995.
7. CON'*FLEX*, manuel de l'utilisateur Laboratoire de Biométrie et d'Intelligence Artificielle, INRA, France, 1996
8. M. Dincbas, H. Simonis, P. Van Hentenryck. Solving the Car-Sequencing Problem In Constraint Logic Programming. In *Proceedings of ECAI'88*. Munich, West Germany, August 1988.
9. D. Dubois, H. Fargier, and H. Prade. The calculus of fuzzy restrictions as a basis for flexible constraint satisfaction. In *Proceedings of IEEE International Conference on Fuzzy Systems*. IEEE, 1993.
10. E.C. Freuder and R.J. Wallace. Partial constraint satisfaction. *AI Journal*, 58, 1992, pp.21–70.
11. L. Gacôgne. Elements de logique floue. Hermes, 1997.

12. M. Lemaître and L. Lobjois. Bibliothèque d'algorithmes de résolution de problèmes et d'optimisation sous contraintes. CERT, FRANCE, 1997.
13. A. K. Mackworth. Consistency in Networks of Relations. *Artificial Intelligence 8 (1977)*, pp 99-118.
14. A.K. Mackworth. Constraint satisfaction. In Stuart C. Shapiro, editor, *Encyclopedia of AI (second edition)*, volume 1, pages 285–293. John Wiley & Sons, 1992.
15. U. Montanari. Networks of constraints: Fundamental properties and application to picture processing. *Information Science*, 7, 1974.
16. A. Rosenfeld, R.A. Hummel, and S.W. Zucker. Scene labelling by relaxation operations. *IEEE Transactions on Systems, Man, and Cybernetics*, 6(6), 1976.
17. Z. Ruttkay. Fuzzy constraint satisfaction. In *Proceedings of 3rd International Conference on Fuzzy Systems*, 1994.
18. T. Schiex, H. Fargier, and G.Verfaillie. Valued Constraint Satisfaction Problems: Hard and Easy Problems. In *Proceedings of IJCAI'95*. Morgan Kaufmann, 1995.
19. P. Van Hentenryck. *Constraint Satisfaction in Logic Programming*. MIT Press, 1989.
20. P. Van Hentenryck, Y. Deville and C-M. Teng. A generic arc-consistency algorithm and its specializations. *Artificial Intelligence 57 (1992)*, pp 291-321.
21. L.A. Zadeh. Calculus of fuzzy restrictions. in K. Tanaka, L.A. Zadeh, K.S Fu and M. Shimura editors, *Fuzzy sets and their applications to cognitive and decision processes*. Academic Press, 1975.

Combining Topological and Qualitative Size Constraints for Spatial Reasoning

Alfonso Gerevini[1] and Jochen Renz[2]

[1] Dipartimento di Elettronica per l'Automazione, Università di Brescia
Via Branze 38, 25123 Brescia, Italy
gerevini@bsing.ing.unibs.it
[2] Institut für Informatik, Albert-Ludwigs-Universität
Am Flughafen 17, 79110 Freiburg, Germany
renz@informatik.uni-freiburg.de

Abstract. Information about the relative size of spatial regions is often easily accessible and, when combined with other types of spatial information, it can be practically very useful. In this paper we combine a simple framework for reasoning about qualitative size relations with the Region Connection Calculus RCC-8, a widely studied approach for qualitative spatial reasoning with topological relations. Reasoning about RCC-8 relations is NP-hard, but a large maximal tractable subclass of RCC-8 called $\widehat{\mathcal{H}}_8$ was identified. Interestingly, any constraint in RCC-8 $-$ $\widehat{\mathcal{H}}_8$ can be consistently reduced to a constraint in $\widehat{\mathcal{H}}_8$, when an appropriate size constraint between the spatial regions is supplied. We propose an $O(n^3)$ time path-consistency algorithm based on a novel technique for combining RCC-8 constraints and relative size constraints, where n is the number of spatial regions. We prove its correctness and completeness for deciding consistency when the input contains topological constraints in $\widehat{\mathcal{H}}_8$. We also provide results on finding a consistent scenario in $O(n^3)$ time both for combined topological and relative size constraints, and for topological constraints alone. This is an $O(n^2)$ improvement over the known methods.

1 Introduction

The Region Connection Calculus (RCC) [13] is a well studied topological approach for qualitative spatial reasoning, where regions are non-empty regular subsets of a topological space. Regions need not be one-piece. Binary relations between regions are based on the "connected" relation $C(a,b)$ which is true if the closure of region a and the closure of region b have a non-empty intersection.

RCC-8 is a set of eight jointly exhaustive and pairwise disjoint relations called basic relations definable in the RCC-theory, and of all possible disjunctions of the basic relations, resulting in 2^8 different RCC-8 relations altogether.

An important reasoning problem in this framework is deciding consistency of a set of spatial constraints of the form xRy where x, y are region variables and R is a relation in RCC-8. Another related problem is finding a consistent scenario for a set of RCC-8 constraints, that is a consistent refinement of all the constraints in the set to one of their basic relations. These problems are in general NP-hard, but they can be solved in polynomial time for a large subset of RCC-8 (denoted $\widehat{\mathcal{H}}_8$) which is a maximal tractable subclass of RCC-8 [15]. In particular, Renz and Nebel [15] proved that the consistency of a set of constraints over $\widehat{\mathcal{H}}_8$ can be decided in $O(n^3)$ time, where n is the number of variables involved.

This paper contains two main contributions. In the first part of the paper we address the problem of finding a consistent scenario for a set of $\widehat{\mathcal{H}}_8$ constraints, and we propose an $O(n^3)$ time algorithm for solving this task. This is an $O(n^2)$ improvement over the bound of the previously known methods.

In the second part of the paper, we study the combination of RCC-8 with qualitative information about region sizes, which is often easily accessible and practically useful. As a very simple example, suppose to have three geographical regions A, B and C for which the only topological information available is that B is contained in A. In addition we know that A is smaller than C, and that C is smaller than B. The combined set of topological and relative size information is inconsistent, but we cannot detect this by just independently processing the two kind of information, or by just expressing the size information as topological constraints.[1]

Specifically, we consider the following qualitative relations between region sizes, which have been largely studied in the context of temporal reasoning (e.g., [17, 16, 6]): $<, \leq, >, \geq, \neq, =, <=>$. Interestingly, any constraint in RCC-8 $-$ $\widehat{\mathcal{H}}_8$ can be consistently refined to a constraint in $\widehat{\mathcal{H}}_8$, when an appropriate size constraint of this class is supplied.

We propose an algorithm, BIPATH-CONSISTENCY, based on a novel technique for dealing with combined topological and qualitative size constraints, and we prove that, despite our extended framework is more expressive than $\widehat{\mathcal{H}}_8$ (and therefore it has a larger potential applicability), the problem of deciding consistency can be solved in cubic time (i.e., without additional worst-case cost). BIPATH-CONSISTENCY is a general algorithm, in the sense that it can be applied not only to spatial relations. For example, in the context of temporal reasoning it can be used to combine relations in Allen's Interval Algebra [1] and qualitative constraints on the duration of the temporal intervals. Of course, different classes of relations might need different completeness and complexity proofs.

The proof of the completeness of this algorithm is based on a particular method of constructing a consistent scenario for a set of constraints over $\widehat{\mathcal{H}}_8$, which is analyzed in the first part of the paper. Moreover, this method can also be used in combination with BIPATH-CONSISTENCY to compute, in cubic time, a consistent topological scenario satisfying an input set of qualitative size constraints between the spatial regions.

The rest of the paper is organized as follows. In the first part we briefly introduce RCC-8 (Section 2) and give the results concerning computing a consistent scenario (Section 3). The second part deals with the combination of topological and size constraints (Sections 4 and 5).

---

[1] Another more complex example illustrating interdependencies between topological and size constraints is given in Section 5.

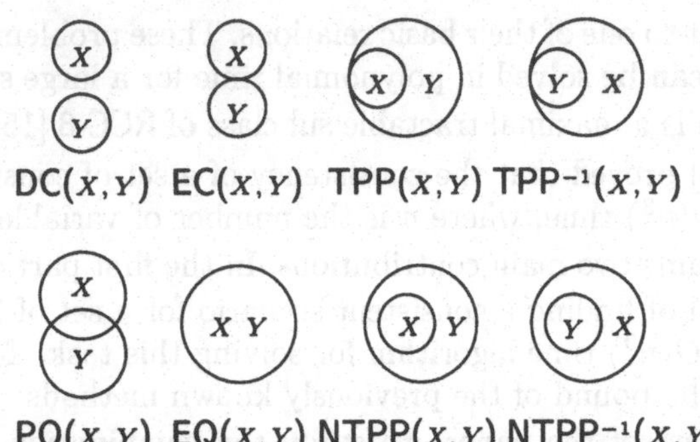

Fig. 1. Two-dimensional examples for the eight basic relations of RCC-8

2 The Region Connection Calculus RCC-8

RCC-8 is a set of binary spatial relations formed by eight jointly exhaustive and pairwise disjoint relations definable in the RCC-theory called *basic relations*,[2] and by all possible disjunctions of the basic relations (resulting in 2^8 different RCC-8 relations altogether). The basic relations are denoted by DC (DisConnected), EC (Externally Connected), PO (Partial Overlap), EQ (EQual), TPP (Tangential Proper Part), NTPP (Non-Tangential Proper Part), and their converse TPP^{-1} and NTPP^{-1} [13]. Figure 1 shows two-dimensional examples of these relations. In the following, an RCC-8 relation will be written as a set of basic relations.

An important reasoning problem in this framework is deciding consistency of a set Θ of spatial constraints of the form xRy where x, y are region variables and R is an RCC-8 relation. Θ is consistent if and only if there is a *model* of Θ, i.e., an assignment of spatial regions to the variables of Θ such that all the constraints are satisfied. This problem (denoted by RSAT) is NP-complete [15]. RSAT is a fundamental reasoning problem since several other interesting reasoning problems can be reduced to it by polynomial Turing reduction [7].

A set of constraints in RCC-8 can be processed using an $O(n^3)$ time *path-consistency* algorithm, which makes the set *path-consistent* by eliminating all the impossible labels (basic relations) in every subset of constraints involving three variables [11, 12]. If the empty relation occurs during this process, the set is not consistent, otherwise the resulting set is path-consistent. Since RSAT is NP-complete, in general imposing path-consistency is not sufficient for deciding consistency of a set of RCC-8 constraints. Renz and Nebel [15] identified a subset of RCC-8 (denoted by $\widehat{\mathcal{H}}_8$) for which RSAT can be solved in polynomial time. They also proved that $\widehat{\mathcal{H}}_8$ is maximal with respect to tractability, i.e., if any RCC-8 relation is added to $\widehat{\mathcal{H}}_8$, then the consistency problem becomes NP-complete. Finally they showed that computing path-consistency for a set of constraints over $\widehat{\mathcal{H}}_8$ is sufficient for deciding its consistency.

$\widehat{\mathcal{H}}_8$ contains 148 relations, i.e., almost 60% of the RCC-8 relations. The following 108 RCC-8 relations are not contained in $\widehat{\mathcal{H}}_8$, where (N)TPP denotes TPP

[2] I.e., between any two regions exactly one of the basic relations holds.

or NTPP:

$$\mathsf{RCC\text{-}8} \setminus \widehat{\mathcal{H}}_8 = \{R \mid (\{\mathsf{(N)TPP}, \mathsf{(N)TPP}^{-1}\} \subset R \text{ and } \{\mathsf{PO}\} \not\subset R) \text{ or } (\{\mathsf{EQ}, \mathsf{NTPP}\} \subset R \text{ and } \{\mathsf{TPP}\} \not\subset R) \text{ or } (\{\mathsf{EQ}, \mathsf{NTPP}^{-1}\} \subset R \text{ and } \{\mathsf{TPP}^{-1}\} \not\subset R)\}$$

We assume that a set of RCC-8 constraints Θ contains one constraint for each pair of variables involved in Θ, i.e., if no information is given about the relation holding between two variables x and y, then the universal constraint $x\{*\}y$ is implicitly contained in Θ ($*$ denotes the *universal relation*, i.e., the union of all the basic relations). Another assumption that we make is that whenever a constraint xRy is in Θ, also $yR^{\smile}x$ is present, where $R^{\smile}$ is the converse of R.

We say that a set of constraints Θ' is a *refinement* of Θ if and only if the same variables are involved in both the sets, and for every pair of variables x, y, if $xR'y \in \Theta'$ then $xRy \in \Theta$ and $R' \subseteq R$. Θ' is said to be a ***consistent refinement*** of Θ if and only if Θ' is a refinement of Θ and both Θ and Θ' are consistent. A ***consistent scenario*** Θ_s of a set of constraints Θ is a consistent refinement of Θ where all the constraints of Θ_s are assertions of basic relations.

3 Finding a Consistent Scenario for RCC-8

In order to decide the consistency of a set of RCC-8 constraints Θ, it is sufficient to find a path-consistent refinement of Θ containing only constraints over $\widehat{\mathcal{H}}_8$.[3] However, for other tasks such as finding a model of Θ this is not sufficient. For these tasks it is rather necessary to have basic relations between any pair of variables involved in Θ, i.e., a consistent scenario for Θ is required.

A naive algorithm for finding a consistent scenario for Θ is based on restricting every relation to a basic relation in a backtrack-like manner by using path-consistency as forward checking after each restriction. This requires $O(n^5)$ time if Θ contains only constraints over $\widehat{\mathcal{H}}_8$, and to the best of our knowledge no algorithm with a better worst-case complexity is known. As in the case of qualitative temporal reasoning (e.g., Ligozat [10], vanBeek [16]), by exploiting some properties of the particular class of used relations, it is possible to design more efficient algorithms. For instance, a more efficient algorithm is possible for a certain set of relations when path-consistency implies minimal labels or strong consistency [4] for this set. However, this is not the case for $\widehat{\mathcal{H}}_8$ [15].

In the following wo will provc that given a consistent set Θ of constraints over $\widehat{\mathcal{H}}_8$, a consistent scenario Θ_s can be obtained in $O(n^3)$ time by reducing all the constraints of Θ to constraints over the basic relations in a very particular way. In order to prove this, we will use several "refinement strategies" of the form "given a particular set $\mathcal{S} \subseteq \widehat{\mathcal{H}}_8$, a relation R', and a path-consistent set Θ of constraints over $\mathcal{S}$, Θ can be consistently refined to Θ' by replacing each constraint xRy in Θ, such that $R' \subset R$, with the constraint $xR'y$." In the following the set $\mathcal{S}$ will be indicated with $\widehat{\mathcal{H}}_{\downarrow_{R'}}$.

[3] This is of course also true for any other tractable subclass of RCC-8 for which path-consistency is sufficient for deciding consistency.

By using the encoding of RCC-8 in classical propositional logic as specified in [15], it is possible to prove that these refinement strategies preserve consistency. In this encoding every set of RCC-8 constraints Θ is transformed to a propositional formula $p(\Theta)$ such that Θ is consistent if and only if $p(\Theta)$ is satisfiable. In particular, every variable x involved in Θ is transformed to a set of propositional atoms $\{X_k \mid k = 1, \ldots, m; m \leq cn^2\}$ (c is a constant), and every constraint $xRy \in \Theta$ is transformed to a set of clauses involving literals over X_k and Y_k for some k. Since each constraint xRy is transformed to a propositional Horn clause if $R \in \widehat{\mathcal{H}}_8$, consistency of a set Θ of constraints over $\widehat{\mathcal{H}}_8$ can be decided by applying positive unit resolution (PUR) to $p(\Theta)$. Here we will use a property which was proved in [15], namely, that a new positive unit clause $\{X_w\}$ can be derived from $p(\Theta)$ by using PUR only if (1) there is a variable y in Θ such that the clause $\{Y_w\}$ is present, and (2) Θ contains a so-called *R_Γ-chain from x to y*. An R_Γ-chain from x to y is a sequence of constraints $xRz, zR'z', \ldots, z''R'''y$, where all relations $R, R', \ldots, R'''$ are from a particular set of relations R_Γ.[4] We also need another property which can be proven by using the same methods as those applied in [15]:

Lemma 1. *Let Θ be a set of constraints over $\widehat{\mathcal{H}}_8$ that contains an R_Γ-chain from x to y for some variables x and y. If for some $w \in \{1, \ldots, m\}$ the clause $\{X_w\}$ can be derived from $p(\Theta)$ and $\{Y_w\}$ by using PUR, then $\{X_k\}$ can be derived from $p(\Theta)$ and $\{Y_k\}$ by using PUR for all $k \in \{1, \ldots, m\}$.*

We will only sketch some of the proofs involving the encoding of RCC-8 in classical propositional logic, and refer to the technical report for the full proofs [5]. We will use refinement strategies for the following sets of relations:

Definition 1.
- $\widehat{\mathcal{H}}_{\downarrow \mathsf{DC}} = \widehat{\mathcal{H}}_8$
- $\widehat{\mathcal{H}}_{\downarrow \mathsf{EC}} = \{R \in \widehat{\mathcal{H}}_8 \mid$ *R does not contain both* DC *and* EC$\}$
- $\widehat{\mathcal{H}}_{\downarrow \mathsf{PO}} = \{R \in \widehat{\mathcal{H}}_8 \mid$ *R does not contain any of* DC, EC, *or* EQ, *unless R is a basic relation*$\}$
- $\widehat{\mathcal{H}}_{\downarrow \mathsf{NTPP}} = \{R \in \widehat{\mathcal{H}}_8 \mid$ *R does not contain any of* DC, EC, EQ, *or* PO, *unless R is a basic relation*$\}$

Lemma 2 (DC-refinement)**.** *Let Θ be a path-consistent set of constraints over $\widehat{\mathcal{H}}_{\downarrow \mathsf{DC}}$. Θ can be consistently refined to Θ' by replacing every constraint $xRy \in \Theta$ such that $\{\mathsf{DC}\} \subset R$ with the constraint $x\{\mathsf{DC}\}y$.*

Proof Sketch. Let xRy with $R = \{\mathsf{DC}\} \cup R'$ be one of the constraints of Θ, and suppose that Θ becomes inconsistent if xRy is replaced with $x\{\mathsf{DC}\}y$ resulting in Θ''. Since the propositional encoding of $x\{\mathsf{DC}\}y$ is $p(x\{\mathsf{DC}\}y) = \bigwedge_{k=1}^{m}(\neg X_k \vee \neg Y_k)$ (see [15]), no new positive unit clause can be derived by using these Horn clauses. Thus, the empty clause can be derived from $p(\Theta'')$ by using PUR only when for some $w \in \{1, \ldots, m\}$ both the unit clauses $\{X_w\}$ and $\{Y_w\}$ can be

[4] R_Γ is the set of relations that contains one of the basic relations $\mathsf{TPP}^{-1}, \mathsf{NTPP}^{-1}$, or EQ, but does not contain any of TPP, NTPP, or PO [15]

derived from $p(\Theta)$. It follows from [15] that if this were possible, then Θ would not be path-consistent. This contradicts our assumptions. Since no new positive unit clause is derivable from $p(\Theta'')$, any constraint xRy of Θ that contains $\{\mathsf{DC}\}$ can be replaced with $x\{\mathsf{DC}\}y$ simultaneously, for any pair of variables x and y in Θ, without applying the path-consistency algorithm after each replacement. □

The proofs of the following three refinement strategies are more complex than the proofs of the previous ones since there are more cases to consider. However, all cases can be handled with the same methods as used in the previous proofs, namely, by looking at whether the changes to the propositional encodings resulting from the refinement of constraints permit to derive the empty clause by using PUR. In all of these cases it turns out (mostly by applying Lemma 1) that if the empty clause is derivable after the refinements, then it was also derivable before the refinement. Therefore the refinements preserve consistency of the set of constraints.

Lemma 3 (EC-refinement). *Let Θ be a path-consistent set of constraints over $\widehat{\mathcal{H}}_{\downarrow\mathsf{EC}}$. Θ can be consistently refined to Θ' by replacing every constraint $xRy \in \Theta$ such that $\{\mathsf{EC}\} \subset R$ with the constraint $x\{\mathsf{EC}\}y$.*

Lemma 4 (PO-refinement). *Let Θ be a path-consistent set of constraints over $\widehat{\mathcal{H}}_{\downarrow\mathsf{PO}}$. Θ can be consistently refined to Θ' by replacing every constraint $xRy \in \Theta$ such that $\{\mathsf{PO}\} \subset R$ with the constraint $x\{\mathsf{PO}\}y$.*

Lemma 5 (NTPP-refinement). *Let Θ be a path-consistent set of constraints over $\widehat{\mathcal{H}}_{\downarrow\mathsf{NTPP}}$. Θ can be consistently refined to Θ' by replacing every constraint $xRy \in \Theta$ such that $\{\mathsf{NTPP}\} \subset R$ with the constraint $x\{\mathsf{NTPP}\}y$.*

In addition to the four refinement strategies described above, we need a further constraint refinement technique for handling relations containing $\{\mathsf{EQ}\}$.

Lemma 6 (EQ-elimination). *Let Θ be a path-consistent set of constraints over $\widehat{\mathcal{H}}_8$. Θ can be consistently refined to Θ' by eliminating $\{\mathsf{EQ}\}$ from every constraint $xRy \in \Theta$ unless $R = \{\mathsf{EQ}\}$.*

Proof Sketch. Let xRy be one of the constraints of Θ, and suppose that Θ becomes inconsistent if $\{\mathsf{EQ}\}$ is eliminated from xRy resulting in Θ''. Since eliminating $\{\mathsf{EQ}\}$ from a relation R is equivalent to intersecting R with the relation $\overline{\{\mathsf{EQ}\}}$ expressible as $\overline{\{\mathsf{EQ}\}} = \{\mathsf{EC}\} \circ \{\mathsf{DC},\mathsf{PO}\}$,[5] Θ'' is equivalent to $\Theta \cup \{x\{\mathsf{EC}\}z, z\{\mathsf{DC},\mathsf{PO}\}y\}$ where z is a fresh variable which is only related with x and y. As neither $\{\mathsf{EC}\}$ nor $\{\mathsf{DC},\mathsf{PO}\}$ are contained in R_Γ, no positive unit clauses for literals of $p(\Theta)$ can be derived from $p(\Theta'')$ by PUR using the clauses resulting from the propositional encoding of the two new constraints. Thus, the empty clause can only be derived from $p(\Theta'')$ by using the unit clauses in the propositional encodings of the new constraints. Because of Lemma 1 there must be a way in which only the unit clauses of the newly added constraints can be used to derive the empty clause, and not the unit clauses derivable from $p(\Theta)$.

[5] $\overline{Rel}$ denotes the complement of Rel, $R_1 \circ R_2$ denotes the composition of R_1 with R_2.

It follows from [15] that this is possible only if Θ contains an R_Γ-chain from x to y and an R_Γ-chain from y to x. But if this were the case, it follows from [15] that Θ would not be path-consistent, and thus the initial assumptions would be contradicted. Since no new R_Γ-chain is introduced in Θ'', {EQ} can be eliminated from all relations simultaneously without applying the path-consistency algorithm after each elimination. □

We can now combine the five strategies to derive an algorithm for determining a consistent scenario for a consistent set of constraints over $\widehat{\mathcal{H}}_8$.

Theorem 1. *For each path-consistent set Θ of constraints over $\widehat{\mathcal{H}}_8$, a consistent scenario Θ_s can be determined in time $O(n^3)$, where n is the number of variables involved in Θ.*

Proof. The following algorithm, SCENARIO(Θ), solves the problem:

(1) apply DC-refinement, (2) apply EC-refinement, (3) apply EQ-elimination, (4) apply PO-refinement, (5) apply NTPP-refinement, (6) return the set of the resulting constraints.
Impose path-consistency after each of the steps (1)–(5).

SCENARIO(Θ) terminates in $O(n^3)$ time since each of the steps (1)–(5) takes time $O(n^2)$ and path-consistency, which takes time $O(n^3)$, is computed 5 times. By Definition 1 we have that $\widehat{\mathcal{H}}_{\downarrow \mathsf{NTPP}} \subset \widehat{\mathcal{H}}_{\downarrow \mathsf{PO}} \subset \widehat{\mathcal{H}}_{\downarrow \mathsf{EC}} \subset \widehat{\mathcal{H}}_8$. It follows from Lemmas 5 and 6 that after applying each refinement step, Θ is refined to a set of constraints containing only relations for which the next refinement step is guaranteed to make a consistent refinement. Since the interleaved applications of the path-consistency algorithm can only refine constraints and never add new basic relations to the constraints, the possible set of relations obtained after each step is not extended by applying the path-consistency algorithm.

Thus, since Θ is consistent and contains only constraints over $\widehat{\mathcal{H}}_8$, the output of SCENARIO(Θ) is consistent. Moreover, since any (non-basic) relation of $\widehat{\mathcal{H}}_8$ contains one of DC, EC, PO, NTPP, or NTPP^{-1} (see the definition of $\widehat{\mathcal{H}}_8$ in Section 2), the interleaved applications of path-consistency and steps (1)–(5) guarantee that the output of SCENARIO(Θ) is a consistent scenario for Θ. □

By applying SCENARIO(Θ) to a path-consistent set of constraints over $\widehat{\mathcal{H}}_8$ we obtain a particular consistent scenario Θ_s of Θ. Since exactly this consistent scenario is used in the proof of the main theorem of Section 5, in the following lemma we explicitly describe the relationship between Θ_s and Θ.

Lemma 7. *Let Θ be a path-consistent set of constraints over $\widehat{\mathcal{H}}_8$ involving the variables x and y, and let Θ_s be the output of* SCENARIO(Θ).

- *The constraint x{EQ}y is contained in Θ_s only if it is also contained in Θ.*
- *The constraint x{TPP}y is contained in Θ_s only if Θ contains either x{TPP}y or x{TPP, EQ}y.*
- *The constraint x{NTPP}y is contained in Θ_s only if Θ contains either x{NTPP}y, x{NTPP, TPP}y or x{NTPP, TPP, EQ}y.*

In all the other cases, $xRy \in \Theta$ is refined to one of $x\{\mathsf{DC}\}y$, $x\{\mathsf{EC}\}y$ or $x\{\mathsf{PO}\}y$ in Θ_s.

Proof Sketch. If the path-consistency algorithm were not applied after each of the steps (1) - (5) in SCENARIO(Θ), the proof would immediately follow from the applications of the refinements in the algorithm. Considering the interleaved path-consistency computations, it might be possible that after refining a constraint of Θ to one of {DC}, {EC}, or {PO} by one of the steps (1), (2), or (4), another constraint $xRy \in \Theta$, such that $R \cap \{\mathsf{DC},\mathsf{EC},\mathsf{PO}\} \neq \emptyset$ and $R \cap \{\mathsf{TPP},\mathsf{TPP}^{-1},\mathsf{NTPP},\mathsf{NTPP}^{-1},\mathsf{EQ}\} \neq \emptyset$, is refined by the path-consistency algorithm to $xR'y$ such that $R' \cap \{\mathsf{DC},\mathsf{EC},\mathsf{PO}\} = \emptyset$. In this case, xRy would be refined by SCENARIO(Θ) to one of $x\{\mathsf{NTPP}\}y$, $x\{\mathsf{TPP}\}y$, $x\{\mathsf{NTPP}^{-1}\}y$, $x\{\mathsf{TPP}^{-1}\}y$, or $x\{\mathsf{EQ}\}y$ in Θ_s which contradicts the lemma. However, by analyzing the composition table of the RCC-8 relations (see, e.g.,[15]) it follows that this is never possible for the sets of relations used by the different refinement strategies. □

4 Combining Topological and Qualitative Size Relations

In this section we introduce $\mathcal{QS}$, a class of qualitative relations between region sizes, and we combine this class with RCC-8. We also give some technical results that will be used in the next section, where we present an algorithm for processing constraints in the combined framework.

In the following we will assume that all the spatial regions are measurable sets in $\mathbb{R}^n$ [2]. Note that this assumption does not compromise the computational properties of $\widehat{\mathcal{H}}_8$, because from [14] it follows that the regions of every consistent set of RCC-8 constraints can always be interpreted as measurable sets (e.g., as sets of spheres in $\mathbb{R}^3$). We will also assume that the size of an n-dimensional region corresponds to its n-dimensional measure [2]. For example, the size of a sphere in $\mathbb{R}^3$ corresponds to its volume.

Given a set V of spatial region variables, a set of $\mathcal{QS}$ constraints over V is a set of constraints of the form $size(x)\ S\ size(y)$, where $S \in \mathcal{QS}$, $size(x)$ is the size of the region x, $size(y)$ is the size of the region y, and $x, y \in V$.

Definition 2. *$\mathcal{QS}$ is the class formed by the following eight qualitative relations between the size of spatial regions: $<$, $>$, $\leq$, $\neq$, $=$, $\geq$, $<=>$ and $\emptyset$, where $<=>$ is the universal relation, and $<$, $>$, and $=$ are the basic relations.*

Proposition 1. *The relations of $\mathcal{QS}$ form a Point Algebra.*

It is obvious that the topological RCC-8 relations and the relative size relations are not independent from each other. Table 1 gives the size relations that are entailed by the basic RCC-8 relations, and the topological relations that are entailed by the basic size relations. $Sizerel(R)$ indicates the strongest size relation entailed by the topological relation R, and $Toprel(S)$ indicates the strongest topological relation entailed by the size relation S.

The dependencies from a non-basic relation R can be obtained by disjunctively combining the relations entailed by each basic relation in R. For example, {TPP,EQ} entails "$\leq$".

r		$Sizerel(r)$	r		$Sizerel(r)$	s		$Toprel(s)$
TPP	$\models$	$<$	DC	$\models$	$<=>$	$=$	$\models$	DC, EC, PO, EQ
NTPP	$\models$	$<$	EC	$\models$	$<=>$	$>$	$\models$	DC, EC, PO, TPP^{-1}, $NTPP^{-1}$
TPP^{-1}	$\models$	$>$	PO	$\models$	$<=>$	$<$	$\models$	DC, EC, PO, TPP, NTPP
$NTPP^{-1}$	$\models$	$>$	EQ	$\models$	$=$			

Table 1. Interdependencies of basic RCC-8 relations (r) and basic $\mathcal{QS}$ relations (s)

Since any topological relation – and any sub-relation thereof – entailed by the basic size relations $<, >, =$ is contained in $\widehat{\mathcal{H}}_8$, the following proposition is true.

Proposition 2. *The relation $R \in$ RCC-8$\setminus\widehat{\mathcal{H}}_8$ of any constraint xRy can be consistently refined to a relation $R' \in \widehat{\mathcal{H}}_8$, if an appropriate size constraint between x and y is given. In particular, if definite size information is given, then R can always be consistently refined to a relation $R' \in \widehat{\mathcal{H}}_8$.*

For example, the RCC-8$\setminus\widehat{\mathcal{H}}_8$ constraint $x\{\text{TPP}, \text{TPP}^{-1}, \text{NTPP}, \text{DC}, \text{EC}\}y$ can be consistently refined to the $\widehat{\mathcal{H}}_8$ constraint $x\{\text{TPP}, \text{NTPP}, \text{DC}, \text{EC}\}y$ if the size constraint $size(x) \leq size(y)$ is given. Before giving an algorithm for processing RCC-8 constraints combined with qualitative size constraints, we need to give some further technical definitions and results that will be used in the next section to prove the formal properties of the algorithm.

Definition 3 (Model for Σ). *Given a set Σ of constraints in $\mathcal{QS}$, we say that an assignment σ of spatial regions to the variables of Σ is a* model *of Σ if and only if σ satisfies all the constraints in Σ.*

Definition 4 (Consistency for $\Theta \cup \Sigma$). *Given a set Θ of constraints in* RCC-8 *and a set Σ of constraints in $\mathcal{QS}$, $\Theta \cup \Sigma$ is* consistent *if there exists a model of Θ which is also a model of Σ.*

We say that a consistent scenario for a set Θ of constraints is *size-consistent* relative to a set Σ of constraints if and only if there exists a model for the scenario that is also a model of Σ.

The next lemma states that non-forced equalities can be omitted from a path-consistent set of size constraints in $\mathcal{QS}$ without losing consistency.

Lemma 8. *Let Σ be a path-consistent set of size constraints over $\mathcal{QS}$ and Σ' the set of size constraints such that, for each constraint size(i) S size(j) in Σ,*

1. *if $S \in \{<, >\}$ then size(i) S size(j) $\in \Sigma'$,*
2. *if S = "$\leq$" then size(i) $<$ size(j) $\in \Sigma'$,*
3. *if S = "$\geq$" then size(i) $>$ size(j) $\in \Sigma'$,*
4. *if S = "$=$" then size(i) $=$ size(j) $\in \Sigma'$,*
5. *if S = "$<=>$" then size(i) $\neq$ size(j) $\in \Sigma'$.*

Σ' is consistent and any model of Σ' is also a model of Σ.

Proof Sketch. It follows from van Beek's method of computing a consistent scenario for a set of relations in the temporal Point Algebra [16]. □

Let Θ be a set of constraints in RCC-8, Σ a set of of constraints in $\mathcal{QS}$, t_{ij} the relation between i and j in Θ, and s_{ij} the relation between $size(i)$ and $size(j)$ in Σ. We say that: t_{ij} entails the negation of s_{ij} ($t_{ij} \models \neg s_{ij}$) if and only if $Sizerel(t_{ij}) \cap s_{ij} = \emptyset$; s_{ij} entails the negation of t_{ij} ($s_{ij} \models \neg t_{ij}$) if and only if $Toprel(s_{ij}) \cap t_{ij} = \emptyset$.

Proposition 3. *A consistent set Θ of constraints in* RCC-8 *entails the negation of a $\mathcal{QS}$ relation s_{ij} between size(i) and size(j) if and only if $Sizerel(\hat{t}_{ij}) \cap s_{ij} = \emptyset$, where $\hat{t}_{ij}$ is the strongest entailed relation between i and j in Θ.*

Proposition 4. *A consistent set Σ of constraints in $\mathcal{QS}$ entails the negation of a* RCC-8 *relation t_{ij} between i and j if and only if $Toprel(\hat{s}_{ij}) \cap t_{ij} = \emptyset$, where $\hat{s}_{ij}$ is the strongest entailed relation between i and j in Σ.*

Lemma 9. *Let Θ be a consistent set of constraints in* RCC-8*, Σ a consistent set of $\mathcal{QS}$ constraints over the variables of Θ, t_{ij} the relation between i and j in Θ, and s_{ij} the relation between size(i) and size(j) in Σ.*

- *$t_{ij} \models \neg s_{ij}$ if and only if $s_{ij} \models \neg t_{ij}$;*
- *$\Theta \models \neg s_{ij}$ if and only if $\Sigma \models \neg t_{ij}$;*

Proof Sketch. It follows from Table 1. □

In the next lemma t_{ij} indicates the *basic* relation between i and j in a consistent scenario Θ_s for a set Θ of topological relations; $\mathcal{S}(i)$ indicates the size of the region assigned to the variable i in a model of Θ.

Lemma 10. *Let Θ_s be a consistent scenario for a (consistent) set Θ of topological constraints in $\widehat{\mathcal{H}}_8$. It is possible to construct a model of Θ such that, for each variable i and j,*

(1) if $Sizerel(t_{ij})$ is one of $<, >, =$, then $\mathcal{S}(i) < \mathcal{S}(j)$, $\mathcal{S}(i) > \mathcal{S}(j)$, and $\mathcal{S}(i) = \mathcal{S}(j)$, respectively;
(2) if $Sizerel(t_{ij})$ is the universal relation ("$<=>$"), then $\mathcal{S}(i)$ and $\mathcal{S}(j)$ can be arbitrarily chosen in such a way that either $\mathcal{S}(i) < \mathcal{S}(j)$ or $\mathcal{S}(i) > \mathcal{S}(j)$.

Proof Sketch. Let Σ be a consistent set of assertions of relations derived from Θ using (1) and (2),[6] and let s_{ij} be the relation between the region sizes $size(i)$ and $size(j)$ in Σ. We show that it is possible to construct a model θ for Θ_s in which the values (spatial regions) assigned to the variables satisfy Σ. Suppose that this were not true. We would have that (a) there would exist h and k such that $\Theta_s \models \neg s_{hk}$, or (b) there would exist h' and k' such that $\Sigma \models \neg t_{h'k'}$ (i.e., there is no model of Θ_s satisfying s_{hk}, or there is no model of Σ consistent with $t_{h'k'}$.) Since by construction of Θ_s, for any pair of variables in Θ_s the strongest relation between i and j is t_{ij}, (a) can hold only if (a') $t_{hk} \models \neg s_{hk}$ holds. For analogous reasons we have that (b) can hold only if (b') $s_{h'k'} \models \neg t_{h'k'}$ holds. But both (a') and (b') cannot hold. In fact, since for any i, j Sizerel(t_{ij}) $\in \{<, >, =, <=>\}$ (because t_{ij} is basic), by (1) it cannot be the case that $t_{hk} \models \neg s_{hk}$, and hence by Lemma 9 also $s_{h'k'} \models \neg t_{h'k'}$ cannot hold. □

[6] E.g., if $Sizerel(t_{ij})$ is "$<$", then $size(i) < size(j) \in \Sigma$.

5 Reasoning about Size and Topology Relations

A natural method for deciding the consistency of a set of RCC-8 constraints and a set of $\mathcal{QS}$ constraints, would be to first extend each set of constraints with the constraints entailed by the other set, and then independently check the consistency of the extended sets by using a path-consistency algorithm. However, as the example below shows, this method is not complete for $\widehat{\mathcal{H}}_8$ constraints.

Another possibility, would be to compute the strongest entailed relations (minimal relations) between each pair of variables before propagating constraints from one set to the other. However, this method has the disadvantage that it is computationally expensive.[7]

Finally, a third method could be based on iteratively using path-consistency as a preprocessing technique and then propagating the information from one set to the other.[8] The following example shows that the information would need to be propagated more than once, and furthermore it is not clear whether in general this method would be complete for detecting inconsistency.[9]

Example. Consider the set Θ formed by the following $\widehat{\mathcal{H}}_8$ constraints

$$x_0\{\mathsf{TPP},\mathsf{EQ}\}x_2,\ x_1\{\mathsf{TPP},\mathsf{EQ},\mathsf{PO}\}x_0,\ x_1\{\mathsf{TPP},\mathsf{EQ}\}x_2,\ x_4\{\mathsf{TPP},\mathsf{EQ}\}x_3,$$

and the set Σ formed by the of following $\mathcal{QS}$ constraints

$$size(x_0) < size(x_2),\ size(x_3) \leq size(x_1),\ size(x_2) \leq size(x_4).$$

We have that Θ and Σ are independently consistent, but their union is not consistent. Moreover, the following propagation scheme does not detect the inconsistency: (a) enforce path-consistency to Σ and Θ independently; (b) extend Σ with the size constraints entailed by the constraints in Θ; (c) extend Θ with the topological constraints entailed by the constraints in Σ; (d) enforce path-consistency to Θ and Σ again. In order to detect that $\Theta \cup \Sigma$ is inconsistent, we need an additional propagation of constraints from the topological set to the size set.

Instead of directly analyzing the complexity and completeness of the propagation scheme illustrated in the previous example, we propose a new method for dealing with combined topological and qualitative size constraints. In particular, we propose an $O(n^3)$ time and $O(n^2)$ space algorithm, BIPATH-CONSISTENCY, for imposing path-consistency to a set of constraints in RCC-8 $\cup$ $\mathcal{QS}$. We prove that BIPATH-CONSISTENCY solves the problem of deciding consistency for any input set Θ of topological constraints in $\widehat{\mathcal{H}}_8$ combined with any set of size constraints

[7] The best known algorithm for computing the minimal network of a set of $\widehat{\mathcal{H}}_8$ constraints requires $O(n^5)$ time.

[8] Note that imposing a path-consistency algorithm is sufficient for consistency checking of $\widehat{\mathcal{H}}_8$ and $\mathcal{QS}$ constraints, but is incomplete for computing the minimal relations [16, 15].

[9] A similar method is used by Ladkin and Kautz to combine qualitative and metric constraints in the context of temporal reasoning [8].

Algorithm: BIPATH-CONSISTENCY
Input: A set Θ of RCC-8 constraints, and a set Σ of $\mathcal{QS}$ constraints over the variables $x_1, x_2, \ldots, x_n$ of Θ.
Output: **fail**, if $\Sigma \cup \Theta$ is not consistent; path-consistent sets equivalent to Σ and Θ, otherwise.

1. Q $\leftarrow \{(i,j) \mid i < j\}$; ($i$ indicates the i-th variable of Θ. Analogously for j)
2. *while* Q $\neq \emptyset$ *do*
3. select and delete an arc (i,j) from Q;
4. *for* $k \neq i, k \neq j$ $(k \in \{1...n\})$ *do*
5.   *if* BIREVISION(i,j,k) *then*
6.   *if* $R_{ik} = \emptyset$ *then* return **fail**
7.   *else* add (i,k) to Q;
8.   *if* BIREVISION(k,i,j) *then*
9.   *if* $R_{kj} = \emptyset$ *then* return **fail**
10.   *else* add (k,j) to Q.

Function: BIREVISION(i,k,j)
Input: three region variables i, k and j
Output: true, if R_{ij} is revised; false otherwise.
Side effects: R_{ij} and R_{ji} revised using the operations $\cap$ and $\circ$ over the constraints involving i, k, and j.

1. *if* one of the following cases hold, *then* return false:[10]
   (a) $Toprel(s_{ik}) \cap t_{ik} = U_t$ *and* $Sizerel(t_{ik}) \cap s_{ik} = U_s$,
   (b) $Toprel(s_{kj}) \cap t_{kj} = U_t$ *and* $Sizerel(t_{kj}) \cap s_{kj} = U_s$
2. oldt $:= t_{ij}$; olds $:= s_{ij}$;
3. $t_{ij} := (t_{ij} \cap Toprel(s_{ij})) \cap ((t_{ik} \cap Toprel(s_{ik})) \circ (t_{kj} \cap Toprel(s_{kj})))$;
4. $s_{ij} := (s_{ij} \cap Sizerel(t_{ij})) \cap ((s_{ik} \cap Sizerel(t_{ik})) \circ (s_{kj} \cap Sizerel(t_{kj})))$;
5. $t_{ij} := (t_{ij} \cap Toprel(s_{ij}))$;
6. *if* (oldt $= t_{ij}$) *or* (olds $= s_{ij}$) *then* return *false*;
7. $t_{ji} := Converse(t_{ij})$; $s_{ji} := Converse(s_{ij})$;
8. return *true*.

Fig. 2. BIPATH-CONSISTENCY

in $\mathcal{QS}$ involving the variables of Θ. Thus, despite this framework is more expressive than $\widehat{\mathcal{H}}_8$ (and therefore has a larger potential applicability), the problem of deciding consistency can be solved without additional worst-case cost.

BIPATH-CONSISTENCY is a modification of Vilain and Kautz's path-consistency algorithm [17] as described by Bessière [3], which in turn is a slight modification of Allen's algorithm [1]. The main novelty of our algorithm is that BIPATH-CONSISTENCY operates on a graph of *pairs* of constraints. The vertices of the graph are constraint variables, which in our context correspond to spatial regions. Each edge of the graph is labeled by a pair of relations formed by a topological relation in RCC-8 and a size relation in $\mathcal{QS}$. The function BIREVISION(i,k,j) has the same role as the function REVISE used in path consistency algorithms for

[10] As in the function REVISE given in [3], this step is used to avoid processing the triple i, j, k when it is known that R_{ij} would not be revised.

constraint networks (e.g., [11]). The main difference is that BIREVISION(i,k,j) considers pairs of (possibly interdependent) constraints, instead of single constraints.

Note that BIPATH-CONSISTENCY is a general algorithm, in the sense that it can be applied not only to spatial reasoning. For example, it can be applied to pairs of temporal relations, where each pair is formed by a relation in the Allen's Interval Algebra [1] and a qualitative constraint on the duration of the intervals. Of course, different classes of relations might need different completeness and complexity proofs.

A formal description of BIPATH-CONSISTENCY is given in Figure 2, where R_{ij} is a pair formed by a relation t_{ij} in RCC-8 and a relation s_{ij} in $\mathcal{QS}$; $R_{ij} = \emptyset$ when $t_{ij} = \emptyset$ or $s_{ij} = \emptyset$; U_t indicates the universal relation in RCC-8 and U_s the universal relation in $\mathcal{QS}$.

Theorem 2. *Given a set Θ of constraints in $\widehat{\mathcal{H}}_8$ and a set Σ of constraints in $\mathcal{QS}$ involving variables in Θ,* BIPATH-CONSISTENCY *applied to Σ and Θ decides the consistency of $\Sigma \cup \Theta$.*

Proof. It is clear that, if the algorithms returns `fail`, then $\Sigma \cup \Theta$ is inconsistent. Otherwise (the algorithm does not return `fail`) both the output set of size constraints Σ_p and the output set Θ_p of topological constraints are independently path-consistent. Hence, by proposition 1 and the fact that a path-consistent set of constraints either in $\widehat{\mathcal{H}}_8$ or in a Point Algebra is consistent [15,9], Σ and Θ are independently consistent.

Let Θ_p be the path-consistent set of topological constraints given as output of BIPATH-CONSISTENCY applied to Σ and Θ, and Σ_p the path-consistent set of the size constraints. We show that $\Sigma_p \cup \Theta_p$ is consistent (and therefore that $\Sigma \cup \Theta$ is consistent). In order to do that, we show that it is possible to construct a consistent scenario Θ_s for Θ_p in which the region variables can be interpreted as regions satisfying the constraints of Σ.

Let Θ_s be a consistent scenario for Θ_p in which, for any pair of variables i and j, the (basic) relation r_{ij} between i and j is

- EQ if $i\{\mathsf{EQ}\}j \in \Theta_p$,
- one of DC, EC, PO, if $R \cap \{\mathsf{DC},\mathsf{EC},\mathsf{PO}\} \neq \emptyset$, where $iRj \in \Theta_p$,
- one of TPP, NTPP, TPP^{-1}, NTPP^{-1}, otherwise.

Lemma 7 guarantees the existence of Θ_s.

From Θ_s we can derive an assignment to the variables of Θ_s satisfying the constraints of Σ_p (and the topological constraints of Θ_s) in the following way. Let Σ'_p be the set of size constraints derived from Σ_p by applying the five transformation rules of Lemma 8, and let σ_p be a consistent scenario for Σ'_p. By Lemma 8 σ_p is also a consistent scenario for Σ_p (and hence for Σ).

For each pair of variables i and j, consider the size relation $Sizerel(r_{ij})$ between i and j. By construction of Θ_s and steps 3–7 of BIREVISION (the subroutine used by BIPATH-CONSISTENCY to revise topological and size constraints), it is clear that if $Sizerel(r_{ij})$ is one of "$<$", "$>$", "$=$", then the relation between i and j in Σ'_p (and in σ_p) is the same as $Sizerel(r_{ij})$. So, any assignment satisfying r_{ij} satisfies also the size relations between i and j in Σ'_p (and in σ_p).

Consider now the case in which $Sizerel(r_{ij})$ is the indefinite relation ("<=>"). (Note that since r_{ij} is a basic relation it cannot be the case that $Sizerel(r_{ij}) \in \{\leq, \geq, \neq\}$ – see Table 1.) We have that r_{ij} must be one of {DC},{EC},{PO}. Since Σ_p is consistent, by construction of σ_p and by Lemma 10 we can consistently assign regions to i and j satisfying r_{ij} *and* the size relations between i and j in σ_p (and hence in Σ'_p). Consequently, by Lemma 8 from Θ_s we can derive a consistent assignment satisfying the relations in Σ_p (and hence in Σ). □

Theorem 3. *Given a set Θ of constraints over* RCC-8 *and a set Σ of constraints in $\mathcal{QS}$ involving variables in Θ, the time and space complexity of* BIPATH-CONSISTENCY *applied to Σ and Θ are $O(n^3)$ and $O(n^2)$ respectively, where n is the number of variables involved in Θ and Σ.*

Proof. Since any relation in $\mathcal{QS}$ can be refined at most three times, any relation in RCC-8 can be refined at most eight times, and there are $O(n^2)$ relations, the total number of edges that can enter into Q is $O(n^2)$. For each arc in Q, BIPATH-CONSISTENCY runs BIREVISION $2n$ times. BIREVISION has a constant time complexity. The quadratic space complexity is trivial. □

Theorem 4. *Given a set Θ of constraints in $\widehat{\mathcal{H}}_8$ and a set Σ of constraints in $\mathcal{QS}$ involving variables in Θ, the consistency of $\Sigma \cup \Theta$ can be determined in $O(n^3)$ time and $O(n^2)$ space, where n is the number of variables involved in Θ and Σ.*

Proof. It follows from Theorems 2 and 3. □

Theorem 5. *Given a set Θ of constraints in $\widehat{\mathcal{H}}_8$ and a set Σ of $\mathcal{QS}$ constraints involving variables in Θ, a size-consistent consistent scenario Θ_s for $\Theta \cup \Sigma$ can be computed in $O(n^3)$ time and $O(n^2)$ space, where n is the number of variables involved in Θ and Σ.*

Proof. From Theorem 1, the proof of Theorem 2 and Theorem 3, it follows that Θ_s can be computed by first applying BIPATH-CONSISTENCY to Θ and Σ, and then running the algorithm described in the proof of Theorem 1 on the set of the topological constraints in the output of BIPATH-CONSISTENCY. □

6 Conclusions

In this paper we have addressed the problem of integrating a basic class of spatial relations, expressing information about the relative size of spatial regions, with RCC-8, a well known class of topological relations. We developed an $O(n^3)$ time algorithm for processing a set of combined topological and relative size constraints, and we proved the correctness and completeness of the algorithm for deciding consistency when the topological constraints are in the $\widehat{\mathcal{H}}_8$ class.

We have also presented an $O(n^3)$ time method for computing a consistent scenario both for combined topological and relative size constraints, and for topological constraints alone.

Future work includes extending the class of size relations to (relative) quantitative size constraints, such as "the size of a certain region is at least two times, and at most six times, the size of another region".

Acknowledgments

The work of the first author has been partly supported by CNR project SCI*SIA, and by a CNR short-term fellowship (1997). The work of the second author has been supported by DFG as part of the project FAST-QUAL-SPACE, which is part of the DFG special research effort on "Spatial Cognition". We thank Brandon Bennett and the anonymous referees for their helpful comments.

References

1. J.F. Allen. Maintaining knowledge about temporal intervals. *Communication of the ACM*, 26(1):832–843, 1983.
2. T. Apostol. *Mathematical Analysis*. Addison Wesley, 1974.
3. C. Bessière. A simple way to improve path-consistency in Interval Algebra networks. In *Proc. AAAI-96*, pages 375–380, 1996.
4. R. Dechter. From local to global consistency. *Artificial Intelligence*, 55:87–108, 1992.
5. A. Gerevini and J. Renz. Combining topological and qualitative size constraints for spatial reasoning. Technical report. To appear.
6. A. Gerevini and L. Schubert. On computing the minimal labels in time point algebra networks. *Computational Intelligence*, 11(3):443–448, 1995.
7. M.C. Golumbic and R. Shamir. Complexity and algorithms for reasoning about time: A graph-theoretic approach. *Journal of the Association for Computing Machinery*, 40(5):1128–1133, November 1993.
8. H.A. Kautz and P.B. Ladkin. Integrating metric and qualitative temporal reasoning. In *Proc. AAAI-91*, pages 241–246, 1991.
9. P.B. Ladkin and R. Maddux. On binary constraint networks. Technical Report KES.U.88.8, Kestrel Institute, Palo Alto, CA, 1988.
10. G. Ligozat. A new proof of tractability for Ord-Horn relations. In *Proc. AAAI-96*, pages 715–720, 1996.
11. A.K. Mackworth. Consistency in networks of relations. *Artificial Intelligence*, 8:99–118, 1977.
12. A.K. Mackworth and E.C. Freuder. The complexity of some polynomial network consistency algorithms for constraint satisfaction problems. *Artificial Intelligence*, 25:65–73, 1985.
13. D.A. Randell, Z. Cui, and A.G. Cohn. A spatial logic based on regions and connection. In *Principles of Knowledge Representation and Reasoning: Proceedings of the 3rd International Conference (KR'92)*, pages 165–176, 1992.
14. J. Renz. A canonical model of the Region Connection Calculus. In *Principles of Knowledge Representation and Reasoning: Proceedings of the 6th International Conference (KR'98)*, pages 330–341, 1998.
15. J. Renz and B. Nebel. On the complexity of qualitative spatial reasoning: A maximal tractable fragment of the Region Connection Calculus. In *Proc. IJCAI'97*, pages 522–527, 1997. Technical Report with full proofs available at `www.informatik.uni-freiburg.de/~sppraum`.
16. P. van Beek. Reasoning about qualitative temporal information. *Artificial Intelligence*, 58(1-3):297–321, 1992.
17. M. Vilain, H.A. Kautz, and P. van Beek. Constraint propagation algorithms for temporal reasoning: a revised report. In D.S Weld and J. de Kleer, editors, *Readings in Qualitative Reasoning about Physical Systems*, pages 373–381. Morgan Kaufmann, San Mateo, CA, 1990.

Constraint Representation for Propagation

Warwick Harvey[1] and Peter J. Stuckey[2]

[1] School of Computer Science and Software Engineering, Monash University, Clayton VIC 3168, Australia (wharvey@cs.monash.edu.au)

[2] Department of Computer Science, The University of Melbourne, Parkville VIC 3052, Australia (pjs@cs.mu.oz.au)

Abstract. Propagation based finite domain solvers provide a general mechanism for solving combinatorial problems. Different propagation methods can be used in conjunction by communicating through the domains of shared variables. The flexibility that this entails has been an important factor in the success of propagation based solving for solving hard combinatorial problems. In this paper we investigate how linear integer constraints should be represented in order that propagation can determine strong domain information. We identify two kinds of substitution which can improve propagation solvers, and can never weaken the domain information. This leads us to an alternate approach to propagation based solving where the form of constraints is modified by substitution as computation progresses. We compare and contrast a solver using substitution against an indexical based solver, the current method of choice for implementing propagation based constraint solvers, identifying the the relative advantages and disadvantages of the two approaches.

1 Introduction

Propagation based finite domain solvers provide a general mechanism for solving combinatorial problems. Different propagation methods can be used in conjunction by communicating through the domains of shared variables. The flexibility that this entails has been an important factor in the success of propagation based solving for solving hard combinatorial problems. The most primitive and common constraints that are used within propagation based solvers are linear integer constraints. Most simple constraints fall into this category and usually they form the bulk of constraints used in modelling a problem. More complicated propagation constraints are nonlinear constraints, usually restricted to a few forms like $X \times Y = Z$ and $X^2 = Z$. Modern propagation based constraint solvers like CHIP and ILOG SOLVER also include libraries of specialized propagation methods for complex constraints such as `cumulative` and `cycle`. Because of the uniform communication mechanism complex multi-faceted combinatorial problems can be handled where different subparts are solved efficiently by specialized propagation mechanisms.

An unnerving and not well studied property of propagation based solvers is that the form of a constraint may change the amount of information that propagation discovers. For example consider the constraint $X = Y \wedge X + Y = Z$, and the equivalent constraint $X = Y \wedge 2Y = Z$. Using the second form, the domain of Z (using domain propagation) or at least its upper and lower bounds (using bounds propagation) will be even integers, but this is not necessary using the first form. Hence the form of constraints changes the result of the solver. The usual pragmatic choice for representing constraints is to represent them in the form they occur in the program that creates them. This can be improved as the above example shows, and propagation solvers will typically make use of binding constraints $X = Y$ (if they occur before both X and Y occur in another form of constraint) and ground variables to produce more efficient forms of constraints. This still leaves much room for improvement: for example the constraint $X + Y = Z \wedge X = Y$ will not be improved under this policy.

In this paper we investigate the effect of different representations of linear integer constraints in terms of propagation, and show how we can use this information to create efficient bounds propagation solvers. The contributions of the paper are

- A number of theorems which relate the form of a linear constraint to the amount of domain information that can be extracted from the constraint.
- The design and implementation of a bounds propagation solver which makes use of the possibilities of changing the form of linear constraints.
- Empirical comparisons of the solver with `clp(FD)`, a state of the art indexical solver.

The rest of the paper is organized as follows: in Section 2 we formally define domain and bounds propagation solvers and show a number of different results regarding the amount of domain information they extract from different forms of constraints. In Section 3 we describe the constraint solver we have built to take advantage of some of these results. Then in Section 4 we give an empirical comparison of the solver, showing the effect of various ways of changing the form of the constraints during execution. Finally in Section 5 we conclude.

2 Propagation Based Solving

In this paper we restrict ourselves to linear integer constraint solving. A *primitive constraint* c is a linear equality ($=$), inequality ($\leq$) or disequation ($\neq$), which may be written $\sum_{i=1}^{n} a_i x_i$ op d where a_i, d are integers and op $\in \{=, \leq, \neq\}$. A *constraint* is a conjunction of primitive constraints, which we will sometimes treat as a set of primitive constraints. An integer (real) valuation θ is a mapping of variables to integer (resp. real) values, written $\{x_1 \mapsto d_1, \ldots, x_n \mapsto d_n\}$. We extend the valuation θ to map expressions and constraints involving the variables in the natural way. Let *vars* be the function that returns the set of (free) variables appearing in a constraint or valuation. A valuation θ is an integer (real) solution of constraint C if $\mathcal{Z} \models_\theta C$ (resp. $\mathcal{R} \models_\theta C$).

A *range* of integers $[l..u]$ is the set of integers $\{l, l+1, \ldots, u\}$, or $\emptyset$ if $l > u$. A *domain* D is a complete mapping from a fixed (countable) set of variables

$\mathcal{V}$ to finite sets of integers. A *false domain* D is a domain where there exists x with $D(x) = \emptyset$. The *intersection* of two domains D_1 and D_2, denoted $D_1 \sqcap D_2$, is defined by the domain $D_3(x) = D_1(x) \cap D_2(x)$ for all x. A domain D_1 is *stronger* than a domain D_2, written $D_1 \sqsubseteq D_2$, if $D_1(x) \subseteq D_2(x)$ for all variables x. A domain D_1 is stronger than (equal to) a domain D_2 w.r.t. variables V, denoted $D_1 \sqsubseteq_V D_2$ (resp. $D_1 =_V D_2$), if for all $x \in V$ $D_1(x) \subseteq D_2(x)$ (resp. $D_1(x) = D_2(x)$). We use the notation $-\{x\}$ to denote the variable set $\mathcal{V} - \{x\}$.

In an abuse of notation, we define a valuation θ to be an element of a domain D, written $\theta \in D$, if $\theta(x_i) \in D(x_i)$ for all $x_i \in vars(\theta)$. We will be interested in determining the infimums and supremums of expressions with respect to some domain D. Define the infimum and supremum of an expression e with respect to a domain D as $\inf_D e = \inf \ \{\theta(e) | \theta \in D\}$ and $\sup_D e = \sup \ \{\theta(e) | \theta \in D\}$.

A propagation solver can be considered as a function $solv(C, D) = D'$ which maps a constraint C and an initial domain D to a new domain D' such that

$$\mathcal{Z} \models C \land \bigwedge_{x \in vars(C)} x \in D(x) \leftrightarrow C \land \bigwedge_{x \in vars(C)} x \in D'(x)$$

The solver determines that the constraint C and domain D are unsatisfiable when it returns a false domain D'.

A domain D is *domain consistent* with constraint C if for each primitive constraint $c \in C$ where $vars(c) = \{x_1, \ldots, x_n\}$ then for each $1 \leq i \leq n$ and each value $d_i \in D(x_i)$ there exists $d_j \in D(x_j), 1 \leq j \leq n, j \neq i$ such that $\{x_1 \mapsto d_1, \ldots, x_n \mapsto d_n\}$ is an integer solution of c. A *domain propagation solver* is such that $solv(C, D)$ is always domain consistent with C.

Define the domain consistency removal function $dc(c, D)$ as returning a domain D' such that $D'(x_j) = D(x_j), x_j \notin vars(c)$, and when $x_j \in vars(c)$

$$D'(x_j) = \{\theta(x_j) \mid \theta \in D \text{ and } \theta \text{ is a solution of } c\}.$$

A domain propagation solver *dsolv* can be defined as

$$diter(C, D) = \bigsqcap_{c \in C} dc(c, D)$$

$$dsolv(C, D) = \text{gfp}(\lambda d.diter(C, d))(D).$$

A domain D is *bounds consistent* with constraint C if for each primitive constraint $c \in C$ where $vars(c) = \{x_1, \ldots, x_n\}$ then for each $1 \leq i \leq n$ and $d_i \in \{\inf_D x_i, \sup_D x_i\}$ there exists *real numbers* $d_j, 1 \leq j \leq n, j \neq i$ where $\inf_D x_j \leq d_j \leq \sup_D x_j$ such that $\{x_1 \mapsto d_1, \ldots, x_n \mapsto d_n\}$ is a *real* solution of c. A bounds propagation solver is such that $solv(C, D)$ is always bounds consistent with C.

Define the bounds consistency removal function $bc(c, D)$ as returning a domain D' such that $D'(x_j) = D(x_j), x_j \notin vars(c)$, and where $x_j \in vars(c)$ as follows. Let l_j and u_j be defined as:

$$l_j = \inf_D \left(\frac{d - \sum_{i=1, i \neq j}^{n} a_i x_i}{a_j} \right) \qquad u_j = \sup_D \left(\frac{d - \sum_{i=1, i \neq j}^{n} a_i x_i}{a_j} \right)$$

– if $c \equiv \sum_{i=1}^n a_i x_i = d$ then $D'(x_j) = [\sup\{\lceil l_j \rceil, \inf_D x_j\} .. \inf\{\lfloor u_j \rfloor, \sup_D x_j\}]$.
– if $c \equiv \sum_{i=1}^n a_i x_i \leq d$, $a_j > 0$ then $D'(x_j) = [\inf_D x_j .. \inf\{\lfloor u_j \rfloor, \sup_D x_j\}]$.
– if $c \equiv \sum_{i=1}^n a_i x_i \leq d$, $a_j < 0$ then $D'(x_j) = [\sup\{\lceil l_j \rceil, \inf_D x_j\} .. \sup_D x_j]$.
– if $c \equiv \sum_{i=1}^n a_i x_i \neq d$, then

$$D'(x_j) = \begin{cases} [\inf_D x_j + 1 .. \sup_D x_j] & \text{if } l_j = u_j = \inf_D x_j \\ [\inf_D x_j .. \sup_D x_j - 1] & \text{if } l_j = u_j = \sup_D x_j \\ [\inf_D x_j .. \sup_D x_j] & \text{otherwise} \end{cases}$$

A bounds propagation solver *bsolv* can be defined as

$$\mathit{biter}(C, D) = \bigsqcap_{c \in C} \mathit{bc}(c, D)$$
$$\mathit{bsolv}(C, D) = \mathrm{gfp}(\lambda d.\mathit{biter}(C, d))(D).$$

With a formal definition of a domain propagation solver and a bounds propagation solver we are in a position to establish results about the behaviour of the solvers on different forms of the same constraint. The following proposition is widely known; effectively it states that the order of applying propagation rules makes no difference to the result. The result is a straightforward application of Cousot's chaotic iteration theorem [2]. We make use of the freedom of computation of $\mathit{solv}(C, D)$ implied by this result in many proofs.

Proposition 1. *Let $C = c_1 \wedge \cdots \wedge c_n$ and let $J_k, k \geq 1$ be an infinite set of subsets of $\{1, \ldots, n\}$ such that for each k and $1 \leq i \leq n$ there exists $l > 0$ such that $i \in J_{k+l}$. When solv $\in \{$dsolv, bsolv$\}$ and iter is the corresponding iteration function, if $D_0 = D$ and $D_{k+1} = \mathit{iter}(\wedge_{i \in J_k} c_k, D_k)$, then $\mathit{solv}(C, D) = \bigsqcap_{k \geq 1} D_k$.*

The first result we present relates the domains of variables occurring in a two variable equation (TVPE). For these constraints we obtain a one to one correspondence between domain elements or bounds. We shall make use of this correspondence in later results.[1]

Lemma 1. *Consider the primitive constraint $c \equiv b_j x_j + b_k x_k = e$, $b_j \neq 0, b_k \neq 0$. Then for any domain D we have (a) there is a one-to-one correspondence between elements of the domains of x_j and x_k in $\mathit{dsolv}(c, D)$; that is $d_j \in \mathit{dsolv}(c, D)(x_j)$ iff $\frac{e - b_j d_j}{b_k} \in \mathit{dsolv}(c, D)(x_k)$ and (b) there is a one to one correspondence between bounds for x_j and x_k in $D' = \mathit{bsolv}(c, D)$; that is $\inf_{D'} b_j x_j + \sup_{D'} b_k x_k = e$ and $\sup_{D'} b_j x_j + \inf_{D'} b_k x_k = e$.*

The following lemma establishes that a ground variable can be eliminated from a constraint without changing propagation behaviour. This justifies the first kind of substitution we use later: replacing ground variables by their values.

Lemma 2. *Consider the primitive constraint $c_1 \equiv \sum_{i=1}^n a_i x_i$ op d where op $\in \{=, \leq, \neq\}$, Let $c_2 \equiv \sum_{i=1, i \neq j}^n a_i x_i$ op $d - a_j d_j$. Then for solv $\in \{$dsolv, bsolv$\}$ and any domain D where $D(x_j) = \{d_j\}$ we have that $\mathit{solv}(c_1, D) = \mathit{solv}(c_2, D)$.*

[1] We omit proofs due to space reasons, see [4] for details.

Often large linear constraints are broken up into smaller parts, in order to reduce the kind of constraints to a small number of forms by introducing new variables. For example the constraint $x_1+x_2-2x_3-2x_4=5$ can be decomposed into $v+x_2-2x_4=5 \wedge v=x_1-2x_3$. The next two theorems show that this splitting process, introducing a new variable to represent a linear subterm of the constraint, does not change the domain information determined by propagation.

Theorem 1. *Consider the primitive constraint* $c_1 \equiv \sum_{i=1}^n a_i x_i$ op d, *where* op $\in \{=,\leq,\neq\}$. *Let v be some variable $v \notin \{x_1,\ldots,x_n\}$. Then for any subset $V \subseteq \{1,\ldots,n\}$ and domain D where $D(v) \supseteq \{\sum_{i\in V} a_i\theta(x_i) \mid \theta \in D\}$ we have* $dsolv(c_1,D) =_{vars(c_1)} dsolv(c_2 \wedge c_3, D)$, *where* $c_2 \equiv v+\sum_{i=1,i\notin V}^n a_i x_i$ op d *and* $c_3 \equiv v=\sum_{i\in V} a_i x_i$.

Theorem 2. *Consider the primitive constraint* $c_1 \equiv \sum_{i=1}^n a_i x_i$ op d, *where* op $\in \{=,\leq,\neq\}$. *Let v be some variable $v \notin \{x_1,\ldots,x_n\}$. Then for any subset $V \subseteq \{1,\ldots,n\}$ and domain D where $D(v) \supseteq [\sum_{i\in V} \inf_D a_i x_i .. \sum_{i\in V} \sup_D a_i x_i]$, we have* $bsolv(c_1,D) =_{vars(c_1)} bsolv(c_2 \wedge c_3, D)$ *where* $c_2 \equiv v+\sum_{i=1,i\notin V}^n a_i x_i$ op d *and* $c_3 \equiv v=\sum_{i\in V} a_i x_i$.

Since breaking up a primitive constraint into two parts by introducing a new variable does not affect the result of propagation, it is interesting to consider when we can perform the reverse operation, substitution, and improve the strength of propagation. We shall concentrate on substitution using two variable equations (TVPEs).

Definition 1. *Let* $c_1 \equiv \sum_{i=1}^n a_i x_i$ op d, *where* op $\in \{=,\leq,\neq\}$, *and let* $c_2 \equiv b_j x_j + b_k x_k = e, j \neq k, b_j > 0, b_k \neq 0$. *Then the* substitution *of x_j using c_2 applied to c_1, denoted $subs(c_1,x_j,c_2)$ is defined as*

$$subs(c_1,x_j,c_2) \equiv (b_j a_k - a_j b_k)x_k + b_j \sum_{i=1,i\notin\{j,k\}}^n a_i x_i \text{ op } b_j d - a_j e.$$

When $b_j < 0$ *we define* $subs(c_1,x_j,c_2) = subs(c_1,x_j,-b_j x_j - b_k x_k = -e)$.

The following theorems show the effects of substitution using a TVPE primitive constraint. The first theorem shows that substitution by a TVPE can never weaken the domain propagation that occurs.

Theorem 3. *Consider the primitive constraints* $c_1 \equiv \sum_{i=1}^n a_i x_i$ op d, *where* op $\in \{=,\leq,\neq\}$, *and* $c_2 \equiv b_j x_j + b_k x_k = e, j \neq k, b_j \neq 0, b_k \neq 0$. *Let* $c_3 = subs(c_1,x_j,c_2)$. *Then for all domains D we have* $dsolv(c_1 \wedge c_2, D) \sqsupseteq dsolv(c_3 \wedge c_2, D)$.

That the result can be strictly stronger can be seen from the example $c_1 \equiv x_1+x_2-2x_3-2x_4=5$, $c_2 \equiv x_1-x_2=0$ and the domain $D(x_1)=D(x_2)=\{0,1,2,3,4,5\}, D(x_3)=D(x_4)=\{0,1,2\}$. $dsolv(c_1 \wedge c_2, D) = D$ but $dsolv(2x_2-2x_3-2x_4=5 \wedge x_1-x_2=0, D)$ returns a false domain.

We can in fact characterize when we may get benefits by substitution. The next theorem defines (negatively) the cases when substitution can lead to improved domain propagation.

Theorem 4. *Consider the primitive constraints* $c_1 \equiv \sum_{i=1}^n a_i x_i$ op d *where* op $\in \{=, \leq, \neq\}$, *and* $c_2 \equiv b_j x_j + b_k x_k = e, j \neq k, b_j \neq 0, b_k \neq 0$. *Let* $c_3 = subs(c_1, x_j, c_2)$. *Then* $dsolv(c_1 \wedge c_2, D) = dsolv(c_3 \wedge c_2, D)$ *for all domains* D *iff*

(a) op $\in \{=, \neq, \leq\}$ *and* $a_j = 0$ *or* $a_k = 0$;
(b) $n = 2$, op $\in \{\leq\}$ *and* $a_j b_j a_k b_k > 0$;
(c) $n = 2$, op $\in \{=\}$ *and* $|a_j b_k / b_j a_k| \neq 1$;
(d) $dsolv(c_1 \wedge c_2, D)$ *gives a false domain for all domains* D; *or*
(e) $c_3 \leftrightarrow true$.

As a consequence of the above theorem we can see there may be disadvantages with splitting constraints into parts: it may remove the advantages of substitution. Considering the previous example, the same propagation behaviour results from replacing c_1 by $v + x_2 - 2x_4 = 5 \wedge v = x_1 - 2x_3$, but then if we use c_2 to substitute for x_1 we obtain $v + x_2 - 2x_4 = 5 \wedge v = x_2 - 2x_3 \wedge x_1 - x_2 = 0$. We are guaranteed by Theorem 4 that propagation is never improved by this substitution. Hence we obtain weaker propagation behaviour than if we had not split c_1 before substitution $(2x_2 - 2x_3 - 2x_4 = 5 \wedge x_1 - x_2 = 0)$.

For bounds propagation we have a similar result to domain propagation: substitution by a TVPE can only improve bounds found in the resulting propagation.

Theorem 5. *Consider the primitive constraints* $c_1 \equiv \sum_{i=1}^n a_i x_i$ op d *where* op $\in \{=, \leq, \neq\}$, *and* $c_2 \equiv b_j x_j + b_k x_k = e, j \neq k$, $b_j \neq 0$, $b_k \neq 0$. *Let* $c_3 = subs(c_1, x_j, c_2)$. *Then for all domains* D *we have* $bsolv(c_1 \wedge c_2, D) \sqsupseteq bsolv(c_3 \wedge c_2, D)$.

Given we can get stronger domain information by substituting using a TVPE constraint, it is natural to ask whether we can use a TVPE constraint to totally eliminate a variable from consideration. The next theorems show when this elimination is guaranteed not to lose information.

Theorem 6. *Given a constraint* C *and TVPE equation* $c_2 \equiv b_j x_j + b_k x_k = e, j \neq k$, $b_j \neq 0$, $b_k \neq 0$. *Let* $C' = \wedge_{c \in C} subs(c, x_j, c_2)$. *Then for all domains* D *we have* $dsolv(C \wedge c_2, D) \sqsupseteq_{-\{x_j\}} dsolv(C', dsolv(c_2, D))$.

Theorem 7. *Given a constraint* C *and TVPE equation* $c_2 \equiv b_j x_j + b_k x_k = e, j \neq k$, $b_j = \pm 1$, $b_k \neq 0$. *Let* $C' = \wedge_{c \in C} subs(c, x_j, c_2)$. *Then for all domains* D *we have* $bsolv(C \wedge c_2, D) \sqsupseteq_{-\{x_j\}} bsolv(C', bsolv(c_2, D))$.

Note that if $b_j \neq \pm 1$, then performing a TVPE elimination may result in weaker bounds propagation. Consider the following example. Let $c_1 \equiv 2x + y = 3$, $c_2 \equiv 2x + z = 4$ and $c_3 = subs(c_1, x, c_2) \equiv y - z = -1$. Let $D(x) = [0..2]$, $D(y) = [0..4]$ and $D(z) = [0..4]$. Let $D' = bsolv(c_1 \wedge c_2, D)$ and $D'' = bsolv(c_3, bsolv(c_2, D))$ (note that $bsolv(c_2, D) = D$). Then $D'(x) = [0..1]$, $D'(y) = [1..3]$ and $D'(z) = [2..4]$ while $D''(x) = [0..2]$, $D''(y) = [0..3]$ and $D''(z) = [1..4]$. Thus the original version is stronger than the transformed: the information that z must be even and y must be odd has been lost. Note that domain propagation eliminates all the odd elements of z when propagating through c_2, and thus does not suffer from this problem.

We conclude this section by remarking that almost no substitution using a three (or more) variable equation will result in propagation which can be guaranteed to be no weaker than the original. This is due to there being no analogue of Lemma 1 for equations with more than two variables. As a result, the domain or bounds corresponding to the expression replacing the substituted variable will often be weaker than those of the variable itself, resulting in weaker propagation on the other variables in the constraint. Consider the following example

$$c_1 \equiv v + w + x - y = 5$$
$$c_2 \equiv x + y + z = 3$$
$$c_3 \equiv v + w - 2y - z = 2$$

Here, x in c_1 has been replaced by $3 - y - z$ in c_3. Suppose we are working with the domain D such that $D(v) = D(w) = [0..15], D(x) = D(y) = D(z) = [0..3]$. Let $D' = solv(c_1 \wedge c_2, D)$, $D'' = solv(c_3 \wedge c_2, D)$. Now, x has domain $[0..3]$, but the expression $3 - y - z$ has domain $[-3..3]$. As a result, while $D'(v) = D'(w) = [0..8]$, we have $D''(v) = D''(w) = [0..11]$, which is weaker (the domains of x, y and z are unchanged in both cases). Note that for the same constraints but a different domain the reverse relationship can hold. Consider $D(v) = D(w) = [0..10], D(y) = [-9..9], D(x) = D(z) = [-3..6]$. Then we have $D'(y) = [-8..9]$, while $D''(y) = [-4..9]$.

3 A Tableau Based Bounds Propagation Solver

Indexicals were introduced in [9] as a mechanism for specifying propagation behaviour. Indexicals have been widely used for implementing finite domain solvers, including that of the `clp(FD)` compiler [3] which is widely accepted as one of the fastest currently available implementations of a finite domain solver for CLP. The idea behind indexicals is that rather than implementing support for a large number of primitive constraints directly, and optimising each separately and in combination, the compiler should only implement a few low-level primitives (indexicals) and implement them well. Higher-level constraints can then be implemented in terms of these primitives. This also has the advantage that if a programmer wants to use a primitive constraint not provided by the libraries that come with the compiler (or wishes to modify the propagation behaviour of a provided constraint), he or she is able to use indexicals to implement the constraint themselves.

The indexical approach builds n indexicals for a n-variable constraint. When one of the variables in an n-variable constraint is modified, $n - 1$ indexicals are woken for propagation. The indexicals woken will often share some redundant computation, which is repeated for each woken indexical. This problem has also been noted in [1], where the solution presented is to break up constraints with many terms into several smaller ones, by introducing new intermediate variables. We have seen in Theorem 1 and Theorem 2 that this breakup of constraints does not reduce the amount of domain information discovered. The breakup reduces the amount of redundant computation, and can in some cases reduce the number of iterations of propagation required.

As a result of Lemma 2, Theorem 5 and Theorem 7 we are interested in being able to manipulate the form of constraints in a bounds propagation solver. In particular we wish to substitute ground variables out of constraints, and substitute variables appearing in unit two variable equations. This is problematic using an indexical representation since each primitive constraint is compiled into multiple indexicals. As a result, we propose an alternative representation of the constraints, based on a constraint tableau.

Given Theorem 4 and the subsequent example, we can see there are disadvantages to splitting primitive constraints when substitutions may be performed. Splitting a primitive constraint may prevent any gain in propagation behaviour. Hence for our alternate approach we will avoid the splitting of primitive constraints, in order to make substitution more effective. But since we deal with a primitive constraint as a whole the redundant computation created by indexicals will not occur in our approach.

3.1 Constraint Representation

The representation we use for our new implementation of a propagation solver is similar to that used in CLP($\mathcal{R}$) [5] for representing real constraints. Essentially, each primitive constraint is represented as a list of terms appearing in the constraint, plus a constant. Each primitive constraint is tagged with its type (equation, inequality, disequation), and a count of the number of terms appearing in it. Each node in a term list stores the value of the coefficient, the ID of the variable, a pointer to the next term, and a pointer to the parent constraint node.

A variable node stores the lower and upper bound of the variable as well as a doubly linked list of excluded values (holes in the domain). In addition there are four lists used for propagation, containing the term node occurrences of the variable in: inequalities where it has a positive coefficient, inequalities where it has a negative coefficient, equations, and disequations. Each term node stores a pointer to the next occurrence of the same variable in the same context (for example, in a disequation, or in an inequality with a negative coefficient). The four lists contain all the primitive constraints which contain the variable. They also respectively hold the primitive constraints that need to be propagated whenever the variable: has its lower bound updated, has its upper bound updated, has either its lower or upper bound updated, and becomes ground.

The primitive constraint itself is used as a propagation rule for all the variables in the constraint, as opposed to indexicals which update only one variable. This means that new bounds on any number of the variables appearing in the primitive constraint can be propagated to all other variables in only two passes over the primitive constraint. Hence propagation is linear in the number of variables in the constraint, compared to quadratic for the indexical scheme. It is also reasonably straightforward to manipulate the constraints if desired, for example substituting out a variable which has become ground, or performing substitutions of one variable by another.

Let $c \equiv \sum_{i=1}^{n} a_i x_i \leq d$. Calculations performed in evaluating $bc(c, D)$ share a great deal of work. Given $a_j > 0$ ($a_j < 0$) we calculate the (possibly new) upper (resp. lower) bound as:

$$\left\lfloor \frac{d - \sum_{i=1, i \neq j}^{n} \inf_D(a_i x_i)}{a_j} \right\rfloor \qquad \left(\text{resp.} \quad \left\lceil \frac{d - \sum_{i=1, i \neq j}^{n} \inf_D(a_i x_i)}{a_j} \right\rceil \right)$$

If we let $S = d - \sum_{i=1}^{n} \inf_D(a_i x_i)$ then we can alternatively calculate this as:

$$\left\lfloor \frac{S + a_j \inf_D x_j}{a_j} \right\rfloor \qquad \left(\text{resp.} \quad \left\lceil \frac{S + a_j \sup_D x_j}{a_j} \right\rceil \right)$$

Thus we can determine all the new bounds in two passes over the constraint: one to compute S, the other to compute the bounds.

For the purposes of computing bounds, equations can be considered as a pair of inequalities. Propagation using disequations only occurs when all but one variable is ground and then they remove an element from the domain of this variable (possibly causing unsatisfiability).

3.2 The Propagation Queue

For indexical solvers the propagation queue contains the indexicals that are waiting to be propagated. In the tableau approach the queue contains primitive constraints waiting to be propagated through. If a primitive constraint is in the propagation queue, it is labelled with the type of the pending propagation and a pointer to the next constraint in the queue. The propagation type is used for testing membership of the propagation queue, as well as for distinguishing which "half" (or both) of an equation needs propagating.

Each time a variable's bound is modified, all the primitive constraints which then need to be propagated are added to the queue. This is achieved by traversing the appropriate occurrence lists and adding the constraints there to the propagation queue, or for an equation possibly modifying which "halves" require propagation. A standard optimisation to avoid redundant work is to not re-add any constraint already in the queue.

Propagating through an inequality cannot result in waking up the same inequality; however, this is not the case for equations. Despite this, in many situations propagating back through the same equality constraint can be guaranteed to give no new information. The following theorem characterises some cases where re-propagation is not necessary. We assume here that the equation is modelled as a pair of inequalities, and that the solver (as happens in practice) alternates between propagating each inequality.

Theorem 8. *Let $c_1 \equiv \sum_{i=1}^{n} a_i x_i = d$, with corresponding inequalities $c_2 \equiv \sum_{i=1}^{n} a_i x_i \leq d$ and $c_3 \equiv -\sum_{i=1}^{n} a_i x_i \leq -d$. Consider evaluating $bc(c_2, D)$ (half of the computation for $bc(c_1, D)$). Let α be the number of tighter bounds created which involved integer rounding. Let β be the number of bounds created which are at least as tight as the existing bounds and did not involve integer rounding. If $bc(c_3, D) = D$ then if $\alpha = 0$ or $\beta \geq 2$ we have $bc(c_2, D) = bc(c_3, bc(c_2, D))$.*

Note that the $bc(c_3, D) = D$ condition is often known to be true without an explicit check. For instance, it is true if we have just propagated through c_3, or if none of the relevant bounds have been modified since the last time such a propagation occurred.

Indexical solvers typically handle the possible repropagation of equations by compiling equations with all unit (± 1) coefficients specially. In this case it is guaranteed that α will always be 0. Hence any indexicals derived from the same equation need not be repropagated. This kind of optimisation is important for the indexical representation, where a primitive constraint generates n rules, $n-1$ of which would be otherwise be woken.

We chose a different approach, which is facilitated by the tableau representation. We repeatedly propagate through an equation until $\alpha = 0$ or $\beta \geq 2$, before doing any other propagation. This may avoid propagating useless bounds elsewhere, but may also do unnecessary work in some cases. Empirical comparisons showed a slight benefit in repropagating immediately. Note that we need to calculate α at run-time unlike an indexical solver, since, due to substitutions, coefficients can change during the computation.

3.3 Variable Substitution

We have identified two kinds of substitution which never reduce the amount of bounds information determined by the solver: substitution of ground variables and substitution of a variable with a unit coefficient in a two variable equation.

The first kind of substitution makes the constraints smaller (fewer variables), thus speeding up their propagation. We can choose to substitute ground variables out of new primitive constraints only, or out of all existing primitive constraints as well. The first case has an extremely low overhead and thus least likely to have a negative impact; one simply adjusts the constant term for the primitive constraint being generated rather than adding a new variable term. The second case involves traversing the occurrence lists for the variable and, for each primitive constraint, adjusting the constant term and deleting the relevant variable term. This obviously has a higher overhead, and thus a greater chance of impacting performance negatively, but it also occurs much more often (typically all variables become ground by the end of a successful computation) and thus has a larger scope for improving performance. The computational results presented in Section 4 indeed show that performing the substitutions often yields a significant improvement in execution time, and only occasionally results in a slight penalty.

Performing ground substitutions of a variable is straightforward. One simply traverses all the occurrence lists for a variable, deleting the relevant term node from each primitive constraint, and updating the constants (if the primitive constraint is now completely ground, we may detect failure). If a substitution causes a primitive constraint to become of a special form (single variable or UTVPE), then it is marked for further processing after the substitution is complete. Any pending propagation then continues as before (the modified primitive constraints will already be in the propagation queue if they need to be there).

Substituting using an equation is more complex. For simplicity, we only substitute using a UTVPE equation where both coefficients are unit (± 1). These are by far the most common kind of equation occurring in finite domain programs (TVPE constraints with non-unit coefficients did not occur in any of the problems studied). If UTVPE substitutions are being performed, some extra information is stored in the variable node. If the variable has been eliminated, the substitution is recorded here. If the variable has been used in eliminating other variables, a list of all the substitutions it occurs in is maintained (so that if this variable is subsequently substituted, those substitutions can be updated).

UTVPE substitution removes a variable from the propagation solver, requiring less variables to be propagated on; it also never increases the size of any constraints. It can be applied using only primitive constraints that are UTVPE when they reach the solver (possibly after ground variables have been substituted out), or in addition using constraints that become UTVPE as the computation progresses (through ground or UTVPE substitution). Since we derive maximum benefit from UTVPE substitution if we completely eliminate a variable from the solver, we perform the substitution on all primitive constraints currently in the solver, as well as any new ones added. As a result, the overheads are much higher than for ground substitutions, and more propagation needs to be saved or pruning achieved to yield a benefit.

To perform a UTVPE substitution $X = aY + c$, we traverse all the occurrence lists for X and in each primitive constraint replace it by Y, updating the variable coefficient and constant term as necessary. If Y already appears in the constraint, then the two terms need to be summed (and both deleted if they sum to zero). Note that if the constraint is an inequality and Y already appears, care needs to be taken that the summed node ends up in the correct occurrence list (min or max). Note also that when adding X's occurrence lists to Y's, the min and max lists need to be exchanged if a is negative. The final thing that needs to be done for a UTVPE substitution is to propagate X's domain information to Y.

Backtracking may cause substitutions to be undone. This is fairly straightforward, basically it amounts to a reverse substitution. This is made easy by not deleting the occurrence lists of substituted variables, which then form the basis for the reverse substitution.

4 Computational Results

The tableau based solver is embedded in the CLP($\mathcal{R}$) interpreter, replacing the usual solver. We compare a number of different variants of the new propagation solver against each other, and against `clp(FD)` [3]. The variants of the new propagation solver are:

`base` Basic version: ground variables are substituted when a new constraint is added to the solver, but no other substitution is performed.
`eqn` Like **`base`**, but equation optimisation is also performed ($\alpha = 0$ case only).
`ground` Like **`eqn`**, but variables which become ground are substituted out of all active constraints.
`utvpe` Like **ground**, but input UTVPE constraints are used to substitute variables in all active constraints as well.
`edetect` Like **`utvpe`**, but constraints which become UTVPE due to substitutions are also used for substitution.
`clp-fd` The `clp(FD)` compiler, version 2.21.

The benchmarks were written in such a way as to minimise any algorithmic differences between the benchmark code for each system (in order to try to compare just the solvers). In particular, this means that heuristics such as first-fail have not been used. This is because different solvers are likely to select different variables to label first, resulting in the systems traversing different trees and solving different sets of constraints, degrading the usefulness of the comparison.

The benchmarks were run on a 167MHz Sun UltraSPARC Enterprise 1. The numbers presented for each benchmark are the minimum times recorded for 20 separate runs.

The first test problems used are scheduling problems (sched-*), with precedence constraints and resource contention. For each problem we computed worst case bounds a priori (the sum of all task durations) and used these as bounds for all variables. sched-bridge-good uses data from the bridge construction example in [8], and searches for a (modestly) good solution. The remainder are job shop scheduling benchmarks, searching for a first solution. These were taken from J.E. Beasley's OR-Library, from the file `jobshop1.txt`.

The second problem set is Fibonacci programs and goals. fib-std-* is the standard (naïve) formulation, with the two recursive calls last. fib-utvpe-* is a slightly reordered formulation such that all the equations are UTVPE (after initial ground substitution) at the time they are passed to the solver. Both were run in the forward (in, out) and backward (out, in) directions, for two different Fibonacci numbers (14/610 and 18/4181).

temp-* are some temporal reasoning problems, taken from [7], using the "shared-track" knowledge base (temp-st-*). hamil-* is a program for calculating Hamiltonian paths described in [6]. The benchmark was run on different data sets, ranging in size from 10 nodes to 50 nodes, searching for a first solution. Entries in the table of the form "?" indicate that the benchmark took in excess of 8 hours to run.

queens-* is the well-known "N Queens" benchmark. We evaluate two versions: the *forward checking* (queens-fc-*) version, and the more usual *generalised forward checking* (queens-gfc-*) version (see [8] for details), searching for all solutions using board sizes of 8, 10 and 12.

	base	eqn	ground	utvpe	edetect	clp_fd
sched-bridge-good	1.26	1.27	1.33	1.25	1.23	1.02
sched-orb03	0.23	0.24	0.24	0.23	0.23	0.18
sched-orb06	0.24	0.24	0.25	0.23	0.23	0.19
sched-la18	0.22	0.24	0.25	0.24	0.21	0.19
sched-la21	0.74	0.74	0.77	0.73	0.71	0.60
fib-utvpe-forw-14	0.02	0.01	0.02	0.01	0.01	0.02
fib-std-forw-14	0.04	0.04	0.02	0.02	0.02	0.03
fib-utvpe-back-14	0.07	0.07	0.05	0.03	0.02	0.04
fib-std-back-14	0.10	0.10	0.07	0.08	0.07	0.07
fib-utvpe-forw-18	0.19	0.16	0.15	0.07	0.07	0.12
fib-std-forw-18	0.32	0.28	0.24	0.24	0.21	0.26
fib-utvpe-back-18	0.59	0.52	0.48	0.26	0.24	0.31
fib-std-back-18	0.86	0.76	0.66	0.69	0.59	0.61
temp-st-sfenabled	0.10	0.10	0.09	0.10	0.09	0.03
temp-st-sfexits	0.50	0.51	0.49	0.50	0.49	0.11
temp-st-path	0.85	0.87	0.87	0.84	0.84	0.18
hamil-10	0.00	0.00	0.00	0.00	0.00	0.00
hamil-20	15.66	13.23	12.63	0.00	0.00	8.34
hamil-30	?	?	?	0.18	0.19	?
hamil-40	?	?	?	0.98	1.00	?
hamil-50	?	?	?	533.21	544.17	?
queens-fc-8	0.09	0.09	0.09	0.09	0.08	0.24
queens-fc-10	1.64	1.67	1.69	1.69	1.71	5.08
queens-fc-12	40.88	41.24	41.06	41.71	42.22	142.63
queens-gfc-8	0.05	0.05	0.05	0.05	0.04	0.13
queens-gfc-10	0.99	0.97	0.99	1.00	0.99	2.86
queens-gfc-12	25.17	25.17	25.15	25.30	25.15	81.43
magic	0.97	0.88	0.77	0.75	0.71	0.59
zebra	0.11	0.11	0.10	0.08	0.08	0.06
crypta	0.09	0.09	0.07	0.07	0.06	0.09
cryptb	0.37	0.34	0.27	0.26	0.25	0.33
alpha	1.98	1.83	1.16	1.15	1.34	1.42
bramsey-12	0.05	0.05	0.05	0.05	0.05	0.04
bramsey-14	1.14	1.08	0.96	0.98	1.32	1.43
bramsey-16	872.84	835.19	762.70	764.83	1053.36	1368.52
perm-11a	0.29	0.26	0.27	0.17	0.19	0.18
perm-11b	0.69	0.66	0.63	0.51	0.50	0.33
perm-11c	1.10	1.04	1.02	0.82	0.82	0.50
perm-12a	4.43	4.15	3.97	3.04	3.07	2.11
perm-12b	4.11	3.90	3.84	3.02	3.03	1.98
perm-12c	7.06	6.61	6.92	5.50	5.46	3.27
eq-10	0.45	0.46	0.34	0.34	0.35	0.44
eq-20	0.50	0.50	0.41	0.42	0.41	0.50

Table 1. Computational results

The next set are small combinatorial problems. magic is a (3x3) magic squares problem (all solutions); zebra is the well known "Who owns the zebra?" problem; crypt* are crypt-arithmetic problems from [8] (crypta is send-more-money), using an explicit carry; alpha is the alpha cipher puzzle, originally from the news group `rec.puzzles`. (The times shown for these benchmarks are for 100 repeats.)

bramsey is a boolean formulation of the problem of finding a 3-colouring of a complete graph with N vertices such that no monochrome triangles exist (note that 16 is the largest N for which a solution exists). perm is the permutation generation example from [8], for which we generated a number of random problems (using the same technique as in [8]). Each eq-* problem is a set of N linear equations on seven variables with domains [0..10], searching for all solutions (though there is only one).

The results appear in Table 1. The optimization of equation handling (eqn vs. base) seems worthwhile, with modest improvements to most of the benchmarks containing equations, and never causing any significant slow down.

It is fairly clear that variables which become ground should always be substituted out of all active constraints (**ground** vs. eqn). Only for a few benchmarks (sched-bridge-good and some perm) does it seem to cause a slight slow-down (presumably due to the extra overhead of checking for substitutions for little or no gain), while it often results in a significant benefit.

Similarly, performing substitution of input UTVPE constraints is almost always worthwhile (**utvpe** vs. **ground**). At the extreme, we have the hamil problems, where performing UTVPE substitution results in orders of magnitude improvement. The success on hamil is because performing UTVPE substitutions on disequations increases the strength of the solver so that it finds unsatisfiability much earlier in the search tree.

The final solver option, detecting new UTVPE constraints, does not seem so useful (edetect vs. utvpe). The only benchmarks where it provides an advantage of any significance are the fib-std benchmarks and magic. On the other hand, for the bramsey problems, it suffers a substantial slow-down. The only other benchmarks where new UTVPE constraints occur through substitution are zebra, crypt and eq. The lack of advantage of this option is probably due to the detected UTVPE constraints being discovered too late in the computation, so that too little work is saved to offset the cost of substitution.

Finally, it is worth noting that the tableau-based solver is competitive with clp(FD). For those problem classes where there was a substantial difference between the two, clp(FD) was faster on three (sched, temp, perm), and our solver was faster on four (hamil, queens, bramsey, eq). In general, it seems that clp(FD) has an advantage when there is a lot of work an intelligent compiler can do, or when the problem is simple. utvpe seems to have an advantage when a significant number of variables appearing in new constraints are ground (thus simplifying the constraints), or where a significant number of the constraints are equations with more than two variables.

5 Conclusion

We have presented theorems that examine when we can safely change the form of a constraint in a propagation solver, and guarantee that there is no loss in propagation information. Using these results we have constructed an efficient bounds propagation solver for linear constraints based on a tableau representation and substitution. The solver competes favourably with clp(FD), one of the fastest currently available finite domain CLP systems. Given the refinedness of the clp(FD) system as well as the fact that the underlying run-time engine of clp(FD) is compiled while that of CLP(R) is interpreted, we feel that this is a significant achievement. We believe the competitiveness of our solver stems from two things. Firstly, the compact representation of linear constraints used (with efficient update of multiple bounds in two passes over the constraint), rather than the multiple propagation rule representation used in the indexicals scheme (with its redundant computation). Secondly, the ability to easily modify constraints on-the-fly, through variable substitutions.

Although we have presented the solver solely for linear integer constraints it is not difficult to use the same methods with non-linear or other complex constraints where we may not be able to make ground or UTVPE substitutions. Ground substitutions are just performed on the linear constraints and nothing further is required. UTVPE substitutions are applied to linear constraints and kept as propagation rules that relate the substituted variable to its replacement expression if the substituted variable occurs in complex constraint. In this case we are unable to totally eliminate variables by UTVPE substitutions but we still restrict the amount of propagation that occurs, and get possibly stronger propagation from the linear constraints.

In this paper we have studied the representation of linear constraints. Non-linear constraints also have different propagation behaviour depending on representation, and are usually broken into parts, each in a standard form, by finite domain solvers. But the equivalent of Theorem 2 does not hold. Hence an interesting problem to investigate is the most appropriate method for handling non-linear constraints in terms of the strength of the resulting information.

References

1. Philippe Codognet and Daniel Diaz. Compiling constraints in clp(FD). *The Journal of Logic Programming*, 27(3):185–226, 1996.
2. P. Cousot and R. Cousot. Automatic synthesis of optimal invariant assertions: Mathematical foundations. In *ACM Symposium on Artificial Intelligence and Programming Languages*, 1977.
3. Daniel Diaz and Phillipe Codognet. A minimal extension of the WAM for clp(FD). In David S. Warren, editor, *Proceedings of the 10th International Conference on Logic Programming*, pages 774–790. MIT Press, 1993.
4. Warwick Harvey and Peter J. Stuckey. Constraint representation for propagation. Computer Science Technical Report 98/10, The University of Melbourne, 1998. Available at `http://www.cs.mu.oz.au/~pjs/papers/papers.html`.
5. Joxan Jaffar, Spiro Michaylov, Peter Stuckey, and Roland Yap. The CLP($\mathcal{R}$) language and system. *ACM Transactions on Programming Languages and Systems*, 14(3):339–395, July 1992.
6. J.H.M. Lee, H.F. Leung, and H.W. Won. Extending GENET for non-binary CSP's. In *Proceedings of the Seventh IEEE International Conference on Tools with Artificial Intelligence*, pages 338–343. IEEE Computer Society Press, 1995.
7. Jonathan S. Ostroff. *Temporal Logic for Real-Time Systems*. Wiley, 1989.
8. Pascal Van Hentenryck. *Constraint Satisfaction in Logic Programming*. Logic Programming Series. MIT Press, Cambridge, MA, 1989.
9. Pascal Van Hentenryck, Vijay Saraswat, and Yves Deville. Constraint processing in cc(FD). manuscript, 1992.

A Unified Framework for Interval Constraints and Interval Arithmetic

T.J. Hickey[1], M.H. van Emden[2], H. Wu[2]

[1] Brandeis University, Waltham, MA 02254, USA
[2] University of Victoria, Victoria, BC, Canada

Abstract. We are concerned with interval constraints: solving constraints among real unknowns in such a way that soundness is not affected by rounding errors.
The contraction operator for the constraint $x + y = z$ can simply be expressed in terms of interval arithmetic. An attempt to use the analogous definition for $x * y = z$ fails if the usual definitions of interval arithmetic are used. We propose an alternative to the interval arithmetic definition of interval division so that the two constraints can be handled in an analogous way. This leads to a unified treatment of both interval constraints and interval arithmetic that makes it easy to derive formulas for other constraint contraction operators.
We present a theorem that justifies simulating interval arithmetic evaluation of complex expressions by means of constraint propagation. A naive implementation of this simulation is inefficient. We present a theorem that justifies what we call the *totality optimization*. It makes simulation of expression evaluation by means of constraint propagation as efficient as in interval arithmetic. It also speeds up the contraction operators for primitive constraints.

1 Introduction

This paper is about the interplay between interval constraints and interval arithmetic. The contraction operators of interval constraints can be succinctly expressed in terms of interval arithmetic, provided that the definition of division in interval arithmetic is suitably modified. Constraint propagation in interval constraints generalizes interval evaluation in interval arithmetic. The totality optimization of interval constraints ensures that in the special case of interval arithmetic no additional computational cost is incurred.

The contributions of this paper are the following: *A unified framework for interval constraints and interval arithmetic.* An advantage of this framework is that it becomes a routine method to derive formulas for a new contraction operator. Examples are the *min* and *max* operators treated in [17]. *A simple definition of interval division in its full generality.* Lack of such a definition has given rise to awkward problems in interval arithmetic. *The totality optimization.* Complex constraints can be decomposed into sets of primitive constraints, if the original constraint is total in one of its variables, then this information can be used to more efficiently solve the constraint.

2 Informal Account of Interval Constraints

In this section we give a brief introduction to interval constraints, beginning with an example. Let us consider the problem of computing the x and y coordinates of the intersection of a circle and a parabola. If we want the solution with nonnegative x-coordinates, then we consider the interval constraint system:

$$x^2 + y^2 = 1 \wedge y = x^2 \wedge 0 \leq x \tag{1}$$

This is a conjunction of three logical formulas related by sharing x and y, which denote unknown reals. The logical formulas are regarded as constraints on the possible values of the unknowns. An interval constraint implementation computes intervals such that all solutions, if any, are contained within the computed intervals.

Complex constraints such as occur in the first formula of interval constraint system (1) are translated to primitive constraints, as shown in formula (2). The translation process introduces the auxiliary variables x_2 and y_2:

$$x^2 = x_2 \wedge y^2 = y_2 \wedge x_2 + y_2 = 1 \wedge x^2 = y \wedge 0 \leq x \tag{2}$$

The most commonly used primitive constraints are

$$x + y = z, \quad x * y = z, \quad x^n = y, \quad x = y, \quad x \leq y$$

where n is an integer. As each of the variables is regarded as an unknown real, it is associated with an interval containing all values of this real that might occur in a solution. To solve such a system according to interval constraints, one starts with intervals large enough to contain all solutions of interest. Then one iterates among the primitive constraints, reducing intervals to subintervals as far as necessary to remove values that are inconsistent with the constraint under consideration.

Consider, for example, constraints of the form $u + v = w$, which is the form of the third constraint in (2). Suppose that the intervals for u, v and w are $[0, 2], [0, 2]$ and $[3, 5]$ respectively. Then all three intervals contain inconsistent values. For example, $v \leq 2$ and $w \geq 3$ imply that $u = w - v \geq 1$. Hence the values less than 1 for u are *inconsistent*, in the conventional sense of the word: it is inconsistent to believe the negation of the conclusion of a logical implication if one accepts the premise. Similar considerations rule out values less than 1 for v and values greater than 4 for w. Removing all inconsistent values from the *a priori* given intervals leaves the intervals $[1, 2]$ for u and v and $[3, 4]$ for w.

To obtain the new intervals from the old ones is to apply the *constraint contraction operator* associated with the constraint, in this case $x + y = z$. The new bounds 1 and 4 are computed according to the rules of interval arithmetic and require the rounding direction to be set appropriately. Thus interval constraints depend on interval arithmetic.

Some standard references on interval arithmetic are [1, 9, 15].

An interval constraint system performs a constraint contraction for each of the primitive constraints. Because typically constraints share variables, contraction usually has to be performed multiple times on any given constraint: every time another constraint causes the interval for a variable to contract, all constraints containing that variable have to have their contraction operators applied again. Because changes are always contractions and because interval bounds are floating-point numbers, a finite number of contractions suffices to reach a state where all constraints yield a null contraction. A constraint propagation algorithm terminates when this is found to be the case.

As interval constraints only remove inconsistent values and may not remove all such values, it may be that the resulting intervals contain no solution. Thus results in interval constraints have the meaning: *if* a solution exists, then it is in the intervals found.

Some references to interval constraints are [4, 5, 18, 10].

3 Machine Numbers and Intervals

In numerical analysis, algorithms are studied in an idealized setting, where the operations are applied to real numbers and yield the correct real-valued results. The theorems that are proved in numerical analysis concern properties of the idealized algorithms such as convergence, stability, condition, etc. It is accepted as inevitable that these theorems are no longer valid when the algorithms are executed on actual hardware. The correct real results have to be approximated by floating-point numbers. Not only are there approximation errors, but even the familiar algebraic laws such as associativity and distributivity fail with floating-point numbers.

In interval constraints the situation is different. Here the computation itself is a proof that the reals that are removed from the intervals during the computation do not belong to a solution. An extreme case is that an interval becomes empty, and then it has been proved that no solution exists. Such a proof is done by means of computations on floating-point numbers on actual hardware. These computations are subject to rounding errors. Ways have been found to make such proofs valid, in spite of the unavoidable rounding errors.

As we have the potential of each interval constraint computation being a proof, it is important to realize that potential. This can only be done if machine arithmetic is considered to a sufficient level of detail. For interval methods these details are more important than for numerical analysis. At the same time it is important to avoid unnecessary detail. One therefore has to find the right abstraction of floating-point arithmetic in terms of real numbers. There are several ways of doing this. As none is universally accepted, we make this paper a self-contained mathematical treatment. Hence the following definitions and lemmas.

Lemma 1. *Let $a \leq b$ be reals. The following are closed connected sets of reals:* $\emptyset$, $\mathcal{R}$, $\{x \in \mathcal{R} \mid a \leq x \leq b\}$, $\{x \in \mathcal{R} \mid a \leq x\}$, $\{x \in \mathcal{R} \mid x \leq b\}$, *where the last three are written as* $[a, b], [a, +\infty], [-\infty, b]$, *respectively. There are no other closed connected sets of reals.*

This lemma is a well-known result in topology; see for example [14].

Note that the fact that we *write*, say, $\{x \in \mathcal{R} \mid x \leq b\}$ as $[-\infty, b]$ does not imply that $-\infty$ is a real number. The same notation suggests that we write $[-\infty, +\infty]$ for $\mathcal{R}$.

From the above lemma, we can define *real intervals*, a fundamental concept in this paper.

Definition 2 Real intervals. A set of reals is defined to be a real interval iff the set is closed and connected. □

Since the computations are applied to the floating-point numbers on actual hardware, it is important that we have an explicit definition for the set of the floating-point numbers of the machine. We call the set of these numbers *machine numbers*.

Definition 3 Machine numbers. The set $\mathcal{M}$ contains the real number 0 as well as finitely many other reals. In addition it contains two elements that are not reals that we denote by $-\infty$ and $+\infty$. $\mathcal{M}$ is totally ordered. Any two real elements in $\mathcal{M}$ are ordered as in $\mathcal{R}$. Moreover, for all real $x \in \mathcal{M}, -\infty < x < +\infty$. □

Definition 4. For any $x \in \mathcal{R}$, x^- is the greatest machine number not greater than x; x^+ is the smallest machine number not smaller than x. Obtaining x^- from x is called *rounding down*, and obtaining x^+ from x is called *rounding up*. [3]

We can obtain a machine interval (defined below) from a real interval $[a, b]$ by rounding down its lower bound a and rounding up its upper bound b.

Definition 5 Machine intervals. A machine interval is one of the following: $\emptyset$, $\mathcal{R}$, $\{x \in \mathcal{R} \mid a \leq x \leq b\}$, $\{x \in \mathcal{R} \mid a \leq x\}$, $\{x \in \mathcal{R} \mid x \leq b\}$, where a and b are machine numbers. The last three are written as $[a, b]$, $[a, +\infty]$, $[-\infty, b]$, respectively, and $[-\infty, +\infty]$ is an acceptable notation for $\mathcal{R}$. □

Let us denote the set of machine intervals as $\mathcal{I}$. $\mathcal{I}$ is finite. $\mathcal{I}$ is a subset of the real intervals. Machine intervals are representable sets of reals. The types of intervals (real or machine) refer to the nature of the end points (in so far as they exist). Both types of intervals are sets of reals.

Definition 6. An n-ary relation (n is a positive integer) is a set of n-tuples of reals. □

For example: $\{< x, y, z > \in \mathcal{R}^3 \mid x \circ y = z\}$ is a ternary relation, where $\circ$ is a binary operation.

[3] In interval arithmetic there is no such error as overflow. If an operation yields a real with an absolute value that exceeds that of all finite machine numbers, then rounding towards the applicable infinity yields an infinity and rounding towards 0 yields a finite machine number. No problem either way.

Definition 7. An n-ary real box (machine box) is the Cartesian product of n real intervals (machine intervals). □

For n = 1, we will not distinguish an n-ary real box (machine box) from a real interval (machine interval).

Lemma 8. *For every n-ary relation, there is a unique least n-ary machine box containing it.*

This existence and uniqueness suggest the definition of a function:

Definition 9. Let r be an n-ary relation. Then bx(r) is defined to be the smallest n-ary machine box containing r. □

Lemma 10. *For all reals a and b,* $bx([a,b]) \subset [a^-, b^+]$. *Inequality holds iff* $b < a$ *and there are zero or one machine numbers k such that* $b \leq k \leq a$. □

As we will see, inequality will translate to deviation from optimality. This happens rarely. To start with, we have equality if $a \leq b$. Otherwise we also have equality, unless a and b are quite close, compared to their magnitude.

Computing the intersection of two intervals is straightforward in principle. Here also rounding introduces some subtlety.

Lemma 11. *For all real intervals* $[r,s]$ *and* $[t,u]$ *we have that* $bx([r,s] \cap [t,u]) \subset [max(r^-, t^-), min(s^+, u^+)]$. *Inequality hold iff (a)* $s < t$ *and* $s^+ \geq t^-$ *or (b)* $u < r$ *and* $u^+ \geq r^-$. □

As noted before, inequality will translate to deviation from optimality. This happens rarely. To start with, we have equality when the left-hand side is non-empty. *If* there is inequality, then the right-hand side is almost empty: it contains at most two machine numbers. Moreover, it often happens that, say, $[r,s]$ is a machine interval, and then the spuriously non-empty right-hand side contains at most *one* machine number, which is either r or s. Similarly for $[t,u]$.

Lemma 12. $\forall r, s \subset \mathcal{R}^n$, *we have* $r \subset s \Rightarrow bx(r) \subset bx(s)$ *(monotonicity of bx).* $\forall r \subset \mathcal{R}^n$, *we have* $bx(r) = bx(bx(r))$ *(idempotence of bx). (See [4].)*

We have now the tools to describe sets of reals in a way that is practical on a computer: as a pair of machine numbers. A great advantage of the IEEE floating-point numbers is that they are machine numbers in our sense because they include the infinities.

4 Interval Constraint Systems

It is the purpose of an interval constraint system to provide information about the unknowns. In the initial state there is no information. Information is gained by applying contraction operators, which cause contraction of the intervals associated with the unknowns.

Information about an unknown is given in the form of a set of reals to which the unknown belongs. These sets are restricted to intervals with machine numbers as bounds. For all unknowns simultaneously, the state is a machine box. The previous section was devoted to define boxes, as well as the necessary preliminary definitions.

We can now define an interval constraint system. It is a system with the following components.

1. **A set of primitive relations** This is the set of relations that occurs in the elements of the set of constraints. The following is a typical set of such relations:

$$sum \stackrel{\text{def}}{=} \{(x,y,z) \in \mathcal{R}^3 \mid x+y=z\}$$
$$prod \stackrel{\text{def}}{=} \{(x,y,z) \in \mathcal{R}^3 \mid x*y=z\}$$
$$eq \stackrel{\text{def}}{=} \{(x,y) \in \mathcal{R}^2 \mid x=y\}$$
$$leq \stackrel{\text{def}}{=} \{(x,y) \in \mathcal{R}^2 \mid x \leq y\}$$
$$power_n \stackrel{\text{def}}{=} \{(x,y) \in \mathcal{R}^2 \mid x^n = y\} \text{ for integer n.}$$

2. **A set of constraints** Each constraint is a formula of the form $p(x_1,\ldots,x_n)$ where p names a relation and $x_1,\ldots,x_n$ are real numbers. They may be known (0, and 1 are typical rational examples) or they may be unknown. In the latter case x_i is an identifier, which may occur in another constraint, where it denotes the same unknown real.
The relation p is a primitive relation; see the applicable component of interval constraint systems.
3. **A sequence of unknowns** This is a sequence of the unknowns occurring in the elements of the set of constraints. In interval constraint systems, the unknowns are usually shared by two or more of the constraints.
4. **A state** A state is a sequence of machine intervals (as defined earlier). For $i = 1,\ldots,n$, the i-th machine interval is the set of real values that are not inconsistent (in this state) as value for the i-th unknown. A state should be thought as a state of information about the sequence of unknowns.
The set of states is partially ordered by pointwise inclusion: $S_1 \preceq S_2$ *iff* each element of S_2 is included (as a set) in the corresponding element of S_1. The symbol is chosen to reflect that in S_2 one has more information about the unknowns than in S_1. The relation $\preceq$ is a partial order. There is one bottom in the partial order: the sequence where all the elements are $[-\infty,+\infty]$. There is a single top in the partial order: the sequence where all the elements are the empty interval $\emptyset$.

Now that the concept of interval constraint systems is defined, we can come back to the purpose of such systems: to contract the intervals of the state as much as possible by applying contraction operators. There is one such operator associated with each of the primitive relations of the system.

The main purpose of this paper is to define these operators in terms of interval arithmetic, and to adapt, as far as necessary, the definitions of interval arithmetic to simplify the connection with interval constraints.

5 The Constraint Contraction Operator

The constraint contraction operator contracts intervals by removing inconsistent values.

Suppose the state of an interval constraint system contains inconsistent values. Then these values are inconsistent with at least one primitive relation, say, r. Ideally we only want values in r. For other reasons, values have already been restricted to some box B, which is the state projected on the arguments of r. However, $r \cap B$ is not in general a machine box. Hence the best we can do in practice is to reduce B to $bx(r \cap B)$. This motivates the following definition ([4]).

Definition 13. The constraint contraction operator γ associated with an n-ary relation r acting on an n-ary machine box B is defined as $\gamma_r(B) = bx(r \cap B)$. □

The operator is sound because its result contains $r \cap B$. It is efficiently representable on a computer because of the bx function.

We are interested in applications of this definition where r is *sum*, *prod*, *eq*, *leq*, or *power*$_n$, and where B is the machine box $abcdef \stackrel{\text{def}}{=} [a,b] \times [c,d] \times [e,f]$ or the machine box $abcd \stackrel{\text{def}}{=} [a,b] \times [c,d]$, for $a,b,c,d,e,f \in \mathcal{M}$ and $a \leq b, c \leq d, e \leq f$. The notations *abcd* and *abcdef* used in this paper are based on their definitions here, unless otherwise specified.

5.1 Interval Arithmetic for Constraints

Interval division Consider a typical contraction operator: the one that contracts the interval $[0,2]$ for x and y and $[3,5]$ for z taking into account the constraint $x+y=z$. As we have explained, the result is $[1,2]$ for x and y and $[3,4]$ for z. The new interval for x can be succinctly computed by the formula $[a,b] \cap ([e,f]-[c,d])$ if $[a,b]$, $[c,d]$ and $[e,f]$ are the old intervals for x, y and z respectively. The interval subtraction is as defined in interval arithmetic.

However, in the analogous situation for the $x * y = z$ constraint, we have to compute $[a,b] \cap ([e,f]/[c,d])$. Implementers of interval constraints [5, 3, 10] have learned to ignore the interval arithmetic definition for $[e,f]/[c,d]$.

According to our definition $[e,f]/[c,d]$ can be of four different forms: a single closed interval, two disjoint closed intervals, a single interval with 0 as open bound, and two disjoint intervals where 0 can occur as an open bound. The first category is the one of standard interval arithmetic. An example of the second category is $[1,1]/[-1,1] = [-\infty,-1] \cup [1,+\infty]$. One can not replace this set by its least surrounding interval; otherwise one will obtain a non-empty result for $[-\frac{1}{2},\frac{1}{2}] \cap [1,1]/[-1,1]$ and one will not achieve optimal contraction in interval constraints.

An example of the third category is $[1,1]/[1,\infty] = (0,1]$. One can not replace this set by its closure, otherwise one will obtain a non-empty result in situations such as $[-1,0] \cap ([1,1]/[1,\infty])$ and one will not achieve optimal contraction in interval constraints.

An example of the fourth category is $[1,1]/[-\infty,1] = [-\infty,0) \cup [1,+\infty]$. Again, if one ignores the open bound, then optimality can be lost.

To implement the constraint contraction operators, we need to further define these operators in terms of interval arithmetic. Therefore, it is important to define the primitive interval arithmetic operations and consider them to a sufficient level of detail.

The operator γ is optimal in the sense that its result is the smallest representable set that contains all possible values. Thus if our implementation formulas achieve equality to rather than containment of γ, we will have obtained optimal implementation.

Definition 14.

$$
\begin{aligned}
[a,b]+[c,d] &\stackrel{\text{def}}{=} \{z \mid \exists x,y.\ x+y=z \wedge x\in[a,b] \wedge y\in[c,d]\}\\
[a,b]-[c,d] &\stackrel{\text{def}}{=} \{z \mid \exists x,y.\ y+z=x \wedge x\in[a,b] \wedge y\in[c,d]\}\\
[a,b]*[c,d] &\stackrel{\text{def}}{=} \{z \mid \exists x,y.\ x*y=z \wedge x\in[a,b] \wedge y\in[c,d]\}\\
[a,b]/[c,d] &\stackrel{\text{def}}{=} \{z \mid \exists x,y.\ y*z=x \wedge x\in[a,b] \wedge y\in[c,d]\}
\end{aligned}
$$

for all real intervals $[a,b]$, $[c,d]$, and $[e,f]$.

Note that the given definition of $[a,b]-[c,d]$ is one of the two possibilities:

$$
\begin{aligned}
[a,b]-[c,d] &\stackrel{\text{def}}{=} \{z \mid \exists x,y.\ z=x-y \wedge x\in[a,b] \wedge y\in[c,d]\}\\
[a,b]-[c,d] &\stackrel{\text{def}}{=} \{z \mid \exists x,y.\ y+z=x \wedge x\in[a,b] \wedge y\in[c,d]\}
\end{aligned}
$$

The corresponding definitions for $[a,b]/[c,d]$ would be:

$$
\begin{aligned}
[a,b]/[c,d] &\stackrel{\text{def}}{=} \{z \mid \exists x,y.\ z=x/y \wedge x\in[a,b] \wedge y\in[c,d]\}\\
[a,b]/[c,d] &\stackrel{\text{def}}{=} \{z \mid \exists x,y.\ y*z=x \wedge x\in[a,b] \wedge y\in[c,d]\}
\end{aligned}
$$

However, in this case there is an important difference: x/y is not always defined. The first alternative, which is invariably chosen in interval arithmetic, needs fixing up. The usual fix is to disallow the occurrence of 0 in $[c,d]$. This has the effect of making interval arithmetic useless exactly in those cases where one needs it most. The other fix in the literature is called "extended interval arithmetic". The reference to this is usually given as [13], which is an elusive publication. Whatever it is, it is unlikely to be as simple as switching to the second formula, as was first pointed out in [17].

For the sake of uniformity, we use the same method for the definition of $[a,b]-[c,d]$, although either alternative will work equally well there.

Definition 15.

$$\leq([a,b]) \stackrel{\text{def}}{=} \{y \mid \exists x.\ y \leq x \wedge x \in [a,b]\}$$
$$\geq([a,b]) \stackrel{\text{def}}{=} \{y \mid \exists x.\ x \leq y \wedge x \in [a,b]\}$$
$$=([a,b]) \stackrel{\text{def}}{=} \{y \mid \exists x.\ y = x \wedge x \in [a,b]\}$$

for all real intervals $[a,b]$ and $[c,d]$.

The unary functions defined here are new for interval arithmetic. The idea comes naturally as we are considering the interval arithmetic operations which are necessary for the implementation of the primitive relations like *eq*, *leq*. The definitions above will lead us to a unified definition format for the constraint contraction operators of *all* the primitive relations, and also simplify the implementation. For example, the unary function $\leq([a,b])$ will just give up the lower bound of the interval, that is $\leq([a,b]) = [-\infty, b]$.

Definition 16.

$$[a,b]^n \stackrel{\text{def}}{=} \{y \mid \exists x.\ x^n = y \wedge x \in [a,b]\}$$
$$[a,b]^{\frac{1}{n}} \stackrel{\text{def}}{=} \{y \mid \exists x.\ y^n = x \wedge x \in [a,b]\}$$

for all real intervals $[a,b]$ and $[c,d]$ and integers n. □

Lemma 17.

$$[a,b] + [c,d] = [a+c, b+d],$$
$$[a,b] - [c,d] = [a-d, b-c],$$

for all real intervals $[a,b]$ *and* $[c,d]$.

The implementation of interval multiplication and division is complicated compared to that of addition and subtraction. It is given in detail in [11].

5.2 Interval Arithmetic Formulas for the Constraint Contraction Operator

The constraint contraction operator requires formulas for $bx(r \cap B)$. As this is a box, we only need to compute its projections. We first consider the projections of $r \cap B$. In the following lemmas, we specify the projections of the primitive relations based on the interval arithmetic operations defined above.

Lemma 18. *For all* $a,b,c,d,e,f \in \mathcal{M}$*:*

$$\pi_1(sum \cap abcdef) = [a,b] \cap ([e,f] - [c,d])$$
$$\pi_2(sum \cap abcdef) = [c,d] \cap ([e,f] - [a,b])$$
$$\pi_3(sum \cap abcdef) = [e,f] \cap ([a,b] + [c,d])$$

$$\pi_1(prod \cap abcdef) = [a,b] \cap ([e,f]/[c,d])$$
$$\pi_2(prod \cap abcdef) = [c,d] \cap ([e,f]/[a,b])$$
$$\pi_3(prod \cap abcdef) = [e,f] \cap ([a,b] * [c,d])$$

where $\pi_i(X)$ is the i-th projection of the relation X.

Proof.

$$\begin{aligned}\pi_1(prod \cap abcdef) &= \pi_1(\{(x,y,z) \mid x * y = z \wedge x \in [a,b] \wedge y \in [c,d] \wedge z \in [e,f]\}) \\ &= \{x \mid \exists y, z.\ x * y = z \wedge x \in [a,b] \wedge y \in [c,d] \wedge z \in [e,f]\} \\ &= \{x \mid x \in [a,b] \wedge (\exists y, z.\ x * y = z \wedge y \in [c,d] \wedge z \in [e,f]\} \\ &= [a,b] \cap \{x \mid \exists y, z.\ x * y = z \wedge y \in [c,d] \wedge z \in [e,f]\} \\ &= [a,b] \cap ([e,f]/[c,d])\end{aligned}$$

Similarly for π_2 and π_3 and for all projections of the relation *sum*.

Lemma 19. *For all $a, b, c, d \in \mathcal{M}$ and all integers n:*

$$\pi_1(eq \cap abcd) = [a,b] \cap = ([c,d])$$
$$\pi_2(eq \cap abcd) = [c,d] \cap = ([a,b])$$

$$\pi_1(leq \cap abcd) = [a,b] \cap \leq ([c,d])$$
$$\pi_2(leq \cap abcd) = [c,d] \cap \geq ([a,b])$$

$$\pi_1(power_n \cap abcd) = [a,b] \cap [c,d]^{\frac{1}{n}}$$
$$\pi_2(power_n \cap abcd) = [c,d] \cap [a,b]^n$$

Where $\pi_i(X)$ is the i-th projection of the relation X.

Proof.

$$\begin{aligned}\pi_1(leq \cap abcd) &= \pi_1(\{(x,y) \mid x \leq y \wedge x \in [a,b] \wedge y \in [c,d]\}) \\ &= \{x \mid \exists y.\ x \leq y \wedge x \in [a,b] \wedge y \in [c,d]\} \\ &= \{x \mid x \in [a,b] \wedge (\exists y.\ x \leq y \wedge y \in [c,d]\} \\ &= [a,b] \cap \{x \mid \exists y.\ x \leq y \wedge y \in [c,d]\} \\ &= [a,b] \cap \leq ([c,d])\end{aligned}$$

Similarly for π_2, π_3 and for all projections of the other relations.

Lemma 20. $bx(\pi_i(r)) = \pi_i(bx(r))$, *where r is an n-ary relation and $i = 1, \ldots, n$.*

From the above lemma and the definitions of the projections over the primitive relations, we are now ready to consider the implementation of the constraint contraction operator γ in detail based on interval arithmetic.

Theorem 21. *For all $a, b, c, d, e, f \in \mathcal{M}$:*

$$\pi_1(\gamma_{sum}(abcdef)) \subset [a,b] \cap [(e-d)^-, (f-c)^+]$$
$$\pi_2(\gamma_{sum}(abcdef)) \subset [c,d] \cap [(e-b)^-, (f-a)^+]$$
$$\pi_3(\gamma_{sum}(abcdef)) \subset [e,f] \cap [(a+c)^-, (b+d)^+]$$

where $\pi_i(X)$ is the i-th projection of the box X. For π_1 there is equality except when $(e-d)^- \leq b < (e-d)$ or $(f-c) < a \leq (f-c)^+$. Similarly for π_2 and π_3. □

Proof.

$$\begin{aligned}
\pi_1(\gamma_{sum}(abcdef)) &= \pi_1(bx(sum \cap abcdef)) \\
&= bx(\pi_1(sum \cap abcdef)) \\
&= bx([a,b] \cap ([e,f] - [c,d])) \\
&= bx([a,b] \cap [e-d, f-c]) \\
&= bx([max(a, e-d), min(b, f-c)]) \\
&\subset [max(a, (e-d)^-), min(b, (f-c)^+)] \\
&= [a,b] \cap [(e-d)^-, (f-c)^+]
\end{aligned}$$

Similarly for π_2 and π_3.

The formulas in this theorem are almost always optimal. Non-optimality occurs when the interval should be empty and the formula returns an interval containing exactly one machine number.

The definition of γ_{prod} in terms of interval arithmetic is different from that of γ_{sum}. The reason for this, as illustrated in the introduction, is that the interval division $[e,f]/[c,d]$ can be of four different forms: a single closed interval, two disjoint closed intervals, a single interval with 0 as open bound, and two disjoint intervals with 0 as open bound(s). One needs to consider the different forms separately to achieve optimal contraction in interval constraints.

Theorem 22. *For all $a, b, c, d, e, f \in \mathcal{M}$:*

$$\begin{aligned}
\pi_1(\gamma_{prod}(abcdef)) &= bx([a,b] \cap (RI_1 \cup RI_2)) \text{ if } [e,f]/[c,d] = RI_1 \cup RI_2 \\
&= bx([a,b] \cap RI_3) \text{ if } [e,f]/[c,d] = RI_3 \\
\pi_3(\gamma_{prod}(abcdef)) &= [e,f] \cap [l^-, u^+]
\end{aligned}$$

where $\pi_i(X)$ is the i-th projection of the box X, and l, u are reals, and where $RI_1 \cup RI_2$ is a union of two disjoint connected sets of reals, not necessarily closed, and RI_3 is a connected, but not necessarily closed, set of reals.

Theorem 23. *For all $a, b, c, d \in \mathcal{M}$:*

$$\begin{aligned}
&\pi_1(\gamma_{eq}(abcd)) = \pi_2(\gamma_{eq}(abcd)) = [a,b] \cap [c,d] \\
&\pi_1(\gamma_{leq}(abcd)) = [a,b] \cap [-\infty, d] \\
&\pi_2(\gamma_{leq}(abcd)) = [c,d] \cap [a, +\infty]
\end{aligned}$$

where $\pi_i(X)$ is the i-th projection of the box X.

The implementation of γ_{power_n} requires considerations similar to those for γ_{prod}. $[a,b]^n$ and $[a,b]^{\frac{1}{n}}$ can be of three different forms: a single closed interval, two disjoint closed intervals, and two disjoint intervals with 0 as open bound(s). The mathematical analysis and the implementation details of γ_{power_n} are given in [20].

Theorem 24. *For all $a, b, c, d \in \mathcal{M}$ and integer n:*

$$\begin{aligned}
\pi_1(\gamma_{power_n}(abcd)) &= bx([a,b] \cap (RI_1 \cup RI_2)) \text{ if } [c,d]^{\frac{1}{n}} = RI_1 \cup RI_2 \\
&\subset [a,b] \cap [l^-, u^+] \text{ if } [c,d]^{\frac{1}{n}} = [l,u] \\
\pi_2(\gamma_{power_n}(abcd)) &= bx([c,d] \cap (RI_1 \cup RI_2)) \text{ if } [a,b]^n = RI_1 \cup RI_2 \qquad (3)\\
&\subset [c,d] \cap [l^-, u^+] \text{ if } [a,b]^n = [l,u]
\end{aligned}$$

where $\pi_i(X)$ is the i-th projection of the box X, $l, u \in \mathcal{R}$ and $RI_1 \cup RI_2$ is a union of two disjoint connected sets of reals, not necessarily closed. Considerations concerning departure from optimality are analogous to those in Theorem 21.

An example of $[a,b]^n = RI_1 \cup RI_2$ is $[-\infty, 1]^{-1} = [-\infty, 0) \cup [1, +\infty]$.

6 Beyond Primitive Constraints

The primitive constraints allow an interval arithmetic system to express equalities or inequalities between real-valued expressions of any complexity. When a complex constraint is "total" in one of its arguments (as described below) it can sometimes be computed more efficiently when treated as a whole, than when viewed as a set of primitive constraints.

Definition 25. The i-th canonical extension $C_{r,i}$ of an n-ary relation r is defined as

$$\begin{aligned}
&C_{r,i}(S_1, \ldots, S_{i-1}, S_{i+1}, \ldots, S_n) \\
&= \{x \mid \exists u_1 \in S_1, \ldots, u_{i-1} \in S_{i-1}, u_{i+1} \in S_{i+1}, \ldots u_n \in S_n. \\
&\quad r(u_1, \ldots, u_{i-1}, x, u_{i+1}, \ldots, u_n)\}
\end{aligned}$$

□

Informally, $C_{r,i}(S_1, \ldots, S_{i-1}, S_{i+1}, \ldots, S_n)$ is the set of all values for the i th argument of r that are consistent with r and with the other arguments being in $S_1, \ldots, S_{i-1}, S_{i+1}, \ldots, S_n$. Canonical extensions can be regarded as generalizations of interval arithmetic operations; at least, if defined in our way. For example:

$$\begin{aligned}
C_{prod,1}([c,d],[e,f]) &= [e,f]/[c,d] \\
C_{prod,2}([a,b],[e,f]) &= [e,f]/[a,b] \\
C_{prod,3}([a,b],[c,d]) &= [a,b] * [c,d]
\end{aligned}$$

Canonical extensions allow the following generalization of lemma 18.

Theorem 26. *Let r be n-ary relation in $\mathcal{R}^n$, and B an n-ary box. For $i = 1,\ldots,n$ we have $\pi_i(r \cap B) = B_i \cap C_{r,i}(B_1,\ldots,B_{i-1},B_{i+1},\ldots,B_n)$, where $B_i = \pi_i(B)$.*

Proof. Consider the case $i = 1$.

$$\begin{aligned}\pi_1(r \cap B) &= \pi_1(\{(x_1,\ldots,x_n) \mid r(x_1,\ldots,x_n) \wedge x_1 \in B_1 \wedge \ldots \wedge x_n \in B_n\}) \\ &= \{x_1 \mid \exists x_2,\ldots,x_n.\, r(x_1,\ldots,x_n) \wedge x_1 \in B_1 \wedge \ldots \wedge x_n \in B_n\}) \\ &= B_1 \cap \{x_1 \mid \exists x_2,\ldots,x_n.\, r(x_1,\ldots,x_n) \wedge x_2 \in B_2 \wedge \ldots \wedge x_n \in B_n\} \\ &= B_1 \cap C_{r,1}(B_2,\ldots,B_n).\end{aligned}$$

The proof is similar for $i = 2,\ldots,n$.

Definition 27. An n-ary relation r is *total* in its i-th argument if the set $C_{r,i}(S_1,\ldots,S_{i-1},S_{i+1},\ldots,S_n)$ is nonempty whenever all arguments are nonempty. □

Example: $r(x_1,\ldots,x_n)$ is defined as $f(x_1,\ldots,x_{n-1}) = x_n$, where f is a function. Then r is total in its n-th argument.

Example: *prod* is total in its third argument. It is not total in its first and second arguments as can be seen from $C_{prod,2}([0,0],[1,1]) = \emptyset$.

Theorem 28 The totality theorem. *Let $S_1,\ldots,S_n$ be nonempty sets. If an n-ary relation r is total in its i-th argument ($i = 1,\ldots,n$) and if $C_{r,i}(S_1,\ldots,S_{i-1},S_{i+1},\ldots,S_n) \subset S_i$, then $S_j \subset C_{r,j}(S_1,\ldots,S_{j-1},S_{j+1},\ldots,S_n)$ for $j = 1,\ldots,i-1,i+1,\ldots,n$.*

Proof. Assume that $i = 1$. Suppose $C_{r,1}(S_2,\ldots,S_n) \subset S_1$ and $u_j \in S_j$, with $j = 2,\ldots,n$. From the totality of r in its first argument (see assumption $i = 1$) we know that $C_{r,1}(\{u_2\},\ldots,\{u_n\})$ is nonempty. It therefore contains an element, say, u_1, and it is in S_1. As a result we have that $(u_1,\ldots,u_n) \in r$. It follows that $u_j \in C_{r,j}(\{u_1\},\ldots,\{u_{j-1}\},\{u_{j+1}\},\ldots,\{u_n\})$, which is contained in $C_{r,j}(S_1,\ldots,S_{j-1},S_{j+1},\ldots,S_n)$.

The totality optimization Suppose the real valued expression E contains the variables $x_1,\ldots,x_{n-1}$ and no others. Suppose E is defined for all values of its variables. Then the relation $r(x_1,\ldots,x_n)$ that is defined to hold whenever $E = x_n$, is total in its last argument. We can obtain a short cut when computing the constraint contraction associated with r. According to theorem 26 we can obtain the result by computing $\pi_i(r \cap B) = B_i \cap C_{r,i}(B_1,\ldots,B_{i-1},B_{i+1},\ldots,B_n)$. Let B be such that $B_n = [-\infty,+\infty]$. Then $C_{r,n}(B_1,\ldots,B_{i-1},B_{i+1},\ldots,B_n) \subset B_n$. Hence $\pi_n(r \cap B)$ is $C_{r,n}(B_1,\ldots,B_{i-1},B_{i+1},\ldots,B_n)$, which is E evaluated in interval arithmetic with B_j substituted for x_j, $j = 1,\ldots,n-1$. Theorem 28 shows that in this case $\pi_j(r \cap B) = B_j$ for $j = 1,\ldots,n-1$. The theorem says that the entire propagation is effected by a single interval arithmetic evaluation.

This is an instance of what we call the *totality optimization*. It optimizes constraint propagation. This optimization is also applicable at the level of the single contraction operator. The constraint *sum* is total in all its arguments. Therefore, if in the course of evaluating the formulas in lemma 18 the first (or the second) interval operation is found to give a result strictly contained in the old interval, then the two remaining projections (or one remaining projection) are unchanged.

The *prod* constraint is total only in its third argument. The totality optimization can therefore only be applied there. Because of this, the third projection should be evaluated first, in case the sole potential opportunity for the totality optimization materializes.

7 Related Work

Interval arithmetic One source of interval constraints, interval arithmetic, started with a bang: almost the first publication was the 1966 book [15] by Ramon E. Moore, published in a prestigious series. It is still referred to as a source for important ideas. Subsequent developments in interval arithmetic are consolidated in books such as [9, 16, 1].

Interval constraints Interval constraints can be traced to the dissertation by Waltz where constraints were propagated to reduce sets of possible values [19]. The CHIP programming language [8] showed that this idea is more widely applicable. The next development was its application to reals by Davis [7]. BNR Prolog [5] can be regarded as an implementation of Davis's ideas with Prolog as front-end programming language. That is, BNR Prolog is to Davis what CHIP is to Waltz. In actual fact, BNR Prolog was inspired by Cleary's relational interval arithmetic [6], which, however, viewed intervals as generalized reals, a view often taken in the interval arithmetic literature. Thus the BNR Prolog team not only merged Cleary's ideas with constraint propagation, but also made the switch from viewing intervals as generalized reals to viewing them as sets of reals. Davis and the BNR Prolog team were not the only ones to independently discover interval constraints; a third one was Hyvönen [12]. The basic interval constraints method can be enhanced by incorporating Newton's method [2, 10].

In this paper we have developed interval constraints from first principles and formulated the main results in terms of interval arithmetic. We have found that it is possible to do this in a uniform way, treating constraints uniformly, independently of whether they arise from the arithmetic operations or relations. Moreover, we showed that a recently reported modification of interval division [17], allows both interval arithmetic and interval constraints to fit in the same framework.

References

1. Götz Alefeld and Jürgen Herzberger. *Introduction to Interval Computations.* Academic Press, 1983.

2. F. Benhamou, D. McAllester, and P. Van Hentenryck. CLP(Intervals) revisited. In *Logic Programming: Proc. 1994 International Symposium*, pages 124–138, 1994.
3. Frédéric Benhamou, Pascal Bouvier, Alain Colmerauer, Henri Garetta, Bruno Giletta, Jean-Luc Massat, Guy Alain Narboni, Stéphane N'Dong, Robert Pasero, Jean-François Pique, Touraïvane, Michel Van Caneghem, and Eric Vétillard. Le manuel de Prolog IV. Technical report, PrologIA, Parc Technologique de Luminy, Marseille, France, 1996.
4. Frédéric Benhamou and William J. Older. Applying interval arithmetic to real, integer, and Boolean constraints. *Journal of Logic Programming*, 32:1–24, 1997.
5. BNR. BNR Prolog user guide and reference manual. 1988.
6. J.G. Cleary. Logical arithmetic. *Future Computing Systems*, 2:125–149, 1987.
7. E. Davis. Constraint propagation with labels. *Artificial Intelligence*, 32:281–331, 1987.
8. M. Dincbas, P. Van Hentenryck, H. Simonis, A. Aggoun, T. Graf, and F. Berthier. The constraint programming language CHIP. In *Proc. Int. Conf. on Fifth Generation Computer Systems*, 1988.
9. Eldon Hansen. *Global Optimization Using Interval Analysis*. Marcel Dekker, 1992.
10. Pascal Van Hentenryck, Laurent Michel, and Yves Deville. *Numerica: A Modeling Language for Global Optimization*. MIT Press, 1997.
11. T. Hickey and M. van Emden. Using the IEEE floating-point standard for implementing interval arithmetic. In preparation.
12. E. Hyvönen. Constraint reasoning based on interval arithmetic. In *Proceedings of the Eleventh International Joint Conference on Artificial Intelligence*, pages 1193–1198, Detroit, USA, 1989.
13. W.M. Kahan. A more complete interval arithmetic. Technical report, University of Toronto, Canada, 1968.
14. Seymour Lipschutz. *General Topology*. Schaum's Outline Series, 1965.
15. Ramon E. Moore. *Interval Analysis*. Prentice-Hall, 1966.
16. Arnold Neumaier. *Interval Methods for Systems of Equations*. Cambridge University Press, 1990.
17. M.H. van Emden. Canonical extensions as common basis for interval constraints and interval arithmetic. In *Proceedings of the Sixth French Conference on Logic and Constraint Programming*, Orléans, France, 1997.
18. M.H. van Emden. Value constraints in the CLP Scheme. *Constraints*, 2:163–183, 1997.
19. D. Waltz. Understanding line drawings in scenes with shadows. In Patrick Henry Winston, editor, *The Psychology of Computer Vision*, pages 19–91. McGraw-Hill, 1975.
20. Huan Wu. Defining and implementing a unified framework for interval constraints and interval arithmetic. Master's thesis. In preparation.

Constrained-Based Problem Decomposition for a Key Configuration Problem

Ulrich Junker

ILOG
9, rue de Verdun, BP 85
F-94253 Gentilly Cedex
junker@ilog.fr

Abstract. Finding good problem decompositions is crucial for solving large-scale key/lock configuration problems. We present a novel approach to problem decomposition where the detection of a subproblem hierarchy is formulated as a constraint satisfaction problem (CSP) on set variables. Primitive constraints on set variables such as an inverse and a union-over-set-constraint are used to formalize properties of trees and to ensure that solutions of these CSPs represent a tree. An objective for optimizing properties of the tree is presented as well. Experimental results from an industrial prototype are reported.

Keywords: constraints on trees, problem decomposition, key configuration, set variables.

1 Introduction

Domain filtering techniques as elaborated in the field of CSPs have successfully been applied to solve combinatorial problems such as job-shop scheduling and car sequencing. An example is the famous edge-finder constraint that allows solving difficult job-shop examples to optimality. The following techniques are crucial for reducing an initially large search space to a smaller space that still contains all solutions or all optimal solutions:

1. Improved filtering by global constraints or good constraint models.
2. Heuristics defining the order in which choices are made.
3. Non-chronological search (e.g. best-first or limited discrepancy search).

The search space is reduced by cutting off inconsistent subtrees having no solution (1), by making inconsistent subtrees small by using first-fail heuristics (2), and by cutting subtrees if lower bounds on the solutions in the subtrees are strictly greater than the costs of the best solution found so far. Finding better solutions first (2,3) thus allows cutting the search space further.

A principal problem, however, is the scalability of these techniques, especially when we face real-world problems such as production scheduling, personnel planning, resource allocation, and others that are large in size. For example, if 1000 tasks have to be allocated to 1000 resources then a complete search to find an optimal solution is no longer practicable. In order to find acceptably good solutions, problem decomposition methods are usually applied in AI and OR. We distinguish three methods:

1. **Solution Synthesis:** a large problem is decomposed into subproblems such that each variable occurs in exactly one of the subproblems. If a constraint belongs to a subproblem then all of its variables belong to this subproblem. For each subproblem, several possible solutions are determined. The master problem then consists of (optimally) selecting one solution of each subproblem s.t. all remaining constraints are satisfied. These are these constraints that do not belong to any subproblem. This method is used, for example, to solve crew scheduling problems [1].
2. **Subproblem Improvement:** a current solution for the complete problem is improved in several steps. In each step, a subproblem is chosen and changes to the current solution are restricted to the variables in this subproblem.
3. **Subproblem Separation:** a large problem is decomposed into subproblems and a common problem, such that each variable appears in exactly one of these problems. There can be constraints between the variables of a subproblem and those of the common problem, but not between variables of two different subproblems. As a consequence, the subproblems can be solved separately after the common problem has been solved. Such an approach has been used, for example, in [2] for resource allocation problems.

In this paper, we study the last method for a particular example, namely the configuration of locking systems for large complexes such as airports, plants, and office buildings. A given locking matrix describes which key should open which lock (of which door). The task is to choose the physical properties of keys and locks (e.g. the tooth lengths) such that this locking matrix is respected. In order to treat large cases, the human planners decompose the problem and build up a hierarchy of subproblems.

In this paper, we address the central question of how to find a good decomposition into subproblems. It turned out that this task can be formulated as a CSP. Different properties of the tree of subproblems can be formalized in terms of constraints on set variables [7]. An objective on the form of the tree and the kind of subproblems can be introduced in the same manner.

The paper is organized as follows: The key configuration problem is presented in section 2. Section 3 gives a short survey on set variables. Analyzing properties of solutions of key configuration problems allows the introduction of a problem decomposition scheme (section 4). The CSP for the configuration of a tree is introduced in section 5 and extended to the subproblem hierarchy in 6. Section 7 describes an algorithm for finding such a hierarchy and section 8 reports results from an industrial prototype.

	l_1	l_2	l_3
k_1	X		X
k_2		X	X

k_1	k_2	l_1	l_2	l_3
$\{t_{1,5}, t_{2,6}\}$	$\{t_{1,7}, t_{2,4}\}$	$\{t_{1,5}, t_{2,6}\}$	$\{t_{1,7}, t_{2,4}\}$	$\{t_{1,5}, t_{1,7}, t_{2,6}, t_{2,4}\}$

Fig. 1. A locking matrix (left side) and a possible solution (right side).

2 The Key Configuration Problem

We briefly present the problem of the configuration of locking systems. Large complexes of buildings can have thousands of different doors that have their respective locks and keys. Obviously, the door of an office should not be opened by the keys of the other offices. Moreover, the entrances of the floors, buildings, and special-purpose rooms are opened by several keys, but not necessarily all. Access to several rooms is provided by master keys. Master keys can open several doors, but not necessarily all. A so-called locking matrix specifies which key opens which lock. An example is given in figure 1. Each row corresponds to a key and each column to a lock. A key opens a lock if there is a cross in the corresponding row and column. Mathematically, a locking matrix can be described by a binary relation between the set of keys and the set of locks.

A locking matrix is technically realized by choosing various physical properties for each key and each lock (e.g. the teeth and the holes of a key). For the sake of simplicity, we summarize all these properties by the term *pin*. A key opens a lock if the pins of the key are a subset of the pins of the lock. For example, a key has several teeth $t_{i,d}$ each of which has a depth d and a unique position i. At each these of positions, a lock has a pin that can be subdivided several times. If a key opens a lock then the depths of the teeth must correspond to the depths of the subdivisions. Key k_1 in figure 1 has a tooth $t_{1,5}$ of depth 5 at position 1 and a tooth $t_{2,6}$ of depth 6 at position 2. Key k_2 has the teeth $t_{1,7}$ and $t_{2,4}$. Since k_1 opens lock l_1 and k_2 opens l_2 those locks have the same pin sets. Since l_3 is opened by both keys its pin set is the union of the pin sets of k_1 and k_2. We now define a key configuration problem as follows:

Definition 1. *A* key configuration problem *is defined by a finite set $\mathcal{K}$ of keys, a finite set $\mathcal{L}$ of locks, a locking relation $\mathcal{O} \subseteq \mathcal{K} \times \mathcal{L}$, and a finite set $\mathcal{P}$ of pins. A* solution *to this problem consists of a pin set $P(k) \subseteq \mathcal{P}$ for each key $k \subset \mathcal{K}$ and of a pin set $Q(l) \subseteq \mathcal{P}$ for each lock $l \in \mathcal{L}$ such that*

1. *$P(k) \subseteq Q(l)$ iff $(k, l) \in \mathcal{O}$ for each $k \in \mathcal{K}$ and $l \in \mathcal{L}$,*
2. *$P(k)$ is legal for each $k \in \mathcal{K}$,*
3. *$Q(l)$ is legal for each $l \in \mathcal{L}$.*

The pin sets $P(k)$ and $Q(l)$ are legal if they satisfy mechanical and security constraints that are manufacturer-specific. Some examples are:

1. *Security constraints:* the difference between the shortest and the longest tooth of a key is at least 3.

2. *Mechanical constraints:* a tooth of depth 0 cannot be between two teeth of depth 8.

A key configuration problem would not be difficult to solve if the number of pins were large. The difficulties stem from the fact that cases with 10000 keys and locks must be realized with less than 100 pins. Even if the number of keys and locks is small the number of used pins should be minimized. A pin is *used* iff it is contained in the pin set $P(k)$ of at least one key $k \in \mathcal{K}$ and if it is not contained in the pin set $Q(l)$ of at least one lock $l \in \mathcal{L}$. In order to find a solution having a minimal number of used pins, we decompose the problem as follows. In the first step, we ignore legality constraints and use anonymous pins.

1. Find an optimal solution that satisfies constraint (1) in def. 1.
2. Assign the anonymous pins to concrete pins by obeying legality constraints.

Whereas the first step leads to a general mathematical model, which is difficult to solve, the second problem requires manufacturer-specific strategies and knowledge, which are beyond the scope of this paper. We therefore restrict further discussion to the first problem.

3 CSPs on Finite Set Variables

The CSPs presented in this paper will be based on constrained set variables as introduced by [7, 3]. Given a finite (element) domain $\mathcal{D}$, the value of a *set variable* is a subset of the element domain $\mathcal{D}$. The domain of a set variable therefore is the power-set $2^{\mathcal{D}}$. Filtering techniques for set variables either add elements of $\mathcal{D}$ to all possible values of the set variable or remove elements from all possible values. The current domain of a set variable X is therefore represented by a set of *required elements* $req(X)$ (those that have been added) and a set of *possible elements* $pos(X)$ (those that have not been removed). A variable X has a single possible value (and is called *instantiated*) iff $req(X)$ is equal to $pos(X)$.

An n-ary *constraint* C on set variables is associated with an n-ary relation $R_C \subseteq 2^{\mathcal{D}^n}$. An n-ary *constraint literal* is an n-ary constraint C applied to an n-ary tuple of variables $(X_1, \ldots, X_n)$ and is written in the form $C(X_1, \ldots, X_n)$.

Definition 2. *A CSP on finite set variables $(\mathcal{D}, \mathcal{X}, \mathcal{C})$ is defined by a finite element domain $\mathcal{D}$, a set of variables $\mathcal{X}$, and a set of constraint literals $\mathcal{C}$. A domain assignment of the CSP is a pair (req, pos) of two mappings $req : \mathcal{X} \to 2^{\mathcal{D}}$ and $pos : \mathcal{X} \to 2^{\mathcal{D}}$. A solution for the CSP under a given domain assignment (req, pos) is a value assignment $val : \mathcal{X} \to 2^{\mathcal{D}}$ satisfying*

$$\begin{array}{l} 1.\ req(X) \subseteq val(X) \subseteq pos(X) \quad \textit{for all } x \in \mathcal{X}, \\ 2.\ (val(X_1), \ldots, val(X_n)) \in R_C \textit{ for all } C(X_1, \ldots, X_n) \in \mathcal{C}. \end{array} \tag{1}$$

As with standard CSPs, filtering techniques can be applied that reduce the domains of set variables. For each constraint C, a specific filtering operation can be defined that exploits the semantics of the relation R_C [4]. We give an example for a simplified union-over-set constraint that is defined for $3n$ set variables with $\mathcal{D} := \{1, \ldots, n\}$. The constraint $union(X_1, Y_1, Z_1, \ldots, X_n, Y_n, Z_n)$ is satisfied by val iff

$$\bigcup_{j \in val(X_i)} val(Y_j) \subseteq val(Z_i)$$

for all $i = 1, \ldots, n$. The following filtering operation defines new sets of required and possible elements:

$$\begin{aligned} req'(Z_i) &:= req(Z_i) \cup \{k \in \mathcal{D} \mid \exists j : j \in req(X_i), k \in req(Y_j)\} \\ pos'(Y_j) &:= pos(Y_j) - \{k \in \mathcal{D} \mid \exists i : j \in req(X_i), k \notin pos(Z_i)\} \\ pos'(X_i) &:= pos(X_i) - \{j \in \mathcal{D} \mid \exists k : k \notin pos(Z_i), k \in req(Y_j)\} \end{aligned} \tag{2}$$

We say that a domain assignment is *locally consistent* iff the filtering operation of each constraint maps the domain assignment to itself.

Throughout this paper, we use constraints with the following semantics. Let X, Y, X_i, Y_i, Z_i be constrained set variables, d be an element of $\mathcal{D}$, and $C(\ldots, X_i, \ldots)$ be a constraint literal having X_i among its variables:

1. unary constraints: $|X|$, $d \in X$, $d \notin X$.
2. binary constraints: $X \subseteq Y$, $X \nsubseteq Y$, $X = Y$.
3. ternary constraints: $X \cap Y = Z$, $X \cup Y = Z$.
4. set-of: $\{i \in \mathcal{D} \mid C(\ldots, X_i, \ldots)\}$.
5. inverse: $j \in X_i$ iff $i \in Y_j$.
6. aggregations: $Z_i = \bigcup_{j \in X_i} Y_j$ and $Z_i = max\{Y_j \mid j \in X_i\}$.

These constraints and the corresponding filtering are provided by the constraint library ILOG SOLVER [5] or have been added as extension [6].

As an example, we introduce a CSP for the key configuration problem. We choose the set $\mathcal{P}$ of pins as the element domain of the CSP. We introduce a set variable X_k for each key k and a set variable Y_l for each lock l denoting the respective pin sets. For each $(k, l) \in \mathcal{O}$, we introduce a constraint literal subset(X_k, Y_l). Furthermore, we introduce a constraint literal not-subset(X_k, Y_l) for each $(k, l) \in \overline{\mathcal{O}}$ where $\overline{\mathcal{O}} := (\mathcal{K} \times \mathcal{L}) - \mathcal{O}$. A value assignment val is a solution of this CSP iff

$$\begin{aligned} &1.\ val(X_k) \subseteq val(Y_l) \text{ for } (k, l) \in \mathcal{O} \text{ (opening)} \\ &2.\ val(X_k) \nsubseteq val(Y_l) \text{ for } (k, l) \in \overline{\mathcal{O}} \text{ (locking)} \end{aligned} \tag{3}$$

Since the current domain assignment (req, pos) is locally consistent, the value assignment $val := req$ satisfies the first constraint. It satisfies also the second constraint if for each pair (k, l) in $\overline{\mathcal{O}}$ there exists a pin p that is in the required set $req(X_k)$, but not in the possible set of $pos(Y_l)$. A possible search strategy is to pick a pair in $\overline{\mathcal{O}}$ and a pin p and then satisfy the constraint by adding p to $req(X_k)$ and removing it from $pos(Y_l)$. We say that the *conflict* $(k, l) \in \overline{\mathcal{O}}$ is solved by the pin p in this case.

In general, the number of pairs in $\overline{\mathcal{O}}$ is large compared to the number of available pins. As a consequence, several of the conflicts are solved by the same pin. The crucial question is which conflicts can be solved by the same pins.

	l_1	l_2	l_3	l_4	l_5	l_6	l_7	l_8
k_1	X		X				X	X
k_2		X	X				X	X
k_3	X	X	X				X	
k_4				X		X	X	X
k_5					X	X	X	
k_6				X	X	X	X	X
k_7	X	X	X	X	X	X	X	X
k_8		X	X	X		X	X	

	l_1	l_2	l_3	l_4	l_5	l_6	l_7	l_8
k_1		4		2	2 4	2		
k_2	3			2 3	2	2		
k_3				2	2	2		6
k_4	1	1 4	1		4			
k_5	1 3	1	1	3				6
k_6	1	1	1					
k_7								
k_8	5				5			5

Fig. 2. A nearly hierarchical example (left) and the chosen conflict areas (right).

4 Problem Decomposition

In this section, we determine which conflicts in $\overline{\mathcal{O}}$ can be solved by the same pins. The result is used to elaborate a problem decomposition scheme that allows a good exploitation of the available pins.

Consider a solution to a key configuration problem (defined by P and Q). For each pin p, we define the set of keys and locks to which the pin has been assigned in the given solution:

$$\begin{aligned} K(p) &:= \{k \in \mathcal{K} \mid p \in P(k)\} \\ L(p) &:= \{l \in \mathcal{L} \mid p \in Q(l)\} \end{aligned} \tag{4}$$

If a key k is in $K(p)$ and a lock l is not in $L(p)$ then $P(k)$ is not a subset of $Q(l)$. As a consequence, k does not open l (i.e. $(k, l) \in \overline{\mathcal{O}}$). Thus, we get the following property of a solution:

$$K(p) \times (\mathcal{L} - L(p)) \subseteq \overline{\mathcal{O}} \tag{5}$$

Suppose that two conflicts (k_1, l_1), (k_2, l_2) are solved by the same pin p. Then the keys k_1, k_2 are elements of $K(p)$ and the locks l_1, l_2 are not elements of $L(p)$. As a consequence, (k_1, l_2) and (k_2, l_1) are conflicts as well.

We conclude that a pin p can be assigned to a set K' of keys and suppressed for a set L' of locks if $K' \times L'$ is a subset of $\overline{\mathcal{O}}$, i.e. none of the keys in K' opens a lock in L'. We call such a pair (K', L') a *conflict area*. The key configuration problem can be formulated as the problem of finding a minimal number of conflict areas that cover all conflicts in $\overline{\mathcal{O}}$.

We discuss some examples for finding large conflict areas. The first example consists of 8 keys and 8 locks. The locking matrix is shown in the left part of figure 2. In total, there are 27 conflicts. All conflicts that are in the same row (or in the same column) can be solved by the same pin. Since 1 row does not contain a conflict, 7 areas would be sufficient. An even better solution is obtained if we explore the (nearly) hierarchical structure of the problem. In fact, we can decompose the complete problem into two subproblems $k_1, k_2, k_3, l_1, l_2, l_3$ and $k_4, k_5, k_6, l_4, l_5, l_6$ and a common problem k_7, l_7, k_8, l_8. There is a conflict area between the keys of the second subproblem and the locks of the first one. The

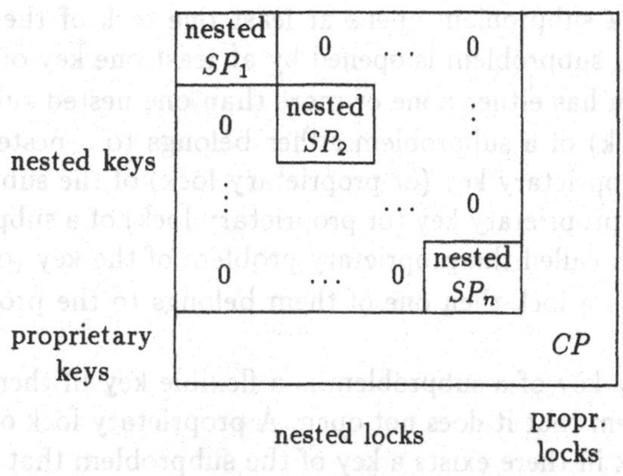

Fig. 3. Structure of (sub)problem

second conflict area is between the keys of the first subproblem and the locks of the second one. Hence, two pins are sufficient to separate both subproblems. Each subproblem consists of two conflicts and two pins are necessary to solve them. However, the pins needed for the first subproblem can be reused for the second one. Since the keys of a subproblem are in conflict with the locks of the other subproblem this does not provide problems. Keys and locks of the common problem that are involved in conflicts are called *flexible keys* and *flexible locks*. In the example, k_8 and l_8 are flexible and one additional pin per flexible object is needed. As a result, we need only 6 pins. Although the gain of 1 is not very impressive, the possibilities of reusing the same pins in different subproblems pays off if they are large.

The second example consists of 2^n keys $k_1, \ldots, k_{2^n}$ and 2^n locks $l_1, \ldots, l_{2^n}$. The key k_i opens the lock l_i, but no other lock. The simplest way is to choose a conflict area per row ending up with 2^n pins. A second solution is to recursively divide the initial problem into two subproblems of same size. Then $2n$ pins are sufficient. For $2^n = 1024$ keys (and locks) we thus need 20 pins. An even better solution is obtained as follows: Consider a set of m pins. We want to choose a maximal number of subsets such that none of the sets is a subset of any other set. Then it is sufficient to assign to each key/lock pair k_i, l_i one of these sets. The subsets of cardinality $\frac{m}{2}$ satisfy the required property. There are $\binom{m}{m/2}$ such subsets. Hence, we determine the smallest m s.t. $\binom{m}{m/2}$ is greater than or equal to 2^n. For the 1024 keys, we thus need only 13 pins. The 20 pins needed for the first approach can be used for 184756 keys, i.e. 180 times more.

We generalize both examples to the following problem decomposition scheme. A given problem can be decomposed into several subproblems and a common part. As illustrated in figure 3, the subproblems are arranged in a diagonal. This decomposition can recursively be applied to the subproblems. Thus, we obtain a hierarchy of subproblems. The root of the hierarchy is the initial problem. We require that all subproblems in the hierarchy satisfy the following properties:

1. Each key of a subproblem opens at least one lock of the subproblem and each lock of a subproblem is opened by at least one key of the subproblem.
2. A subproblem has either none or more than one nested subproblem.
3. A key (or lock) of a subproblem either belongs to a nested subproblem or it is called proprietary key (or proprietary lock) of the subproblem. If a key (or lock) is a proprietary key (or proprietary lock) of a subproblem then this subproblem is called the proprietary problem of the key (or the lock).
4. If a key opens a lock then one of them belongs to the proprietary problem of the other.
5. A proprietary key of a subproblem is a flexible key iff there exists a lock of the subproblem that it does not open. A proprietary lock of a subproblem is a flexible lock iff there exists a key of the subproblem that does not open it.

Such a problem decomposition exists if and only if each key of the key configuration problem opens at least one lock and each of the locks is opened by at least one key.

We determine the number of pins needed for a subproblem. Suppose a subproblem s has n nested subproblems $s_1, \ldots, s_n$ and s_i needs n_i pins. Furthermore, let m be the smallest number s.t. $\binom{m}{m/2}$ is greater than or equal to n. Then s needs m pins for separating the subproblems. Since pins can be reused in the nested subproblems, s needs only $max\{n_i \mid i = 1, \ldots, n\}$ pins inside the subproblems. Furthermore, s needs 1 pin for each flexible key and flexible lock. The sum of these numbers gives the number of pins needed for s. The number of pins needed for the complete problem is obtained at the root of the subproblem hierarchy.

5 Tree Configuration

The crucial problem now is to find a subproblem hierarchy for a given key configuration problem that minimizes the number of pins. This problem again is a combinatorial problem and it is therefore convenient to formulate it as a CSP. This CSP has a general part namely that of the configuration of a tree which will be presented in this section. In the next section, we add further constraints for ensuring that the resulting tree has the properties of a subproblem hierarchy as introduced in the last section.

The tree configuration problem (TCP) consists in arranging a given set of objects $\mathcal{V} := \{v_1, \ldots, v_n\}$ in form of a tree. Several of these objects can belong to the same node in the tree. In this case, we say that they are *equivalent*. We suppose that there is one distinguished object r in $\mathcal{V}$ that belongs to the root node. An object is an ancestor (descendant) of another object if the node of the first object is an ancestor (descendant) of the node of the second object. An object is related to another object if there is a path between the nodes of both objects in the tree. If there is no such path the objects exclude each other and can be separated. In order to determine these relations, we introduce the following constrained set variables for each $v_i \in \mathcal{V}$:

$$\begin{array}{ll} \mathrm{A}_i & \text{the set of ancestors of } v_i. \\ \mathrm{D}_i & \text{the set of descendants of } v_i. \\ \mathrm{E}_i & \text{the set of objects equivalent to } v_i. \\ \mathrm{S}_i & \text{the set of descendants or equivalent objects of } v_i. \\ \mathrm{R}_i & \text{the set of objects related to } v_i. \\ \mathrm{X}_i & \text{the set of excluded objects of } v_i. \end{array} \tag{6}$$

There are two reasons for choosing a representation in terms of ancestors instead of parents. First, initial constraints on ancestors and related nodes can be expressed directly. Second, this allows less strict decisions and is less prone to failure. After deciding that v is an ancestor of w, it is possible to insert additional objects between v and w.

We now introduce the constraint (literals) of the CSP. For the sake of readability, we only present the semantics of these constraints and write $A(v_i)$, $D(v_i)$, $E(v_i)$, $S(v_i)$, $R(v_i)$, $X(v_i)$ for the values $val(\mathrm{A}_i)$, $val(\mathrm{D}_i)$, $val(\mathrm{E}_i)$, $val(\mathrm{S}_i)$, $val(\mathrm{R}_i)$, $val(\mathrm{X}_i)$ of the variables A_i, D_i, E_i, S_i, R_i, X_i.

Union: $S(v)$ has been defined as the union of $D(v)$ and $E(v)$. The set of related objects is the union of $D(v)$, $E(v)$, and $A(v)$. The excluded objects are the complement of the related nodes.

$$S(v) = D(v) \cup E(v) \quad R(v) = S(v) \cup A(v) \quad \mathcal{V} = R(v) \cup X(v) \tag{7}$$

Disjointness: The set of ancestors, the set of equivalent objects, the set of descendant objects, and the set of excluded objects of an object v are mutually disjoint. Three constraints are sufficient to express this property:

$$D(v) \cap E(v) = \emptyset \quad S(v) \cap A(v) = \emptyset \quad R(v) \cap X(v) = \emptyset \tag{8}$$

Reflexivity: Each object is equivalent to itself:

$$v \in E(v) \tag{9}$$

Inverse: If an object v is an ancestor of an object w then the w is a descendant of v and vice versa. Furthermore, if v is equivalent to w then w is equivalent to v. The same property holds for related nodes.

$$\begin{array}{c} v \in A(w) \text{ iff } w \in D(v) \\ v \in E(w) \text{ iff } w \in E(v) \\ v \in R(w) \text{ iff } w \in R(v) \end{array} \tag{10}$$

Transitivity: If v is an ancestor of w then all ancestors of v are ancestors of w. Furthermore, if v is equivalent to w then all objects that are equivalent to v are also equivalent to w. We formulate both properties by a union-over-set-constraint:

$$\bigcup_{w \in A(v)} A(w) \subseteq A(v) \qquad \bigcup_{w \in E(v)} E(w) \subseteq E(v) \tag{11}$$

Tree properties: The root r has no ancestors and no excluded objects:

$$A(r) = \emptyset \quad X(r) = \emptyset \tag{12}$$

If an object v has two ancestors w_1, w_2 then these ancestors are related. This property guarantees the existence of a unique parent of v. We express it by a union-over-set-constraint in the following way:

$$\bigcup_{w \in D(v)} A(w) \subseteq R(v) \tag{13}$$

Definition of Equivalence: If a node in the tree has only a single son then there is no reason to put these two objects in different nodes. We avoid this case by the following property: Two objects v and w have the same sets of related objects iff they are equivalent. We formulate this by the setof-constraints:

$$E(v) := \{w \in \mathcal{V} \mid R(v) = R(w)\} \tag{14}$$

Properties of Equivalence: If two nodes are equivalent then they have the same set of related nodes, of ancestors, and so on. It is sufficient to state:

$$\bigcup_{w \in E(v)} R(w) \subseteq R(v) \quad \bigcup_{w \in E(v)} S(w) \subseteq S(v) \quad \bigcup_{w \in E(v)} A(w) \subseteq A(v) \tag{15}$$

Ancestors: The following constraint is implied by the others, but allows more propagation: An object w' is an ancestor of an object v iff they are related and there exists an excluded object w of v such that w' is also related to w. We formulate this by a union-over-set-constraint:

$$A(v) = R(v) \cap \bigcup_{w \in X(v)} R(w) \tag{16}$$

We obtain a further implied constraint: If w is a descendant of v then all objects related to w are also related to v:

$$\bigcup_{w \in D(v)} R(w) \subseteq R(v) \tag{17}$$

The TCP-CSP for $\mathcal{V}$ and r consists of the variables (6) and the constraints (7 - 17). The solutions of the TCP-CSP are trees that are labelled with sets of objects and don't have nodes with only one son.

Definition 3. *A labelled tree for $\mathcal{V}$ and r is defined by a set of nodes $\mathcal{N}$, a root $r' \in \mathcal{N}$, a mapping $\pi : \mathcal{N} - \{r'\} \rightarrow \mathcal{N}$ defining the parent of a node, and a mapping $\nu : \mathcal{V} \rightarrow \mathcal{N}$ defining the node of an object*[1] *such that*

1. *The graph $(\mathcal{N}, \{(\pi(n), n) \mid n \in \mathcal{N})$ is a directed tree,*
2. *$\nu(r) = r'$,*
3. *ν is surjective,*
4. *if $n_1 \in \mathcal{N} - \{r'\}$ then there exists $n_2 \in \mathcal{N} - \{r', n_1\}$ s.t. $\pi(n_1) = \pi(n_2)$.*

(18)

[1] In fact, each node $n \in \mathcal{N}$ is labelled with the set of objects v satisfying $\nu(v) = n$.

Each solution of the CSP corresponds to a unique labelled tree:

Proposition 1. *There exists a bijective mapping from the set of solutions of the TCP-CSP for $\mathcal{V}$ and r to the set of labelled trees for $\mathcal{V}$ and r.*

A tree can be extracted as follows from a solution of the TCP-CSP. Each equivalence class $E(v)$ is a node of the tree. A node $E(v)$ is the parent of node $E(w)$ iff $|A(w)| = |A(v)| + |E(v)|$.

6 Tree of Subproblems

In this section, we apply the CSP for tree configuration to the problem of finding a subproblem hierarchy for the key configuration problem. We apply the TCP-CSP to the given key and lock objects (plus an additional root object $r \notin \mathcal{K} \cup \mathcal{L}$) and add further constraints that are based on the locking relation $\mathcal{O}$. Hence, we consider the following set of objects:

$$\mathcal{V} := \mathcal{K} \cup \mathcal{L} \cup \{r\} \tag{19}$$

Each object v then defines a subproblem containing the objects $S(v)$. In section 4, we called it the proprietary subproblem of v. The proprietary keys and locks of this subproblem are in $E(v)$. The keys and locks of the nested subproblems are in $D(v)$.

Locking relation: Given any object v in $\mathcal{V}$, we are interested in the objects that are either opened by v or that v opens.

$$O(v) := \begin{cases} \{w \in \mathcal{K} \mid (w, v) \in \mathcal{O}\} & \text{if } v \in \mathcal{L} \\ \{w \in \mathcal{L} \mid (v, w) \in \mathcal{O}\} & \text{if } v \in \mathcal{K} \\ \mathcal{V} & \text{if } v = r \end{cases} \tag{20}$$

If an object w is in $O(v)$ then one of these objects must be in the proprietary subproblem of the other. This means that both objects must be related (by a path in the resulting tree):

$$O(v) \subseteq R(v) \tag{21}$$

Non-empty subproblems: An object w can only be in the proprietary subproblem $S(v)$ of another object v if it opens or is opened by another object of the subproblem (i.e. $O(w) \cap S(v) \neq \emptyset$ for all $w \in S(v)$). We formulate this condition in terms of *setof*-constraints:

$$S(v) \subseteq \{w \in \mathcal{V} \mid O(w) \cap S(v) \neq \emptyset\} \tag{22}$$

Subsumption: (implied constraint) If the set of opened/opening objects of an object v is a subset of the set of opened/opening objects of an object w then these both objects are related:

$$\text{if } O(v) \subseteq O(w) \text{ then } v \in R(w) \tag{23}$$

Flexible Keys/Locks: Given any object v in $\mathcal{V}$, we are interested in the forbidden objects of v, i.e. the objects that are not opened by v or that v does not open.

$$\overline{O}(v) := \begin{cases} \{w \in \mathcal{K} \mid (w, v) \in \overline{O}\} & \text{if } v \in \mathcal{L} \\ \{w \in \mathcal{L} \mid (v, w) \in \overline{O}\} & \text{if } v \in \mathcal{K} \\ \emptyset & \text{if } v = r \end{cases} \tag{24}$$

A proprietary object w of a subproblem is flexible iff this subproblem contains a forbidden object of w. Again, we use *setof*-constraints to formulate this condition:

$$F(v) := \{w \in E(v) \mid \overline{O}(w) \cap S(v) \neq \emptyset\} \tag{25}$$

Objective: The set of flexible objects allows us to define the objective. We use a simplified objective that counts only the number of flexible objects and neglects the number of pins needed for separating the subproblems.

$$c(v) = \mid F(v) \mid + max\{c(w) \mid w \in D(v)\} \tag{26}$$

The CSP for the key configuration decomposition problem (KDP-CSP) is a CSP that consists of the variables(6), the constraints (7 - 17) and (20 - 26), and the objective of minimizing $c(r)$. Each solution of this CSP corresponds to a subproblem hierarchy for our key configuration problem.

7 Algorithm

We briefly describe a non-deterministic algorithm for finding the solutions of the KDP-CSP. It is sufficient to consider the decision variables $X(v)$ for all objects v. All other sets are uniquely determined by a value assignment to the $X(v)$s according to the constraints (7), (8), (14), (16), and (10).

A trivial solution of the KDP-CSP consists in setting all the $req(X(v))$s to the empty set. In this case, none of the objects exclude each other and there is a single subproblem that contains all objects. This solution has the highest number of flexible keys and locks. In order to reduce the number of flexible objects, we try to separate as many objects as possible by maximizing the sets $X(v)$. Our algorithm consists of two loops. In the outer loop, the algorithm chooses a non-instantiated $X(v)$. It instantiates it $X(v)$ by considering all possible elements w that are not required. A non-deterministic choice is made: Either w is added to the required set of $X(v)$ (the preferred choice) or removed from the possible set of $X(v)$. The algorithm finds a solution iff all variables $X(v)$s can be instantiated with success:

1. **while** there are non-instantiated variables $X(v)$ **do**
2. select a $v \in \mathcal{V}$ s.t. $req(X(v)) \neq pos(X(v))$.
3. **while** $req(X(v)) \neq pos(X(v))$ **do**
4. select a $w \in pos(X(v)) - req(X(v))$.
5. **choose:** add w to $req(X(v))$ or remove w from $req(X(v))$.
6. apply filtering algorithm to update current domain assignment.
7. **if** this domain assignment is inconsistent **then** return with failure.
8. return with success.

Such a non-deterministic algorithm is easy to implement by the search programming facilities of tools such as ILOG SOLVER.

A big concern, however, is the efficiency of this approach. If there are n objects in $\mathcal{V}$ then maximal n^2 decisions are taken by one non-deterministic execution of the algorithm. For each of these decisions, two alternatives are considered. This means that we can obtain maximal 2^{n^2} different executions. Despite these worst-case considerations, the CSP has several good properties that reduce effort:

1. **Unary constraints:** The constraints 21, 23 involve a single variable and allow reducing the domain of this variable initially (i.e. before any non-deterministic choice has been made).
2. **Variable ordering:** In order to find larger subproblems first, we select a v with largest $req(R(v))$ (i.e. smallest $pos(X(v))$) first (in line 2).
3. **Value ordering:** The same principle can be applied when selecting a value w. Thus, we determine relations between larger subproblems first.
4. **Separation of subproblems:** Once $X(v)$ is instantiated, the set of ancestors of v is determined as well. There remain two subproblems, which are independent and can be solved separately: First, determine the relations among the objects in $S(v)$ and second, the relations among the objects in $X(v) \cup A(v)$.

The first three principles have been used in an industrial prototype for key configuration and helped to find good solutions quickly. More work is needed to explore the last principle. This could allow treating examples of large size efficiently, supposing that these examples have a nearly hierarchical structure.

Ex.	#initial objects	#groups	#flexible objects	height	#leaves	# choice points	#fails	CPU time
1	51	15	2	4	6	105	176	4sec.
2	46	33	4	6	12	803	1828	33sec.
3	1672	318	4	7	92	262	563	2222sec.
4	4444	252	36	12	94	3706	8158	837sec.

Fig. 4. Results of Industrial Prototype

8 Preliminary Experimental Results

In this section, we report preliminary experimental results that were obtained by an industrial prototype, which was developed for a manufacturer of locking systems. The need for problem decomposition methods was discovered quite early in the development phase. Even for smaller examples, initial experiments

	1	3	4	5	6	8	9	10	14	15	17	23	26	28	29	30	31	33	34
350	X	X	X	X	X	X	X	X	X	X	X	X	X	X	X	X	X	X	X
501	X	.	X	.	.	.	.	.	X	.	.	.	.	.	.	.	.	.	.
502	.	.	.	.	.	.	.	.	X	.	X	.	X	.	.	.	.	.	.
503	.	.	.	.	.	X	.	.	.	.	.	X	.	.	.	.	.	.	.
504	.	.	.	.	.	X	.	.	.	.	.	.	.	X	.	.	.	X	.
505	.	.	.	.	.	.	.	.	X	X	.	.	.	.	.	.	.	.	.
506	X	.	.	X	.	.	X	.	X	.	.	.	X	.	.	.	.	.	.
507	.	.	.	.	.	X	X	.	.	.	.	.	.	.	.	.	.	.	.
508	.	.	.	.	X	.	.	.	.	.	.	.	.	X	X	X	X	X	.
509	.	.	.	.	.	.	.	.	.	.	.	.	.	X	X	.	.	.	.
510	.	.	.	.	.	.	.	.	.	.	.	.	.	X	.	X	.	.	.
511	.	.	.	.	.	.	.	.	.	.	.	.	.	X	.	.	.	X	.
512	.	.	.	.	.	.	.	.	.	.	.	.	.	.	.	.	.	.	X
513	.	.	.	.	X	.	.	X	.	.	.	.	.	.	.	.	.	.	.

Fig. 5. Locking matrix for example 2.

showed that the assignment of pins to keys and locks should be guided by hierarchical relations between these objects. First attempts were made to find subsumption relations between keys/locks in a procedural way and to directly build a tree. This approach lacked flexibility (e.g. no backtracking possible) and a clear mathematical specification and worked only for smaller examples. Based on this experience, we developed a first CSP for finding a subproblem hierarchy.

Compared to the CSP presented in this paper, the prototype has some drawbacks. First, equivalence classes $E(v)$ and some of the constraints were missing. As a consequence, inner nodes could have a single son, which led to weird trees. Second, the objective was to minimize the total number of flexible keys/locks, which was simpler to express and which is an upper bound of the objective $c(r)$. Third, keys to doors of offices were not allowed to be flexible due to manufacturer-specific conventions.

In order to find good solutions quickly, search occurs in two phases. In a first phase, the search tree is artificially cut. Heuristics are used to estimate whether only one of the alternatives is promising or whether all have to be considered. In the second, all alternatives are considered, but the best solution of the first phase puts an upper bound on the objective.

Figure 4 shows the results for some selected examples. In order to treat larger examples efficiently, keys/locks of offices that belong to the same floor are grouped together. The second columns contains the number of objects before preprocessing and the third column contains the number after this operation. We discuss two of the examples briefly. The second example is small, but lacks a clear hierarchical structure. Figure 5 shows the locking matrix of this example, whereas figure 6 gives the resulting tree[2]. Example 3 is large, but has a clear hierarchical structure and thus a small number of flexible keys/locks.

[2] The equivalence relation is depicted by horizontal links.

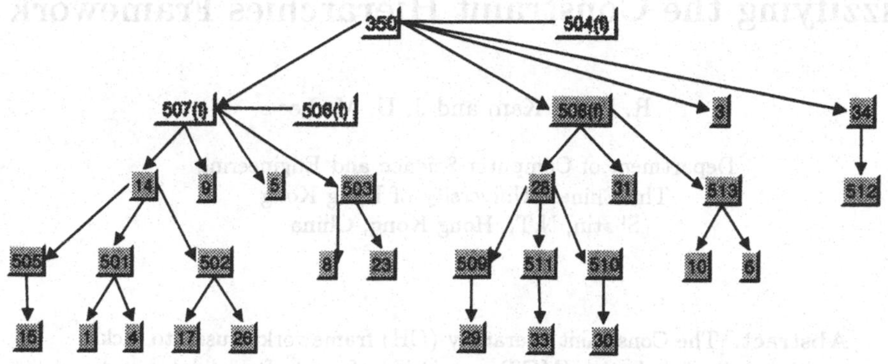

Fig. 6. Subproblem hierarchy for example 2.

9 Conclusion

We presented a novel approach to problem decomposition for key configuration problems. An initially large problem is recursively divided into subproblems and a common problem such that the subproblems can be treated independently after the common problem has been solved. Most key configuration problems in practice have this hierarchical structure and can thus be treated efficiently.

The novelty of our approach is the use of constraint satisfaction techniques for finding a subproblem hierarchy. This CSP-approach has several advantages over a procedural or purely heuristic decomposition method. Mathematical properties of the subproblem hierarchy can be stated clearly and added easily. Search algorithms allow exploring several solutions and finding a good or a best subproblem hierarchy. The CSP makes a sophisticated usage of constrained set variables (cf. [7, 3]) and clearly shows the usefulness of constraints such as set-of, inverse, max-over-set, and union-of-sets-over-set [6].

References

1. E. Andersson, E. Housos, N. Kohl, and D. Wedelin. Crew pairing optimization. In Gang Yu, editor, *OR in Airline Industry*, Kluwer Academic Publishers, Boston/London/Dordrecht, 1998.
2. B.Y. Choueiry, B. Faltings, and R. Weigel. Abstraction by interchangeability in resource allocation. In *Proc. IJCAI'95*, Montréal, 1995.
3. C. Gervet. Interval propagation to reason about sets: Definition and implementation of a practical language. *Constraints. An International Journal*, 1, 1997.
4. P. van Hentenryck, Y. Deville, and C.-M. Teng. A generic arc-consistency algorithm and its specializations. *Artificial Intelligence*, 57, 1992.
5. ILOG. Ilog Solver. V4.0. Reference manual and user manual, ILOG, 1997.
6. D. Mailharo. A classification and constraint based framework for configuration. *AI-EDAM: Special Issue on Configuration*, 12(4), 1998.
7. J.F. Puget. Programmation par contraintes orientée objet. In *Intl. Conference on Expert Systems*, Avignon, 1992.

Fuzzifying the Constraint Hierarchies Framework

R. W. L. Kam and J. H. M. Lee

Department of Computer Science and Engineering
The Chinese University of Hong Kong
Shatin, N.T., Hong Kong, China

Abstract. The Constraint Hierarchy (CH) framework is used to tackle *multiple criteria selection* (MCS), consisting of a set of candidates and a set of, possibly competing, criteria for selecting the "best" candidate(s). In this paper, we identify aspects of the CH framework for further enhancement so as to model and solve MCS problems more accurately. We propose the Fuzzy Constraint Hierarchies framework, which allows constraints to belong to, possibly, more than one level in a constraint hierarchy to a varying degree. We also propose to replace the standard equality relation = used in valuation comparators of the CH framework by the α-approximate equality relation $=_{a(\alpha)}$ for providing more flexible control over the handling of valuations with close error values. These proposals result in three new classes of valuation comparators. Formal properties of the new comparators are given, wherever possible.

1 Introduction

An *over-constrained system* [3] is a set of constraints with no solution, caused by some of the constraints contradicting others. From the users' point of view, no-solution is hardly a satisfactory answer. Users normally want solutions of some sort, even if they are *partial* in the sense that the solutions can cause some constraints to be violated. The task becomes how to relax or weaken some of the constraints in an over-constrained system so as to obtain useful partial solution.

New solution techniques, well summarized in [3], are developed to model and tackle over-constrained systems. In particular, the *Constraint Hierarchies* (CH) framework by Borning *et al.* [2] allows constraints to be *required* and *preferential*. While the required constraints must be satisfied, satisfaction of preferential constraints are not mandatory but they should be satisfied as much as possible. Each preferential constraint has a strength and, together with the required constraints, they form a *constraint hierarchy*. A *better* comparator is used to rank and select among competing possible solutions.

The problem at hand is that of *multiple criteria selection* (MCS), which consists of a set of candidates and a set of, possibly competing, criteria for selecting the "best" candidate(s). MCS is a common decision process in answering such questions as which presidency candidate to vote for, which applicants to admit to the graduate programme, and so on. The CH framework is chosen to model and solve MCS problems since selection criteria are like preferential constraints:

(1) criteria have relative priorities and (2) candidates are most likely not able to satisfy all criteria anyway and we would like to select the candidate that satisfy the most constraints in some sense. There are two issues in tackling MCS problems by the CH framework. First, it is sometimes difficult to determine the relative strength of some criteria with absolute certainty. Second, the standard equality relation used in *better* comparators is sometimes too rigid and presents problems in handling competing solutions with very close error values.

In this paper, we show how simple application of fuzzy techniques can resolve the issues. To help better model MCS problems, we propose to fuzzify the levels of constraint hierarchies, allowing constraints to belong to a level with a certain degree of membership. To deal with valuations with close error values, we propose to use the α-approximate equality relation $=_{a(\alpha)}$, a relaxed form of equality, in the comparators, obtained by fuzzifying and de-fuzzifying the standard equality relation $=$. The result is the *Fuzzy Constraint Hierarchy* framework plus three new classes of valuation comparators, each of which improves upon their counterparts in the CH framework.

The paper is organized as follows. We first give a brief overview of the CH framework and two motivating scenarios for our work, followed by an exposition of the Fuzzy Constraint Hierarchies framework, its related class of comparators, and formal properties of these comparators. We also show how another class of comparators is defined using the α-approximate equality relation. A seamless integration of the two new classes of comparators gives the best of both worlds. Last but not least, we conclude the paper by listing our contributions and discussing future work and implementation issues.

2 The Constraint Hierarchies Framework

In this section, we give a brief introduction to the CH framework. Interested readers are referred to [2] for full details. Two example scenarios are used to illustrate aspects of the framework opted for further enhancement.

2.1 Constraint Hierarchies

Let $\mathcal{D}$ be the domain. An *n-ary constraint* c is a relation over $\mathcal{D}^n$. A *labeled constraint* is a pair (c, k), where c is a constraint and k is a label stating the *strength* of c. The strength labels are totally ordered. Without loss of generality, we map the strengths to non-negative integers. A *constraint hierarchy* H is a multiset of labeled constraints with a finite number of labels. According to the associated labels, constraints are classified into different disjoint multisets H_k, called *levels*, for each label k: level H_k contains the set of labeled constraints with label k. Given a constraint hierarchy, we use H_0 to denote the set of *required* (or *hard*) constraints. The levels $H_1, H_2, \ldots, H_n$ denote different sets of *preferential* (or *soft*) constraints, ranging from the strongest strength to the weakest.

A *valuation* for a set of constraints is a function that maps the free variables in the constraints to elements in the domain over which the constraints are defined.

Let c be a constraint and θ a valuation. The expression $c\theta$ is the boolean result of applying θ to c. We say that $c\theta$ *holds* if the value of $c\theta$ is **true**.

We define $S_0 = \{\theta \mid \forall c \in H_0 \text{ s.t. } c\theta \text{ holds}\}$ to be the set of valuations that satisfy the required constraints. The solution set to a constraint hierarchy H depends on the definition of a valuation comparator $better(\theta, \sigma, H)$ that compares two valuations θ and σ for the constraints in H. Many definitions of *better* are possible as long as the comparator is irreflexive, transitive, and respect the hierarchy [2] in the loose sense that a "better" valuation must indeed satisfy "more" constraints in H. Note that *better* does not define a total order since some valuations can be *incomparable* according to this definition. In other words, it is possible that a valuation θ is *not better* than valuation σ and vice versa. The *solution set* of a constraint hierarchy H is obtained by eliminating all potential valuations that are worse than some other potential valuations: $S = \{\theta \mid \theta \in S_0 \wedge \forall \sigma \in S_0 \text{ s.t. } \neg better(\sigma, \theta, H)\}$.

In the following, we give several definitions of *better*, which require an *error function* $e(c\theta)$ to measure how well a constraint c is satisfied by valuation θ. The error function returns non-negative real numbers and must satisfy the property: $e(c\theta) = 0 \Leftrightarrow c\theta$ holds. Given a constraint Hierarchy H and two valuations θ and σ, the comparator *locally-better* *l-b* is defined as follows:

$$\begin{aligned} l\text{-}b(\theta, \sigma, H) \equiv\ & \exists k > 0 \text{ such that} \\ & \forall i \in \{1, \ldots, k-1\} \forall p \in H_i\ e(p\theta) = e(p\sigma) \\ & \wedge \exists q \in H_k\ e(q\theta) < e(q\sigma) \\ & \wedge \forall r \in H_k\ e(r\theta) \leq e(r\sigma) \end{aligned}$$

The *globally-better* schema *g-b* defines a class of global comparators, parametrized by a function g that combines the errors of all constraints in a level H_i.

$$\begin{aligned} g\text{-}b(\theta, \sigma, H, g) \equiv\ & \exists k > 0 \text{ such that} \\ & \forall i \in \{1, \ldots, k-1\}\ g(\theta, H_i) = g(\sigma, H_i) \\ & \wedge g(\theta, H_k) < g(\sigma, H_k) \end{aligned}$$

Suppose we assign also a positive real number w_p to each constraint p to denote the *weight* of p. Three global comparators, namely *weighted-sum-better* *w-s-b*, *worst-case-better* *w-c-b*, and *least-square-better* *l-s-b* can be defined using different combining functions g.

$$\begin{aligned} & w\text{-}s\text{-}b(\theta, \sigma, H) \equiv g\text{-}b(\theta, \sigma, H, g) \\ & \text{where } g(\tau, H_i) \equiv \sum_{p \in H_i} w_p e(p\tau) \end{aligned} \qquad \begin{aligned} & l\text{-}s\text{-}b(\theta, \sigma, H) \equiv g\text{-}b(\theta, \sigma, H, g) \\ & \text{where } g(\tau, H_i) \equiv \sum_{p \in H_i} w_p e(p\tau)^2 \end{aligned}$$

$$\begin{aligned} & w\text{-}c\text{-}b(\theta, \sigma, H) \equiv g\text{-}b(\theta, \sigma, H, g) \\ & \text{where } g(\tau, H_i) \equiv \max\{w_p e(p\tau) \mid p \in H_i\} \end{aligned}$$

Different specific comparators can be defined by choosing the appropriate error function e. We call this class of comparators *classical comparators* to differentiate them from the ones introduced later in this paper,

2.2 Dominance of Strong Constraints

What millions died—that Caesar might be great!
Thomas Campbell (1777–1844)

In the CH framework, two valuations are compared level by level, starting from the strongest level. If two valuations are equivalent in one level, then comparison proceeds to the next level. The comparison process stops once a valuation is found to be better than the other at a certain level, or when none of the two valuations are better than the other. Constraints in weaker levels are completely ignored. There are two problems. First, it is sometimes difficult to determine the relative strengths among constraints with absolute certainty in practice. Second, a constraint c_1 being more important than another constraint c_2 may not imply that the satisfaction of c_1 should take *strict* precedence over that of c_2. Failure to cope with these phenomena may result in counter-intuitive solutions.

Example 1 Suppose a company wants to promote a sales representative to become the general sales manager from a pool of candidates. The ideal candidate must be a degree holder. (S)he should have at least 5 years of working experience and be able to meet a sales quota of 1 million per annum. Being in a supervisory role, the potential manager should also be familiar with and be able to sell at least 20 products of the company. While the education background is a firm requirement, working experience and sales performance are, in general, considered to be more important than versatility in product range. In considering candidates with similar working experience and sales performance, the last criterion should also be taken into account, although to a lesser degree, to differentiate the best candidate from the rest.

The last criterion is common sense but is difficult to model in the CH framework. We model the problem to its nearest approximation as follows. There are four variables: D to denote if the candidate is a degree holder, Y to denote the candidate's working experience in number of years, Q to denote the candidate's sales figure in thousands of dollars, and P to denote the number of products that the candidate can sell. We get the following constraint hierarchy H.

Level	Constraints
H_0	$(c_1)\ D = \textbf{degree}$
H_1	$(c_2)\ Y \geq 5$, $(c_3)\ Q \geq 1000$
H_2	$(c_4)\ P \geq 20$

The following error function e measures how well the constraints are satisfied:

$$e(c_1\theta) = \begin{cases} 1 \text{ if } D\theta = \textbf{degree} \\ 0 \text{ Otherwise} \end{cases} \qquad e(c_2\theta) = \begin{cases} \dfrac{5 - Y\theta}{5} & \text{if } Y\theta < 5 \\ 0 & \text{if } Y\theta \geq 5 \end{cases}$$

$$e(c_3\theta) = \begin{cases} \dfrac{1000 - Q\theta}{1000} & \text{if } Q\theta < 1000 \\ 0 & \text{if } Q\theta \geq 1000 \end{cases} \quad e(c_4\theta) = \begin{cases} \dfrac{20 - P\theta}{20} & \text{if } P\theta < 20 \\ 0 & \text{if } P\theta \geq 20 \end{cases}$$

Consider two competing candidates A and B with their corresponding qualifications encoded in the valuations θ_A and θ_B respectively:

$$\theta_A = \{D \mapsto \textbf{degree}, Y \mapsto 5, Q \mapsto 1000, P \mapsto 2\}$$
$$\theta_B = \{D \mapsto \textbf{degree}, Y \mapsto 5, Q \mapsto 990, P \mapsto 30\}$$

Applying the valuations to the constraints in H and using the error function e just defined, we obtain the error sequences of the two candidates.

θ	$e(c_1\theta)$	$e(c_2\theta)$	$e(c_3\theta)$	$e(c_4\theta)$
θ_A	0	0	0	0.9
θ_B	0	0	0.01	0

Assuming the weight of all constraints to be 1.0, we can easily check that any classical comparators would conclude A to be the better candidate. According to the requirement of the selection criteria and common sense, however, candidate B should be selected since B can sell many more products than A while A's edge over B in sales performance is only marginal (ten thousand in one million is negligible in a big corporation!). We call this the *dominance* problem. In this example, the slight minimization of the error of one stronger constraint precedes the consideration of weaker constraints even if the resulting valuation will cause very large error in the weaker constraint.

The dominance problem cannot be solved by simply adjusting the weight since the error of c_2 is 0 in both cases. One might argue changing the error function to

$$e(c_3\theta) = \begin{cases} \frac{1000 - Q\theta}{1000} & \text{if } Q\theta < 1000 - 100 \\ 0 & \text{if } Q\theta \geq 1000 - 100 \end{cases}$$

or some similar function to increase the "tolerance" of the constraint c_3. Candidates A and B are now equal up to level 1 and their comparison has to be resolved using c_4 in level 2. This seems to solve the dominance problem for the current scenario.

Example 2 What if candidate B can sell only 3 products instead?

$$\theta_A = \{D \mapsto \textbf{degree}, Y \mapsto 5, Q \mapsto 1000, P \mapsto 2\}$$
$$\theta_B = \{D \mapsto \textbf{degree}, Y \mapsto 5, Q \mapsto 990, P \mapsto 3\}$$

With the new error function, candidate B will always be selected using *all* comparators defined. Depending on how errors are compared, however, candidate A, who is slightly better in sales performance and slightly worse in the number of products, should be as competitive as, if not better than, candidate B. The new error function blindly concludes that the error of a valuation for c_3 is 0 if the error is less a certain value. There are two problems. First, this method fails if both candidates have sizable but close error values. Second, the errors of c_4 for the valuations are not taken into account. This violates the last requirement of the promotion criteria.

We cannot massage the relative strengths of the constraints either since sales performance is in general more important than number of products as stated in the requirement. We propose to solve the dominance problem by allowing constraints to belong to different levels with varying membership grade so that weak constraints can have influence in stronger levels.

2.3 Stiff Equality in Better Comparators

Equality is in the eyes of the beholder.

In comparing valuations in the CH framework, comparison proceeds from one level to the other in the hierarchy only when the valuations are concluded to be equivalent in the current level. In a local comparator, two valuations are *equivalent* in a level if the errors computed from the two valuations for every constraint in the level are equal. In a global comparator, two valuations are *equivalent* in a level if the errors computed from the two valuations for all constraints in the level using the combining function g are equal. Both notions of equivalence use the standard equality relation $=$, which governs that any individual x can only be equal to itself and nothing else. In daily experience, however, we are sometimes satisfied with things that are "approximately equal to" each other. In many real-life situations, we cannot afford to be too rigid since physical data always contain errors so that absolute equality can never be attained.

Given two valuations. There could be cases in which the errors of two valuations for a level are very close to each other and yet one valuation is concluded to be better than the other or incomparable to the other. The errors are, however, so close that the conclusion is drawn only in the numerical, but not common, sense. There could well be more useful information in the next level to help make a better decision. We call this the *stiff equality problem*.

Example 3 Let us use the sales representative promotion problem for illustration again. We assume the same modeling of the problem as in examples 1 and 2. In our first scenario, the competing candidates have the following valuations:

$$\theta_A = \{D \mapsto \texttt{degree}, Y \mapsto 2.9, Q \mapsto 700, P \mapsto 30\}$$
$$\theta_B = \{D \mapsto \texttt{degree}, Y \mapsto 3, Q \mapsto 690, P \mapsto 2\}$$

Applying the valuations to the constraints in H gives the following error sequences.

θ	$e(c_1\theta)$	$e(c_2\theta)$	$e(c_3\theta)$	$e(c_4\theta)$
θ_A	0	0.42	0.3	0
θ_B	0	0.4	0.31	0.9

The *l-b* comparator would find the candidates to be incomparable. Assuming all constraint weights to be 1.0, the global comparators would conclude B to be the better candidate.

Example 4 Worst yet, in our second scenario, the candidates' profiles become:

$$\theta_A = \{D \mapsto \texttt{degree}, Y \mapsto 2.9, Q \mapsto 690, P \mapsto 30\}$$
$$\theta_B = \{D \mapsto \texttt{degree}, Y \mapsto 3, Q \mapsto 700, P \mapsto 2\}$$

θ	$e(c_1\theta)$	$e(c_2\theta)$	$e(c_3\theta)$	$e(c_4\theta)$
θ_A	0	0.42	0.31	0
θ_B	0	0.4	0.3	0.9

All comparators will conclude B to be the better candidate.

Common sense would suggest the contrary for both examples since the two candidates are close to indistinguishable in level H_1. The abysmal differences in the error values are inconclusive. The candidates should better be differentiated using information in level H_2. An approach to solve the stiff equality problem is to relax the equality relationship in the comparators so that two error values of similar magnitude are considered equal.

3 Fuzzifying Hierarchy Levels

The closer one looks, the fuzzier things are.

Our first extension aims to solve the dominance problem. We propose to generalize the CH framework by allowing a constraint to belong to possibly more than one level in the hierarchy to a varying degree. In the following, we briefly introduce some basic machineries of the fuzzy set theory [4], followed by the definition of the *Fuzzy Constraint Hierarchies* (FCH) framework and its formal properties.

3.1 Basic Fuzzy Set Theory

Every *crisp set* A is associated with a *characteristic function* $\mu_A : \mathcal{U} \rightarrow \{0,1\}$, which determines whether an individual from the universal set $\mathcal{U}$ is a member or non-member of A:

$$\mu_A(x) = \begin{cases} 1 \text{ if and only if } x \in A \\ 0 \text{ if and only if } x \notin A \end{cases}$$

Fuzzy sets are usually obtained by generalizing the characteristic function so that $\mu_A : \mathcal{U} \rightarrow [0,1]$. Given an element $x \in \mathcal{U}$, $\mu_A(x)$ denotes the degree of membership of x in the fuzzy set A. A larger value indicates a higher degree of membership. The generalized μ_A is called a *membership function*. Thus, each element of a fuzzy set A is a pair $(x, \mu_A(x))$. We write $(x, \mu_A(x)) \in A$ to mean that x belongs to A with *membership grade* $\mu_A(x)$. In practice, the membership function μ_A of a fuzzy set has to be estimated from partial information sampled from, possibly, incomplete data.

3.2 Fuzzy-Labeled Constraints

The FCH framework inherits most of the structure of the CH framework. The domain $\mathcal{D}$ and the notions of constraints c and strengths k remain unchanged. The strengths are totally ordered and we use non-negative integers as strengths. In the FCH framework, we generalize the *level* H_k of each strength k from a crisp set to a fuzzy set for $k \geq 1$. The required level remains a crisp set. A *fuzzy-labeled constraint* is a tuple $(c, k, \mu_k(c))$, where c is a constraint, $k \geq 1$ is the strength of c, and $\mu_k(c)$ is a real number in $[0,1]$ indicating the membership grade of c

in H_k. The function μ_k is the membership function associated with the fuzzy set H_k. A *fuzzy constraint hierarchy* H consists of a multiset H_0 of required constraints and a multiset of fuzzy-labeled constraints with a finite number of labels. It is important to note that a constraint c can belong to more than one level with varying degree of membership.

The solution set S of a fuzzy constraint hierarchy is defined similarly: $S_0 = \{\theta \mid \forall c \in H_0 \text{ s.t. } c\theta \text{ holds}\}$ and $S = \{\theta \mid \theta \in S_0 \wedge \forall \sigma \in S_0 \text{ s.t. } \neg \mathit{better}(\sigma, \theta, H)\}$, except that the valuation comparator *better* must now take the membership grade of constraints into account. Assuming the same notion of error function $e(c\theta)$, we present the *fuzzy-locally-better* comparator *f-l-b* as follows:

$$
\begin{aligned}
&\textit{f-l-b}(\theta, \sigma, H) \equiv \exists k > 0 \text{ such that} \\
&\quad \forall i \in \{1, \ldots, k-1\} \forall (p, \mu_i(p)) \in H_i \; e(p\theta)\mu_i(p) = e(p\sigma)\mu_i(p) \\
&\wedge \exists (q, \mu_k(q)) \in H_k \; e(q\theta)\mu_k(q) < e(q\sigma)\mu_k(q) \\
&\wedge \forall (r, \mu_k(r)) \in H_k \; e(r\theta)\mu_k(r) \leq e(r\sigma)\mu_k(r)
\end{aligned}
$$

The terms $\mu_i(p)$, $\mu_k(q)$, and $\mu_k(r)$ can be canceled out on both sides of the equality and inequalities. We leave the terms in the definition since they are essential for a further generalization of the comparator. Disregarding the terms for the moment, this definition is almost identical to that of the *l-b* comparator in the CH framework. There is a subtle difference between the two comparators: a constraint can appear in possibly more than one level in the hierarchy.

The *fuzzy-globally-better* schema *f-l-g-b* is similar to the classical version except that the combining function g must now incorporate the membership of the constraints in each level:

$$
\begin{aligned}
&\textit{f-g-b}(\theta, \sigma, H, g) \equiv \exists k > 0 \text{ such that} \\
&\quad \forall i \in \{1, \ldots, k-1\} \; g(\theta, H_i, \mu_i) = g(\sigma, H_i, \mu_i) \\
&\wedge g(\theta, H_k, \mu_k) < g(\sigma, H_k, \mu_k)
\end{aligned}
$$

The three classical global comparators can be fuzzified as follows:

$$
\begin{aligned}
&\textit{f-w-s-b}(\theta, \sigma, H) \equiv \textit{f-g-b}(\theta, \sigma, H, g) \\
&\text{where } g(\tau, H_i, \mu_i) \equiv \sum_{(p, \mu_i(p)) \in H_i} w_p e(p\tau)\mu_i(p)
\end{aligned}
$$

$$
\begin{aligned}
&\textit{f-w-c-b}(\theta, \sigma, H) \equiv \textit{f-g-b}(\theta, \sigma, H, g) \\
&\text{where } g(\tau, H_i, \mu_i) \equiv \max\{w_p e(p\tau)\mu_i(p) \mid (p, \mu_i(p)) \in H_i\}
\end{aligned}
$$

$$
\begin{aligned}
&\textit{f-l-s-b}(\theta, \sigma, H) \equiv \textit{f-g-b}(\theta, \sigma, H, g) \\
&\text{where } g(\tau, H_i, \mu_i) \equiv \sum_{(p, \mu_i(p)) \in H_i} w_p e(p\tau)^2 \mu_i(p)
\end{aligned}
$$

We call the newly defined comparators *fuzzy comparators*.

3.3 Illustrative Examples

The sales representative promotion problem can be more accurately formulated in the FCH framework as follows:

Level	Constraints
H_0	$(c_1, 1.0)$
H_1	$(c_2, 1.0)$, $(c_3, 1.0)$, $(c_4, 0.02)$
H_2	$(c_4, 1.0)$

Using the same error functions and weight 1.0 for all constraints, we yield the following table of results for the two candidate valuations in example 1.

	$\theta = \theta_A$ $i = 1$	$\theta = \theta_B$ $i = 1$	$\theta = \theta_A$ $i = 2$	$\theta = \theta_B$ $i = 2$
$e(c_2\theta)\mu_i(c_2)$	0	0	0	0
$e(c_3\theta)\mu_i(c_3)$	0	0.01	0	0
$e(c_4\theta)\mu_i(c_4)$	0.018	0	0.9	0
$e(c_2\theta)^2\mu_i(c_2)$	0	0	0	0
$e(c_3\theta)^2\mu_i(c_3)$	0	0.0001	0	0
$e(c_4\theta)^2\mu_i(c_4)$	0.0162	0	0.81	0

If the *f-l-b* local comparator is used, we find that the two valuations are incomparable. Assuming a weight of 1.0 for all constraints in each level, the global comparators *f-w-s-b*, *f-w-c-b*, and *f-l-s-b* all conclude sales representative B to be the more desirable candidate for promotion.

In the new hierarchy, the constraint c_4 appears, besides in H_2, in H_1 with a membership of 0.02. In general, errors of c_2 and c_3 take precedence in the decision-making process since they both have a membership of 1.0. The influence of c_4 becomes effective only when the errors in c_4 for the candidate valuations are significant enough to overcome the suppression by the 0.02 membership factor. We use the same hierarchy to compare the valuations in example 2. The error of each constraint for each valuation and its product with the corresponding membership grades are summarized in the following tables:

	$\theta = \theta_A$	$\theta = \theta_B$
$e(c_1\theta)$	0	0
$e(c_2\theta)$	0	0
$e(c_3\theta)$	0	0.01
$e(c_4\theta)$	0.9	0.85

	$\theta = \theta_A$ $i = 1$	$\theta = \theta_B$ $i = 1$	$\theta = \theta_A$ $i = 2$	$\theta = \theta_B$ $i = 2$
$e(c_2\theta)\mu_i(c_2)$	0	0	0	0
$e(c_3\theta)\mu_i(c_3)$	0	0.01	0	0
$e(c_4\theta)\mu_i(c_4)$	0.018	0.017	0.9	0.85
$e(c_2\theta)^2\mu_i(c_2)$	0	0	0	0
$e(c_3\theta)^2\mu_i(c_3)$	0	0.0001	0	0
$e(c_4\theta)^2\mu_i(c_4)$	0.0162	0.01445	0.81	0.7225

Again, the local comparator finds the two valuations incomparable. The global comparator *f-w-s-b* recommends candidate A for promotion. The *f-w-c-b* comparator presents a biased view by looking at only the extreme case of a level. The *f-l-s-b* comparator amplifies error differences by comparing the square of the errors. In both cases, the errors of c_4 become more prominent in level H_1 and candidate B is recommended.

3.4 Remarks

Weight and membership grade of a constraint seem to be similar concepts and might be combined in the definition of the example global comparators. They are different for two reasons, one conceptual and one pragmatic. First, the weight of a constraint is a measure of the relative importance of the constraint as compared to other constraints within a level, whereas the membership grade of a constraint denotes the degree that the constraint belong to a level. Second, as can be seen from examples 1 and 2, the dominance problem persists no matter how we adjust the weights of constraints in the original constraint hierarchy: strong constraints still dominate over the weaker ones. On the other hand, membership grade allows a generally weak constraint to exercise its influence in stronger levels. Since the two concepts describe two different properties of a constraint with respect to a level, we suggest to keep them as two separate values instead of combining them into a single constant.

The relationship between local and global comparators in the CH framework carries forward to their fuzzy counterparts in the FCH framework. In other words, the solution set found using the fuzzy-locally-better comparator contains both of those found using the fuzzy-weighted-sum-better and the fuzzy-least-square-better comparators.

Proposition 1. *For a given error function e,*

$$\forall\theta\forall\sigma\forall H\ \ f\text{-}l\text{-}b(\theta,\sigma,H)\rightarrow f\text{-}w\text{-}s\text{-}b(\theta,\sigma,H)$$
$$\forall\theta\forall\sigma\forall H\ \ f\text{-}l\text{-}b(\theta,\sigma,H)\rightarrow f\text{-}l\text{-}s\text{-}b(\theta,\sigma,H).$$

Corollary 1. *For a given fuzzy constraint hierarchy, let S_{FLB} denote the set of solutions found using the f-l-b comparator, and S_{FWSB} and S_{FLSB} those found using the f-w-s-b and f-l-s-b comparators respectively. We have $S_{FWSB}\subseteq S_{FLB}$ and $S_{FLSB}\subseteq S_{FLB}$.*

We skip the proofs of the results since they are similar to those of the corresponding results for the CH framework found in [2]. As expected, the *f-l-b* comparator does not imply the *f-g-b* schema instantiated with an arbitrary combining function *g*. For example, the *f-l-b* comparator does not imply the *f-w-c-b* comparator.

4 Fuzzifying the Equality Relation

To equal or not to equal, that is the question.

Our second extension aims to solve the stiff equality problem. We formalize the notion of *approximately-equal-to* and define new valuation comparators using the modified equality relation. The α-approximate-equality relation $=_{a(\alpha)}$ is obtained by computing the α-cut [4] of the fuzzified equality relation, where α is a user-defined constant that controls the degree of approximation or tolerance.

A relation is a set of tuples. To fuzzify a crisp relation R, we need to devise a meaningful membership function that conforms to the intended interpretation of the relation. The membership function for the fuzzified relation, say R^f, should also provide a metric to measure how "well" an element tuple belongs to R^f. Thus the function must assign a membership of 1.0 to elements of R and the membership grade assigned to a non-member x of R should reflect the degree of x satisfying the property described by the intended interpretation of R. We are interested in only a subset of the standard equality relation $=$ since we only test the equality of non-negative real numbers. While many membership functions are possible, we propose to use the following membership function for the fuzzy relation $=^f(x, y)$:

$$\mu_{=^f}((x,y)) = \begin{cases} 1 & \text{if } x = y = 0 \\ 1 - \left|\frac{x-y}{x+y}\right| & \text{Otherwise} \end{cases}$$

for any non-negative real numbers x and y.

The function $\mu_{=^f}$ provides a measure on how close two real numbers are. The fuzzy relation $=^f$, however, cannot be used directly in decision-making. We need to extract the set of elements of $=^f$, the membership of which exceeds a certain user supplied *approximation threshold* $\alpha \in [0, 1]$, by computing the α-cut of $=^f$. An *α-cut* of a fuzzy set A is a crisp set A_α that contains all the elements of the universal set $\mathcal{D}$ that have a membership grade in A greater than or equal to the specified value of α, written as:

$$A_\alpha = \{x \in \mathcal{D} \mid \mu_A(x) \geq \alpha\}.$$

We define the *α-approximate equality relation* $=_{a(\alpha)}$ to be $=^f_\alpha$. We say that x is *α-approximately equal to* y, written $x =_{a(\alpha)} y$ (by abusing notation), if $(x, y) \in =_{a(\alpha)}$.

By replacing $=$ by $=_{a(\alpha)}$ in the definition of the *l-b* comparator and simple mathematics, we yield the *approximate-locally-better* comparator *a-l-b* as follows:

$$\begin{aligned} a\text{-}l\text{-}b(\theta, \sigma, H, \alpha) \equiv \exists k > 0 \text{ such that} \\ \forall i \in \{1, \ldots, k-1\} \forall p \in H_i \; e(p\theta) =_{a(\alpha)} e(p\sigma) \\ \wedge \exists q \in H_k \; (e(q\theta) \neq_{a(\alpha)} e(q\sigma) \wedge e(q\theta) < e(q\sigma)) \\ \wedge \forall r \in H_k \; (e(r\theta) < e(r\sigma) \vee e(r\theta) =_{a(\alpha)} e(r\sigma)) \end{aligned}$$

The *approximate-globally-better* schema *a-g-b* is obtained by modifying the *g-b* schema in a similar fashion.

$$\begin{aligned} a\text{-}g\text{-}b(\theta, \sigma, H, g, \alpha) \equiv \exists k > 0 \text{ such that} \\ \forall i \in \{1, \ldots, k-1\} \; g(\theta, H_i) =_{a(\alpha)} g(\sigma, H_i) \\ \wedge \; (g(\theta, H_k) \neq_{a(\alpha)} g(\sigma, H_k) \wedge g(\theta, H_k) < g(\sigma, H_k)) \end{aligned}$$

We get three global comparators *approximate-weighted-sum-better a-w-s-b*, *approximate-worst-case-better a-w-c-b*, and *approximate-least-square-better a-l-s-b* by instantiating the *a-g-b* schema with the same combining functions g for their classical counterparts. We call this class of comparators *approximate comparators*.

4.1 Illustrative Examples

In the following, we show how the new comparators can be used to solve the stiff equality problem as exemplified in examples 3 and 4. Note that the new comparators have no connection to the FCH framework (yet). In the following, we assume that the sales representative promotion problem is modeled using the CH framework as in example 1. We first give a table containing the membership grade of the number pairs for the fuzzy relation $=^f$ needed for our further discussion.

x	y	$\mu_{=^f}(x,y)$
0.42	0.4	0.976
0.31	0.3	0.984
$0.72\ (= 0.42 + 0.3)$	$0.71\ (= 0.4 + 0.31)$	0.993
$0.73\ (= 0.42 + 0.31)$	$0.7\ (= 0.4 + 0.3)$	0.979
$0.2664\ (= 0.42^2 + 0.3^2)$	$0.2561\ (= 0.4^2 + 0.31^2)$	0.980
$0.2725\ (= 0.42^2 + 0.31^2)$	$0.25\ (= 0.4^2 + 0.3^2)$	0.957

Suppose we set the approximation threshold α to 0.95. All approximate comparators defined are able to conclude that the valuations for both examples are equivalent at level H_1, leaving the decision to level H_2. Therefore, candidate A is recommended.

The threshold α can be adjusted to the user's liking and need. Suppose now that α is 0.98. The following table summarizes the recommendation made by each of the approximate comparators for both scenarios.

Example	*a-l-b*	*a-w-s-b*	*a-w-c-b*	*a-l-s-b*
3	$B\ (H_1)$	$A\ (H_2)$	$B\ (H_1)$	$A\ (H_2)$
4	$B\ (H_1)$	$B\ (H_1)$	$B\ (H_1)$	$B\ (H_1)$

Each row contains the recommendations for each problem scenario; while each column corresponds to recommendations from each approximate comparator. We also record the level at which the decision is made in brackets beside each recommendation. By increasing the threshold, the equality becomes more stiff and more undesirable recommendations are made using information solely in level H_1.

4.2 Remarks

The threshold α offers fine control over the stiffness of the α-approximate equality relation. On one end of the spectrum, when $\alpha = 1$, the α-approximate equality relation is reduced to the standard equality relation. All approximate comparators are also reduced to the original comparators. On the other end of the spectrum, when $\alpha = 0$, any pair of error values are considered to be α-approximately equal to each other. In this case, all valuations are incomparable no matter which comparator is used. The solution set is always S_0, which is the set of solutions for the required constraints. In other words, the soft constraints have no effect in the calculation of the solution set.

As shown in the rework of example 3 with $\alpha = 0.98$, the comparator *a-l-b* implies neither *a-w-s-b* nor *a-l-s-b* in general. Thus, solution sets computed from the new comparators do not inherit the solution set subsumption properties of their classical counterparts.

The proposed membership function $\mu_{=^f}((x,y))$ for the fuzzy relation $=^f$ aims to measure and compare the order of magnitude of the difference between x and y against that of the sum of x and y. While this measure works well in general, it can give results that may be counter-intuitive to some. For example, the function will assign the same membership grade to the pairs $(0.02, 0.03)$, $(2,3)$, and even $(2.0 \times 10^6, 3.0 \times 10^6)$. The phenomenon is due to the fact that the difference between the two numbers in each pair all appears in the same significant digit, in this case the first digit, and the digits differ by the same amount. In addition, the membership grade of $(x, 0)$ is always 0 for all $x > 0$. Thus, even $(1.0 \times 10^{-9}, 0)$ will have a membership grade of 0. This is because the difference between any quantity and void is infinite. From being nothing to something does constitute a quantum jump. If one finds this membership function not suitable, other membership functions, such as,

$$\mu_{=^f}((x,y)) = 1 - \left|\frac{x-y}{x+y+c}\right|, \text{ for some constant } c > 0$$

$$\mu_{=^f}((x,y)) = \begin{cases} |x-y| & \text{if } |x-y| < 1 \\ 1 - \left|\frac{x-y}{x+y}\right| & \text{Otherwise} \end{cases}$$

are possible as long as the function provides a reasonable measure of how similar two nonnegative numbers are.

5 Combining the Frameworks

The FCH framework and the approximate comparators address different aspects of the CH framework. The fuzzy comparators still suffer from the stiff equality problem and the approximate comparators do not solve the dominance problem. Since the two generalizations complement each other, the next natural step is to incorporate the α-approximate equality relation into the fuzzy comparators, yielding a new class of fuzzy comparators. We use the same naming convention for the comparators. Their abbreviated names should be self-explanatory.

The straight-forward generalization of the fuzzy local comparator follows.

$$\begin{aligned} &a\text{-}f\text{-}l\text{-}b(\theta, \sigma, H, \alpha) \equiv \exists k > 0 \text{ such that} \\ &\quad \forall i \in \{1, \ldots, k-1\} \forall (p, \mu_i(p)) \in H_i \ e(p\theta)\mu_i(p) =_{a(\alpha)} e(p\sigma)\mu_i(p) \\ &\wedge \exists (q, \mu_k(q)) \in H_k \ (e(q\theta)\mu_k(q) \neq_{a(\alpha)} e(q\sigma)\mu_k(q) \ \wedge e(q\theta)\mu_k(q) < e(q\sigma)\mu_k(q)) \\ &\wedge \forall (r, \mu_k(r)) \in H_k \ (e(r\theta)\mu_k(r) < e(r\sigma)\mu_k(r) \ \vee e(r\theta)\mu_k(r) =_{a(\alpha)} e(r\sigma)\mu_k(r)) \end{aligned}$$

This definition should explain why the terms $\mu_i(p)$, $\mu_k(q)$, and $\mu_k(r)$ are essential: they do not cancel out under the α-approximate equality relation.

The definitions of the global schema follows.

$$a\text{-}f\text{-}g\text{-}b(\theta, \sigma, H, g, \alpha) \equiv \exists k > 0 \text{ such that}$$
$$\forall i \in \{1, \ldots, k-1\}\ g(\theta, H_i, \mu_i) =_{a(\alpha)} g(\sigma, H_i, \mu_i)$$
$$\wedge\ (g(\theta, H_k, \mu_k) \neq_{a(\alpha)} g(\sigma, H_k, \mu_k) \wedge g(\theta, H_k, \mu_k) < g(\sigma, H_k, \mu_k))$$

We get three global comparators *a-f-w-s-b*, *a-f-w-c-b*, and *a-f-l-s-b* by instantiating the global schema with the same combining functions g for their fuzzy counterparts. We call this class of operators *combined operators*.

Assuming an approximation threshold of $\alpha = 0.95$, we obtain the following tables of recommendations from each of the combined comparators for the scenarios described in examples 1 to 4.

Example	*a-f-l-b*	*a-f-w-s-b*	*a-f-w-c-b*	*a-f-l-s-b*
1	$A, B\ (H_1)$	$B\ (H_1)$	$B\ (H_1)$	$B\ (H_1)$
2	$A\ (H_1)$	$A\ (H_1)$	$A, B\ (H_2)$	$B\ (H_1)$
3	$A\ (H_1)$	$A\ (H_2)$	$A\ (H_2)$	$A\ (H_2)$
4	$A\ (H_1)$	$A\ (H_2)$	$A\ (H_2)$	$A\ (H_2)$

The level at which the recommendation is made is enclosed in brackets. The recommendation "A, B" means that the two valuations are incomparable. The recommendations made by the combined comparators are at least as good as and, in some cases, better than the ones made by either class of the previously defined new comparators.

6 Concluding Remarks

The contribution of this paper is four-fold. First, we review the CH framework and use realistic examples to illustrate the dominance problem and the stiff equality problem. We also pinpoint aspects of the framework for further enhancement. Second, we propose the FCH framework to solve the dominance problem. In the new framework, each constraint can belong to more than one level of a hierarchy and to a varying degree of membership. New local and global comparators, which take the membership grade of constraints into account, are introduced. Following the style of [2], we also show the formal properties and relationship of the new comparators. Third, we give a fuzzy version $=^f$ of the equality relation and define the α-approximate equality relation to be the α-cut of $=^f$. Another new class of comparators is defined based on the α-approximate equality for solving the stiff equality problem. Fourth, we show a seamless integration of the the α-approximate equality relation and the FCH framework. The combined framework allows more flexibility in the modeling and handling of MCS problems. In particular, the solutions computed from the combined framework correspond more to how human makes decision, at least for the four example problems presented.

Our approach in adopting fuzzy techniques in constraint research differs from that of previous work (such as [1]) in that we fuzzify, instead of constraints,

(1) the level membership of constraints and (2) the equality relation used in *better* comparators. Further work is needed to study the connection between our framework and the closely related Multiple Attribute (or Criteria or Objective) Decision-Making (MADM) methods in the fuzzy system [6] and operations research [8] literature. As with other fuzzy-based systems, experimentation and experience are needed to determine the membership grades of constraints and the approximation threshold α for a particular application. The efficient knowledge elicitation technique by Slany [7] and the learning technique by Rossi and Sperduti [5] are good starting points.

We have demonstrated how the FCH framework can be used to better model a large class of over-constrained problems, namely those in MCS. More experience in using the FCH framework is needed to understand how the framework can help better tackle other over-constrained problems. There is also need to study if the FCH framework exhibits undesirable behavior in other problem instances.

Two implementations of FCH for the finite domain are available, one in spreadsheet and one using C. A more sophisticated implementation in Prolog of the combined framework for the finite domain is in progress. Existing solution algorithms for constraint hierarchies should also be easily adapted for solving fuzzy constraint hierarchies since the difference between the two frameworks lies mainly in the definition of the comparators.

Acknowledgement

This research is supported in part by The Croucher Foundation Research Grant (CF94/21), 1996–1998. We thank L.W. Chan, H.F. Leung, and K.S. Leung for useful discussions on fuzzy set theory. K.H. Lee and Tony Lee helped to locate the quote by Thomas Campbell.

References

1. S. Bistarelli, U. Montanari, and F. Rossi. Semiring-based constraint solving and optimization. *Journal of the ACM*, 44(2):201–236, 1997.
2. A. Borning, B. Freeman-Benson, and M. Wilson. Constraint hierarchies. *Lisp and Symbolic Computation*, 5(3):223–270, 1992.
3. M. Jampel. A brief overview of over-constrained systems. In M. Jampel, E. Freuder, and M. Maher, editors, *Over-Constrained Systems*, pages 1–22. LNCS 1106, Springer-Verlag, 1996.
4. G.J. Klir and T.A. Folger. *Fuzzy Sets, Uncertainty, and Information*. Prentice Hall, 1992.
5. F. Rossi and A. Sperduti. Learning solution preferences in constraint problems. *Journal of Theoretical and Experimental Artificial Intelligence*, 10, 1998.
6. Marc Roubens. Fuzzy sets and decision analysis. *Fuzzy Sets and Systems*, 90(2):199–206, 1997.
7. Wolfgang Slany. Scheduling as a fuzzy multiple criteria optimization problem. *Fuzzy Sets and Systems*, 78:197–222, 1996.
8. M. Tamiz, editor. *Multi-objective programming and goal programming : theories and applications*. LNEMS 432, Springer-Verlag, 1996.

Constraints for Object Recognition in Aerial Images — Handling of Unobserved Features

Thomas H. Kolbe

Institute for Environmental Sciences
University of Vechta
P.O. Box 1553, 49364 Vechta, Germany
Thomas.Kolbe@uni-vechta.de

Abstract. In this paper we will show how constraint solving methods can be applied for the recognition of buildings in aerial images. Object models are transformed to constraint representations which are matched against extracted image features. To cope with disturbances caused by occlusions and noise, we distinguish between the unobservability of a) relations between object parts and b) object parts themselves. Whereas other approaches for solving over-constrained problems suggest to reduce the relaxation of a variable to the relaxation of its incident constraints, we argue that both cases have to be treated separately. Information theory is applied to derive constraint weights on a probabilistic basis. We extend constraints and variables in a way which provides for an adequate integration of constraint violation and variable elimination on the one hand, and allows the determination of the maximum likelihood estimation for the matching between model and image on the other hand.

1 Introduction

The automation of 3D object extraction, esp. buildings, is an issue of high importance due to the increasing demand for 3D city models. 3D data are needed for various applications including geo-information systems, transmitter placement, urban planning, cartography, and environmental related investigations.

The complexity and variability of buildings makes the use of strict models and low level image matching techniques like template matching and pattern classification unfeasible [24]. Relational matching was identified to be the appropriate scheme, where model and image are decomposed into graph structures and matched against each other [23, 26]. In section 2 we explain the employed models in detail.

To cope with the huge number of involved image features and the high complexity of building models, we have to apply efficient techniques in order to solve the underlying subgraph isomorphism problem. The application of constraint solving techniques [18], which has a long tradition in computer vision [28, 10, 23], proved to achieve good efficiency on large images [16]. However, they rely on the fact that all variables can be assigned values and all constraints can be fulfilled. Unfortunately this is often not the case, because of disturbances in the image like occlusions, noise and segmentation errors. Thus the problem often is over-constrained.

In recent years different methods for solving over-constrained systems have been developed [7, 19, 30]. Although several frameworks were proposed which have these methods as special cases [8, 15], the specific techniques concentrate either on the relaxation of constraints or on the elimination of variables. Unobservability of objects in aerial images occurs rather often, and sometimes it can even be predicted (for example, when we know about low contrast). Clearly in these cases the unobservability of an object may not be punished as hard as the violation of constraints between observed objects. Therefore a more natural model is required which makes this distinction explicit.

We developed a modeling scheme, which distinguishes between the unobservability of objects and the violation of relations between objects. Above, it integrates both effects into one evaluation function. Our concept is based on information theory and is motivated by work on relational matching [1, 26]. It is explained in section 4. The evaluation function gives the best matching a probabilistic semantic, namely the maximum likelihood estimation. The relaxation of constraints is achieved by program transformation, namely augmentation of the constraints by an additional variable which rates the violation resp. satisfaction of that constraint. Our concept can further be used in conjunction with standard consistency techniques and thus can be implemented i.e. on top of a CLP(FD) system. This is explicated in section 5.

At the end of the article (section 6) we finally show that our proposed modeling scheme also builds a natural link between MaxCSP and Dynamic CSP.

2 Building Recognition as a CSP

For the recognition of buildings we basically apply two models. On the one hand we have a (3D) object model, describing the shape and geometry of buildings. The model primitives consist of volumetric building parts that can be combined to more or less complex building structures. On the other hand we have a (2D) image model, which describes the objects and their relations that can be observed in the image. Here the primitives consist of points, lines and faces. Relations include (among others) line parallelism, neighbourhood, and collinearity.

The gap between the 3D object model and the 2D image model is bridged using aspect graphs. Aspect graphs enumerate all topologically invariant views on an object model, and can be efficiently computed for polyhedral 3D objects. Every aspect is represented in terms of the image model. Relations are propagated from the object model to the 2D aspects.

The modeling is presented in detail in [2]. The strategy, esp. how building hypotheses are generated and selected, is described in [5].

To identify an aspect and thus the underlying building in an image, the aerial raster image is segmented to derive a symbolic image description [6]. The extracted image features are also represented in terms of the image model. The features and their interrelationships form the feature relation graph FRG.

Now, the model and the extracted image features both are given as relational structures (graphs), where the nodes represent objects and the edges relations. The aim is to find the (small) model graph in the (huge) feature relation graph

FRG. To solve this subgraph isomorphism problem, we transform the model graph into a constraint satisfaction problem CSP(V, D, C), where the variables V represent the model primitives, and the constraints C the model relations. The variable domains D consist of the set of extracted image features. The task then is to find a valid assignment of extracted image features to the model variables, which satisfies all model constraints. This combinatorial problem is also known as the consistent labeling problem [10, 11].

As we have shown in [16], constraint logic programming over finite domains CLP(FD) [25, 13] has proved to be an appropriate platform for representing the different models and performing the search. The application of consistency techniques (forward checking and look-ahead) [17, 9, 18] provided an acceptable efficiency.

Applied constraints. For the task of building recognition we employ four different types of constraints. Fig. 1 shows the geometric constraints and fig. 2 the topological constraints.

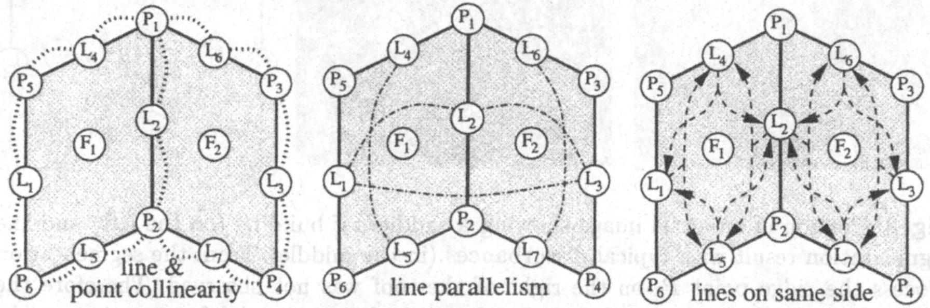

Fig. 1. Geometric constraints being used to describe a building roof consisting of points $P_1, \ldots, P_6$, lines $L_1, \ldots, L_7$, and faces F_1, F_2.

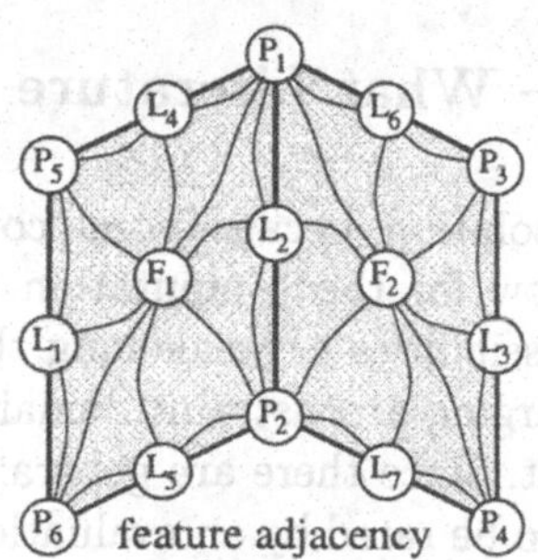

Fig. 2. Topological constraints used for the roof model.

The `collinear`(L, P) constraint states that a line segment L and a point P have to be collinear. This is realized by measuring the distance between the point and the straight line that goes through the line segment. The constraint now checks whether the distance is below a given threshold.

The `line_parallel`(L_1, L_2) constraint states that two line segments L_1 and L_2 have to be parallel. It is realized by computing the angle difference between both lines and the test whether it is smaller than a given threshold value.

`same_side_line`(L_{ref}, L_1, L_2) is a ternary constraint, stating that two line segments L_1 and L_2 have to lie in the same halfplane which is defined by the straight line going through a third line segment L_{ref}.

`feature_adjacent`(F_1, F_2) is a topological constraint, demanding that two image features F_1 and F_2 have to be neighboured, where features can be points, lines and faces. Since the feature adjacency graph is derived during the image segmentation and all neighboured feature pairs are enumerated, the test of this constraints reduces to a simple look-up.

Unobserved features and violation of constraints. The application of standard constraint solving methods demands that every variable can be assigned a value and all constraints can be satisfied. However, occlusions, low contrast, noise, and image segmentation errors often cause disturbances, which in the last consequence have two different effects: 1) relations that are expected in the model do not hold between the corresponding image features, and 2) expected model features are not observed in the image and therefore objects are missing (see fig. 3 for an example). Thus the given CSPs are over-constrained and the employed techniques have to be adapted to reflect these problems.

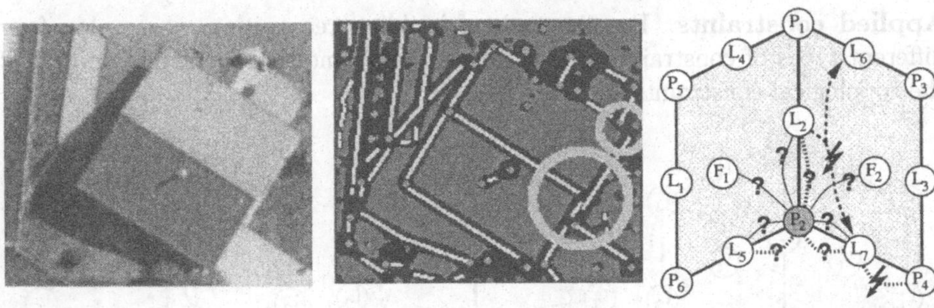

Fig. 3. Portion of an aerial image showing a saddleroof building (on the left) and the segmentation result with typical disturbances (in the middle). From the segmentation process the ridge point P_2 on the right of the roof was not observed. Therefore the incident relations cannot be observed either, which is indicated by question marks in the right image. Furthermore the `same_side_line`(L_2, L_6, L_7) constraint and the `collinear`(L_7, P_4) constraint is violated. This is indicated by the two flash symbols in the right image.

3 The Problem is Over-Constrained – What Literature Offers

An over-constrained system OCS is a CSP with no solution, because some constraints contradict others [14]. Nevertheless, to allow for the computation of (a somewhat sub-optimal) result, there are four possibilities of weakening the problem [7]: 1) enlarging a variable domain, 2) enlarging a constraint domain, 3) removing a variable, and 4) removing a constraint. Since there are generally different possibilities to weaken one CSP, they have to be rated by an evaluation function, allowing the definition of an ordering on them.

In literature several methods with specific evaluation functions for solving OCS have been proposed. They can be basically classified into two categories:

1. Relaxation of constraints (HCLP [30], MaxCSP [8])
2. Elimination of variables (Dynamic CSP [19])

Above, different frameworks (PCSP [8], GOCS [15]) have been suggested. These frameworks abstract from concrete evaluation functions and the way of weakening the original problem. As we will explain below, they have HCLP and/or

MaxCSP as instances. To clarify the relation between the mentioned methods, we have arranged them in a taxonomy as shown in fig. 4. In the following we will give a brief overview of each method, explain their position in the taxonomy, and discuss their use for our task of object recognition.

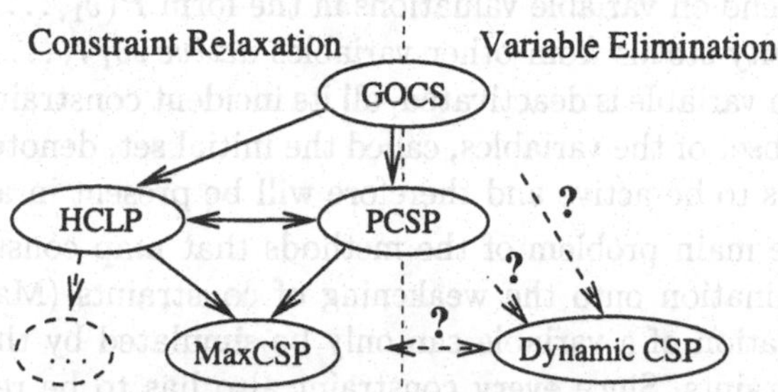

Fig. 4. Taxonomy of OCS methods. The only method focussing on variable elimination, DCSP, has not been cast in a general framework yet.

Maximum Constraint Satisfaction (MaxCSP) is the most simple and yet best-known method. It has been investigated in detail by Freuder and Wallace in [8]. The underlying (natural) metric simply counts the number of satisfied constraints. The best solutions are those with the smallest number of constraint violations.

Hierarchical Constraint Logic Programming (HCLP) was developed by Wilson, Borning et al. ([29, 30]), and expresses preferences by employing a constraint hierarchy. Constraints on the highest level of the hierarchy always have to be satisfied. Constraints on lower levels may be violated. The lexicographic ordering of the hierarchy levels ensures that the satisfaction of a more important constraint is always rated higher than alternatively satisfying an arbitrary number of constraints from lower levels.

HCLP can be considered as a framework for the relaxation of constraints, because it allows different ways to construct the evaluation function. For example, in [15] MaxCSP is shown to be an instance of HCLP.

Partial Constraint Satisfaction (PCSP) is a framework developed by Freuder and Wallace [7, 8] that regards any modification of the original CSP as a change of the problem space PS. It is general in the sense that any distance function that is a metric can be used to measure the difference of a modified problem space PS' to the original PS.

In [8] several concrete metrics are proposed, with MaxCSP being investigated in detail. However, none of them dealt explicitly with the relaxation of variables.

General framework for Over-Constrained Systems (GOCS) has been proposed by Jampel in his PhD thesis [15] as an abstraction from HCLP and PCSP. First it is shown that (most) problems expressed in HCLP can be transformed to PCSP and vice versa, when the evaluation function is expressed in terms of constraint augmentations (weakening method 2) from above). The main focus of GOCS lies on the compositionality of evaluation functions and solving schemes. Unfortunately, the relation to Dynamic CSP was only raised as a question of future research in the conclusion of the thesis.

Dynamic CSP (DCSP) was developed by Mittal and Falkenhainer [19] and is, to the best of our knowledge, the only scheme that explicitly handles the elimination of variables. In DCSP variables can be activated or switched off by special activity constraints. The circumstances under which variables are activated can depend on variable valuations in the form $P(v_1, \ldots, v_n) \rightarrow active\!: v_j$ or on the activity status from other variables $active\!: v_1 \wedge \ldots \wedge active\!: v_n \rightarrow active\!: v_j$. When a variable is deactivated, all its incident constraints also become deactivated. A subset of the variables, called the initial set, denotes the variables which have always to be active and therefore will be present in any solution.

Discussion. The main problem of the methods that map constraint violation and variable elimination onto the weakening of constraints (MaxCSP, HCLP) is that the elimination of a variable can only be simulated by the relaxation of its incident constraints. Since every constraint also has to be relaxable due to a simple violation of the underlying relation, what costs should be assigned to each constraint? These two cases have to be distinguished, because otherwise the cost for variable elimination would be equal to the violation of all its incident constraints, which does not necessarily reflect the importance of the variable and thus will often be over-estimated.

The same applies to the frameworks PCSP and GOCS. Although they are not restricted to the weakening of constraints, the authors state that any of the four weakening possibilities enumerated above may be reduced to the augmentation of constraints by new, compatible relation tuples. Whereas logically correct, this leads to the problems mentioned when defining an evaluation function. Moreover, augmenting constraint or variable domains to resolve the inconsistencies is not feasible, if we further want to use consistency techniques. They rely on the fact that 1) variable domains become monotonically smaller as search proceeds, and 2) the set of relation tuples defining compatible value combinations remains constant.

The problem of DCSP as the only available method for handling variable elimination is, that if variables are active, all constraints between them have to be satisfied. This clearly is too restrictive for our application domain (cf. fig. 3).

We will therefore need a scheme which explicitly distinguishes between the unobservability of objects (realised by variable elimination + relaxation of incident constraints) and relations between objects (by single constraint relaxations). Starting point for the integration of both effects into one evaluation function is the work of Vosselman on relational matching [26]. He was the first who succeeded to provide for a sound integration of unobservability of objects and their relations in an evaluation function for relational matching.

4 An Evaluation Function Based on Information Theory

In literature several evaluation functions for measuring the similarity of two relational descriptions (graph structures) $D_1 = (V_1, E_1)$ and $D_2 = (V_2, E_2)$ have been proposed. We will briefly review the crucial aspects of three important established schemes in chronological order, and explain how they overcome the deficencies (which are closely related to those of the reviewed OCS methods) of their ancestors.

Shapiro and Haralick [22] suggested a (still popular) metric to measure the structural error $\mathcal{E}$ of a mapping between two relational descriptions D_1 and D_2. They simply count the number of relation tuples that are not mapped by the mapping function $h : V_1 \mapsto V_2$ from E_1 to E_2 and vice versa: $\mathcal{E}(h) = |E_1 \circ h - E_2| + |E_2 \circ h^{-1} - E_1|$. Later they extended their metric by allowing normalized, weighted relation attributes (cf. [11]). There are two main problems with this metric: 1) Graph nodes in V_1 that have no mapping partner in V_2 are mapped to a dummy element (the so-called *wildcard*, symbolized by $*$). As we have discussed above with using constraint relaxation methods for variable elimination, it is difficult to assign costs for such wildcard mappings. Costs cannot be 0, because then the best mapping would only consists of wildcard mappings. 2) It is difficult to determine constraint weights, because relations can have attributes of different types (real, integer, symbolic).

Boyer and Kak [1] proposed to regard relational matching as a communication problem, where the first description D_1 is transmitted over a discrete, noisy communication channel and is received as a somewhat distorted description D_2 (see fig. 5). In 1948 Shannon introduced a quantitative measure for the information contained in a transmitted message [21]. The relation between the information contained in a symbol a and the probability that a will be chosen from an alphabet is defined by the equation $I(a) = -\log P(a)$. It can be regarded as a measure of surprise that a was observed: the higher the probability, the lower the information content we get. The conditional information $I(a|b) = -\log P(a|b)$ measures the surprise if we know that a was sent whereas we receive b. It is a measure for the uncertainty of the transmission.

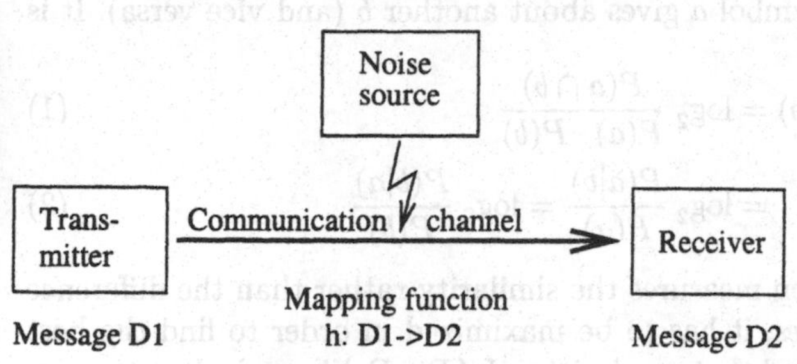

Fig. 5. Information theoretic modeling of a discrete communication channel

Boyer and Kak showed that the information content of a relational description is $I(D) = I(V) + I(E)$, with $I(V) = \sum_{v \in V} I(v)$ being the sum of the information contained in the nodes, and $I(E) = \sum_{e \in E}$ the information contained in the relations. The information of a node v_i itself consists of the sum[1] of the information contained in each attribute a_j: $I(v_i) = \sum_{a_j \in v_i} I(a_j)$. The information contributed by an attribute a depends on the probability of a taking a certain $value_l$: $I(a = value_l) = -\log P(a = value_l)$. The information of a relation e_i is defined as the sum over the information of all relation tuples $I(e_i) = \sum_{tup_j \in e_i} I(tup_j)$. Finally, the information contained in a relation tuple is the sum over the relation tuple attributes $I(tup_j) = \sum_{a_j \in tup_j} I(a_j)$, where $I(a_j)$ has the same definition as above.

[1] Assuming that all attributes are statistically independent.

Now the conditional information between two description $I(D_2|D_1)$ is defined in an analogous manner by replacing the probabilities by conditional probabilities. Since the conditional information measures the uncertainty of a transmission (and here also the quality of a channel), the task of finding the best mapping $\hat{h}$ from D_1 to D_2 can be reduced to the minimization $\hat{h} : \min_h I_h(D_2|D_1)$. The authors showed that $\hat{h}$ maximizes $P(h|D_1 \cap D_2)$, expressing that $\hat{h}$ is the most likely mapping under the given descriptions, the maximum likelihood estimation (cf. [4]) between D_1 and D_2.

The most important contribution of the proposed scheme for our purposes is that (in contrast to the first method presented above) weights now reflect the probabilistic nature of attribute values, and that they easily combine to an evaluation function having a probabilistic semantic. However, it does not solve the problem of wildcard mappings, because it is not possible to define the conditional information $I(*|a)$ between an attribute a and a wildcard.

Here the work of Vosselman [26] begins, who switched from using the conditional information to the mutual information, which is a symmetrical measure of the information that a symbol a gives about another b (and vice versa). It is defined as [12]:

$$I(a\,;\,b) = \log_2 \frac{P(a \cap b)}{P(a) \cdot P(b)} \tag{1}$$

$$= \log_2 \frac{P(a|b)}{P(a)} = \log_2 \frac{P(b|a)}{P(b)} \tag{2}$$

Since the mutual information measures the similarity rather than the difference between relational structures, it has to be maximized in order to find the best mapping $\hat{h}$. Vosselman showed that maximizing $I_h(D_1; D_2)$ is equivalent to maximizing $P(h|D_1 \cap D_2)$. Still, $\hat{h}$ is the maximum likelihood estimation between the relational descriptions D_1 and D_2.

The crucial improvement wrt. the model of Boyer and Kak consists in the evaluation of wildcard mappings. Since a relation attribute from an object model r_m and a wildcard are statistically independent, following eqn. 1 this leads to

$$I(r_m\,;\,*) = \log \frac{P(r_m) \cdot P(*)}{P(r_m) \cdot P(*)} \qquad \text{(because } r_m \text{ and } * \text{ are independent)}$$

$$= 0 \tag{3}$$

This means that wildcard mappings neither support nor contradict to a mapping. A matching consisting only of wildcard mappings therefore would contain no (mutual) information.

To see how the modeling scheme can be applied to the constraint representation of object models we have presented in section 2, suppose that our model relations are denoted by r_m, and the relations that can be observed in the segmented image by r_i. Then the mutual information between every pair (r_m, r_i) can be calculated from eqn. 2 by applying *Jeffrey's Rule* [20]:

$$I(r_i\,;\,r_m) = \log_2 \frac{P(r_i|r_m)}{P(r_i)} = \log_2 \frac{P(r_i|r_m)}{\sum_{r'_m} P(r_i|r'_m) \cdot P(r'_m)} \tag{4}$$

The mutual information has to be computed for every value combination of r_m and r_i, which in this case are the four tuples $(true, true)$, $(true, false)$, $(false, true)$, and $(false, false)$. Eq. 5 shows the calculation for the first tuple:

$$I(r_i = t\,;\, r_m = t) = \log_2 \frac{P(r_i = t|r_m = t)}{P(r_i{=}t|r_m{=}t)P(r_m{=}t)+P(r_i{=}t|r_m{=}f)P(r_m{=}f)} \quad (5)$$

The following example (tab. 1 and tab. 2) demonstrates the computation of the mutual information, when the a priori probabilities for the model relation and the conditional probabilities for the image relation wrt. the model relation are given:

Table 1. Example for a priori probabilities for model relation r_m (left) and conditional probabilities of image relation r_i wrt. model relation r_m (right).

r	$P(r)$
true	0.17
false	0.83

$P(r_i\|r_m)$	$r_m = true$	$r_m = false$
$r_i = true$	0.95	0.00
$r_i = false$	0.05	1.00

Table 2. Resulting mutual information calculated from table 1 using equation 4. The upper left value was computed using eqn. 5 which is derived from eqn. 4 for the case $(r_i = true\,,\, r_m = true)$.

$I(r_i\,;\,r_m)$ [bits]	$r_m = true$	$r_m = false$
$r_i = true$	2.56	$-\infty$
$r_i = false$	−4.07	0.25

From this example we can see that if a predicted model relation can be observed in the image, it supports the matching by 2.56 bits. Otherwise, if the same relation would not hold for the image, it contradicts the matching by 4.07 bits. If the relation could not be observed, because of a wildcard mapping of an incident variable, it would be rated 0.

Before we now proceed with the definition of our CSP modeling scheme we will summarize the four main points from this section, because we will explicitly refer to them later:

1. The mutual information between a (relation or object) attribute and a wildcard is 0.
2. The combination of the ratings of objects and relations is done by simply building the sum over the mutual information of all attributes.
3. For relations having no other attributes except for *true*/*false* the mutual information is given as a 2×2-table.
4. The mapping $\hat{h}$ with the highest mutual information corresponds to the maximum likelihood estimation.

5 Combining Variable Elimination and Constraint Relaxation

We assume that the model which should be matched with the extracted image features is given as a CSP(V, D, C) with variables V, associated domains D, and constraints C. Now, to distinguish between the relaxation of a constraint due to a simple violation or due to the unobservability of an incident variable every constraint $c(v_1, \ldots, v_n) \in C$ is extended by a three-valued domain variable $b \in \{-1, 0, 1\}$ to a constraint $c'(v_1, \ldots, v_n, b)$ with

$$\begin{aligned} c'(v_1, \ldots, v_n, b) \Leftrightarrow & (b = 1 \wedge c(v_1, \ldots, v_n)) \vee \\ & (b = -1 \wedge \neg c(v_1, \ldots, v_n)) \vee \\ & (b = 0) \end{aligned} \tag{6}$$

This variable can be seen both as an indicator and a control switch for the constraint. If on the one hand the original constraint c becomes entailed, b will be set to one. On the other hand, if b is set to 1, c has to be satisfied in order to satisfy c', thus the original constraint c will be enforced. Analogously, if c becomes contradictory[2], b will be set to -1, and if b is set to -1, the negation of c is enforced. The third case ($b = 0$) allows for an unconditional relaxation of c' wrt. the original constraint c.

Each variable domain $d \in D$ is extended by the wildcard value '$*$' (comparable to an explicit null value in record fields of databases) to a domain $d' = d \cup \{*\}$ with

$$\forall v_i \in V : \ (v_i = * \ \Leftrightarrow \ \forall c'_j(\ldots, v_i, \ldots, b_j) \in C' : \ b_j = 0) \tag{7}$$

This condition relates the indicator variables to the original CSP variables. It expresses that if a wildcard is assigned to a variable, the b variables of all incident constraints have to be 0, to satisfy the constraints c'. The other way around, if the b variables of all constraints which are incident to a variable are set to 0, the variable has to be assigned the wildcard value.

As one might already suspect the three-valued variable b is closely related to the wildcard mapping and the mutual information. In fact it covers main point 1) from the end of the last section. The values -1 and 1 are inspired from point 3), esp. from the mutual information in the left column of tab. 2. A satisfied constraint supports a matching ($b = 1$), a violated constraint gives a malus ($b = -1$).

According to point 2) from last section, the evaluation function is defined as the sum over the b variables of the transformed constraints:

$$f(C') = \sum_{i=1}^{|C'|} b_i \ \text{ with } c'_i(\ldots, b_i) \in C' \tag{8}$$

Maximization of this function leads to the best matching (cf. point 4) from last section).

---

[2] Contradiction here has the same definition as in [15]: there does not exist any model (in the logical sense) in which all constraints without c are true, and c is also true.

Up to now, constraints have been unweighted. If a maximum likelihood estimation is desired, two things have to be done:

1. The values 1 and -1 of the b variables have to be replaced by the mutual information $I(r_m = true; r_i = true)$ resp. $I(r_m = true; r_i = false)$ (cf. left column of tab. 2).
2. The set of complementary constraints $\bar{C}$ has to be determined. When the set of all possible (binary) constraints is $\mathcal{C} = \{c(v_i, v_j) \mid v_i, v_j \in V, i \neq j\}$, the set of complementary constraints then is $\bar{C} = \{\neg c \mid c \in \mathcal{C} \wedge c \notin C\}$. These are the constraints which state that relations which are not true in the object model must also be false in the image. The values 1 and -1 of their indicator variables have to be replaced by the mutual information $I(r_m = false; r_i = false)$ resp. $I(r_m = false; r_i = true)$ (shown in the right column of tab. 2).

The problem here is that we get a quadratic number of constraints wrt. the number of variables, because $|C \dot{\cup} \bar{C}| = |\mathcal{C}|$. We therefore omit the complementary constraints in the following, knowing that the best matching is related to but not guaranteed to be the maximum likelihood estimation. It is an issue of future research to estimate and limit the error.

Application to building recognition. Adding the b variables significantly enlarges the search space (by a factor of $3^{|C|}$). However, a careful modeling in the context of an application domain allows a priori reductions of the search space. We will exemplify this in the following for the definition of geometric constraints and the knowledge about the observability of image features.

The geometric constraints `line_parallel` and `collinear` play an important role wrt. the quality of a reconstructed building. Violations of these constraints are not tolerated, because it can be observed that in all of these cases one of the participating image features is not correctly extracted from the image. As explained in section 2 the constraints were defined using thresholds. If we now set the threshold to the maximum difference we find in a (large) set of training matches, the constraint will be true for all training examples[3]. Thus the conditional probability $P(r_i = true | r_m = true)$ that can be derived from the training data set will be 1 and therefore $P(r_i = false | r_m = true) = 0$. This means the constraint will not be violated in any acceptable matching. It can only be relaxed due to the unobservability of an incident variable. Therefore we can remove the -1 from the domains of the b variables of `line_parallel` and `collinear` constraints.

If one has knowledge about the observability of certain model parts, this can be exploited by the a priori elimination of wildcards from the resp. variable domains. In the system we have described in [5], the generation of building models is indexed by previously reconstructed 3D corners. Since the reconstruction of the corners uses the same image(s) as the final recognition of the complete building, the observability of the resp. building corners is propagated via the building model to the resulting CSP.

[3] We assume that the training matches were done by an expert, who can decide in every case, wether a certain deviation is acceptable.

Although a detailed explanation of the implementation is out of the scope of this paper, we will drop a few words on this topic. The modeling scheme is implemented by extending the CLP(FD) solver of the ECLIPSE system [27]. We adapted the inference rules for forward checking (FCIR) and look ahead (LAIR) as defined by van Hentenryck in [25], and provide a language interface similar to the constraint declarations of CHIP [3]. At the moment we only use the values -1 and 1 for the b variables, but we are currently evaluating test data sets to gain the probability distributions needed to compute the mutual information. Fig. 6 shows three example matchings that were determined using the proposed scheme.

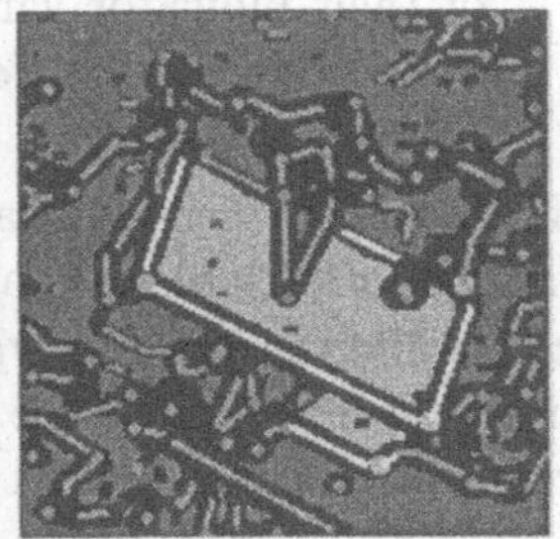

Fig. 6. Matching results for three buildings. The left building already was shown in fig. 3. The proposed evaluation function (correctly) decides that most violations of geometric constraints are best reflected by assuming the unobservability of incident variables. On the left one corner point and the right ridge point were mapped to a wildcard. Note that the right edge of the upper roof face is mapped correctly although it violates a `same_side_line` constraint (cf. fig. 3). In the middle one roof edge and the incident corner point were mapped to a wildcard, because the `line_parallel` and `collinearity` constraint could not be satisfied. Finally, on the right two corner points and the left edge of the lower roof face have a wildcard mapping.

6 Related Work

In section 3 we have pointed out that MaxCSP only considers the relaxation of constraints whereas Dynamic CSP is restricted to the elimination of variables. Here we show that both MaxCSP and Dynamic CSP may be regarded as special cases of our evaluation function. We show this by simulating MaxCSP and Dynamic CSP in terms of our model.

To implement the MaxCSP metric, one simply has to remove the 0 from the domains of the b variables and the wildcard $*$ from the variable domains. Thus constraints can only be relaxed, if the underlying relation is violated. Clearly, maximizing eqn. 8 then maximizes the number of satisfied constraints.

Dynamic CSP forbids the violation of constraints between active variables. Therefore we remove the -1 from the domains of the b variables. The initial variable set is always active and thus present in any solution. This is ensured by removing the wildcard $*$ from the variables in this set. Activity constraints of the form $P(v_1, \ldots, v_j) \rightarrow active : v_k$ are transformed to $P'(v_1, \ldots, v_j, b) \Leftrightarrow (b = 0) \vee (b = 1 \wedge (P(v_1, \ldots, v_j) \rightarrow v_k \neq *))$. The other activity constraints can be transformed in a analogous way. This simulation of Dynamic CSP is similar to the one mentioned in [19].

Finally, we demonstrate the use of the proposed scheme with an example given by Freuder and Wallace for PCSP in [8] (which can be seen as a simple version of a configuration problem). The problem is that we have a minimal wardrobe and some restrictions which clothes can be worn together with others. It is shown in fig. 7 and has under the given conditions no solution. When applying the MaxCSP metric to solve the over-constrained problem, every variable has to be assigned a clothing article, because MaxCSP is not capable of variable relaxation[4]. In this example this leads to the two "best" solutions which suggest to wear Cordovans, a grey shirt, a grey tie, and dress blue slacks or Cordovans, a green shirt, a grey tie, and dress grey slacks. Both solutions obviously are inacceptable. Allowing also for the elimination of variables, we instead get a solution that suggests to drop the tie, which is not only the most comfortable but also the least eye-offending proposal.

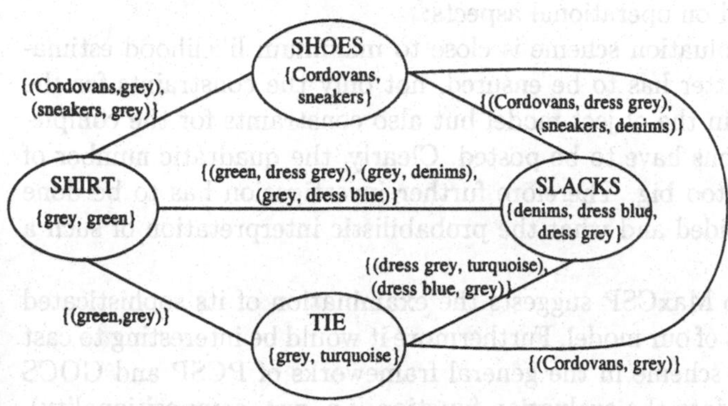

Fig. 7. Robot clothing example adopted from [8] and extended by a tie. The MaxCSP approach finds two best-rated solutions with two constraint violations each: 1) Cordovans, grey shirt, grey tie, dress blue slacks (yuck!), and 2) Cordovans, green shirt, grey tie, dress grey slacks (which is not much better). Our evaluation function in contrast decides that it is best to wear sneakers, denims, and a grey shirt and to drop the tie.

7 Conclusion and Future Work

We have presented a modeling scheme for CSPs which provides a smart integration of the unobservability of object parts and their interrelationships in the context of object recognition. The proposed evaluation function has a probabilistic basis. Information theory is applied to derive constraint weights from probability distributions of relations. These probabilities can be empirically derived from training matchings. This concept allows the definition of the best matching in a probabilistic sense, namely the maximum likelihood estimation between model and image data. Over-constrained systems which are modeled using this concept can be solved by the application of standard constraint solving methods.

We have implemented the scheme in CLP(FD) by extending the solver of the ECLIPSE system and have succesfully applied it for the recognition of buildings in aerial images. We have shown how domain specific restrictions can be used to

[4] The same applies to HCLP, which also cannot handle the elimination of variables.

sharpen the modeling of constraints and how a priori knowledge can be used for initial pruning of the search space.

Finally, by demonstrating that MaxCSP and DCSP are special cases of our concept we have established an up to now missing (natural) link between them.

Future work has two main focuses, the first concentrating on the evaluation function and the second on operational aspects:

1) The proposed evaluation scheme is close to maximum likelihood estimation. However, if the latter has to be ensured, not only the constraints for the relations that are true in the object model but also constraints for the complementary negated relations have to be posted. Clearly, the quadratic number of required constraints is too big. Therefore further investigation has to be done on how this can be avoided and what the probabilistic interpretation of such a reduced model will be.

2) The proximity to MaxCSP suggests the examination of its sophisticated heuristics in the context of our model. Furthermore it would be interesting to cast the proposed modeling scheme in the general frameworks of PCSP and GOCS to gain further insights into the evaluation function (i.e. wrt. compositionality).

Acknowledgements. This work was mainly done within the project "Semantic Modeling and Extraction of Spatial Objects from Images and Maps", especially in the subproject "Building Extraction" funded by the German Research Council (DFG). Thanks go to Lutz Plümer, Armin B. Cremers, Wolfgang Förstner, Gerd Gröger and Ingo Petzold who helped with many discussions and critical comments to develop these ideas. We thank the DFG for supporting our work.

References

[1] K. L. Boyer and A. C. Kak. Structural Stereopsis for 3D-Vision. *IEEE Transactions on Pattern Analysis and Machine Intelligence*, 10(2):144–166, 1988.

[2] C. Braun, T. H. Kolbe, F. Lang, W. Schickler, V. Steinhage, A. B. Cremers, W. Förstner, and L. Plümer. Models for Photogrammetric Building Reconstruction. *Computer & Graphics*, 19(1):109–118, 1995.

[3] M. Dincbas, P. van Hentenryck, H. Simonis, A. Aggoun, T. Graf, and F. Berthier. The Constraint Logic Programming Language CHIP. In ICOT, editor, *Proceedings of the International Conference on Fifth Generation Computer Systems*, pages 693–702, 1988.

[4] R. O. Duda and P. E. Hart. *Pattern Classification and Scene Analysis.* Wiley & Sons, New York, 1973.

[5] A. Fischer, T. H. Kolbe, and F. Lang. Integration of 2D and 3D Reasoning for Building Reconstruction Using a Generic Hierarchical Model. In W. Förstner and L. Plümer, editors, *Semantic Modeling for the Acquisition of Topographic Information from Images and Maps.* Birkhäuser Verlag, Basel, 1997.

[6] W. Förstner. A Framework for Low Level Feature Extraction. In J.-O. Eklundh, editor, *Computer Vision, ECCV '94, Vol. II*, number 801 in Lecture Notes in Computer Science, pages 383–394. Springer-Verlag, 1994.

[7] E. C. Freuder. Partial Constraint Satisfaction. In N. Sridharan, editor, *Proc. of the 11. Int. Joint Conf. on Artificial Intelligence IJCAI'89 in Detroit, MI, USA.* Morgan Kaufmann, 1989.

[8] E. C. Freuder and R. J. Wallace. Partial Constraint Satisfaction. In M. Jampel, E. Freuder, and M. Maher, editors, *Over-Constrained Systems*, number 1106 in LNCS, pages 63–110. Springer-Verlag, Berlin, 1996.

[9] R. M. Haralick and G. L. Elliott. Increasing Tree Search Efficiency for Constraint Satisfaction Problems. *Artificial Intelligence*, 14:263–313, 1980.

[10] R. M. Haralick and L. G. Shapiro. The Consistent Labeling Problem: Part I. *IEEE Transactions on Pattern Analysis and Machine Intelligence*, 1:173–184, 1979.

[11] R. M. Haralick and L. G. Shapiro. *Computer and Robot Vision*, volume II. Addison-Wesley Publishing Company, 1993.

[12] F. M. Ingels. *Information and Coding Theory.* Intext Educational Publishers, San Francisco, Toronto, London, 1971.

[13] J. Jaffar and M. J. Maher. Constraint Logic Programming: A Survey. *Journal of Logic Programming*, 19/20:503–581, 1994.

[14] M. Jampel. A Brief Overview of Over-Constrained Systems. In M. Jampel, E. Freuder, and M. Maher, editors, *Over-Constrained Systems*, number 1106 in LNCS, pages 1–22. Springer-Verlag, Berlin, 1996.

[15] M. B. Jampel. *Over-Constrained Systems in CLP and CSP.* PhD thesis, Dep. of Computer Science, City University London, UK, September 1996.

[16] T. H. Kolbe, L. Plümer, and A. B. Cremers. Using Constraints for the Identification of Buildings in Aerial Images. In *Proceedings of the 2. Int. Conf. on Practical Applications of Constraint Technology PACT'96 in London*, pages 143–154. The Practical Application Company Ltd., 1996.

[17] A. K. Mackworth. Consistency in Networks of Relations. *Artificial Intelligence*, 8:99–118, 1977.

[18] P. Meseguer. Constraint Satisfaction Problems: An Overview. *AICOM*, 2(1):3–17, March 1989.

[19] S. Mittal and B. Falkenhainer. Dynamic Constraint Satisfaction Problems. In *Proc. of AAAI 1990 in Boston*, pages 25–31, 1990.

[20] J. Pearl. *Probabilistic Reasoning in Intelligent Systems: Networks of Plausible Inference.* Morgan Kaufmann, San Mateo, California, 2. edition, 1988.

[21] C. E. Shannon. A Mathematical Theory of Communication. *Bell System Journal*, 27, 1948.

[22] L. G. Shapiro and R. M. Haralick. A Metric for Comparing Relational Descriptions. *IEEE Trans. on Pattern Analysis and Machine Intell.*, 7(1):90–94, 1985.

[23] L. G. Shapiro and R. M. Haralick. Relational Matching. *Applied Optics*, 26(10):1845–1851, 1987.

[24] P. Suetens, P. Fua, and A. J. Hanson. Computational Strategies for Object Recognition. *ACM Computing Surveys*, 24(1):5–61, 1992.

[25] P. van Hentenryck. *Constraint Satisfaction in Logic Programming.* Logic Programming Series. MIT Press, Cambridge, MA, 1989.

[26] G. Vosselman. *Relational Matching.* Number 628 in LNCS. Springer-Verlag, Berlin, 1992.

[27] M. Wallace, S. Novello, and J. Schimpf. ECLiPSe: A Platform for Constraint Logic Programming. Technical report, IC-Parc London, UK, August 1997.

[28] D. L. Waltz. Understanding Line Drawings of Scenes with Shadows. In P. H. Winston, editor, *Psychology of Computer Vision.* McGraw-Hill, New York, 1975.

[29] M. Wilson and A. Borning. Extending Hierarchical Constraint Logic Programming: Nonmonotonicity and Inter-Hierarchy Comparison. In *Proceedings of the 1989 North American Conference on Logic Programming in Cleveland, Ohio*, 1989.

[30] M. A. Wilson. *Hierarchical Constraint Logic Programming.* PhD thesis, Dept. of Computer Science, University of Washington, May 1993.

SALSA : A Language for Search Algorithms

François Laburthe
Thomson-CSF Corporate Research Laboratory
Domaine de Corbeville, 91404 Orsay
laburthe@dmi.ens.fr

Yves Caseau
Bouygues - D.T.N.
1 av. E. Freyssinet 78061 St Quentin en Y.
caseau@dmi.ens.fr

Abstract: Constraint Programming is a technique of choice for solving hard combinatorial optimization problems. However, it is best used in conjunction with other optimization paradigms such as local search, yielding hybrid algorithms with constraints. Such combinations lack a language supporting an elegant description and retaining the original declarativity of Constraint Logic Programming. We propose a language, SALSA, dedicated to specifying (local, global or hybrid) search algorithms. We illustrate its use on a few examples from combinatorial optimization for which we specify complex optimization procedures with a few simple lines of code of high abstraction level. We report preliminary experiments showing that such a language can be implemented on top of CP systems, yielding a powerful environment for combinatorial optimization.

1. Introduction

Today, combinatorial problem solving is one of the most successful fields of application for Constraint Programming (CP). In the past few years, on problems such as scheduling, resource allocation, crew rostering, fleet dispatching, etc., the CP technology has risen to a state-of-the-art level on academic problems as well as on some real-life industrial ones (see the *PACT* and *Ilog Users* conferences).

However, in many cases where the constraint approach has proven really successful, the standard resolution procedure was not used and a more customized search was applied. In some sense, many CP approaches have left the framework of Constraint Logic Programming (CLP) [JL 87], and belong to the more general case of hybrid optimization algorithms.

Indeed, the default search procedure offered by today's CP systems is inherited from logic programming systems (Prolog's SLD resolution strategy [Llo 87]). Since constraint propagation is incomplete for most finite domain constraints used in combinatorial problem solving (e.g. other global constraints), a search tree is explored, where each node corresponds to the labeling of one of the variables involved in the goal by one of the values in its domain). Upon failure in one of the branches, the algorithm backtracks to the previous node and tries to assign to the variable the next value from its domain. This search tree is visited by a depth-first exploration, in order to limit memory requirements. In the case of optimization problems, two strategies are available, either a new search is started each time a solution is found (constraining the objective function to take a better value), or one dynamically impose that the objective be better than the best solution found so far (branch&bound search). Many Constraint Programming applications have considered other search strategies for the following reasons :

- Such a global search may not be the best method for obtaining a first solution (tailored greedy heuristics performing a limited amount of look-ahead search may be more efficient, for example in scheduling [DT 93] or routing [CL 98]).

- It may be a good idea to incorporate a limited amount of breadth-first search (such as the "shaving" mechanism used for scheduling [MS 96]),
- Other visiting orders of the search tree may somtimes be worthwhile (e.g. LDS [HG 95], [CL 98], A* [LM 97]),
- It may be interesting to express topological conditions on the shape of the subtree that is explored (unbalanced trees, limited number of nodes, limited number of choices along a branch, ...)

This is actually an old idea of logic programming to separate logic and control and to specify both with a separate language [HS 98]. The recent work on CP tools (such as Oz explorer [Sch 97]) belong to this trend of providing the user with the ability to specify the way the global search tree is visited.

Moreover, combinatorial problem solving with constraints is also expanding beyond the scope of global search by considering hybrid combinations of constraint propagation and global search with other paradigms, such as local optimization and greedy heuristics. This shift can be easily understood for two reasons :

- Global search may be applied successfully only if the algorithm is given enough time to visit a significant portion of the solution space. For large problems, such a thorough exploration is out of reach, hence other approaches should be considered.
- In the past decades, Operations Researchers have proposed a variety of algorithms dedicated to specific optimization problems, many of which are extremely efficient. This wealth of knowledge should be used as much as possible within CP.

There are many ways in which CP may be combined with local optimization : one can find a first solution by global search and further optimize it by local search; one can explore part of a global search tree and apply a local search to optimize the partial solution at each node of the tree [CL 98]; one can use global search to find one local move [LK 73], for instance by an exhaustive branch and bound exploration of the neighborhood [PG 96], or by keeping a fragment of the solution and trying a limited global search to extend it,

In practice, programming such algorithms is a tedious and error-prone task, for lack of a high-level language : CP tools do not offer the ability to perform non-monotonic operations (which are the basis of local search algorithms) and other tools dedicated to a specific optimization paradigm (MIP [FG 93] or local optimization [MVH 97]) do not offer the possibility to post constraints or to perform hypothetical reasoning. Hence, the programmer is left with an imperative language which most of the time lacks abstraction and declarativity (such as C++).

In order to offer an environment for programming such hybrid algorithms, we propose to consider logic and control separately and to use a specific language in order to control the search for solutions. To this aim, we propose a language, SALSA, dedicated to programming search algorithms. SALSA is not a standalone language but works in cooperation with a host programming language. We will demonstrate how SALSA can be used to program local, global and hybrid search procedures.

The paper is organized as follows : section 2 discusses the basis of search algorithms, neighborhoods and choices, and informally introduces the main ideas of SALSA, while section 3 presents the language. Section 4 is the main part of the paper in which we review a set of examples of hybrid algorithms from combinatorial optimization that illustrate the expressive power of SALSA. Section 5 gives an overview of a formal operational semantics and briefly presents the prototype implementation.

2. Transitions, choices and neighborhoods

Local and global search algorithms have many features in common. First of all, they search for solutions (configurations of a system) within some search space. Thus, an execution of a search algorithm may be represented by a sequence of states (those points in the search space which have been visited). In local search, states are solutions (they can be interpreted as answers to the optimization problem), whereas in global search, states may be incomplete or partial solutions (which is the case, in CP, when only a fraction of the variables have been instantiated). A search algorithm can hence be described by the mechanism responsible for driving the execution from one state to the next one. Such moves from one configuration to another are chosen among several possible ones : local search only considers one move among the set, whereas global search comes back to the choice point until all possible branches (moves) have been considered. If we describe such a system by an undeterministic automaton, each visited state can be traced back from the start state by a sequence of transitions. Moreover, global search also considers backward moves (going back in time to a previously visited state).

2.1 Global search

Global search algorithms are usually specified by goals describing the state to be reached (the solution). For a given goal, the user can specify the order in which the variables should be instantiated. Thus, the user is left with two possibilities in order to customize the search procedure : decomposing the global goal into a series of smaller sub-goals and specifying a labeling procedure for each sub-goal.

A completely different standpoint consists of describing the search algorithms in a framework of distributed computation : the state corresponds to the computation environment (the "constraint store"), and branching corresponds to process cloning. A process is associated with each node; copies of the current process are made at a choice point (one copy per branch), and the corresponding transitions are evaluated in the computation environment of the new process. Such a formalism (offered in Oz [SS 94]), by giving explicit access to the state (processes are named and can be stored in variables or passed as arguments to functions), enables the user to program any exploration strategy, such as A* [Pea 84].

2.2 Local search

The LOCALIZER language has been proposed for local search algorithms [MVH 97]. Such algorithms programmed in this elegant framework feature three components :

1. *Invariants* : these invariants are used to introduce functional dependencies between data structures. In addition to the basic data structures used to represent a solution, some additional data structures are used to store redundant information. Their values is specified by means of a formula called an invariant. Such formulae, which are in a sense similar to constraints, are used to maintain consistent values in the additional data structures each time a value of the basic

data structures is modified. Unlike constraints, invariants specify in a declarative manner the non-monotonic evolution of data structures.

2. *Neighborhoods* : they correspond to the moves that can be applied to go from one state to another. They are described by imperative updates which trigger some computations, in order to maintain the invariants.

3. *Control* : the control flow of the algorithm is described in two places. The global search procedure is always made of two nested loops (at most *MaxTries* random walks, each of which is composed of at most *MaxIter* moves). In addition, one may specify some local conditions (affecting one single neighborhood) that will be used for selecting the move : the moves in the neighborhood may be sorted or selected according to a given probability, etc.

Hence, with such a description, a local search algorithm can be easily adapted from hill-climbing to tabu search or from a random walk to simulated annealing, by adding a few conditions specifying when to accept a move.

2.3 Hybrid search

The formalisms for global and local search differ : in global search, goals and constraints describe properties of final states, while in local search, invariants and neighborhoods describe properties of all states. However, if we further decompose global search algorithms, the basic branching mechanism is very much like that of local search : from a state, we consider several decisions (labeling a variable by one of its values, or enforcing one among a set of constraints), each leading to a different state, and we only choose one of them at a time. Thus, a language expressing neighborhoods (in local search) and choices (in global search) in the same formalism would be able to express hybrid combinations. This is what SALSA does :

- Choices are specified in a manner similar to LOCALIZER's neighborhoods. Transitions correspond to the evaluation of an expression, and some local control can be specified at the choice level (by specifying which such transitions are valid ones, in what order they should be considered, recognizing local optima, etc.).

- Such choices are reified as objects, which can in turn, be composed by a set of operators, in order to specify search algorithms.

The result is a language for search algorithms, which can describe elegantly local search procedures, global search algorithms, and many combinations.

3. The SALSA language

This section describes in an informal manner the SALSA language. A detailed presentation is available in [CL97]. To keep this presentation simple, we start by a simple example : default search procedures for a finite domain constraint solver.

3.1 Defining choices

We start by an example of a choice named *L*, responsible for labeling a logic variable with one of the values in its domain (SALSA keywords are typed in bold).

```
L :: Choice(
    moves post(FD, x == v)
    with x = some(x in Variable | unknown?(value,x)),
         v ∈ domain(x) )
```

A choice definition contains two parts. The first part follows the *moves* keyword and defines the set of transitions representing all branches of the choice. The second part follows the *with* keyword and defines local variables. Such variables may either be bound to a value or be associated to a set of possible values.

Several comments can be made on this example. First of all, the expression that gets evaluated in a branch of the choice (*post(FD, x == v)*, for some substitution of *x* and *v*) posts a constraint to a constraint solver (*FD*). Throughout this article, for lack of space, we will refer to such "solvers" without describing them. Each time we use the syntax *post(S,e)*, *S* will be responsible for triggering some computations after the evaluation of the expression *e* (by means of constraints, invariants, rules, or any other consistency mechanism). In our example, the choice uses two local variables *x* and *v*. At run-time, each time the choice *L* is used, the value of *v* will be chosen among the set (*domain(x)*) while the value of *x* will be uniquely determined (the expression *some(x in E | P(x))* will iterate the set *E* until it finds an element such that *P(x)* is true and returns that first element, like in the ALMA programming language [AS 97]). There will be as many branches to the choice generated by *L*, as there are possible values to be substituted to the pair *(x,v)* in the expression *post(FD, x == v)*.

The next example describes another possibility for restricting the domains of variables when the domains contain many values : instead of assigning a value to a variable, we use a dichotomic splitting mechanism. Note here, that the set of transitions is given explicitly by means of the *or* keyword, separating the enumerated branches of the choice. Such a choice has only two branches since the local variables *x* and *mid* are bound to a unique value.

```
R :: Choice(
    moves post(FD, x <= mid) or post(FD, x > mid)
    with x = some(x in Variable | unknown?(value,x) & card(x) > 4),
         mid = (x.sup + x.inf) / 2 )
```

3.1 Composing choices in order to define search algorithms

In order to describe complete search algorithms, choices need to be composed. In the finite domain constraint solver example, all variables need be assigned. For instance, one can take decisions following the choice *L* until all variables are instantiated. In order to express such algorithms, we introduce two composition mechanisms.

If *C* and *D* have been defined as two choices, we represent by the expression $C \times D$ the algorithm that applies first a transition from choice *C* and, from the new state, applies a transition from choice *D*. In such a composition, *C* and *D* need not be different : one can apply the same branching mechanism over a whole search tree : C^n represent *C* composed *n* time with itself, and C^* represents an infinite expression $C \times C \times$... Hence, in our example, a standard labeling strategy can be described by the term L^*.

Another strategy would consist of first reducing the domains by dichotomic splits until no more domains of size greater than 4 remain, and then, to apply the labeling procedure. Such an algorithm can be described as the composition of R^* and L^*. However, it cannot be denoted $R^* \times L^*$ since this expression would have to generate an infinite number of R-transitions before performing the first L-transition. Hence, we introduce a new composition mechanism : if C and D are two choices $C \lozenge D$ tries to apply a transition of C; whenever C is unable to branch (when C does not manage to produce one single valid tuple of values for its free variables), a transition of D is applied. Both composition mechanisms ($\times$ and $\lozenge$), are generalized to the composition of arbitrary expressions involving choices. Thus, in our example, the new labeling procedure should be denoted $R^* \lozenge L^*$, since it applies transitions from R, and when it is no longer able to do so, it applies transitions from L, until it is no longer able to do so.

We have described the syntax of the language for creating such choices as well as for composing them. We complete this brief presentation by focusing on the control flow of such algorithms. Choices are responsible for generating branches leading to new states which are organized into a search tree. There are two implicit rules for the visit of this tree. First, when a failure occurs (when an uncaught exception is raised), the control backtracks to the father node, which, in turn, expands the next branch. Second, when all branches of a node have been explored, the control returns to the father node.

An algorithm is executed by calling the *SOLVE* primitive on a SALSA expression. There are two ways to exit from such an algorithm, either when one comes to a leaf of a search tree and there is no more transition to follow, or, when one should apply a transition, but the choice is unable to branch. We introduce two special SALSA terms, called terminators, used to specify the behavior of the algorithm when it comes to such exits. The *cont* terminator continues the exploration and the *exit* terminator commits to the current state and discards any further exploration. These terminators can be composed as any other terms. Hence, in our example, the complete procedure for finding one solution can be expressed as follows :

```
SOLVE(R* ◊ L* ◊ exit)
```

We now illustrate how such an algorithm can be easily modified in order to perform a branch and bound optimization (say, minimization) instead of a simple search for a solution. For the purpose of the example, we describe two functions which store the value of the objective function (the logical variable *OBJ*) in an imperative global variable (*UB*) and which post the constraint that the objective be strictly smaller than the smallest solution found so far. We now describe how SALSA terms can be enriched with the evaluation of function calls. There are three ways to compose a term T with a function f. T *where* f calls f at each internal node of the tree and discards the sub-trees where this evaluation has returned the value *false*, or where it has lead to failure (raising an exception). T and f can also be composed with the constructs $\times$ and $\lozenge$, in which case f is called before each exit of T.

```
registerUB() -> UB := OBJ.value
enforceUB() -> post(FD, OBJ < UB)
```

The branch and bound algorithm described below builds the same search tree as the algorithm searching for one solution, except that it now calls *enforceUB* at each internal node and *registerUB* at each solution.

```
SOLVE((R* ◊ L*) where enforceUB ◊ registerUB ◊ cont)
```

It is often useful in CP to use dedicated algorithms for lower bounds, which may be more acute than those computed by the constraint solver (for example, the weight of a minimal spanning tree for the traveling salesman problem [PGPR 96]). In this case, we can keep the SALSA term for optimization, all we have to do is change the *enforceUB* function.

```
enforceUB() : boolean -> (computeLowerBound() < UB)
```

We can see on this introductory example a benefit from the SALSA formulation : it is easy to experiment variations on a search algorithm, to replace a choice mechanism by another, or to customize the way the search tree should be explored.

4. Examples

This section is devoted to the illustration of the SALSA language on real examples taken from combinatorial optimization. The first example consists of a simple customized procedure for a combinatorial toy problem solved by CP (*n* queens on a chessboard). The second example is a classical example from local optimization, GSAT; since this example was developed in [MVH 97], we show how the SALSA formulation is a natural extension of the LOCALIZER approach. The third example shows how SALSA can be used in order to experiment with greedy heuristics and limited backtracking on a simple scheduling problem. The fourth example shows how SALSA can help the programmer to code some complex local optimization algorithms, such as Lin&Kernighan's heuristic for the TSP, for which the search for the best local moves is done by a global search algorithm. Finally, the last example addresses a complex vehicle routing problem, which is solved by a hybrid algorithm combining various forms of local optimization, look-ahead evaluation, greedy heuristic and constraint propagation.

4.1 The n queens problem

In order to place *n* queens on an *n*×*n* chessboard, such that no two of them attack each other, we represent the position of each queen by a logical variable. We store these variables in an array named *queens* (*queens[i]=j* means that there is a queen in the cell at the intersection of line *i* and row *j*). We denote by *FD* the solver constraining the rows and diagonals of the various queens to be different. A useful heuristic consists in selecting the variable on which to branch by the first-fail criterion and iterating the values in its domain, starting from the center of the row. Such a branching procedure can be described by a SALSA choice which sorts the values of its local variables *(i,j)* by increasing distance to the middle of the row.

```
Q :: Choice(
  moves post(FD, queens[i] == j)
     with i = some(i in {i in (1 .. n) | unknown?(value,queens[i])}
                          minimizing card(domain(queens[i])) )
          j ∈ domain(i)
  ordered by increasing abs(n/2 - j))
```

We can now easily describe an algorithm which looks for all solutions and displays them all (by calling each time the function *display*) with the following

```
SOLVE(Q* ◊ display ◊ cont)
```

4.2 GSAT

We now come to a famous example from local optimization. The GSAT algorithm was proposed in [SLM 92] in order to solve the 3-SAT problem. Such a problem is defined by a set of Boolean variables and a set of clauses which are conjunctions of three literals (variables or negations of variables). The problem consists of finding an assignment of values to variables such that all clauses are satisfied. The algorithm starts with an assignment drawn at random and flips some variables (changing them to their opposite value). The algorithm tries to repair the solution by performing such flips which decrease the number of violated clauses). Such a local move can thus easily be described by :

```
SimpleFlip :: Choice(
  moves x.value := not(x.value)
    with x = some(x in Litteral |
                  exists(c in Clause | involves(c,x) & unsatisfied(c))
  such that delta(card({c in Clause | unsatisfied(c)}) <= 0
  until {c in Clause | unsatisfied(c)} = {})
```

Note here that we have enriched (following the design of LOCALIZER) the choice description with a condition (after the *such that* keyword) constraining the number of violated clauses decrease along the transition (with the *delta* keyword). A random walk can then easily be described by the following expression which applies at most *MaxIter* times a move from the *SimpleFlip* choice. In order for this algorithm not to backtrack, we need to retain only one move from this choice. In order to do so, we introduce the *C/n* which keeps only up to *n* moves from the choice *C*. Moreover, the last line specifies that whenever *penalty() = 0*, the choice should not branch. This is the equivalent of the stopping conditions of LOCALIZER, but it is associated here to the choice (or neighborhood) and not to the global loop. We can then describe a simple random walk by the following expression :

```
SOLVE((SimpleFlip/1)^MaxIter ◊ exit)
```

Note here, that at each choice point, several literals may be flipped until we come to one which decreases the number of unsatisfied clauses. Once this first feasible move has been found, all further branches are discarded.

As has been noted in [MVH 97], such an algorithm is inefficient since the set of unsatisfied clauses is recomputed from scratch for each move. It is wiser to perform more incremental computations and to maintain a few additional structures. An elegant specification of such consistency mechanisms by means of invariants is proposed in [MVH 97]. Such invariants can easily be taken into account in an improved version of the SimpleFlip choice.

We can also define another choice responsible for generating at most *MaxTries* random configurations as well as the full GSAT algorithm described in [MVH 97] :

```
Init :: Choice(
moves   for x in Litteral x.value := random(Boolean),
        post(SAT, initInvariants())
  with i in (1 .. MaxTries)

SOLVE((Init × (SimpleFlip/1)^MaxIter × cont) ◊ exit)
```

What we have done here is to replace the implicit nested loop iteration of LOCALIZER by a limited exploration in a search tree. Although this may not seem an improvement for pure local optimization procedure, it will prove useful for more complex search algorithms. The next table reports some results obtained on a few instances (times are measured on a Spard Ultra 1) :

	MaxIter	*MaxTries*	*time*
pb1 (301 clauses)	300	30	0.17 s.
pb2 (645 clauses)	1500	100	2.8 s.
pb3 (860 clauses)	2000	300	34 s.

Figure 1: GSAT in CLAIRE/SALSA

A few words may be said about the running times. A first version of the GSAT algorithm was coded in CLAIRE (http://www.ens.fr/~laburthe/claire.html). The invariant declaration of LOCALIZER were transformed (by hand) into the few incremental computations necessary for their maintenance : this step transformed 10 lines of LOCALIZER into 30 lines of CLAIRE. This first algorithm ran faster than LOCALIZER for two reasons : the first reason is that the CLAIRE code did not have to interpret at run-time the invariants in order to maintain them; the second reason is that the set operations have been heavily optimized in CLAIRE and may be more efficient than those used in [MVH 97]. The algorithm presented here, replaced the simple iteration loop of our CLAIRE algorithm by its SALSA expression. This resulted in slow down by a factor of 1.5 (over the imperative CLAIRE version). This slow down is due to the fact that the transitions are now considered in a framework where they could be potentially backtracked, which implies an overhead. However, the final running time is competitive, which suggest that using a common language in order to specify local and global search algorithms is a plausible approach from an efficiency point of view.

4.3 Greedy heuristics for disjunctive scheduling

We now describe a few scheduling heuristics which build a schedule in a chronological manner, selecting tasks one after the other and scheduling them as early as possible. Such heuristics are the basis of many algorithms for cumulative [De 92], and job-shop [DT 93] scheduling. An instance of such a heuristic consists of selecting at each step the task which can start earliest among all unscheduled tasks. The basic step of the algorithm can be described by a choice, selecting one task *t* such that for all precedence constraints enforcing that some task *t'* must be performed before *t*, *t'* has already been scheduled.

```
Ins :: Choice(
  moves post(schedule, t.start == t.start.inf)
    with t ∈ {t in Tasks | available(t)}
  sorted by increasing t.start.inf )
```

In order to consider only the best task at each choice point, we sort the moves (i.e., the tasks) by increasing earliest starting time and we limit the exploration of the choice to one branch. Thus, only the task which can start earliest will be considered by the choice. This yields a naïve heuristic (*H1*) which never backtracks :

```
SOLVE((Ins/1)* ◊ exit)
```

This heuristic can be improved if we try to schedule the tasks before assessing their priority. For instance, at each point we can evaluate a lower bound of the makespan of the schedule and we can try to schedule, at each iteration, the task which causes this lower bound to increase the least. Such an improved greedy heuristic performs a limited look-ahead search. We introduce a new SALSA construct : *smallest(T,e,n)* explores all branches of *T* and retains only those yielding the *n* smallest values for the evaluation of *e*. If we take as a lower bound the minimal possible value for the logical variable *Makespan*, the look-ahead greedy heuristic (*H2*) can be described as follows :

```
SOLVE(smallest(Ins,Makespan.inf,1)* ◊ exit)
```

Both these greedy heuristics have been described as partial visits in a search tree. They can hence be improved with the addition of a limited amount of backtracking. We can hence propose a kind of "limited discrepancy search" [HG 95], when two tasks *t* and *t'* yield the same lower bound, instead of breaking the tie arbitrarily, we set a choice point and explore both branches (*schedule t* or *schedule t*). In order to limit the complexity of the algorithm, we may limit such branching to the first 6 levels of the search tree and consider at most two tasks per tie. This yields the *H3* algorithm :

```
SOLVE(smallest(Ins, bound, 2, 0%)⁶ ×
      smallest(Ins, bound, 1)* ◊ display ◊ exit)
```

Note here, that we have added a parameter to the first look-ahead search which specifies that we keep at most two branches from the choice *Ins* and that we only keep those branches which are no more than 0% away from the minimal value of *bound* (thus, we only keep at most 2 tied optimal branches).

A simple comparison of those algorithms *H1* to *H3* is proposed in figure 2 on a few benchmarks from job-shop scheduling. Running times are given on a Sparc Ultra 1 and should be considered as indicative because the lower bound function is not optimized (very naïve). As expected, results get better and running times longer when more exploration is performed. The purpose of SALSA is to enable the user to experiment easily with such variations.

instance	*size*	*optimum*	*H1*	*H2*	*H3*
MT06	6×6	55	88 (0.02s.)	68 (0.05s.)	60 (0.6s.)
MT10	10×10	930	1265 (0.1s.)	1262 (0.5s.)	1220 (39s.)
ORB1	10×10	1059	1478 (0.08s.)	1456 (0.4s.)	1344 (3.8s.)
ORB2	10×10	888	1157 (0.07s.)	1157 (0.3s.)	1038 (4.2s.)
ORB3	10×10	1005	1281 (0.09s.)	1297 (0.4s.)	1229 (9.6s.)

Figure 2: various greedy heuristics on job-shop scheduling problems

4.4 The Lin and Kernighan heuristic for the traveling salesman problem

We now describe a famous local optimization procedure proposed in [LK 73] for the traveling salesman problem (TSP). This procedure is based on *k-opt* moves which remove *k* edges from the circuit and reconnect the *k* disconnected components (chains of vertices or single vertices) by *k* new edges. For most such *k-opt* moves, the set of those *k* old and *k* new edges forms an alternating cycle. The algorithm constructs this cycle progressively, by augmenting an alternating path until a cycle is obtained. A global search algorithm is developped in order to find the best alternating cycle. The cost of the alternating cycle (the sum of the distances of the old edges minus the sum of the distances of the new edges) must be positive in order for the move to improve the tour. The procedure constrains the cost of all alternating paths to be positive, in order to limit the exploration.

Such an algorithm can be easily described my means of SALSA choices. Let *Cities* be the set of vertices, and *d* the distance matrix, let *pred* be the relation encoding the solution (associating to a vertex its predecessor in the tour), and let *possPred* be the relation encoding the graph (associating to a vertex all its possible predecessors). We represent the alternating path by a vector *l* of vertices such that each edge *pred(l[i]),l[i]* is replaced by *pred(l[i+1]),l[i]*. We use a solver (*LK*), which maintains (say, by means of an invariant) the gain of the alternating path (the sum over all vertices *i* in *l*, of *f(i) = d[pred(l[i]), l[i]] - d[pred(l[i+1]), l[i]]*) and which triggers a failure whenever this gain becomes negative. We introduce two choices, initiating and augmenting the alternating cycle, by adding a vertex to the vector *l* :

```
  Init :: Choice(
    moves post(LK, l := list(x))
       with x ∈ {x in Cities |
                              exists(y in possPred(x) | d[y,x] <
d[pred(x),x]]})

  Augment :: Choice(
    moves   post(LK, l :add x)
       with x ∈ Cities
    until  (length(l) > 1 & l[1] = l[length(l)]) )
```

The global search algorithm for finding one local move, as it is proposed in the original paper [LK 73], backtracks on the first two levels of the search tree (considering all possibilities for the two first vertices of *l*), and from then on, only considers the addition of the vertex yielding maximal gain. It can thus be described as follows :

```
  SOLVE(largest(Init × Augment × largest(Augment,gain,1)*, gain, 1))
```

Once the best move has been found, we can perform it (flipping the edges along the alternating cycle) by calling the *performMove* function. The full algorithm is a standard hill-climbing procedure which applies such local moves until no more improvement can be made and can be easily specified as follows :

```
  SOLVE( (largest(Init × Augment × largest(Augment,gain,1)*, gain, 1)
                × performMove)* ◊ exit)
```

Hence, using SALSA, we have proposed a simple description of a well-known complex algorithm. Moreover, with such a description, it is easy to experiment with variations of this algorithm.

4.5 Hybrid insertion heuristics for vehicle routing

This section is devoted to a real hybrid algorithm mixing local and global search intended for vehicle routing. The problem can be stated as follows : given a set of points and a central depot, find a set of routes covering all points, each route starting and ending in the depot, and respecting some side constraints (limited route length, limited amount of goods transported along a route, time windows, etc.). The objective is to find a solution with minimal total length. The insertion algorithm starts with empty routes and selects the tasks one by one and inserts them in a route (such algorithms are widely used heuristics in practical routing because they are able to handle many additional constraints). The performance of such insertion heuristics can be significantly improved if a limited amount of local optimization is performed after each insertion [GHL 94], [Ru 95], [CL 98]. This leads to a complex algorithm using global search as a general framework (a greedy heuristic with a limited look-ahead exploration of the branches for each insertion), and using local search at each node of the search tree. We show here how SALSA can be used to program a simplified version of this algorithm; we refer the reader to [CL 98] for more details.

We start by describing the simple greedy heuristic. Inserting a task *t* in a route *r* can be described as a choice. We consider all pairs of adjacent vertices *(x,y)* in *r* and try to insert *t* between *x* and *y* (by posting to a "*dispatch*" solver the information that *x* and *t* are now linked by an edge in the route *r* as well as *t* and *y*). Note that we define a parametric choice (*t* and *r* are its two parameters) :

```
Insert(t:Task, r:Route) :: Choice(
  moves post(dispatch, (link(x,t,r), link(t,y,r)))
    with (x,y) ∈ edges(r)
  sorted by increasing insertionCost(t,x,y) )
```

From such a choice, we will retain only the edge *(x,y)* with the least insertion cost, by limiting the number of branches to 1 (since the branches are sorted by increasing insertion costs).

In order to specify the procedure used for selecting the route in which a task is inserted, we need to introduce a new SALSA control structure : choices can be made from SALSA terms using the *moves from* keyword followed by a choice expression. This SALSA expression must be either a straightforward choice, the union of choices or the lookahead exploration (*smallest/greatest*) of a SALSA expression. A union of choices $U_{x \in E}(C(x))$ is the choice which yields all transitions of the choices *C(x)*for *x* in the set *E*.

In order to insert one task *t*, we only keep, for each route, the best possible insertion place : this can be described by keeping for each route *r*, only one branch of the choice *Insert(t,r)*) and taking the union of these choices.

```
Insert(t:Task) :: Choice(
  moves from ∪r ∈ Routes (Insert(t,r) / 1) )
```

Among all these possibilities of insertion, we select only the one yielding the minimal total cost. And the greedy algorithm can hence be described as follows :

```
OneInsert :: Choice(
  moves from smallest(Insert(t), TotalLength(), 1)
    with t = some(t in Tasks | unaffected(t)) )

SOLVE(OneInsert* ◊ exit)
```

We now come to incremental local optimization, which will be performed after each insertion. Below, we describe two choices responsible for local moves. The first choice is responsible for a 2-opt local move on the route to which *t* belongs (2-opt is a standard optimization procedure for routing problems which amounts to erase 2 edges *xy* and *uz* from a route to replace them by the edges *xu* and *yz*). The second choice is responsible for a 3-opt optimization which concerns edges from 2 or 3 different routes (we replace the edges *tu*, *xy* and *zw* by *xu*, *zy* and *tw*). Both kinds of local moves, are accepted only when they yield an improvement in the total length of the solution.

```
TwoOpt(t:Task) :: Choice(
   moves post(dispatch, (link(x,u,r), link(y,z,r)))
      with r = route(t),
           ((x,y), (u,z)) ∈ SortedPairsOf(edges(r))
   such that delta(Length(r)) < 0 )

ThreeOpt(t:Task) :: Choice(
   moves post(dispatch, (link(x,u,r1), link(z,y,r2), link(t,w,r)))
      with r = route(t), u = next(t),
           r1 ∈ RoutesCloseTo(r), r2 ∈ RoutesCloseTo(r),
           (x,y) ∈ edges(r1), (z,w) ∈ edges(r2)
   such that delta(TotalLength) < 0 )
```

We can now describe an enriched version of the heuristic which performs a limited amount of local optimization during the insertion : for each route *r*, after having found the best pair of points between which *t* should be inserted and before evaluating the insertion cost, we perform at most *n* steps of 2-opt in order to optimize *r*. This enables us to perform a more informed choice among all possible insertions. Then, once the best insertion has been chosen and performed, we further optimize the solution by performing at most *m* steps of 3-opt optimization, which may recombine the route in which the task has been inserted with other routes.

```
SmartInsert:: Choice(
  moves from smallest(Insert(t) × (TwoOpt(t)/1)ⁿ,TotalLength(),1)
                       × (ThreeOpt(t)/1)ᵐ
   with t = some(t in Tasks | unaffected(t)) )
```

The final procedure can then be described as

```
SOLVE((SmartInsert/1)* ◊ exit)
```

We have just described here, with 25 lines of SALSA code a hybrid algorithm for vehicle routing. By looking from top down at this specification, one can see that it is a greedy algorithm (it is of the form $C/1^*$), that the basic step performs a look-ahead exploration of a choice, and that the basic choice uses various moves and hill-climbing random walks. Compared to an imperative implementation of such a hybrid algorithm, it is much more concise and it gives a global view of the algorithm (which is useful for understanding what the algorithm does). This SALSA specification is independant from the data structures, the consistency mechanisms, as well as the computation environment (distributed or sequential). It is thus a high-level description of the control of the algorithm, complementary with a logic statement of the problem.

5. Operational Semantics

An operational semantics has been proposed for SALSA in [CL97]. The execution of SALSA expressions is described formally by a set of transition rules in a calculus of distributed processes. A process is created each time a new node is expanded in the search tree. The processes have access to two different kinds of data : local data which is associated to the search node (for example, the state of the domains) and global data which is used for communication between processes (for example, in branch and bound optimization, when a process comes to a solution, a variable shared by all processes and containing the value of the best solution found so far is updated).

In this semantics, the evaluation of a SALSA expression corresponds to the evolution of a set of processes which represent the frontier of the tree (those nodes which are the limit between the part of the tree which has been explored and what has not yet been explored). The different processes are not synchronized, which means that the exploration can follow any strategy (depth first, breadth first, or anything else). Since the processes are not fully independent (because of the synchronization performed by the global environment), this leaves the possibility of undeterministic executions for SALSA programs (for instance, different executions yielding different sequences of solutions can be obtained from a single SALSA branch and bound optimization).

A proprietary prototype has been implemented at Thomson/CSF after this semantics. It is implemented as a code generator : SALSA expressions are compiled into CLAIRE code, which, in turn is compiled into C++ code. On average, one line of SALSA generates 10-15 lines of CLAIRE which, in turn, generate about 50-100 lines of C++.

Conclusion

In this paper, we have stressed the importance of hybrid algorithms for combinatorial problem solving with constraints and we have proposed a language for specifying the control of such algorithms. We have illustrated the use of the SALSA language on various examples from combinatorial optimization, from standard CP programs or local optimization algorithms to complex combinations of local and global search. For those examples, the SALSA code yields a concise specification of the control of the algorithm. Hence, SALSA is a step in the quest for elegant and declarative descriptions of complex algorithms.

In addition, we have implemented a prototype, generating CLAIRE code from SALSA expressions. Such a tool gives the programmer the ability to experiment easily many variations of an algorithm, which is valuable for experimenting new ideas or tuning hybrid algorithms. SALSA can be implemented on other systems than CLAIRE and we hope that this preliminary work will motivate other proposals from the CP community concerning languages and environments for algorithms combining local and global search.

Acknowledgments

The theoretical fondations of SALSA were developped within the ESPRIT CHIC-2 project that studies hybrid algorithms. We would like to thank Éric Jacopin, Pascal van Hentenryck, Laurent Michel, Laurent Perron and Jean-François Puget for fruitful discussions.

References

[AS 97] K.R. Apt, A. Schaerf, *Search and Imperative Programming*, Proc. of the 24th ACM Symposium on Principles of Programming Languages (POPL'97), ACM Press, 1997

[CL 98] Y. Caseau, F. Laburthe, *Heuristics for Large Constrained Vehicle Routing Problems*, submitted for publication, march 1998.

[CL 97] Y. Caseau, F. Laburthe, *SaLSA: A Specification Language for Search Algorithms*, LIENS report 97-11, École Normale Supérieure, 1997.

[DT 93] M. Dell'Amico & M. Trubian. *Applying Tabu-Search to the Job-Shop Scheduling Problem.* Annals of Op. Research, **41**, p. 231-252, 1993.

[De 92] E. Demeulemeester, *Optimal Algorithms for various classes of multiple resource constrained project scheduling problems*, unpublished PhD. dissertation, Université Catholique de Louvain, Belgique, 1992.

[FG 93] R. Fourer, D. MacGay, B.W. Kernighan, *AMPL: A Modelling Language for Mathematical Programming,* Brook/Cole Publishing Company, 1993.

[GHL94] M. Gendreau, A. Hertz, G. Laporte. *A Tabu Search Heuristic for the Vehicle Routing Problem,* Management Science, **40**, p. 1276-1290, 1994.

[HS 98] M. Hanus, F. Steiner, *Controlling Search in Functional Logic Programs*, technical report, RWTH Aachen, 1998.

[HG 95] W. Harvey, M. Ginsberg, *Limited Discrepancy Search*, Proceedings of the 14th IJCAI, p. 607-615, Morgan Kaufmann, 1995.

[JL 87] J. Jaffar, J.-L. Lassez, *Constraint Logic Programming*, Proceedings of the ACM symposium on Principles of Programming Languages, 1987.

[LK 73] S. Lin, B.W. Kernighan, *An Effective Heuristic for the Traveling Salesman Problem.* Operations Research **21**, 1973.

[Llo 87] J.W. Lloyd, *Foundation of Logic Programming,* Spinger, 1987.

[MS 96] D. Martin, P. Shmoys, *A time-based approach to the Jobshop problem*, Proc. of IPCO'5, M. Queyranne ed., LCNS 1084, Springer, 1996.

[MVH 97] L. Michel, P. Van Hentenryck, *Localizer: A Modeling Language for Local Search.* Proc. of CP'97, LNCS 1330, Springer, 1997.

[ML 97] J.-M. Labat, L. Mynard, *Oscillation, Heuristic Ordering and Pruning in Neighborhood Search.* Proc. of CP'97, G. Smolka ed., LNCS 1330, Springer, 1997.

[Pea 84] J. Pearl, *Heuristics: Intelligent Search Strategies for Computer Problem Solving*, Addison-Wesley, 1984.

[PG 96] G. Pesant, M. Gendreau, *A View of Local Search in Constraint Programming*, proc. of CP'96, LNCS 1118, p. 353-366, Springer 1996.

[PGPR 96] G. Pesant, M. Gendreau, J.-Y. Potvin, J.-M. Rousseau, *An Exact Constraint Logic Programming Algorithm for the Travelling Salesman with Time Windows*, to appear in Transportation Science, 1996.

[Ru 95] R. Russell, *Hybrid Heuristics for the Vehicle Routing Problem with Time Windows*, Transportation Science, **29** (2), may 1995.

[SS 94] C. Schulte, G. Smolka, *Encapsulated Search for Higher-order Concurrent Constraint Programming,* Proc. of ILPS'94, M. Bruynooghe ed., p. 505-520, MIT Press, 1994.

[Sch 97] C. Schulte, *Oz explorer: A Visual Constraint Programming Tool,* Proc. 14th ICLP, L. Naish ed., p. 286-300, MIT Press, 1997.

[SLM 92] B. Selman, H. Levesque, D. Mitchell, *A New Method for Solving Hard Satisfiability Problems* Proc. of AAAI-92, p. 440-446, 1992.

Random Constraint Satisfaction: Theory Meets Practice*

Ewan MacIntyre[1], Patrick Prosser[1], Barbara Smith[2], and Toby Walsh[1]

[1] The APES Research Group, Department of Computer Science, University of Strathclyde, Glasgow, United Kingdom. Email {em,pat,tw}@cs.strath.ac.uk
[2] The APES Research Group, School of Computer Studies, University of Leeds, United Kingdom. Email bms@scs.leeds.ac.uk

Abstract. We study the experimental consequences of a recent theoretical result by Achlioptas *et al.* that shows that conventional models of random problems are trivially insoluble in the limit. We survey the literature to identify experimental studies that lie within the scope of this result. We then estimate theoretically and measure experimentally the size at which problems start to become trivially insoluble. Our results demonstrate that most (but not all) of these experimental studies are luckily unaffected by this result. We also study an alternative model of random problems that does not suffer from this asymptotic weakness. We show that, at a typical problem size used in experimental studies, this model looks similar to conventional models. Finally, we generalize this model so that we can independently adjust the constraint tightness and density.

1 Introduction

One of the most exciting areas in AI in recent years has been the study of phase transition behaviour. In a seminal paper that inspired many later researchers, Cheeseman, Kanefsky, and Taylor demonstrated that the hardest search problems often occur around a rapid transition in solubility [2]. Problems from such transitions in solubility are routinely used to benchmark algorithms for many different NP-complete problems. Experimental results about phase transition behaviour have come thick and fast since the publication of [2]. For example, in random 3-SAT, the phase transition was quickly shown to occur when the ratio of clauses to variables is approximately 4.3 [14]. Unfortunately, theory has often proved more difficult. A recent result proves that the width of the phase transition in random 3-SAT narrows as problems increases in size [3]. However, we only have rather loose but hard won bounds on its actual location [4, 13]. For random constraint satisfaction problems, Achlioptas *et al.* recently provided a more negative theoretical result [1]. They show that the conventional random models are almost surely trivially insoluble for large enough problems. This paper studies the impact of this theoretical result on experimental studies.

* Supported by EPSRC awards GR/L/24014 and GR/K/65706. The authors wish to thank other members of the APES research group. We are especially grateful to Ian Gent who derived the expected number of cliques in a random graph.

2 Constraint satisfaction

A binary constraint satisfaction problem consists of a set of variables, each with a domain of values, and a set of binary constraints. Each constraint rules out a subset of the possible values for a pair of variables. Each assignment of values to variables ruled out is called a nogood. Associated with each problem is a constraint graph. This has variables as vertices and edges between variables that appear in nogoods. The constraint satisfaction decision problem is to decide if there is an assignment of values to variables so that none of the constraints are violated.

Four models of random problems are used in most experimental and theoretical studies. In each model, we generate a constraint graph G, and then for each edge in this graph, choose pairs of incompatible values. The models differ in how we generate the constraint graph and how we choose incompatible values. In each case, we can describe problems by the tuple $\langle n, m, p_1, p_2 \rangle$, where n is the number of variables, m is the uniform domain size, p_1 is a measure of the density of the constraint graph, and p_2 is a measure of the tightness of the constraints.

model A: with probability p_1, we select each one of the $n(n-1)/2$ possible edges in G, and for each edge with probability p_2 we pick each one of the m^2 possible pairs of values as incompatible;

model B: we uniformly select exactly $p_1 n(n-1)/2$ edges for G, and for each edge we uniformly pick exactly $p_2 m^2$ pairs of values as incompatible;

model C: with probability p_1, we select each one of the $n(n-1)/2$ possible edges in G, and for each edge we uniformly pick exactly $p_2 m^2$ pairs of values as incompatible;

model D: we uniformly select exactly $p_1 n(n-1)/2$ edges for G, and for each edge with probability p_2 we pick each one of the m^2 possible pairs of values as incompatible.

3 Phase transitions

Constraint satisfaction algorithms are now routinely benchmarked using random problems from one of these four models. To help unify experimental studies with different problems, Gent *et al.* [8] define the constrainedness, κ of an ensemble of combinatorial problems as,

$$\kappa =_{\text{def}} 1 - \frac{\log_2(\langle Sol \rangle)}{N}$$

where N is the log base 2 of the size of the state space, and $\langle Sol \rangle$ is the expected number of these states that are solutions. Since $0 \leq \langle Sol \rangle \leq 2^N$, it follows that $\kappa \in [0, \infty)$. If $\kappa \approx 0$ then problems are very under-constrained and soluble. It is usually very easy to find one of the many solutions. If $\kappa \approx \infty$ then problems are very over-constrained and insoluble. It is usually relatively easy to prove their insolubility. If $\kappa \approx 1$ then problems are on the "knife-edge" between solubility and insolubility. It is often difficult to find solutions or prove the insolubility of such problems. This definition of constrainedness has been used to locate phase transitions behaviour both in NP-complete problems like constraint satisfaction, and in polynomial problems like enforcing arc consistency [5].

Consider, for example, binary constraint satisfaction problems from model B. The state space has m^n states, one for each possible assignment of values to the n variables. Each of the $p_1 n(n-1)/2$ edges in the constraint graph rules out a fraction $(1-p_2)$ of the possible assignments of values to variables. Thus,

$$\langle Sol \rangle = m^n (1-p_2)^{p_1 n(n-1)/2} \qquad N = n \log_2(m)$$

Substituting these into the definition of constrainedness gives,

$$\kappa = \frac{n-1}{2} p_1 \log_m \left(\frac{1}{1-p_2}\right)$$

Gent *el al.* [7] show experimentally that rapid transitions in solubility occur around $\kappa \approx 1$ for a selection of model B problems with between 10 and 110 variables and domains of sizes between 3 and 50. Problem hardness for a wide variety of algorithms tends to peak around these transitions.

4 The problem with random problems

Achlioptas *et al.* [1] identify a shortcoming of all four random models. They prove that if $p_2 \geq 1/m$ then, as n goes to infinity, there almost surely exists a *flawed* variable, one which has every value *unsupported*. A value for a variable is unsupported if, when the value is assigned to the variable, there exists an adjacent variable in the constraint graph that cannot be assigned a value without violating a constraint. A problem with a flawed variable cannot have a solution. They argue that therefore "*... the currently used models are asymptotically uninteresting except, perhaps, for a small region of their parameter space ...*" (when $p_2 < 1/m$). Further, they claim that "*... the threshold-like picture given by experimental results [with these models] is misleading, since the problems with defining parameters in what is currently perceived as the underconstrained region (because a solution can be found fast) are in fact overconstrained for large n (obviously, larger than the values used in experiments) ...*". Note that this result does not apply to problems in which the constraints have certain types of structure. For example, if each constraint only allows variables to take different values then problems encode graph colouring, which has good asymptotic properties.

Achlioptas *et al.* [1] propose an alternative random problem class, model E which does not suffer from this asymptotic shortcoming, and which does not separate the generation of the constraint graph from the selection of the nogoods. In this model, we select uniformly, independently and with repetitions, $pm^2n(n-1)/2$ nogoods out of the $m^2n(n-1)/2$ possible. They prove that if a random instance generated using this model has less than $n/2$ nogoods then it almost surely has a solution (theorem 6, page 113). They conjecture that substantially stronger bounds could be derived to increase the number of allowed nogoods. We note that model E is not entirely novel since Williams and Hogg study random problems with both a fixed number of nogoods picked uniformly, and with an uniform probability of including a nogood [15]. As Achlioptas *et al.* themselves remark [1], the expected number of repetitions in model E is usually insignificant (for instance, it is $O(1)$ when the number of nogoods is $\Theta(n)$), and repetitions are only allowed to simplify the theoretical analysis. The differences between model E and the models of Williams and Hogg are therefore likely to be slight.

5 Experimental practice

Achlioptas *et al.*'s result does not apply to random problems for which $p_2 < 1/m$. To study the practical significance of this restriction, we surveyed the literature from 1994 (when phase transition experiments with random constraint satisfaction problems first started to appear), covering all papers in the proceedings of CP, AAAI, ECAI and IJCAI which gave details of experiments on random constraint satisfaction problems. The results of this survey are summarized in Tables 1 and 2. An experimental study is deemed "inapplicable" if the problem sets tested include an ensemble of problems with $p_2 < 1/m$.

Conference	Inapplicable studies	Total studies
AAAI-94	2	3
ECAI-94	0	4
CP-95	3	4
IJCAI-95	1	5
AAAI-96	0	4
CP-96	3	5
ECAI-96	1	5
AAAI-97	2	4
CP-97	0	7
IJCAI-97	0	1
totals	12	42

Table 1. Summary of results of the literature survey.

Just over a quarter of papers include problems to which the results of [1] do not apply. The most common exception are random problems with $m = 3$ and $p_2 = 1/9$ or $2/9$. Model B is the most common model of generation, followed by model A. Whilst a significant number of papers use problems outside the scope of [1], nearly three quarters use problem sets that are vulnerable to these criticisms. In addition, all of the papers which included inapplicable problem sets also used some instances with $p_2 \geq 1/m$. In conclusion therefore, the results of [1] apply to most published experiments.

Conference	Author initials	Model	$\langle n, m\rangle$	$p_2 < 1/m$?
AAAI-94	[DF,RD]	B	$\langle 25-250, 3\rangle$	$p_2 = 1/9, 2/9$
	[DF,RD]	B	$\langle 25-275, 3\rangle$	$p_2 = 1/9, 2/9$
			$\langle 15-60, 6\rangle$	$p_2 = 4/36$
			$\langle 15-35, 9\rangle$	no
	[NY,YO,HH]	B	$\langle 20, 10\rangle$	no
ECAI-94	[PP]	D	$\langle 20, 10\rangle$, $\langle 20, 20\rangle$, $\langle 30, 10\rangle$	no
	[BMS]	B	$\langle 8, 10\rangle$	no
	[DL]	B	$\langle 10, 20\rangle$	no
	[DS,ECF]	A	$\langle 50, 8\rangle$	no
CP-95	[IPG,EM,PP,TW]	B	$\langle 10-110, 3\rangle$	$p_2 = 2/9$
			$\langle 10, 10\rangle$, $\langle 20, 10\rangle$, $\langle 10, 5-50\rangle$, ...	no
	[JL,PM]	A	$\langle 10, 10\rangle$	no
	[FB,PR]	B	$\langle 25, 3\rangle$	$p_2 = 1/9$
			$\langle 35, 6\rangle$, $\langle 50, 6\rangle$	$p_2 = 4/36$
			$\langle 15, 9\rangle$, $\langle 35, 9\rangle$	no
	[FB,AG]	B	$\langle 25, 3\rangle$	$p_2 = 2/9$
			$\langle 25, 6\rangle$, $\langle 15, 9\rangle$	no
IJCAI-95	[ECF,PDH]	A	$\langle 50, 8\rangle$	no
	[DF,RD]	B	$\langle 125, 3\rangle$	$p_2 = 1/9$
			$\langle 35, 6\rangle$	$p_2 = 4/36$
			$\langle 250, 3\rangle$, $\langle 50, 6\rangle$, $\langle 35, 9\rangle$, ...	no
	[PM,JL]	D	$\langle 10, 10\rangle$, $\langle 20, 10\rangle$, $\langle 30, 10\rangle$	no
	[KK,RD]	B	$\langle 100, 8\rangle$	no
	[BMS,SAG]	B	$\langle 20, 10\rangle$, $\langle 50, 10\rangle$	no
AAAI-96	[AC,PJ]	B	$\langle 16, 8\rangle$, $\langle 32, 8\rangle$	no
	[ECF,CDE]	B	$\langle 100, 6\rangle$	no
	[IPG,EM,PP,TW]	B	$\langle 20, 10\rangle$	no
	[KK,RD]	B	$\langle 100, 8\rangle$, $\langle 125, 6\rangle$, $\langle 150, 4\rangle$	no
CP-96	[CB,JCR]	B	$\langle 35, 6\rangle$	$p_2 = 4/36$
			$\langle 125, 3\rangle$, $\langle 350, 3\rangle$	$p_2 = 1/9$
			$\langle 35, 9\rangle$, $\langle 50, 6\rangle$, $\langle 50, 20\rangle$, ...	no
	[DAC,JF,IPG,EM,NT,TW]	B	$\langle 20, 10\rangle$	no
	[IPG,EM,PP,BMS,TW]	B	$\langle 20-50, 10\rangle$	no
	[JL,PM]	B	$\langle 15, 5\rangle$	$p_2 = 1/25 - 4/25$
			$\langle 10, 10\rangle$	$p_2 = 1/100 - 9/100$
	[RJW]	A	$\langle 30, 5\rangle$, $\langle 100, 5\rangle$	$p_2 = 0.1$
ECAI-96	[JEB,EPKT,NRW]	B	$\langle 50, 10\rangle$	no
	[BC,GV,DM,PB]	B	$\langle 50, 10\rangle$, $\langle 20, 5\rangle$	no
	[SAG,BMS]	B	$\langle 30-70, 10\rangle$	no
	[ACMK,EPKT,JEB]	B	$\langle 30, 5\rangle$	$p_2 = 0.12$
			$\langle 40, 5\rangle$	$p_2 = 0.08$
			$\langle 60, 5\rangle$	$p_2 = 0.04$
			$\langle 10, 5\rangle$, $\langle 20, 5\rangle$, $\langle 10, 10\rangle$, ...	no
	[JL,PM]	B	$\langle 10, 10\rangle$	no
AAAI-97	[AM,SES,GS]	B	$\langle 6-12, 9\rangle$	no
	[DRG,WKJ,WSH]	B	$\langle 10, 5\rangle$	no
	[IPG,EM,PP,TW]	B	$\langle 10-120, 3\rangle$	$p_2 = 2/9$
			$\langle 10, 10-100\rangle$	no
	[DF,IR,LV]	B	$\langle 20, 4\rangle$	$p_2 = 0.125$
			$\langle 150, 3\rangle$	$p_2 = 0.222$
			$\langle 20-75, 6\rangle$, $\langle 20, 10\rangle$	no
CP-97	[IPG,JLU]	D	$\langle 10, 10\rangle$	no
	[IR,DF]	B	$\langle 100, 8\rangle$	no
	[DS,ECF]	B	$\langle 20, 20\rangle$, $\langle 40, 20\rangle$	no
	[BMS,SAG]	B	$\langle 10, 10\rangle$	no
	[PG,JKH]	B	$\langle 50, 10\rangle$, $\langle 100, 15\rangle$, $\langle 250, 25\rangle$, ...	no
	[ED,CB]	B	$\langle 100, 20\rangle$	no
	[IPG,EM, PP, PS, TW]	B	$\langle 20-70, 10\rangle$	no
IJCAI-97	[RD, CB]	B	$\langle 20, 10\rangle$	no

Table 2. Parameters and models used in some previous studies of random constraint satisfaction problems.

6 Probability of flawed variables

As Achlioptas *et al.* themselves suggest [1], previous experimental studies will not have been greatly influenced by the existence of flawed variables since problem sizes are usually too small. Using the Markov inequality, they give a first moment bound on the probability of a flawed variable,

$$\Pr\{\text{problem has a flawed variable}\} \leq n(1-(1-p_2^m)^n)^m$$

For example, for the popular $\langle n, 10, 1, 1/2\rangle$ problem class, they calculate that the probability of a flawed variable is less than 10^{-5} even for n as large as 200. At what size of problem and sample do flawed variables start to occur?

By making a few simplifying assumptions, we can estimate the probability of a flawed variable with reasonable accuracy. This estimate might be used to determine parameters for experimental studies. Our first assumption is that each variable is connected to exactly $p_1(n-1)$ others. In practice, some variables have a greater degree, whilst others have a lesser degree. Fortunately, our experiments show that this mean-field approximation does not introduce a large error into the estimate. We also assume independence between the probabilities that the different variables have at least one unflawed value. The probability that there are no flawed variables is then simply the product of the probabilities that the variables have at least one unflawed value. For model A problems, we have,

$$\begin{aligned}
&\Pr\{\text{problem has a flawed variable}\}\\
&= 1 - \Pr\{\text{there are no flawed variables}\}\\
&= 1 - (\Pr\{\text{a variable has at least one unflawed value}\})^n\\
&= 1 - (1 - \Pr\{\text{every value for the variable is flawed}\})^n\\
&= 1 - (1 - (\Pr\{\text{a value for the variable is flawed}\})^m)^n\\
&= 1 - (1 - (\Pr\{\text{value inconsistent with every value of an adjacent variable}\})^m)^n\\
&= 1 - (1 - (1 - \Pr\{\text{value consistent with a value of every adjacent variable}\})^m)^n\\
&= 1 - (1 - (1 - (\Pr\{\text{value consistent with a value of an adjacent variable}\})^{p_1(n-1)})^m)^n\\
&= 1 - (1 - (1 - (1 - \Pr\{\text{value inconsistent with every value of adjacent variable}\})^{p_1(n-1)})^m)^n\\
&= 1 - (1 - (1 - (1 - (\Pr\{\text{value inconsistent with a value of adjacent variable}\})^m)^{p_1(n-1)})^m)^n
\end{aligned}$$

For model A, the probability that a given value is inconsistent with every value of an adjacent variable is p_2. Hence, we obtain the estimate,

$$\Pr\{\text{problem has a flawed variable}\} = 1 - (1 - (1 - (1 - p_2^m)^{p_1(n-1)})^m)^n$$

A similar derivation can be made for model B problems. In this model each constraint is picked uniformly from the ${}_{m^2}C_{p_2 m^2}$ possible binary constraints. If we assign a value to one of the variables involved in a constraint, then ${}_{m^2-m}C_{p_2 m^2-m}$ of the possible constraints have nogoods that rule out all the values for the other variable. Hence, the probability that a particular value for a variable is inconsistent with every value for an adjacent variable is given by,

$$\Pr\{\text{value inconsistent with every value of adjacent variable}\} = \binom{m^2-m}{p_2 m^2 - m} \Big/ \binom{m^2}{p_2 m^2}$$

Thus, for model B problems, we obtain the estimate,

$$\Pr\{\text{problem has a flawed variable}\} = 1-(1-(1-(1-\binom{m^2-m}{p_2m^2-m}/\binom{m^2}{p_2m^2})^{p_1(n-1)})^m)^n$$

Note that we have assumed independence between the probabilities that the m different values for a given variable are flawed. The probability that every value for a variable is flawed is then simply the product of the probabilities that each individual value is flawed. Whilst this independence assumption is valid for model A, it is not strictly true for model B.

7 Problem size

We can use these estimates for the probability of flawed variables to determine when flawed variables will start to occur in experimental studies. To test the accuracy of these estimates and to compare them with the simpler first moment bound, we generated random problems from the popular model B and calculated the fraction with a flawed variable. Since flawed variables are more likely in dense constraint graphs, we generated problems with complete constraint graphs (i.e. with $p_1 = 1$). As in other studies (e.g. [12, 6]), we also generated a separate set of problems in which the average degree of the vertices in the constraint graph is kept constant. That is, we vary p_1 as $1/(n-1)$. As we argue in Section 9, the constraint tightness at the phase transition then remains roughly constant. Keeping the average degree constant also reduces the probability of flawed variables occurring. In Table 3, we give the results for $\langle n, 10, 1, 1/2\rangle$ and $\langle n, 10, 19/(n-1), 1/2\rangle$ with n from 200 to 4000. In this (and indeed all the subsequent experiments) our estimate for the probability of a problem having a flawed variable is very close to the observed fraction of problems with flawed variables, and much closer than the first moment bound to the observed fraction of flawed variables.

With complete constraint graphs, flawed variables are observed in samples of 1000 when the problems have 500 or more variables. This is beyond the size of problems typically solved with systematic procedures but potentially within the reach of approximation or local search algorithms. By comparison, with constraint graphs of constant average degree, flawed variables are not observed in samples of 1000 even when the problems have thousands of variables. Because of the greater homogeneity of model B problems, we expect flawed variables to be less likely than in model A. Our estimates for the probability of a flawed variable support this conjecture. For example, for $\langle 1000, 10, 1, 1/2\rangle$ problems, our estimate for the probability that a model A problem has a flawed variable is 0.99986 whilst for a model B problem it is 0.275.

With constraint graphs of constant average degree, we can estimate when we expect to observe flawed variables. If $p_1 = \gamma/(n-1)$ and a fraction f of problems contain flawed variables then, by rearranging our estimates for the probability of a flawed variable, the number of variables n_f in model A problems is,

$$n_f = \frac{\log(1-f)}{\log(1-(1-(1-p_2^m)^\gamma)^m)}$$

n	sample size	fraction with flawed variables	estimate for Pr{flawed variable}	1st moment bound
200	10^6	0.000000	0.000000	0.000006
500	10^4	0.0005	0.0006	0.0370
1000	10^3	0.272	0.275	>1
1200	10^3	0.753	0.755	>1
1500	10^3	1.000	0.999	>1
2000	10^3	1.000	1.000	>1
4000	10^3	1.000	1.000	>1

(a) $\langle n, 10, 1, 1/2\rangle$

n	sample size	fraction with flawed variables	estimate for Pr{flawed variable}	1st moment bound
200	10^3	0.000	0.000	0.000
500	10^3	0.000	0.000	0.037
1000	10^3	0.000	0.000	>1
1500	10^3	0.000	0.000	>1
2000	10^3	0.000	0.000	>1
4000	10^3	0.000	0.000	>1

(b) $\langle n, 10, 19/(n-1), 1/2\rangle$

Table 3. The impact of flawed variables on model B problems with a domain size of 10 and: (a) complete constraint graphs; (b) constraint graphs of constant average degree.

And in model B problems,

$$n_f = \frac{\log(1-f)}{\log(1-(1-(1-\binom{m^2-m}{p_2 m^2 - m}/\binom{m^2}{p_2 m^2})^{\gamma})^m)}$$

For instance, for model B problems with similar parameters to those of Table 3 (i.e. $m = 10$, $\gamma = 19$ and $p_2 = 1/2$), $n_{1/1000} \approx 3.2 * 10^{17}$ and $n_{1/2} \approx 2.2 * 10^{19}$. That is, problems need more than 10^{17} variables before we start to observe flawed variables in samples of 1000 problem instances, and more than 10^{19} variables before half contain a flawed variable. As a consequence, at this domain size, constraint tightness, and degree of the constraint graph, experimental studies can safely ignore flawed variables.

With smaller domain sizes, we expect flawed variables to be more prevalent. To test this hypothesis, we generated problems with $m = 3$, $p_2 = 1/m$ and either complete constraint graphs or constraint graphs of constant average degree. Note that, for model B, $p_2 = 1/m$ is the smallest possible value which gives flawed variables. If $p_2 < 1/m$ then at least one value for each variable *must* be supported as each constraint rules out strictly less than m possible values. Note also that these problems have the same domain size and same constraint tightness as 3-colouring problems. Table 4 gives the results for $\langle n, 3, 1, 1/3\rangle$ and $\langle n, 3, 19/(n-1), 1/3\rangle$ with $n = 10$ to 2000. With complete constraint graphs, flawed variables occur with a significant frequency in problems with as few as 20 variables. This is despite p_2 being given the minimal possible value. With constraint graphs of constant average degree, although flawed variables occur in problems with as few as 20 variables, their frequency increases much more slowly with n. We need a thousand or more variables to ensure that problems almost always include a flawed variable. By comparison, with complete constraint graphs, we need just 60 or so variables. Some of the experiments surveyed in Section 5 used random problems containing hundreds of variables with $m = 3$ and $p_2 = 1/3$. Flawed variables may therefore have had a significant impact on these experiments.

n	sample size	fraction with flawed variables	estimate for Pr{flawed variable}	1st moment bound
10	10^3	0.006	0.011	0.311
20	10^3	0.143	0.156	> 1
30	10^3	0.504	0.536	> 1
40	10^3	0.869	0.882	> 1
50	10^3	0.987	0.990	> 1
60	10^3	1.000	1.000	> 1

(a) $\langle n, 3, 1, 1/3 \rangle$

n	sample size	fraction with flawed variables	estimate for Pr{flawed variable}	1st moment bound
20	10^3	0.143	0.156	> 1
50	10^3	0.318	0.345	> 1
100	10^3	0.524	0.571	> 1
200	10^3	0.796	0.816	> 1
500	10^3	0.986	0.985	> 1
1000	10^3	0.999	1.000	> 1
2000	10^3	1.000	1.000	> 1

(b) $\langle n, 3, 19/(n-1), 1/3 \rangle$

Table 4. The impact of flawed variables on model B problems with a small domain size and: (a) complete constraint graph; (b) constraint graph of constant average degree.

8 Model E

At the sizes typically used in previous experimental studies, how does model E differ from the conventional models? To explore this issue, we compared problems from model E with $n = 20$ and $m = 10$ against problems of a similar size from the popular model B. As we argue in the next section, model E quickly gives problems with complete constraint graphs. We therefore used model B problems with $p_1 = 1$ as a comparison. For model B, we generated 1000 problems at each value of p_2 between 1/100 and 99/100. For model E, we generated 1000 problems at each value of p from 1/190 to 500/190 in steps of 1/190. Note that model E allows for repetitions when selecting nogoods so p can be greater than 1.

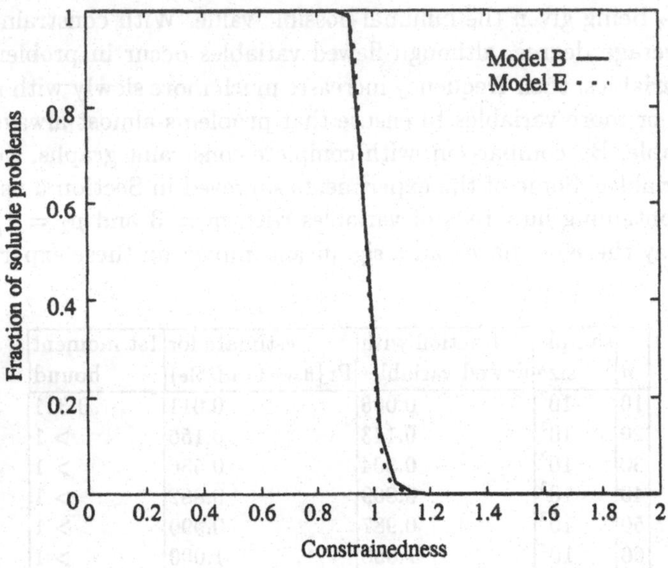

Fig. 1. Fraction of soluble problems against constrainedness, κ

To aid comparison, we estimated the constrainedness, κ of the generated problems. We have found κ a useful measure for comparing algorithm performance across a wide variety of different problem classes [9]. Since the nogoods in model E are selected independently and with repetitions, κ is approximately proportional to p. In Figure 1, we plot the fraction of soluble problems against the constrainedness. In both models, we see a rapid transition between soluble and insoluble problems at around $\kappa \approx 1$ as predicted. Associated with this transition is a peak in search cost. In Figure 2, we plot the median consistency checks performed by the forward checking algorithm with conflict-directed backjumping and the fail-first heuristic (FC-CBJ-FF). The search cost for the two models is very similar, depending almost entirely on their constrainedness and size. The only slight difference is that at very small values of p, model E problems do have complete constraint graphs and are easier to solve. We discuss the size of the constraint graph in more detail in the next section.

9 Constraint graph

Some of the experimental studies listed in Section 5 keep p_1 constant as n increases. Even if problem and sample sizes are small enough that flawed variables are unlikely, this may not be a very good idea. The transition between soluble and insoluble problems occurs around $\kappa \approx 1$. That is, when $-\frac{n-1}{2} p_1 \log_m(1-p_2) \approx 1$. If we fix m and p_1 then p_2 decreases as we increase n. Eventually p_2 is less than $1/m^2$ and, in model B at least, we are unable to generate any non-empty constraints. For instance, with $p_1 = 1$, $m = 3$ and $\kappa \approx 1$, p_2 is smaller than $1/m^2$

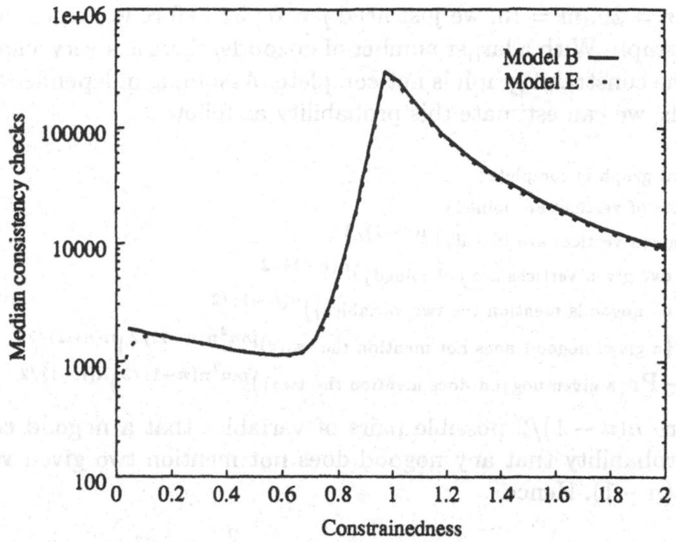

Fig. 2. Median search cost for FC-CBF-FF against constrainedness, κ

for n larger than about 20. In other words, even though flawed variables cannot occur since $p_2 < 1/m$, we cannot run an experiment at the phase transition with $m = 3$ and $p_1 = 1$ for n larger than about 20.

It may be better experimental practice to maintain the topology of the constraint graph by keeping the average degree constant. That is, to vary p_1 as $1/(n-1)$. If $\kappa \approx 1$ and $p_1 = \gamma/(n-1)$, then $p_2 \approx 1 - m^{-2/\gamma}$ which is constant. Hence the phase transition is expected to occur at a roughly constant value of p_2 as n varies. Experimental data for small n supports this conclusion. For example, Figure 2 of [12] shows that the transition in solubility for model B problems with $m = 10$ and $p_1 = 4.9/(n-1)$ occurs at $p_2 \approx 1 - m^{-2/4.9} \approx 0.6$ as n increases from 10 to 50. Of course, since $p_2 \geq 1/m$, such problems contain flawed variables and are trivially insoluble for large enough n. However, as we argued before, n needs to be so large that our experiments can safely ignore this fact. For instance, for $m = 10$, $p_1 = 4.9/(n-1)$, and $p_2 = 0.6$, we calculate that $n_{1/1000} \approx 5.6 * 10^{13}$ and $n_{1/2} \approx 3.8 * 10^{16}$. That is, problems need more than 10^{13} variables before we expect to observe flawed variables in samples of 1000 problem instances, and more than 10^{16} variables before half contain a flawed variable.

One shortcoming of model E is that it generates complete constraint graphs for quite small values of p, even though each constraint contains just a few nogoods. It is hard therefore to generate sparse constraint graphs with tight constraints. By comparison, in models A to D we can independently adjust the constraint tightness and density. In model E, we randomly select $pm^2n(n-1)/2$ nogoods independently and with repetitions. By a coupon collector's argument, we expect a complete constraint graph when $p \approx \log(n(n-1)/2)/m^2$. For example, for $n = 20$, $m = 10$, we just need $p \approx 0.052$ before we expect a complete constraint graph. With a larger number of nogoods, there is a very small probability that the constraint graph is not complete. Assuming independence between the nogoods, we can estimate this probability as follows,

$$\begin{aligned}
&\Pr\{\text{constraint graph is complete}\} \\
&= \Pr\{\text{all pairs of vertices are joined}\} \\
&= (\Pr\{\text{two given vertices are joined}\})^{n(n-1)/2} \\
&= (1 - \Pr\{\text{two given vertices are not joined}\})^{n(n-1)/2} \\
&= (1 - \Pr\{\text{no nogoods mention the two variables}\})^{n(n-1)/2} \\
&= (1 - (\Pr\{\text{a given nogood does not mention the two}\})^{pm^2n(n-1)/2})^{n(n-1)/2} \\
&= (1 - (1 - \Pr\{\text{a given nogood does mention the two}\})^{pm^2n(n-1)/2})^{n(n-1)/2}
\end{aligned}$$

As there are $n(n-1)/2$ possible pairs of variables that a nogood could mention, the probability that any nogood does not mention two given variables is simply $2/n(n-1)$. Hence,

$$\Pr\{\text{constraint graph is complete}\} = (1 - (1 - \frac{2}{n(n-1)})^{pm^2n(n-1)/2})^{n(n-1)/2}$$

For example, for $n = 20$ and $m = 10$, the probability that the constraint graph is incomplete is less than 10^{-2} when $p = 1/m$, and less than 10^{-18} when $p = 1/2$.

We can generalize model E to tackle this problem by reversing the usual process of generating a constraint graph and then selecting nogoods within it. In model F, we select uniformly, independently and with repetitions, $p_1p_2m^2n(n-1)/2$ nogoods out of the $m^2n(n-1)/2$ possible. We then generate a constraint graph with exactly $p_1n(n-1)/2$ edges and throw out any nogoods that are not between connected vertices in this graph. Note that model E is a special case of model F in which $p_1 = 1$. Using similar arguments to [1], we can show that model F (like model E) is not trivially insoluble as we increase problem size. In addition, by setting p_1 small but p_2 large, we can generate sparse constraint graphs with tight constraints. We leave it as an open question if there are models with good asymptotic properties which admit problems with a few tight constraints, but which do not throw out nogoods.

10 Non-random problems

Random problems provide a plentiful and unbiased source of problems for benchmarking. However, we must be careful that our algorithms do not become tuned to solve random problems and perform poorly on real problems. All of the models discussed here generate simple binary constraints, but real problems can contain structures that occur very rarely in these models. For example, in a graph colouring problem derived from a real exam time-tabling problem at Edinburgh University, Gent and Walsh found a 10 clique of nodes with only 9 colours available [10]. This was in a 59 node graph with 594 edges. The presence of this clique dominated the performance of their graph colouring algorithm. Random graphs of similar size and density are very unlikely to contain such a large clique.

The probability that m given nodes in a random graph with n nodes and e edges are connected by the right $m(m-1)/2$ edges to form a m-clique is,

$$\Pr\{m \text{ given nodes form a } m\text{-clique}\} = \prod_{i=0}^{\frac{m(m-1)}{2}-1} \frac{e-i}{\frac{n(n-1)}{2}-i}$$

Multiplying this probability by ${}_nC_m$, the number of sets of m nodes in a n node graph, we get the expected number of m-cliques. By the Markov inequality, this gives a bound on the probability of the graph containing a m-clique,

$$\Pr\{m\text{-clique in graph of } n \text{ nodes \& } e \text{ edges}\} \leq \frac{n!}{m!(n-m)!} \prod_{i=0}^{\frac{m(m-1)}{2}-1} \frac{e-i}{\frac{n(n-1)}{2}-i}$$

For $n = 59$, $m = 10$ and $e = 594$, the probability of clique of size 10 or larger is less than 10^{-10}. It is thus very unlikely that a random graph of the same size and density as the graph in the exam time-tabling problem would contain a regular structure like a 10-clique. However, cliques of this size are very likely in the real data due to the module structure within courses.

As another example, Gomes *et al.* have proposed quasigroup completion as a constraint satisfaction benchmark that models some of the structure found in time-tabling problems [11]. Quasigroup completion is the problem of filling in the missing entries in a Latin square, a multiplication table in which each entry appears once in every row and column. An order n quasigroup problem can be formulated as n-colouring a graph with n^2 nodes and $n^2(n-1)$ edges. The edges form $2n$ cliques, with each clique being of size n and representing the constraint that each colour appears once in every row or column. For example, an order 10 quasigroup has 20 cliques of size 10 in a 100 node graph with 900 edges. With a random graph of this size and edge density, the probability of a clique of size 10 or larger is less than 10^{-20}. It is thus unlikely that a random graph of this size and density would contain a regular structure like a 10-clique, let alone 20 of them linked together. The random models are thus unlikely to generate problems like the exam time-tabling problem or quasigroup completion.

11 Conclusions

We have performed a detailed study of the experimental consequences of a recent theoretical result of Achlioptas *et al.* [1]. This result shows that, as we increase problem size, the conventional models of random problems almost surely contain a flawed variable and are therefore trivially insoluble. Our survey of previous experimental studies shows that most meet the restriction on their result that $p_2 \geq 1/m$. Fortunately, most (but not all) of these studies use too few variables and too large domains to be affected by the result. As expected, flawed variables occur most often with dense constraint graphs and small domains. With constraint graphs of fixed average degree and large domains, flawed variables can be safely ignored. Achlioptas *et al.* propose an alternative random model which does not suffer from this asymptotic problem. We show that, at a typical problem size used in experiments, this model gives problems of a similar solubility and hardness to conventional models. However, it has a small experimental weakness since we cannot run tests with sparse but tight constraints. We therefore generalized the model so that we can independently adjust the constraint tightness and density. Finally, we showed that some of the structures that occur in real problems like large cliques are very rare in these random models.

What general lessons can be learnt from this study? First, experiments can benefit greatly from theory. Flawed variables are likely to have occurred in a small but significant number of previous experimental studies. A simple arc consistency algorithm would therefore have solved some of these problems. Experimental practice can now be improved to ensure that either we use an alternative model without this asymptotic problem, or we use a conventional model but choose parameters so that flawed variables are unlikely. Second, theory can benefit greatly from experiments. Theory provided an estimate for the probability of problems having flawed variables. Experiments quickly determined the accuracy of this estimate. Third, we must continue to improve and extend our random models so that we can generate a wide range of hard problems with which to test our algorithms.

References

1. D. Achlioptas, L.M. Kirousis, E. Kranakis, D. Krizanc, M.S.O. Molloy, and C. Stamatiou. Random constraint satisfaction: A more accurate picture. In *Proceedings of Third International Conference on Principles and Practice of Constraint Programming (CP97)*, pages 107–120, 1997.
2. P. Cheeseman, B. Kanefsky, and W.M. Taylor. Where the really hard problems are. In *Proceedings of the 12th IJCAI*, pages 331–337. International Joint Conference on Artificial Intelligence, 1991.
3. E. Friedgut. Sharp thresholds for graph properties and the k-SAT problem, 1998. Unpublished manuscript.
4. A. Frieze and S. Suen. Analysis of two simple heuristics on a random instance of k-SAT. *Journal of Algorithms*, 20:312–355, 1996.
5. I.P. Gent, E. MacIntyre, P. Prosser, P. Shaw, and T. Walsh. The constrainedness of arc consistency. In *3rd International Conference on Principles and Practices of Constraint Programming (CP-97)*, pages 327–340. Springer, 1997.
6. I.P. Gent, E. MacIntyre, P. Prosser, B.M. Smith, and T. Walsh. An empirical study of dynamic variable ordering heuristics for the constraint satisfaction problem. In *2nd International Conference on Principles and Practices of Constraint Programming (CP-96)*, pages 179–193, 1996.
7. I.P. Gent, E. MacIntyre, P. Prosser, and T. Walsh. Scaling effects in the CSP phase transition. In *1st International Conference on Principles and Practices of Constraint Programming (CP-95)*, pages 70–87. Springer-Verlag, 1995.
8. I.P. Gent, E. MacIntyre, P. Prosser, and T. Walsh. The constrainedness of search. In *Proceedings of the 13th National Conference on AI*, pages 246–252. American Association for Artificial Intelligence, 1996.

9. I.P. Gent, E. MacIntyre, P. Prosser, and T. Walsh. The scaling of search cost. In *Proceedings of the 14th National Conference on AI*, pages 315–320. American Association for Artificial Intelligence, 1997.
10. I.P. Gent and T. Walsh. Phase transitions from real computational problems. In *Proceedings of the 8th International Symposium on Artificial Intelligence*, pages 356–364, 1995.
11. C. Gomes and B. Selman. Problem structure in the presence of perturbations. In *Proceedings of the 14th National Conference on AI*, pages 221–226. American Association for Artificial Intelligence, 1997.
12. S. Grant and B.M. Smith. The phase transition behaviour of maintaining arc consistency. Research Report 95.25, School of Computer Studies, University of Leeds, 1995. A revised and shortened version appears in Proceedings of 12th ECAI, pages 175–179, 1996.
13. L.M. Kirousis, E. Kranakis, and D. Krizanc. Approximating the unsatisfiability threshold of random formulas. In *Proceedings of the 4th Annual European Symposium on Algorithms (ESA'96)*, pages 27–38, 1996.
14. D. Mitchell, B. Selman, and H. Levesque. Hard and Easy Distributions of SAT Problems. In *Proceedings of the 10th National Conference on AI*, pages 459–465. American Association for Artificial Intelligence, 1992.
15. C. Williams and T. Hogg. Exploiting the deep structure of constraint problems. *Artificial Intelligence*, 70:73–117, 1994.

A Tableau Based Constraint Solving Toolkit for Interactive Graphical Applications

Kim Marriott, Sitt Sen Chok and Alan Finlay[1]

School of Computer Science & Software Engineering,
Monash University,
Clayton 3168 Vic.,
Australia
{marriott,css}@csse.monash.edu.au

Abstract. We describe an object-oriented constraint solving toolkit, QOCA, designed for interactive graphical applications. It has a simple yet powerful interface based on the *metric space model* for constraint manipulation. Currently QOCA supports linear arithmetic constraints and two different metrics: the square of the Euclidean distance and the Manhattan distance. It provides three solvers, all of which rely on keeping the constraints in solved form and relies on novel algorithms for efficient resolving of constraints during direct manipulation. We provide a thorough empirical evaluation of QOCA, both of the interface design and the speed of constraint solving.

1 Introduction

Since the very infancy of computer graphics there has been interest in the use of constraints [16]. The reason being that constraints allow graphical objects to behave more intelligently since they capture the semantic relationships between diagram components. However, despite the utility of constraints, they are not widely used in interactive graphical applications. Apart from CAD systems, most applications provide at best rudimentary constraint solving abilities. We feel that the reasons for this are twofold. First there is the problem of efficiency. Efficient constraint solving techniques, such as those based on local propagation, are suitable for some applications such as simulation but are not powerful enough for many graphical application since these require inequalities or cyclic constraints. On the other hand, general arithmetic constraint solving techniques are sufficiently expressive but naive implementations are too slow, in particular for real time direct manipulation. The second reason is that, perhaps because of concerns about efficiency, most existing constraint solvers are tightly integrated with the graphical application making reuse of the solver in other applications difficult. This means that an application builder who wishes to provide constraints must spend considerable effort and time building their own specialized

[1] Current affiliation: Ericsson Australia, 198 Bell St, Preston 3072, Australia.

constraint solver, something most graphical application programmers do not have the time or necessary background in constraint solving to do.

Over the last 7 years we have been developing an object-oriented constraint solving toolkit, called QOCA, which is expressly designed for interactive graphical applications and which is intended to overcome the above two problems. It is written in C++ and consists of about 17,000 lines of code. A major design goal has been to provide an interface which is simple yet flexible enough to be used in a wide variety of applications and which treats constraints as first class objects. The other goal has been to provide constraints which are expressive enough to be useful and yet which can be solved sufficiently quickly for real-time direct manipulation. To some extent there is a synergy between these two goals since, because of the many possible tradeoffs between efficiency and expressiveness, QOCA provides a variety of solvers and a simple common interface allows the application programmer to readily experiment with the different solvers, choosing the appropriate one for their application.

Currently QOCA provides three different solvers. All are based on keeping the current constraints in a tableau and using pivoting to keep them in a solved form. The first, `LinEqSolver`, provides linear equalities and uses the square of the the (weighted) Euclidean distance to compare solutions. The second, `LinIneqSolver`, also uses the square of the Euclidean distance but also allows linear inequalities. It is based on linear complementary pivoting [8]. The third, `CassSolver`, is based on the Cassowary algorithm [5]. It also provides linear equalities and inequalities but instead uses the (weighted) Manhattan distance to compare solutions.

We provide a systematic evaluation of QOCA. We demonstrate the utility of the interface by describing how it has been employed in four widely varying graphical applications: graphic editors, error correction in visual language parsing, graph layout and interactive document layout on the Internet. Our empirical results also demonstrate that the three solvers are sufficiently fast for practical applications.

The most closely related work are our earlier papers on other aspects of QOCA. In [11] we focused on how it could be integrated with an existing graphical editor, Idraw, and in [5] we gave the Cassowary algorithm. The current paper extends these by detailing new constraint solving algorithms, the metric space model for interaction, the architecture of QOCA and providing the first empirical evaluation of QOCA. Other related work on constraint solving algorithms for graphical applications are largely formalized in terms of constraint hierarchies. Early solvers provided only local propagation. More recent solvers include UltraViolet [1,2] which supports linear equations and certain types of linear inequalities and DETAIL [13,12] which supports linear equations. QOCA extends these by supporting arbitrary linear inequalities. In addition we provide an empirical evaluation of our algorithms in the context of a concrete application.

2 The Interface of QOCA

One of the most striking features of QOCA is its simple interface. To understand the interface design, consider a simple application, that of a constraint-based graphics editor. The editor essentially provides three operations: the user may add objects or constraints, the user may delete an object or constraint, and finally the user may edit or directly manipulate an object. At any point in time, the configuration of the editor consists of a set of graphic objects, a set of constraints over variables in the objects and a current solution which is an assignment to the variables that satisfies the constraints. The variables correspond to graphical attributes of the objects in the diagram and the diagram on the graphics display is, therefore, simply a visual representation of the current solution.

Reflecting this discussion, the QOCA toolkit is based on the *metric space model*, a new metaphor for constraint interaction. In this model, there is a metric which gives the distance between two assignments to the variables, and at any time there is a current set of constraints and a current solution. Mirroring the operations in the graphic editor, interaction in the metric space model can occur in three ways. First, a constraint may be added to the current set of constraints in which case the new solution is the assignment which is closest to the old assignment and which satisfies the new constraint set. Second, a constraint may be deleted from the current set of constraints, in which case the current solution remains unchanged. Finally, the current solution may be manipulated by "suggesting" values for some of the variables. The new solution is the assignment which is closest to the old assignment and to the requested variable values and which satisfies the constraint set. The constraint set remains unchanged.

The metric space model is closely related to the now classic *hierarchical constraints* approach [3]. The reason that we have based the toolkit on the metric space model rather than directly on the constraint hierarchy model is that in the metric space model editing a variable value is viewed as a different operation to constraint deletion and addition while the natural way to model variable editing in the constraint hierarchy approach is as a sequence of constraint deletion and additions. The advantage of having an explicit operation for editing is that the speed requirements for editing are much more stringent than for constraint deletion and addition because of the need to provide continuous feedback during direct manipulation. Thus for efficiency it is important to provide a specialized algorithm for editing which can take advantage of the fact that the current solution is "close" to the next solution rather than using algorithms for arbitrary constraint deletion and addition. A related advantage of the metric space model is that we believe it more directly matches the application program needs, so it provides a simpler and more natural interface for the application programmer.

QOCA implements the metric space model by means of three main components: constrained variables, called `CFloats`, linear arithmetic constraints, called `LinConstraints`, and constraint solvers, called `Solvers`.

Internally a `CFloat`, v, has a *value*, $v.val$, a *desired value*, $v.des$, both of which are floating point numbers as well as a *stay weight*, $v.weight$, and and an *edit weight*, $v.eweight$, which, respectively, indicate the importance of leaving the variable unchanged if it is not being edited and the importance of changing it to the desired value when the variable is being edited. Both weights are non-negative floats. The weights are set by the application programmer when the **CFloat** is created and cannot be subsequently changed. Applications set the desired value when the variable is created and also when the variable is selected for editing. The solver is responsible for setting the actual value and will also update the desired value to be the actual value when appropriate. To the application programmer the **CFloat** appears to have a single value, since they set the desired value using the method **SuggestValue**, call the solver, and then read the actual value using **GetValue**. However, for book keeping reasons, the solver requires **CFloats** to keep the two values separate.

There are a number of different types of **CFloats**. The standard **CFloat** used by the application programmer is the *unrestricted* **CFloat** whose value can range over all reals. Internally the solvers also make use of *restricted* **CFloats** whose value must be non-negative and which are used to represent slack variables and artificial variables.

Linear arithmetic constraints, that is **LinConstraints**, can be constructed from **CFloats**. They have the standard form:

$$a_1 \times x_1 + \ldots + a_n \times x_n \;\; op \;\; c$$

where *op* is one of <, >, >=, <= or ==, c is a float and the a_is are floats and the x_is are **CFloats**. Note that QOCA takes advantage of the C++ facilities for overloading operators so as to allow the natural specification of constraints.

Actually, neither **CFloats** nor **LinConstraints** are directly manipulated by the programmer. Instead, for efficiency and safeness they are manipulated by means of the reference-counted "handles," **CFloatHandle** and **ConstraintHandle** respectively. These can be assigned and constructed in the obvious ways.

Constraint solvers form the heart of QOCA. Interaction with a solver has two modes: *constraint manipulation* and *editing*.

Each solver provides the following Boolean methods for constraint manipulation. Linear constraints can be added to the solver one at a time using **AddConstraint**. Each time the solver checks that the new constraint is compatible with the current constraints. If it is not, the constraint is not added and *false* is returned. The solver methods **RemoveConstraint** and **ChangeConstraint** respectively allow the application programmer to remove a constraint which is currently in the solver or indicate that it has been changed. **ChangeConstraint** behaves as if it does a **RemoveConstraint** followed by an **AddConstraint** but the actual implementation may do considerably less work, in particular when only the RHS constant in the constraint has changed. After the application programmer has finished adding or removing constraints from the solver they must call the solver method **Solve** to find a new assignment for the variables which is as close as possible to the current solution. The desired values are then updated to the new solution. The reason for requiring the programmer to perform an explicit call to **Solve** rather than implicitly calling **Solve** after each addition or deletion is that it may be quite expensive, so should only be called when needed.

The editing mode is used to modify the values of the "edit" variables. Typically this occurs during direct manipulation. First the application programmer tells the solver which variables are to be edited using multiple calls to **SetEditVar**. Next **BeginEdit** is called. This initializes internal data structures for fast "resolving" of the constraints. Now during manipulation the application programmer repeatedly sets the desired values of the edit variables and then calls the solver function **Resolve** which efficiently computes the new solution to the constraints which is as close as possible to the old solution and to the new desired values of the edit variables. Finally the application programmer calls **EndEdit** to signal the end of the edit phase.

In more detail, the assignment found by **Solve** for the variables $v_1, ...v_n$ is the solution to the current constraints which minimizes the objective function $\sum_{i=1}^{n} v_i.weight \times ||v_i - v_i.des||$ where the precise metric $||\cdot||$ employed is solver dependent. The objective function employed in **Resolve** is similar except that the weighting for each variable, v, being edited is $v.eweight$ rather than $v.weight$. Given that the edit weights are uniformly greater than the stay weights, this reflects the desire to move the variables being edited to the new value at the expense of keeping the value of the other variables unchanged.

Example 1. Consider a diagram consisting of a point (xm, ym) and a line from (xl, yl) to (xu, yu) in which the point is constrained to lie at the midpoint of the line. The following program fragment creates the variables and constraints, adds them to the solver and calls **Solve** to compute the initial position. The constructor for **CFloatHandles** takes three arguments: the stay and edit weights together with an initial desired value. Note that both xm and ym have a stay weight of zero indicating that they are "dependent variables," although they have a non-zero edit weight (otherwise, editing could never change their value!). Next the program chooses xm and ym to be the edit variables, and then repeatedly samples the mouse to find the desired values and calls **Resolve** to compute the new value until the user releases the mouse button, which finishes the edit cycle.

```
CFloatHandle xl(1,1000,45.5), xm(0,1000,0), xu(1,1000,60),
             yl(1,1000,45.5), ym(0,1000,0), yu(1,1000,60);
ConstraintHandle xcon = (1*xl + 1*xu - 2*xm == 0),
                 ycon = (1*yl + 1*yu - 2*ym == 0);
LinEqSolver  solv;

solv.AddConstraint(xcon);  solv.AddConstraint(ycon);
solv.Solve();
DrawLine(xl.GetValue(),yl.GetValue(),xu.GetValue(),yu.GetValue());
solv.SetEditVar(xm);  solv.SetEditVar(ym);
solv.BeginEdit();
while (mouse.button.down) {
  xm.SuggestValue(mouse.x);  ym.SuggestValue(mouse.y);
  solv.Resolve();
  DrawLine(xl.GetValue(),yl.GetValue(),xu.GetValue(),yu.GetValue());
}
solv.EndEdit();
```

3 The Solvers

The QOCA toolkit is designed to provide a variety of solvers. These may provide different types of constraints, use different metrics or employ different algorithms and time/space tradeoffs in constraint solving. Currently QOCA provides three true solvers and two auxiliary solvers.

All of the solvers are based on transforming the original constraints into a *solved form.* Each constraint c_i in the solved form is either of the form $0 = 0$ or of the form $x_i + \sum_{j=1}^{m} a_{ij} y_j = b_i$ where the variable x_i occurs only in c_i and the $y_1, ..., y_m$ are variables and the a_{ij} and b_i are constants. If the variable x_i is restricted, i.e. a slack variable, the RHS constant b_i is required to be non-negative. The variable x_i is said to be *basic* and the $y_1, ..., y_m$ are *parameters.* A constraint of the form $0 = 0$ indicates that a *redundant* constraint is present, that is a constraint implied by the other constraints in the system.

To support manipulation of constraints into their solved form QOCA provides the `Tableau` class. Conceptually, a tableau contains three parts: the original constraints, the solved form, and the *quasi-inverse.* The quasi-inverse is a matrix detailing the elementary row operations which have been performed on the original constraints to obtain the normal form. The primary reason for computing the quasi inverse is that it allows incremental deletion of constraints. Careful implementation of the tableau class is vital for reasonable performance. Indeed, because of the multiple uses of the tableau class, the QOCA toolkit provides a variety of different implementations. One of the most important implementation decisions is whether to explicitly compute the solved form or rather to implicitly compute it as needed by multiplying the original constraints by the quasi-inverse.

3.1 The Simple Linear Equality Solver: `LinEqSystem`

The most basic solver is `LinEqSystem`. This provides incremental addition and deletion of linear equations. Although it provides `Solve` and `Resolve` the suffix "`System`" indicates that it does not directly support the metric system model. Instead the application programmer should use the solver `LinEqSolver`. This, however, is implemented using `LinEqSystem` so we will first explain how this works.

`LinEqSystem` is built around a single tableau. The key invariant is that after each operation the constraints are left in solved form. We now briefly describe the solver's implementation.

`AddConstraint`: Incremental addition of a linear equation is performed by using an incremental version of Gauss-Jordan elimination (see for instance [15]).
`RemoveConstraint`: Constraint removal is handled by using the quasi-inverse, similarly to the algorithm given in [14].
`ChangeConstraint`: In most cases this calls `RemoveConstraint` followed by a `AddConstraint`. However, if only the RHS constant has changed in the constraint, then the original constraint in the tableau is modified and by employing

the quasi-inverse the differential change to the RHS values of the solved form is efficiently computed.
BeginEdit: First this performs pivots to make edit variables parameters, if this is possible, and then computes **DepVars**, the set of basic variables which depend on the edit variables.
Solve and **Resolve**: These do not directly support the metric space model. Instead the solution computed depends on the current solved form. The solver simply uses the value of the parametric variables to compute the value of the basic variables. The effect of this is to ignore the desired values for basic variables. One subtlety is that **Resolve** computes the new values of the basic variables in **DepVars** differentially. We note that in theory this may lead to a buildup of rounding errors, but this does not seem to occur in practice.
EndEdit: This sets the desired values of all variables to be their actual values.

3.2 Linear Equality Solver: LinEqSolver

The solver **LinEqSolver** is implemented in terms of **LinEqSystem**. It provides incremental addition and deletion of linear equalities as well as a **Solve** and **Resolve** which support the metric system model. The square of the Euclidean distance between the variable values is used as the metric.

Constraints are kept inside a private **LinEqSystem**. Thus, **AddConstraint**, **RemoveConstraint**, and **ChangeConstraint**, are directly provided by the underlying **LinEqSystem**.
Solve: Intuitively this is quite simple, we must find the solution which minimizes:

$$\sum_{i=1}^{n} v_i.weight \times (v_i.val - v_i.des)^2,$$

with respect to the constraints C in the solver where $v_1, ..., v_n$ are the **CFloats**. We do this by using the solved form of C to eliminate the basic variables, $\mathbf{x}$. This gives a quadratic polynomial, say $f'(\mathbf{y})$, over the parametric variables $y_1, ..., y_m$. The minimal value for f' will occur at the point in which all derivatives are equal to zero. Thus to find the value for the parameters which minimizes the original system we set up another **LinEqSystem** this time with a constraint $\partial f'/\partial y_i = 0$ for each parameter y_i. Once the values for each y_i are found these can be passed as desired values into the original **LinEqSystem** to find the overall solution.
Resolve: This is quite similar to **Solve**. One difference is that edit weights are used for edit variables and that the parameters dependent upon the edit variables are found first. When constructing the partial derivatives we need only consider these, since the other parameters will maintain their current value. One difficulty is that the constraint system $\nabla f'(\mathbf{y}) = \mathbf{0}$ actually depends on the desired values for the variables, in particular the desired values for the edit variables. Unfortunately, these change each time **Resolve** is called. Clearly we do not want to create and solve a new system $\nabla f'(\mathbf{y}) = \mathbf{0}$ for each call. Instead in **BeginEdit** we compute the parametric derivative $\nabla f'(\mathbf{y}, \mathbf{d})$ where $\mathbf{d}$ is a vector of variables, one for each edit variable's desired value. We are careful to ensure

that when pivoting the ds remain parameters. Then in **Resolve** we simply solve for the parameters **y** given the new values for the **ds** (which is simply the new desired value of the corresponding edit variable). In turn we resolve for the values of the **x** given values for the **y** in the original tableau. Thus **Resolve** in **LinEqSolver** actually calls **Resolve** for each of its internal **LinEqSystems**.

3.3 The Simplex Solver: LinIneqSystem

The most basic solver provided by QOCA which supports linear inequalities as well as linear equalities is **LinIneqSystem**. Like **LinEqSystem**, this solver is not intended for direct use by the application programmer since it does not support the metric space model, rather it is used to implement the two solvers for inequalities, **LinIneqSolver** and **CassSolver**, which do support the metric space model. **LinIneqSystem** contains a single tableau to which constraints are added. The interesting methods are described below.
AddConstraint: Incremental addition of a linear equation or inequality is performed by using an incremental version of Gauss-Jordan elimination and phase I of the simplex algorithm (see for instance [15, 5]). An invariant of the constraint addition algorithm is that the solved form will always have the form

$$\mathbf{x}^{\mathbf{ur}} + \mathbf{A}^1\mathbf{y}^{\mathbf{ur}} + \mathbf{A}^2\mathbf{y}^{\mathbf{sl}} = \mathbf{b}^{\mathbf{ur}} \wedge \mathbf{x}^{\mathbf{sl}} + \mathbf{A}^3\mathbf{y}^{\mathbf{sl}} = \mathbf{b}^{\mathbf{sl}}$$

where $\mathbf{x}^{\mathbf{ur}}$ is the vector of "unrestricted" basic variables, $\mathbf{y}^{\mathbf{ur}}$ is the vector of "unrestricted" parameters, $\mathbf{x}^{\mathbf{sl}}$ is the vector of basic variables which are slacks, $\mathbf{y}^{\mathbf{sl}}$ is the vector of parameters which are slacks and the RHS constants $\mathbf{b}^{\mathbf{sl}}$ are required to be non-negative.
RemoveConstraint: The algorithm for constraint removal is given in [14].
ChangeConstraint: In most cases this calls **RemoveConstraint** followed by **AddConstraint**. However, if only the RHS constant has changed in the constraint, then the new RHS values of the solved form are computed. If any of the RHS constants associated with slack basic variables have become non-negative, phase I of the simplex is called.
Solve: This doe not directly support the metric space model. Instead it uses phase II of the simplex algorithm to minimize $\sum_{i=1}^{n} v_i.weight \times (v_i.val - v_i.des)$ with respect to the linear constraints C in the solver with **CFloats** $v_1, ..., v_n$.

3.4 Linear Complementary Pivoting: LinIneqSolver

QOCA provides two solvers which support linear inequalities as well as equalities and which provide a **Solve** and **Resolve** which support the metric system model. They differ in the choice of metric used to find the closest solution and the underlying algorithms. The first solver we shall look at, **LinIneqSolver**, like **LinEqSolver** uses the square of the Euclidean distance as the metric.

In this solver, constraints are kept inside a private **LinIneqSystem**. This means **AddConstraint**, **RemoveConstraint** and **ChangeConstraint** are directly provided by the underlying **LinIneqSystem**.

Solve: This must find the solution which minimizes

$$\sum_{i=1}^{n} v_i.weight \times (v_i.val - v_i.des)^2$$

with respect to the constraints in the solver. This is an example of a convex quadratic problem. Arguably the simplest approach to solving such problems is a simple modification of the simplex algorithm that finds the local optimum of a quadratic problem, which since the problem is convex, is the global optimum.

Now, a solution is a local minimum if in every direction either the optimization value increases or the region becomes infeasible. The information about infeasibility is captured by the constraints in the original problem (called the *primal problem*). Information about how the optimization function decreases is captured in the so-called *dual problem* which is obtained by looking at the derivative of the optimization function. The idea is, therefore, to combine the primal and dual problems and solve these together. Any solution to their combination will be a feasible optimal solution for the original problem. Since the derivative of a quadratic optimization function is linear, both the dual and the primal problem consist of linear arithmetic constraints and so a variant of the simplex can be used to solve their conjunction.

We first consider the simpler case in which all variables are restricted to take non-negative values. Let the constraints in the primal problem be in (basic feasible) solved form:

$$PP: \quad \mathbf{x} + \mathbf{A}\mathbf{y} = \mathbf{b}$$

where $\mathbf{x}$ are the basic variables and $\mathbf{y}$ are the parameters and let f' be the function to be minimized after basic variables have been eliminated from it. Then the dual problem is

$$DP: \quad \mathbf{t} - \mathbf{A}^T\mathbf{z} = \nabla f'(\mathbf{y})$$

where $\mathbf{z} \geq \mathbf{0}$ are the dual variables (one for each equation in the primal problem) and $\mathbf{t} \geq \mathbf{0}$ are the dual slack variables. The combined problem CP is the conjunction of the dual and primal problem plus the constraints that $\mathbf{x} \cdot \mathbf{z} = \mathbf{0}$ and $\mathbf{y} \cdot \mathbf{t} = \mathbf{0}$. These last constraints mean that in the combined problem every variable has a *complementary* variable which is not allowed to be positive if it is.

Example 2. Imagine that we have three variables, x_l, x_r and x_m, which are restricted to take non-negative values, x_m is in the middle of x_l and x_r, x_l is to the left of x_r and x_r is less than 100. After rewriting into solved form, our primal problem is:

$$\begin{array}{llll} x_m & -\frac{1}{2}x_l & -\frac{1}{2}x_r = & 0 \\ s_1 & +x_l & -x_r = & 0 \\ s_2 & & +x_r = & 100 \end{array}$$

and that $x_l.des = 40$, $x_m.des = 60$ and $x_r.des = 60$. After elimination we obtain the function $f' = (x_l - 40)^2 + (\frac{1}{2}x_l + \frac{1}{2}x_r - 60)^2 + (x_r - 60)^2$. Putting the primal and dual together we obtain:

$$\begin{array}{llr} x_m -\frac{1}{2}x_l -\frac{1}{2}x_r & = & 0 \\ s_1 +x_l -x_r & = & 0 \\ s_2 +x_r & = & 100 \\ t_1 -\frac{5}{2}x_l -\frac{1}{2}x_r +\frac{1}{2}z_1 -z_2 & = & -150 \\ t_2 -\frac{1}{2}x_l -\frac{5}{2}x_r +\frac{1}{2}z_1 +z_2 -z_3 & = & -180 \end{array}$$

where the variables in the problem and their complements are given by:

$$x_l \leftrightarrow t_1 \; x_m \leftrightarrow z_1 \; x_r \leftrightarrow t_2 \; s_1 \leftrightarrow z_2 \; s_2 \leftrightarrow z_3.$$

Unfortunately the complete problem is not in solved form since some of the RHS constants are negative. To transform it into a solved form we subtract an artificial variable v from every equation and then pivot on the row with the largest negative constant, making v basic in that row. We obtain:

$$\begin{array}{llr} x_m -t_2 \quad +2x_r -\frac{1}{2}z_1 \quad -z_2 +z_3 & = & 180 \\ s_1 -t_2 +\frac{3}{2}x_l +\frac{3}{2}x_r -\frac{1}{2}z_1 \quad -z_2 +z_3 & = & 180 \\ s_2 -t_2 +\frac{1}{2}x_l +\frac{7}{2}x_r -\frac{1}{2}z_1 \quad -z_2 +z_3 & = & 280 \\ t_1 -t_2 -2x_l +x_r \quad -2z_2 +z_3 & = & 30 \\ v -t_2 +\frac{1}{2}x_l +\frac{5}{2}x_r -\frac{1}{2}z_1 \quad -z_2 +z_3 & = & 180 \end{array}$$

We have now obtained a solved form which is feasible and which satisfies the complementary conditions. The only problem is that the artificial variable v is in the basis. We continue pivoting until v leaves the basis. At each pivot we choose to make basic the variable which is complementary to the variable which just left the basis. Thus in the next stage we would choose to move x_r into the basis since this is the complement of t_2. We use the standard simplex row selection rule to determine which variable to move out of the basis. This ensures that feasibility is maintained. Because we only move a variable into the basis once its complementary variable has been moved out of the basis this means that the solution corresponding to any of the solved forms will satisfy the complementary conditions.

Unfortunately our case is more complex because we also have unrestricted variables. Now our primal problem will have the special form identified above:

$$\mathbf{x^{ur}} + \mathbf{A^1 y^{ur}} + \mathbf{A^2 y^{sl}} = \mathbf{b^{ur}} \wedge \mathbf{x^{sl}} + \mathbf{A^3 y^{sl}} = \mathbf{b^{sl}}$$

Naive computation of the dual problem gives

$$-\mathbf{A^1}^T \mathbf{z^{ur}} = \nabla f'(\mathbf{y^{ur}}) \wedge \mathbf{t} - \mathbf{A^2}^T \mathbf{z^{ur}} - \mathbf{A^3}^T \mathbf{z^{sl}} = \nabla f'(\mathbf{y^{sl}})$$

where $\mathbf{z^{ur}}$ are the dual unrestricted variables (the dual variable of an equation is unrestricted) and $\mathbf{z^{sl}}$ are the dual restricted variables. However from the complementary condition it essentially follows that the $\mathbf{z^{ur}}$ will always remain parameters, thus they can be ignored. Thus the dual problem is equivalent to:

$$0 = \nabla f'(\mathbf{y^{ur}}) \wedge \mathbf{t} - \mathbf{A^3}^T \mathbf{z^{sl}} = \nabla f'(\mathbf{y^{sl}})$$

We solve this by first using the complementary pivot algorithm to find values for $\mathbf{y}^{\mathbf{sl}}$, $\mathbf{y}^{\mathbf{ur}}$ and $\mathbf{x}^{\mathbf{sl}}$ by solving

$$0 = \nabla f'(\mathbf{y}^{\mathbf{ur}}) \wedge \mathbf{x}^{\mathbf{sl}} + \mathbf{A}^3\mathbf{y}^{\mathbf{sl}} = \mathbf{b}^{\mathbf{sl}} \wedge \mathbf{t} - \mathbf{A}^{3^T}\mathbf{z}^{\mathbf{sl}} = \nabla f'(\mathbf{y}^{\mathbf{sl}})$$

and then performing back substitution of the parameter values into the original **LinIneqSystem** in order to find values for $\mathbf{x}^{\mathbf{ur}}$.
Resolve: It is straightforward to modify the algorithm for **Solve** so that it is incremental for resolving. Changing the desired variable values only changes the RHS constants in the solved form. There are two possibilities. If the solved form remains feasible, then we just read the new solution directly from the solved form. Otherwise, the solved form is now infeasible. In this case we proceed as above, first introducing an artificial variable v and making the solved form feasible, then pivoting until v leaves the basis. In order to be able to update the RHS efficiently, as in **LinEqSolver**, we introduce a new variable for each edit variable which acts as a placeholder for the desired value.

3.5 Cassowary Solver: CassSolver

The final solver provided in the QOCA toolkit is **CassSolver**, based on the Cassowary algorithm described in [5]. Like **LinIneqSolver** this provides linear inequality and equality constraints and makes use of a private **LinIneqSystem**. Unlike **LinIneqSolver**, **CassSolver** measure the distance between two solutions using the Manhattan distance rather than the square of the Euclidean distance.

The key idea behind the Cassowary algorithm is to minimize the objective function

$$\sum_{i=1}^{n} v_i.weight \times |v_i.val - v_i.des|$$

by solving a related linear programming problem. This problem is obtained by first adding to the original problem new restricted variables δ_i^+ and δ_i^- for each of the original **CFloats** v_i. These are the positive and negative error respectively of the variable v_i. Then for each v_i we associate an *error equality*

$$v_i + \delta_i^+ - \delta_i^- = v_i.des.$$

The solution to the original problem is found by minimizing the linear objective function

$$\sum_{i=1}^{n} v_i.weight \times (\delta_i^+ + \delta_i^-)$$

with respect to the original constraints together with the error equalities. We now briefly describe the interesting methods:
AddConstraint: This adds the constraint together with an error equality for each new variable to an internal **LinIneqSystem**.
RemoveConstraint: This removes the constraint as well as the associated error equalities from the internal **LinIneqSystem**.

`Solve`: Uses phase II of the simplex algorithm to solve the objective function using the internal `LinIneqSystem`.
`BeginEdit`: Modifies the objective function so that the edit weight is used to multiply the error variables associated with edit variables rather than the stay weight.
`Resolve`: Changing the desired value for an edit variable means that the RHS constant of the error equation must be changed. This is achieved by calling the `ChangeConstraint` method of the internal `LinIneqSystem`. If this causes the RHS of any restricted variable in the solved form to become negative, the dual simplex algorithm is used to restore feasibility.
`EndEdit`: This sets the desired value of each variable to its actual value. In order to reflect this change, the `ChangeConstraint` method of the internal `LinIneqSystem` is used to appropriately modify the RHS constants of the error equations.

We note that the algorithms for `Resolve` and `EndEdit` are significantly simpler than those given in [5]. This is because we can simply change the RHS constants of the error equations and then use the `ChangeConstraint` method of the internal `LinIneqSystem` to appropriately update the RHS constants in the solved form. This is easy because the tableau contains the quasi-inverse. In contrast the algorithm in [5] must explicitly modify the solved form.

4 Evaluation

There are two aspects of the toolkit which warrant evaluation. The first is the design of the interface, the second is performance of the constraint solvers. We look at these in turn.

Clearly the interface is reasonably simple. The question is whether it is sufficiently flexible to be used in a variety of applications. The original motivation for the interface design and the associated metric space model came from the integration with the graphic editor Idraw [11]. Since then we have used QOCA in a number of other graphical applications which we now detail.

QOCA has been employed for two different purpose in the Penguins system [6,7]. Given a grammatical specification of a visual language, such as state transition diagrams or mathematical equations, the Penguins system automatically generates an incremental parser for the visual language which is integrated into a graphics editor. One use of QOCA is for geometric error correction during parsing. The second use of QOCA in Penguins is to support direct manipulation during editing of diagrams. Constraints inferred during parsing are maintained during manipulation, thus providing an editor which behaves as if it understands the semantics of the visual language. One pleasing observation has been that linear equations and inequalities have proven sufficient to approximate the constraints in a very wide variety of visual languages, namely, state transition diagrams, flow charts, mathematical equations, trees and message sequence charts.

Another application in which we have employed QOCA (more exactly, a Java implementation of the Cassowary algorithm with the same interface) is for the dynamic layout of multiple column web documents composed of text, images and tables [4]. As the viewer changes font selection or resizes the browser, the layout of the document is modified. Geometric constraints ensure that the layout is appropriate. Again linear equality and inequality constraints have proven powerful enough.

The final applications we have used QOCA for are in graph layout. Currently QOCA is not suitable for arbitrary graph layout since this requires minimization of a complex non-quadratic objective function which captures aesthetics like reducing the number of edge crossings. However, QOCA has proven suitable for tree layout. Since it also allows arbitrary linear constraints on node placement it is more flexible than other approaches to tree layout. QOCA has also proven useful for quickly finding an initial graph layout, before using more expensive optimization techniques to improve the layout [9]. Finally, it has proven useful for removing node overlapping from a graph layout [10].

The second aspect of QOCA requiring evaluation is the speed of constraint solving, in particular whether it is fast enough to be used in real applications. Our test data comes from two applications generated by the Penguins system. The first is an incremental parser for recognizing state transition diagrams and the associated graphics editor. The second is similar except that the visual language is that of binary trees. The first application only requires equalities, so we have used it to compare all three solvers, while in the second application inequality constraints are used to preserve the ordering of the node's children and that parents are above their children. Thus we have used this to compare `LinIneqSolver` and `CassSolver`. We have tried QOCA on a variety of diagrams with up to 150 graphics objects.

We have timed the various calls to QOCA made during the incremental recognition of each of these diagrams and during direct manipulation. In each application, after each graphic object is drawn, the incremental parser is called. This calls `AddConstraint` to add constraints to the solver and also `Solve` to perform error correction. It may also call `RemoveConstraint` since adding new objects may invalidate earlier recognition of objects. Direct manipulation with the graphic editor calls `EditVar` and `BeginEdit` to begin editing, `Resolve` during manipulation and `EndEdit` at the end of the direct manipulation. We have deliberately chosen diagrams which will exhibit worst-case behaviour of `Resolve` and `BeginEdit` since virtually all components of the diagram are connected and so almost all variables are dependent upon the edit variables.

Table 1 details our findings. All times are for a Pentium-II 266MMX running Windows95 and are in milliseconds. We give the number of graphical components in the diagram (Size), the number of constraints (C) and the number of variables (V) generated by the application program (this does not include auxiliary constraints and variables generated within the solvers). For each operation and solver `LinEqSolver` (Eq), `LinIneqSolver` (In) and `CassSolver` (Cs) we give the average and then in brackets the maximum elapsed time taken to perform the operation.

		50	100	150	50	100	150
	Size	50	100	150	50	100	150
	C	177	379	573	228	452	664
	V	255	513	768	252	498	747
BeginEdit	Eq	14 (76)	68 (327)	140 (731)			
	In	29 (107)	122 (467)	254 (1050)	84 (282)	327 (1784)	796 (2813)
	Cs	2 (7)	6 (30)	11 (60)	0 (0)	3 (18)	10 (34)
EndEdit	Eq	0 (0)	0 (0)	0 (0)			-
	In	0 (0)	0 (0)	0 (0)	0 (0)	0 (0)	0 (0)
	Cs	7 (23)	39 (110)	90 (268)	3 (15)	45 (120)	122 (288)
Solve	Eq	25 (74)	102 (312)	233 (701)	-		
	In	38 (109)	149 (453)	339 (1016)	47 (208)	229 (1111)	733 (2612)
	Cs	24 (194)	75 (439)	154 (920)	12 (55)	52 (217)	123 (727)
Resolve	Eq	0 (13)	0 (28)	0 (56)	-	-	
	In	0 (13)	3 (26)	11 (55)	1 (13)	7 (41)	27 (81)
	Cs	0 (13)	1 (119)	2 (141)	0 (4)	0 (11)	1 (40)
Add-Constraint	Eq	0 (2)	0 (25)	0 (82)			
	In	0 (3)	0 (24)	0 (81)	0 (6)	0 (29)	1 (94)
	Cs	3 (209)	7 (417)	13 (603)	0 (18)	2 (28)	6 (892)
Remove-Constraint	Eq	0 (0)	0 (0)	0 (0)	-	-	
	In	0 (0)	0 (0)	0 (0)	0 (0)	0 (0)	0 (2)
	Cs	0 (0)	0 (3)	0 (3)	0 (0)	0 (3)	0 (3)

(a) State transition application (columns 3–5) (b) Binary tree application (columns 6–8)

Table 1. Speed of Constraint Solving

The performance of all three solvers is very satisfactory when adding or removing constraints. All three perform well when only equalities are used. **`LinEqSolver` is slightly faster than `LinIneqSolver`, and quicker than `CassSolver`** during `Resolve` and `EndEdit` but slower (because of the overhead of constructing a second tableau) in `Solve` and `BeginEdit`. When inequalities are used the performance of `LinIneqSolver` is a little slow for diagrams with more than 600 constraints. The performance of `CassSolver`, however, is impressive. Thus, `LinEqSolver` is the method of choice for equalities, while `CassSolver` is the method of choice if inequalities are also required.

Acknowledgements

Many people have helped in the development of the various QOCA versions. They include Richard Helm, Tien Huynh, John Vlissides, Toby Sargeant, Tania Armstrong, Andrew Kelly and Yi Xiao.

References

1. A. Borning and B. Freeman-Benson. The OTI constraint solver: A constraint library for constructing interactive graphical user interfaces. In *Proceedings of the First International Conference on Principles and Practice of Constraint Programming*, pages 624–628, Cassis, France, September 1995.
2. A. Borning and B. Freeman-Benson. Ultraviolet: A constraint satisfaction algorithm for interactive graphics. *Constraints*, 3(1):9–32, 1998.
3. A. Borning, B. Freeman-Benson, and M. Wilson. Constraint hierarchies. *Lisp and Symbolic Computation*, 5(3):223–270, September 1992.
4. A. Borning, R. Lin, and K. Marriott. Constraints for the Web. In *Proceedings of the Fifth ACM International Multi-Media Conference*, pages 173–182, November 1997.
5. A. Borning, K. Marriott, P. Stuckey, and Y. Xiao. Solving linear arithmetic constraints for user interface applications. In *Proceedings of the 10th ACM Symposium on User Interface Software and Technology*, pages 87–96, 1997.
6. S.S. Chok and K. Marriott. Automatic construction of user interfaces from constraint multiset grammars. In *IEEE Symposium on Visual Languages*, pages 242–250, 1995.
7. S.S. Chok and K. Marriott. Automatic construction of intelligent diagram editors. In *Proceedings of the 11th ACM Symposium on User Interface Software and Technology*, 1998.
8. R. Fletcher. *Practical Methods of Optimization.* John Wiley & Sons, Chichester, 1987.
9. W. He and K. Marriott. Constrained graph layout. In *Graph Drawing '96*, volume 1190 of *LNCS*, pages 217–232. Springer-Verlag, 1996.
10. W. He and K. Marriott. Removing node overlapping using constrained optimisation. In *Twenty-First Australasian Computer Science Conf.*, pages 169–180. Springer-Verlag, 1998.
11. R. Helm, T. Huynh, K. Marriott, and J. Vlissides. An object-oriented architecture for constraint-based graphical editing. In C. Laffra, E. Blake, V. de Mey, and X. Pintado, editors, *Object-Oriented Programming for Graphics*, pages 217–238. Springer-Verlag, 1995.
12. H. Hosobe, S. Matsuoka, and A. Yonezawa. Generalized local propagation: A framework for solving constraint hierarchies. In *Proceedings of the Second International Conference on Principles and Practice of Constraint Programming*, pages 237–251. Springer-Verlag LLNCS 1118, 1996.
13. H. Hosobe, K. Miyashita, S. Takahashi, S. Matsuoka, and A. Yonezawa. Locally simultaneous constraint satisfaction. In *Proceedings of the 1994 Workshop on Principles and Practice of Constraint Programming*, pages 51–62. Springer-Verlag LLNCS 874, 1994.
14. T. Huynh and K. Marriott. Incremental constraint deletion in systems of linear constraints. *Information Processing Letters*, 55:111–115, 1995.
15. K. Marriott and P. Stuckey. *Programming with Constraints: An Introduction.* The MIT Press, 1998.
16. I. Sutherland. Sketchpad: A man-machine graphical communication system. In *Proceedings of the Spring Joint Computer Conference*, pages 329–346. IFIPS, 1963.

Safe Datalog Queries with Linear Constraints*

Peter Z. Revesz

Department of Computer Science and Engineering
University of Nebraska-Lincoln, Lincoln NE 68588, USA,
revesz@cse.unl.edu

Abstract. In this paper we consider Datalog queries with linear constraints. We identify several syntactical subcases of Datalog queries with linear constraints, called safe queries, and show that the least model of safe Datalog queries with linear constraints can be evaluated bottom-up in closed-form. These subcases include Datalog with only positive and upper-bound or only negative and lower bound constraints or only half-addition, upper and lower bound constraints. We also study other subcases where the recognition problem is decidable.

1 Introduction

Constraint databases is an active area of current research. In particular, linear constraint databases have been used for modeling geometric data and in other applications [3, 14, 15, 22, 23]. There are several proposals to define query languages for linear constraint databases.

Most query language proposals are based on first-order logic. However, it has been found that first-order languages even with real polynomial constraint databases are incapable of expressing many simple recursive queries like finding the transitive closure of an input graph [2].

Other query language proposals are based on fixpoint-logic [1, 29]. Unfortunately, the evaluation of fixpoint queries with linear constraint databases is not guaranteed. This is a major drawback for database use, where non-expert users should be allowed to express new queries without having to worry about termination problems. For example, Kuijpers et al. [22] prove for a five-rule stratified Datalog program that defines topological connectivity that it terminates for any rational linear constraint database input. However, the proof is quite complicated and works only for that single program.

Recently, Grumbach and Kuper [12] have proposed a tractable language with a bounded inflationary fixpoint operator. This is advantageous from the point of guaranteed termination for any query expressible in the language. However, the query language has a syntax and semantics which is not particularly elegant.

In this paper we consider restricted subsets of fixpoint-logic with linear constraint databases. For these restricted cases, we show that termination of the

* This work was supported in part by NSF grants IRI-9625055 and IRI-9632871.

query evaluation can be guaranteed. In addition, the correctness of the syntax of the language is easy to check even by beginning users, while the semantics of the language is based on standard fixpoint-logic.

An important problem that occurs in database applications is the recognition problem. Given a query program, an input database, a defined relation name R, and a tuple t of constants (rationals or integers) the recognition problem asks whether t is in R within the least fixpoint of the query program and the input database.

The recognition problem is known to be undecidable in general for fixpoint queries and linear constraint databases. In this paper we identify several syntactical subcases of fixpoint queries for which the recognition problem can be solved in finite time. We call these syntactical subcases safe queries.

The primary language based on fixpoint logic is Datalog. Theorem 1 shows that the least fixpoint of any Datalog query with only positive and upper bound constraints or only negative and lower bound constraints is evaluable in PTIME. Theorems 2 shows that the least fixpoint of Datalog queries with integer half-addition constraints is also evaluable in finite time. These theorems extend the known cases of Datalog with constraint queries whose least fixpoints can be found in finite time.

In both cases the least fixpoints will be computed in a constraint form, where the output relations are a set of constraint tuples. Each constraint tuple is a shorthand description for the set of constant tuples that satisfy the constraint. Therefore, it is easy to test whether t is in relation R by testing whether t satisfies any constraint tuple of R. We also consider the complexity of the recognition problem for any fixed program on a variable size input database. This measure, often used in databases, is referred to as the *data complexity* of queries [6, 30]. Theorem 3 shows that Datalog with half-addition constraints has a DEXPTIME-complete data complexity. Theorems 4 and 6 show that the recognition problem is also decidable for two subcases of Datalog with addition and Datalog with linear equation constraints.

This paper is organized as follows. Section 2 lists some basic definitions, including various types of constraints and Datalog queries with constraints. Section 3 describes the evaluation procedure for Datalog queries for positive and upper bound, negative and lower bound and half-addition constraints and analyzes the data complexity of the recognition problem. Sections 4 and 5 study the recognition problem for subcases of Datalog with addition and Datalog with equation constraints. Finally, Section 6 discusses related work and conclusions.

2 Basic Concepts

2.1 Atomic Constraints

In this paper we consider several types of atomic constraints, which are all subcases of *linear constraints* of the form

$$c_1 x_1 + \ldots + c_k x_k \,\theta\, b$$

where c_i is a constant and x_i is a variable for each $1 \leq i \leq k$, the θ is either $\geq$ or $>$ and b is any constant. We call b the *gap-value* in each linear constraint.

We distinguish between two cases of linear constraints depending on the domain of the variables and constants: the domain of *rational linear constraints* is the set of rationals $\mathbf{Q}$ and the domain of *integer linear constraints* is the set of integers $\mathbf{Z}$.

We consider the following subcases of (rational or integer) linear constraints.

Positive Constraint: A positive constraint is an atomic constraint where each coefficient is non-negative.

Negative Constraint: A negative constraint is an atomic constraint where each coefficient is non-positive.

Lower Bound Constraint: A lower bound constraint is an atomic constraint of the form $x \; \theta \; b$.

Upper Bound Constraint: An upper bound constraint is an atomic constraint of the form $-x \; \theta \; b$.

Equality Constraint: An equality constraint is a conjunction of an upper and a lower bound constraint of the form $x \geq b$ and $-x \geq -b$. We abbreviate such a conjunction by $x = b$.

Half-Addition Constraint: A half-addition constraint is an atomic constraint of the form $x_1 + x_2 \geq b$ or $x_1 - x_2 \geq b$ or $-x_1 + x_2 \geq b$ or $-x_1 - x_2 \geq b$ where b is non-negative.

Addition Constraint: An addition constraint is a conjunction of two atomic constraints of the form $-x_1 + x_2 \geq b$ and $x_1 - x_2 \geq -b$. We abbreviate such a conjunction by $x_2 = x_1 + b$.

Equation Constraint: An equation constraint has the same form as an atomic constraint except θ is $=$. An equation constraint can be expressed by a conjunction of two atomic constraints.

Note: An addition constraint can be expressed as $\exists x_3 \quad x_2 + x_3 \geq b$ and $-x_2 - x_3 \geq -b$ and $x_1 + x_3 \geq 0$ and $-x_1 - x_3 \geq 0$. Notice that addition constraints cannot be expressed by half-addition constraints when $b \neq 0$, because either $-b$ or b is negative.

2.2 Datalog with Constraints

The following definition of the syntax and semantics of Datalog programs with constraints extends the definition of Datalog without constraints in [1, 29] and was also given in [18].

Facts: Each input database is a set of facts (also called constraint tuples) that have the form,

$$R_0(x_1, \ldots, x_k) :\!-\; \psi. \qquad (fact)$$

where ψ is a conjunction of atomic constraints on $x_1, \ldots, x_k$ which are not necessarily distinct variables or constants.

Rules: Each Datalog program is a set of rules that have the form,

$$R_0(x_1, \ldots, x_k) :\!\!- R_1(x_{1,1}, \ldots, x_{1,k_1}), \ldots, R_n(x_{n,1}, \ldots, x_{n,k_n}), \psi. \qquad (rule)$$

where $R_0, \ldots, R_n$ are not necessary distinct relation symbols and the xs are not necessarily distinct variables or constants and ψ is a conjunction of atomic constraints. We call the left hand side of :— the *head* and the right hand side of :— the *body* of a fact or rule. Several facts or several rules can have the same left-hand relation name. In the facts all variables in the body also appear in the head. In the rules some variables in the body may not appear in the head.

Query: Each Datalog query consists of a Datalog program and an input database.

Example 1 The following query checks whether at least k out of n formulas $f_1(x_1, \ldots, x_m), \ldots, f_n(x_1, \ldots, x_m)$ of atomic constraints can be simultaneously satisfied. We assume that the formulas are in disjunctive normal form and that $f_{i,j}(x_1, \ldots, x_m)$ is the jth disjunct of the ith formula.

Let $C(y, x_1, \ldots, x_m)$ be an input database relation which contains a constraint tuples of the form $y = i, f_{i,j}(x_1, \ldots, x_m)$ for each $f_{i,j}$.

Let $Next(x, y)$ be an input database relation that contains the constraint tuples $x = i, y = i + 1$ for each $0 \leq i \leq n$. Let $Need(x)$ and $Out\_Of(y)$ be the relations that contains $x = k$ and $y = n$, respectively. Then, the query can be expressed as follows.

$$Sat(x_1, \ldots, x_m) \quad :\!\!- Test(x_1, \ldots, x_m, n, k),\ Out\_Of(n)\ Need(k).$$

$$Test(x_1, \ldots, x_m, i_1, j_1) :\!\!- Test(x_1, \ldots, x_m, i, j),\ Next(i, i_1),\ C(i_1, x_1, \ldots, x_m),\ Next(j, j_1).$$

$$Test(x_1, \ldots, x_m, i_1, j) \quad :\!\!- Test(x_1, \ldots, x_m, i, j),\ Next(i, i_1).$$

$$Test(x_1, \ldots, x_m, 0, 0).$$

The query defines the relation *Test* such that $Test(x_1, \ldots, x_m, i, j)$ is true for some values of $x_1, \ldots, x_m, i, j$ if and only if out of the first i formulas at least j can be simultaneously satisfied.

Semantics: Let Q be any Datalog query with constraints. We call an *interpretation* of Q any assignment I of a finite or infinite number of tuples over $\delta^{\alpha(R_i)}$ to each R_i that occurs in Q, where δ is the domain of the attribute variables and $\alpha(R_i)$ is the arity of relation R_i.

The *immediate consequence operator* of a Datalog query Q, denoted T_Q, is a mapping from interpretations to interpretations as follows. For each interpretation I:

$R_0(a_1, \ldots, a_k) \in T_Q(I)$ iff there is an instantiation σ of all variables by constants from δ, including variables $x_1, \ldots, x_k$ by constants $a_1, \ldots, a_k$, in either a fact of the form $(fact)$ such that $\sigma(\psi)$ is true, or a rule of the form $(rule)$ such that $R_i(\sigma(x_{i,1},\ldots,x_{i,k_i})) \in I$ for each $1 \le i \le n$ and $\sigma(\psi)$ is true.

Let $T_Q^0(I) = T_Q(I)$. Also let $T_Q^{i+1}(I) = T_Q^i(I) \cup T_Q(T_Q^i(I))$. An interpretation I is called a *least fixpoint* of a query Q iff $I = \bigcup_i T_Q^i(\emptyset)$.

The above is a general definition of the syntax and the semantics of Datalog programs with constraints. In this paper, we will be interested in particular with the following cases of Datalog with constraints:

Datalog^{pos}: positive and upper bound constraints.

Datalog^{neg}: negative and lower bound constraints.

Datalog^{ha}: half-addition, upper and lower bound constraints.

Datalog^{VA}: addition constraints defining vector addition.

Datalog^{MM}: equation constraints defining matrix multiplication.

For the last two types of queries some special restrictions apply that are detailed in Sections 4 and 5.

2.3 Stratified Datalog with Constraints

Semipositive Datalog queries [1, 29] extend Datalog with negation. Syntactically, they are composed of facts of the form $(fact)$ and rules of the form $(rule)$ where a negation symbol may occur before any relation symbol R_i that is the head of some fact.

Semantically, each semipositive Datalog program is a mapping from interpretations to interpretations similarly to Datalog programs except if R_i is negated in a rule, then the consequence operator requires that $R_i(\sigma(x_{i,1},\ldots,x_{i,k_i})) \notin I$.

Example 2 We can modify Example 1 to test whether exactly k formulas are satisfied by inserting $\neg\, C(i_1, x_1, \ldots, x_m)$ into the body of the third rule.

Another extension of Datalog is the class of *stratified Datalog* programs. Each stratified Datalog program Π is the union of semipositive programs $\Pi_1, \ldots, \Pi_k$ satisfying the following property: no relation symbol R that occurs negated in a Π_i is a head of a rule in any Π_j with $j \ge i$. We call P_i the ith stratum of the program.

Each stratified Datalog program is a mapping from interpretations to interpretations. In particular, if Π is the union of the semipositive programs $\Pi_1, \ldots, \Pi_k$ with the above property, then the composition $\Pi_k(\ldots \Pi_1() \ldots)$ is its semantics.

The above is a general definition for semipositive and stratified Datalog programs. In this paper, we will be interested in the following:

Stratified Datalog$^{pos/neg}$: that is, stratified Datalog programs in which:

- Each input database relation is either positive, that is, it contains only positive or upper bound constraints, or negative, that is, it contains only negative or lower bound constraints.

- Each odd stratum contains only unnegated positive input database relations or relations defined in earlier odd strata and negated negative input database relations or relations defined in earlier even strata.
- Each even stratum contains only unnegated negative input database relations or relations defined in earlier even strata and negated positive input database relations or relations defined in earlier odd strata.

3 Evaluation of Datalog with Constraints

In this section we show that the least fixpoint of Datalog^{pos}, Datalog^{neg} and Datalog^{ha} queries can be evaluated bottom-up.

3.1 Constraint Least Fixpoints and Least Models

Constraint Rule Application: Let us assume that we have a rule of the form (*rule*) and we also have given or derived facts for each $1 \leq i \leq n$ of the form:

$$R_i(x_{i,1}, \ldots, x_{i,k_i}) :\!\!- \psi_i(x_{i,1}, \ldots, x_{i,k_i}).$$

where formula ψ_i is a conjunction of constraints. A *constraint rule application* of this rule given these facts as input produces the following derived fact:

$$R_0(x_1, \ldots, x_k) :\!\!- \phi(x_1, \ldots, x_k).$$

where ϕ is a quantifier-free formula that is equivalent to

$$\exists * \psi_1(x_{1,1}, \ldots, x_{1,k_1}), \ldots, \psi_n(x_{n,1}, \ldots, x_{n,k_n}), \psi.$$

where $*$ is the list of the variables in the body of the rule which do not occur in the head of the rule.

The ***bottom-up constraint fixpoint evaluation*** of Datalog queries starts from the input facts and rules and repeatedly applies one of the rules until no new facts can be derived and added to the database. We call the set of input and derived facts the constraint least fixpoint of the query.

Remember that a constraint tuple is equivalent to a possibly infinite number of regular tuples of constants from the domain. Hence a finite number of constraint tuples could represent an infinite least fixpoint. Proposition 1, which relies on this observation, was proven in many instances in constraint logic programming and constraint databases [16–18].

Proposition 1 For any Datalog with constraints query the bottom-up constraint least fixpoint is equivalent to the least fixpoint.

Observation 1: The evaluation of stratified Datalog queries can be reduced to the evaluation of Datalog queries. We evaluate each stratum by at first replacing in it each negated occurrence of a constraint relation R_i by its complement constraint relation co_R_i. This evaluation gives a constraint least model for the stratified Datalog query.

Proposition 1 gives some idea for computing even infinite least fixpoints in finite time. However, the termination of the constraint least fixpoint evaluation has to be proven for each particular case of constraints. For several cases of constraints termination is not possible. However, we can show termination for Datalog^{pos}, Datalog^{neg}, stratified Datalog$^{pos/neg}$ and Datalog^{ha} queries.

3.2 Termination Proof for Datalog^{pos}, Datalog^{neg} and Stratified Datalog$^{pos/neg}$

Observation 2: For integers we can rewrite each $>$ constraint with gap-value b into an equivalent $\geq$ constraint with gap-value $b+1$ and the same left hand sides. Hence we will assume that we have only $\geq$ constraints in the case of integers. Otherwise, the statements in this section apply to both rationals and integers with small differences that we point out as appropriate.

At first, we prove two quantifier elimination results, the first for positive and upper bound constraints, and the second for negative and lower bound constraints.

Lemma 1 Let S be any conjunction of positive and upper bound constraints over $x, y_1, \ldots, y_n$. Then we can rewrite $\exists x S$ into a logically equivalent conjunction S' of positive and upper bound constraints over $y_1, \ldots, y_n$.

The symmetric case of the above is also closed under quantifier-elimination.

Lemma 2 Let S be any conjunction of negative and lower bound constraints over $x, y_1, \ldots, y_n$. Then we can rewrite $\exists x S$ into a logically equivalent conjunction S' of negative and lower bound constraints over $y_1, \ldots, y_n$.

We can now show the following theorem in case of Datalog with positive or Datalog with negative constraints.

Theorem 1 The least fixpoint of any Datalog^{pos} or Datalog^{neg} query is evaluable in closed form in PTIME in the size of the input database.

By Observation 1 we can reduce the evaluation of stratified Datalog$^{pos/neg}$ queries to evaluating for each stratum either a Datalog^{pos} or Datalog^{neg} query by finding the complement relations before the evaluation of each stratum.

Lemma 3 Let R be any constraint relation with n number of tuples and at most m number of atomic constraints in each tuple. Then the complement relation of R can be found in PTIME in the size of the relation.

The proof of the above Lemma uses the fact that in any fixed k-dimension n number of hyperplanes cut the space into a polynomial in n number of k-dimensional polyhedra, each of which either belongs to R or to its complement. From Lemma 3 follows:

Corollary 1 The least model of any stratified fixed Datalog$^{pos/neg}$ program and variable input database is evaluable in closed form, where relations defined in odd strata will have positive and relations defined in even strata will have negative constraint forms, in PTIME in the size of the input database.

3.3 Termination Proof for Datalog^{ha}

Datalog^{ha} with Integer Domain: By Observation 2 we can again assume that each θ is $\geq$. We can transform any conjunction S of half-addition, lower bound and upper bound constraints over a set of variables $x_1, \ldots, x_{n-1}$ into a S' with only half-addition constraints over $x_1, \ldots, x_{n-1}, d$ where d is the largest absolute value of the gap-values in S. This is because we can replace each $x \geq b$ by $x + d \geq (b + d)$ and each $-x \geq b$ by $-x + d \geq (b + d)$.

We consider d as if it were an nth variable x_n. We could have any distinct pair of the n variables on the left hand side of a half-addition constraint. It does not matter which element of a pair is written first and which is written second. Without loss of generality we can insist that if $\pm x_i \pm x_j$ is on the left hand side, then $i < j$. It is easy to see that there can be only $4n(n-1)/2 = 2n(n-1)$ different left hand sides because there are four distinct cases considering whether x_i and x_j has positive or negative signs.

We further simplify S' so that it contains at most one half-addition constraint with each different left hand side. If S' has several half-addition constraints with the same left hand side all but the one with the highest gap-value is superfluous and is deleted. We call S' the *normal form* of S.

Lemma 4 Let S be any normal form conjunction of half-addition constraints over $x, y_1, \ldots, y_n$ and d. Then we can rewrite $\exists x S$ into a logically equivalent normal form S' of half-addition constraints over $y_1, \ldots, y_n$ and d.

Let us fix any ordering of the $2n(n-1)$ possible left hand sides. Using this fixed ordering, we can represent any S in normal form as a $2n(n-1)$-dimensional point in which the ith coordinate value will be $(b+1)$ if S contains a half-addition constraint with the ith left hand side and b is the gap-value in it, and 0 otherwise.

We say that a point *dominates* another point if it has the same dimension and all of its coordinate values are $\geq$ the corresponding coordinate values in the other point.

Suppose that relation $R(x_1, \ldots, x_{n-1})$ is defined in some Datalog^{ha} program. As the constraint fixpoint evaluation derives new constraint tuples for R, the right hand side of these constraint tuples will be conjunctions of half-addition constraints over the n variables, including d. The sequence of derived constraint tuples can be represented as described above using a point sequence:

$p_1, p_2, \ldots$

It is easy to see that if point p_i dominates point p_j, then p_i and p_j represent conjunctions S_i and S_j of half-addition constraints such that the set of solutions of S_i is included in the set of solutions of S_j. This shows that the fixpoint evaluation could be modified to add only points that do not dominate any earlier point in the sequence. By the geometric Lemma in [24], in any fixed dimension any sequence of distinct points with non-negative integer coordinates must be finite, if no point dominates any earlier point in the sequence. This shows that using a modified constraint fixpoint evaluation:

Theorem 2 The least fixpoint of any Datalog^{ha} query is evaluable in half-addition constraint form when the domain is the integer numbers.

For the recognition problem we can say the following.

Theorem 3 The recognition problem for any fixed Datalog^{ha} program and variable input database has a DEXPTIME-complete data complexity when the domain is the integer numbers.

Datalog^{ha} with Rational Domain: We can assume without loss of generality that the gap-values and the absolute value d are integer numbers, because if they are not, then we can multiply all gap-values by the least common multiple m of all the denumerators. Clearly, $(a_1, \ldots, a_k)$ satisfies a transformed conjunction of constraints if and only if $(\frac{a_1}{m}, \ldots, \frac{a_k}{m})$ satisfies the original constraint.

For dealing with rational numbers we will also treat as a special variable x_{n+1} the value $d + \frac{1}{2}$. Otherwise, the normal form will be defined as in the integer case except we allow both $\geq$ and $>$ comparisons within the half-addition constraints.

Lemma 5 Let S be any normal form conjunction of half-addition constraints over $x, y_1, \ldots, y_n, d, d + \frac{1}{2}$. Then we can rewrite $\exists x S$ into a logically equivalent normal form S' of half-addition constraints over $y_1, \ldots, y_n, d, d + \frac{1}{2}$.

For the rest of the section, the proof is similar to the integer case. Hence we have that:

Corollary 2 The least fixpoint of any Datalog^{ha} query is evaluable in half-addition constraint form when the domain is the rational numbers.

For the recognition problem we can say the following.

Corollary 3 The recognition problem for any fixed Datalog^{ha} program and variable input database has a DEXPTIME-complete data complexity when the domain is the rational numbers.

4 The Recognition Problem for Datalog^{VA} Queries

Datalog^{VA} queries are composed of regular relational database facts (sets of constant tuples) and rules of the form:

$$\begin{aligned} R(x_1, \ldots, x_m, y_1, \ldots, y_k) :- \; & F_1(y_{1,1}, \ldots, y_{1,k_1}), \ldots, F_n(y_{n,1}, \ldots, y_{n,k_n}), \\ & P(z_1, \ldots, z_m, y_{p,1}, \ldots, y_{p,k_p}), \\ & x_1 = z_1 + c_1, \; \ldots, \; x_m = z_m + c_m. \end{aligned}$$

where the F_is are input database relations, R and P are relation symbols occuring in the head of rules. Relation P and each relation F_i is optional in the rule. The ys are not necessarily distinct variables among themselves but they are all distinct from the x_is and z_is, which are all different.

The domain of the x_i and z_i variables is the set of non-negative integers numbers $\mathbf{N}$, but each c_i and any constant in the input database can be any integer.

The following theorem is proven by reduction of the recognition problem for Datalog^{VA} to the recognition problem in *vector addition systems with states*, VASS, which is shown to be decidable in [21]. VASS is a generalization the reachability problem in Petri nets, for which the containment problem is undecidable. This implies for Datalog^{VA} queries the following.

Theorem 4 The recognition problem for Datalog^{VA} queries is decidable and for semipositive Datalog^{VA} queries is undecidable.

Nevertheless, it is possible to prove the following.

Theorem 5 It can be decided whether a Datalog^{VA} query is safe, i.e., its output can be represented in constraint form for any valid input database.

5 The Recognition Problem for Datalog^{MM} Queries

Datalog^{MM} queries are composed of regular relational database facts and rules of the form:

$$\begin{aligned} R(x_1,\ldots,x_m) :\!\!- \; & R(y_1,\ldots,y_m), \\ & -x_1 + c_{1,1}y_1 + \ldots + c_{1,m}y_m = 0, \\ & \vdots \\ & -x_m + c_{m,1}y_1 + \ldots + c_{m,m}y_m = 0. \end{aligned}$$

or

$$R(x_1,\ldots,x_m) :\!\!- \; F(x_1,\ldots,x_m).$$

where F is a regular input relation (sets of constant tuples), the x_is and y_is are all different variables, and each $c_{i,j}$ is a rational constant. The domain of the variables is the set of rational numbers.

It can be seen that Datalog^{MM} queries can express sets of *Markov processes* when we make the restriction that for each j the $\sum_{1 \leq i \leq m} c_{i,j} = 1$ and use only a single recursive rule. We call this condition (1).

Further, it is known that the value of Markov processes approach a steady state when all the $c_{i,j}$s are positive. We call this condition (2).

Therefore, when conditions (1&2) hold, then after some finite number of rule applications we will only get $R(a_1,\ldots,a_m)$ tuples such that $\mid a_i - b_i \mid < \epsilon$ where $(b_1,\ldots,b_n)$ is the steady state value and ϵ is an arbitrarily small positive rational number.

We define the recognition problem with ϵ tolerance the task of deciding whether there is a tuple in the least fixpoint of the query such that each of its elements is within an ϵ distance from the corresponing element in the given tuple. Taking advantage of the steady state convergence of Markov processes [28], we can prove the following.

Theorem 6 The recognition problem with ϵ tolerance for Datalog^{MM} quereis satisfying conditions (1&2) is decidable.

6 Related Works and Conclusion

Datalog^{pos}, Datalog^{neg} and Datalog^{ha} queries are cases of constraint logic programs whose syntax and semantics was defined in a general way in [16]. Constraint bottom-up evaluations for constraint queries (both constraint logic programs and constraint relational calculus queries) were considered within a constraint database framework in [18] and many recent papers (see [17, 26] for surveys on constraint logic programming and constraint databases).

A *gap-order constraint* is a lower bound constraint, an upper bound constraint or a constraint of the form $x + b \leq y$ where $b \geq 0$. Note that all gap-order constraints are half-addition constraints, but some half-addition constraints are not gap-order constraints. For example, $x + y \geq 5$ is a half-addition constraint but it is not expressible by gap-order constraints. A least fixpoint evaluation for Datalog with gap-order constraints is described in [24]. The recognition problem is also studied in [8]. The DISCO system [5] implements Datalog queries with integer gap-order constraints. Adding negation in a safe way to Datalog with gap-order queries is studied in [25].

A *temporal constraint* is like a gap-order constraint but the gap-value can be any integer (both negative and non-negative). Temporal constraints can express addition constraints. Hence the recognition problem for Datalog with temporal constraints is undecidable. However, an evaluation of relational calculus queries with temporal constraints is possible and is considered by Koubarakis in [19, 20]. Efficient tests for temporal constraint satisfaction are described in [9] and for monotone two-variable constraints in [11].

Chomicki and Imielinski [7] consider the language Datalog$_{1S}$ which is like Datalog extended with an increment operator which may occur only in the first argument of relations. Linear recursive Datalog$_{1S}$ is a subcase of Datalog^{VA}. The least fixpoint is evaluable for Datalog$_{1S}$ queries [7].

Fribourg and Olsén [10] consider the connection between Petri nets and a subset of Datalog^{VA} programs. [10] shows that the least fixpoint of those queries that can be represented by a special case of Petri nets, called BPP-nets, is evaluable in finite time.

There is a growing number of implementations of first-order constraint queries with linear constraint databases, for example CCUBE [4], DEDALE [13] and MLPQ [27]. The query evaluation algorithms described in this paper could be useful extensions of these systems as well as some constraint logic programming systems, for example CLP(R), that implement linear constraints. We already started implementing safe recursive queries in MLPQ.

References

1. S. Abiteboul, R. Hull and V. Vianu. *Foundations of Databases*. Addison-Wesley, 1995.
2. M. Benedikt, G. Dong, L. Libkin, L. Wong. Relational Expressive Power of Constraint Query Languages. *Journal of the ACM*, vol. 45, 1–34, 1998.
3. A. Brodsky, J. Jaffar, M.J. Maher. Toward Practical Query Evaluation for Constraint Databases. *Constraints*, vol. 2, no. 3&4, 279–304, 1997.
4. A, Brodsky, V.E. Segal, J. Chen, P.A. Exarkhopoulo. The CCUBE Constraint Object-Oriented Database System. *Constraints*, vol. 2., no. 3&4, 245–278, 1997.
5. J. Byon, P.Z. Revesz, DISCO: A Constraint Database System with Sets, *Proc. Workshop on Constraint Databases and Applications*, Springer-Verlag LNCS 1034, 68–83, 1995.
6. A.K. Chandra, D. Harel. Structure and Complexity of Relational Queries. *Journal of Computer and System Sciences*, vol. 25, 99–128, 1982.
7. J. Chomicki, T. Imielinski. Finite Representation of Infinite Query Answers. *ACM Transactions of Database Systems*, vol. 18, no. 2, 181–223, 1993.
8. J. Cox, K. McAloon. Decision Procedures for Constraint Based Extensions of Datalog. In: F. Benhamou, A. Colmerauer, eds., *Constraint Logic Programming*, MIT Press, 1993.
9. R. Dechter, I. Meiri, J. Pearl. Temporal Constraint Networks. *Artificial Intelligence*, vol. 49, 61–95, 1991.
10. L. Fribourg, H. Olsén. A Decompositional Approach for Computing Least Fixed-Points of Datalog Programs with $\mathcal{Z}$-Counters. *Constraints*, vol. 2, no. 3&4, 305–336, 1997.
11. D. Goldin, P.C. Kanellakis. Constraint Query Algebras. *Constraints*, vol. 1, no. 1&2, 54-83, 1996.
12. S. Grumbach, G. M. Kuper. Tractable Recursion over Geometric Data. *Proc. Third International Conference on Principles and Practice of Constraint Programming*, Springer-Verlag LNCS 1330, 450-462, 1997.
13. S. Grumbach, P. Rigaux, L. Segoufin. The DEDALE System for Complex Spatial Queries. *Proc. ACM SIGMOD International Conference on Management of Data*, ACM Press, 213–224, 1998.
14. S. Grumbach, J Su, C. Tollu. Linear Constraint Query Languages: Expressive Power and Complexity. *Proc. Logic and Computational Complexity*, Springer-Verlag LNCS 960, 1994.
15. M. Gyssens, J. Van den Bussche, D. Van Gucht. Complete Geometrical Query Languages. *Proc. 16th ACM Symposium on Principles of Database Systems*, 62–67, 1997.
16. J. Jaffar, J.L. Lassez. Constraint Logic Programming. *Proc. 14th ACM Symposium on Principles of Programming Languages*, 111–119, 1987.
17. J. Jaffar, M.J. Maher. Constraint Logic Programming: A Survey. *Journal of Logic Programming*, vol. 19 & 20, 503–581, 1994.
18. P. C. Kanellakis, G. M. Kuper, P. Z. Revesz. Constraint Query Languages. *Journal of Computer and System Sciences*, vol. 51, no. 1, 26-52, 1995.

19. M. Koubarakis. Database Models for Infinite and Indefinite Temporal Information. *Information Systems*, vol. 19, no. 2, 141–173, 1994.
20. M. Koubarakis. The Complexity of Query Evaluation in Indefinite Temporal Constraint Databases. *Theoretical Computer Science*, vol. 171, no. 1&2, 25–60, 1997.
21. S. R. Kosaraju. Decidability of Reachability in Vector Addition Systems. *Prof. 14th ACM Symposium on Theory of Computing*, 267-281, 1982.
22. B. Kuijpers, J. Paredaens, M. Smits, J. Van den Bussche. Termination Properties of Spatial Datalog Programs. In: D. Pedreschi and C. Zaniolo, eds., *Logic in Databases*, Springer-Verlag LNCS 1154, 101–116, 1997.
23. J. Paredaens, J.V.D. Bussche, D.V. Gucht. First-Order Queries on Finite Structures over the Reals. *Proc. Symp. on Logic in Computer Science*, 1995.
24. P. Z. Revesz. A Closed Form Evaluation for Datalog Queries with Integer (Gap)-Order Constraints. *Theoretical Computer Science*, vol. 116, no. 1, 117-149, 1993.
25. P. Z. Revesz. Safe Query Languages for Constraint Databases. *ACM Transactions on Database Systems*. vol. 23, no. 1, 1–43, 1998.
26. P. Z. Revesz. Constraint Databases: A Survey. In: L. Libkin and B. Thalheim, eds., *Semantics in Databases*, Springer-Verlag LNCS 1358, 209–246, 1998.
27. P. Z. Revesz, Y. Li. MLPQ: A Linear Constraint Database System with Aggregate Operators. *Proc. International Database Engineering and Applications Symposium*, IEEE Press, 132–137, 1997.
28. H. Schneider, G. P. Barker. *Matrices and Linear Algebra.* 2nd ed., Holt, Rinehart and Winston, 1973.
29. J.D. Ullman. *Principles of Database and Knowledge-Base Systems*, vols 1&2. Computer Science Press, 1989.
30. M. Vardi. The Complexity of Relational Query Languages. *Proc. 14th ACM Symposium on the Theory of Computing*, 137–145, 1982.

Proof of Lemma 1: First, simplify the positive constraints by deleting all variables with zero coefficients. Now, S' will contain the set of constraints that do not contain the variable x and all constraints that can be derived from some upper bound constraint of the form $-x\theta_1 b$ and a positive constraint of the form $c_0x + c_1y_1 + \ldots + c_ny_n\theta_2 a$ where c_i is a positive rational number for $0 \leq i \leq n$. The new constraint created will be $c_1y_1 + \ldots + c_ny_n\theta_3 a + c_0 b$, where θ_3 is $\geq$ if θ_1 and θ_2 are both $\geq$ and $>$ otherwise. This is still a positive constraint and if a, b and c_0 are integers, then the new gap-value created will be also an integer. Therefore, upper bound and positive constraints are closed under existential quantifier elimination in the case of both rationals and integers. We can prove the soundness of the quantifier elimination similarly to the proof of Lemma 4.

Proof of Lemma 2: This case is symmetric to the case of Lemma 1. All constraints created will be between a lower bound constraint and a negative constraint.

Proof of Theorem 1: Let us consider any relation $R(x_1, \ldots, x_k)$. Each fact of R will contain a conjunction of positive and upper bound constraints. Note that the left hand side of each positive constraint will be the same as the left hand side of a positive constraint in the input database or one of the rules except that some coefficients can be changed to zero. Therefore, the number of different left hand sides of positive constraints is a finite number (if we have m variables in a positive constraint, then there could be 2^m different left hand sides that could be generated from it).

Let C be the set of positive coefficients in any positive constraint in the input database or the rules. Let B be the set of gap-values in any upper bound constraint. Let D denote the set of all possible products of an element in B and and element in C. Now, consider any positive constraint with m variables. As we eliminate any variable from it by adding it to an upper bound constraint we always add an element of D to the gap-value of the positive constraint. Further we can add only m times. Hence the number of possible gap-values that can be created is finite. In fact, if there are at most m variables in any positive constraint, then the set of possible gap-values that can be created are $S = \{b + d_1 + \ldots + d_m \;:\; b \in B, d_i \in D \cup \{0\}, 1 \leq i \leq m\}$. For any fixed program, m will be a constant equivalent to the maximum number of variables in any rule or fact. Hence the number of possible gap-values that can be created is polynomial in the size of B and C and hence also in the size of the input database.

Since both the set of left hand sides and the set of right hand sides that could occur in any constraint in any fact of R is a polynomial in the input database size, the number of possible constraints and the number of possible facts of R is also polynomial in it. The fixpoint evaluation needs to continue at most the number of different constraint tuples that could be added to the database. Since that is a polynomial number in the input database size, after that many iterations the fixpoint evaluation can stop. Hence each fixed Datalog^{pos} query can be evaluated in PTIME in the size of the input database.

A similar argument can show that Datalog^{neg} is also evaluable in PTIME data complexity.

Proof of Lemma 4: S' will be the conjunction of all the half-addition constraints in S that do not contain the variable x and all the half-addition constraints that can be derived from any pair of half-addition constraints in S using the implication table below.

	$x - z \geq b$	$-x + z \geq b$	$x + z \geq b$	$-x - z \geq b$
$x - y \geq a$		$-y + z \geq a + b$		$-y - z \geq a + b$
$-x + y \geq a$	$y - z \geq a + b$		$y + z \geq a + b$	
$x + y \geq a$		$y + z \geq a + b$		$y - z \geq a + b$
$-x - y \geq a$	$-y - z \geq a + b$		$-y + z \geq a + b$	

Given any two half-addition constraints with opposite signs for x, their sum is returned by the implication table. It is easy to see that if S consisted of half-addition constraints, then S' will contain only half-addition constraints because in each constraint created using the implication table the gap-value will be the sum of two gap-values already present in S. Therefore only non-negative gap-values will be created using the implication table. The only case that merits special mention is when y and z are the same variables. In that case we may obtain either $2y \geq a+b$ or $-2y \geq a+b$. These two cases can be rewritten into half-addition constraint form as $y+d \geq floor(\frac{a+b}{2})+d$ and $-y+d \geq floor(\frac{a+b}{2})+d$ respectively, where the floor function takes the smallest integer value that is greater than or equal to any given rational value.

For any instantiation, if two half-addition constraints are both true, then their sum also must be a true half-addition constraint. Hence if S is true, then S' must be also true for any instantiation of the variables $x, y_1, \ldots, y_n$.

For the other direction, suppose that S' is true for some instantiation of the variables $y_1, \ldots, y_n$. Then make the same instantiation into S. After the instantiation, x will be the only remaining variable in S. Wherever x occurs positively, the constraint implies a lower bound for x, and wherever x occurs negatively the constraint implies an upper bound for x.

Suppose that the largest lower bound l is implied by some constraint f and the smallest upper bound u is implied by some constraint g. Since the sum of f and g under the current instantiation is equivalent to $l \leq u$ and is in S', which is true, we can find a value between l and u inclusively for x that will make S also true.

Proof of Theorem 2: We can modify the basic fixpoint evaluation method by adding for each relation R only "points" that do not dominate any earlier point added to relation R. This shows that the number of points added to R must be finite. By reasoning similarly to R for each defined relation, we can see that the modified fixpoint evaluation must terminate. The correctness of the modification follows from the observation that points that are not added are not new (in the sense that there is no instantiation which makes them true but does not make any other input or already derived fact true).

Non-systematic Search and Learning: An Empirical Study

E Thomas Richards and Barry Richards

IC-Parc, Imperial College, London SW7 2AZ
Email: {etr,ebr}@icparc.ic.ac.uk

Abstract. This paper explores the performance of a new complete non-systematic search algorithm *learn-SAT* on two types of 3-SAT problems, (i) an extended range of AIM problems [1] and (ii) structured unsolvable problems [2]. These are thought to present a difficult challenge for non-systematic search algorithms. They have been extensively used to study powerful special purpose SAT algorithms. We consider two of these, viz. the tableau-based algorithm of Bayardo & Schrag [2] and *relsat*. We compare their performance with that of *learn-SAT*, which is based on restart-repair and learning no-goods. Surprisingly, *learn-SAT* does very well. Sometimes it does much better than the other two algorithms; at other times they are broadly equivalent; and then there are some "anomalies". One thing at least is clear, *learn-SAT* solves problems which many would predict are beyond its scope. The relative performance of the three algorithms generates several interesting questions. We point to some of them with a view to future research. The empirical paradigm in this paper reflect some of the views outlined by Mammen & Hogg [10].

1 Introduction

This paper builds on the work initiated in Richards & Richards [15, 16], which are focused on assessing the viability of a complete non-systematic search technique based on restart-repair and learning-by-merging. Non-systematic search algorithms are generally thought to be ill-suited to problems with few solutions. In Richards & Richards [16] we show that this is not the case for an algorithm here called *learn-SAT*. We ran *learn-SAT* on a range of 3-SAT problems having just one solution, i.e. on problems generated using the method of Asahiro et al. [1]. Its performance is compared with that of the tableau-based algorithm of Bayardo & Schrag [2]. Using constraint checks as a measure of performance, we discovered that *learn-SAT* performs significantly better at lower clause densities, and only slightly worse (with one exception) at higher clause densities. These results led us to conjecture that *learn-SAT* performs in similarly on other 3-SAT problems. That is, it typically outperforms systematic algorithms at lower clause densities and approximate performance elsewhere.

One key issue for *learn-SAT* is memory. In the worse case, as we explain below, *learn-SAT* requires exponential space. This will certainly be a problem in some instances, but it is not clear precisely where this limitation affects performance. For single solution 3-SAT problems, *learn-SAT* performs well in comparison with the best current algorithms. Memory is efficiently managed in these cases and perhaps, we are tempted to hypothesise, this will be so for all *solvable* problems. Where the limitation will be felt, however, is on unsolvable problems. Whether these cases are typical or not is an issue we begin to address below.

To this end we investigate structured unsolvable problems generated by the method of Bayardo & Schrag [2]. These problems consist of a randomly generating unsolvable problem inserted into a randomly generated larger problem. This approach allows scaleability of algorithms to be investigated on two dimensions, one relating to the size of the "inner" problem, the other relating to the size of the "outer" problem.

We show below that *learn-SAT* scales very well on the size of the outer problem, in comparison with the best known algorithm *relsat* [3]. In general, *learn-SAT* performs much better than *relsat* at lower clause densities, and only marginally worse at higher clause densities. As the outer problem grows, the relative performance of *learn-SAT* becomes even better. It outperforms *relsat* at ever higher clause densities.

One might expect the situation to be different with respect to the size of the inner problem. That is, as the inner unsolvable problem becomes larger, the relative performance of *learn-SAT* might get progressively worse. We look at unsolvable inner problems of four different sizes, from 10 to 25 variables. Perhaps surprisingly, *learn-SAT* performs significantly better than *relsat* on all problems at clause density 4 or below, and again at most 5 times worse at higher clause densities. But there is an interesting trend. As the size of the inner problem increases, the relative performance of *relsat* becomes ever better. It progressively outperforms *learn-SAT* at ever lower clause densities. The conclusion here is that *relsat* scales better with respect to the size of the inner problem Nevertheless, it does not overtake *learn-SAT* at 3.5 until the inner problem is half the size of the outer problem. The performance profile of *learn-SAT* on the inner unsolvable problems reflects the burden on memory generated by search. Sometimes search imposes a very light burden, e.g. at lower clause densities, and sometimes it creates a heavier burden, although not in general an excessive one.

What emerges from the empirical studies in this paper is that memory management in *learn-SAT* for 3-SAT problems is a burden that can be handled effectively. Overall *learn-SAT* performs very well relative to *relsat*. But there are circumstances where their performances diverge, one outperforming the other by a significant margin. This raises some interesting questions, which we cannot pursue here.

The structure of the paper is as follows. In Section 2 we describe *learn-SAT* and its origins. In Section 3 we report the results of a comparative study on the AIM problems. In Section 4 we extend the empirical study to structured unsolvable problems [2]. For reference in Section 5 we compare *learn-SAT* and *relsat* on certain benchmarks and in Section 6 we summarise the conclusions.

2 *Learn-SAT*

Learn-SAT has two basic components: restart-repair and learning-by-merging. Restart-repair seeks to build incrementally a complete consistent assignment to the variables of a problem. If it encounters a dead-end, a partial assignment which cannot be consistently extended to a variable, the search is abandoned and restarts from the beginning. This process is implemented as part of a repair strategy guided by a complete "tentative" assignment to the variables.

Learning-by-merging identifies a new constraint at each dead-end. This is added to the constraint store and prunes the subsequent search. Learning-by-merging ensures the completeness of *learn-SAT*. This form of learning originates from the work of Maruyama et al. [11] and Jiang et al. [9]; it is fully described in Richards et al. [14]. Similar learning techniques have been developed independently by a number of people, among them Dechter [6], Schiex & Verfaillie [17, 18], Ginsberg [8] and Frost & Dechter [7]. These investigate no-good learning in the context of backtrack search. In contrast, we apply no-good learning in the context of non-systematic search. The origins of *learn-SAT* lie in *ng-backmarking* [14] and *weak-commitment* [19]. *Ng-backmarking* is based on a very weak form of search driven mainly through learning-by-merging. *Weak-commitment* uses a stronger form of search with weaker no-good learning. *Learn-SAT* combines the search of *weak-commitment* with learning-by-merging.

Before describing the components of *learn-SAT*, we first define some key concepts. A *constraint satisfaction problem* (CSP) is expressed in terms of a set of variables $\mathcal{V}$, where each $v \in \mathcal{V}$ has an associated finite domain $\mathcal{D}$ of possible values, and a set of constraints C involving some subset of the set of variables. A constraint $c \in C$, involving variables $v_1, v_2, \ldots, v_k$ is represented as a subset of $\mathcal{D}_1 \times \mathcal{D}_2 \ldots \mathcal{D}_k$ which specifies the set of prohibited n-tuples. An *assignment* is a labelling of values to a subset of the set of variables. A *complete assignment* is a labelling of values to all the variables of the CSP. A *consistent assignment* is a labelling to a subset of the variables such that no constraint is violated. A *solution* is a complete and consistent assignment. Given an assignment, a *conflict variable* is a variable involved in a constraint violated by the assignment.

Given a CSP, a *no-good* is an assignment to a set of variables that either violates a constraint or cannot be extended to a solution. Note that all n-tuples prohibited by the initial problem constraints, i.e. those which define the problem, are no-goods; these are called *simple* no-goods. For an assignment $\mathcal{P}$ and a no-good $\mathcal{NG}$, $\mathcal{P}$ *violates* $\mathcal{NG}$ if $\mathcal{NG} \subseteq \mathcal{P}$. Any assignment that violates a no-good is also a no-good.

Let us now turn to restart-repair, a constructive search technique. This seeks to build a consistent partial assignment incrementally by repairing a complete but inconsistent assignment to the variables. The algorithm splits this assignment into two partial assignments *VarsLeft* and *VarsDone*. It begins with *VarsDone* being empty and *VarsLeft* consisting of the complete inconsistent assignment. As long as *VarsDone* is consistent and *VarsLeft* is inconsistent, the following process repeats: a variable whose assignment is involved in a constraint violation is randomly selected from *VarsLeft* and a value is then chosen that is consistent with *VarsDone*. The process either terminates in a complete consistent solution or encounters a dead-end, i.e. a variable that cannot be assigned a value consistent with *VarsDone*. Restart-repair restarts with *VarsDone* again empty and *VarsLeft* consisting of all the variables with their current assignments. Restart-repair is specified in detail in Figure 1. Note that restart-repair is incomplete.

```
Restart-repair
VarsDone:= a consistent partial assignment (initially empty)
VarsLeft:= an assignment to all variables not in VarsDone
until VarsDone ∪ VarsLeft is a solution do
Randomly select variable/value pair (v,val) in conflict from VarsLeft
if assign v a value val' consistent with VarsDone
then VarsDone ← VarsDone ∪ (v,val'), and VarsLeft ← VarsLeft-(v,val)
else VarsLeft ← VarsDone ∪ VarsLeft and VarsDone ← ø
```

Fig. 1. *Restart-repair*

The second component of *learn-SAT*, viz. **learning-by-merging**, takes the form specified in Richards et al. [14], and is defined as follows: Given a CSP, let $\mathcal{P}$ be a dead-end assignment and v be the dead-end variable. For each value χ_i ($1 \leq i \leq m$) in the domain of v, there exists a constraint c_i and a no-good ng_i that prohibits that value. Learning-by-merging generates a new no-good ng by merging the no-goods $ng_1, ng_2, \ldots, ng_m$ at v, $ng = \cup(ng_i - v)$. Note that $\mathcal{P}$ violates ng.

```
Restart-repair + Learning-by-merging
VarsDone:= a consistent partial assignment (initially empty)
VarsLeft:= an assignment to all variables not in VarsDone
until VarsDone ∪ VarsLeft is a solution do
Randomly select variable/value pair (v,val) in conflict from VarsLeft
if assign v a value val' consistent with VarsDone
then VarsDone ← VarsDone ∪ (v,val'), and VarsLeft ← VarsLeft-(v,val)
     else ng ← merge-learn(VarsDone, v),
     if ng = ø then return fail, no solution exists
     else record ng, and let VarsLeft ← VarsDone ∪ VarsLeft
     and VarsDone ← ø
```

Fig. 2. *Restart-repair + Learning-by-merging*

Learning-by-merging is integrated with restart-repair to yield the basic search component of *learn-SAT*; see Figure 2. It is important to note that this composite algorithm is complete. This follows directly from the fact that the search space pruned by the no-good set (constraint store) is monotonically increasing. At each dead-end a new no-good is added to the constraint store which is not subsumed by any other no-good. As a result, each no-good learned prunes more of the search space.

Learn-SAT incorporates a heuristic called binary ordering which is specifically tailored for SAT problems. This heuristic drives the search towards discovering dead-ends, i.e. no-goods, as early as possible. It is "biased" towards removing parts of the search space where there are no solutions. This is unlike hill-climbing heuristics like the min-conflicts strategy of Minton et al. [12], which seeks to minimise the number of constraint violations at each repair step.

Restart-repair + Learning-by-merging + Binary-ordering

1-3 As above

4* Let *VarsConf* be the set of conflict variables in *VarsLeft*
   Select variable v from *VarsConf* with maximum bin count $C(v)+C(\neg v)$
   where $C(v)$ is the number of binary clauses involving v
   and $C(\neg v)$ is the number of binary clauses involving $\neg v$

5* **if** assign v a value val' consistent with *VarsDone* such that
   the number of resulting binary clauses is maximised

6-7* As above

Fig. 3. *Restart-repair + Learning-by-merging + Binary-ordering*

The binary-ordering heuristic is specified in lines 4* and 5* of Figure 3. The basic strategy is to look at all the variables in *VarsLeft* which are involved in a constraint violation. For each such variable count the number of binary clauses in which the variable occurs, and add this to the number of binary clauses in which the negation of the variable occurs. Select the variable with the highest sum to be reassigned in *VarsDone*.

The final component of *learn-SAT* is forward checking. The implementation here is somewhat subtle since it must be integrated with learning. The basic requirement is explained as follows. Suppose *learn-SAT* is attempting to extend *VarsDone* to another variable v. Suppose that v is a dead-end variable. When *learn-SAT* tries one possible value for v, forward checking eliminates the remaining element(s) in the domain of some other variable, domain wipe-out. A set of assignments in *VarsDone* which cause this are stored as a set. The same holds when *learn-SAT* tries each of the other possible values for v. Forward checking leads to domain wipe-out, not necessarily for the same variable in each case. Again assignments in *VarsDone* which cause this are stored for each possible value for v. The no-good generated when all the values in the domain of v have been tried is the union of all of these "elimination" sets. This procedure is fully described in Richards & Richards [15] .

3 AIM Problems

3.1 Experimental strategy

We now explore the performance of *learn-SAT* on the so-called AIM problems. These problems are generated using the method of Asahiro et al. [1]. Each instance has exactly one solution. One might expect that *learn-SAT* will have to do a very considerable amount of search before finding the solution. As a result, it would have to manage an excessively heavy burden on memory, thereby degrading the quality of performance.

The tableau-based algorithm of Bayardo & Schrag [2] is thought to be one of the best for solving hard SAT problems, among them the AIM problems. This algorithm uses the *Tableau* method of Crawford & Auton [5] and incorporates conflict-directed backjumping [13] and 3rd order jump-back learning [7]. We refer to this algorithm as *Tableau*{CBJ+3rdLrn}, reflecting its three main components.

It is has been said that *Tableau*{CBJ+3rdLrn} solves the AIM problems trivially. On some measures this may be true. But it is not the case if performance is measured in terms of constraint checks. In this paper we shall calibrate the performance of an algorithm in terms of the number of constraint checks executed during search. Since constraint checking is involved at every stage in the search, this provides a more reliable and sensitive measure of the overall work undertaken. It also allows very different kinds of algorithms to be compared, not only the two algorithms under investigation but also the *weight* strategy of Cha & Iwama [4].[1]

3.2 Problem set and empirical results

We compare the performances of *learn-SAT* and *Tableau*{CBJ+3rdLrn} on AIM problems across different clause densities. To enhance the "granularity" of the study we consider more clause densities than were addressed in the original problem set.[2] We look at instances generated at 9 clause densities, ranging from 1.6 to 6.8. At each clause density we consider 4 different problems, each with 100 randomly generated initial complete assignments. Each data point represents the average

---

[1] In the case of *Tableau*{CBJ+3rdLrn} constraint checking takes two forms. First, every instance of unit propagation is counted as a constraint check; that is, every clause involved in unit propagation represents a constraint check. Second, every elimination or reduction of a clause due to a value assignment is counted as a constraint check.

[2] We are grateful to Yuichi Asahiro for extending the problem set as required.

number of constraint checks executed in solving 400 problem instances.[3] Figure 4 shows the performance of *learn-SAT* and *Tableau*{CBJ+3rdLrn} on problems involving 50, 100, and 200 variables.

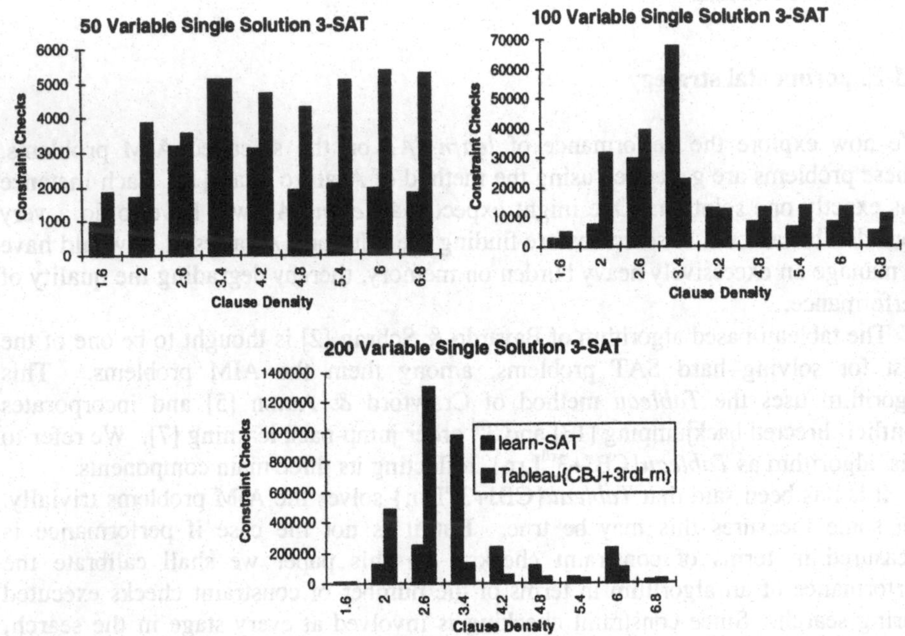

Fig. 4. *Tableau*{CBJ+3rdLrn} and *learn-SAT* on AIM problems

Between 1.6 and 2.6 *learn-SAT* does better than *Tableau*{CBJ+3rdLrn}. This becomes more pronounced as the problem size increases. In effect, *learn-SAT* seems not only to perform better, but also to scale better, than *Tableau*{CBJ+3rdLrn} at lower clause densities. One might wonder how robust this phenomenon is. That is, will *learn-SAT* always outperform *Tableau*{CBJ+3rdLrn} at lower clause densities? We explore this question further in the next section.

The relative performance at clause densities between 4.2 and 6.8 is more mixed. On the 50 variable problems *learn-SAT* does considerably better, but as the problem

[3] One may feel that this is a relatively small data set, particularly in comparison with empirical studies which consider many thousands of problems. In the case of this study, however, we address a very specific kind of problem. At each clause density we consider randomly generated instances of four problems. This represents a much more extensive sampling than would be achieved in any less focused study. Moreover, the results of the study constitute only one view of the phenomenon we are exploring. See next section.

size increases, *Tableau*{CBJ+3rdLrn} improves. It is only marginally worse on the 100 variable problems and slightly better on the 200 variable problems. This suggests that at these clause densities *Tableau*{CBJ+3rdLrn} scales better than *learn-SAT*. We look at this phenomenon again with respect to unsolvable problems.

The trend which we see between 4.2 and 6.8 is much more pronounced at 3.4. For the smallest problems the two algorithms are basically equivalent, but on the 100 variable problems *Tableau*{CBJ+3rdLrn} performs roughly three times better than *learn-SAT*, and on the 200 variable problems an order of magnitude better. Here *Tableau*{CBJ+3rdLrn} is clearly the more scaleable algorithm.

For the extended set of AIM problems, it is remarkable that *learn-SAT* performs so well at every clause density in comparison to *Tableau*{CBJ+3rdLrn}, with the single exception of clause density 3.4. This is not as one might predict. In the worst case the memory burden of *learn-SAT* is exponential and therefore progressively insupportable. AIM problems might be expected to approximate the worst case for *learn-SAT*. The algorithm should have to undertake an excessive amount of search, exploring a large number of dead-ends. The algorithm adds a no-good to the constraint store at each dead-end, the resulting burden on memory should become progressively difficult to manage. Curiously, this does not happen, at least not uniformly. Relatively speaking, *learn-SAT* is managing the burden on memory at least as well as *Tableau*{CBJ+3rdLrn} is managing its overheads, except at clause density 3.4.

We conjecture that *learn-SAT* will perform much better than *Tableau*{CBJ+3rdLrn} at lower clause densities, and will scale very much better there. We also conjecture that *Tableau*{CBJ+3rdLrn} will scale better than *learn-SAT* at higher clause densities, and will very significantly outperform it at a particular clause density, here roughly 3.4. We call this the ***transition point*** for *learn-SAT* since its performance generally improves as we move away from this point.[4]

Significantly 3.4 is not the only transition point. There is another one at approximately 2.6 for *Tableau*{CBJ+3rdLrn}. How is this to be explained? One might suspect that it is a combination of the topology of the problems and the methods of search. Seeking an explanation, however, seems premature. The leading question here is whether the phenomenon is stable. We address this question in the next section.

Before doing so, we consider whether other non-systematic search techniques, particularly incomplete algorithms, might approximate or even outperform *learn-SAT* on the AIM problems. Cha & Iwama [4] conducted experiments on instances of these problems using various non-systematic, incomplete algorithms including *GSAT*, *walk-SAT* and *weight*. They found *weight* to be the best of these. We discovered, however, that *weight* performed very much worse than *learn-SAT*. For all problem instances, regardless of size, and at all clause densities *learn-SAT* typically outperformed *weight* by 2 or 3 orders of magnitude.

---

[4] This should not be confused with the concept of a phase transition which relates to randomly generated problem sets containing both solvable and unsolvable problem instances. Here all the problem instances are solvable.

Finally, we tested the conjecture that *learn-SAT* scales well relative to *Tableau*{CBJ+3[rd]Lrn} on problems at lower clause densities. We looked at problems with 400 variables at clause density 2. As before, we addressed four different problems of this size and density, and considered 100 randomly generated initial assignments for each problem. The relative performance of *learn-SAT* and *Tableau*{CBJ+3[rd]Lrn} is unambiguous: *learn-SAT* requires approximately 500,000 constraint checks on average for these problems. In contrast *Tableau*{CBJ+3[rd]Lrn} fails to solve 60% of these problems within a pre-set limit of 10,000,000 constraint checks.

4 Structured Unsolvable 3-SAT Problems

4.1 Experimental strategy

In this section we explore the issue of scaleability with respect to unsolvable problems. Again one might expect that *learn-SAT* will not scale well on these problems. Proving a problem is unsolvable requires that the whole search space be eliminated; in the case of *learn-SAT* this means finding a set of no-goods which prunes all possible assignments. This should typically generate a very heavy burden on memory management, thereby making it difficult to prove unsolvability. Moreover, as the problems become larger, the burden on memory should grow sharply and hence, the performance should degrade steeply.

However, the "picture" which emerges from studying the structured unsolvable problems of Bayardo & Schrag [2] conforms only partly to this prediction. For problem instances of a certain type, explained below, *learn-SAT* shows the anticipated difficulties. These impose a significant burden on memory, and as the problems increase in size, the performance of *learn-SAT* deteriorates. However, for problem instances of another type the situation is very different. For these instances *learn-SAT* scales very much better than both *Tableau*{CBJ+3[rd]Lrn} and a related algorithm *relsat* [3], which has been shown to perform better than *Tableau*{CBJ+3[rd]Lrn}.

This result is not only surprising but instructive. It indicates that memory can be efficiently managed for certain unsolvable problems, particularly relative to the burden carried by systematic search algorithms like *Tableau*{CBJ+3[rd]Lrn} and *relsat*. The rate at which the performance of these algorithms deteriorates as the problems become larger is far greater than that for *learn-SAT*. This is a clear manifestation that search in *learn-SAT* imposes a much more confined overhead on memory than the "corresponding" burden generated by the two systematic search algorithms, *Tableau*{CBJ+3[rd]Lrn} and *relsat*.

4.2 Problem sets and empirical results

The method of Bayardo & Schrag [2] constructs unsolvable problems by inserting an unsolvable sub-problem into a larger problem. Each component, i.e. the inner problem and the outer problem, can have different clause densities and will typically be of different size. We let *n* and *d* designate the size and clause density of the problem as a whole (the outer problem), and *n'* and *d'* the size and density of the inner unsolvable sub-problem. In the experiments below we explore the relative performance of *learn-SAT* and *relsat* on two dimensions: one, the size of the outer problem, and the other, the size of the inner problem.

First, we compare the performance of *relsat* and *Tableau*{CBJ+3rdLrn}, and another special purpose algorithm *sizesat*, also developed by Bayardo & Schrag [3]. The point here is to indicate that the three algorithms do not differ much in their performance on these unsolvable problems. To this end we consider problem instances of "average" size with respect to both the outer problem and the inner unsolvable sub-problem. For all problem instances the inner unsolvable sub-problem consists of 15 variables ($n' = 15$) with clause density *d'* given by the equation $n' * d' = (3.5 * n') + 5$.[5] The size of the outer problem is also fixed, all instances consist of 100 variables ($n = 100$), and the clause density *d* varies in the range 3 to 10. Each data point represents the average performance of each algorithm on 100 instances; both the inner sub-problem and the outer problem are randomly generated. As before, we measured the average number of constraint checks executed. Although *relsat* is uniformly the best of the three algorithms, the margin of difference is not very great. For structured unsolvable problems we can reasonably assume that the performance profiles will be relatively similar. For this reason we focus our subsequent empirical studies on *relsat*.

The first study explores the issue of scaleability with respect to the outer problem. We look at problems where the outer problem consists of 75, 100 or 150 variables (*n*) and we consider a range of clause densities *d* from 3 to 10. In all cases the size *n'* and density *d'* of the inner unsolvable sub-problem is the same; $n' = 15$ variables, and *d'* is fixed by the formula $n' * d' = (3.5 * n') + 5$. Figure 6 gives the average performance of *learn-SAT* and *relsat* on 100 randomly generated problems at each data point.

Three striking things emerge from Figure 6. First, the overall performance of *learn-SAT* relative to *relsat* is far better than one might expect. When *learn-SAT* fails to reach the performance of *relsat*, which is only at the higher clause densities, it is by a modestly small margin. We saw something similar in the case of the AIM problems. Second, at the lower clause densities the performance of *learn-SAT* is very much better than that of *relsat*, again there are notable similarities between these results and the results of the AIM problems.

Perhaps the most striking phenomenon concerns scaleability. As we move from the lower to the higher clause densities, the relative performance of the two algorithms "crosses over"; that is, *learn-SAT* performs better than *relsat*. We call

---

[5] This equation ensures that the randomly generated sub-problem is unsolvable and relatively hard to prove to be so. The phase transition for these problems lies at 3.4 roughly, where 50% of the problems generated are unsolvable. The problems are certain to be unsolvable at a slightly higher clause density, which is given by the equation. These are thought to be very hard to prove inconsistent.

this the *performance cross-over*.[6] Interestingly, the cross-over moves as the size of the outer problem increases. For 75 variable problems the cross-over lies between densities 4 and 5, for 100 variable problems it lies between 5 and 6, and for 150 variable problems between 6 and 7. This "right shift" is a clear manifestation of relative scaleability.

The conclusion here is unmistakable. For these problems the burdens of *relsat* rise much more steeply than the burden on memory in *learn-SAT*. *Learn-SAT* performs better on an ever increasing set of problems. This raises an interesting question: Does there exist a cross-over for all outer problems sizes or is there an outer problem size with no cross-over?

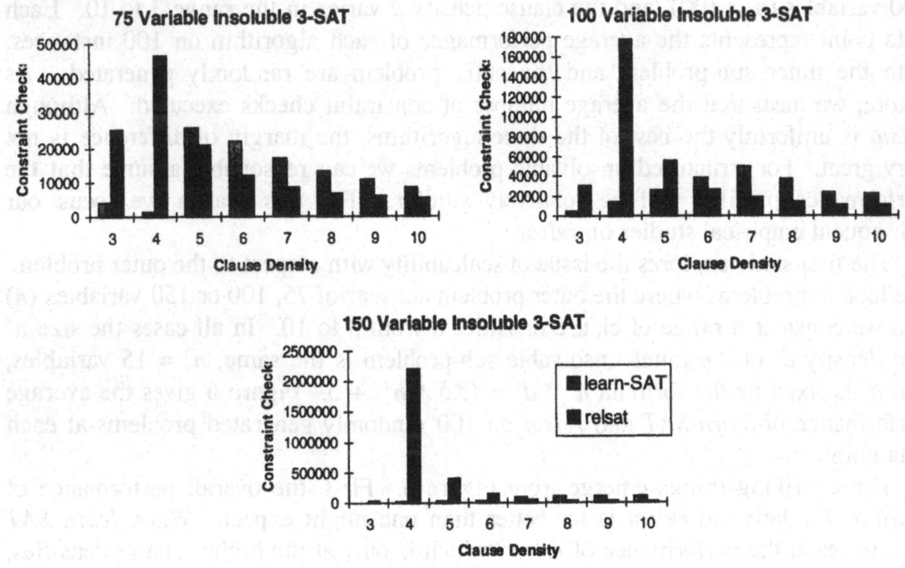

Fig. 6. *Relsat* and *learn-SAT* for structured insoluble problems

There is another view of the above results, connected with transition points. Note that the transition point for *relsat* is uniformly at clause density 4, roughly. In contrast, the transition point for *learn-SAT* moves from 5 to 7 to 9 on the three different problem sizes. In effect, transition points are not always stable. Sometimes they are; sometimes they are not. In addition, the peak at the transition point is relatively small for *learn-SAT* whereas the peak is much greater for *relsat*. This is

---

[6] This is not to be confused with the phase transition crossover where randomly generated problems have a 50% probability of being either solvable or unsolvable.

clearly significant in seeking an explanation for these phenomena. We do not speculate further here on this question.

As for scaleability, this too is not uniform. In particular, *learn-SAT* does not always scale better than *relsat*. Above we fixed the size of the inner unsolvable sub-problem while varying the outer problem size. Let us now vary the size of the inner problem and fix the outer problem size. For the next study the outer problem always involves 100 variables. Again we explore different clause densities, ranging from 3 to 10. We consider inner sub-problems of four different sizes: 10, 15, 20 and 25 variables. For all sub-problems we again use $n' * d' = (3.5 * n') + 5$ to fix clause density. For each data point we randomly generate 100 problem instances. The results are given in Figure 7.

Here the results are more as one might expect, although the overall performance of *learn-SAT* is surprisingly good, even on the largest sub-problems. Moreover, *learn-SAT* again outperforms *relsat* at the lower clause densities by a large margin. But here the cross-over point moves to the left as the size of the inner sub-problem grows. For sub-problems consisting of 10 variables, the cross-over point is between clause density 6 and 7. For 15 variable sub-problems it is between 5 and 6, and finally for 25 variable sub-problems between 4 and 5.

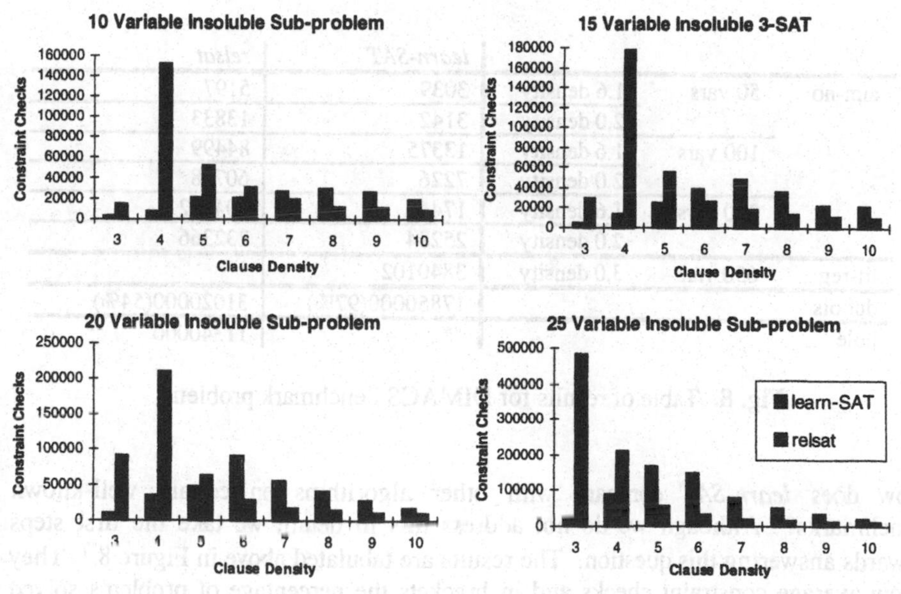

Fig. 7. *Relsat* and *learn-SAT* for structured insoluble 3-SAT problems

Again the conclusion is unmistakable. *Relsat* outperforms *learn-SAT* as the size of the sub-problem grows. In effect, *relsat* scales better than *learn-SAT* on these problems. However, when *relsat* performs poorly relative to *learn-SAT* it performs very poorly indeed. Between clause densities 3 and 4 its performance is far below that of *learn-SAT*. Note that again the transition points are shifting. The *Learn-SAT* transition moves from approximately 8 to 7 to 6 to 5, while *relsat* moves from 4 to 3 approximately. Instability seems a characteristic of transition points.

In view of the trend with respect to sub-problem size one might expect that *relsat* will eventually overtake the performance of *learn-SAT* at a clause density below 4. To explore this we consider three sets of 100 problems with 100 variables and clause density 3.5. In the first set each problem contains an unsolvable sub-problem where the number n' of variables is 40 and the clause density d' is determined by the equation $n' * d' = (3.5 * n') + 5$. In the second set of problems n' is 45, and in the third set n' is 50, again the above formula is used to determine clause density d'. Where n' is 40, *learn-SAT* requires approximately 400,000 constraint checks, less than half of the count for *relsat*, approximately 1,000,000 on average. When n' is 45, the two algorithms require approximately the same number of constraint checks on average, roughly 1,100,000. But when n' is 50, *relsat* requires 900,000 constraint checks on average, which is approximately two times better than *learn-SAT*.

5 Some Benchmarks

			learn-SAT	*relsat*
aim-no	50 vars	1.6 density	3039	5197
		2.0 density	3142	13833
	100 vars	1.6 density	13375	84499
		2.0 density	7226	60768
	200 vars	1.6 density	17446	104382
		2.0 density	25284	232366
lit-reg	650 vars	3.0 density	3840102	**
dubois			17850000(97%)	31020000(54%)
hole			**	11340000

Fig. 8. Table of results for DIMACS benchmark problems

How does *learn-SAT* compare with other algorithms on certain well-known benchmarks? Although we do not address this in detail, we take the first steps towards answering this question. The results are tabulated above in Figure 8.[7] They show average constraint checks and in brackets the percentage of problems solved within a cut-off bound, if less than 100%.[8]

[7] Problems are from ftp://dimacs.rutgers.edu/pub/challenge/satisfiability

[8] The cut-off bound for the aim-no and the literal regular problems is 10,000,000 constraint checks, and for the dubois and hole problems it is 50,000,000. ** shows that no problems were solved within the cut-off.

6 Explanation of Performance Profiles

The relative performance profiles of the algorithms compared here raise an interesting question: How are these differences to be explained? Two key related phenomena are performance cross-over and shifting transition points. These appear to challenge the usual algorithm independent explanations based on problem topology. This is a topic for future research.

Acknowledgements

We are grateful to Yuichi Asahiro, Roberto Bayardo, Hani El-Sakkout and Jonathan Lever for their help in developing the experimental paradigm, and to an anonymous referee for constructive criticism of an earlier draft.

References

1. Y. Asahiro, K. Iwama and E. Miyano, Random generation of test instances with controlled attributes, Cliques, Colouring and Satisfiability. DIMACS Series in Disc. Math. and Theory Comp. Sci., 1995
2. R. J. Bayardo and R. Schrag, Using CSP look-back techniques to solve exceptionally hard SAT instances. Proceedings CP96, Cambridge, MA, USA, August 1996
3. R. J. Bayardo and R. Schrag, Using CSP look-back techniques to solve real-world SAT instances. Proceedings AAAI-97, Providence, RI, USA, July 1997
4. B. Cha and K. Iwama, Performance test of local search algorithms using new types of random CNF formulas. Proceedings IJCAI-95, 1995
5. J.M. Crawford and L.D, Auton, Experimental results on the crossover point in random 3SAT. Artificial Intelligence 81, 1996.
6. R. Dechter, Enhancement schemes for constraint processing: backjumping, learning and cutset decomposition. Artificial Intelligence 41, 1990
7. D. Frost and R. Dechter, Dead-end driven learning, Proceedings AAAI-94, 1994
8. M. Ginsberg, Dynamic Backtracking. Journal of Artificial Intelligence Research, 1:25-46, 1993
9. Y. Jiang, E. T. Richards, and B. Richards, No-good backmarking with min-conflict repair in constraint satisfaction and optimisation. Proceedings PPCP-94 2nd International Workshop, Washington State USA, 1994
10. D. L. Mammen and T. Hogg, A New Look at the Easy-Hard-Easy Pattern of Combinatorial Search Difficulty. Journal of Artificial Intelligence Research, 6:47-66, 1997
11. F. Maruyama, Y. Minoda, S. Sawada, Y. Takizawa, and N, Kawato, Solving Combinatorial Constraint Satisfaction and Optimization Problems Using Sufficient Conditions for Constraint Violation. ISAI-91 4th International Symposium on AI, 1991
12. S. Minton, M. D. Johnston, A. B. Phillips and P. Laird, Minimising conflicts: a heuristic repair method for constraint satisfaction and scheduling problems. Artificial Intelligence 58, 1992

13. P. Prosser, Hybrid algorithms for the constraint satisfaction problem. Computational Intelligence 9, 1993
14. E. T. Richards, Y. Jiang and B. Richards, Ng-backmarking - an algorithm for constraint satisfaction. AIP Techniques for Resource Scheduling and Planning, BT Technology Journal Vol. 13 No 1 January, 1995
15. E. T. Richards and B. Richards, No-good Learning for Constraint Satisfaction. Proceedings CP-96 Workshop on Constraint Programming Applications, 1996
16. E. T. Richards and B. Richards, Restart-Repair and Learning: An empirical study of single solution 3-SAT problems. Proceedings CP-97 Workshop on the Theory and Practice of Dynamic Constraint Satisfaction, 1997
17. T. Schiex and G. Verfaillie, No-good Recording for Static and Dynamic Constraint Satisfaction Problems. Proceedings IEEE 5th International Conference on Tools with Artificial Intelligence, 1993
18. T. Schiex and G. Verfaillie, Stubbornness: a possible enhancement for backjumping and no-good recording. Proceedings ECAI-94, 1994
19. M. Yokoo, Weak-commitment search for solving constraint satisfaction problems. Proceedings AAAI-94, 1994

A Generic Model and Hybrid Algorithm for Hoist Scheduling Problems

Robert Rodošek and Mark Wallace

IC-Parc, Imperial College, SW7-2AZ London
E-mail: {rr5, mgw}@icparc.ic.ac.uk

Abstract. This paper presents a robust approach to solve Hoist Scheduling Problems (HSPs) based on an integration of Constraint Logic Programming (CLP) and Mixed Integer Programming (MIP). By contrast with previous dedicated models and algorithms for solving classes of HSPs, we define only one model and run different solvers.
The robust approach is achieved by using a CLP formalism. We show that our models for different classes of industrial HSPs are all based on the same generic model. In our hybrid algorithm search is separated from the handling of constraints. Constraint handling is performed by constraint propagation and linear constraint solving. Search is applied by labelling of boolean and integer variables.
Computational experience shows that the hybrid algorithm, combining CLP and MIP solvers, solves classes of HSPs which cannot be handled by previous dedicated algorithms. For example, the hybrid algorithm derives an optimal solution, and proves its optimality, for multiple-hoists scheduling problems.

1 Introduction

1.1 The Hoist Scheduling Problem

Many industrial processes employ computer-controlled hoists for material handling [2, 4, 14, 16, 22]. The hoists are programmed to perform a fixed sequence of moves repeatedly. Each repetition of the sequence of moves is called a *cycle* and the total time required by the hoists to complete the cycle is called a *cycle time*. A typical application is an automated electroplating line for processing printed circuit boards (jobs). The importance of minimising the cyclic time is evident by the fact that the lot sizes for electroplating jobs are usually large and a production run may require weeks between changeovers [22]. Even a small reduction in the cycle time can result in a significant saving of time and cost.

Due to the nature of different industrial processes, specific approaches for different classes of HSPs have been developed. There are two drawbacks of the proposed approaches. First, the models and solution algorithms are dedicated to each class of problems, and second, an optimal solution and the proof of optimality has been shown only for restricted classes of HSPs [10].

1.2 A Generic Model and Solver for HSPs

This paper addresses all the different classes of HSPs using a single generic approach. This approach uses Constraint Logic Programming (CLP) as the modelling language, and models the different classes of HSPs by extending a single underlying model with extra constraints. The models are handled by a generic algorithm which uses a combination of constraint propagation and linear solving.

The HSP problem involves both linear constraints and logical constraints, and CLP is a powerful language for modelling such problems. The language used in this paper to model HSPs is CLP(R)[1], an instance of the CLP scheme [13]. However while the CLP Scheme envisages a single constraint solver for all the constraints, this paper follows [3] and passes constraints to either (or both) of two different solvers. In this setup, we can separate the definition and the behaviour of constraints. A practical consequence is that the programmer can concentrate on modelling of the problem and any problems with the performance of the default behaviour can be ironed out afterwards.

The hybrid algorithms for solving HSPs combines a CLP solver and a MIP solver such that both solvers share the variables and constraints to cooperate in finding an optimal solution. The experiments on HSPs have shown that there are problem classes which can be solved neither by constraint propagation nor MIP alone, but which succumb to this combination of the two.

Moreover the combination is not an exclusive one, where some constraints are handled by one solver and the remainder by the other solver. Indeed every constraint is passed to both solvers. This application, therefore, shows the value of allowing a single constraint to be handled by more than one solver.

1.3 Outline of the Paper

In this paper two contributions are presented. First, models for classes of HSPs can be defined independently of any solver which will be used during the search for an optimal solution. Second, the proposed hybrid algorithm derives a schedule with the minimal cyclic time and proves its optimality for classes of HSPs which cannot be handled by previous dedicated CLP and MIP solvers.

The remainder of this paper is organised as follows. Section 2 presents related work. Section 3 models different classes of HSPs. Section 4 demonstrates how to use a CLP formalism to apply different solvers on the same model. Section 5 presents the computational experience with the proposed hybrid approach. Finally, Section 6 concludes the paper.

[1] By CLP(R) we mean constraint logic programming over numerical equations and inequations. The implementation we use is ECLiPSe [9], which supports not only linear constraint solving, but also finite domain propagation, and various other constraint handling facilities.

2 Related Work

2.1 Hoist Scheduling Models and Programs

Previous approaches to minimise the cycle time of HSPs are mostly mathematical programming-based approaches [15, 16, 18, 22]. Recently, several constraint programming-based approaches have been developed [2, 4]. In the following we present classes of HSPs, the models, and the solution algorithms which have been used in the proposed approaches.

Phillips and Unger [18] used a mixed integer programming model to determine a schedule with the minimum cyclic time for a real *one-hoist* scheduling problem with 12 chemical treatment tanks. The Phillips and Unger's (P&U's) HSP has become a benchmark problem in several follow-up studies.

Shapiro and Nuttle [22] introduced a branch-and-bound procedure and used linear programming on different subproblems to bound the search space.

Lei and Wang [15] introduced a heuristic algorithm for *two-hoists* scheduling problems with both hoists on the same track. The algorithm uses a *partitioning* approach by which the production line is partitioned into two sets of contiguous tanks and each hoist is assigned to a set. Lei et. al. [14] introduced also another heuristic algorithm for the class of *two-hoists* scheduling problems with both hoists on the same track. In contrast to the algorithm in [15], the movements of both hoists must be scheduled to *avoid traffic collisions*. The algorithm is not able to guarantee the optimal solution.

Baptiste et. al. [2] presented advantages and drawbacks of different kinds of constraint programming-based approaches. All approaches demonstrated that the good versatility of CLP language allows one to develop very rapidly computational models for different classes of HSPs. The empirical results show that CLP with a linear solver (Prolog III) is more effective than constraint propagation over finite domains in dealing with the HSPs. Prolog III was able to produce an optimal one-hoist schedule for the P&U's problem in 30 minutes and the finite domain solver in 306 minutes on SUN station Sparc 4/60. To increase the power of consistency control within the constraints solver, the disjunctive constraints have been used in an active way to reduce the domain of each variable. This modification of the CLP approach helps the rational solver to derive the optimal schedule in 40 seconds.

All HSPs introduced above have been shown by the authors to belong to the class of NP-hard problems [10]. Existing approaches which derive the minimal cycle time are limited to the single-hoist cases and use branch-and-bound procedures, whose efficiency quickly diminishes as the number of tanks in the system increases. Scheduling two or more hoists further expands the search space, and makes the task of searching for the global optimal solution extremely difficult.

2.2 MIP, CLP and Hybrid Algorithms

Hoist scheduling problems involve both logical and linear constraints. A pioneer in the combination of logical constraint solving and OR techniques is

Hooker [11]. An implemented system which combines logic and linear programming is 2LP [17]. A mathematical modelling language and implementation that interfaces to both CLP and linear solvers is presented in [1].

One of the first CLP platforms to support both constraint propagation and linear solving was CHIP [5]. However the solvers were not designed to handle constraints with shared variables. A CLP implementation supporting the combination of constraint propagation and linear programming with shared constraints and variables was described in [3].

The linear constraint solvers of these two systems were internal ones, and lacked the scaleability of commercial matrix-based implementations such as CPLEX [6] and XPRESS-MP [23]. Nevertheless several researchers identified problems and problem classes that could not be handled by the major MIP packages, but could be solved using constraint propagation. Examples were party planning [20] and machine allocation [8].

In 1995 an integration was developed between the CLP platform ECLiPSe and the commercial packages CPLEX and XPRESS-MP [21]. This was used to build a hybrid algorithm solving a fleet scheduling problem [12]. Subsequently an automatic translator was built to map models expressed in ECLiPSe to MIP models [19]. The resulting MIP model can be solved using constraint propagation and search in ECLiPSe; linear solving and search in an external MIP package; or linear solving in an external package, and propagation and search in ECLiPSe. The paper [19] describes how this system was used to improve on the CLP results of [8, 20], and to solve a number of other problems.

The current paper uses the same implementation to solve to optimality some problem classes that have never previously been solved, neither using CLP nor MIP techniques.

3 Modelling the Different HSP Classes

In this section we present natural models for several classes of HSPs. The models are not tailored for any solver, and models for different classes are obtained by simply adding or changing the relevant constraints: no remodelling is attempted.

The modelling language syntax is based on Edinburgh Prolog, with some extensions to make the models easier to read.[2]

- `for(El,Min:Max) do Goal`, applies the goal to each number in the range.
- A functional syntax can be used where an integer is expected. For example the goal `plus(2,1) < 5` is expanded into the goal `plus(2,1,N), N<5`.
- Finally an array syntax is defined such that `Array[N]` picks out the `N`th member of the array `Array`, for example: `Var = f(5,3,1), X is Var[2]` which instantiates `X` to 3.

3.1 Single Cyclic Scheduling

Informal Description The simplest cyclic HSP contains a single hoist and the number of sequential chemical treatment tanks in the production line. Each

[2] These extensions have been implemented in ECLiPSe.

tank applies chemical or plating treatments, such as H_2SO_4 activating or Nickel plating, to the jobs. A large number of identical jobs is placed at the initial stage of the production line and these jobs have to be processed in the order that tanks are sequenced. The hoist is programmed to handle the inter-tank moves of the jobs, where each move consists of three simple hoist operations: (i) lift a job from a tank; (ii) move to the next tank; and (iii) submerge the job in that tank. Upon completion of a move, a hoist travels to another tank for the next scheduled move. Both the hoist travelling times and the times to perform moves are given constants. The time of each move is independent of the move direction. A hoist can carry one job at a time, and no buffer exists between tanks. A job must remain in each tank for a certain amount of time, between a minimum and a maximum: this is the tank's *time window*. The fixed sequence of moves that the hoist performs in each cycle is defined by a *one-hoist* cyclic schedule [18]. Exactly one job is removed from each tank in a cycle, and therefore, one job enters and one job leaves the production line in a cycle. Figure 1 represents a one-hoist scheduling problem with 6 tanks and three jobs present in the system simultaneously.

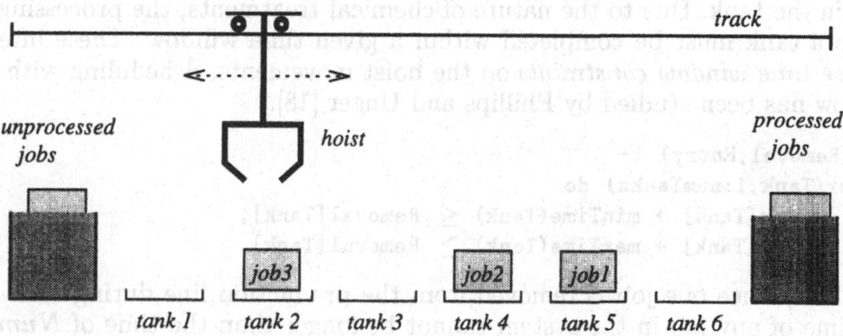

Fig. 1. A one-hoist scheduling problem

CLP Model This class of one-hoist scheduling problems can be captured by the following model. The model is expressed in CLP syntax: input data is expressed as facts; constraints as clauses; variables start with an upper-case letter. We use a bold font for types; for example **numTanks(Integer)** means that the predicate **numTanks** takes a single argument which is an integer.

- **numTanks(Integer)**. The number (=12) of chemical treatment tanks in the production line.
- **empty(Tank, Tank, Time)**. **Tank** is an integer denoting a tank. **Time** is also an integer. The predicate **empty** is used to record the times of travel from tank to tank for the hoist when empty. It records times for every pair of tanks.
- **full(Tank, Time)**. The transport times of jobs from a tank to the next tank on the production line.
- **numJobs(Integer)**. The number (=3) of jobs in the production line.

– `minTime(Tank, Time)`. The minimum time a job can stay in each tank.
– `maxTime(Tank, Time)`. The maximum time a job can stay in each tank.

The problem variables are those whose value is found during the search for the shortest possible cycle:

– `Entry`. An array of the times at which the jobs are put into the tanks.
– `Removal`. An array of the times at which the jobs are removed from the tanks.
– `Period`. The time of a cycle.

A single cyclic HSP with time windows can be defined by four types of constraints.

First, we relate the array of variables `Entry` to the array of decision variables `Removal`. For each tank, the entry time is the removal time from the previous tank, plus the transportation time between the two tanks. The "0th" tank is the stack of unprocessed jobs.

```
lin1(Removal,Entry):-
   for(Tank,1:numTanks) do
      Removal[Tank-1] + full(Tank-1) = Entry[Tank].
```

Second, the entry time of a job to a tank is related straightforwardly to its removal time from this tank: the difference between them is equal to the treatment time in the tank. Due to the nature of chemical treatments, the processing of a job in a tank must be completed within a given time window. These intervals impose *time window constraints* on the hoist movements. Scheduling with time window has been studied by Phillips and Unger [18].

```
lin2(Removal,Entry) :-
   for(Tank,1:numTanks) do
      Entry[Tank] + minTime(Tank) ≤ Removal[Tank],
      Entry[Tank] + maxTime(Tank) ≥ Removal[Tank].
```

Third, since one job is removed from the production line during each cycle the time of any job in the system cannot be longer than the time of $NumJobs$ cycles.

```
lin3(Removal,Period) :-
   Removal[numTanks] + full(numTanks) ≤ numJobs * Period.
```

Fourth, the hoist can only do one thing at a time. Thus a constraint is required to prevent the hoist transporting a job from tank T_1 to $T_1 + 1$ at the same time as it is transporting the same, or another, job from tank T_2 to $T_2 + 1$. A clash will obviously occur if a task is being performed on a job at the same time as any other task on the same job. Less obviously a clash will occur if a task is being performed on a job at time `Time`, and another task is being performed on the same job at time `Time+Period`. In this case the clash will be between the first task on one job and the second task on the following job. In fact a clash will occur if two tasks are being performed on a job at any pair of times `Time` and `Time+N*Period`, for N up to but not including the number of jobs at the same time on the production line.

To ensure no clash between the transportation from T_1 to $T_1 + 1$ and T_2 to $T_2 + 1$, either one job must be removed from tank T_1 after the other was placed in tank $T_2 + 1$, leaving time for the hoist to travel empty from tank $T_2 + 1$ to tank T_1; or the job must be placed in tank $T_1 + 1$ before being removed from tank T_2, leaving time for the hoist to travel empty from $T_1 + 1$ to T_2.

This constraint is the core of the generic HSP model. It is expressed in terms of the following clauses:

```
disj(Removal,Entry,Period) :-
   for(T1,1:numTanks-1) do  for(T2,T1+1:numTanks) do
      for(K,1:numJobs-1) do
         disj1(T1,T2,K,Removal,Entry,Period).
disj1(T1,T2,K,Removal,Entry,Period) :-
   Entry[T1+1] + empty(T1+1,T2) + K * Period ≤ Removal[T2].
disj1(T1,T2,K,Removal,Entry,Period) :-
   Entry[T2+1] + empty(T2+1,T1)  ≤ Removal[T1] + K * Period.
```

This disjunctive constraint is superficially similar to the resource constraints encountered in disjunctive scheduling, which enforce that one task is performed either before or after another task [7]. However the disjunctive constraints in hoist scheduling involve not just the two task variables, `Entry[T1]` and `Removal[T2]` for example, but they also involve a third variable `Period`. The occurrence of a third variable makes the handling of the hoist scheduling disjunctive constraints quite different. In case there are only two variables, choosing one alternative for each disjunctive constraint, together with propagation, suffices to decide the global consistency of the constraints. In case three variable are involved, by contrast, choosing disjuncts and propagating without failing, no longer suffices to guarantee global consistency.

The whole single cyclic scheduling problem with time windows, denoted by **hsp1**, is defined as follows:

```
problem hsp1:
   minimize  Period
   subject to lin1(Removal,Entry), lin2(Removal,Entry),
              lin3(Removal,Period), disj(Removal,Entry,Period).
```

Other classes of HSPs can be defined by an extension or a small modification of this generic HSP model.

3.2 Scheduling with Tank Capacity

Each tank has a finite capacity. There is a limit to the number of jobs it can treat at any one time. The papers on one-hoist scheduling problems consider usually the maximum capacity of each tank equal to one.

- **tankCapacity(Tank, Integer)**. The capacity of each tank.

The tanks must never contain more jobs than their capacities. So for tank T_1, a job must be removed before the arrival of the job which is `tankCapacity(I)` jobs (=cycles) behind it on the production line. We introduce the following constraint:

```
lin4(Removal,Entry,Period) :-
    for(Tank,1:numTanks) do
        Removal[Tank] - Entry[Tank] ≤ tankCapacity(Tank) * Period.
```

The P&U's problem with tank capacity is denoted by **hsp2** and it contains constraints lin1, lin2, lin3, lin4, disj.

3.3 Scheduling with Multiple Hoists on One Track

HSP can use two or more hoists on the same track. In the multiple hoist problem we need a variable which associates a hoist to each activity - transporting a job from one tank to the next. Data:

- **numHoists(Integer)**. The number of hoists (=2) in the system.

Variable:

- **Hoist** An array recording which hoist is assigned to each activity. **Hoist[T]** is the hoist which transports a job from tank **T** to **T+1**.

The multiple hoist problem can be modelled by changing only the disjunctive constraint disj from the previous model. The new disjunctive constraint only differs by allowing an extra alternative: the case where the two activities are performed by different hoists.

We assume the hoists are numbered, with the hoists further along the track towards the higher-numbered tanks also having higher numbers. Because the hoists cannot pass each other, if two activities do overlap in time, the activity involving the higher-numbered tank must be performed by the higher-numbered hoist.

```
mhdisj(Removal,Entry,Hoist,Period) :-
    for(T1,1:numTanks-1) do  for(T2,T1+1:numTanks) do
        for(K,1:numJobs-1) do
            mhdisj1(T1,T2,K,Removal,Entry,Hoist,Period).

mhdisj1(T1,T2,K,Removal,Entry,_H,Period) :-
    Entry[T1+1] + empty(T1+1,T2) ≤ Removal[T2] + K * Period.
mhdisj1(T1,T2,K,Removal,Entry,_H,Period) :-
    Entry[T2+1] + empty(T2+1,T1) + K * Period ≤ Removal[T1].
mhdisj1(T1,T2,K,Removal,Entry,Hoist,Period) :-
    /* Comment: T2>T1 */
    Hoist[T2] ≥ Hoist[T1] + 1.
```

The whole P&U's problem with multi hoists on one track is denoted by **hsp3** and it contains constraints lin1, lin2, lin3, lin4, mhdisj.

Notice that Lei and others introduced two quite different models for the 2-hoist problem, the *partitioning* model [15], and the *traffic-collision* approach [14]. **hsp3** models the traffic-collision approach. The weaker partition approach could be modelled by adding the single constraint

```
partition(Hoist) :-
    for(I,1:numTanks-1) do  for(J,I+1:numTanks) do
        Hoist[J] ≥ Hoist[I].
```

3.4 Scheduling with Multiple Tracks

HSPs can contain hoists on more than one track. Previous approaches toward solving cyclic HSPs have been limited to single-track cases. Our model for that problem is very similar to the model for the previous class of HSPs. Since the hoists use different tracks it is enough to force that the hoists for each tank are different. We adapt the model of **hsp3** by adding a single extra clause to the procedure for `mhdisj1`, viz:

```
mhdisj1(T1,T2,K,Removal,Entry,Hoist,Period) :-
    Hoist[T1] ≥ Hoist[T2] + 1.
```

The whole P&U's problem with multi hoists on different tracks is denoted by **hsp4** and it contains `lin1`, `lin2`, `lin3`, `lin4`, and the modified `mhdisj`.

4 Deriving Models for Different Solvers

We use the CLP formalism for modelling and solving HSPs. Once a CLP program has been developed for a class of HSPs it is relatively easy, compared with the mathematical programming approach, to adapt the model for other classes of HSPs and run different solution algorithms.

4.1 Modelling

CLP has greater expressive power than traditional mathematical programming models in two ways:

- Constraints involving disjunction can be represented directly
- Constraints can be encapsulated (as predicates) and used in the definition of further constraints

However, a CLP model can be automatically translated into a traditional MIP model by

- Eliminating disjunctions in favour of auxiliary boolean variables
- Unfolding predicates into their definitions

This translation is only applicable on condition that any recursively defined constraints can be fully unfolded at the time of translation. This condition is satisfied in the HSP model, and all the other large scale industrial optimisation problems we have addressed. The translation is presented in detail in [19]. We briefly summarise the key steps, and present a toy example.

- For each possible top level goal, `p(X1, ..., Xn)` add to the program a single clause

  ```
  p(X1...Xn) :- p(X1...Xn,1).
  ```

  The extra final argument is an input boolean (1 imposes the constraint, whilst 0 would relax it).

– Each predicate definition

```
disj(X1...Xn) :- Body1.
...
disj(X1...Xn) :- BodyN.
```

is translated into a single-clause predicate

```
disj(X1...Xn,B) :- Body1[B1], ..., BodyN[BN], B1+...+BN=B.
```

The bodies **Bodyi[Bi]** are produced by adding an extra argument `Bi` to every goal.

– Each linear constraint `X` $\leq$ `Y` is translated into another linear constraint `X + m * B` $\leq$ `Y + m` where `m` is the number $(hi(X) - lo(Y))$. Value $hi(X)$ is the upper bound of X and $lo(Y)$ is the lower bound of Y. Note, every translated linear constraint is equivalent to the original constraint if the auxiliary binary variable is instantiated to 1; and it is true for every value of X and Y within their ranges, if it is instantiated to 0.

After translation, the resulting CLP program has no choice points. When the input data of a given problem are supplied, the translated program is automatically unfolded into a conjunction of linear constraints.

4.2 Example

The program

```
prog(X, Y) :-  X::1..10, Y::1..10, diff(X, Y).
diff(X, Y) :-  Y+2 ≤ X.
diff(X, Y) :-  X+2 ≤ Y.
```

is translated into the program:

```
prog(X, Y) :- prog(X, Y, 1).
prog(X, Y, B) :-  X::1..10, Y::1..10, diff(X, Y, B).
diff(X, Y, B) :-  Y+2+B1 ×11 ≤ X+11, X+2+B2 × 11 ≤ Y+11, B1+B2 = B.
```

The goal `prog(3,Y)` is unfolded into the constraints:

```
1 ≤ Y ≤ 10, Y+2+B1 × 11 ≤ 14, 5+B2 × 11 ≤ Y+11, B1+B2 = 1.
```

4.3 Solving

The proposed evaluation algorithm allows an integration of MIP with CLP using a *unique model* for a problem. The derived linear constraints are treated either by the MIP solver, or the CLP solver, or by both solvers. Our hybrid algorithm combines both solvers such that search is separated from the handling of constraints. Search is applied by labelling of boolean and integer variables. Constraint handling is performed by constraint propagation of the CLP solver and linear constraint solving of the MIP solver.

We have implemented the integration of CLP with MIP by using the ECLiPSe constraint logic programming platform and the XPRESS-MP mathematical programming package [9, 23]. This allows XPRESS to be used to solve problems modelled in ECLiPSe. The control of the search process and the constraint propagation is handled by CLP while the linear constraint solving is handled by MIP. The constraint propagation is performed by a consistency algorithm on finite domains and it represents a component of the ECLiPSe package. On the other hand, the linear constraint solving is performed by the simplex algorithm which is a component of the XPRESS package.

Communication between the solvers is supported by the attributed variables of ECLiPSe. For the purposes of the hoist scheduling problem, the information communicated is just the upper and lower bounds of the variables.

Naturally the main performance benefit of the hybrid solver is due to the early detection of failure by the different solvers. Each solver detects certain failures which would not have been detected by the other solver until a later node in the search tree. For example constraint propagation fails immediately with constraints,

```
X::0..2, Y::0..2, X+2*Y = 3, X-Y = 1.
```

but cannot detect any inconsistency in the constraints:

```
X::1..10, Y::1..10, 2*X+2*Y ≥ 20, X+Y ≤ 11.
```

A linear solver has precisely the complementary behaviour, detecting the inconsistency of the second constraint set, but not the first.

On the HSP problem, we apply the following three solvers:

- **CLP solver.** The constraints are considered only by ECLiPSe. The search is done by labelling binary variables first. Constraint handling is performed by constraint propagation on finite domains.
- **MIP solver.** The constraints are considered only by XPRESS. The search is done by performing the default XPRESS branch-and-bound procedure. Constraint handling is performed by linear constraint solving (simplex). The optimal solution of the whole problem is returned to ECLiPSe.
- **CLP&MIP solver.** The constraints are considered by ECLiPSe and XPRESS. The search is done by labelling binary variables first. Constraint handling is performed by constraint propagation on finite domains and linear constraint solving.

5 Empirical Results

Let us discuss the empirical results of the hybrid CLP&MIP solver relative to the results of the CLP and MIP solvers on the following HSPs from Section 2:

The empirical results in Table 2 show that HSPs are hard for our CLP solver. However, the flexibility of CLP gives the programmer the choice of a variety

Table 1. Hoist scheduling problems

hsp1	the P&U's problem with 12 tanks and 4 jobs
hsp2	the P&U's problem with the tank capacity equal to 2
hsp3	the collision-based P&U's problem with 2 hoists on one track
hsp4	the P&U's problem with 2 hoists on two tracks

of constraint solvers and variable domains. Baptiste et al. [2] compared two domains and associated constraint solvers from different CLP languages: CHIP's finite domains and Prolog III's rational numbers. Their empirical results show when a constraint solver should be chosen in preference to another constraint solver and how to control the search towards an efficient running program.

The MIP solver has difficulties to derive an optimal solution to all HSPs. The solver is very efficient for problems **hsp1** and **hsp2**, and inefficient for problems **hsp3**, and **hsp4**.

Table 2. Characteristics of the solvers on different HSPs

The CLP solver:

	Time (1st sol.)	Time (opt.sol.)	Time (proof opt.)	Min. cycle time	FD fails
hsp1	1204 sec	> 60 min	-	-	> 20000
hsp2	3371 sec	> 60 min	-	-	> 20000
hsp3	> 60 min	-	-	-	> 20000
hsp4	> 60 min	-	-	-	> 20000

The MIP solver:

	Time (1st sol.)	Time (opt.sol.)	Time (proof opt.)	Min. cycle time	Nodes processed
hsp1	4 sec	6 sec	7 sec	521	1200
hsp2	6 sec	8 sec	8 sec	521	1521
hsp3	7 sec	> 60 min	-	-	> 50000
hsp4	6 sec	> 60 min	-	-	> 50000

The CLP&MIP solver:

	Time (1st sol.)	Time (opt.sol.)	Time (proof opt.)	Min. cycle time	FD fails	LP fails
hsp1	19 sec	73 sec	105 sec	521	1338	502
hsp2	28 sec	76 sec	102 sec	521	1399	521
hsp3	218 sec	926 sec	961 sec	395	4179	1768
hsp4	36 sec	68 sec	185 sec	379	1300	92

By applying the CLP&MIP solver, simplex and the constraint propagation on finite domains helped to derive an optimal solution and to prove its optimality. It follows that the proposed constraint handling is very useful procedure by cutting the solution space and deriving an optimal solution to the HSPs in reasonable time. There is a certain level of orthogonality between constraint propagation and linear constraint solving. The number of FD-failures and the number of LP-failures show that both constraint handling procedures are needed to prune the search space. Since constraint propagation is performed before linear constraint solving it is difficult to say which procedure is more important.

All timings in Table 2 are in CPU seconds running on a SUN-SPARC/20. "FD-fails" denotes the number of failures by performing constraint propagation and "LP-fails" denotes the number of failures by linear constraint solving.

We show the robustness of the hybrid approach by solving 100 randomly generated two-hoists HSPs with multiple tracks. The problems represent modifications of problem *hsp4* in Section 2. The limits on processing times, $Min(i)$ and $Max(i)$, $i = 1, ..., NumTanks$, are determined by drawing values from two sampling functions, $f_{Min}(i) = Min(i) - 10 + 20 * r_1$ and $f_{Max}(i) = Max(i) - 10 + 20 * r_2$, where r_1 and r_2 are $(0,1)$ uniform random numbers [15]. Once the values of these processing time limits are computed, they are used as constants. The hoist travelling times are also determined in a similar way using a sampling function $f_{Full}(i) = Empty(i, i+1) + 15 + 10 * r_3$.

Table 3. The CLP&MIP solver on 100 randomly generated hsp4

Derived optimal solutions	100
Min. time	167 sec
Max. time	1146 sec
Avg. time	314 sec

Table 3 represents the minimum, maximum, and average computation times needed to derive optimal schedules of the generated HSPs. The results demonstrate that the hybrid solver is a robust algorithm and successfully derives an optimal solution and proves its optimality to all HSPs with two hoists on different tracks.

6 Conclusions

We have presented models for several classes of industrial HSPs and an efficient translation to a generic model for different solution techniques, i.e. the CLP solver, the MIP solver, or hybrid CLP&MIP solvers. These models and solvers have been benchmarked on some problems which have been the subject of previous research both using CLP, MIP and heuristic algorithms.

The proposed CLP&MIP solver can solve several classes of HSPs which have never previously been solved to optimality. Neither the CLP solver nor the MIP solver alone are able to solve them in reasonable time. The experimental results demonstrated that constraint propagation and linear constraint solving are orthogonal up to certain degree. An infeasibility of several HSPs is recognised by only one of the procedures. The proposed integration of CLP with MIP allows comparisons between the two approaches and gives a clearer idea of when CLP should be chosen in preference to MIP, and when an integrated solver is quicker than the CLP solver or the MIP solver.

However the HSP experiments have revealed an unexpected, but very important, benefit of hybrid solvers. The experiments show that, if constraints are passed to both a constraint propagation engine and a linear solver, the robustness of the model may be dramatically enhanced. The same generic model can be easily and naturally adapted for all the different classes of HSPs, and they can all be solved.

Using either MIP or CLP solvers alone, problem modelling is made harder because models must be designed specifically for the solver, as for example in [14, 15, 16, 18, 22]. In fact, when the same generic model is solved by a CLP or an MIP solver alone, only a subset of the different problem classes can be effectively handled. Our hope is that hybrid solvers may make it possible to simplify problem modelling, by reducing the need to address issues of solver efficiency at the modelling stage.

Our work makes a contribution to the long-term objective of separating the modelling and solving of combinatorial problems. With the powerful modelling facilities of CLP, with multiple solvers and flexible search control, the encoding of a correct model of the problem can indeed be a guaranteed step towards an efficient running program. The consequences can be revolutionary - with programmers actually taking modelling seriously.

Acknowledgements Many thanks to the IC-PARC group who has contributed to the writing of this paper through helpful discussions and criticisms.

References

1. Barth, P., Bockmayr, A.: Modelling Mixed-Integer Optimisation Problems in Constraint Logic Programming. *MPI Report Nr. I-95-2-011* (1995)
2. Baptiste, P., Legeard, B., Manier, M.A., Varnier, C.: A Scheduling Problem Optimisation Solved with Constraint Logic Programming. *Proc. of the PACT Conf.* (1994) 47-66
3. Beringer, H., De Backer, B.: Combinatorial Problem Solving in Constraint Logic Programming with Cooperating Solvers. Chapter 8 in *Logic Programming: Formal Methods and Practical Applications* ed. C. Beierle and L. Pluemer Elsevier (1995)
4. Cheng, C.C., Smith, S.F.: A Constraint Satisfaction Approach to Makespan Scheduling. *Proc. of the AIPS Conf.* (1996) 45-52
5. Dincbas, M., Van Hentenryck, P., Simonis, H., Aggoun, A., Graf, T., Berthier, F.: The Constraint Logic Programming Language CHIP. *Proc. of the FGCS Conf.* (1988) 693-702
6. CPLEX. Using the CPLEX Callable Library. *CPLEX Optimization, Inc.* (1997)
7. Dincbas, M., Simonis, H., Van Hentenryck, P.: Solving Large Combinatorial Problems in Logic Programming. *Journal of Logic programming* **8** (1995) 75-93
8. Darby-Dowman, K., Little, J., Mitra, G., Zaffalon, M.: Constraint Logic Programming and Integer programming Approaches and their Collaboration in Solving an Assignment Scheduling Problem. *Constraints* **1(3)** (1997) 245-264

9. ECLiPSe User Manual Version 3.7.1. *IC-PARC, Imperial College, London* (1998)
10. Hanen. C.: Study of a NP-Hard Cyclic Scheduling Problem: The Recurrent Job-Shop. *European Journal of Operations Research* **72** (1994) 82-101
11. Hooker, J.N., Osorio, M.A.: Mixed Logical/Linear Programming. *Proc. of the INFORMS CSTS Conf.* Atlanta (1996)
12. Hajian, M., Sakkout, H.El, Wallace, M., Richards, E.: Towards a Closer Integration of Finite Domain Propagation and Simplex-Based Algorithms. *Proc. of the AI Maths Conf.* Florida (1995) **www.icparc.ic.ac.uk/papers.html**
13. Jaffar, J., Lassez, J.L.: Constraint Logic Programming. *Proc. of the ACM POPL Symposium* Munich (1997)
14. Lei, L., Armstrong, R., Gu, S.: Minimizing the Fleet Size with Dependent Time-Window and Single-Track Constraints. *Operations Res. Letters* **14** (1993) 91-98
15. Lei, L., Wang, T.J.: The Minimum Common-Cycle Algorithm for Cycle Scheduling of Two Material Handling Hoists with Time Window Constraints. *Management Science* **37(12)** (1991) 1629-1639
16. Lei, L., Wang, T.J.: Determining Optimal Cyclic Hoist Schedules in a Single Hoist Electroplating Line. *IEE Transactions* **26(2)** (1994) 25-33
17. McAloon, K., Tretkoff, C.: *Optimization and Computational Logic.* Wiley-Interscience (1996)
18. Phillips, L.W., Unger, P.S.: Mathematical Programming Solution of a Hoist Scheduling Problem. *AIIE Transactions* **8(2)** (1976) 219-255
19. Rodošek, R., Wallace, M.G., Hajian, M.T.: A New Approach to Integrating Mixed Integer Programming with Constraint Logic Programming. *Annals of Operational Research. Recent Advance in Combinatorial Optimization: Theory and Applications* (to appear) **www.icparc.ic.ac.uk/papers.html**
20. Smith, B.M., Brailsford, S.C., Hubbard, P.M., Williams, H.P.: The Progressive Party Problem: Integer Linear Programming and Constraint Programming Compared. *Constraints* **1(2)** (1996) 119-138
21. Schimpf. J.: ECLiPSe Approach to Solver Integration and Cooperation. *Proc. of the INFORMS CSTS Conf.* Monterey (1998)
22. Sharpio, G.W., Nuttle, H.: Hoist Scheduling for a PBC Electroplating Facility. *IIE Transactions* **20(2)** (1988) 157-167
23. Dash Associates. XPRESS-MP Reference Manual. *Dash Associates UK* (1993)

Linear Concurrent Constraint Programming over Reals

Vincent Schachter

L.I.E.N.S., Ecole Normale Supérieure
45, rue d'Ulm 75005 Paris
schachte@dmi.ens.fr

Abstract. We introduce a constraint system $\mathcal{LC}$ that handles arithmetic constraints over reals within the linear concurrent constraint programming (`lcc`) framework. This approach provides us with a general, extensible foundation for linear programming algorithm design that comes with a (linear) logical semantics. In particular, it allows us to build a 'glass-box' version of the (constraint solver) simplex algorithm by defining (monotone) `cc ask` and `tell` agents over a higher-level constraint system as `lcc`($\mathcal{LC}$) programs. We illustrate at the same time the use of the `lcc`framework as a non-trivial concurrent algorithm specification tool.

1 Introduction

Constraint-based programming languages are based on a functional separation between a program that successively generates pieces of partial information called constraints, and a constraint solver that collects, combines, simplifies and detects inconsistencies between these constraints. Initially, constraint solvers were monolithic programs written in a low-level language (the 'black-box' approach), making it hard not only to modify or extend the solver, but also to reason about it or debug it. A few proposals [6, 16] have been made over the years to allow more flexibility and customization of constraint solvers, as well as provide them with an interesting semantics, ideally on par with that of the language : the so-called 'glass-box' (or 'open-box') approaches. In particular, a significant success of the concurrent constraint (`cc`) paradigm has been the rational reconstruction of the finite-domain constraint propagators of CLP(FD) by `cc`-agents [6].

In the `cc` paradigm, concurrent agents communicate asynchronously via a shared store : they add constraints to the store (`tell` agents) and synchronize by asking the store whether a given constraint is entailed (`ask` agents). However, the store evolves *monotonically* during computations, making the `cc` framework ill-suited to the expression of *global constraints* that use inherently *non-monotonic* (imperative, backtrackable) data structures.

This is precisely the case for another prominent domain of application of constraint technology : constraint programming over reals. The simplex algorithm is typically non-monotonic in that the information computed along a failed branch

of the search procedure (i.e. one that leads to a non-optimal vertex) is used to perform the rest of the search.
Indeed, although many systems for handling linear constraints over reals have been proposed (see [12] for a survey), we are not aware of any attempt to reconstruct the corresponding family of constraint solving algorithms in the spirit of cc(FD), i.e. from a set of elementary, combinable primitives aimed at abstracting its fundamental operations. In this paper, we show how Linear `cc` (`lcc`) – a *non-monotonic* extension of `cc` languages introduced in [14], in a spirit similar to [1], where the constraint system is axiomatized in linear logic and constraints are consumed by **ask** agents without maintenance or recomputation – may be used to overcome the 'non-monotony obstacle', and in so doing we provide the first example of practical use of the `lcc` framework. We illustrate `lcc` expressiveness and programming style by first building a low-level constraint system to handle equations and inequations over reals, and then programming one (of many possible) constraint solvers faithful to the `cc` ask & tell paradigm as an `lcc` program on top of that constraint system.
The rest of the paper is organized as follows. Section 2 gives the necessary background on the `lcc` framework as developed in [13, 4], and describes the tight correspondance between `lcc` computations and proofs in linear logic. Section 3 then introduces the constraint system $\mathcal{LC}$ designed to serve as a base for (non-monotonic) constraint computing over reals. Section 4 illustrates the use of $\mathcal{LC}$ by expressing a constraint solver that is complete with respect to satisfiability and entailment of linear equations and inequations as a couple of `lcc` agents, effectively defining a cc($\mathbb{R}$) language.

2 The `lcc` Framework

We recall below the main features of the linear concurrent constraint framework as defined in [4, 13]

2.1 Syntax

Definition 21 (Linear constraint system) *A* linear constraint system *is a pair* $(C, \vdash_C)$*, where:*

– C *is a set of formulas of intuitionistic linear logic (ILL) (see for example [5]), called the* linear constraints, *built from a set* V *of variables, a set* Σ *of function and relation symbols, with logical operators:* $\otimes, 1, \exists, !$

– $\Vdash_C$ *is a subset of* $C \times C$ *which defines the non-logical axioms of the constraint system.*

– $\vdash_C$ *is the least subset of* $C^* \times C$ *containing* $\Vdash_C$ *and closed by the rules of ILL for* $1, \otimes, \exists$ *and* $!$.

The classical constraint systems of `cc` languages [15] can be recovered with the usual translation of classical or intuitionistic logic into linear logic, by writing all constraints under a ! [5]. In general, linear constraints are not erasable in the sense that $d \not\vdash 1$. However, explicit erasure of constraints through the ask operator of lcc agents constitutes one of the main features of the formalism, and opens up the possibility of writing non-monotonic algorithms.

lcc *agents* are defined by the grammar $A ::= p(x) \mid tell(c) \mid (A \parallel A) \mid A + A \mid \exists x A \mid \forall x(c \rightarrow A)$ where $\parallel$ stands for parallel composition, + for non-deterministic choice, $\exists$ for variable hiding and $\rightarrow$ for blocking ask. The atomic agents $p(x)\ldots$ are ***procedure calls***. Recursion is obtained by ***declarations*** : $D ::= p(x) = A$ and $\mathcal{D} :: \epsilon \mid [\mathcal{D}]_{\sim}, \mathcal{D}$ where $[\mathcal{D}]_{\sim}$ denotes congruence classes of $\mathcal{D}$ up to variable renaming.

An lcc ***program*** is a delclarations-agent couple. In the following, both the constraint system $\mathcal{C}$ and the set of declarations $\mathcal{D}$ will be implicit.

Definition 22 (Configurations) *A* configuration *is a triple* $(x;\ c;\ \Gamma)$, *where* x *is a set of variables,* c *is a constraint, and* Γ *a multi-set of agents.*

In a configuration $(x;\ c;\ \Gamma)$, x denotes the set of hidden variables and c is the store. We shall use the notation x, y to denote the union of the disjoint sets x and $\{y\}$, $fv(A)$ to denote the set of free variables of an agent or formula A, and $v(A)$ to denote the set of all variables occurring in A. The operational semantics of lcc programs can be presented by a congruence and a transition relation between configurations.

Definition 23 *The* structural congruence $\equiv$ *is the least congruence satisfying the rules of Table 1.*

Table 1. Structural congruence

α-Conversion	$\dfrac{z \notin v(A)}{\exists y A \equiv \exists z A[z/y]}$	
Parallel composition	$(x;\ c;\ A \parallel B, \Gamma) \equiv (x;\ c;\ A, B, \Gamma)$	
Hiding	$\dfrac{y \notin x \cup fv(c, \Gamma)}{(x;\ c;\ \exists y A, \Gamma) \equiv (x, y;\ c;\ A, \Gamma)}$	$\dfrac{y \notin fv(c, \Gamma)}{(x, y;\ c;\ \Gamma) \equiv (x;\ c;\ \Gamma)}$

The transition *relation* $\longrightarrow$ *is the least transitive relation on configurations satisfying the rules of Table 2.*

The only difference with monotonic cc is that constraints are formulas of linear logic and that the communication rule *ask* consumes information. In the *ask* rule, the resulting store d is the part of the store which remains after some necessary consumptions for entailing the guard e. Without restriction,

Table 2. Transition relation

Tell	$(x;\ c;\ tell(d), \Gamma) \longrightarrow (x;\ c \otimes d;\ \Gamma)$
Ask	$\dfrac{c \vdash_{\mathcal{C}} d \otimes e[t/y]}{(x;\ c;\ \forall y(e \to A), \Gamma) \longrightarrow (x;\ d;\ A[t/y], \Gamma)}$
Procedure calls	$\dfrac{[p(y) = A]_{\sim} \in \mathcal{D}}{(x;\ c;\ p(y), \Gamma) \longrightarrow (x;\ c;\ A, \Gamma)}$
$\equiv$	$\dfrac{(x;\ c;\ \Gamma) \equiv (x';\ c';\ \Gamma') \quad (x';\ c';\ \Gamma') \longrightarrow (y';\ d';\ \Delta') \quad (y';\ d';\ \Delta') \equiv (y;\ d;\ \Delta)}{(x;\ c;\ \Gamma) \longrightarrow (y;\ d;\ \Delta)}$
Guarded choice	$\dfrac{(x;\ c;\ A, \Gamma) \longrightarrow (y;\ d;\ \Delta)}{(x;\ c;\ A + B, \Gamma) \longrightarrow (y;\ d;\ \Delta)} \qquad \dfrac{(x;\ c;\ B, \Gamma) \longrightarrow (y;\ d;\ \Delta)}{(x;\ c;\ A + B, \Gamma) \longrightarrow (y;\ d;\ \Delta)}$

`lcc` computation is thus intrinsically non-deterministic, even without the choice operator $+$, since several constraints can satisfy the condition of the *ask* rule. Note that **ask** agents are written with a universal quantifier to indicated the variables which are bound in the guard.

Of particular interest, especially for control purposes, are linear atomic constraints without entailment, i.e.'tokens'[1]. In that case, entailment by a store is simply multiset inclusion. Note also that we chose the one-step guarded choice rule to express non-determinism, the main reason being that we will need to keep a tight rein on the production of suspensions in the programs of Section 4. As noted in [4], this choice has no effect on the semantics as long as only successes and accessible stores are observed.

Definition 24 (Observables) *The* store *of a configuration* $(x;\ c;\ \Gamma)$ *is the constraint* $\exists x c$. *An* accessible store *from A is a constraint d such that there exist a constraint c and a multi-set Γ of agents such that* $(\emptyset;\ 1;\ A) \longrightarrow (x;\ c;\ \Gamma)$ *and* $\exists x c \vdash d \otimes \top$.

A success *for an agent A is a configuration* $(x;\ c;\ \emptyset)$ *such that* $(\emptyset;\ 1;\ A) \longrightarrow (x;\ c;\ \emptyset)$*;*

A suspension *for A is a configuration* $(x;\ c;\ d_1 \to A_1, \ldots, d_n \to A_n)$, $n \geq 0$, *such that* $(\emptyset;\ 1;\ A) \longrightarrow (x;\ c;\ d_1 \to A_1, \ldots, d_n \to A_n)$ *and for no i*, $c > d_i$ *(a success is a suspension with* $n = 0$*).*

2.2 Logical semantics

One of the main attractive features of the lcc framework is its logical semantics, i.e. the existence of a direct translation between lcc and linear logic, following

---

[1] Tokens are practically the only type of constraints that `lcc` examples in the literature have used so far.

the 'Programs=Formulas and Computation = Proof Search' paradigm. We summarize below the main features of this correspondance, as presented in [4, 13].

Let $(\mathcal{C}, \Vdash_{\mathcal{C}})$ be a linear constraint system and $\mathcal{D}$ be a set of declarations.

Definition 25 *lcc agents are translated into formulas in the following way:*

$$\begin{array}{ll} tell(c)^{\dagger} = c & \forall x(c \rightarrow A)^{\dagger} = \forall x c \multimap A^{\dagger} \\ p(x)^{\dagger} = p(x) & (\exists x A)^{\dagger} = \exists x A^{\dagger} \\ (A \parallel B)^{\dagger} = A^{\dagger} \otimes B^{\dagger} & (A + B)^{\dagger} = A^{\dagger} \,\&\, B^{\dagger} \end{array}$$

If Γ is the multi-set of agents $(A_1 \dots A_n)$, define $\Gamma^{\dagger} = A_1^{\dagger} \otimes \dots \otimes A_n^{\dagger}$. If $\Gamma = \emptyset$ then $\Gamma^{\dagger} = 1$.

The translation of a configuration $(x;\ c;\ \Gamma)$ is the formula $\exists x(c \otimes \Gamma^{\dagger})$.

Let us denote by ILL($\mathcal{C}$,$\mathcal{D}$) the deduction system obtained by adding to ILL:

- the non-logical axiom $c \vdash d$ for every $c \Vdash_{\mathcal{C}} d$ in $\Vdash_{\mathcal{C}}$,
- the non-logical axiom $p(x) \vdash A^{\dagger}$ for every declaration $p(x) = A$ in $\mathcal{D}$.

Theorem 26 (Soundness) *Let $(x;\ c;\ \Gamma)$ and $(y;\ d;\ \Delta)$ be LCC configurations.*

If $(x;\ c;\ \Gamma) \equiv (y;\ d;\ \Delta)$ then $(x;\ c;\ \Gamma)^{\dagger} \dashv\vdash_{ILL(\mathcal{C},\mathcal{D})} (y;\ d;\ \Delta)^{\dagger}$.

If $(x;\ c;\ \Gamma) \longrightarrow (y;\ d;\ \Delta)$ then $(x;\ c;\ \Gamma)^{\dagger} \vdash_{ILL(\mathcal{C},\mathcal{D})} (y;\ d;\ \Delta)^{\dagger}$.

Conversely, one can characterize the observation of successes, even in presence of the operator of explicit choice + (the proofs are given in [13, 4]):

Theorem 27 (Observation of successes) *Let A be an lcc agent and c be a linear constraint.*

If $A^{\dagger} \vdash_{ILL(\mathcal{C},\mathcal{D})} c$, then there exists a success $(x;\ d;\ \emptyset)$ for A such that $\exists x d \vdash_{\mathcal{C}} c$.

Theorem 28 (Observation of stores [11]) *Let A be an lcc agent and c be a linear constraint. If $A^{\dagger} \vdash_{ILL(\mathcal{C},\mathcal{D})} c \otimes \top$, then c is a store accessible from A.*

2.3 Programming in lcc

lcc as we envision it is to cc what linear logic is to classical logic : a lower-level machinery giving explicit control over resources (constraints and formulas), therefore allowing greater expressivity as well as finer theoretical analysis. With this added expressive power comes, however, the usual drawback of 'lower level' formalisms : writing complex programs can get somewhat unwieldy. In particular, concurrency and asynchrony notoriously require explicit and heavy-handed handling of the necessary synchronizations, *especially in a non-monotonic framework.* We list below the main features of the corresponding programming discipline, and also add some syntactic sugar to the framework.

Programming Style Non-monotony in the concurrent constraint framework has several consequences :

- Constraint consumption allows a form of imperative programming : for example, by using a constraint eq(x,v) that is a placeholder for the real value v of variable x, on may erase (**ask**) or update (**ask** followed by **tell**) the 'value' of x that may be read by the $\forall$-rule. This, in turn, precludes the need for data structures such as streams to hold simpler, but inherently non-monotonic, information.
- One must distinguish between *permanent* constraints (i.e. the monotonic, or 'banged', subset of the constraint system) that behave exactly as in the cc framework, and constraints that may be removed either by *internal actions* of the constraint system, that is linear deductions defined by the $\vdash$ relation, or by **ask** at the level of agents.
- The fact that the $\vdash$ relation deduces non-monotonically forces the program designer to think – at least in part – procedurally about the store when programming the agents :
  - The rules of the constraint system must be designed with 'defeasibility' in mind, i.e. consequences of a constraint c must not be left behind after its erasure or update, as they may become inconsistent with, for example, a newer version of c.
  - External consumption of constraints through the **ask** effectively actualizes[2] the potential non-determinism of the $\vdash$ relation, i.e. it forces the store into one of a set of possible equivalence classes of states.
    For example, let c, d, d', e, e', f be linear constraints such that $c \vdash d \otimes d'$ and $c \otimes e \otimes e'$. Agents $d \longrightarrow f$ and $e \longrightarrow f$ force the store in respective states $f \otimes d'$ and $f \otimes e'$.
    The store may thus be seen as 'looping' through the equivalence-class of possible deductions, this equivalence class being modified by a **tell** action or reduced (measured) by an **ask** action.
  - The framework is of course not confluent in general : non-joinable 'critical pairs' in the rules defining the constraint system may lead to non-confluent behavior of programs, as may non-deterministic agents whose alternatives are 'non-joinable'. Note that since we work here with what is essentially a certain class of rewriting rules, a confluence theorem such as the one developed for the Constraint Handling Rules (CHR) formalism in [16], based on joinability of critical pairs, may help define a 'well-behaved' subclass of linear constraint systems.

Bracket Notation : When describing constraint system rules or lcc agents, one very often wishes *not* to consume a given constraint in a specific rule or query, effectively designing a rule 'monotonic' relatively to that constraint. We will use the following notation :

$$[\![c]\!] \otimes d \vdash e \text{ stands for } c \otimes d \vdash c \otimes e$$

and similarly for $\longrightarrow$.

[2] It is hard to avoid thinking of the analogy with the act of measuring a micro-state in quantum mechanics...

3 A Constraint System for Linear (In)Equalities

We wish to capture in the definition of a linear constraint system the most general – the less 'context dependent' – pieces of information needed and operations performed by algorithms dealing with linear equations and inequations. To describe and modify a 'state of affairs' in such a context, we need to manipulate three types of information (from the 'highest level' to the 'lowest level') :

1. ***The system S of equations and inequations*** representing the mathematically meaningful information on the real-valued variables, in the usual linear-algebraic or geometric interpretation of the language.
2. ***Sets of variables and indices*** : constraints in S must be manipulated and combined explicitly to yield useful information, typically satisfiability or entailment of other constraints. In particular, S may be represented in many ways equivalent with respect to the geometric interpretation : search through the space of representations is the core of the simplex algorithm.

   To maintain and modify this representational information, we use *sets* of variables and indices. The purpose is that a given 'point of view' on S be entirely described by a few sets such as the sets of upper-bounded and lower-bounded variables, the set of base variables, and the set of all variables in S.
3. To carry actual computations in a concurrent constraint setting, we finally need some extra information in the store :
   - ***synchronization constraints***, i.e. tokens that play their usual synchronization role between concurrent processes acting on the same variables.
   - a way to store intermediate (numerical) results of calculations : a mere binary ***'placeholder' constraint*** eq(x,v) with arithmetic evaluation of its value-argument v by the store is sufficient.

We now move on to a more formal description of the $(\mathcal{LC}, \vdash_{\mathcal{LC}})$ constraint system for elementary manipulation of linear equations and inequations[3].

3.1 'Classical' Foundations

To handle linear equations and inequations over reals[4], we need to carry basic arithmetic computations : evaluate the coefficients of linear combinations of con-

[3] Since we wish to recover monotony in the cc framework later on, we do not include rules for disequations. Their treatment *within* the constraint system, similar to that of equations, entails no special difficulty. Of course, to test efficiently for satisfiability and entailment with disequations in the system, one has to do some extra work. The constraint solver reconstruction that we present in Section 4 is designed so that detection of implicit equalities and corresponding improvements in the entailment test for equations may be added easily to the 'core' agents

[4] Actually, we compute only over rationals. We suppose given a (countable) set of definitions for integer constants (one may see them as mere syntactic conventions), and any rational number may be expressed as a basic arithmetic term.

straints, test wether their value is positive, or zero, etc.
Therefore, we need definitions for the basic arithmetic function and predicate symbols $\{0, 1, +, *, -, /, =, \leq, \geq, \neq\}$[5]. We rely for this on the usual axioms of *elementary field theory*, together with the 5 axioms defining the order relation on an ordered field.
Note that these axioms constitute[6] a complete theory [9] : satisfiability of any formula built with the above predicates is decidable, using a quantifier elimination method. Moreover, it is the 'natural' theory when dealing with constraints on reals or rationals, and it enjoys the standard mathematical structures R as a model: we shall refer to it as $\mathcal{CT}$ in the rest of the paper. Of course, we cannot use $\mathcal{CT}$ 'directly' for our constraint system : besides its computational intractability, it gives no explicit control over the constraints and the 'state of deductions'.

3.2 Constraints on Sets

Sets are represented by constraints $set(E,T)$ where E is a variable and T a set-term, represented modulo set equality ('$=_{set}$' is defined by the usual 'classical' axioms, as term equality augmented with associativity and commutativity properties). Table 3 gives the rules on set manipulation.
The **element** equivalence allows to add an element to a set, or pluck it from a set to work with it, while the **assign** rule deals with set copying.

Table 3. $\mathcal{LC}$ **set constraints**

Evaluate	$set(E, A) \otimes A =_{set} B \vdash_{\mathcal{LC}} set(E, B)$
Element	$set(E, \{x_1, \ldots, x_n\}) \otimes (x \in E) \dashv\vdash_{\mathcal{LC}} set(E, \{x, x_1, \ldots, x_n\})$
Assign	$set(E, \{x_1, \ldots, x_n\}) \otimes (E' := E) \vdash_{\mathcal{LC}} set(E, \{x_1, \ldots, x_n\}) \otimes set(E', \{x_1, \ldots, x_n\})$

We will note $E = \{x_1, \ldots, x_n\}$ for $set(E, \{x_1, \ldots, x_n\})$ and $E = \emptyset$ for $set(E, \{\})$ when the context is unambiguous.
We use this set machinery in the following as a privileged way of implementing the information removal capabilities of `lcc`. For example, if E is a set of variables of unknown cardinality to which a treatment T must be applied :

1. E is copied to E' using the **assign** rule ; E' will be used for T to prevent interference with other processes that need to access E

[5] These axioms are formulas of 'classical logic' (we suppose them translated in linear logic, i.e. suitably 'banged') : the predicates $\{=, \leq, \geq, \neq\}$ will behave like 'usual', *non-consumable* constraints.

[6] Together with the axiom of existence of a square root and the axiom schema of existence of a zero for any odd-degree polynomial.

2. agents of the form '$(\forall e((e \in E') \longrightarrow T(e)))$' remove elements from E' and apply the treatment T
3. a test $E' \neq \emptyset$ guards a 'termination agent' that 'cleans up' and posts a token to signal completion to other processes

3.3 Linear Arithmetic Constraints

The $\mathcal{LC}$ constraint system uses the following constraints, in addition to those defined above :

- **Tokens :** as necessary.[7]
- **Unary :** `vars`, `base`
- **Binary :** `line`, `eq`, `leq`, `geq`, `vareq`, `const`
- **Ternary :** `co`

Equations in $\mathcal{LC}$ are represented as $line(i, a)$ constraints, where i is the equation number and a is a linear arithmetic term $a_1x_1 + \ldots a_nx_n + b$. A constraint $line(i, a)$ may be read as : ' equation (i) states that a=0 ' and thought of as a line in a simplex matrix. Inequations are limited to one variable, and represented by : $leq(x, \beta)$ for $x \leq \beta$ and $geq(x, \alpha)$ for $x \geq \alpha$
The `eq(x,v)` constraint stands for :'x has current value v' and is a placeholder for values of variables that evaluates its second argument.
The $\mathcal{LC}$ rules[8] for linear equations and inequations are given in Table 4. They are designed to maintain the system of equations in Gauss normal form and deduce the corresponding coefficients so that agents may access them.
Two distinguished sets, the set V of all variables in the linear system and the set B of base variables, are used to direct the gaussian elimination process carried through the **Scalar** and **Simplify** rules. These sets are recognized and maintained through the **vars** and **base** predicates.
An equation holds two types of non-monotonically varying information : the set of its non-zero-coefficient variables and the values of the coefficients. Through the **Dissect-Rebuild** equivalence, a line may be dissected into the multiset of its coefficients (represented as constraints $co(i, x, a)$ – or $const(i, a)$ for the constant subterm – where i is the equation number, x the variable and a the value of the coefficient) and the set of its variables V_i (distinguished by the `vareq` constraint), and subsequently rebuilt if none of the necessary information has been consumed . The existence of two distinct states ('dissected' versus 'whole') stems from the need to prevent modification of a line while its coefficients are being used, since those coefficients would then lose their logical meaning.

[7] As tokens do not appear in deductions of $\mathcal{LC}$, defining new tokens as needed for the specific application has no impact on the workings of the constraint system. Alternatively, one can define a generic unary constraint `token(i)` and use the '$\exists$' mechanism to generate new indices

[8] Depending on the presentation, these rules should be taken either as axioms or axiom schemas, universally quantified over the intended range of the variables (Q or N) or over the number of terms in the linear sums.

Table 4. $\mathcal{LC}$ axioms for linear equations and inequations

Evaluate	$\mathtt{line}(i,s)\otimes(s=s')\vdash_{\mathcal{LC}}\mathtt{line}(i,s')$ $\quad eq(x,v)\otimes(v=v')\vdash_{\mathcal{LC}} eq(i,v')$
Scalar	$\mathtt{line}(i,s)\vdash_{\mathcal{LC}}\mathtt{line}(i,\lambda s)$
Simplify	$\llbracket base(B)\otimes(x_l,i)\in B\otimes\mathtt{line}(i,\sum a_{ik}x_k+b_i)\rrbracket\otimes\mathtt{line}(j,\sum a_{jk}x_k+b_j)$
	$\vdash_{\mathcal{LC}}\mathtt{line}(j,\sum(a_{jk}-\frac{a_{jl}}{a_{il}}*a_{ik})x_k+(b_j-\frac{a_{jl}}{a_{il}}*b_i))$
Dissect-Rebuild	$\llbracket base(B)\otimes B=\{x_1,\ldots,x_p\}\otimes Vars(V)\otimes V=\{x_1,\ldots,x_n\}$
	$\otimes vareq(i,V_i)\rrbracket\otimes\mathtt{line}(i,a)\dashv\vdash_{\mathcal{LC}}\mathrm{co}(i,x_{i_1},a_{i_1})\otimes\ldots\otimes\mathrm{co}(i,x_{i_k},a_{i_k})$
	$\otimes co(i,x_{i_{k+1}},0)\otimes\ldots\otimes co(i,x_{i_n},0)\otimes const(i,b)\otimes V_i=\{x_{i_1},\ldots,x_{i_k}\}$
	where $(x_{i_1},\ldots,x_{i_k})=fv(a)$, b is the constant in a,
	$\exists n_1,\ldots,n_k s.t.\ (x_{i_1},n_1)\in B$, and $(x_{i_2},n_2),\ldots,(x_{i_k},n_k)\notin B$
Instantiate	$\llbracket\mathtt{line}(i,x+b)\rrbracket\vdash_{\mathcal{LC}}!(x=-b)$
Faileq	$\mathtt{line}(i,a)\otimes(a\neq 0)\vdash_{\mathcal{LC}}\bot$
Failineq	$geq(x,a)\otimes leq(x,b)\otimes(b<a)\vdash_{\mathcal{LC}}\bot$
	$leq(x,a)\otimes(x>a)\vdash_{\mathcal{LC}}\bot$ $\quad geq(x,a)\otimes(x<a)\vdash_{\mathcal{LC}}\bot$

Moreover, the coefficients we are interested in are those of lines in Gauss normal form relatively to set B : the conditions of application of the rule are meant to ensure that coefficients are deduced only when the elimination process has terminated.

The **Instantiate** rule, together with **Evaluate**, allows replacement of variables that are constrained to one value by that value in the other equations. Finally, the failure rules catch trivial inconsistency or incompatibility of equations or inequations.

The two following properties of $\mathcal{LC}$ are easily shown by reasoning on the possible deductions from an initial state consisting in a store S of m `line` constraints, with `leq`, and `geq` constraints and a base B of m variables.

Theorem 1. *$\mathcal{LC}$ is consistency-complete with respect to systems of* equations.

Proof: 'Consistency-complete' means here that if the system composed of the `line` constraints of S has no solution under its standard mathematical interpretation – i.e. model of $\mathcal{CT}$ – than store S is inconsistent under $\vdash_{\mathcal{LC}}$. This is just a consequence of the completeness of the gaussian elimination process.

Theorem 2. *$\mathcal{LC}$ is sound : satisfiability in $\mathcal{CT}$ implies satifiability in $\mathcal{LC}$.*

Proof: Once again, this is a consequence of the nature of the elimination process. The `Faileq` rule can only be activated if the subsystem of equations is inconsistent. The first inequation failure rule may be activated only through trivially incompatible inequations on the same variable, while the other failure rules may be activated only if variable x is instantiated to a value v, which happens only if `line(i,x-v)` is a linear combination of the initial equations.

The $\mathcal{LC}$ constraint system thus provides a set of elementary tools to manipulate information about linear arithmetic constraints, together with a logical interpretation of these manipulations. The only 'active' behavior of $\mathcal{LC}$ consists in applying gaussian elimination to equations, effectively keeping the system in 'dereferenced' form. Although trivial conflicts are detected and lead to failure, global satisfiability of a system of equations and inequations corresponding to the usual mathematical interpretation is, of course, not tested. How to implement such a test, effectively recreating a higher-level constraint solver over reals in the common sense of the term, is the object of the next section.

4 Rebuilding the Simplex

In this section, we illustrate the expressive power of $\mathcal{LC}$ and the `lcc` framework by showing how one can rebuild a –fairly– classical simplex-based constraint solver by programming the ask and tell agents in lcc($\mathcal{LC}$). This solver can be easily modified, extended, or tailored to specific applications (for instance, reactivity – dynamic removal of equations or inequations – may be implemented with little extra work).

We also show that the higher level **ask** and **tell** `lcc`($\mathcal{LC}$) primitives defined may be seen as *monotonic* operators over the $\mathcal{CT}$ constraint system, where the $\mathcal{CT}$ language is construed as an abstraction of the $\mathcal{LC}$ constraint system , while completeness of $\mathcal{LC}$ w.r.t. the linear existential formulas of $\mathcal{CT}$ is recovered precisely through the **ask** and **tell**.
We start by giving minimal background and notations on linear programming, as well as some properties of the representation of linear systems we use to test satisfiability and entailment of linear constraints. Next, we describe the structure of the ask and tell procedures and give some flavor of the (hopefully simple) `lcc` programming style. We finish by showing how monotonicity is recovered by abstracting away tokens, sets, and indices from $\mathcal{LC}$ and considering a more familiar, higher level, entailment relation over the abstract constraint system $\mathcal{CT}$.

4.1 A Simplex Algorithm

We choose to represent linear programming problems in a way very similar to the one presented in Refalo's work [12] on resolution and implication of linear constraints in the CLP framework. Let us recall briefly the main notations and results that sustain this approach.

Any system of equations, inequations and disequations may be rewritten in *normal form*, defined as a pair $(F_{G(auss)}, F_{S(implex)})$ where F_G holds the equations and disequations over unbounded variables, while F_S holds inequations and equations over bounded variables. The details of the decomposition are given in [12], the main result being that a system in normal form has a solution.

We concentrate here on the F_S subsystem[9], for which a 'solvable form' is defined.

Definition 41 *A system of linear constraints is in* solvable *form if it is written :*

$$\begin{cases} x_b = M_{*L}x_{*L} + M_{*U}x_{*U} \\ l \leq x \leq u \end{cases}$$

and verifies :

$$l_B \leq M_{*L}l_{*L} + M_{*U}u_{*U}$$

where :

- *M is an m*n matrix, and* $M_{*B} = -I$
- *x is a vector of n variables*
- *B,L,U are disjoint index sets, B representing the base variables, L and U the lower and upper-bounded variables*
- *l and u are vectors of* $\bar{\mathcal{R}}^m$ *s.t.* $\langle l_i, u_i\rangle \neq \langle -\infty, +\infty\rangle$ *and* $l_i \neq -\infty$ *for* $i \in L$, $u_i \neq +\infty$ *for* $i \in U$.

One shows easily that a system of equations and inequations over bounded variables has a solution iff it may be put in solvable form. We define the *base solution* associated with a solvable form S as a variable affectation σ_S :

$$\sigma_S(x_i) = \begin{cases} l_i & \text{if } i \in L \\ u_i & \text{if } i \in U \\ \sigma_S(ax_L + a'x_U) & \text{if } i \in B \text{ and } x_i \text{ is in base} \end{cases}$$

A *standard linear program* is of the form *min* $a_Lx_L + a_Ux_U + b$ under conditions S, where S is a system in solvable form. It is *solved* when $a_L \geq 0$ and $a_U \leq 0$, as the base solution associated with S is then optimal for the cost function.

4.2 Description of the ask and tell Agents

To program a naturally usable constraint system for equations and inequations over reals in a concurrent constraints setting entails defining :

- a `tell`(c) agent that checks for satisfiability of $\sigma \cup c$ when executed in store σ and updates the store accordingly

[9] Let us just mention that handling the F_G subsystem requires maintenance of two extra variable sets J and K and incremental detection of implicit equalities [12, 8], and that disequations may be treated one by one [7].

– an ask(c) agent that checks wether $\sigma \vdash_{CT} c$

where c ranges over equations ($ax = b$) and inequations ($ax \leq b$). Furthermore, ask(c) and tell(c) should be atomic operations.
Most of the notations used in our code come directly from the above definition of solvable form ; sets B[10],U,L are maintained by the tell agents.
The tell($ax \leq b$) procedure (Table 5) tests satisfiability of a constraint $ax \leq b$ in store S by adding an equation line(i, ax) to the store (to take advantage of the built-in elimination mechanism that maintains ax as a combination of the variables of L and U), and then minimizing ax with limit b, i.e. using a 'partial' simplex algorithm that stops as soon as $ax \leq b$, or when the minimum m is reached and $m > b$, or ax proves to be unbounded. tell($ax = b$) functions similarly, minimizing ax with limit b or $-ax$ with limit -b, depending on the value of ax under the current base solution. In cases where the constraint is satisfiable, partialsimplex returns the token ***satisfiable*** and tell adds the constraint to the store permanently by updating the B,U and L sets, else (***unsatisfiable*** case) it fails.
Similarly, the ask($ax \leq b$) procedure tests entailment of $ax \leq b$ by minimizing $-ax$ with limit -b when ax contains only bounded variables [11] In case elimination of implicit equalities from the system is implemented, than ask($ax = b$) merely tests wether $ax = b$ is trivially solvable ; if it is not, than the simplex must be used again. In indecisive cases, ask suspends, guarded by a $((base(B) \otimes B \neq B_0) \longrightarrow \ ask(...))$ agent that detects variation of the base relative to base B_0 where the previous computation was carried.
The core of the program, used both in the ask and tell agents, is the partialsimplex(ax,b) procedure, partly shown in Table 6. Agent Selectinvar(i) fills in global set X_i with candidate entering variables, and then calls Selectionrule that reduces it to a singleton, according to ,e.g., Bland's rule. Agent Selectoutvars fills set X_o with candidate exiting variables, i.e. variables $x \in B$ such that the variation caused by a pivot is compatible with inequality constraints. Agent Pivot just updates B,U,L using the entering variable and one of the $x \in X_o$.

The following programming techniques ensure graceful combination of concurrency and non-determinism with non-monotony :

– sets are used to control recursion and check for termination (a.k.a. $\emptyset$)
– guarded choices are designed to avoid suspensions that might awaken later in a store where the (non-monotonically varying) values currently computed have lost meaning
– atomicity of ask and tell is guaranteed by guarding their execution with the distinguished token *update*

The most striking use of ***linearity*** (non-monotonicity) here resides perhaps in the Pivot procedure, where $\forall k\ (((x_o, k) \in B) \longrightarrow\ tell((x_i, k) \in B)$ removes variable x_o from the base and replaces it by x_i, both variables being instantiated through the same equation k.

[10] B holds couples (x,i)
[11] If ax contains unbounded variables, than $ax \leq b$ is ***not*** implied by the store.

Table 5. `tell`**(ax≤b) agent**

$$\begin{array}{l}
\mathtt{tell}(ax \leq b) :: (sup(Eqs,N) \;\; \| \;\; \mathtt{tell}(line(N+1,ax)) \;\; \| \\
\quad (\llbracket line(N+1,ax)\rrbracket \longrightarrow \;\; partialsimplex(N+1,b)) \;\; \| \\
\quad (unsatisfiable \longrightarrow \;\; \mathtt{tell}(\bot)) \\
\quad + \\
\quad satisfiable \longrightarrow \;\; \exists x_s(\mathtt{tell}(leq(x_s,b)\otimes(x_s \in U) \;\; \| \\
\qquad (line(N+1,ax) \longrightarrow \;\; line(N+1,ax-x_s)) \;\; \| \\
\qquad \forall B, \forall x_e \llbracket (base(B)\rrbracket \otimes (x_e \in X_e) \longrightarrow \\
\qquad\quad \mathtt{tell}((x_e,N+1) \in B)) \;\; \| \\
\qquad\quad ((x_e \in U) \longrightarrow \;\; \mathtt{tell}(update)) \\
\qquad\quad + \;\; ((x_e \in L) \longrightarrow \;\; \mathtt{tell}(update)))
\end{array}$$

4.3 Monotony Recovered

Once the **ask** and **tell** agents are defined as atomic operators, we wish to recover their intended meaning with respect to the natural interpretation arithmetic constraints (see 3.1 above). To do so, we need to abstract away the extra information stored in $\mathcal{LC}$ for control purposes, i.e. the lower level information types mentioned in Section 3.
We define a correspondance between $\mathcal{LC}$ and $\mathcal{CT}$ as follows :

- α : $\mathcal{LC} \longrightarrow \mathcal{CT}$ abstracts away mathematically meaningless information by mapping constraints **line, eq, leq, geq** to the corresponding constraints written with $=, \leq, \geq$ and 'forgetting' all other information in $\mathcal{LC}$
- β: cc($\mathcal{CT}$) $\longrightarrow$ lcc($\mathcal{LC}$) where $tell(c), ask(c) \mapsto$ implementation in lcc($\mathcal{LC}$)

We can then relate the derivations in lcc($\mathcal{LC}$) and cc($\mathcal{CT}$) as follows by (tedious !) reasoning on the complete code for **ask** and **tell** :

Theorem 3 (Abstraction).
If $(x;\ s;\ \beta(tell(c))) \longrightarrow_{\mathcal{LC}} (x';\ s';\ \emptyset)$ *then*

$$(y;\ \alpha(s);\ tell(c)) \longrightarrow_{\mathcal{CT}} (y';\ \alpha(s');\ \emptyset)$$

If $(x;\ s;\ \beta(ask(c) \longrightarrow\ A)) \longrightarrow_{\mathcal{LC}} (x';\ s';\ \beta(A))$ *then* $\alpha(s) \vdash_{\mathcal{CT}} c$

Conversely, an lcc($\mathcal{LC}$) configuration is **$\mathcal{CT}$-reachable** if it is accessible from the β-translation of a cc($\mathcal{CT}$) initial configuration.

Theorem 4 (Implementation).
If $(x;\ s;\ \beta(tell(c))$ *is reachable and* $(y;\ \alpha(s);\ tell(c)) \longrightarrow_{\mathcal{CT}} (y';\ \alpha(s');\ \emptyset)$ *then* $(x;\ s;\ \beta(tell(c))) \longrightarrow_{\mathcal{LC}} (x';\ s';\ \emptyset)$
If $\alpha(s) \vdash_{\mathcal{CT}} c$ *and* $(x;\ s;\ \beta(ask(c) \longrightarrow\ A))$ *is reachable then* $(x;\ s;\ \beta(ask(c) \longrightarrow\ A)) \longrightarrow_{\mathcal{LC}} (x';\ s';\ \beta(A))$

Table 6. Partialsimplex agent

$$
\begin{array}{l}
\mathit{partialsimplex}(i,\beta) :: \mathit{eval}(i,\alpha) \;\; \| \;\; \mathit{trueval}(\alpha) \longrightarrow \;\; (\exists C(\mathit{eq}(C,\alpha) \;\; \| \;\; \mathit{pivots}(i,C,\beta))) \\
\mathit{pivots}(i,C,\beta) :: \exists d(\mathit{selectinvar}(i) \;\; \| \;\; \mathit{selectoutvars}(i,d) \;\; \| \\
\quad (X_i = \emptyset \longrightarrow \;\; \mathtt{tell}(\mathit{unsatisfiable})) + \; \forall v_d \;\; (\llbracket \mathit{eq}(d,v_d) \rrbracket \otimes (X_i \neq \emptyset)) \\
\quad \longrightarrow \\
\quad ((v_d = +\infty) \longrightarrow \;\; \mathtt{tell}(\mathit{satisfiable}) \\
\quad + \\
\quad (v_d \neq \infty) \otimes \mathit{switchtoken} \longrightarrow \;\; (\mathit{switch} \;\; \| \;\; \mathit{switchtoken} \longrightarrow \mathit{pivots}(i,C,\beta)) \\
\quad + \\
\quad (v_d \neq \infty) \otimes \mathit{pivottoken} \longrightarrow \;\; \forall \alpha \;\; (\mathit{eq}(C,\alpha) \\
\quad \longrightarrow \\
\qquad ((\alpha - v_d \leq \beta) \longrightarrow \;\; \mathtt{tell}(\mathit{satisfiable})) \\
\qquad + \\
\qquad ((\alpha - v_d > \beta) \\
\qquad \longrightarrow \\
\qquad ((X_i \neq \emptyset \longrightarrow \\
\qquad \mathit{pivot} \;\; \| \;\; ((X_i = \emptyset) \otimes \llbracket \forall \alpha \mathit{eq}(C,\alpha) \rrbracket \longrightarrow \;\; \mathit{pivots}(i,C,\beta))))))
\end{array}
$$

In other words, the **ask** and **tell** agents defined above behave exactly as classical (monotonic) cc agents over the $\mathcal{CT}$ constraint system. Thus, while linearity – the possibility to remove information from the store – is necessary to program these agents over the elementary constraint system $\mathcal{LC}$, and will still be necessary for example to extend the simplex algorithm or combine it with other resolution procedures, one may chose to hide it at the higher level of abstraction corresponding to the usual black-box specification of solvers over reals. In particular, the functional separation between language and solver, breached *a priori* by the extra expressiveness of the lcc framework, is recovered : the box has been opened and closed again.

5 Conclusion and Future Work

The dual motivation of this paper leads to two correlated but distinct research tracks. First, we have built a linear constraint system $\mathcal{LC}$ designed to handle equations and inequations over reals, and showed its faithfulness to the intended goal. We have illustrated its expressive power by defining a complete constraint solver for linear arithmetic constraints as a couple (ask, tell) of lcc($\mathcal{LC}$) agents. The other contribution of this paper is that it provides the first example of practical use of the lcc framework, and makes the case of its interest as a programming paradigm.
On the first track, possible research directions include :

- explicit extension of the reconstructed constraint solver to allow full reactivity/defeasibility for linear equations and disequations

– comparison of non-standard pivot algorithms – such as criss-cross methods [10] – with simplex methods as a source of potential algorithmic insight.

The second track addresses more general language design issues. The specificity of the `lcc` framework resides in its combination of declarative and imperative programming in a concurrent context, and in its logical semantics that follows very closely *both* the constraint system description formalism – indeed, solvers are described *in* linear logic – and the programming language itself. It is worthwhile to note the emergence of a natural separation between three levels : rules for which no strategy is specified (the 'classical' rules of the solver), linear rules that allow specification of an 'execution' strategy through **ask** agents, and the 'strategy specification' language itself (`lcc` programs). This separation is related to the separation typical of another generalized constraint programming paradigm, based on (rewriting) rules, the CHR/ELAN framework [16, 3, 2] :

1. a – classically specified, black-box – constraint solver
2. constraint rewriting rules that operate above this solver
3. strategies that govern the application of these rules.

As a first step towards a better understanding of this stratification, and its interaction with concurrency, we plan on investigating links between the two frameworks. For example, building a simple translation of CHR into the lower-level `lcc` formalism could facilitate transport of the confluence properties proven in [16].
Finally, one of the main promises of a concurrent 'constraints + states' programming paradigm is the possibility to combine solvers *within the same framework*, for instance, global, complete algorithms such as the simplex with local, incomplete algorithms such as those underlying finite-domain or real solvers that use interval arithmetic.

Acknowledgements

We are grateful to François Fages and Sylvain Soliman for many fruitful discussions and comments. We also thank the anonymous referees for their remarks, that helped us write the final version of this paper.

References

[1] E. Best, F.S. de Boer, and C. Palamidessi. Concurrent constraint programming with information removal. In *Proceedings of Coordination*, LNCS. Springer-Verlag, 1997.

[2] P. Borovansky, C. Kirchner, H. Kirchner, P.-E. Moreau, and M. Vittek. Elan : a logical framework based on computational system. In *Proceedings of the First International Workshop on Rewriting Logic*, volume Volume 4 of electronic notes in TCS, 1996.

[3] C.Kirchner and C.Ringeissen. Rule-based constraint programming. Preprint, 1998.

[4] F.Fages, P.Ruet, and S.Soliman. Phase semantics and verification of concurrent constraint programs. In *LICS*, 1998.

[5] J.Y. Girard. Linear logic. *Theoretical Computer Science*, 50(1), 1987.

[6] P. Van Hentenryck, V.A. Saraswat, and Y. Deville. Constraint processing in cc(FD). Draft, 1991.

[7] J-L.Lassez and K.McAloon. Independance of negative constraints. In Springer, editor, *Proceedings of TAPSOFT*, LNCS, 1989.

[8] J.L.Lassez and K.McAloon. A canonical form for generalized linear constraints. *Journal of Symbolic Computation*, 1989.

[9] J.R.Shoenfield. *Mathematical Logic*. Addison-Wesley, 1967.

[10] K.Fukuda and T.Terlaky. Criss-cross methods : a fresh view on pivot algorithms. *Submitted to Elsevier Preprint*, 1997.

[11] P. Lincoln and V.A. Saraswat. Proofs as concurrent processes. Draft, 1991.

[12] P.Refalo. *Resolution et implication de contraintes lineaires en programmation logique par contraintes*. PhD thesis, Universite de la Mediterrannee, 1997.

[13] P. Ruet. *Logique non-commutative et programmation concurrente par contraintes*. PhD thesis, Université Denis Diderot, Paris 7, 1997.

[14] V.A. Saraswat and P. Lincoln. Higher-order linear concurrent constraint programming. Technical report, Xerox Parc, 1992.

[15] V.A. Saraswat, M. Rinard, and P. Panangaden. Semantic foundations of concurrent constraint programming. In *POPL'91: Proceedings 18th ACM Symposium on Principles of Programming Languages*, 1991.

[16] T.Fruhwirth, S.Abdennadher, and H.Meuss. Confluence and semantics of constraint handling rules. *Constraint Journal (submitted)*, 1997.

Using Constraint Programming and Local Search Methods to Solve Vehicle Routing Problems

Paul Shaw*

ILOG S.A.
9, rue de Verdun, BP 85
94253 Gentilly Cedex, FRANCE.
shaw@ilog.fr

Abstract. We use a local search method we term Large Neighbourhood Search (LNS) to solve vehicle routing problems. LNS is analogous to the shuffling technique of job-shop scheduling, and so meshes well with constraint programming technology. LNS explores a large neighbourhood of the current solution by selecting a number of "related" customer visits to remove from the set of planned routes, and re-inserting these visits using a constraint-based tree search. Unlike similar methods, we use Limited Discrepancy Search during the tree search to re-insert visits. We analyse the performance of our method on benchmark problems. We demonstrate that results produced are competitive with Operations Research meta-heuristic methods, indicating that constraint-based technology is directly applicable to vehicle routing problems.

1 Introduction

A vehicle routing problem (VRP) is one of visiting a set of customers using a fleet of vehicles, respecting constraints on the vehicles, customers, drivers, and so on. The goal is to produce a low cost routing plan specifying for each vehicle, the order of the customer visits they make. (In academic problems cost is generally proportional to the number of vehicles, or total travel distance/time.) Industrial VRPs tend to be large, and so local search techniques are used extensively as they scale well and can produce reliably good solutions.

Constraint programming appears to be a good technology to apply to VRPs because of the ubiquity of complex constraints in real problems, such as legislation on driver breaks, or complex pay provisions. However, search in constraint programming is usually based upon complete tree-based techniques, which can at the present moment only solve problems of up to 30 customers reliably.

A natural conjecture is that a combination of local search and constraint programming should work well for VRPs. Such a method would hopefully provide the advantages of both: *exploration* and *propagation*.

---

* This work was carried out while the author was working in the Department of Computer Science, University of Strathclyde, as part of the APES research group. The author wishes to thank all members of APES for their help and support.

We apply a technique we refer to as Large Neighbourhood Search (LNS) to VRPs. LNS makes moves like local search, but uses a tree-based search with constraint propagation to evaluate the cost and legality of the move. The moves made are generally very powerful, changing a large portion of the solution. The potential for changing large parts of the solution gives LNS its name, as a neighbourhood's size typically varies exponentially with the number of basic elements of the solution changed by the move.

One way of applying LNS to a VRP is by defining a move to be the removal and re-insertion of a set I of customer visits. We define a "relatedness" measure between customer visits and use this as a basis for choosing the set I at each step. We use Limited Discrepancy Search (LDS) to re-insert the customer visits into the current set of routes. The size of I increases over time, stepping up when search is deemed to have stagnated at the current size of set I.

Experiments are carried out on benchmark problems, with and without time windows. We analyse solutions produced by LNS over a range of parameter settings. LNS is shown to have excellent average performance and produces many new best solutions to these benchmark problems.

The paper is organised as follows: Section 2 describes LNS as applied to the VRP, compares it with related work, and assesses its benefits. Section 3 presents computational experiments on benchmark problems. Section 4 concludes.

2 Large Neighbourhood Search

LNS is based upon a process of continual relaxation and re-optimization. For the VRP, the positions of some customer visits are *relaxed* (the visits are removed from the routing plan), and then the routing plan *re-optimised* over the relaxed positions (by re-inserting these visits). One iteration of removal and re-insertion can be considered as the examination of a neighbourhood move. If a re-insertion is found that results in a cost below that of the best routing plan found so far, this new solution is kept as the current one.

The re-insertion process uses heuristics and constraint propagation. The *minimum* cost re-insertion can be evaluated via branch and bound, or techniques that only partially explore the search tree can be used.

Two factors affect the way in which LNS operates when applied to the VRP: how customer visits are chosen for removal, and the re-insertion process. These are now examined in more detail.

2.1 Choosing Customer Visits

We describe a possible method for choosing the customer visits that are removed and re-inserted. We would not be surprised if better techniques are found. However, we believe in a general choice strategy: that of choosing *related* visits. *Related* has to be suitably defined. A good measure is one that results in opportunities for the re-insertion to improve the routing plan. *i.e.* the measure should discount (by labelling as unrelated or loosely related), sets of visits that are likely to maintain their previous positions when re-inserted. There is no point in removing visits whose re-insertion is independent of the others', and the relatedness concept attempts to capture this.

One observation is that visits geographically close to one another are more related than remote ones. (Alternatively, visits that it is cheap to travel between should be more related than those with a high travel cost.) It is unlikely that remote visits will have inter-changes in position due to the high costs involved.

If two visits occur in the same route, we can also consider them to be related. Removing multiple visits from the same route should be encouraged when reducing the number of vehicles used is important, as removing all visits from a route is the only way to reduce the number of routes. (This happens when all visits are removed from a route, and are then re-inserted into existing routes.) Related visits might also have similar allowable visiting hours, or be visited at similar times in the current routing plan.[1]

Here, for simplicity, we assume a *binary* relatedness operator $\mathcal{R}(i, j)$ taking two visits and delivering a non-negative value indicating how closely they are related. Ideally, this function should include domain knowledge about side constraints (*e.g.* see section 2.4 for a discussion of a pickup and delivery example).

We do not address problems with side constraints[2] here, and define:

$$\mathcal{R}(i, j) = 1/(c_{ij} + V_{ij})$$

where c_{ij} is the cost of getting to j from i (travel distance in this paper), and V_{ij} evaluates to 1 if i and j are served by different vehicles ***and*** reduction of the number of vehicles is important in the cost function (see section 3.2 on problems with time windows). V_{ij} evaluates to 0 otherwise. We assume that all c_{ij} are normalised in the range [0..1].

Figure 1 describes how visits are chosen. If the relatedness measure $\mathcal{R}(i, j)$ perfectly captured which visits should be removed together, then one would imagine that visits should be drawn from the routing plan using only the relatedness concept. In reality, the relatedness measure is never perfect, and relying on it too heavily can cause search to be too short-sighted (for example, see section 3.1). We therefore include a random element. In the algorithm, D controls determinism. With $D = 1$, relatedness is ignored and visits are chosen randomly. With $D = \infty$, visits relaxed are maximally related to some other relaxed visit. In between, there is a mixture. (Also note that there is always *some* random element to the search even at $D = \infty$, as a *random* visit maximally related to a previously relaxed visit is chosen.)

There are other ways that $\mathcal{R}(i, j)$ could be used to choose customer visits. In figure 1, a visit is chosen that is related to *one* visit in the already chosen set. Alternatively, one could rank the visits by relatedness to all (or some) visits in the chosen set. Moreover, the ranking system is not ideal when the relatedness of some pairs of visits is much larger than others (this is addressed in [10]).

---

[1] For the job-shop scheduling problem, [4] uses a shuffling technique (analogous to LNS) that relaxes the start times of all operations within a certain range.

[2] See [10] for a study of LNS when side constraints are added.

```
RemoveVisits(RoutingPlan plan, integer toRemove, real D)
    VisitSet inplan := GetVisits(plan)
    Visit v := ChooseRandomVisit(inplan)
    inplan := inplan - {v}
    RemoveVisit(plan, v)
    VisitSet removed := {v}
    while |removed| < toRemove do
        v := ChooseRandomVisit(removed)
        // Rank visits in plan with respect to relatedness to v
        // Visits are ranked in decreasing order of relatedness
        VisitList lst := RankUsingRelatedness(v, inplan)
        // Choose a random number, rand, in [0, 1)
        real rand := Random(0,1)
        // Relax the visit that is rand^D of the way through the rank
        v := lst[integer(|lst|*rand^D)]
        removed := removed + {v}
        inplan := inplan - {v}
    end while
end RemoveVisits
```

Fig. 1. How visits are removed using relatedness

Control of the Neighbourhood Size For efficiency, one wants to remove the smallest set of visits that will improve the cost when the visits are re-inserted. We use the following scheme to attempt to ensure this: Initially, start the number of visits r to remove at 1. Then, during search, if a consecutive attempted moves have not resulted in an improvement in the cost, increase r by one. An upper limit of 30 was placed on the value of r. This scheme increases r only when the search has deemed to have become "stuck" for the smaller value of r. The value of a determines how stubbornly LNS seeks improvements at smaller values of r. [3] used a similar technique for shuffling in job-shop scheduling.

2.2 Re-inserting Visits

The re-insertion process uses branch and bound, with constraint propagation and heuristics for variable and value selection. The upper bound is set to the cost of the best solution found so far. In its simplest form, the search examines the whole tree for the re-insertion of all visits at minimum cost.

We view each of the relaxed (removed) visits as the constrained variables, that can take values corresponding to their available insertion points. (An insertion point is a point between two adjcacent visits in the same route that may accommodate the visit.) For any particular visit, some insertion points may be ruled out as illegal via simple propagation rules. For example, a visit v cannot be inserted between visits i and j if this would cause the vehicle to arrive at v or j after their latest deadlines. Additionally, propagation rules maintain the load on the vehicle, and bounds on start of service time for all visits along a route, based on the pickup quantity, the travel times between visits, and customer time windows. For a detailed description of such rules, see [15].

Insertion positions for visits can also be ruled out if they would take the lower bound on the cost of the plan over the upper bound defined by the best solution found so far. We form the lower bound as the *current* cost of the routing plan. (We do not compute a lower bound on the cost of including as yet unrouted visits.) This makes the procedure fast, but the search tree is larger than it would be if the bound was better. Improving the bound is a subject of future work.

Branching Heuristics We follow the general rules of of "most constrained variable", "least constrained value" to choose a visit to insert and its insertion point. A visit could be considered constrained if it is far from the rest of the routing plan (and so will bring the cost of the plan more quickly towards the upper bound when inserted). When choosing a position, we could consider an insertion point less constraining if it increases the cost of the routing plan less.

Assume that visit v has a set of insertion points $\mathcal{I}_v = \{p_1, \ldots, p_n\}$, and that the cost $\mathcal{C}_p$ of an insertion point p is the increase in cost of the routing plan resulting from inserting v at p. We then define the *cheapest* insertion point $c_v \in \mathcal{I}_v$ of v as the one for which $\mathcal{C}_{c_v}$ is a minimum. As a heuristic, we choose visit v to insert for which the cost $\mathcal{C}_{c_v}$ of its cheapest insertion is largest. This choice of visit is known as the *farthest insertion* heuristic. We then try to insert this visit at each of its insertion points, cheapest to most expensive, in increasing order. The sub-problem of inserting the remaining visits is solved after each insertion of v. If any visit has only one legal insertion point, it is immediately inserted at this point. This is performed as a propagation rule: a so-called "unit propagation".

The farthest insertion heuristic works well, but like any heuristic, has its problems. The main one is it only addresses one constraint: the bound on the cost function. When other constraints are added, its guidance is poorer. Ideally, one wants the heuristic to take account of all (or the more important) constraints.

Limited Discrepancy Search In many cases, the branch and bound re-insertion procedure can find a better solution or prove that none exists for about 25 removed visits in a few seconds for problems with time windows. For problems without time windows, the optimal re-insertion for only around 15 visits can be computed in this time as the reduced number of constraints results in less pruning of the search space. Unfortunately, the distribution of solution times has a heavy tail, and some re-insertions take a long time to compute. To alleviate this problem, we used Limited Discrepancy Search [9] (LDS). LDS explores the search tree in order of an increasing number of *discrepancies*, a discrepancy being a branch against the value ordering heuristic. We count a single discrepancy as the insertion of a customer visit at its *second* cheapest position. We count as two discrepancies either one insertion at the third cheapest position, or two insertions at their second cheapest positions, and so on. We use only *one phase* of LDS, with the discrepancy limit set to a pre-defined value d. In this way, we explore all leaf nodes from 0 to d discrepancies, without re-visiting leaf nodes. Our re-insertion algorithm is shown in figure 2. The management of legal insert positions is not mentioned—we assume they are handled by automatically triggered propagation rules, as previously discussed. The parameter d trades the coverage of the the search tree with the speed of re-insertion. When d is small, we opt for large numbers of attempted re-insertions with little search tree coverage for each one. For high values of d, the opposite situation holds. The presence of a "trade off" is investigated in section 3.

```
Reinsert(RoutingPlan plan, VisitSet visits, integer discrep)
    if |visits| = 0 then
        if Cost(plan) < Cost(bestplan) then
            bestplan := plan
        end if
    else
        Visit v := ChooseFarthestVisit(visits)
        integer i := 0
        for p in rankedPositions(v) and i ≤ discrep do
            Store(plan) // Preserve plan on stack
            InsertVisit(plan, v, p)
            Reinsert(plan, visits - v, discrep - i)
            Restore(plan) // Restore plan from stack
            i := i + 1
        end for
    end if
end Reinsert
```

Fig. 2. How visits are re-inserted

2.3 Related Work

LNS is analogous to the shuffling technique used in job-shop scheduling [1,4]. To perform a shuffle, start times for operations on the majority of machines are relaxed, and a tree-based search procedure reconstructs the schedule. We have not used the term "shuffling" in this paper to avoid confusion with job-shop scheduling. Moreover, the basic idea is easily generalizable to other problem classes, where the natural visualization of the move is not a shuffling of positions.

In [1], a simple shuffle is presented, but in [4], various types of shuffle are used. The shuffles differ by the criteria for selecting the operations that will be relaxed. These selections use common machines, common start times, and so on. Interestingly, each of the shuffles can be seen as exploiting the relatedness of operations. The authors also use an *incomplete* search technique to reconstruct the schedule by limiting the number of backtracks available. We tried such an approach, but it proved inferior to LDS, with virtually no advantages in implementation simplicity or efficiency.

Other work on routing problems [14, 16] also advocates the use of constraint programming within local search. Here, move operators from the routing literature are used (for instance generalised insertion), but a constraint programming branch and bound search evaluates the neighbourhood to find the best legal move. One can see the similarities with LNS, but there are differences. The main one is that only *traditional* move operators are being used, and so constraint programming only improves the efficiency of the evaluation of the neighbourhood, and not the power of the move operators themselves. Secondly, the whole neighbourhood is being explored, requiring a complete branch and bound search. With LNS, any method can be used to perform the re-insertion of visits, for instance, a heuristic method, local or complete search, LDS, or another discrepancy-based approach (*e.g.* [13]).

Some work has been performed in solving quadratic assignment problems using a similar technique to LNS [12].

Constraint programming and local search were applied to routing problems in [2], using a technique of filtering out certain moves which violate core constraints, allowing the constraint engine to check the remainder. The operation of the method is therefore unlike LNS.

2.4 Discussion

There are advantages to using LNS over traditional local search. The main advantage is that side constraints can be better handled. For instance, in the VRP, different models such as the pickup and delivery problem (PDP) can be easily dealt with. Using traditional local search, this is more difficult: special-purpose operators need to move both the pickup and delivery to a different route simultaneously. With LNS, the pickup and delivery are simply made strongly related. The normal PDP constraints of *same vehicle* and *time(pickup) < time (delivery)* then constrain where the visits can be re-inserted. Making these visits highly related is important here. If only one visit of the pair was removed, it would be highly restricted in where it could be re-inserted.[3]

Kindervater and Savelsbergh [11] discuss ways of efficiently introducing side constraints into local search. Their methods, however, are complex and dedicated to particular move operators and side constraints. Moreover, they do not suggest how to extend their methods to different move operators or side constraints.

A difficulty with problems with many side constraints is that many of the simple local search move operations normally used (such as moving a single visit to a new position) will be illegal due to violation of these constraints. Increasing

[3] The above discussion brings about a difficulty with LNS. When many different *types* of side constraints are operating, how strongly should any constraint relate visits in comparison to the others? This question, one of tuning, seems to plague all sufficiently complex heuristic algorithms. Automatically determining relative relatedness values is a subject of future work.

numbers of side constraints constantly reduce the number of feasible moves. This can make local search difficult, as the search space becomes more restricted or even disconnected. LNS alleviates this problem somewhat by providing far-reaching move operators that allow the search to move over barriers in the search space created by side constraints.

In local search, evaluation of cost differences is time consuming. In idealised models, one often uses travel distance as the cost function, since for most simple moves, cost differences can be computed in constant time. (Savelsbergh [19] has also introduced ways of computing route time differences for such operators in constant time.) However, for real VRPs, cost functions are seldom this simple. With LNS, the full cost of a move is evaluated during constraint propagation. Cost differences are *not* used, and there is no need to invent clever methods to compute them. We did mention, however, that our heuristics for choosing the next visit to insert and its favoured position operate on cost differences. Since this information is just a *hint* to the search, and most cost functions are generally related to distance, we can simply use distance as an approximation.

3 Computational Results

We report the results of applying LNS to benchmark problems with and without time windows. All problems have an unlimited number of identical limited capacity vehicles located at a single depot. Time and distance between customers is Euclidean. Each customer has a specified load, and for problems with time windows, a service time and a time window during which it must be visited. For all problems, we chose an initial solution with the number of vehicles equal to the number of customers, with one customer visit performed by each vehicle. The initial neighbourhood size is set so that only one visit is removed and re-inserted. We examine the quality of solutions obtained by LNS over various parameter settings. We also report new best solutions obtained. Finally, we perform CPU-intensive runs of LNS to compare results with the best Operations Research methods. We used a 143 MHz Ultra Sparc running Solaris for all experiments. All code was written in C++ and compiled using the Sun C++ compiler.

3.1 Capacitated VRPs

Following [18], we use three types of capacitated VRP: classic test problems, non-uniform problems, and those derived from real data. The classic problems (C50, C75, C100, C100B, C120, C150, C199) are due to [6]. The non-uniform problems (TAI100A–TAI100D, TAI150A–TAI150D) were created by Rochat and Taillard [18] to capture structure inherent in real problems: loads are exponentially distributed, and customers are realistically clustered. Finally, problems reflecting real data are taken from [8] (F71 and F134) and [22] (TAI385). In all these problems, the number in the name indicates the number of customers. The objective is to minimise the total distance travelled.

LNS as presented has 3 parameters. First, we can vary the number of discrepancies d used by LDS. Second, we can vary the number of unsuccessful moves a that must be made to increase the number of visits to re-insert. Finally, we can change the determinism parameter D. We chose $d \in \{0, 1, 2, 3, 5, 10, \infty\}$ ($d = \infty$ performs complete search), $a \in \{250, 500, 1000\}$, and $D \in \{1, 5, 10, 15, 30, \infty\}$ ($D = 1$ ignores relatedness, while $D = \infty$ uses maximal relatedness).

For each combination of parameter settings, we ran LNS three times (with different random seeds) on all problems, with a time limit of 900 seconds. When $d = \infty$ some re-insertions can take a long time, and so a time limit of 20 seconds was placed on the re-insertion process, which is in force for all experiments. (The number of timeouts that occurred for $d \leq 10$ was negligable.)

Table 1 shows the results of running LNS over all capacitated problems: three times for each parameter combination. We show the percentage difference in cost between solutions obtained by LNS and the best published solution. We computed these percentages as follows: for each combination of parameters, we take the costs of all the solutions provided by LNS and divide them by the cost of the best published solution for the corresponding problem. This delivers a set of *cost ratios*. We then form a ratio which is the geometric mean of this set: the global cost ratio. By subtracting one and multiplying by 100, we attain the average percentage figure above the best published solutions. We used this method to produce all averages of percentages.

The average costs produced by LNS are close to the best published ones. All average results are within 7% of the best published solution, and for the best parameter settings, 2.2% from the best published solution on average. The number of attempts a has the smallest impact on the quality, but results for $a = 1000$ are slightly worse. From examination of, for instance, the results for $a = 250$, it is clear that the worst results are produced at the extremities of the ranges of discrepancies and determinism. Determinism set at 5 or 10 and a discrepancy limit around 2 appear to give the best results. Relatedness is useful, as at unit determinism (visits chosen for re-insertion at random), results are poorer. However, over reliance on relatedness also produces a degradation of results (seen at infinite determinism). LDS is also playing a role: at 0 and infinite discrepancies, results are worse than for values such as 2 or 3.

Best Published Solutions Table 2 compares the lowest costs obtained by LNS with the best published ones. A +, -, or = indicates whether LNS bettered, could not match, or matched these solutions. LNS has tied the best in 8 cases, bettered it in 3, and not attained it in 7 of the cases. We attribute the largest deviation of around 1.5% in problem TAI385 to the large problem size. We believe a longer running time is required than we allowed in our experiments.

3.2 VRPs with Time Windows

We performed experiments on some of Solomon's instances [20], the classic benchmark VRPs with time windows. Each problem has 100 customers, time

		discrepancies						
attempts	determinism	0	1	2	3	5	10	∞
250	1	4.3	3.8	4.8	4.2	5.0	5.6	6.0
	5	3.0	2.5	2.3	2.2	3.3	3.7	2.6
	10	2.8	2.3	2.2	2.3	2.5	3.5	3.2
	15	2.8	2.4	2.2	2.7	2.6	3.4	3.8
	30	3.3	2.8	2.7	2.6	3.4	3.2	4.2
	∞	5.5	3.6	4.1	4.3	5.1	5.3	4.5
500	1	5.1	4.4	3.8	4.6	5.0	5.3	5.3
	5	3.0	2.4	2.9	2.7	2.4	2.9	3.8
	10	2.8	2.1	2.3	2.6	2.9	3.9	3.7
	15	2.9	2.5	2.5	2.3	2.6	3.3	3.6
	30	2.6	2.7	3.0	2.6	3.2	3.9	4.2
	∞	4.9	5.0	4.6	3.9	4.2	5.8	4.6
1000	1	4.8	5.3	5.2	4.6	5.3	6.0	5.4
	5	2.9	2.9	2.9	3.0	2.7	3.4	3.6
	10	3.1	3.1	2.9	3.1	3.1	3.2	3.9
	15	3.1	2.8	2.7	2.9	2.6	3.0	3.6
	30	3.5	3.0	2.6	3.7	3.2	3.4	4.1
	∞	6.1	4.4	5.0	4.6	5.7	6.0	5.2

Table 1. Performance of LNS on simple capacitated problems over various parameter settings. Each problem without time windows was solved three times. Mean *percentages* above the best published solutions are shown.

windows and capacity constraints. A scheduling horizon is defined by placing a time deadline on the return time to the depot. The problems are divided into two main classes: "series 1" and "series 2" with different scheduling horizons. The series 1 problems have a shorter scheduling horizon than those of series 2. On average, around 3 vehicles are required to serve the 100 customers in the series 2 problems, whereas around 12 are needed for series 1. Experiments were performed only on the series 1 problems, of which there are 29. For the series 2 problems, the re-insertion procedure was not able to optimise the insertion of the large number of visits required to reduce the number of routes to 4 or under. As future work, we plan to tackle this problem by providing some guidance in the cost function to encourage at least one short route. In this way, less visits will need to be re-optimised to reduce the number of routes.

The series 1 problems are split into subclasses: R1, with customers distributed randomly, C1, with customers in well-defined clusters, and RC1, with a mixture. The objective function for VRPs with time windows is normally a hierarchical one: minimise the number of vehicles, and within this, minimise total travel distance. We associate a high cost with the use of each vehicle, and then LNS automatically reduces vehicles when it can. We performed the same analysis as for problems without time windows.

The average percentages above the best published values are shown in table 3. Since we now take vehicles into account, we show the average percentages of

Problem	Best	LNS	
C50	524.61	524.61	=
C75	835.26	835.26	=
C100	826.14	826.14	=
C100B	819.56	819.56	=
C120	1042.11	1042.97	-
C150	1028.42	1032.61	-
C199	1291.45	1310.28	-
TAI100A	2047.90	2047.90	=
TAI100B	1940.61	1939.90	+

Problem	Best	LNS	
TAI100C	1407.44	1406.86	+
TAI100D	1581.25	1586.08	-
TAI150A	3055.23	3055.23	=
TAI150B	2727.99	2732.27	-
TAI150C	2362.79	2361.62	+
TAI150D	2655.67	2661.72	-
F71	241.97	241.97	=
F134	1162.96	1162.96	=

Table 2. Comparison of best solutions obtained by LNS against best published solutions for simple capacitated problems.

vehicles (left) and distance (right) above the best published solution. Only results for classes R1 and RC1 are included in the table. Results for class C1 were not included as these problems are easy. Nearly all runs produced the best known solution to their corresponding problem and so including class C1 in the table would have skewed the results. Further evidence of the easiness of some of the C1 benchmarks is that problems C101 and C102 can be solved to optimality by our branch and bound insertion procedure in a few seconds. The optimal solution to both problems is 10 vehicles, distance 828.94, correcting previous results in [7] that claim the optimal has distance 827.3 using 10 vehicles. [7] uses distances truncated at the first decimal place, leading to the error. We use real-valued distance and time values.

Results again indicate that LNS performs well, attaining average solutions (in terms of numbers of vehicles) as good as just over 3% from the best published solution. However, some quite bad solutions (up to around 12% from the best published solution) are produced when relatedness is ignored ($D = 1$).

One can see that good solutions are created when the number of discrepancies is higher than for the problems without time windows. There are reasons for this. First, when more constraints are present, more pruning occurs, making more intensive search cheaper than for problems with no time windows (this effect can also been observed in [5,15]). Second, our farthest insertion heuristic makes more mistakes for these problems for two reasons: time windows are not taken into account, and the heuristic provides poor guidance in reducing the number of routes. Thus, more discrepancies are necessary to repair heuristic errors.

The attempts a plays an important role—results are poorer for increasing a. This is because the neighbourhood size is still low by the end of the search. For instance, with $a = 1000$, little search is done with medium to large numbers (> 15) of visits are being re-inserted. The worsening of results as a increases is probably due to the fact that to reduce the number of routes by one, often two or even three routes have to be removed from the routing plan. For the series 1 problems, this means that around 20 visits or more must be removed.

		discrepancies													
att.	det.	0		1		2		3		5		10		∞	
250	1	9.4	2.1	8.5	1.3	9.5	1.4	10.5	1.5	9.5	1.5	12.7	1.4	10.6	1.6
	5	5.4	1.9	4.4	1.0	3.7	0.7	4.2	0.6	3.8	0.9	3.3	0.4	3.7	0.4
	10	5.6	2.0	4.2	1.5	3.8	1.0	3.8	0.8	3.2	0.6	4.1	0.4	3.4	0.4
	15	5.0	2.8	3.5	1.6	4.1	0.9	3.6	0.7	3.3	0.6	3.6	0.3	3.3	0.6
	30	6.6	4.2	3.1	2.2	3.6	0.8	3.3	0.8	3.8	0.1	5.0	-0.0	4.3	0.5
	∞	6.0	4.2	6.0	1.4	4.5	1.6	4.2	0.4	3.7	0.5	3.6	0.6	4.2	0.2
500	1	9.9	1.8	9.0	1.0	10.5	1.4	10.2	1.1	9.2	1.2	8.1	1.7	10.8	1.1
	5	5.6	1.4	4.4	0.8	4.3	0.7	4.2	0.5	4.1	0.6	3.6	0.2	3.9	0.4
	10	5.2	2.1	3.8	1.3	3.5	0.7	3.7	0.6	4.4	-0.1	4.4	0.1	4.2	0.4
	15	5.0	2.2	4.7	0.7	3.7	0.5	3.7	0.7	3.4	0.4	3.4	0.1	4.0	0.1
	30	5.1	3.0	3.8	1.4	4.7	0.7	3.2	0.7	3.9	0.4	3.4	0.7	4.6	0.0
	∞	6.1	4.2	5.1	1.4	3.9	0.8	4.1	0.5	3.8	0.6	3.7	0.8	3.6	0.7
1000	1	9.9	2.3	11.6	2.1	9.3	1.9	10.4	1.9	13.8	2.1	11.0	1.9	10.0	1.8
	5	6.1	1.3	5.0	0.8	5.1	0.3	5.3	0.4	5.0	0.5	4.2	0.1	5.0	0.4
	10	6.1	1.3	4.8	0.6	5.1	0.4	4.3	0.8	5.4	0.2	3.4	0.4	4.1	0.6
	15	5.8	2.1	4.7	0.8	5.1	0.3	4.2	0.6	5.7	0.1	3.5	1.1	4.4	0.3
	30	6.2	2.4	5.7	0.7	3.9	0.3	4.9	0.4	5.0	0.3	3.9	0.1	5.7	0.1
	∞	7.2	2.7	5.4	2.2	4.1	1.7	4.3	0.8	5.4	0.1	5.2	0.3	5.2	0.3

Table 3. Performance of LNS on VRPs with time windows over various parameter settings. Each problem was solved three times. Mean *percentages* of vehicles (left) and distance (right) above the best published solutions are shown.

Finally, unlike the problems without time windows, relying heavily on relatedness does not appear to be as detrimental to the quality of results. Without time windows, cost rose noticeably when D was too high, but only a mild increase (if any) can be seen for the problems with time windows. It would thus appear that the relatedness function for problems with time windows (which concentrates on relating visits in the same route) is a good guide.

Best Published Solutions Table 4 compares the best solutions obtained by LNS with the best published ones taken from [7, 17, 18, 21, 23]. We show in the table the best published solution, and the best solution obtained by either Rochat and Taillard [18] (hereafter referred to as RT) or Taillard *et al.* [21] (hereafter referred to as TAI) if the best published solution was not generated by RT or TAI. We do this as RT and TAI (unlike the others) use real, double precision distances. As stated in [21], a consequence of using limited precision distances is that solutions found using these methods may not be feasible when higher precision distances are used to check their validity. A +, -, or = indicates whether LNS bettered, could not match, or matched the best solution from RT or TAI.

LNS has tied RT or TAI in 16 of the 29 cases, bettered them in 10, and not matched them in 3 of the cases. In two of these three cases, LNS could not match the number of vehicles used by TAI. All new best solutions produced by LNS are available at http://www.math.sintef.no/GreenTrip.

Prob.	Best Pub.	RT & TAI	LNS	
C101	10 827.3	10 828.94	10 828.94	=
C102	10 827.3	10 828.94	10 828.94	=
C103	10 828.06		10 828.06	=
C104	10 824.78		10 824.78	=
C105	10 828.94		10 828.94	=
C106	10 827.3	10 828.94	10 828.94	=
C107	10 827.3	10 828.94	10 828.94	=
C108	10 827.3	10 828.94	10 828.94	=
C109	10 828.94		10 828.94	=
R101	18 1607.7	19 1650.80	19 1650.80	=
R102	17 1434.0	17 1486.12	17 1486.12	=
R103	13 1207	13 1294.24	13 1292.68	+
R104	10 982.01		9 1007.31	+
R105	14 1377.11		14 1377.11	=
R106	12 1252.03		12 1252.03	=

Prob.	Best Pub.	RT & TAI	LNS	
R107	10 1126.69		10 1104.66	+
R108	9 968.59		9 963.99	+
R109	11 1214.54		11 1197.42	+
R110	11 1080.36		10 1135.07	+
R111	10 1104.83		10 1096.73	+
R112	10 953.63		10 953.63	=
RC101	14 1669	14 1696.94	14 1696.95	-
RC102	12 1554.75		12 1554.75	=
RC103	11 1110	11 1262.02	11 1261.67	+
RC104	10 1135.83		10 1135.48	+
RC105	13 1643.38		14 1540.18	-
RC106	11 1448.26		12 1376.26	-
RC107	11 1230.54		11 1230.48	+
RC108	10 1139.82		10 1139.82	=

Table 4. Comparison of best solutions obtained against best published solutions for Solomon's problems

Comparison of Improvement Over Time In both RT and TAI, tables of the mean number of vehicles and distances as the search progresses are given. We use this opportunity to compare LNS with these approaches. However, these approaches use more CPU time than the experiments reported so far. We therefore performed longer runs of LNS using parameter settings of $a = 250$ and $D = 15$ (which we considered reasonable from examination of table 3). We solved all problems in R1 and RC1 6 times with different random seeds, using a time limit of 1 hour. For half of these runs we set $d = 5$, and for the other half, $d = 10$.

Table 5 shows, for each method, the CPU time used at three points during the algorithm, and the mean solution quality for each class at that point. This quality is expressed as the mean number of vehicles used per problem over the class, and the mean distance travelled per problem over the class. We use a faster machine than either RT or TAI, and to give a better comparison of resources used, have divided their times by the ratio of our clock rate to theirs.

We can see that the results for $d = 5$ are better than those for $d = 10$, and so a smaller discrepancy is better here. LNS performs well in comparison with the best Operations Research meta-heuristic techniques: the number of vehicles and distance is reduced to approximately the same level as TAI using a roughly equivalent amount of CPU time.

4 Conclusion

Large Neighbourhood Search, a method analogous to the shuffle of job-shop scheduling, has been applied to VRPs. LNS operates by making powerful reinsertion based moves, which are evaluated using constraint programming.

Class	RT			TAI			LNS				
	CPU	Quality		CPU	Quality		CPU	Quality ($d = 5$)		Quality ($d = 10$)	
R1	315	12.83	1208.43	803	12.64	1233.88	900	12.45	1198.37	12.48	1196.07
	909	12.58	1202.31	2408	12.39	1230.48	1800	12.35	1201.47	12.45	1195.30
	1888	12.58	1197.42	4816	12.33	1220.35	3600	12.33	1201.79	12.42	1195.71
RC1	301	12.75	1381.33	656	12.08	1404.59	900	12.05	1363.67	12.05	1360.89
	909	12.50	1368.03	1969	12.00	1387.01	1800	12.00	1363.68	12.03	1358.40
	1818	12.38	1369.48	3938	11.90	1381.31	3600	11.95	1364.17	12.00	1358.26

Table 5. Comparison of solution quality over time for Solomon's problems

Selecting visits for re-insertion based upon a "relatedness" concept leads to significantly better results than random selection. LDS was used to re-insert visits, giving better results than complete search or limiting the the number of backtracks in depth-first search.

On benchmark problems, LNS is highly competitive with leading Operations Research methods, while being much simpler. Furthermore, we believe LNS holds more promise for real problems than traditional local search methods due to its ability to better address side constraints.

Acknowledgment

I wish to thank members of the APES group for their thought provoking conversations, and Ian Gent in particular for encouraging me to write this paper.

The production of this paper was supported by the GreenTrip project, a research and development undertaking partially funded by the ESPRIT Programme of the Commission of the European Union as project number 20603. The partners in this project are Pirelli (I), ILOG (F), SINTEF (N), Tollpost-Globe (N), and University of Strathclyde (UK).

References

1. D. Applegate and W. Cook. A computational study of the job-shop scheduling problem. *ORSA Journal On Computing*, 3:149–156, 1991.
2. B. De Backer, V. Furnon, P. Prosser, P. Kilby, and P. Shaw. Local search in constraint programming: Application to the vehicle routing problem. In A. Davenport and C. Beck, editors, *Proceedings of the CP-97 workshop on Industrial Constraint-based Scheduling*, 1997.
3. P. Baptiste, C. Le Pape, and W. Nuijten. Constraint-based optimization and approximation for job-shop scheduling. In *Proceedings of the AAAI-SIGMAN Workshop on Intelligent Manufacturing Systems, IJCAI-95, Montreal, Canada*, 1995.
4. Y. Caseau and F. Laburthe. Disjunctive scheduling with task intervals. Technical report, LIENS Technical Report 95-25, École Normale Supérieure Paris, France, July 1995.

5. Y. Caseau and F. Laburthe. Solving small TSPs with constraints. In L. Naish, editor, *Proceedings the 14th International Conference on Logic Programming*. The MIT Press, 1997.
6. N. Christofides, A. Mingozzi, and P. Toth. The vehicle routing problem. *Combinatorial Optimization*, pages 315–338, 1979.
7. M. Desrochers, J. Desrosiers, and M. Solomon. A new optimization algorithm for the vehicle routing problems with time windows. *Operations Research*, 40(2):342–354, 1992.
8. M. Fisher. Optimal solution of vehicle routing problems using minimum K-trees. *Operations Research*, 42:626–642, 1994.
9. W. D. Harvey and M. L. Ginsberg. Limited discrepancy search. In *Proceedings of the 14th IJCAI*, 1995.
10. P. Kilby, P. Prosser, and P. Shaw. A comparison of traditional and constraint-based heuristic methods on vehicle routing problems with side constraints. Submitted to the *Constraints* Special Issue on Industrial Scheduling, 1998.
11. G. A. P. Kindervater and M. W. P. Savelsbergh. Vehicle routing: Handling edge exchanges. In E. H. L. Aarts and J. K. Lenstra, editors, *Local Search in Combinatorial Optimization*, pages 337–360. Wiley, Chichester, 1997.
12. T. Mautor and P. Michelon. MIMAUSA: A new hybrid method combining exact solution and local search. In *Proceedings of the 2nd International Conference on Meta-heuristics*, 1997.
13. Pedro Meseguer and Toby Walsh. Interleaved and discrepancy based search. In *Proceedings of the 13th European Conference on AI—ECAI-98*, 1998. To appear.
14. G. Pesant and M. Gendreau. A view of local search in constraint programming. In *Proceedings of CP '96*, pages 353–366. Springer-Verlag, 1996.
15. G. Pesant, M. Gendreau, J.-Y. Potvin, and J.-M. Rousseau. An exact constraint logic programming algorithm for the traveling salesman problem with time windows. *Transportation Science*, 1998. To appear.
16. G. Pesant, M. Gendreau, and J.-M. Rousseau. GENIUS-CP: A generic single-vehicle routing algorithm. In *Proceedings of CP '97*, pages 420–433. Springer-Verlag, 1997.
17. J.-Y. Potvin and S. Bengio. A genetic approach to the vehicle routing problem with time windows. Technical Report CRT-953, Centre de Recherche sur les Transports, University of Montreal, 1994.
18. Y. Rochat and E. D. Taillard. Probabilistic diversification and intensification in local search for vehicle routing. *Journal of Heuristics*, 1(1):147–167, 1995.
19. M. W. P. Savelsbergh. The vehicle routing problem with time windows: Minimizing route duration. *ORSA Journal on Computing*, 4(2):146–154, 1992.
20. M. M. Solomon. Algorithms for the vehicle routing and scheduling problem with time window constraints. *Operations Research*, 35:254–265, 1987.
21. E. Taillard, P. Badeau, M. Gendreau, F. Guertain, and J.-Y. Potvin. A tabu search heuristic for the vehicle routing problem with soft time windows. *Transportation Science*, 32(2), 1997.
22. E. D. Taillard. Parallel iterative search methods for vehicle routing problems. *Networks*, 23:661–676, 1993.
23. S. R. Thangiah, I. H. Osman, and T. Sun. Hybrid genetic algorithm, simulated annealing, and tabu search methods for vehicle routing problems with time windows. Working paper UKC/OR94/4, Institute of Mathematics and Statistics, University of Kent, Canterbury, 1994.

A Polynomial Time Local Propagation Algorithm for General Dataflow Constraint Problems

Gilles Trombettoni

Artificial Intelligence Laboratory, E.P.F.L.
CH-1015 Lausanne, Switzerland
trombe@lia.di.epfl.ch

Abstract. The multi-way dataflow constraint model allows a user to describe interactive applications whose consistency is maintained by a local propagation algorithm. Local propagation applies a sequence of *methods* that solve the constraints individually. The local aspect of this solving process makes this model sensitive to cycles in the constraint graph. We use a formalism which overcomes this major limitation by allowing the definition of *general methods* that can solve several constraints simultaneously. This paper presents an algorithm called General-PDOF to deal with these methods which has a polynomial worst case time complexity. This algorithm therefore has the potential to tackle numerous real-life applications where cycles make local propagation unfeasible. Especially, general methods can implement "ruler and compass" rules to solve geometric constraints.

1 Introduction

Dataflow constraints are used in interactive systems, such as graphical user interfaces, graphical layout systems and animation. They simplify the programming task, are conceptually simple and easy to understand. They are capable of expressing relationships over multiple data types, including numbers, strings, bitmaps, fonts, and colors [Vander Zanden, 1996].

Local propagation was first applied to graphical layout systems [Sutherland, 1963], [Gosling, 1983] but is not used in this field anymore. Indeed, cycles in the constraint graph often make local propagation unfeasible for these applications which involve non-linear equations and dense constraint graphs. Instead, many researchers in the CAD field have designed more powerful algorithms reasoning at the geometric level, that is, considering relations between geometric objects (see [Bouma *et al.*, 1995], [Fudos and Hoffmann, 1997], [Dufourd *et al.*, 1998], [Kramer, 1992], [Hsu and Brüderlin, 1997]). Some of them use a *propagation of degrees of freedom* approach which can be viewed as a propagation mechanism working at the geometric level [Hsu and Brüderlin, 1997], [Kramer, 1992].

The model used in this paper remains at the algebraic level and generalizes the notion of *method* specific to local propagation: in the standard model, a method solves one constraint; here, a *general method* solves *a set* of constraints.

The paper describes General-PDOF, a simple, complete and polynomial time algorithm to planify the (general) methods to apply. The contribution of this generalization is twofold:

- For general-purpose interactive applications, this allows a designer to incrementally define new general methods whose constraints form a cycle when the current definitions led to a failure.
- In the CAD field, executing a general method (at the algebraic level) corresponds to applying a "ruler and compass" rule which is traditionnally a basic operation to solve geometric constraints. Thus, General-PDOF can maintain a system of geometric constraints while working at the algebraic level with a simple and general scheme.

2 Background

A *multi-way dataflow constraint problem* can be denoted by (V, C, M). V is a set of variables with a current value each. C is a set of dataflow constraints and M is a set of *methods* that can satisfy the constraints.

Definition 1 *A* **constraint** *c in C is a relation between a set of variables V_c in V. It has a predicate $\Re_c$ to check whether a valuation of V_c satisfies it. (i.e., $\Re_c(\overline{V_c}) = true$; $\overline{V_c}$ denotes a tuple of values, one for each variable in V_c.)*

Constraint c has a set M_c of methods that must be used to satisfy it[1].

A *method* satisfies a constraint by calculating values for its *output variables* in function of the other variables of the constraint.

Definition 2 *A* **method** *m in M_c is a function that can satisfy a constraint c. V_c can be partitioned into two disjoint subsets: the* **input variables** *$V_{c,m}^{in}$ and the non empty subset of* **output variables** *$V_{c,m}^{out}$. (m* **outputs to** *the variables of $V_{c,m}^{out}$.)*

Method m is defined by $\overline{V_{c,m}^{out}} = m(\overline{V_{c,m}^{in}})$ such that constraint c is satisfied. Method m is **executed** *when m is applied and the variables of $V_{c,m}^{out}$ are bound with the new values. Method m is* **free** *if no variable v in $V_{c,m}^{out}$ is connected to a constraint in C (except c). Thus, the execution of a free method does not violate other constraints.*

A dataflow constraint system is often represented by a *constraint graph G_c* as shown in Figure 1 (a).

Definition 3 *A* **constraint graph** *is a bipartite graph where nodes are constraints and variables represented by rectangles and circles respectively. Each constraint is connected to its variables.*

[1] Hence the name *multi-way dataflow* constraint.

Local propagation is the technique used to maintain the consistency of multi-way constraint systems, typically when new constraints are incrementally added. It works in two phases:

- The *planning phase* assigns one method to each constraint. The result of this phase is a *valid* directed graph G_m called *method graph* (see Definition 4 and Figure 1).
- When the method graph G_m contains no directed cycles, the *evaluation phase* executes the methods in some topological order. Otherwise, *strongly connected components, i.e.*, cycles, are collected and evaluated by an external solver.

Definition 4 *A* **method graph** *is a directed graph where nodes are the methods selected by the planning phase. There is an arc (m_i, m_j) iff at least one output variable of m_i is linked to a constraint satisfied by m_j.*

This definition differs from the usual one [Sannella, 1994]. It is more general [Trombettoni, 1997] and will be useful in the following.

Definition 5 *A method graph G_m is* **valid** *iff (1) every constraint has exactly one method associated with it in G_m, and (2) G_m has no variable conflicts, that is, each variable is an output variable of, at most, one method.*

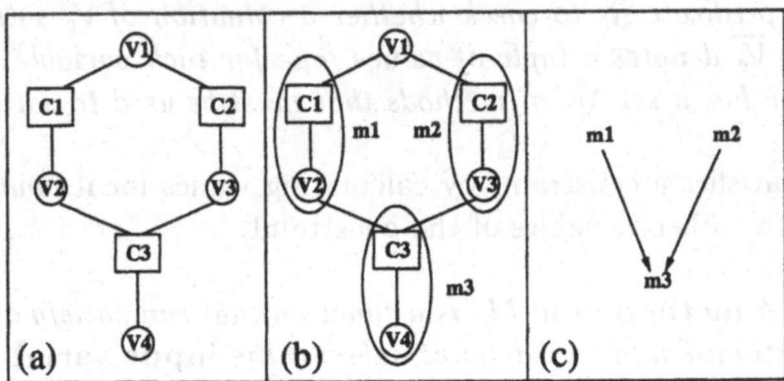

Fig. 1. (a) A (cyclic) constraint graph. (b) Methods selected during the planning phase. A method is represented by an ellipse that encloses both the output variables and the constraint. (c) Valid acyclic method graph formed by these methods. Method m_3, also denoted by m_{c3}^{v4}, is free.

Planning algorithms can be divided into three main categories.

DeltaBlue [Freeman-Benson *et al.*, 1990] and SkyBlue [Sannella, 1994] work by propagating the conflicts from the perturbations to the leaves of the constraint graph.

The propagation of degrees of freedom scheme (in short PDOF) selects the methods in reverse order, *i.e.*, first executing the methods that were chosen last. This algorithm has been used in SketchPad [Sutherland, 1963] and QuickPlan [Vander Zanden, 1996].

A third approach is related to the graph problem of bipartite maximum-matching [Gangnet and Rosenberg, 1992], [Serrano, 1987].

3 Definition and Use of General Methods

Most of the systems based on local propagation only allow *single-output* methods that solve *one* constraint by changing the value of *one* of its variables. For example, the constraint $x = y \times z$ has three single-output methods, *e.g.*, $y \leftarrow \frac{x}{z}$. SkyBlue and QuickPlan accept *multi-output* methods that solve *one* constraint (also called multi-output) by changing the value of *several* variables. [Trombettoni, 1995] introduces *general* methods that solve *one or more* constraints by changing the value of *one or more* output variables. These variables must be connected to at least one of the constraints.

Definition 6 *A* **general** *method m can satisfy a set of constraints C_m. Let V_m be the set of variables linked to a constraint in C_m. V_m is partitioned into two disjoint subsets V_m^{out} and V_m^{in}.*

Method m is defined by $\overline{V_m^{out}} = m(\overline{V_m^{in}})$ such that the constraints in C_m are satisfied[2].

3.1 Example

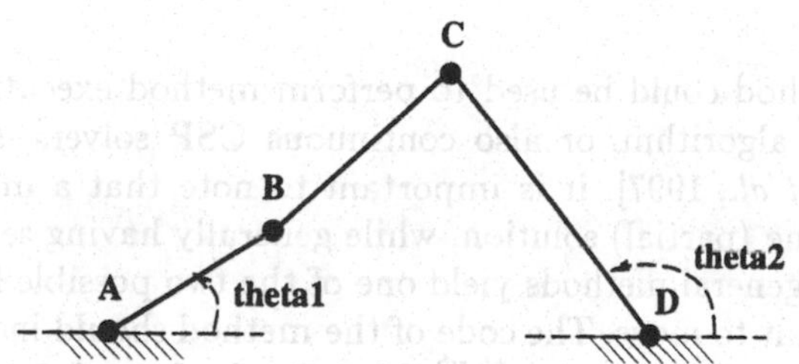

Fig. 2. A mechanism made of three bars *AB*, *BC* and *CD* in 2 D.

The example in Figure 2 is inspired from a linkage described in [Kramer, 1992]. It can be modeled as follows: Points $A\,(x_a; y_a)$ and $D\,(x_d; y_d)$ are fixed in the plane (gray constraints in Figure 3). Bars only impose distance constraints that are quadratic equations. The user can drive the mechanism by moving the bar AB (resp. CD) by an angle Θ_1 (resp. Θ_2).

The corresponding constraint graph is shown in Figure 3 (left), along with the defined methods: Method $m_{c1}^{\Theta_1}$ is a single-output method that can calculate Θ_1 when the location of B is known. Method $m_{c1,c2}^{xb,yb}$ is a general method which gives a new position for the point B. In a sense, this method intersects a line (constraint c_1) and a circle centered in A (constraint c_2) when the location of A and Θ_1 are known. Method $m_{c2,c3}^{xb,yb}$ is a general method giving a new position for the point B which, in a sense, intersects two circles centered in A and C when these points are known. The other methods are symmetric to those above.

[2] The definitions of Section 2 remain unchanged or can be trivially extended.

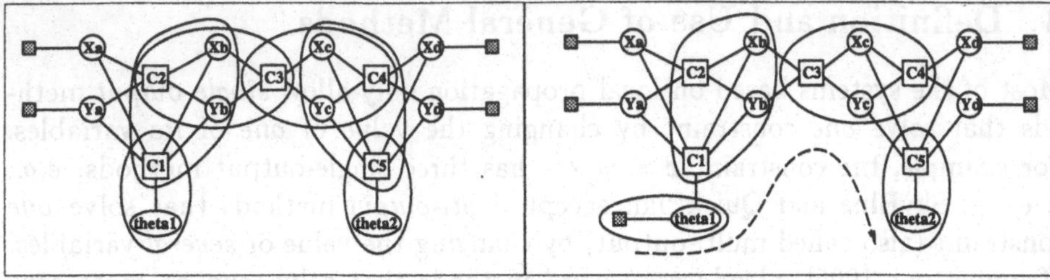

Fig. 3. Left: constraint graph and defined methods of the linkage example. A general method is depicted by an ellipsoid that includes the set of solved constraints and the output variables. Right: the sequence of methods to execute when the user changes the angle Θ_1: to recover the consistency of the linkage, point B is moved, next, point C is moved and finally the angle Θ_2 is modified.

In general, the methods may be either defined by the user or automatically defined from the corresponding constraints. Single-output methods can generally be automatically defined in graphical applications. This is also the case for the general methods of the example that are based on distance and angular constraints.

Remarks

Any numeric method could be used to perform method execution, such as the Newton-Raphson algorithm, or also continuous CSP solvers, such as Numerica [Hentenryck *et al.*, 1997]. It is important to note that a method execution must yield only one (partial) solution, while generally having several choices. In the example, the general methods yield one of the two possible locations for the corresponding point to move. The code of the method should indicate which one to choose. For example, method $m_{c1,c2}^{xb,yb}$ "keeps" only the point with a positive y_b when Θ_1 is comprised in $[0, \Pi]$. This refers to the general and crucial problem of solution predictibility in graphical systems [Kramer, 1992], [Bouma *et al.*, 1995], [Hsu and Brüderlin, 1997]. When one method execution fails, *e.g.*, in case of null intersection between two circles, we consider that the whole propagation process fails.

This problem cannot be modeled with multi-output constraints and shows that the multi-output formalism is a *strict* restriction of the general formalism. See [Trombettoni, 1997] for other examples. To model method $m_{c2,c3}^{xb,yb}$ as a multi-output method, we could consider the conjunction of c_2 and c_3. However, it is then impossible to model method $m_{c3,c4}^{xc,yc}$ in the same way. Indeed, these two methods cannot be defined together as multi-output methods because they both solve constraint c_3, but one solves c_2 while the other solves c_4. Also, methods $m_{c1,c2}^{xb,yb}$ and $m_{c1}^{\Theta_1}$ cannot be defined together in the multi-output method formalism. If only single-output methods are defined in the problem, it can be seen that there is no acyclic method graph able to solve the problem. This means that the PDOF algorithm cannot find a method graph and fails.

4 The General-PDOF Algorithm

We consider the problem of finding a valid acyclic method graph for a dataflow constraint problem with general methods. [Trombettoni, 1997] shows cases where this problem has no solution, whereas solutions exist when considering, not only the defined methods, but also certain implicit *submethods* that are deduced automatically from defined general methods. If these submethods are not known by the propagation algorithm, the solution may be missed. Thus, we would like to design an algorithm that can solve the problem of *finding a valid acyclic method graph by planning with both defined methods and their submethods.* It is important to note that the user does not really care with submethods which will only enable our algorithm to be complete.

Intuitively, the notion of a submethod has the following meaning. When a general method is defined, this may imply that other general methods, called submethods, also exist. A submethod satisfies a subset C' of the constraints of the method and outputs to a subset V' of its output variables. The projection of the result of the method execution on V' satisfies the constraints in C'. For example, consider the general method $m_{c2,c3}^{xb,yb}$ of the previous example. This method induces submethods $m_{c2}^{xb,yb}$ and $m_{c3}^{xb,yb}$. $m_{c2,c3}^{xb,yb}$ calculates the intersection between two circles centered in A and C, and chooses one of the two possible locations (if any). We can also select this point for method $m_{c2}^{xb,yb}$ which could theoretically yield any point on the circle centered in A. Figure 6 will show an example where such submethods are needed to find a valid method graph.

Since submethods are not defined explicitly and may be numerous, it cannot be guessed *a priori* whether a polynomial algorithm can be obtained. This problem is more general than finding a valid acyclic method graph to a system with multi-output constraints. [Vander Zanden, 1996] shows that PDOF remains polynomial when handling multi-output constraints. [Trombettoni, 1995] has presented an exponential algorithm to handle general methods. This section presents the General-PDOF algorithm that solves this problem in polynomial time.

4.1 Submethods

A general method m, given as input of a problem, may induce a method m' that satisfies a subset of the constraints in m and that is not an input of the problem. Figure 4 shows an example.

Definition 7 *Let m be a general method that solves the constraints C_m, with input variables V_m^{in} and output variables V_m^{out}.*

m', a **submethod** *of method m, is defined by m, a subset C'_m of C_m, and a subset $V_m^{out'}$ of V_m^{out}: m' is a function from V_m^{in} to $V_m^{out'}$ such that $m'(\overline{V_m^{in}}) = \Pi_{V_m^{out'}}(m(\overline{V_m^{in}}))$, where Π is the projection on $V_m^{out'}$ of the values returned by m. The submethod m' is* **correct**, *i.e., m' is a method, if calling m' yields values for $V_m^{out'}$ that satisfy the constraints in C'_m.*

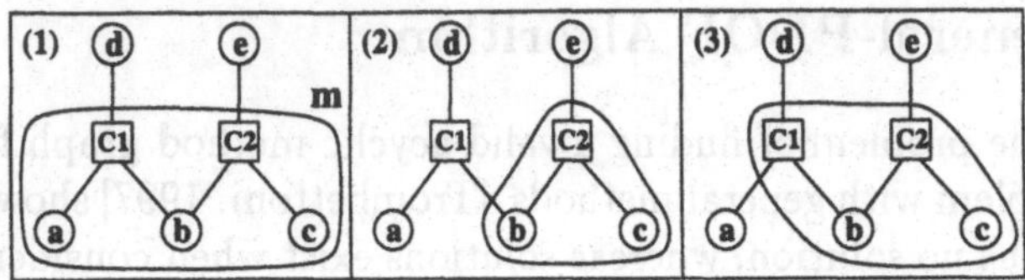

Fig. 4. (1) A general method m that solves constraints c_1 and c_2 and outputs to variables a, b and c. (2) Correct submethod of m. (3) Incorrect submethod of m. Indeed, m changes the value of variable a to satisfy c_1. Thus, there is no guarantee that, for every possible input values for d and e, the projection of the computation of m, only on variable b, satisfies c_1.

This example highlights sufficient syntactical conditions for which a method is correct:

Proposition 1 *Let m be a general method that solves the constraints C_m and outputs to variables V_m. Let m' be a submethod of m that handles constraints $C'_m \subset C_m$ and outputs to variables $V'_m \subset V_m$.*

Submethod m' is correct if no constraint in C'_m is linked to an output variable of V_m which is not in V'_m.

A correct submethod m' means that there exists at least one procedure to perform it, that is, the one given by the defined method m. For instance, the submethod $m_{c2}^{xb,yb}$ previously mentionned in the example can use the result of $m_{c2,c3}^{xb,yb}$ (intersecting the two circles centered in A and C), even if c_2 does not constrain A. However, using method m is not necessary and another procedure can be generated from scratch for m' according to the constraints implied. For instance, another procedure can be used for $m_{c2}^{xb,yb}$ that chooses an arbitrary point on the circle centered in A or that chooses on this circle the closest point from the old position of B.

4.2 Presentation of the Algorithm

Algorithm 1 describes General-PDOF. Its completeness is not trivial and the proof can be found in Section 6. Section 4.3 shows examples. Let us first recall the classical PDOF algorithm.

The key idea behind PDOF is to focus on how to terminate the propagation process, instead of propagating the initial perturbations. It is performed by iteratively selecting a free method, that will be executed after those not yet selected in the remaining constraint graph, and removing its constraints and output variables from the current constraint graph. The process ends when the constraint graph does not contain anymore constraints, and the (directed) method graph formed by the selected methods, *i.e.*, *MG*, is valid and acyclic.

Except that our algorithm can take into account general methods, it is very close to the classical PDOF scheme: only the *Connect* procedure has been added. In the classical PDOF algorithm, the set of defined methods that can currently be selected, including the free ones, evolves as follows when a method is selected

```
algorithm General-PDOF (G: a constraint graph): a valid method graph
  let free be the set of free methods in G
  let MG be an empty acyclic method graph
  while G contains a constraint do
    if free = ∅ then
      exit and return ∅ /* no solution */
    else
      - choose a method m from free and remove it from this set
      - add m to MG (along with the corresponding arcs)
      - remove from G the constraints and the output variables of m
      - Connect (G, m)
      - add to free the free methods of G that previously output to an input
        variable of m
    end
  end
  return MG
end.
procedure Connect (G, m)
  let C_m be the set of constraints solved by m
  let V_m be the set of output variables of m
  for every general method m_i that satisfies a constraint in G connected to an
  input variable of m do
    m'_i ← SubMethod (m_i, C_m, V_m)
    if m'_i ≠ m_i and m'_i has non empty sets of constraints and output variables
    then
      M_i ← Generate-connected-methods (m'_i)
      remove m_i and add the set M_i of connected methods to the set of meth-
      ods (see Definition 8)
    end
  end
end.
```

Algorithm 1: The General-PDOF algorithm.

and its constraint c is removed: the set of methods that satisfy c is not available anymore and the remaining set is unchanged. We also find these two basic cases in General-PDOF, but an additional non trivial case may occur. When a method (general or not) is selected and its constraints C_m and output variables V_m are removed, certain general methods may be neither rejected, nor kept in the current set: those that have a part of their constraints and output variables removed. Lemma 2 will show that their submethods are still correct: *SubMethod* (m_i, C_m, V_m), called by the *Connect* procedure, adds a new (sub)method m'_i to the whole set by removing from m_i the constraints in C_m and the output variables in V_m. Moreover, if m'_i is not *connected*, it is split into the set of its connected subparts by the function *Generate-connected-methods*. Note that since method connectivity is maintained during the planning phase, this requires that defined methods are initially connected.

Definition 8 *Let m be a general method that solves constraints C_m and that outputs to variables V_m. Let g_m be the bipartite graph that represents the dependencies between V_m and C_m in m.*

The method m is **connected** *if g_m is connected, i.e., there exists a path between any two nodes in g_m.*

4.3 Examples

The reader can easily check that General-PDOF can build the method graph of the example in Section 3.1: method $m_{c5}^{\Theta_2}$ is first selected, which frees method $m_{c3,c4}^{xc,yc}$. The selection of that method frees method $m_{c1,c2}^{xb,yb}$. Selecting $m_{c1,c2}^{xb,yb}$ finally frees the input method modifying Θ_1 which is selected at the end.

The example in Figure 5 illustrates the subtleties of the *Connect* procedure and their importance in guaranteeing completeness.

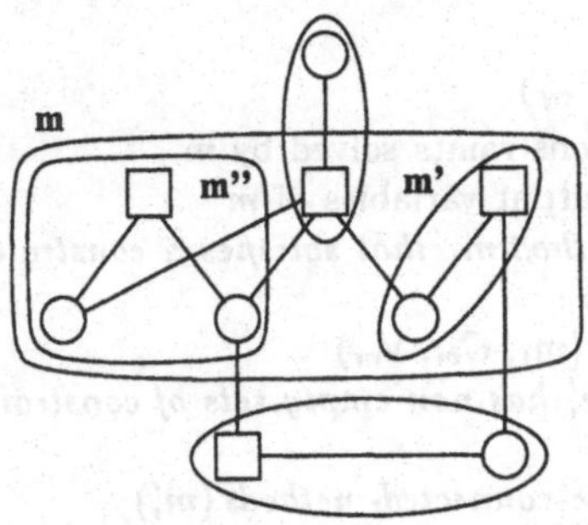

Fig. 5. Role of the *Connect* procedure. At first, the only free method is the single-output method at the top of the figure. When it is selected and removed from the graph, the general method m is replaced by its two connected submethods m' and m''. The free method m' is then selected and removed. This frees the single-output method at the bottom of the figure which is selected next. Finally, the method m'' is selected. If m had not been split into m' and m'', no solution would have been found. Indeed, the "conjunction" of m' and m'' would not have been free (because of m'').

Figure 6 details a geometric example solvable by General-PDOF which highlights the importance of taking into account submethods.

The submethod $m_{c1}^{xb,yb}$ is executed first by placing B in the location calculated by $m_{c1,c2}^{xb,yb}$. This corresponds to one of the two possible locations coming from the intersection between the two circles centered in the new position of A and the old position of C. Using this old position for C, it will be given B a new position close to the old one, in case of a small move of A. Then C will be moved by executing the method $m_{c2,c3}^{xc,yc}$, using the new positions of B and D.

5 Time Complexity

The worst-case time complexity of General-PDOF is $O(n \times dc \times dv \times r \times (g \times dc + g^2))$. n is the number of constraints, r is the maximum number of methods per

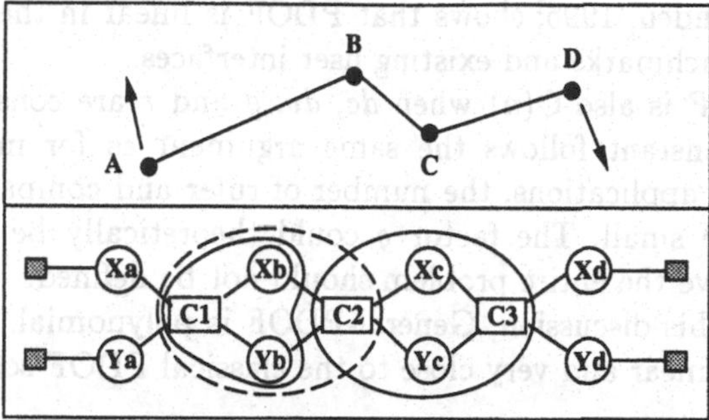

Fig. 6. Another linkage example where the user freely moves A and D simultaneously. All general methods are defined which compute one point given the location of two adjacent ones (intersection of two circles). The methods selected by General-PDOF are shown on the constraint graph. In particular, no solution could be found if the submethod $m_{c1}^{xb,yb}$ of $m_{c1,c2}^{xb,yb}$ was not taken into account.

constraint, dc and dv are the maximum degrees of respectively a constraint and a variable in the constraint graph, and g is the maximum number of constraints and output variables involved in a general method. This complexity is a polynomial function of the input parameters: $dv \leq n$; $g \leq n$; $dc \leq |V|$; $r \leq |M|$.

Details: At each step of General-PDOF, at least one constraint is removed, so that the maximum number of calls to the while loop is n. The other factors correspond to the calls at each iteration, *i.e.*, within the while loop. The complexity of an iteration is dominated by the two last items (see Algorithm 1). In both cases, $dc \times dv \times r$ methods are visited, that is, all of the methods satisfying a constraint at distance 2 of the removed constraints in the bipartite constraint graph[3]. The *Connect* procedure is $O(g \times dc)$ because a method m_i' can be split in at most g connected methods. Checking that a visited method is newly free is $O(g^2)$. These two results are obtained by managing marks for the constraints and output variables of the visited method.

The same analysis gives a more precise time complexity for PDOF which is $O(n \times dv \times dc^2)$ and $O(n \times dv \times dc^2 \times r)$ for multi-output constraints.

Note that this polynomial complexity only concerns the planning phase. The execution phase complexity cannot be evaluated without considering specific types of constraints.

5.1 Discussion

PDOF is $O(n)$ when dc and dv are considered constant, which is the case for the sparse constraint graphs encountered in real user interfaces [Sannella, 1994].

PDOF applied to multi-output methods is $O(n)$ when r is also considered constant. The number r of multi-output methods per constraint could theoretically be very large, but it is a small constant for user interfaces [Sannella *et al.*, 1993].

[3] The data structures follow the existing implementations where entities are implemented as records [Vander Zanden, 1996], [Sannella, 1994].

Also, [Vander Zanden, 1996] shows that PDOF is linear in the number of constraints using benchmarks and existing user interfaces.

General-PDOF is also O(n) when dc, dv, g and r are considered constant. Considering r constant follows the same argument as for multi-output constraints. In CAD applications, the number of ruler and compass rules per constraint should be small. The factor g could theoretically be equal to n, but methods that solve the entire problem should not be defined.

To conclude this discussion, General-PDOF is polynomial. We believe that, in practice, it is linear and very close to the classical PDOF scheme.

6 Completeness

The following completeness property validates General-PDOF.

Proposition 2 *Let $P = (V, C, M)$ be a dataflow constraint problem that contains general methods.*

If there exist valid acyclic method graphs that correspond to P (that may contain submethods of methods in M), then General-PDOF can find one of them.

The proof uses the following two lemmas which are proven in [Trombettoni, 1997].

Lemma 1 *Let P be a dataflow constraint problem that contains general methods and let m be one of the methods of P.*

If m is connected then m has no submethod that is both correct and free.

Lemma 2 *Let us consider any step of General-PDOF applied to a given problem. Let m_1 be a free method that solves the constraints C_1 and outputs to the variables V_1. Let m_2 be another method of the problem.*

After having removed m_1, the submethod $m'_2 = SubMethod(m_2, C_1, V_1)$ is correct.

Proof of Proposition 2 (sketch). The completeness proof of General-PDOF is based on: (1) a confluence property coming from PDOF that remains valid for General-PDOF, and (2) the fact that all of the existing free methods are available at each step of the algorithm.

A confluence property of PDOF states that, considering two free methods m_1 and m_2 at a given step, removing a free method m_1 does not prevent the further selection of m_2. This property remains true for General-PDOF. Indeed, Lemma 2 applied to m_2 proves that m'_2 is correct, and a submethod of a free method is also free. Thus, when method m_1 is selected and removed, m_2 (more precisely m'_2) remains available for a further selection.

The two lemmas are necessary to prove that all of the existing free methods are available at each step of the algorithm. Lemma 1 shows that General-PDOF does not need to consider the submethods of the current connected methods because they cannot be selected. This justifies the connectivity condition maintained during the process. Lemma 2 shows that the submethod m'_i, calculated by the procedure *Connect* of General-PDOF, is correct. This explains why the algorithm adds all of the connected submethods deduced from m'_i since these are all correct and may be free.□

7 Qualitative comparison with Maximum-matching

In the dataflow constraint field, the maximum-matching algorithm (MM) can be used as follows [Gangnet and Rosenberg, 1992]. The planning phase applies MM on the constraint graph. Each pair (c, v) in the matching corresponds to the selection of the single-output method m_c^v. A method graph is thus obtained. The evaluation phase collects the strongly connected components, topologically sorts the *condensed* graph and solves each component in this order: the corresponding method is executed or an external solver is called when a component is made of several methods (a cycle).

MM is close to General-PDOF in that a strongly connected component may correspond to a general method. We highlight here several differences.

7.1 Advantages of MM

First, MM does not require to define general methods, but only single-output methods, which is simpler.

Second, MM finds the same decomposition as General-PDOF when tackling a "structurally well-constrained" problem of equations[4], *i.e.*, for which there exists a perfect matching. Indeed, [König, 1916] has shown that, in this case, the decomposition in strongly connected components is unique. One can check this on the example presented in Section 3.1.

Third, MM always terminates giving a method graph, whereas General-PDOF may fail if there is no acyclic method graph with the defined methods. Indeed, General-PDOF can use only the defined methods and their submethods.

7.2 Advantages of General-PDOF

First, when the problem is under-constrained, such as in most of graphical applications, the result of König does not hold anymore, so that MM may generate (strongly connected) components of arbitrary "semantics" and size. Indeed, MM may generate larger components than General-PDOF would do. *In particular, MM may create a cyclic method graph which needs to be evaluated by an external solver even though an acyclic method graph exists which would lead to a less time-consuming solution.* Moreover, the components created by MM may not correspond to a "real" general method.

For instance, suppose that an additional degree of freedom is allowed in the problem described in Section 3.1: point A can now "roll" horizontally, *i.e.*, x_a is free. In this case, after having changed Θ_1, MM may create the component which corresponds to the general method $m_{c1,c2}^{xa,xb}$. However, this method has no sense geometrically and corresponds to a contradictory system of equations. General-PDOF cannot make this bad choice if $m_{c1,c2}^{xa,xb}$ is not defined.

Second, and even if the problem is well-constrained, MM builds only components which contain as many constraints as variables since there exists a perfect

[4] except if non-square general methods are defined (see below).

matching of the corresponding subgraph. Thus, MM is not able to planify non-square components[5], such as the ones solving inequalities or method $m_{c1}^{xb,yb}$ of the example in Figure 6.

Finally, a component built arbitrarily by MM may yield a solution which is not intuitive for the user, whereas the definition of a general method handled by General-PDOF should precise which solution to choose, according to the semantics of the corresponding ruler and compass rule for example.

7.3 Taking the Best of the Two Algorithms

The confrontation between these two algorithms is not necessary in fact because MM and PDOF can easily be brought together. This can be done as follows:

1. Apply MM on the constraint graph. Let A be the set of arcs in the matching.
2. Apply PDOF on the constraint graph. Two cases may occur at each step:
   (a) There exists a free method m_c^v: m_c^v is selected by PDOF and c and v are removed from the graph. Arcs sharing v or c are removed from A.
   (b) There exists no free method (PDOF is blocked):
      i. Topologically sort the (condensed) directed graph corresponding to A. One obtains a DAG D of components.
      ii. Choose a leaf of D as next free method to select with PDOF.

Thus, this MM-PDOF algorithm can find an acyclic method graph with defined methods if possible (because of PDOF) but never fails and builds new components when no free method is available (because of MM).

The correctness of this algorithm is trivial to check.

We believe that MM-PDOF can be extended to a MM-GPDOF algorithm which makes collaborate MM and General-PDOF. MM-GPDOF will be described in a future work.

8 Conclusion

This paper has described a new local propagation algorithm, called General-PDOF, that can take into account methods solving several constraints simultaneously. This formalism especially allows a system to solve geometric constraints at the algebraic level while keeping a bridge between the two levels.

General-PDOF is simple, complete and has a polynomial time complexity. From a theoretical point of view, it shows that the constraint planning problem with general methods is in P when acyclic solutions are sought. There is no computational jump from simpler problems (with only single-output or multi-output constraints [Trombettoni and Neveu, 1997]). In practice, this complexity should be linear in the number of constraints for user interfaces or CAD applications and General-PDOF should be almost as efficient as PDOF.

[5] These components generally correspond to general methods which choose a solution among an infinite set...

The algorithm given in [Trombettoni, 1995] solves the same problem. However, it is complicated and has an exponential time complexity. The comparison between the two algorithms suggests that the *propagation of conflicts* scheme is not suitable to handle general methods [Trombettoni, 1997].

9 Future Works

Many systems based on local propagation, such as DeltaBlue, SkyBlue and QuickPlan, allow the user to define both *required* constraints that must be satisfied and *preferential* constraints that are satisfied if possible [Borning *et al.*, 1992]. QuickPlan, based on PDOF, removes preferential constraints with a low priority until an acyclic solution is obtained. However, this technique may fail when cycles only contain required constraints. General-PDOF could easily replace the PDOF procedure of QuickPlan in order to take into account both general methods and *constraint hierarchies* [Borning *et al.*, 1992]. A brief analysis shows that the *locally-graph-better* criterion still holds for this hybrid algorithm [Trombettoni, 1997].

We intend to design a MM-GPDOF algorithm which will allow a simple and pertinent collaboration between maximum-matching and General-PDOF: MM-GPDOF would planify defined (general) methods if possible and would build non-defined general methods (corresponding to strongly connected components) only when necessary.

The main contribution of this paper is "theoretical", formally describing a new general-purpose local propagation algorithm and its properties. The potential of General-PDOF to maintain systems of geometric constraints must be validated. We intend to develop a prototype suitable for such applications and especially compare it to the propagation of (geometric) degrees of freedom approach [Hsu and Brüderlin, 1997], [Kramer, 1992]. It will be desirable to allow this tool to automatically define the set of ruler and compass general methods based on the given geometric constraint graph.

In this paper, local propagation has been presented as a technique for incrementally maintaining a set of constraints. However, it could also be used to decompose a set of numeric constraints before satisfaction. [Bliek *et al.*, 1998] presents a distance problem made of tetrahedra and additional bars. In that example, General-PDOF could be used to find the decomposition in small blocks.

Acknowledgments

Special thanks to Christian Bliek and Bertrand Neveu for many useful discussions. Also thanks to Nicolas Chleq and Steven Wilmott for comments on earlier versions of the paper.

References

[Bliek *et al.*, 1998] Christian Bliek, Bertrand Neveu, and Gilles Trombettoni. Using Graph Decomposition for Solving Continuous CSPs. In *these proceedings*, 1998.

[Borning *et al.*, 1992] Alan Borning, Bjorn Freeman-Benson, and Molly Wilson. Constraint hierarchies. *Lisp and Symbolic Computation*, 5(3):223–270, September 1992.

[Bouma *et al.*, 1995] William Bouma, Ioannis Fudos, Christoph Hoffmann, Jiazhen Cai, and Robert Paige. Geometric constraint solver. *Computer Aided Design*, 27(6):487–501, 1995.

[Dufourd *et al.*, 1998] Jean-François Dufourd, Pascal Mathis, and Pascal Schreck. Geometric Construction by Assembling Solved Subfigures. *Artificial Intelligence*, 99(1):73–119, 1998.

[Freeman-Benson *et al.*, 1990] Bjorn Freeman-Benson, John Maloney, and Alan Borning. An incremental constraint solver. *Communications of the ACM*, 33(1):54–63, January 1990.

[Fudos and Hoffmann, 1997] Ioannis Fudos and Christoph Hoffmann. A graph-constructive approach to solving systems of geometric constraints. *ACM Transactions on Graphics*, 16(2):179–216, 1997.

[Gangnet and Rosenberg, 1992] Michel Gangnet and Burton Rosenberg. Constraint programming and graph algorithms. In *Second International Symposium on Artificial Intelligence and Mathematics*, January 1992.

[Gosling, 1983] James Gosling. *Algebraic Constraints*. PhD thesis, Carnegie–Mellon University, 1983.

[Hentenryck *et al.*, 1997] Pascal Van Hentenryck, Laurent Michel, and Yves Deville. *Numerica : A Modeling Language for Global Optimization*. MIT Press, 1997.

[Hsu and Brüderlin, 1997] Ching-Yao Hsu and Beat Brüderlin. A degree-of-freedom graph approach. In , editor, , pages 132–155. Springer Verlag, 1997.

[König, 1916] D. König. Über Graphen und ihre Anwendung auf Determinantentheorie und Mengenlehre. In *Math Ann 77*, pages 453–465, 1916.

[Kramer, 1992] Glenn Kramer. *Solving Geometric Constraint Systems*. MIT Press, 1992.

[Sannella *et al.*, 1993] Michael Sannella, John Maloney, Bjorn Freeman-Benson, and Alan Borning. Multi-way versus one-way constraints in user interfaces. *Software – Practice and Experience*, 23(5):529–566, May 1993.

[Sannella, 1994] Michael Sannella. *Constraint Satisfaction and Debugging for Interactive User Interfaces*. PhD thesis, Department of Computer Science and Engineering, University of Washington, Seattle, 1994. Also available as Technical Report 94-09-10.

[Serrano, 1987] D. Serrano. *Constraint Management in Conceptual Design*. PhD thesis, Massachusetts Institute of Technology, Cambridge, Massachusetts, October 1987.

[Sutherland, 1963] Ivan Sutherland. *Sketchpad: A Man-Machine Graphical Communication System*. PhD thesis, Department of Electrical Engineering, MIT, 1963.

[Trombettoni and Neveu, 1997] Gilles Trombettoni and Bertrand Neveu. Computational complexity of multi-way, dataflow constraint problems. In *International Joint Conference on Artificial Intelligence, IJCAI'97*, pages 358–363, 1997.

[Trombettoni, 1995] Gilles Trombettoni. Formalizing local propagation in constraint maintenance systems. In 7th *Portuguese Conference on Artificial Intelligence, EPIA'95*, pages 83–94, 1995. Lecture Notes in Artificial Intelligence 990.

[Trombettoni, 1997] Gilles Trombettoni. *Solution Maintenance of Constraint Systems Based on Local Propagation*. PhD thesis, University of Nice-Sophia Antipolis, 1997. In french.

[Vander Zanden, 1996] Bradley Vander Zanden. An incremental algorithm for satisfying hierarchies of multi-way, dataflow constraints. *ACM Transactions on Programming Languages and Systems*, 18(1):30–72, January 1996.

Stable Solutions for Dynamic Constraint Satisfaction Problems *

Richard J. Wallace and Eugene C. Freuder

University of New Hampshire, Durham, NH 03824

Abstract. An important extension of constraint technology involves problems that undergo changes that may invalidate the current solution. Previous work on dynamic problems sought methods for efficiently finding new solutions. We take a more proactive approach, exploring methods for finding solutions more likely to remain valid after changes that temporarily alter the set of valid assignments (*stable* solutions). To this end, we examine strategies for tracking changes in a problem and incorporating this information to guide search to solutions that are more likely to be stable. In this work search is carried out with a min-conflicts hill climbing procedure, and information about change is used to bias value selection, either by distorting the objective function or by imposing further criteria on selection. We study methods that track either value losses or constraint additions, and incorporate information about relative frequency of change into search. Our experiments show that these methods are generally effective in finding stable solutions, and in some cases handle the tradeoff between solution stability and search efficiency quite well. In addition, we identify one condition in which these methods markedly reduce the effort to find a stable solution.

1 Introduction

Constraint satisfaction problems (CSPs) involve assigning values to variables in order to satisfy constraints among subsets of variables. Dynamic constraint satisfaction problems (DCSPs) are CSPs that change intermittently over time, by loss or gain of values, variables or constraints. Such change may make the current solution invalid, as when a value is lost, or the number of acceptable tuples in a constraint is reduced, or a new constraint added.

A potentially important distinction is between temporary and permanent changes in the problem. Earlier research has been oriented toward the latter case [1] [2] [6]. In this work, a DCSP was construed as a sequence of CSPs to be solved, and this may have reflected the assumption that changes were permanent. (In the work in which the sequential model was first proposed [2], this assumption was made explicitly.) But there are situations in which current conditions (e.g., machine breakdown or employee absence) preclude certain possibilities that may again be realized when these conditions no longer hold. In the present research,

* supported by the National Science Foundation under Grant No. IRI-9504316.

we emphasize the case of temporary change and introduce methods specifically suited for it. We call these problems *recurrent DCSPs* to distinguish them from DCSPs in which changes are permanent.

If problem alterations are temporary, then changes may occur repeatedly, and different changes may occur with different frequencies. In this case it should be possible to go beyond corrective strategies studied in earlier work to more proactive strategies. Instead of re-solving the problem after a solution has been lost, we would like to avoid losing our solution in the first place. In this way, we can forestall extra search as well as other undesirable aspects of solution failure (downtime, frustration, etc. [3]). This can be done if we can find solutions that are *stable* in the face of change, i.e., that remain valid for the altered problem.

Two criteria for evaluating performance have been suggested earlier, and these can be carried over to the present work: (i) efficiency in finding a new solution, (ii) solution similarity or consistency, i.e. finding a new solution that shares as many values as possible with the old one [6]. We add a third criterion, (iii) solution stability in the face of problem alteration. (In [6] the term "stability" was used for criterion (ii). But, since "similarity" is a more transparent term for this feature, it seems appropriate to use "stability" for the third criterion.)

Some earlier work mentions proactive methods for dynamic CSPs, using a probabilistic model for constraint inclusion [4]. There are, however, critical differences between the specific context for which this model is intended and the situation treated in the present paper, as discussed elsewhere [8].

The next section, 2, describes the methods used in this work to find stable solutions. Section 3 describes our experimental testbed and basic methods for testing strategies for finding stable solutions. Section 4 gives the basic results of empirical tests of stability methods with value loss and constraint addition. Section 5 gives results pertaining to number of stable solutions available and rate of information gain. Section 6 gives conclusions.

2 Methods for Finding Stable Solutions

2.1 Hill Climbing for Recurrent DCSPs

In the DCSPs we are considering, changes to the problem are unpredictable and can also occur during search, i.e. before a solution has been found to replace the one lost before the original change. Under these circumstances, heuristic repair techniques seem like a natural choice, as they do for DCSPs in general. With these methods, problem alteration during search can be incorporated gracefully. An unassigned variable may need to be relabeled, and the resulting assignment may have more conflicts than before. Hill-climbing can then proceed as usual, trying to find a better assignment by heuristic repair, and since adjustments begin at the points of alteration, it may be possible to obtain a new solution with a minimum of revision.

Complete methods face more daunting problems in this situation: (i) if a value in the partial assignment is lost, the partial solution must be retracted back to the point of change before proceeding, (ii) if values are added as well as deleted, the algorithm must start over to be certain of finding an existing solution (pointed out by D. Clancey). Under these conditions, the chief deficiency of hill climbing, that it cannot determine whether a solution is optimal, may be overshadowed by the difficulty of otherwise finding a solution at all.

The procedure used in this work was min-conflicts augmented by a "random walk" strategy in which a random assignment is made with a certain probability (here, 0.10) to a variable in conflict, regardless of whether the new assignment is better or worse than the previous one (Figure 1). This gets min-conflicts out of local minima, and the augmented procedure is effective in finding global minima for random CSPs [7].

```
{PREPROCESSING}
    For each successive variable
        choose value that minimizes conflicts with previous values chosen
{HILL CLIMBING}
    Repeat
        1. randomly select a variable x with ≥ 1 conflicts
        2. with probability p
               choose a value v at random from the domain of x
        2'. with probability 1 − p
               find all min-conflicts values in domain of x
               choose value v at random from min-conflicts set
        3. assign v to x
    until cutoff time reached or complete solution found
```

Fig. 1. Basic hill climbing procedure used in this work: min-conflicts augmented with a random walk feature. In this work p always equals 0.1.

Methods for collecting information relevant to stability that are described in the next section do not require local search procedures. But they seem well-suited to such an approach, as will be indicated.

2.2 Strategies for Finding Stable Solutions

Having chosen a search procedure, we must then consider how to extend it for the purpose of finding stable solutions. This extension necessarily involves two steps, collecting information about change and incorporating this information into the search process (through elaborations of the procedure in Figure 1).

Collecting Information On Change Recurrent DCSPs have these properties:

- Values or tuples may be lost or constraints added temporarily.
- There are differences in the likelihood of change for different elements of the same type.
- These differences are not known *a priori*.

Our basic goal is to avoid choosing values for assignment that are likely to make our solution invalid in the future. To accomplish this under the specified conditions, we must collect information about changes as they occur and use it to decide which value to assign to a given variable during subsequent search.

Data collection can proceed in either of two ways: (i) we can track changes directly, e.g. recording values that are lost, or (ii) we can track solution loss resulting from problem change and relate this to values that participate in solutions of varying stability. In this paper we examine methods for tracking change. This is because in some ways these are the most straightforward and intuitive strategies and because the resulting distributed information about change seems to mesh well with local search. (The alternative, which includes Bayesian methods, will be discussed elsewhere.) The changes we consider here are value losses and constraint additions.

Perhaps the simplest collection strategy is to flag any element that changes. But in this case we cannot discriminate between elements subject to different rates of change. A better method is to tally the number of changes for each element of a given type over time. More sophisticated measures can be envisaged, such as the time that a constraint is present or a value is unavailable, or the number of steps required to find a new solution after a given change has occurred. However, in this paper we will stick to counting changes.

In fact, simply counting the number of times that an element changes is likely to be a very good strategy and, therefore, one worth examining in detail. This is because these counts can be related to relative frequencies and the latter to parent probabilities, in accordance with Bernoulli's Theorem [5]. So, if there are differences in rates of failure that can be considered probabilistically, simple counts such as these may be the best representation of these differences. This also means that, for our purposes, no function of these counts is likely to improve on the identity function.

On the other hand, we don't wish to overemphasize the probabilistic interpretation of these tallies. Their essential feature is that they provide a total ordering among the elements of a given type, so that any two elements can be compared on this basis. As will become clear in the next section, this is all we need to use this information during hill climbing search. In this way, we limit the assumptions required to use this information. Moreover, because we do not have to specify how this information must be combined, we are free to use it in a variety of ways to guide search toward more stable solutions. The tradeoffs in using this approach versus one that allows us to combine local information, e.g. to define more global concepts of goodness, must be the subject of later work.

Incorporating Information into Search We first consider the case of value loss because counts of this type, or "penalties", are directly related to the elements considered in decision making in the min-conflicts procedure. In this context, we evaluate two methods for incorporating penalties into local search.

In the first method, at the point where we compare conflicts among values of a domain, we add the penalty for each value to its current conflicts. (We call this

a. Penalty-Adding
    2′. with probability $1 - p$
        find all values in domain of x with minimum (conflicts + scaled penalty)
        choose value v at random from this biased min-conflicts set

b. Penalty Selection
    2′. with probability $1 - p$
        find all min-conflicts values in domain of x
        repeat
            select and remove value v at random from min-conflicts set
        until penalty for $v <$ cutoff or no more values
        if penalty for $v <$ cutoff
            choose v for assignment
        else
            assign a value chosen at random from original min-conflicts set

Fig. 2. Adjustments made to min-conflicts procedure to incorporate information about value loss (penalties).

penalty-adding.) Therefore, our min-conflicts set is based on this biased value for conflicts (Figure 2a). This should certainly bias search heavily in favor of stable values, but if penalties, or tallies, are used in their original form, the conflicts themselves will have an ever-diminishing influence, and this will eventually undermine hill climbing. To ameliorate this problem, the original penalties can be scaled to be commensurate with the range of conflicts. In this work, penalites were rescaled from the current range (0 to the largest penalty) to a range from 0 to the degree of the variable currently considered for repair.

In the second method (termed *penalty selection*), the set of min-conflicts values is found as usual. Then a value is chosen at random from this set, but it is not chosen for assignment unless its penalty is less than some criterion or cutoff. This process is repeated until an acceptable value is found or all values have been tested; in the latter case, we revert to the usual selection procedure (Figure 2b). In tests described in this paper, the cutoff for selection was the current average penalty. This method should retain much of the efficiency of the original hill climbing procedure. At the same time, it is not evident that one method will be better than the other in finding stable solutions.

In both cases, a selection or cutoff method is also used with the random walk. That is, if the procedure decides to choose a value at random, then values are chosen successively and at random from the remaining, untested subdomain until one is found that meets the selection criterion. If no such value can be found, walk gives up.

Constraint penalties (tallies of constraint addition) can be incorporated into hill climbing by checking them during value selection to avoid values that violate potential constraints with high penalties (Figure 3). In this case, a value chosen from the min-conflicts set is tested against potential constraints that are not part of the current problem. If none of these constraints are violated or if any violated constraints have penalties below a cutoff value, then this value is ac-

```
SELECTION BASED ON CONSTRAINT PENALTIES
  2'. with probability 1 - p
  find all min-conflicts values in domain of x
  repeat
      select and remove value v at random from min-conflicts set
      for each potential constraint not currently present
          if value is incompatible with other value(s) in constraint
          and constraint-penalty > cutoff
              reject value and exit for-loop
  until v not rejected or no more values
  if v not rejected
      choose v for assignment
  else
      assign a value chosen at random from original min-conflicts set
```

Fig. 3. Adjustments made to min-conflicts procedure to incorporate information about constraint additions.

cepted. Otherwise, another value is chosen. If no acceptable value is found, then a random selection is made from the min-conflicts set. Again, a corresponding procedure is used for selection in the walk condition.

As penalties accrue for different elements, hill climbing may be constrained to the point where it is difficult to find a complete solution. This is an interesting and important problem that requires further study. In the present work, we relaxed the selection criterion a bit each time that hill climbing had not found a solution after k seconds. (In experimental work described below, k was high enough that it was rarely necessary to employ this feature; but it was needed to ensure that hill climbing could always find a solution.)

3 Evaluating Penalty Strategies

3.1 A Testbed for Evaluation

To examine the effectiveness of the strategies described in Section 2 experimentally, we tested the procedures with a simulated recurrent DCSP. The simulation occurs in two steps:

- a setup phase in which a probability of change is assigned to each element
- a runtime phase, during which a succession of changes occurs in combination with repeated periods of search

The setup phase turns a CSP into a recurrent DCSP, guided by information given by the user. In most work to date we have used a two-tiered distribution of probabilities based on three user-supplied values: (i) a value representing the expected (i.e. not fixed) proportion of elements associated with more likely events (here, value loss or constraint addition), (ii) and (iii) values for the higher and lower probabilities of change. For each element (i.e. each domain value or each non-fixed constraint), if a number generated by a pseudo-random generator is less than value (i), the element is assigned the high-probability number, (ii), otherwise it is assigned the low-probability number, (iii). For constraint additions, the user also supplies a value for the (expected) proportion of constraints in the original problem that are to be fixed.

In the runtime phase, changes are made periodically by scanning the entire set of relevant elements and, for each element, deciding whether a change should be made with respect to the original problem. (The entire scan is called an *occasion* for change.) For a domain value, the decision is whether it should be deleted; for a non-fixed constraint, the decision is whether it should be added. This is done within either: (i) a *solution-to-solution* format, in which changes occur each time that hill climbing finds a new solution, (ii) a *fixed-time* format in which changes occur after fixed intervals, regardless of the state of search. In all cases, with each occasion for change the altered problem is not accepted unless it has a complete solution. Therefore, changes may be made repeatedly according to the procedure just described until this criterion is met. (This allows clearcut stopping points for hill climbing, which makes experimental evaluation more straightforward.)

The hill climbing procedure, of course, knows nothing about the underlying probabilities associated with the problem elements. It simply tries to find a solution for the current problem. If, in addition, a penalty condition is specified (see below), it uses the current counts of the number of changes for each element, as described in Section 2, to avoid assigning values or violating constraints with higher penalties.

3.2 Overview of Experiments

Most work to date has used the two-tiered scheme to represent DCSPs with a small proportion of elements that are likely to be lost or added and which should, therefore, be avoided (in the case of domain values) or satisfied (in the case of constraints) to enhance stability. Remaining elements have a small, non-zero probability of change. (Hence, there are no fully stable solutions.) In addition, most work has used the solution-to-solution format.

In all experiments every problem was tested twice, once with hill climbing alone, and once with penalty information incorporated into search. (Order of testing was random.) Such a within-problems design insures a higher degree of experimental control than a design with two sets of problems.

Tests were made with coloring problems because the latter are often used in connection with scheduling and resource allocation. In many cases random CSPs have also been tested. Since we have not observed any differences in results for the two types of problem, we restrict our account to the former.

Performance was measured both in terms of the quality of solutions obtained by hill climbing under penalty and non-penalty conditions and the efficiency of finding a solution. For experiments with value loss, the simplest quality measure was the number of high-probability ('bad') values per solution. A global measure of solution stability was the ratio of solutions to occasions for change. Low values for this measure indicate that solutions remained valid after many such occasions, i.e. that stability was relative high. Statistics for both measures were based on all solutions after the first. Efficiency was measured by the total search time during the entire run of k occasions for change. (Setup times at the beginning of a run and in connection with each new set of changes were excluded.)

The testbed and hill climbing procedures were coded in Common Lisp (Lispworks by Harlequin). The experiments were run on a DEC Alpha (DEC3000 M300LX) using compiled code.

4 Experimental Tests of Penalty Strategies

4.1 Experiment 1: Tests with Value Loss

In the first set of tests, changes were limited to value loss. This experiment (like the next) had a two-sided purpose: (i) to assess effectivenes of strategies for combining local failure information and hill climbing, (ii) to see if the effects of these techniques are detectable when 'bad' values were chosen without regard to problem structure. Under these conditions it is impossible to improve solution quality in every case, since in some cases the bad values may not be part of a solution, or they might be either impossible to replace or easily replaced by ordinary hill climbing. A positive result would therefore mean that these methods are likely to have some generality of application. It would also make experimentation much easier, since one would not have to set up carefully contrived situations to see effects.

Methods Random 3-color problems with 100 variables were used in these tests. Presence of complete solutions was guaranteed by repeatedly generating problems until one with a complete solution was found. The density of the constraint graph, in terms of edges added to a spanning tree, was constant for each experiment and was either 0.010, 0.016 or 0.022. (The last-mentioned density is at the edge of the critical complexity region.) All tests were based on 100 problems generated during testing.

For these DCSPs, the higher value for deletion probability, p_h, was 0.3, the lower value, p_l, was 0.003. This gave a large difference between likelihood of loss for high- and low-probability values, without making the former too extreme or the latter so low that these values were rarely deleted. The probability, p_p, that a domain value was associated with the higher deletion probability was 0.025, so the expected number of 'bad' values was 7.5.

In the runtime phase, there were 250 occasions for change (value deletion) in both penalty and non-penalty conditions. During the penalty condition, tallies were kept for each domain value of the number of times it was deleted, for use during subsequent hill climbing, as described in Section 2. At the time of deletion, deleted values were compared with the current instantiation of their associated variables, and assignment losses noted. If there were no assigment losses, deleted values were returned to their domains, and the next deletion occasion began immediately. If at least one assignment was lost after a deletion occasion, then hill climbing recommenced.

Separate tests were made with penalty-adding and penalty selection. In addition, a "solution reuse" and a "restart" condition were tested with each penalty strategy. In the reuse condition, if an assignment had been lost, hill climbing started with the remaining assignments. Lost assignments were first replaced by valid values using the min-conflicts criterion; if there were still conflicts, hill climbing continued to look for a better solution. In the restart condition, after each assignment loss hill climbing began with preprocessing using the same variable ordering. This condition was included to evaluate solution reuse *per se*.

For the two lower constraint graph densities, penalty-discounting occurred after every 100 seconds of hill climbing; for density = 0.022, it occurred after every 1000 seconds. For penalty addition, the effective penalty was halved each time. For penalty selection (and for random walk with either strategy), the cutoff, originally the average penalty value, was doubled.

Results With values penalized after each deletion, both penalty strategies guided hill climbing to solutions with appreciably fewer 'bad' values (Figure 4). It should be noted that the means in Figure 4 are based on an entire run, during which time penalties were increasing from zero. As already indicated, there was also no attempt to select bad values that could be replaced or, conversely, that actually formed part of a solution. This intentional indifference to conditions for success suggests that these strategies are likely to be useful in practice, at least for comparable problems and distributions of failure.

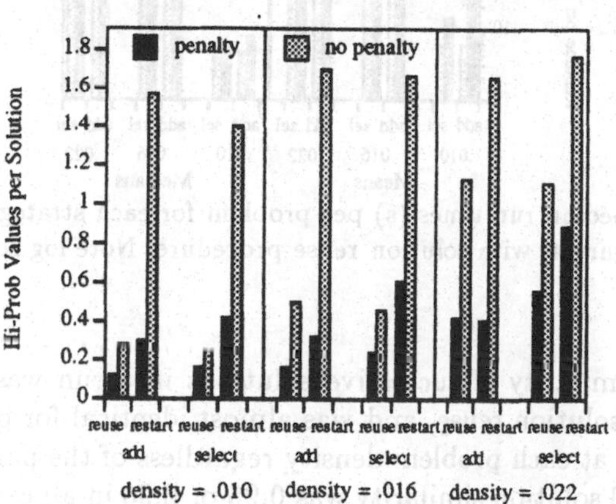

Fig. 4. Number of 'bad' (high-probability-of-deletion) values per solution. Columns are means of 100 test-means (one per problem). Each column-pair is from a separate experiment with tandem runs under penalty and non-penalty conditions. Solution reuse, restart, penalty-adding and penalty selection conditions (as described in text).

Adding penalties to the number of conflicts was somewhat more effective in avoiding high-probability values than selecting from among the true min-conflicts on the basis of penalties. However, penalty-adding was more costly in terms of run time (Figure 5): for most problems at each density, search was faster in the non-penalty condition, and there were always a few problems where incorporating penalties slowed hill climbing down appreciably. In contrast, for the penalty selection strategy there were no consistent differences between penalty and non-penalty conditions across problems, and occasional large differences in run time favored the penalty condition as often as the control.

In these tests, penalty strategies effected only a small decrease (10-15%) in mean value for the ratio of solutions to deletion occasions (a measure of overall solution stability). As noted above, a large difference could not be expected when high-probability-of-deletion values were chosen at random. In addition, in these experiments assignments could be lost following deletion of low-probability values, and an assignment included a third of the possible values. Subsidiary tests carried out in the same way as Experiment 1 showed that increasing p_p and decreasing p_l both led to larger reductions in the ratio of solutions to deletion occasions (up to 50% for individual problems), although there were also larger differences in run time.

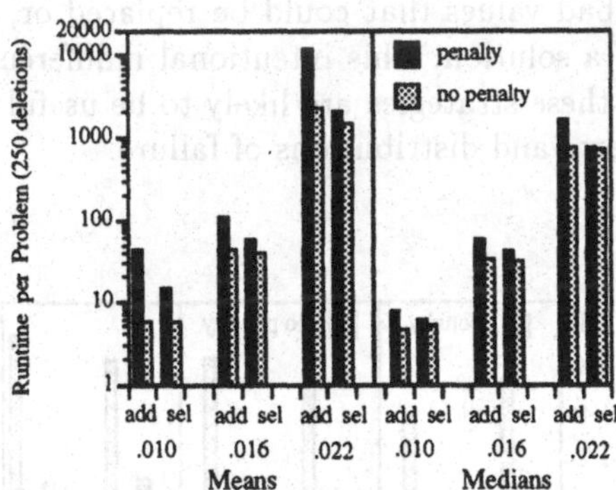

Fig. 5. Mean and median run times (s) per problem for each strategy and its control. Same tests as in Figure 4, with solution reuse procedure. Note log scale on ordinate.

The average similarity of successive solutions in a run was always high in experiments with solution reuse, and was almost identical for penalty and non-penalty conditions at each problem density regardless of the particular strategy. At density = 0.010 solution similarity was 0.95 or 0.96 in all cases, at density = 0.016 it was 0.89 or 0.90, and at density = 0.022 it was 0.69–0.72.

In comparison with "restarting" after assignment loss, solution reuse was very successful in avoiding bad values in solutions (Figure 4). Average similarity of successive solutions was also much lower with restart (0.75-6, 0.56-8, and 0.37-42 for successively higher densities (both strategies)), although hill climbing always began with an initial assignment based on the same variable and value ordering.

4.2 Experiment 2: Tests with Constraint Addition

Methods Random 3-color problems were used, with 100 variables and density = 0.035. No attempt was made to insure that the original problem had solutions, and for this density this was unlikely. In each test 100 problems were generated.

In setting up DCSPs, a probability of 0.6 was used for *fixed* constraints. For non-fixed constraints, p_p, here the probability that a constraint is associated with the higher probability of addition, was either 0.3 or 0.35. Two sets of high- and low-probability values were used: 0.2/0.002 and 0.3/0.003. These conditions were crossed, to give four tests in all. These combinations of probability-values give expected constraint graph densities of 0.014-0.015.

In the runtime phase, there were 250 occasions for change (constraint addition) in both penalty and non-penalty conditions. On each occasion, all non-fixed constraints were considered for addition, using the above probabilities. As in Experiment 1, if the existing solution remained valid after this procedure, the next occasion began immediately, and this was done until at least one variable assignment was made invalid, at which point hill climbing recommenced. During the penalty condition, tallies were kept for each constraint of the number of times it was added to the problem. Because of time constraints, only the solution reuse condition was tested. Penalty discounting was carried out as with the penalty selection procedure for lost values, using a time interval of 100 seconds. The measure of solution quality was the ratio of solutions to occasions for change.

Results With all four probability combinations, penalties improved the general measure of solution quality (Figure 6). The average degree of improvement was somewhat better than with value deletion for problems of comparable density (0.016). But in the present tests mean run time was 2-3 times greater under penalty conditions. Solution similarity was high in both penalty and non-penalty conditions, the average differing by 0.01 in each case.

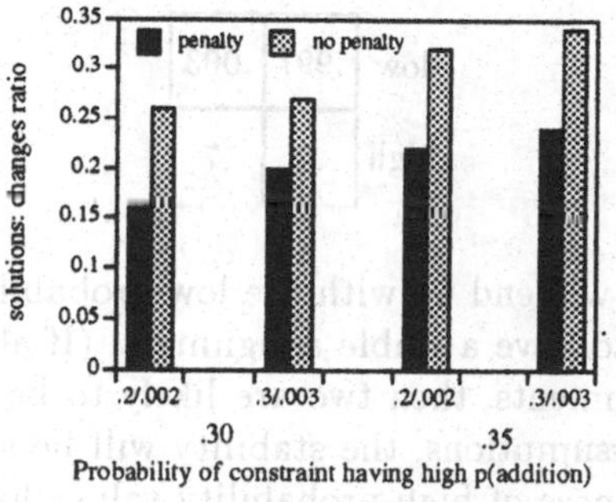

Fig. 6. Ratio of solutions to occasions for change for various probabilities of constraint addition (means of 100 test-means).

4.3 Discussion of Experiments 1 and 2

Strategies based on tracking changes with frequency tallies can improve stability. The experiments show that improvements occur frequently enough so that, in this respect, these techniques may have some generality of application. Of course, tests still need to be made on other types of problems.

With value loss, the penalty selection strategy for incorporating information into search sometimes handled the tradeoff between solution quality (stability) and efficiency very well. In particular, for the most difficult problems (density = 0.022) there was no essential difference in either summary measure (Figure 5).

Unfortunately, for constraint addition, the same type of strategy did incur a sizeable cost, while improving solution stability across the set of problems. Effects on cost were also found with value loss when the number of bad values was higher. Experience with a greater range of problems and conditions will be necessary to better determine when efficiency is markedly impaired.

Experiment 1 showed that, even without penalty information, solution reuse has a marked effect on stability, reflected in comparisons with the restart condition. (As expected, the former was also much more efficient.) Preliminary analysis suggests that two aspects of this procedure improve solution stability.

The first is an "avoidance" or "tabu" effect, which also holds for restart and any other DCSP procedure. During the time that a value is unavailable, it is tabooed for purposes of finding a solution. Since high probability-of-deletion values are more likely to be on the 'tabu list', this reduces the likelihood of their showing up in successive solutions. This effect was evaluated by running a variation on the restart condition in which lost values were put back before search was resumed. Under these conditions, for problems with density = 0.016, the number of bad values per solution increased from 1.5 to 2.5.

The second factor is a conservation of stable values by the reuse procedure. For example, consider a simple situation in which a high- and a low-probability value can both be assigned to a variable. For probability-values in Experiment 1, the transition probabilities for deletion occasions are:

	low	high
low	.997	.003
high	.3	.7

Obviously, this system will end up with the low-probability value assigned most often, i.e. it will tend to have a stable assignment. (If all three values can form part of complete assignments, then two are likely to be low-probability values, and under the same assumptions, the stability will be slightly greater.) In Experiment 1, if all instances of high-probability values had this character, there would be about eight of these transition matrices on average and 92 in which all transitions from a value to itself have probabilities of 0.997. When all variables have low-probability assignments, the probability of no-loss after deletion is 0.740. In this state, the probability of shifting to a high-probability value is

$1 - 0.976 = 0.024$. This simple model does not take account of transitions due to hill climbing, but it shows that, *ceteris paribus*, solution reuse should result in a fair degree of solution stability.

5 Further Experiments on Tracking Change

5.1 Finding Stable Solutions when Solution Cover is High

Experiments 1-2 show that techniques for tracking change can effect a general albeit modest improvement in solution stability. An important question is whether there are situations where improvement is more substantial. One possibility amenable to experimentation is the case where only a small proportion of the solutions are relatively stable. Without special strategies for finding these solutions, hill climbing may be unlikely to encounter them. The independent variable here will be called the *cover* of the solution set by the set of high-probability-of-deletion values. For purposes of experimentation, we simplify the situation by setting p_l to zero; coverage is then defined as the proportion of solutions that include at least one value subject to deletion.

Methods Like the experiments in the previous section, these experiments were based on tandem runs of penalty and non-penalty procedures over identical problems and deletion conditions. The differences were, (i) the high-probability-of-deletion values were the only values with a non-zero probability of deletion (fixed deletion set), (ii) a run ended when a fully stable solution was found, i.e., one with no assignments in the deletion set. For historical reasons, tests to date have only been run with the penalty-adding strategy.

Coloring problems with 100 variables and three colors were generated and tested as in Experiment 1. These problems had a density of 0.028, and the maximum number of solutions was 5 million. These specifications were made because solutions had to be counted repeatedly in generating deletion sets with specified degrees of cover.

For each double run, a deletion set of size 7 was chosen at random and the coverage calculated; this procedure was repeated until the coverage was in the specified range. Then hill climbing was carried out much as in the first set of experiments. After the first solution was found, a value in the deletion set was selected at random and deleted from the domain of its associated variable. If the current solution was made invalid by this deletion, then hill climbing recommenced and continued until it found a new solution. Then the value that had been deleted was replaced and another value was selected from the set. And so forth, until a solution was found that did not include any values in the deletion set. Three ranges of coverage were tested: 0.65-0.75, 0.85-0.95 and ≥ 0.99. Fifty problems were generated for each test. (For the 0.99 coverage, in four cases no deletion set giving this degree of coverage could be found within 1000 tries. As a result, statistics are based on 46 problems in this case.)

The measure of quality/stability in this experiment was the number of complete solutions found before finding a fully stable solution.

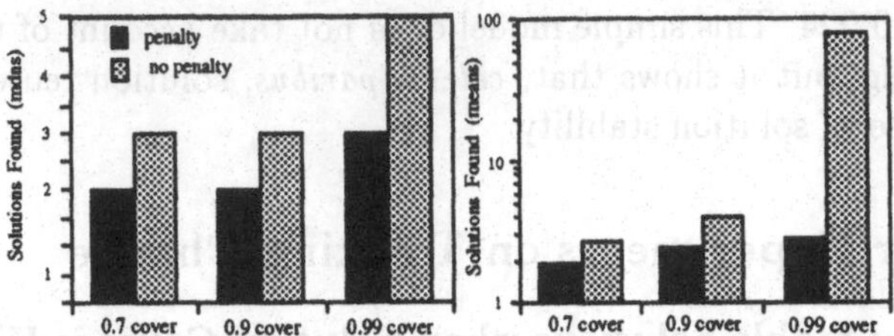

Fig. 7. Number of solutions found before finding one that is fully stable. Medians (left graph) and means (right graph) for penalty and non-penalty conditions as a function of degree of cover of the deletion set. Note log scale on ordinate of graph on right.

Results and Discussion The results show that, on average, use of penalties allows hill climbing to find a stable solution more efficiently, i.e., fewer solutions need to be found before finding one that is completely stable. This effect was found across a fairly wide range of cover (Figure 7).

With very high coverage there was considerable divergence between penalty and non-penalty conditions in mean number of solutions found before finding a stable one (Figure 7). This difference was largely due to cases in which hill climbing without penalties found a very large number of solutions (up to 2200). Although such cases formed a minority, they were by no means rare: for eight of the 46 tests, the ratio of solutions found for non-penalty and penalty conditions, respectively, was $\geq$ 10:1. This indicates that the penalty function was most effective in just those cases that posed the greatest problems for hill climbing. These effects carried over to run times, since for each condition differences in both medians and means were in favor of hill climbing with penalties.

5.2 Tests of Efficiency of Information Collection

If we have no *a priori* information about relative rates of change among elements, it is important to know something about the number of changes required before we can make intelligent decisions about stability. In particular, is it necessary for penalties to converge to basic rates (or probabilities) of change before they are useful? In addition, if the basic likelihood of loss is changing, we may only want to use the most recent information, and we would like to know how little information we need to track changes under these conditions.

Information on these questions was obtained empirically with a procedure like that of Experiment 1 in which penalties were only incremented on the first k deletion occasions. Since there were 250 occasions in all, then for 250 − k occasions, penalties remained constant. k was either 50, 10 or 3. These experiments were done with penalty selection and solution reuse; 50 problems with density = 0.016 were tested for each value of k.

With penalties based on 50 deletion occasions, the results were the same as in Experiment 1, where penalties accrued for all 250 sets of deletions. The average number of 'bad' values per solution was 0.48 with the basic hill climbing procedure and 0.15 with penalties. With penalties based on 10 deletion sets, the corresponding averages were 0.49 and 0.23, and with three sets they were 0.54 and 0.35.

We conclude that tracking value loss is an efficient way to gather information for finding stable solutions. Moreover, it is effective even when assumptions about convergence to underlying probabilities are clearly violated. In the present tests, after three sets of deletions the expected penalty for a high-probability value is about 1, while the expected number of low-probability values with penalties > 0 is between 2 and 3. So some high- and low-probability values will have penalties that are equal or in the 'wrong' direction, although their probabilities differ by a factor of 1000. Despite their poor quality as estimates in this case, penalties served to bias local search in the direction of more stable solutions.

6 Conclusions

In this paper we introduce the concept of solution stability for CSPs and consider one important application, recurrent DCSPs. In addition, we describe a set of methods that are successful in finding stable solutions and, in some cases, in dealing with the tradeoff between solution quality and search efficiency. We have also identified new concepts, such as solution cover, and considered basic issues such as efficiency in gaining information about change. Further issues raised by this work include complete vs. incomplete search for recurrent DCSPs, tracking solution loss vs. problem change, and optimization with respect to solution stability.

References

1. C. Bessière. Arc-consistency in dynamic constraint satisfaction problems. In *Proceedings AAAI-91*, pp. 221–226, 1991.
2. R. Dechter and A. Dechter. Belief maintenance in dynamic constraint networks. In *Proceedings AAAI-88*, pp. 37–42, 1988.
3. M. Drummond, J. Bresina, and K. Swanson. Just-in-case scheduling. In *Proceedings AAAI-94*, pp. 1098–1104, 1994.
4. H. Fargier and J. Lang. Uncertainty in constraint satisfaction problems: a probabilistic approach. In M. Clarke, R. Kruse, and S. Moral, editors, *Symbolic and Quantitative Approaches to Reasoning and Uncertainty, ECSQARU'93*, LNCS Vol. 747, pp. 97–104. Springer-Verlag, Berlin, 1993.
5. W. L. Hays. *Statistics for the Social Sciences (2nd Edit.)*. Holt, Rinehart and Winston, New York, NY, 1973.
6. G. Verfaillie and T. Schiex. Solution reuse in dynamic constraint satisfaction problems. In *Proceedings AAAI-94*, pp. 307–312, 1994.
7. R. J. Wallace. Analysis of heuristic methods for partial constraint satisfaction problems. In E. C. Freuder, editor, *Principles and Practice of Constraint Programming - CP'96*, LNCS Vol. 1118, pp. 482–496. Springer, Berlin, 1996.
8. R. J. Wallace and E. C. Freuder. Stable solutions for dynamic constraint satisfaction problems. In *CP-97 Workshop on Theory and Practice of Dynamic Constraint Satisfaction*, pp. 73–80, 1997.

Generation of Test Patterns for Differential Diagnosis of Digital Circuits

Francisco Azevedo and Pedro Barahona
{fa,pb}@di.fct.unl.pt
Dep. Informática, Universidade Nova de Lisboa, 2825 Monte da Caparica, Portugal

Objective. In a faulty digital circuit, many (single) faulty gates may explain the observed findings. It may be not practical (e.g. in VLSI chips) to test points in the circuit other than their input and output bits, so constraint technology was used to obtain input patterns that identify single faulty gates. However, two alternative faulty gates often have a large number of test patterns, but only a few, if any, differentiate them. We focus on obtaining test patterns that discriminate alternative faulty gates.

Technique. The technique of [2] to generate a test pattern for a faulty gate introduces new values, *d* and *notd*, and assigns d to the gate output. New truth tables cope with the new values, and the patterns generated force a *d* (or *notd*) to reach an output bit.

We adapted the technique to differentiate two faulty gates, not both faulty. The output of a gate is either independent of the faulty state of both gates, or depends on the faulty state of one of the gates alone or depends on either faulty states. We denote this latter case as m-X, meaning that the gate output takes value *X* if both gates are normal and *not X* if any of the gates is faulty. Similarly, d_1-X (d_2-X) denotes the output of a gate that depends solely on the faulty state of gate g_1 (g_2) and takes value X if g_1 (g_2) is normal and not X if it is faulty. We developed truth tables to cope with these new values, which depend on whether the gate is one of the potentially faulty.

For example, the table aside shows the output of faulty gate g_1, a not gate, both for stuck-at-0 and stuck-at-1 faults.

input	0	1	d_2-0	d_2-1
g_1 st.-at-0	d_1-1	0	m-1	d_2-0
g_1 st.-at-1	1	d_1-0	d_2-1	m-0

A differential test pattern produces either a d_1 or a d_2 signal at some output bit, and can be regarded as letting such signals propagate from gates g_1 and g_2 where they are produced to the output bit. Naïve analysis suggests that the output of a gate whose inputs depend on faults at both gates will not differentiate the two faults, but this is not correct. For example, a d_1-X signal "xor-ed" with a m-Y signal results in d_2-Z (where Z = X xor Y, and "and-ing" a d_1-1 with an m-0 results in d_2-0).

Results. We implemented the truth tables of the gates as constraints in an HCLP(FD) language [1], and obtained promising results in some ISCAS benchmarks. Circuit 'd3540' with 50 input bits and 22 output bits, 14 alternative faults were classified in 6 indistinguishable classes and differential patterns produced for them in 21.42 secs.

Future. The program has since been modified to differentiate two sets of faulty gates. We are developing a new version of the program where the gates are implemented as user-defined constraints in CLP over finite domains (0,1 plus m- and d-signals).

References

1. F. Menezes and P. Barahona, Defeasible Constraint Solving, in Over-Constrained Systems: Selected Papers, LNCS, vol.1106, Springer-Verlag, pp. 151-170, 1996.
2. H. Simonis, Test Generation using the Constraint Logic Programming Language CHIP, Procs 6th Int. Conf. on Logic Programming, MIT Press, pp 101-112, 1989.

Combine & Conquer: Genetic Algorithm and CP for Optimization

Nicolas Barnier and Pascal Brisset

École Nationale de l'Aviation Civile, 7 avenue Édouard Belin, B.P. 4005, F-31055 Toulouse Cedex 4, France, E-mail: {barnier,brisset}@recherche.enac.fr

Summary

We introduce a new optimization method based on a Genetic Algorithm (GA) combined with Constraint Satisfaction Problem (CSP) techniques. The approach is designed for combinatorial problems whose search spaces are too large and/or objective functions too complex for usual CSP techniques and whose constraints are too complex for conventional genetic algorithm. The main idea is the handling of sub-domains of the CSP variables by the genetic algorithm. The population of the genetic algorithm is made up of strings of sub-domains whose adaptation are computed through the resolution of the corresponding "sub-CSPs" which are somehow much easier than the original problem. We provide basic and dedicated recombination and mutation operators with various degrees of robustness. The first set of experimentations adresses a naïve formulation of a Vehicle Routing Problem (VRP). The results are quite encouraging as we outperform CSP techniques and genetic algorithm alone on these formulations.

Genetic algorithms are well suited to the quick and global exploration of a large search space to optimize any objective function (even a "black box" one, *i.e.* no hypothesis is required on the function) and are able to provide several solutions of "good quality".

Constraints satisfaction techniques are fitted to highly constrained problems for which the exhaustive exploration of their search spaces are conceivable. Such a method provides naturally feasible solutions.

We suggest to take advantage of the two approaches by combining hybridizing them:

- use of constraint satisfaction to compute feasible solutions on a subspace of the search space;
- use of a genetic algorithm to explore the space formed by the set of these subspaces and perform the optimization.

The ratio ρ of the size of a subspace to the size of the whole search space is the essential parameter of the hybridization : one can continuously pass from a pure CSP search ($\rho = 1$) to a pure stochastic search ($\rho = 0$, *i.e* a subspace is reduced to a single value).

Some Experiments on Learning Soft Constraints

Alessandro Biso, Francesca Rossi, and Alessandro Sperduti

Università di Pisa, Dipartimento di Informatica
Corso Italia 40, 56125 Pisa, Italy
E-mail: bisoale@cli.di.unipi.it {rossi,perso}@di.unipi.it

Classical constraint problems (CSPs) are a very expressive and natural formalism to specify many kinds of real-life problems. However, sometimes they are not very flexible when trying to represent real-life scenarios where the knowledge is not completely available nor crisp. For this reason, many extensions of the classical CSP framework have been proposed in the literature: fuzzy, partial, probabilistic, hierarchical. More recently, all these extensions have been unified in a general framework [1], called SCSP, which uses a semiring to associate with each tuple of values for the variables of each constraint an appropriate "degree of preference", which can also be interpreted as a cost, or an award, or others.

Sometimes, however, even SCSPs are not expressive enough, since one may know his/her preferences over some of the solutions but have no idea on how to code this knowledge into the SCSP. That is, one has a global idea about the *goodness* of a solution, but does not know the contribution of each single constraint to such a measure. In [2] this situation is addressed by using learning techniques based on gradient descent: it is assumed that the level of preference for some solutions (the *examples*) is known, and it is proposed to learn, from these examples, values to be associated with each constraint tuple, in a way that is compatible with the examples.

Here we make the technique proposed in [2] concrete: we identify its features, and we show the results of several experiments run by choosing various values of these features. The SCSP problems on which the experiments are run are randomly generated, in a way which is similar to the random generation of classical CSPs. The results are encouraging, and show that the proposed technique is both reasonable and promising. In fact, the final error in the levels of preferences which are learnt by our approach is small.

We also develop a variation of the basic learning technique which allows to get a reasonable result with a smaller number of examples, thus making the user role in the modeling phase even easier. This new technique is based on an incremental and interactive process, composed of several learning phases in sequence, which have new test sets each time, and training sets larger and larger.

References

1. S. Bistarelli, U. Montanari, and F. Rossi. Semiring-based Constraint Solving and Optimization. *Journal of the ACM*, 44(2):201–236, March 1997.
2. F. Rossi and A. Sperduti. Learning solution preferences in constraint problems. *Journal of Experimental and Theoretical Computer Science*, 1998. Vol 10.

Scheduling Multi-capacitated Resources Under Complex Temporal Constraints

Amedeo Cesta[1], Angelo Oddi[1], and Stephen F. Smith[2]

[1] IP-CNR, National Research Council of Italy
{amedeo,oddi}@pscs2.irmkant.rm.cnr.it
[2] The Robotics Institute, Carnegie Mellon University, Pittsburgh, PA (USA)
sfs@cs.cmu.edu

Extended Abstract. In this paper we develop and analyse CSP-based procedures for solving scheduling problems with metric temporal constraints (e.g. jobs' deadlines or separation constraints between couple of consecutive activities in a job) and multiple capacitated resources, referred to formally as the Multiple Capacitated Metric Scheduling Problem (MCM-SP). This work follows two different solution approaches used to identify resource capacity conflicts. (1) *Profile-based approaches* (e.g. [1]) - They consist of characterizing a resource demand as a function of time, identifying periods of overallocation in this demand profile, and incrementally performing "leveling actions" to (hopefully) ensure that resource usage peaks fall below the total capacity of the resource. (2) *Clique-based approaches* [3, 2] - Given a current schedule, this approach builds up a *conflicts graph* whose nodes are activities and whose edges represent overlapping resource capacity requests of the connected activities. Fully connected subgraphs (cliques) are identified and if the number of nodes in the clique is greater than resource capacity a conflict is detected.

Clique-based approaches perform more global analysis and offer greater accuracy in conflict detection in comparison with local pairwise profile-based analysis, but at a potentially much higher computational cost. In a previous paper [1], several profile-based solution procedures were developed and evaluated (in particular the ESTA algorithm), some of them descending from an approach proposed in the planning literature. Here we complete our analysis with a set of experiments which evaluate cost/performance tradeoffs on problems of increasing scale, varying both the tightness of temporal constraints and the size of resource capacity levels. In problem space regions which are highly constrained, clique-based approaches produces more and better quality solutions, even if they have a much higher computational cost than profile-based approaches, and the differential increases as resource capacity levels increase. In this less constrained circumstance, both methods perform comparably wrt solution quality, suggesting the advantage of the profile-based approaches over the clique-based ones.

References

1. A. Cesta, A. Oddi and S.F. Smith. Profile Based Algorithms to Solve Multiple Capacitated Metric Scheduling Problems. Proceedings of the Fourth International Conference on Artificial Intelligence Planning Systems (AIPS-98).
2. A. Cesta, A. Oddi and S.F. Smith. Scheduling Multi-Capacitated Resources under Complex Temporal Constraints. Technical Report CMU-RI-TR-98-17, The Robotics Institute - Carnegie Mellon University, Pittsburgh, PA 15213 USA.
3. P. Laborie and M. Ghallab. Planning with Sharable Resource Constraints. Proceedings of the International Joint Conference on Artificial Intelligence (IJCAI-95).

Implementing Global Constraints with Index-Sets and Constraint Templates

Yves Colombani

Dash Associates, Quinton Lodge, Binswood Av.
Leamington Spa, CV32 5TH, U.K.
yc@dash.co.uk

In order to improve the deductive power of finite domain constraint solvers usually redundant and global constraints are added to the constraint system. The objective of this work [2] is to develop a new constraint solving scheme designed as an extension of a classical arc-consistency algorithm. Associated to a declarative language, it allows the user to implement his own global relations without the need of manipulating internal structures of the solver or modifying in depth the original model of the studied problem. This system relies on two new structures: *index-sets* and *constraint templates*. The former consist in sets of integers used as indices over tables. They collect variables sharing some properties (for instance tasks in a scheduling problem assigned to the same machine). The latter are descriptions of constraints that must be applied (possibly) over selected sets of variables (for instance the fact that a set of tasks must be scheduled before another set). Both, set-index and constraint template definitions are evaluated dynamically and depend on the variables' domains. Indeed, the new constraints are automatically generated by the constraint solver based on the set contents and variable domain values. The index-set and constraint definition language uses a mathematic style notation. The definitions are compiled to the solver representation which can be directly handled by the propagation mechanism. This organisation guarantees a high level of efficiency.
A prototype based on these structures has been implemented [3] and is currently being tested on various problem types (*e.g.* [1, 4, 5]). The first results are promising.

References

[1] Y. Colombani. Constraint Programming: an Efficient and Practical Approach to Solving the Job-Shop Problem. In *Proceedings of CP'96*, LNCS 1118, Cambridge, MA, 1996. Springer-Verlag.

[2] Y. Colombani. *Un modèle de résolution de contraintes adapté aux problèmes d'ordonnancement. Un prototype et une application.* PhD thesis, LIM, Université Aix-Marseille II, 1997.

[3] Y. Colombani and S. Heipcke. The Constraint Solver SchedEns. Tutorial and Documentation. Technical Report 241, LIM, 1997.

[4] Y. Colombani and S. Heipcke. Julian's Problem: Personnel Assignment with Individual Skills and Preference Profiles. In *Proceedings of PACT'98*, London, 1998.

[5] S. Heipcke and Y. Colombani. A Global Constraint for Scheduling under Labour Resource Constraints. ECAI'98 Workshop on non binary constraints, 1998.

Generating Feasible Schedules for a Pick-Up and Delivery Problem

Eric Domenjoud, Claude Kirchner & Jianyang Zhou
{Eric.Domenjoud, Claude.Kirchner, Jianyang.Zhou}@loria.fr
Inria & Crin, 615, rue du jardin botanique, 54602 Villers-lès-Nancy, France

In this research, we study a transportation problem which is concerned with vehicle routing and driver scheduling for a bus station. The problem requires drivers to provide pick-up and delivery services to customers, subject to vehicle capacity limitation and time constraints. The objective is to efficiently schedule the fleet of vehicles for customer demand so as to reduce costs.

We present a complete constraint model and a solution method for solving the problem. For vehicle routing, a permutation constraint is used to obtain a total order for visiting all customer locations regardless of different vehicle routes; this provides a global planning over all routes. For driver scheduling, set partitioning constraints are used for assigning vehicles to requests. Based on this constraint model, efficient real-time response and optimization algorithms are constructed to generate feasible schedules for the problem.

Our specific problem comes from GIHP (Groupement pour l'insertion des personnes handicapées physiques) which provides transport services to handicapped people. The bus station possesses about 20 vehicles and receives up to 400 requests (800 locations to visit) daily. For GIHP, a transport scheduling system called ROUTER [2] has been developed using the constraint solver of NCL [4]. On a Pentium/300, real-time response for inserting a new request into an existing schedule for about 350 requests is kept under 30 seconds. Optimal insertion is kept under 2.5 minutes. Our algorithm improves average service time per request from about 25 minutes to 15-20 minutes.

References

[1] E. Domenjoud, C. Kirchner and J. Zhou. *A method for solving vehicle routing and scheduling problems.* ERCIM/COMPULOG Workshop on Constraints, Schloss Hagenberg, Austria, Oct. 1997.

[2] E. Domenjoud, C. Kirchner and J. Zhou. *Generating feasible schedules for a pick-up and delivery problem.* Technical report 98-R-142, Loria, 1998.

[3] J. Zhou. *A permutation-based approach for solving the job-shop problem.* Constraints, 2(2): 185-213, Oct. 1997.

[4] J. Zhou. *Designing and implementing a natural constraint language for solving combinatorial problems.* Technical report 97-R-199, Loria, 1997.

An Impartial Efficiency Comparison of FD Constraint Systems

Antonio J. Fernández[1]* and Patricia M. Hill[2]

[1] Departamento de Lenguajes y Ciencias de la Computación, E.T.S.I.I., 29071 Teatinos, Málaga, Spain afdez@lcc.uma.es

[2] School of Computer Studies, University of Leeds, Leeds, LS2 9JT, England hill@scs.leeds.ac.uk

CLP systems differ significantly in the efficiency of their execution so that a wrong choice for an application may be disastrous relative to the necessary performance. Thus, efficiency should be taken into account when choosing the best system for a particular application. In spite of this, there appeared to be no impartial efficiency information concerning CLP systems. In the research described here[1], we have compared, as fairly as possible, eight systems and provided detailed results concerning their speed and robustness.

Eight systems were compared, four black box: ECL^{i}PS^e 3.5.2, Oz 2.0, the Ilog SOLVER 3.1 and B-Prolog 2.1; and four glass box: clp(FD) 2.21, CHR (built on top of ECL^{i}PS^e 3.5.2), SICStus 3#5 and IF/Prolog 5.0. These were compared with respect to the performance of their constraint propagation. For a fair comparison, two very different labeling strategies were used: the naive labeling and the first fail labeling. As far as possible, the variable and value ordering was kept the same for all the systems. In addition, for the robustness comparison, the garbage collection was kept switched on in all the systems.

Seven (mostly well-known) benchmarks were used. The solutions (finding both the first answer and all possible answers) we chose were either supplied with the system, by the system implementers or first written by us and then improved by the implementers. All seven benchmarks were used in the efficiency tests but just two scalable ones were used for the robustness tests.

Ilog was the fastest system and also extremely robust. clp(FD) was also very fast but did not scale well with respect to the number of FD variables. Oz, SICStus and IF/Prolog had very similar performance figures and were about two to three times faster than ECL^{i}PS^e. IF/Prolog worked particularly well for first solution search (even sometimes better than clp(FD) and Ilog). SICStus and IF/Prolog were more robust than clp(FD), Oz, and ECL^{i}PS^e. However, of the two, SICStus has the greater robustness. B-Prolog was comparable to clp(FD) when there was only a small number of FD variables although, as B-Prolog lacked garbage collection, the performance deteriorated rapidly as the number increased. The slowest system was CHR. Two reasons for this: (1) the version used had been built on top of ECL^{i}PS^e (which itself had poor results) and (2) it was not designed for efficiency but for defining adequate constraints solvers for particular problems on specific domains.

* This work was partly supported by EPSRC grant GR/L19515.

[1] See also http://apolo.lcc.uma.es/~afdez/comparison/Efficiency.html

Optimizing with Constraints: A Case Study in Scheduling Maintenance of Electric Power Units

Daniel Frost and Rina Dechter

Dept. of Information and Computer Science,
University of California, Irvine, CA 92697-3425 U.S.A
{frost, dechter}@ics.uci.edu

A well-studied problem in the electric power industry is that of optimally scheduling preventative maintenance of power generating units within a power plant [1, 3]. The general purpose of determining a maintenance schedule is to determine the duration and sequence of outages of power generating units over a given time period, while minimizing operating and maintenance costs over the planning period, subject to various constraints. We show how maintenance scheduling can be cast as a constraint satisfaction problem and used to define the structure of randomly generated non-binary CSPs. These random problem instances are then used to evaluate several previously studied backtracking-based algorithms, including backjumping and dynamic variable ordering augmented with constraint learning and look-ahead value ordering [2].

We also define and report on a new "iterative learning" algorithm which solves maintenance scheduling problems in the following manner. In order to find an optimal schedule, the algorithm solves a series of CSPs with successively tighter cost-bound constraints. For the solution of each problem in the series constraint learning is applied, which involves recording additional constraints that are uncovered during search. However, instead of solving each problem in the series independently, after a problem is solved successfully with a certain cost-bound, the new constraints recorded by learning are used in subsequent attempts to find a schedule with a lower cost-bound. We show empirically that on a class of randomly generated maintenance scheduling problems iterative learning reduces the time required to find a good schedule.

References

1. J. F. Dopazo and H. M. Merrill. Optimal Generator Maintenance Scheduling using Integer Programming. *IEEE Trans. on Power Apparatus and Systems*, PAS-94(5):1537–1545, 1975.
2. Daniel Frost. *Algorithms and Heuristics for Constraint Satisfaction Problems.* PhD thesis, University of California, Irvine, CA 92697-3425, 1997.
3. J. Yellen, T. M. Al-Khamis, S. Vemuri, and L. Lemonidis. A decomposition approach to unit maintenance scheduling. *IEEE Trans. on Power Systems*, 7(2):726–731, 1992.

Some Surprising Regularities in the Behaviour of Stochastic Local Search

Holger H. Hoos and Thomas Stützle

FB Informatik, FG Intellektik, TU Darmstadt
Alexanderstr. 10, D-64283 Darmstadt, Germany
{hoos,stuetzle}@informatik.tu-darmstadt.de

This abstract gives a brief overview of our work presented in [3]. Our approach for characterising the run-time behaviour of stochastic local search (SLS) algorithms is based on a novel and adequate empirical methodology for evaluating SLS algorithms first used in [1] and presented in more detail in [2]: Instead of collecting simple statistics averaged over a large number of runs and large sets of instances, we are estimating and functionally characterising *run-time distributions* on single instances. The data thus obtained provides the basis for formulating hypotheses on the behaviour of SLS algorithms on problem distributions and across several domains. These hypotheses are then tested using standard statistical methodology like parameter estimation methods and goodness-of-fit tests.

Using this methodology, we obtain some novel and surprisingly general empirical results concerning the run-time behaviour of the most popular SLS algorithms for SAT and CSP. Our main result establishes that *on hard instances from a variety of randomised problem classes (Random-3-SAT at the phase transition) as well as encoded problems from other domains (like blocks world planning or graph colouring), the run-time behaviour of some of the most powerful SLS algorithms for both SAT and CSP can be characterised by exponential distributions.* This result has a number of significant implications, the most interesting of which might be the fact that *SLS algorithms displaying this type of behaviour can be easily parallelised with optimal speedup, or, equivalently, their performance cannot be improved by using restart.* As another consequence, the search performed by these algorithms can be interpreted as random picking in a dramatically reduced search-space. Therefore, besides the practical implications of our findings, these also suggest a new interpretation of the behaviour of SLS algorithms and raise a number of interesting questions.

For details, we refer the interested reader to the full paper [3], which is available at `http://www.intellektik.informatik.tu-darmstadt.de/~kipr/1998`.

References

1. H.H. Hoos. Aussagenlogische SAT-Verfahren und ihre Anwendung bei der Lösung des HC-Problems in gerichteten Graphen. *Masters Thesis, Darmstadt University of Technology, Computer Science Department*, 1996. English summary available at `http://www.intellektik.informatik.tu-darmstadt.de/ hoos/publ-ai.html`.
2. H.H. Hoos and T. Stützle. Evaluating Las Vegas Algorithms — Pitfalls and Remedies. *Proc. of UAI'98*, pages 238–245, 1998.
3. H.H. Hoos and T. Stützle. A Characterisation of the Run-time Behaviour of Stochastic Local Search. *Tech. Report AIDA-98-01, Darmstadt University of Technology*, 1998.

Modelling CSP Solution Algorithms with Petri Decision Nets

Stephan Pontow

TU Hamburg-Harburg, Dept. of Process Automation Techniques, 21071 Hamburg, Germany
Email : pontow@tu-harburg.de

Abstract. The constraint paradigm provides powerful concepts to represent and solve different kinds of planning problems. Typically a large and conflicting set of restrictions, objectives and preferences has to be considered for real planning problems. We introduce a unified formalism - called Petri decision nets - for representation and implementation of complex CSP solution algorithms. The formalism enables the consideration of the problem structure as well as given objectives and the usage of problem specific heuristics or expert knowledge. It is based on the fundamental assumption that *designing CSP solution algorithms means designing decision networks.*

Petri Decision Nets (PDN)

We use a synthesis of different Petri net approaches to represent decision networks. Each decision activity necessary to solve a CSP is represented as a single place within a PDN. The marking of a place denotes the execution of the associated decision process. Each place generates an output vector according to the result of the decision. Transitions control the decision flow. For each transition a firing condition is defined. It depends on the output vectors of the pre- and postplaces of the transition. A transition fires if all its preplaces are marked, all its postplaces are unmarked and the Boolean condition evaluates to *true*. The firing of the transitions in PDN is deterministic, controlled by the output vectors of the places. Integrating the concept of hierarchical Petri nets enables hierarchical structuring in PDN as well. Using the PDN formalism allows a more detailed and explicit representation of CSP solution algorithms. An example of a PDN is shown in Fig. 1.

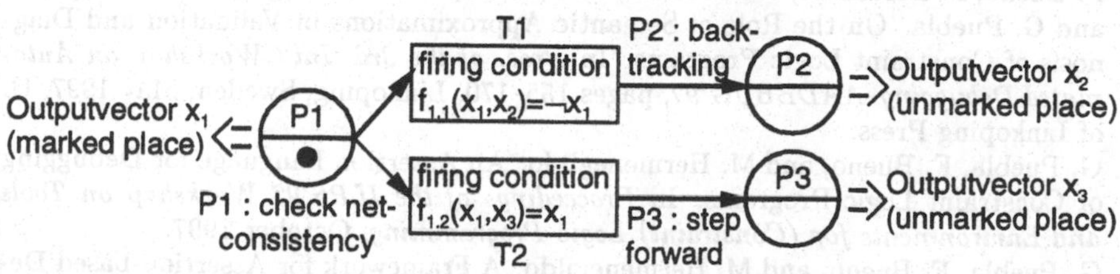

Fig. 1. Decision flow in Petri decision nets

A Framework for Assertion-Based Debugging in Constraint Logic Programming

Germán Puebla, *Francisco Bueno*, and *Manuel Hermenegildo*

{german,bueno,herme}@fi.upm.es
Department of Computer Science
Technical University of Madrid (UPM)

As constraint logic programming matures and larger applications are built, an increased need arises for advanced development and debugging environments. Assertions are linguistic constructions which allow expressing properties of programs. Classical examples of assertions are type declarations. However, herein we are interested in supporting a more general setting [3, 1] in which, on one hand assertions can be of a more general nature, including properties which are statically *undecidable*, and, on the other, only a small number of assertions may be present in the program, i.e., the assertions are *optional*. In particular, we do not wish to limit the programming language or the language of assertions unnecessarily in order to make the assertions statically decidable. Consequently, the proposed framework needs to deal throughout with *approximations* [2].

The framework we propose (see [4]) is aimed at detecting deviations of the program behavior (symptoms) w.r.t. the given assertions, either *statically* (at compile-time) or *dynamically* (at run-time). Our approach is strongly motivated by the availability of analyzers for constraint logic programs which can statically infer a wide range of properties, from types to determinacy or termination.

We provide techniques for using information from global analysis both to detect at compile-time assertions which do not hold (i.e., static symptoms) and assertions which hold for all possible executions (i.e., statically proved assertions). We also provide program transformations which introduce tests in the program for checking assertions at run-time. Both the static and the dynamic checking are provably safe in the sense that all errors flagged are definite violations of the specifications. A preliminary implementation and evaluation of the framework has been performed. Details can be found in [4].

References

1. F. Bueno, D. Cabeza, M. Hermenegildo, and G. Puebla. Global Analysis of Standard Prolog Programs. In *European Symposium on Programming*, number 1058 in LNCS, pages 108–124, Sweden, April 1996. Springer-Verlag.
2. F. Bueno, P. Deransart, W. Drabent, G. Ferrand, M. Hermenegildo,J. Maluszynski, and G. Puebla. On the Role of Semantic Approximations in Validation and Diagnosis of Constraint Logic Programs. In *Proc. of the 3rd. Int'l Workshop on Automated Debugging–AADEBUG'97*, pages 155–170, Linkoping, Sweden, May 1997. U. of Linkoping Press.
3. G. Puebla, F. Bueno, and M. Hermenegildo. An Assertion Language for Debugging of Constraint Logic Programs. In *Proceedings of the ILPS'97 Workshop on Tools and Environments for (Constraint) Logic Programming*, October 1997.
4. G. Puebla, F. Bueno, and M. Hermenegildo. A Framework for Assertion-based Debugging in Constraint Logic Programming. In *Proceedings of the JICSLP'98 Workshop on Types for CLP*, Manchester, UK, June 1998.

Parallel Execution Models for Constraint Propagation *

Alvaro Ruiz-Andino, Lourdes Araujo, Fernando Sáenz, and Jose Ruz

Department of Computer Science, University Complutense of Madrid
e-mail: alvaro@sip.ucm.es

Constraint propagation algorithms present inherent parallelism. Each constraint behaves as a concurrent process triggered by changes in the store of variables, updating the store in its turn. There is an inherent sequentiality, as well, since a constraint must be executed only as the consequence of a previous execution of another constraint. We have developed different parallel execution models of constraint propagation for MIMD distributed memory machines. We have adopted the *indexical scheme*, an adequate approach to achieve consistency for n-ary constraints. The proposed models arise from two techniques, dynamic and static, for scheduling constraint executions (assignment of constraint executions to processing elements). In the static scheduling models the constraint graph is divided into N partitions, which are executed in parallel on N processors. We have investigated an important issue affecting performance, the criterion to establish the graph partition in order to balance the run-time workload. In the dynamic scheduling models, any processor can execute any constraint, improving the workload balance. However, a coordination mechanism is required to ensure a sound order in the execution of constraints. We have designed coordination mechanisms for both centralised and distributed control schemes. Several parallel processing methods for solving Constraint Satisfaction Problems have been proposed. [1] and [3] must be remarked in relation with our work.

These execution models have been implemented in C, developed and tested on a CRAY T3E multiprocessor. Benchmarks considered so far exhibit a speedup between three and five, though better results may be expected for larger problems. The study of the distribution of constraints among processors has shown that a strongly connected partitioning is worse than a heuristic distribution that balances the ready set. Tests on broadcast frequency revealed the convenience of an immediate update. The dynamic model exhibits lower speedups than the static model.

References

1. Baudot, B., Deville, Y.: Analysis of Distributed Arc-Consistency Algorithms. Technical Report 97-07. University of Louvain. Belgium (1997).
2. Ruiz-Andino, A., Araujo, L., Ruz, J.: Parallel constraint satisfaction and optimisation. The PCSO system. Technical Report 71.98. Department of Computer Science. Universidad Complutense de Madrid, Spain. (1998).
3. Zhang, Y., Mackworth, K.: Parallel and Distributed Finite Constraint Satisfaction: Complexity, Algorithms and Experiments. Parallel Processing for Artificial Intelligence. Elsevier (1993).

* Supported by project TIC95-0433.

Using Blocks for Constraint Satisfaction

B. Seybold[1], F. Metzger[2], G. Ogan[2], and K. Simon[1]

[1] Institute for Theoretical Computer Science
[2] Institute for Manufacturing Technology and Machine Tools
ETH Zurich
{seybold,simon}@inf.ethz.ch, {metzger,ogan}@iwf.bepr.ethz.ch

The assembly problem is the spatial joining of separate rigid bodies within a CAD/CAM-system. The solution to the assembly does not only need to contain one consistent instantiation, but also qualitative information. In particular, this covers the localization of redundancy and remaining degrees of freedom in the mechanism. Although it is natural to model the assembly as a constraint satisfaction problem (CSP), solving remains a difficult task.

In general, a CSP can be attacked by two strategies: consistency enforcement and search. Algorithms work best if they combine these strategies in a clever way. When modeling the assembly problem as a CSP, one is confronted with two special conditions. First, the variable domains are continuous. Second, constraints are not arbitrary, but are conjunctions of instantiated predefined constraint types. Thus, search is not possible because of the continuous domains and numeric iterative or interval approaches deliver no information on degrees of freedom and redundancy. Therefore, pure consistency enforcement, which has many drawbacks in general CSPs, is the best choice.

In this poster, we discuss how consistency can be enforced in assembly problems while preserving redundancy information. For this purpose, we introduce k-block-consistency (k-BC), which only requires support for tuples of the same biconnected component (block). BC is weaker than ordinary consistency and can therefore be computed more efficiently. Nevertheless, k-block-consistency is sufficient for k-consistency if the used variable ordering is prefix-connected, i.e. the subgraphs induced by the prefixes of the ordering are connected.

Redundancy and inconsistency can be located on the block level. Due to the fact that each solution as a whole can be moved arbitrarily in space without becoming inconsistent, each value for each variable will always have a support in any other variable. Furthermore, BC does preserve the block structure. During BC enforcement, redundancy and inconsistency are not spread across block borders and can therefore be located properly.

The width is an important indicator for the complexity of constraint satisfaction problems. The width of the block induced subgraphs and of the whole graph are closely related. The width k of a graph is bounded by $k_{max} \leq k \leq k_{max} + 1$ where k_{max} is the maximum width of the block induced subgraphs.

Full paper: *Using Blocks for Constraint Satisfaction*, B. Seybold, F. Metzger, G. Ogan, and K. Simon. Technical Report 297, ETH Zurich, Institute of Theoretical Computer Science, May 1998.

Adaptive Solving of Equations over Rational Trees*

Armin Wolf

GMD – German National Research Center for Information Technology
GMD FIRST, Rudower Chaussee 5, D-12489 Berlin, Germany
E-mail: **armin@first.gmd.de** URL: **http://www.first.gmd.de**

The solution of *Dynamic Constraint Satisfaction Problems* (DCSPs) in *Constraint Logic Programming* (CLP) basically requires a solution of dynamically changing systems of syntactical equations over the rational trees.

For instance, let U, V, X, Y, Z be variables, c be a constant, f, g be function symbols and $\{X \doteq f(X,Y), f(Z,c) \doteq X, U \doteq V, V \doteq U, g(c) \doteq Z\}$ be a set of syntactical equations. Suppose that all but the last equations are considered and the rational solved form

$$X \doteq f(X,Y), Z \doteq f(X,Y), Y \doteq c, U \doteq V.$$

is calculated. Given the last equation, inconsistency is detected, because the two equations $g(c) \doteq Z$ and $Z \doteq f(X,Y)$ are unsolvable. For an adaptation of the rational solved form and the decision about the consistency after the deletion of the equation $f(Z,c) \doteq X$ in CLP we have the opportunity to backtrack to the first equation $X \doteq f(X,Y)$ and then recalculate the solution. A closer examination shows that backtracking is not really necessary. Only the bindings $Z \doteq f(X,Y)$ and $Y \doteq c$ depend on the deleted equation. The binding $U \doteq V$ and the equation $V \doteq U$ are completely independent. Thus, for an adaptation it is sufficient to keep the bindings $X \doteq f(X,Y), U \doteq V$ and reconsider the equation $g(c) \doteq Z$.

Based on this deeper understanding we developed an unification algorithm, which uses truth maintenance techniques to maintain a solved form of a set of equations over the rational trees. Therefore, each given equation is marked with a set of arbitrary identifiers, called label, to distinguish equations or sets of equations one potentially wants to delete. Furthermore, each derived binding is marked with the union of the labels of the equations and bindings it depends on. The unification algorithm keeps track of which input equations influence which output bindings in the rational solved form. The algorithm also keeps the input equations that were needed to adapt the bindings after any deletions, e. g.

$$\begin{aligned}&\mathsf{unify}([\langle X \doteq f(X,Y)\rangle^{\{1\}}, \langle f(Z,c) \doteq X\rangle^{\{2\}}, \langle U \doteq V\rangle^{\{3\}}, \langle V \doteq U\rangle^{\{4\}}, \langle g(c) = Z\rangle^{\{5\}}])\\ &= (\underbrace{\bot}_{\textbf{inconsistency}}, \underbrace{\{\langle X \doteq f(X,Y)\rangle^{\{1\}}, \langle Z \doteq f(X,Y)\rangle^{\{1,2\}}, \langle Y \doteq c\rangle^{\{1,2\}}, \langle U \doteq V\rangle^{\{3\}}\}}_{\textbf{rational solved form}},\\ &\quad \underbrace{[\langle f(Z,c) \doteq X\rangle^{\{2\}}, \langle V \doteq U\rangle^{\{4\}}, \langle g(c) = Z\rangle^{\{5\}}]}_{\textbf{equations required for adaptation}}) .\end{aligned}$$

* The full paper is available at **ftp://ftp.first.gmd.de/pub/plan/cp98-wolf.ps**.

Optimal Placement of Base Stations in Wireless Indoor Telecommunication*

Thom Frühwirth[1] Pascal Brisset[2]

[1] Ludwig-Maximilians-Universität München (LMU)
Oettingenstrasse 67, D-80538 Munich, Germany
fruehwir@informatik.uni-muenchen.de
http://www.informatik.uni-muenchen.de/~fruehwir/
[2] Ecole Nationale de l'Aviation Civile (ENAC)
7 Av. Edouard Belin, BP 4005, F-31055 Toulouse Cedex, France
Pascal.Brisset@recherche.enac.fr

Abstract. Planning of local wireless communication networks is about installing base stations (small radio transmitters) to provide wireless devices with strong enough signals. POPULAR is an advanced industrial prototype that allows to compute the minimal number of base stations and their location given a blue-print of the installation site and information about the materials used for walls and ceilings. It does so by simulating the propagation of radio-waves using ray tracing and by subsequent optimization of the number of base stations needed to cover the whole building. Taking advantage of state-of-the-art techniques for programmable application-oriented constraint solving, POPULAR is among the first practical tools that can optimally plan wireless communication networks.

1 Introduction

Mobile communication has become literally ubiquitous these days. According to a press release of British Telecommunications Plc and MCI Communications Corp of September 1996, there are 60 Mill. mobile phones worldwide (compare this figure to the world's 50 Mill. fax numbers and 40 Mill. email addresses). More and more, mobile communications also comes to company sites by means of local, indoor wireless communication networks. No cabling is required and the employees can be reached at any time at any place.

Current systems are cellular in that a base station (sender, transmitter) controls the links to the tranceivers. A (radio) cell is the space that is covered by a single base station. For buildings, multi-cellular systems are required, because walls and floors absorb part of the radio signal.

Today, the number and positioning of base stations is estimated by an experienced sales person. Computer-aided planning promises to ease some of the

* Work was done while the authors were at ECRC, Munich, Germany

difficulties encountered. An advanced prototype, POPULAR (Planning of Picocellular Radio) [3, 4], was developed in collaboration with industry and research institutions in Germany: The Siemens Research and Development Department (ZFE), the Siemens Personal Networks Department (PN), the European Computer-Industry Research Center (ECRC) and the Institute of Communication Networks at the Aachen University of Technology.

Given a blue-print of the building and information about the materials used for walls and ceilings, POPULAR computes the minimal number of base stations and their location by simulating the propagation of radio-waves using ray tracing and subsequent optimization of the number of base stations needed to cover the whole building.

The authors implemented a first protoype in a few months in the constraint logic programming language ECL^{i}PS^e [6] while at ECRC in 1995. The language includes a library for Constraint Handling Rules (CHR) [5], which are a high-level language extension to implement arbitrary constraint systems. The CHR library was essential for a rapid, flexible and efficient implementation of the constraints that appear in this optimization problem. Based on this prototype, J.-R. Molwitz, a student from the University of Aachen, implemented POPULAR within one man-year while at Siemens.

2 Simulation of Radio Cells by Ray-Tracing

Radio wave propagation suffers mainly from the following effects:

- attenuation (weakening) of the signal due to distance,
- shadowing (absorption) through obstacles,
- multipath propagation due to reflection and diffraction.

The COST[3] Subgroup 'Propagation Models' proposed the so-called *path loss model* [1] to describe these effects. The model is based on the power balance of wireless transmission. It combines a distance dependent term with correction factors for extra path loss due to floors and walls of the building in the propagation path. To take reflection and multipath effects into account, a *fading reserve* (fade margin) is introduced. We also extended the model to take the directional effect of an antenna into account, since antennas do not beam with the same energy in every direction.

In the simulation phase, the characteristics of the building are computed using of test points. Each test point represents a possible receiver position. The test points are placed on a 3-dimensional grid inside the volume that should be covered. For each test point the space where a base station can be put to cover the test point, the "radio cell", is calculated. If the test grid is sufficiently small (several per squaremeter), we can expect that if two neighbouring test points are covered, the space inbetween - hence the whole building - can also be covered.

Ray tracing simulates the propagation of radio waves through the walls and ceilings of the building. To get to the point of minimal sensitivity (i.e. maximal

[3] European Cooperation in the field Of Scientific and Technical research

permissible path loss), each path must be followed through the whole building. The values of antenna attenuation in the direction of the path, the path loss due to the distance and the insertion losses due to intersections of the path with walls and floors are added up to the maximal permissible path loss. The resulting end points are used to describe the hull of the radio cell. Note that the radio cell will usually be a rather odd-shaped object, since the received power may exhibit discontinuities because of tiny changes in the location - such as a move around the corner.

3 Constraint-Based Optimization

For each of the resulting radio cells a constraint is set up that there must be a location of a base station (geometrically speaking, a point) somewhere in that space. Then, we try to find locations that are in as many cells at the same time as possible. This means that a base station at one of these locations will cover several test points at once. Thus the possible locations are constrained to be in the intersections of the cells covered. In this way, a first solution is computed. Next, to minimize the number of base stations, we use a *branch-and-bound method.* It consists in repeatedly searching for a solution with a smaller number of base stations until the minimal number is found. The constraint solver was implemented using Constraint Handling Rules (CHR) [5], which are essentially multi-headed guarded rules that rewrite constraints into simpler ones until they are solved.

In a first attempt restricted to two dimensions, we approximated a cell by a single rectangle. The 2-D coordinates are of the form `X#Y`, rectangles are orthogonal to the coordinate system and are represented by a pair, composed of their left lower and right upper corner coordinates. For each cell, simply a constraint `inside(Sender, Rectangle)` is imposed, where `Sender` refers to a point that must be inside the `Rectangle`.

```
not_empty @ inside(S,A#B-C#D) ==> A<C,B<D.
intersect @ inside(S,A1#B1-C1#D1),inside(S,A2#B2-C2#D2) <=>
        A is max(A1,A2), B is max(B1,B2),
        C is min(C1,C2), D is min(D1,D2),
        inside(S,A#B-C#D).
```

The first rule (named `not_empty`) says that the constraint `inside(S,A#B-C#D)` is only valid if also the condition `A<C,B<D` is fulfilled, so that the rectangle has a non-empty area. The `intersect` rule says that if a base station location `S` is constrained by two `inside` constraints to be in two rectangles at once, we can replace these two constraints by a single `inside` constraint whose rectangle is computed as the intersection of the two initial rectangles.

To compute a solution, after we have set up all the `inside` constraints, we try to equate as many base stations as possible. Equating base stations causes the `intersect` rule to fire with the constraints associated with the base stations. As a result of this labeling procedure, a base stations location will be constrained more and more and thus the `intersect` rule will be applied again and again until the rectangle becomes very small and finally empty. Then the `not_empty` rule applies, causes failure and so initiates chronological backtracking that will lead to another choice.

It took just 10 minutes to extend this solver so that it works with union of rectangles, that can describe the cell more accurately - actually to any desired degree of precision. The union corresponds to a disjunctive constraint of the form `inside(S,R1) or inside(S,R2) or ... or inside(S,Rn)` which is more compactly implemented as `inside(S,[R1,R2,...,Rn])`. The subsequent lifting to 3 dimensions just amounted to adding a third coordinate and code analogous to the one for the other dimensions.

4 Evaluation

Taking advantage of state-of-the-art techniques for programmable application-oriented constraint solving, POPULAR was among the first practical tools that could optimally plan wireless communication networks. While we worked on POPULAR, without knowing from each other, the WiSE tool [2] was developed with exactly the same functionality. WiSE is written in about 7500 lines of C++. For optimization WiSE uses an adaptation of the Nelder-Mead direct search method that optimizes the percentage of the building covered. WiSE has been patented and is in commercial use by Lucent Technologies since 1997 to plan their DEFINITY Wireless Business System - PWT. Another approach [7] uses the Nelder-Mead method for continuous space and Hopfield Neural Networks for a modelling in discrete space. The authors shortly mention a tool called IWNDT written in C.

For a typical office building, an optimal placement is found by POPULAR within a few minutes. This is impressive since everything (including ray tracing and a graphical user interface) was implemented in a CLP language. The CLP code is just about 4000 lines with more than half of it for graphics and user interface. The overall quality of the placements produced is comparable to that of a human expert. The precision is influenced by the underlying path loss model with its the fading reserve, the number of rays used in the simulation and the approximation of radio cells by unions of rectangles.

The result of covering a medieval monastery is shown in Figure 1, where four base stations are needed. If more than one base station covers a region, it is attributed to the base station that provides the strongest signal.

References

[1] COST 231 'Propagation Models' Subgroup, Building Penetration Losses, Report COST 231 TD (90) 116, Darmstadt, Germany, December 1990.

[2] S. J. Fortune, D. M. Gay, B. W. Kernighan et al., WiSE Design of Indoor Wireless Systems, IEEE Computational Science and Engineering, Vol. 2, No. 1, pp. 58-68, Spring, 1995.

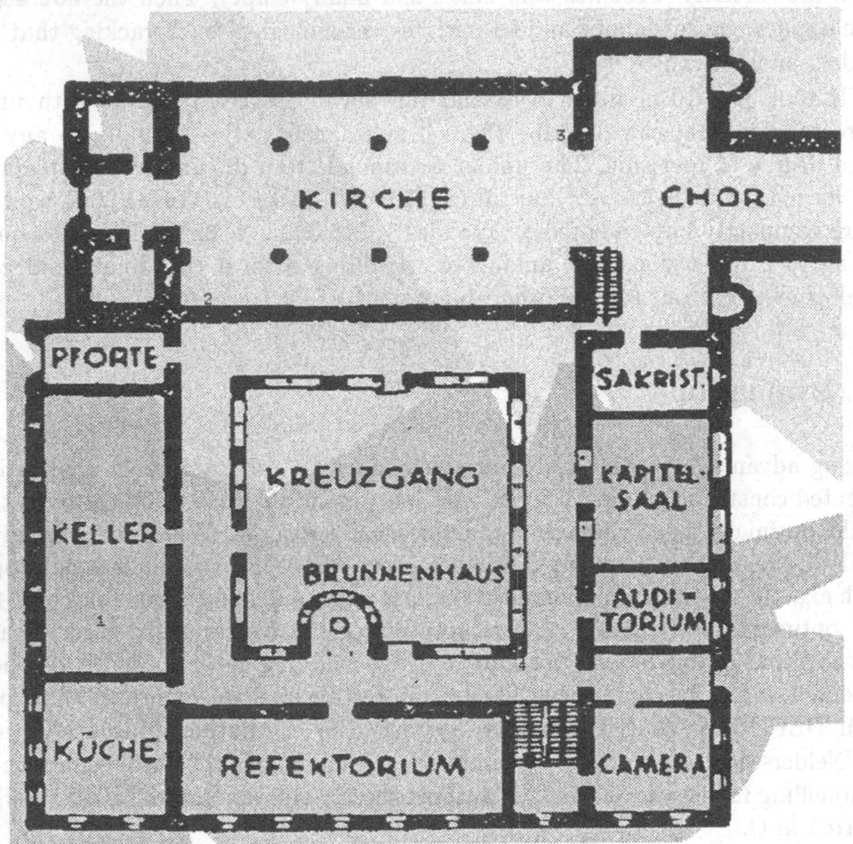

Fig. 1. Covering a medieval monastery

[3] T. Frühwirth, J.-R. Molwitz and P. Brisset, Planning Cordless Business Communication Systems, IEEE Expert Magazine, Special Track on Intelligent Telecommunications, February 1996.

[4] T. Frühwirth and P. Brisset, Optimal Planning of Digital Cordless Telecommunication Systems, Third International Conference on The Practical Application of Constraint Technology (PACT97), London, U.K., April 1997.

[5] T. Frühwirth, Theory and Practice of Constraint Handling Rules, Special issue on constraint logic programming (K. Marriott and P. J. Stuckey, Eds.), Journal of Logic Programming, Vol 37(1-3), pp 95-138, October 1998.

[6] M. Wallace, St. Novello and J. Schimpf, ECLiPSe: A Platform for Constraint Logic Programming, Technical Report, IC-Parc, Imperial College, London, August 1997.

[7] D. Stamatelos and A. Ephremides, Spectral Efficiency and Optimal Base Placement for Indoor Wireless Networks, IEEE Journal on Selected Areas in Communications, Vol. 14, No.4, May 1996.

Author Index

Springer and the environment

At Springer we firmly believe that an international science publisher has a special obligation to the environment, and our corporate policies consistently reflect this conviction.

We also expect our business partners – paper mills, printers, packaging manufacturers, etc. – to commit themselves to using materials and production processes that do not harm the environment. The paper in this book is made from low- or no-chlorine pulp and is acid free, in conformance with international standards for paper permanency.

Lecture Notes in Computer Science

For information about Vols. 1–1436

please contact your bookseller or Springer-Verlag

Vol. 1437: S. Albayrak, F.J. Garijo (Eds.), Intelligent Agents for Telecommunication Applications. Proceedings, 1998. XII, 251 pages. 1998. (Subseries LNAI).

Vol. 1438: C. Boyd, E. Dawson (Eds.), Information Security and Privacy. Proceedings, 1998. XI, 423 pages. 1998.

Vol. 1439: B. Magnusson (Ed.), System Configuration Management. Proceedings, 1998. X, 207 pages. 1998.

Vol. 1440: K.S. McCurley, C.D. Ziegler (Eds.), Advances in Cryptology 1981 – 1997. Proceedings. Approx. XII, 260 pages. 1998.

Vol. 1441: W. Wobcke, M. Pagnucco, C. Zhang (Eds.), Agents and Multi-Agent Systems. Proceedings, 1997. XII, 241 pages. 1998. (Subseries LNAI).

Vol. 1442: A. Fiat. G.J. Woeginger (Eds.), Online Algorithms. XVIII, 436 pages. 1998.

Vol. 1443: K.G. Larsen, S. Skyum, G. Winskel (Eds.), Automata, Languages and Programming. Proceedings, 1998. XVI, 932 pages. 1998.

Vol. 1444: K. Jansen, J. Rolim (Eds.), Approximation Algorithms for Combinatorial Optimization. Proceedings, 1998. VIII, 201 pages. 1998.

Vol. 1445: E. Jul (Ed.), ECOOP'98 – Object-Oriented Programming. Proceedings, 1998. XII, 635 pages. 1998.

Vol. 1446: D. Page (Ed.), Inductive Logic Programming. Proceedings, 1998. VIII, 301 pages. 1998. (Subseries LNAI).

Vol. 1447: V.W. Porto, N. Saravanan, D. Waagen, A.E. Eiben (Eds.), Evolutionary Programming VII. Proceedings, 1998. XVI, 840 pages. 1998.

Vol. 1448: M. Farach-Colton (Ed.), Combinatorial Pattern Matching. Proceedings, 1998. VIII, 251 pages.1998.

Vol. 1449: W.-L. Hsu, M.-Y. Kao (Eds.), Computing and Combinatorics. Proceedings, 1998. XII, 372 pages. 1998.

Vol. 1450: L. Brim, F. Gruska, J. Zlatuška (Eds.), Mathematical Foundations of Computer Science 1998. Proceedings, 1998. XVII, 846 pages. 1998.

Vol. 1451: A. Amin, D. Dori, P. Pudil, H. Freeman (Eds.), Advances in Pattern Recognition. Proceedings, 1998. XXI, 1048 pages. 1998.

Vol. 1452: B.P. Goettl, H.M. Halff, C.L. Redfield, V.J. Shute (Eds.), Intelligent Tutoring Systems. Proceedings, 1998. XIX, 629 pages. 1998.

Vol. 1453: M.-L. Mugnier, M. Chein (Eds.), Conceptual Structures: Theory, Tools and Applications. Proceedings, 1998. XIII, 439 pages. (Subseries LNAI).

Vol. 1454: I. Smith (Ed.), Artificial Intelligence in Structural Engineering. XI, 497 pages. 1998. (Subseries LNAI).

Vol. 1456: A. Drogoul, M. Tambe, T. Fukuda (Eds.), Collective Robotics. Proceedings, 1998. VII, 161 pages. 1998. (Subseries LNAI).

Vol. 1457: A. Ferreira, J. Rolim, H. Simon, S.-H. Teng (Eds.), Solving Irregularly Structured Problems in Prallel. Proceedings, 1998. X, 408 pages. 1998.

Vol. 1458: V.O. Mittal, H.A. Yanco, J. Aronis, R-. Simpson (Eds.), Assistive Technology in Artificial Intelligence. X, 273 pages. 1998. (Subseries LNAI).

Vol. 1459: D.G. Feitelson, L. Rudolph (Eds.), Job Scheduling Strategies for Parallel Processing. Proceedings, 1998. VII, 257 pages. 1998.

Vol. 1460: G. Quirchmayr, E. Schweighofer, T.J.M. Bench-Capon (Eds.), Database and Expert Systems Applications. Proceedings, 1998. XVI, 905 pages. 1998.

Vol. 1461: G. Bilardi, G.F. Italiano, A. Pietracaprina, G. Pucci (Eds.), Algorithms – ESA'98. Proceedings, 1998. XII, 516 pages. 1998.

Vol. 1462: H. Krawczyk (Ed.), Advances in Cryptology - CRYPTO '98. Proceedings, 1998. XII, 519 pages. 1998.

Vol. 1463: N.E. Fuchs (Ed.), Logic Program Synthesis and Transformation. Proceedings, 1997. X, 343 pages. 1998.

Vol. 1464: H.H.S. Ip, A.W.M. Smeulders (Eds.), Multimedia Information Analysis and Retrieval. Proceedings, 1998. VIII, 264 pages. 1998.

Vol. 1465: R. Hirschfeld (Ed.), Financial Cryptography. Proceedings, 1998. VIII, 311 pages. 1998.

Vol. 1466: D. Sangiorgi, R. de Simone (Eds.), CONCUR'98: Concurrency Theory. Proceedings, 1998. XI, 657 pages. 1998.

Vol.1467: C. Clack, K. Hammond, T. Davie (Eds.), Implementation of Functional Languages. Proceedings, 1997. X, 375 pages. 1998.

Vol. 1468: P. Husbands, J.-A. Meyer (Eds.), Evolutionary Robotics. Proceedings, 1998. VIII, 247 pages. 1998.

Vol. 1469: R. Puigjaner, N.N. Savino, B. Serra (Eds.), Computer Performance Evaluation. Proceedings, 1998. XIII, 376 pages. 1998.

Vol. 1470: D. Pritchard, J. Reeve (Eds.), Euro-Par'98: Parallel Processing. Proceedings, 1998. XXII, 1157 pages. 1998.

Vol. 1471: J. Dix, L. Moniz Pereira, T.C. Przymusinski (Eds.), Logic Programming and Knowledge Representation. Proceedings, 1997. IX, 246 pages. 1998. (Subseries LNAI).

Vol. 1473: X. Leroy, A. Ohori (Eds.), Types in Compilation. Proceedings, 1998. VIII, 299 pages. 1998.

Vol. 1474: F. Mueller, A. Bestavros (Eds.), Languages, Compilers, and Tools for Embedded Systems. Proceedings, 1998. XIV, 261 pages. 1998.

Vol. 1475: W. Litwin, T. Morzy, G. Vossen (Eds.), Advances in Databases and Information Systems. Proceedings, 1998. XIV, 369 pages. 1998.

Vol. 1476: J. Calmet, J. Plaza (Eds.), Artificial Intelligence and Symbolic Computation. Proceedings, 1998. XI, 309 pages. 1998. (Subseries LNAI).

Vol. 1477: K. Rothermel, F. Hohl (Eds.), Mobile Agents. Proceedings, 1998. VIII, 285 pages. 1998.

Vol. 1478: M. Sipper, D. Mange, A. Pérez-Uribe (Eds.), Evolvable Systems: From Biology to Hardware. Proceedings, 1998. IX, 382 pages. 1998.

Vol. 1479: J. Grundy, M. Newey (Eds.), Theorem Proving in Higher Order Logics. Proceedings, 1998. VIII, 497 pages. 1998.

Vol. 1480: F. Giunchiglia (Ed.), Artificial Intelligence: Methodology, Systems, and Applications. Proceedings, 1998. IX, 502 pages. 1998. (Subseries LNAI).

Vol. 1481: E.V. Munson, C. Nicholas, D. Wood (Eds.), Principles of Digital Document Processing. Proceedings, 1998. VII, 152 pages. 1998.

Vol. 1482: R.W. Hartenstein, A. Keevallik (Eds.), Field-Programmable Logic and Applications. Proceedings, 1998. XI, 533 pages. 1998.

Vol. 1483: T. Plagemann, V. Goebel (Eds.), Interactive Distributed Multimedia Systems and Telecommunication Services. Proceedings, 1998. XV, 326 pages. 1998.

Vol. 1484: H. Coelho (Ed.), Progress in Artificial Intelligence – IBERAMIA 98. Proceedings, 1998. XIII, 421 pages. 1998. (Subseries LNAI).

Vol. 1485: J.-J. Quisquater, Y. Deswarte, C. Meadows, D. Gollmann (Eds.), Computer Security – ESORICS 98. Proceedings, 1998. X, 377 pages. 1998.

Vol. 1486: A.P. Ravn, H. Rischel (Eds.), Formal Techniques in Real-Time and Fault-Tolerant Systems. Proceedings, 1998. VIII, 339 pages. 1998.

Vol. 1487: V. Gruhn (Ed.), Software Process Technology. Proceedings, 1998. VIII, 157 pages. 1998.

Vol. 1488: B. Smyth, P. Cunningham (Eds.), Advances in Case-Based Reasoning. Proceedings, 1998. XI, 482 pages. 1998. (Subseries LNAI).

Vol. 1489: J. Dix, L. Fariñas del Cerro, U. Furbach (Eds.), Logics in Artificial Intelligence. Proceedings, 1998. X, 391 pages. 1998. (Subseries LNAI).

Vol. 1490: C. Palamidessi, H. Glaser, K. Meinke (Eds.), Principles of Declarative Programming. Proceedings, 1998. XI, 497 pages. 1998.

Vol. 1493: J.P. Bowen, A. Fett, M.G. Hinchey (Eds.), ZUM '98: The Z Formal Specification Notation. Proceedings, 1998. XV, 417 pages. 1998.

Vol. 1494: G. Rozenberg, F. Vaandrager (Eds.), Lectures on Embedded Systems. Proceedings, 1996. VIII, 423 pages. 1998.

Vol. 1495: T. Andreasen, H. Christiansen, H.L. Larsen (Eds.), Flexible Query Answering Systems. IX, 393 pages. 1998. (Subseries LNAI).

Vol. 1496: W.M. Wells, A. Colchester, S. Delp (Eds.), Medical Image Computing and Computer-Assisted Intervention – MICCAI'98. Proceedings, 1998. XXII, 1256 pages. 1998.

Vol. 1497: V. Alexandrov, J. Dongarra (Eds.), Recent Advances in Parallel Virtual Machine and Message Passing Interface. Proceedings, 1998. XII, 412 pages. 1998.

Vol. 1498: A.E. Eiben, T. Bäck, M. Schoenauer, H.-P. Schwefel (Eds.), Parallel Problem Solving from Nature – PPSN V. Proceedings, 1998. XXIII, 1041 pages. 1998.

Vol. 1499: S. Kutten (Ed.), Distributed Computing. Proceedings, 1998. XII, 419 pages. 1998.

Vol. 1501: M.M. Richter, C.H. Smith, R. Wiehagen, T. Zeugmann (Eds.), Algorithmic Learning Theory. Proceedings, 1998. XI, 439 pages. 1998. (Subseries LNAI).

Vol. 1502: G. Antoniou, J. Slaney (Eds.), Advanced Topics in Artificial Intelligence. Proceedings, 1998. XI, 333 pages. 1998. (Subseries LNAI).

Vol. 1503: G. Levi (Ed.), Static Analysis. Proceedings, 1998. IX, 383 pages. 1998.

Vol. 1504: O. Herzog, A. Günter (Eds.), KI-98: Advances in Artificial Intelligence. Proceedings, 1998. XI, 355 pages. 1998. (Subseries LNAI).

Vol. 1507: T.W. Ling, S. Ram, M.L. Lee (Eds.), Conceptual Modeling – ER '98. Proceedings, 1998. XVI, 482 pages. 1998.

Vol. 1508: S. Jajodia, M.T. Özsu, A. Dogac (Eds.), Advances in Multimedia Information Systems. Proceedings, 1998. VIII, 207 pages. 1998.

Vol. 1510: J.M. Zytkow, M. Quafafou (Eds.), Principles of Data Mining and Knowledge Discovery. Proceedings, 1998. XI, 482 pages. 1998. (Subseries LNAI).

Vol. 1511: D. O'Hallaron (Ed.), Languages, Compilers, and Run-Time Systems for Scalable Computers. Proceedings, 1998. IX, 412 pages. 1998.

Vol. 1512: E. Giménez, C. Paulin-Mohring (Eds.), Types for Proofs and Programs. Proceedings, 1996. VIII, 373 pages. 1998.

Vol. 1513: C. Nikolaou, C. Stephanidis (Eds.), Research and Advanced Technology for Digital Libraries. Proceedings, 1998. XV, 912 pages. 1998.

Vol. 1514: K. Ohta,, D. Pei (Eds.), Advances in Cryptology – ASIACRYPT'98. Proceedings, 1998. XII, 436 pages. 1998.

Vol. 1515: F. Moreira de Oliveira (Ed.), Advances in Artificial Intelligence. Proceedings, 1998. X, 259 pages. 1998. (Subseries LNAI).

Vol. 1516: W. Ehrenberger (Ed.), Computer Safety, Reliability and Security. Proceedings, 1998. XVI, 392 pages. 1998.

Vol. 1517: J. Hromkovič, O. Sýkora (Eds.), Graph-Theoretic Concepts in Computer Science. Proceedings, 1998. X, 385 pages. 1998.

Vol. 1518: M. Luby, J. Rolim, M. Serna (Eds.), Randomization and Approximation Techniques in Computer Science. Proceedings, 1998. IX, 385 pages. 1998.

Vol. 1520: M. Maher, J.-F. Puget (Eds.), Principles and Practice of Constraint Programming - CP98. Proceedings, 1998. XI, 482 pages. 1998.

Vol. 1522: G. Gopalakrishnan, P. Windley (Eds.), Formal Methods in Computer-Aided Design. Proceedings, 1998. IX, 529 pages. 1998.